EUROPEAN CONTRACT LAW

European Contract Law

by
HEIN KÖTZ
M.C.L. (Mich.), F.B.A., Emeritus Professor of Law, University of Hamburg
Emeritus Director, Max Planck Institute for Comparative and International Private Law

Second Edition

translated from the German by
GILL MERTENS
and
TONY WEIR

OXFORD
UNIVERSITY PRESS

Great Clarendon Street, Oxford, OX2 6DP,
United Kingdom

Oxford University Press is a department of the University of Oxford.
It furthers the University's objective of excellence in research, scholarship,
and education by publishing worldwide. Oxford is a registered trade mark of
Oxford University Press in the UK and in certain other countries

© Hein Kötz 2017
© Originally published in German as 'Europäisches Vertragsrecht 2'
by Mohr Siebeck GmbH & Co. KG Tübingen 2015

The translation of this work was funded by Geisteswissenschaften International—Translation
Funding for Humanities and Social Sciences from Germany, a joint initiative of
the Fritz Thyssen Foundation, the German Federal Foreign Office, the collecting society
VG WORT and the Börsenverein des Deutschen Buchhandels
(German Publishers & Booksellers Association)

Translation © Gill Mertens & Tony Weir 2017

The moral rights of the authors have been asserted

First Edition published in 1997
Second Edition published in 2017
Impression: 1

All rights reserved. No part of this publication may be reproduced, stored in
a retrieval system, or transmitted, in any form or by any means, without the
prior permission in writing of Oxford University Press, or as expressly permitted
by law, by licence or under terms agreed with the appropriate reprographics
rights organization. Enquiries concerning reproduction outside the scope of the
above should be sent to the Rights Department, Oxford University Press, at the
address above

You must not circulate this work in any other form
and you must impose this same condition on any acquirer

Crown copyright material is reproduced under Class Licence
Number C01P0000148 with the permission of OPSI
and the Queen's Printer for Scotland

Published in the United States of America by Oxford University Press
198 Madison Avenue, New York, NY 10016, United States of America

British Library Cataloguing in Publication Data
Data available

Library of Congress Control Number: 2017943888

ISBN 978-0-19-880004-0

Printed and bound by
CPI Group (UK) Ltd, Croydon, CR0 4YY

Links to third party websites are provided by Oxford in good faith and
for information only. Oxford disclaims any responsibility for the materials
contained in any third party website referenced in this work.

Preface to the Second Edition

Authors rarely say at the outset that the subject of their book does not exist. There is indeed no such thing as a 'European Contract Law': It is in force nowhere, and there is no court in Europe that would apply it. It is true that the contract law of the Member States of the European Union has, to some extent, been unified by the implementation of directives and the case law of the Court of Justice. But the directives only address a limited number of problems of contract law, and mainly seek to ensure that the Member States afford a minimum level of consumer protection. 'European Contract Law' is discussed in this book in a wider context. It takes the national rules of contract law as a starting point, and tries to find which of those rules are sufficiently alike and may therefore be accepted throughout Europe as a 'common' European law of contract. While national contract laws will be taken into account, they are only viewed as local variations of a common European theme. Most of today's law students will spend their professional lives in a world in which knowledge of only one jurisdiction is not enough. This book is intended to help them go beyond the intricacies of their own legal systems, look at the similarities and differences among European jurisdictions, and speculate on the extent to which a 'European Contract Law' may indeed exist.

The first edition of this book was published by Clarendon Press in 1997. It was limited to certain parts of contract law, while the remaining parts were to be contributed by Axel Flessner. As time went by it became clear that he would publish his part separately and on a more ambitious scale. So I decided to bring the first edition up-to-date and complete the text myself.

Since this book is for students of different nationalities, it had to avoid technical jargon and be as down-to-earth as possible. Every time I wrote a sentence in German, I had to ask myself whether it would be capable of being translated into English (and possibly other languages) without too much difficulty. This may have involved some loss of technical precision, but to rid one's thought and language of the exuberant technicalities which flourish all too rampantly in the walled enclosures of national legal systems may be no bad thing. Nonetheless, the translation into English was a formidable task. The first edition was translated by Tony Weir, who alas died in 2011 at the age of seventy-five. He did an outstanding job, and it has been said that there are many places where the translation makes for better reading than the original. The second edition was translated by Gill Mertens. I am sure that she will come up to the same high standard, and I am very grateful to her for a most difficult work. I am also grateful to 'Geisteswissenschaften International'* which funded a major part of

---

* Geisteswissenschaften International—Translation Funding for Humanities and Social Sciences from Germany, a joint initiative of the Fritz Thyssen Foundation, the German Federal Foreign Office, the collecting office VG Wort and the Börsenverein des Deutschen Buchhandels (German Publishers & Booksellers Association).

the costs of translation. Finally, I should like to thank Mrs Angelika Okotokro who steered the manuscript through all the perils of electronic data processing.

Hein Kötz

Hamburg
November 2016

Translator's Note

When Professor Kötz asked me to take on the translation of the second edition of his acclaimed book on *European Contract Law*, I was both honoured and a little nervous. As Professor Kötz states in his preface, Tony Weir's translation of the first edition had been extremely well received.

I discussed how to tackle the second English edition with Professor Kötz, and suggested an approach inspired by modern architectural extensions to older buildings. Trying to copy Tony Weir's English style for the extensive updates and amendments to the text of the first edition could only ever result in an inauthentic pastiche of his prose. We decided to let the two styles sit side by side, while seeking to allow much of Tony Weir's original text to shine through. In places, I found it in need of some re-pointing—not least in terms of some awkward gender referencing in the text. These have not been removed entirely, and there are many places where 'he' is still used for ease of reference. Hopefully, readers of the first edition will not feel challenged by juxtaposition of prose styles in the second.

This second English edition is not just a word-for-word translation of the second German edition of the book, which was published as *Europäisches Vertragsrecht* (2nd edition) by Mohr Siebeck in 2015. Professor Kötz has made many updates and revisions since then, not least in light of the changes made to the French *Code civil*.

The text includes many hundreds of translated extracts of legislation, cases, or academic literature. Had we referenced every single translation, this book may well have been a hundred pages longer, and far less readable. Where parallel texts have been published by the European Union, we have used the official English EU wording. Where other text is derived from a statutory provision, case, or academic literature of a non-English legal system, it is self-evident that this must be in translation. We have used translations provided by official public authorities and institutions, although these are only informative and non-binding.

Our aim was to produce a book that will be an invaluable resource and inspiration for the widest possible range of readers, not all of whom may speak English as their native tongue, and not just within the geographical boundaries of Europe. I salute Professor Kötz for the dedication he has invested in this new edition, and trust that it will be received to the same acclaim as the first.

Gill Mertens *LLB, LLM, MA*

Hamburg
November 2016

Summary Table of Contents

Table of British Cases	xvii
List of Abbreviations	xxiii
1. Development of European Contract Law	1
2. Negotiation and Formation of Contracts	17
3. The Definiteness of the Contract	41
4. Tests of Earnestness	49
5. Formalities	73
6. Interpretation of Contracts	91
7. Unfair, Illegal, and Immoral Contracts	109
8. The Control of Unfair Contract Terms	131
9. Mistake	149
10. Deceit and Duress	173
11. Rights of Withdrawal	191
12. Claims for Performance	197
13. Termination of Contracts	215
14. Damages	241
15. The Effect of Unexpected Circumstances	279
16. Agency and Representation	293
17. Contracts for the Benefit of Third Parties	319
18. Assignment	337
Index	357

Detailed Table of Contents

Table of British Cases	xvii
List of Abbreviations	xxiii

1. Development of European Contract Law — 1
- A. Introduction — 1
- B. Contract Law and Economic Order — 5
- C. European Union Contract Law — 8
- D. A European Code of Contract Law? — 11

2. Negotiation and Formation of Contracts — 17
- A. The Consent of the Parties — 17
- B. The Offer — 19
    - I. Definiteness of the offer — 19
    - II. Intention to be bound — 19
    - III. Effect of the offer — 21
    - IV. Termination of the offer — 21
        1. Refusal or failure to accept an offer — 21
        2. Expiry of time for acceptance — 22
        3. Revocation of the offer — 22
        4. Death or incapacity — 24
- C. Acceptance — 25
    - I. Declaration of acceptance — 25
        1. Acceptor's intention to be bound — 25
        2. Effectiveness of declaration of acceptance — 25
    - II. Acceptance by conduct — 26
        1. Acceptance by commencing performance — 26
        2. Acceptance by silence — 27
    - III. Qualified acceptance — 29
    - IV. Delayed acceptance — 31
- D. Liability for Breaking Off Negotiations — 32

3. The Definiteness of the Contract — 41
- A. Introduction — 41
- B. Types of Case — 42
    - I. Agreements to agree — 43
    - II. Unilateral price-fixing — 45

4. Tests of Earnestness — 49
- A. Introduction — 49
- B. *Cause* as a Requirement for Validity? — 51
- C. Gifts — 52
    - I. Formal requirements in continental law — 53
    - II. The consideration doctrine in English law — 53
    - III. Executed gifts — 54
    - IV. The enforcement of informal promissory gifts — 56
        1. Pledges of contributions — 56
        2. Maintenance payments — 57
        3. Payment for services rendered — 59

D.	Other Gratuitous Transactions		60
	I. Contracts of guarantee		61
	II. Contracts for the use of property		61
	III. Contracts for the management of affairs		62
	IV. Offers to contract		63
	V. Modification of contracts		63
E.	The Intention to Enter a Legal Obligation		66
F.	Summary		69

5. Formalities   73
A.	Introduction		73
B.	Reasons for Formal Requirements		75
C.	Types of Formalities		76
D.	Sanctions		78
	I. Exclusion of oral evidence		78
	II. Invalidity		80
		1. Guarantees	80
		2. Sales of land	83
	III. Other sanctions		84
E.	Enforcement of Contracts Lacking the Requisite Form		84

6. Interpretation of Contracts   91
A.	Introduction	91
B.	Intention and Expression: the Two Theories	91
C.	Objective Interpretation	93
D.	Maxims of Interpretation	98
E.	Forms of Constructive Interpretation	100
	I. Implication of terms by default rules	102
	II. Constructive interpretation	103
	III. Collateral duties	106

7. Unfair, Illegal, and Immoral Contracts   109
A.	Introduction	109
B.	Inequality between Performance and Counterperformance	110
C.	Undue Restraints on Personal or Economic Freedom	117
	I. Basics	117
	II. Long-term contractual relationships	118
	III. Non-compete agreements	119
	IV. Partial invalidity	121
D.	Breach of the Law	122
E.	Restitution of Benefits Conferred	125

8. The Control of Unfair Contract Terms   131
A.	Introduction	131
B.	Judicial Control	134
C.	Legislative Options	136
	I. Unfair contract terms in contracts between businesses	136
	II. Standard terms and individually negotiated terms	139
	III. When is a contract term unfair?	140
	IV. Partial invalidation of terms	143
D.	Preventive Control	145
	I. Criminal sanctions	145

| | | | | II. Group actions | 146 |
| | | | | III. Administrative controls | 147 |

9. Mistake — 149
A. Introduction — 149
B. Avoidance for Mistake — 151
  I. There must be a contract — 151
  II. Avoidance and liability — 152
    1. Claims by buyer for non-conforming goods — 152
    2. Other claims for non-performance — 154
C. Preconditions of Avoidance for Mistake — 155
  I. Historical background — 155
  II. Mistakes as to the qualities of the thing or person — 156
    1. General — 156
    2. Causality — 158
    3. Mistaken motive — 159
    4. Mistake as to the value of the thing — 161
    5. Risk in transactions — 162
    6. Negligent mistakes — 162
    7. Offer to make good the consequences of a mistake — 163
  III. Mistakes caused by the other party — 163
  IV. Recognisable mistakes — 165
  V. Shared mistakes — 166
  VI. A European law on mistake? — 167
    1. Primacy of the contract — 168
    2. 'Special reasons' for allowing avoidance — 169
D. Effecting Avoidance for Mistake — 171

10. Deceit and Duress — 173
A. Deceit — 173
  I. Elements — 173
  II. Non-disclosure as deceit — 175
    1. Duties to inform in general — 175
    2. Attribution of duties to inform — 177
    3. Negligent breach of duties to inform — 179
    4. 'Duties of disclosure' in English law — 180
  III. Deceit by third party — 182
  IV. Claims for damages — 184
B. Duress — 185
  I. Duress and exploitation — 185
  II. Elements of duress — 185
  III. Duress by third party — 188

11. Rights of Withdrawal — 191
A. Introduction — 191
B. Basis and Reasons for Withdrawal — 192
  I. Doorstep selling — 192
  II. Loan agreements, timeshare contracts — 193
  III. Distance-selling contracts — 194
C. Consequences of Withdrawal — 195

12. Claims for Performance — 197
A. Introduction — 197

	B.	Solutions of National Legal Systems	198
		I. Continental law	198
		II. Common law	202
	C.	Harmonised Rules in Europe	205
		I. Claims for performance	205
		1. Impossibility of performance	206
		2. Unreasonably high cost	207
		3. Personal performance	208
		4. Concluding a substitute transaction	209
		5. Timely claim for performance	209
		II. Claims for supplementary performance	210
	D.	The Efficient Breach of Contract	212

13. Termination of Contracts — 215

- A. Introduction — 215
- B. Interests of the Parties — 216
- C. Solutions — 218
  - I. French law — 219
  - II. English law — 220
  - III. German law — 223
- D. Requirements — 224
  - I. Basic requirements — 224
  - II. Impossibility of performance — 226
  - III. Anticipatory non-performance — 228
  - IV. Delayed performance — 229
  - V. Incomplete performance — 231
  - VI. Defective performance — 233
- E. Restitution — 237

14. Damages — 241

- A. Non-Performance of the Contract — 242
- B. Attribution — 244
  - I. Fault principle — 244
  - II. *Obligations de moyens* and *obligations de résultat* — 248
  - III. Breach of contract — 252
  - IV. International rules — 254
- C. Link Between Non-Performance and Damage — 257
  - I. Liability for remote damage — 257
  - II. Contributory responsibility of the creditor — 261
- D. Nature and Extent of Damages — 264
  - I. Liability for expectation interest — 264
  - II. Calculating damages for non-performance of contracts of sale — 266
  - III. Liability for lost profits and lost expectations — 268
  - IV. Liability for disgorgement of profits — 270
  - V. Liability for intangible loss — 271
  - VI. Agreements on limitation of damages — 275

15. The Effect of Unexpected Circumstances — 279

- A. Introduction — 279
- B. Solutions — 280
  - I. French law — 280
  - II. German law — 281
  - III. English law — 285
- C. International Sets of Rules — 288

16. Agency and Representation — 293
- A. Historical Development and Economic Importance — 293
- B. Statutory Representatives — 297
- C. Grant, Extent, and Termination of Authority or the Power to Represent — 298
  - I. Grant — 298
  - II. Implied grant — 299
  - III. Formalities — 300
  - IV. Extent — 301
  - V. Self-dealing by agent — 303
  - VI. Termination — 305
  - VII. Revocability — 305
- D. Dealing without Authority — 307
  - I. Ratification — 307
  - II. Apparent or ostensible authority — 308
    1. Giving the appearance of authority — 308
    2. Justifiable reliance by the third party — 310
  - III. Liability of the supposed agent — 311
- E. The Effects of Agency — 312
  - I. Disclosed agency — 312
  - II. Undisclosed agency — 314
    1. Claims by the principal — 315
    2. Claims by the third party — 317

17. Contracts for the Benefit of Third Parties — 319
- A. Historical Development and Economic Importance — 319
- B. Requirements — 323
  - I. The intention of the parties — 323
  - II. Contracts protective of third parties — 325
  - III. Claims by third parties not based on contractual intention — 328
    1. *Action directe* — 328
    2. Contract chains — 329
  - IV. Limitations of liability and third parties — 331
- C. Effects — 332
  - I. Rights of the promisee — 332
  - II. Defences available to the promisor — 333
  - III. Modification or termination of third party rights — 334

18. Assignment — 337
- A. Historical Development and Economic Importance — 337
- B. Requirements for an Effective Transaction — 340
  - I. Substantive validity — 341
  - II. Non-assignable rights — 342
    1. Rights to wages, maintenance, and support — 342
    2. Personal rights — 342
    3. Parts of debts — 343
    4. Future debts — 343
    5. No-assignment clauses — 346
  - III. Formal requirements — 348
  - IV. Priorities — 350
- C. Effects — 352
  - I. Between assignor and assignee — 352

II. Protection of the debtor 353
    1. Payment to the original creditor 353
    2. Defences available to the debtor 353
    3. Waiver of defences by debtor 354

Index 357

Table of British Cases

Adams v. Lindsell (1818) 23
Adler v. Dickson (1955) 331
Aerial Advertising Co. v. Batchelor's Peas, Ltd. (1938) 103, 234
Alan & Co. Ltd. v. El Nasr Export and Import Co. (1972) 65
Albert v. Motor Insurers' Bureau (1972) 68
Alderslade v. Hendon Laundry (1945) 253
Allied Maples Group Ltd. v. Simmons & Simmons (1995) 268, 269
Amalgamated Investment & Property Co. v. John Walker & Sons (1977) 287
Archbolds (Freightage) Ltd. v. S. Spanglett Ltd. (1961) 124
Armagas Ltd. v. Mundogas S.A. (1986) 309
Ashmore Benson Peace & Co. Ltd. v. A.V. Dawson Ltd. (1973) 123
Associated Japanese Bank (International) Ltd. v. Crédit du Nord S.A. (1988) 154, 166, 169
Atlas Express Ltd. v. Kafco Ltd. (1989) 188
Attorney General v. Blake (2001) 271
Attorney General of Belize v. Belize Telecom Ltd. (2009) 101
Attorney General of Hong Kong v. Humphreys Estate Ltd. (1987) 86
Attwood v. Lamont (1920) 121
Avon Finance Co. Ltd. v. Bridger (1985) 189

Backhouse v. Backhouse (1978) 113
Balfour v. Balfour (1919) 67
Banque Financière v. Westgate Insurance Co. 182
Barclays Bank Plc v. O'Brien (1994) 114, 183, 189
Barton v. Armstrong (1976) 186
Bedford Insurance Co. Ltd. v. Instituto de Resseguros do Brasil (1985) .. 122
Bell v. Lever Brothers (1932) 166, 167
Bigos v. Bousted (1951) 128
Bissett v. Wilkinson (1927) 164
Blackpool Aero Club v. Blackpool Borough Council (1990) 35
Bolton Partners v. Lambert (1889) 308
Bowmakers Ltd. v. Barnet Instruments Ltd. (1945) 129
Box v. Midland Bank Ltd. (1979) 36
Bridge v. Deacons (1984) 120
Briess v. Woolley (1954) 183
Brinkibon Ltd. v. Stahag Stahl (1983) 23
British Bank for Foreign Trade Ltd. v. Novinex Ltd. (1949) 43
British Columbia Saw Mill Co. Ltd. v. Nettleship (1868) 257
British School of Motoring Ltd. v. Simms (1971) 103
British Steel Corp. v. Cleveland Bridge and Engineering Co. Ltd. (1984) ... 33
British Westinghouse Co. v. Underground Electric Railways Co. of London Ltd. (1912) 264, 265
B.R.S. v. Arthur V. Crutchley Ltd. (1968) 30
Brown v. Gould (1971) 44
Bunge Corp. v. Tradax SA (1981) 221, 222
Business Computers Ltd. v. Anglo-African Leasing Ltd. (1977) 354
Butler Machine Tool Co. Ltd. v. Ex-Cell-O Corp. (England) Ltd. (1979) 30
Byrne v. Leon van Tienhoven & Co. (1880) 22

Caparo Industries Plc v. Dickman (1990) 62, 327
Carlill v. Carbolic Smoke Ball Co. (1892) 20
Casey's Patents, Re (1892) 59
Cavendish Square Holding BV v. Talal el Makdessi, ParkingEye Ltd. v. Beavis (2015) 277
Cehave N.V. v. Bremer Handelsgesellschaft m.b.H. (The Hansa Nord) (1975) 236
Central London Property Trust Ltd v. High Trees House Ltd. (1947) 64, 65
Chamber Colliery Co. Ltd. v. Twyerould (1915) 99
Chapelton v. Barry Urban District Council (1940) 134
Chaplin v. Hicks (1911) 269
Chartbrook Ltd. v. Persimmon Houses Ltd. (2009) 95
Cobbe v. Yeoman's Row Management Ltd. (2008) 86
Coldunell v. Gallon (1986) 189
Collen v. Wright (1857) 311
Coombe v. Coombe (1951) 58
Co-operative Insurance Society Ltd. v. Argyll Stores (Holdings) Ltd. (1998) 204, 205
Cory, Re (1912) 57
Couturier v. Hastie (1856) 151
Coward v. Motor Insurers' Bureau (1983) 68
Crabb v. Arun District Council (1976) 86
Craddock v. Hunt (1923) 93
Cresswell v. Potter (1978) 113

Daniels v. White & Son (1938) 253
Darlington Borough Council v. Wiltshier Northern Ltd. (1995) 322
Davis v. London & Provincial Marine Insurance Co. (1878) 181
Davis Contractors Ltd. v. Fareham Urban DC (1956) 287
Dearle v. Hall (1828) 351
Derry v. Peek (1889) 174
Dibbins v. Dibbins (1896) 308
Dickinson v. Dodds (1876) 22
Dimmock v. Hallett (1866) 164, 181
Dimskal Shipping Co. S.A. v. International Transport Workers' Federation (1991) 186, 188
Drew v. Nunn (1879) 305

Elder, Dempster & Co. v. Paterson, Zochonis & Co. (1924) 332
Entores Ltd. v. Miles Far East Corp. (1955) 23
Esso Petroleum Co. Ltd. v. Harper's Garage (Stourport) Ltd. (1968) 119
Eurymedon, The (1975) 332
Evia Luck (No. 2), The (1983) 188
Eyre v. Measday (1986) 254

F.A. Tamplin Steamship Co. Ltd. v. Anglo-Mexican Petroleum Products Co. Ltd. (1916) 286
Fairley v. Skinner (2002) 274
Foakes v. Beer (1884) 66
Freeman & Lockyer v. Buckhurst Park Properties (1964) 316
Frost v. Aylesbury Dairy Co. Ltd. (1905) 253

George Mitchell (Chesterhall) Ltd. v. Finney Lock Seeds Ltd. (1983) 135, 143
G.H. Myers v. Brent Cross Service Co. (1934) 253
Giles Co. v. Morris (1972) 204
Goldsoll v. Goldman (1915) 121
Grant v. Edwards (1986) 88
Gray v. Southouse (1949) 127

Greasley v. Cooke (1980) 86, 88
Great Peace Shipping Ltd. v. Tsavliris Salvage (International) Ltd. (2003) 167
Greaves & Co. Ltd. v. Baynham Meikle & Partners (1975) 103, 254
Gregg v. Scott (2005) 270
Griffith v. Tower Publ. Co. (1897) 342

Hadley v. Baxendale (1854) 258
Hamilton Jones v. David & Snape (2004) 274
Harbutt's 'Plasticine' Ltd. v. Wayne Tank and Pump Co. Ltd. (1970) 265
Harris v. Watson (1791) 64
Harrison and Jones v. Burton and Lancaster (1953) 167
Hedley Byrne & Co. v. Heller & Partners (1964) 37, 62
Helstan Securities Ltd. v. Hertfordshire County Council (1978) 346
Henderson v. Merrett Syndicates Ltd. (1994) 250
Herne Bay Steamboat v. Hutton (1903) 287
Heywood v. Wellers (1976) 274
Hillas & Co. v. Arcos Ltd. (1932) 41
Holman v. Johnson (1775) 126
Hong Kong Fir Shipping Co. Ltd. v. Kawasaki Kishen Kaisha Ltd. (1962) 223
Horwood v. Millar's Timber and Trading Co. (1917) 118
Household Fire & Carriage Acc. Ins. Co. Ltd. v. Grant (1879) 26
Howell v. Coupland (1876) 286
Hudson, Re (1885) 57
Hughes v. Metropolitan Railway (1877) 64

Interfoto Library Ltd. v. Stiletto Ltd. (1989) 134
Investors Compensation Scheme Ltd. v. West Bromwich Building Society (1998) 94, 95, 97
Inwards v. Baker (1965) 86, 88

James Talcott Ltd. v. John Lewis & Co. Ltd. (1940) 353
Jarvis v. Swans Tours Ltd. (1975) 274
Johnson v. Gore Wood Co. (2002) 274
Jones v. Padavatton (1969) 67

Kaufmann v. Gerson (1904) 187
Keighley, Maxstead & Co. v. Durant (1901) 307
Kemp v. Baerselman (1906) 343
Kennedy v. Panama, New Zealand and Australian Royal Mail Co. Ltd. (1867) 151
King v. Michael Faraday & Partners Ltd. (1939) 344
Kingsnorth Trust Ltd. v. Bell (1986) 183
Kiriri Cotton Co. Ltd. v. Dewani (1960) 127
Kitchen v. Royal Air Force Association (1958) 269
Kleinwort Benson Ltd. v. Malaysia Mining Corp. Ltd. (1988) 35
Krell v. Henry (1903) 287

Lake v. Bayliss (1974) 271
Langston v. Langston (1834) 98
Leaf v. International Galleries (1950) 167
Leage, The (1984) 352
Lewis Emanuel & Son Ltd. v. Sammut (1952) 286
Linden Gardens Trust Ltd. v. Lenesta Sludge Disposals Ltd. (1993) 346
Lister v. Romford Ice & Storage Co. (1957) 103
Liverpool City Council v. Irwin (1977) 103

Lloyd's Bank Ltd. v. Bundy (1975) 114, 115
Lombard North Central Ltd. v. Butterworth (1987) 221
Lombard Tricity Finance Ltd. v. Paton (1989) 45
London County Freehold v. Berkeley Property Co. Ltd. (1936) 183
Lucas (T.) & Co. Ltd. v. Mitchell (1974) 121
Luxor (Eastbourne) Ltd. v. Cooper (1941) 104

Mahmoud and Ispahani, Re (1921) 123
Mannai Investment Co. v. Eagle Star Life Assurance Co. (1997) 97
Maskell v. Horner (1915) 186
Mason v. Provident Clothing & Supply Co. Ltd. (1913) 121
Matthews v. Kuwait Bechtel Corp. (1959) 103
McArdle, Re (1951) 59
McRae v. Commonwealth Disposals Commission (1951) 155, 266
Merritt v. Merritt (1970) 67
Moorcock, The (1889) 104
Murphy v. Brentwood (1990) 329
Mutual Finance Ltd. v. John Wetton & Sons Ltd. (1937) 198

Nash v. Halifax Building Society (1979) 125
National Westminster Bank v. Morgan (1985) 115
Nicolene Ltd. v. Simmonds (1952) 253
Nordenfelt v. Maxim Nordenfelt (1894) 120
North Ocean Shipping Co. v. Hyundai Construction Co. (1978) 188

Ocean Tramp Tankers Corp. v. V/O Sovfracht (1964) 288
Office of Fair Trading v. Abbey National plc and others (2010) 140
Olley v. Marlborough Court Ltd. (1949) 134
Oscar Chess Ltd. v. Williams (1957) 167

Page One Records v. Bitton (1968) 204
Pao On v. Lau Yiu Long (1980) 59, 188
Paradine v. Jane (1647) 252
ParkingEye Ltd. v. Beavis 141, 277
Pascoe v. Turner (1979) 86, 88
Patel v. Ali (1984) 208
Philipps Products Ltd. v. Hyland and Hamstead Plant Hire Co. Ltd. (1987) 143
Phoenix General Insurance Co. of Greece S.A. v. Halvanon Insurance Co. Ltd. (1987) 122, 123
Photo Production Ltd. v. Securicor Transport Ltd. (1980) 142, 143
Pioneer Shipping Ltd. v. BTP Tioxide Ltd., The Nema (1982) 286, 288
Port Caledonia, The (1903) 186
Powell v. Brent London Borough Council (1987) 203
Printing and Numerical Registering Co. v. Sampson (1875) 7

Queensland Electricity Generating Board v. New Hope Collieries Ltd. (1989) 44

Raffles v. Wichelhaus (1864) 98
Rainbow v. Hawkins (1904) 311
Raineri v. Miles (1981) 253
Ramsgate Victoria Hotel Co. Ltd. v. Montefiore (1866) 22
Raven, The (1980) 354
Redford v. De Froberville (1978) 265
Redgrave v. Hurd (1881) 175
Reed v. Dean (1949) 103

Robinson v. Davison (1871) 286
Robinson v. Harman (1848) 264
Rose & Frank Co. v. Crompton & Bros. Ltd (1925) 66
Routledge v. Grant (1828) 22
Royal Bank of Scotland v. Etridge (No. 2) (2001) 114
Ruxley Electronics and Construction Ltd. v. Forsyth (1996) 208, 265, 274
Ryan v. Mutual Tontine Westminster Chambers Ass. (1893) 204

Said v. Butt (1920) 315
Samuels v. Davis (1943) 254
Scally v. Southern Health and Social Services Board (1992) 104
Scammel v. Ouston (1941) 42
Schroeder Music Publishing Co. v. Macaulay (1974) 118
Schuler v. Wickman Machine Tool Sales Ltd. (1974) 95, 221
Scruttons Ltd. v. Midland Silicones Ltd. (1962) 332
Seager v. Copydex Ltd. (1967) 33
Shelley v. Paddock (1980) 128
Shirlaw v. Southern Foundries Ltd. (1939) 104
Simaan General Contracting Co. v. Pilkington Glass Ltd. (No. 2) (1988) 331
Simpkins v. Pays (1955) 68, 69
Sky Petroleum Ltd. v. VIP Petroleum Ltd. (1974) 203
Smith v. Eric S. Bush (1990) 62, 327
Smith v. Hughes (1871) 181
Smith v. Land and House Property Corp. (1884) 164
Soames, Re (1897) 57
Solnit, The (1983) 263
South Australia Asset Management Corp. v. York Montague (1997) 254, 260
St. John Shipping Corp. v. Joseph Rank Ltd. (1957) 124
Stewart Gill Ltd. v. Horatio Myer & Co. Ltd. (1992) 144
Stilk v. Myrick (1809) 64
Sudbrook Trading Estate Ltd. v. Eggleton (1982) 44
Swain v. Law Society (1983) 322
Swan, The (1968) 313

Tailby v. Official Receiver (1888) 345
Taylor v. Caldwell (1863) 252
Taylors Fashions Ltd. v. Liverpool Victoria Trustees Co. Ltd. (1982) 88
Thake v. Maurice (1986) 254
Thomas v. Thomas (1842) 59
Thornton v. Shoe Lane Parking Ltd. (1971) 134
Tinsley v. Milligan (1992) 125
Tito v. Waddell (No. 2) (1977) 265
Tolhurst v. Associated Portland Cement Co. (1903) 343
Transfield Shipping Inc. v. Mercator Shipping Inc. (2009) 260
Tsakiroglou & Co. Ltd. v. Noblee Thörl GmbH (1962) 288

Union Eagle Ltd. v. Golden Achievement Ltd. (1997) 229
Universal Steam Navigation Co. v. McKelvie (1923) 313
Universe Tankships Inc. of Monrovia v. International Transport Workers' Federation (1983) 186

Victoria Laundry (Windsor) Ltd. v. Newman Industries Ltd. (1949) 259

Wales v. Wadham (1977) 181
Walford v. Miles (1992) 38

Ward v. Byham (1956) 57, 63
Warner Brothers Pictures Inc. v. Nelson (1937) 204
Watson v. Davies (1931) 308
Watts v. Morrow (1991) 274
Weir v. Bell (1878) 182
White v. Jones (1995) 327
Whitworth Street Estates Ltd. v. James Miller & Partners (1970) 95
William Lacey (Hounslow) Ltd. v. Davis (1957) 35
William Sindall plc v. Cambridgeshire County Council (1994) 153
Williams v. Roffey Brothers & Nicholls (Contractors) Ltd. (1991) 65, 66, 188
Williams v. Williams (1957) 58
With v. O'Flanagan (1936) 181
Wolverhampton Corp. v. Emmons (1901) 203
Wyatt v. Kreglinger (1933) 59

Yianni v. Edwin Evans & Sons (1982) 327
Yonge v. Toynbee (1910) 311
Young & Marten Ltd. v. McManus Childs Ltd. (1969) 253

List of Abbreviations

ABGB	Allgemeines Bürgerliches Gesetzbuch (Austrian Civil Code)
AC	Law Reports, Appeal Cases, House of Lords and Privy Council
AcP	Archiv für die civilistische Praxis (Germany)
AGB	Allgemeine Geschäftsbedingungen (General Terms and Conditions)
AktG	Aktiengesetz (German Stock Corporation Act)
All ER	All England Law Reports
ALR	Allgemeines Landrecht für die Preussischen Staaten (1794)
Am J Comp L	American Journal of Comparative Law
App.Cas.	Law Reports, Appeal Cases, House of Lords and Privy Council (1875–1890)
Aranzadi	Aranzadi, Repertorio de Jurisprudencia (Spain)
art.	article
Ass.plén.	Cour de cassation, Assemblée plénière (France)
Austr. LJ	Australian Law Journal
BAG	Bundesarbeitsgericht (German Federal Labour Court)
BB	Betriebsberater (Germany)
BG	Bundesgericht (Swiss Federal Court)
BGB	Bürgerliches Gesetzbuch (German Civil Code)
BGBl.	Bundesgesetzblatt (German Federal Gazette)
BGE	Entscheidungen des schweizerischen Bundesgerichts (Decisions of the Swiss Federal Court)
BGH	Bundesgerichtshof (German Federal Court)
BGHZ	Entscheidungen des Bundesgerichtshofs in Zivilsachen (Decisions of the German Federal Court in Civil Matters)
BlZüRspr.	Blätter für Zürcherische Rechtsprechung (Switzerland)
Brussels I	Regulation (EU) No. 1215/2012 of the European Parliament and the Council of 12 December 2012 on Jurisdiction and the Recognition and Enforcement of Judgments in Civil and Commercial Matters
Bull.cass.	Bulletin des arrêts de la Cour de cassation (France)
BVerfG	Bundesverfassungsgericht (German Federal Constitutional Court)
BW	Burgerlijk Wetboek (Dutch Civil Code)
CA	Court of Appeal (England and Wales)
Cal. LR	California Law Review (USA)
Camb. LJ	Cambridge Law Journal
Can. BJ	Canadian Bar Journal
Cass.	Suprema Corte di Cassazione (Italian Court of Cassation)
CC	Civil Code
CEC	Accademia dei Giurisprivatisti Europei (ed), *Code européen des contrats*, Livre premier (Milano 2002)

CESL	Proposal for a Common European Sales Law (Annex I to European Commission, Proposal for a Regulation of the European Parliament and the Council on a Common European Sales Law of 11 October 2011)
Ch.	High Court of Chancery; or Law Reports, Chancery Division (since 1890)
Ch.App.	Law Reports, Chancery Appeals
Ch.D.	Law Reports, Chancery Division (1875–1890)
Ch. mixte	Cour de cassation, chambre mixte (France)
CISG	United Nations Convention on Contracts for the International Sale of Goods (Vienna, 11 April 1980)
Civ.	Cour de cassation, chambre civile (France)
CJEU	Court of Justice of the European Union
CLR	Commonwealth Law Reports (Australia)
Cmnd.	Command papers (United Kingdom)
Col J Transnat L	Columbia Journal of Transnational Law (USA)
Col. LR	Columbia Law Review (USA)
Com.	Cour de cassation, chambre commerciale et financière (France)
Cornell LR	Cornell Law Review (USA)
C.P.D.	Law Reports, Common Pleas Division
Curr Leg Probl	Current Legal Problems (United Kingdom)
D.	Recueil Dalloz de doctrine, de jurisprudence et de législation (1945–1964); Recueil Dalloz et Sirey de doctrine, de jurisprudence et de législation (since 1965) (France)
D.A.	Recueil Dalloz analytique de jurisprudence et de législation (1941–1944) (France)
DCFR	Draft Common Frame of Reference; Christian von Bar, Eric Clive, Hans Schulte-Nölke (eds), *Principles, Definitions and Model Rules of European Private Law, Draft Common Frame of Reference*, Interim Outline Edition (2008)
D.H.	Dalloz, Recueil hebdomadaire de jurisprudence (1924–1940) (France)
D.P.	Dalloz, Recueil périodique et critique de jurisprudence, de législation et de doctrine (1825–1940) (France)
Dr prat com int	Droit et pratique du commerce international (France)
D.S.	Recueil Dalloz et Sirey de doctrine, de jurisprudence et de législation (France)
EC	European Community
ECJ	Court of Justice of the European Union
EEC	European Economic Communities
EFSlg.	Ehe- und familienrechtliche Entscheidungen (Decisions on family law and the law of husband and wife) (Austria)
Eng.Rep.	English Reports
ERCL	European Review of Contract Law
ERPL	European Review of Private Law
EU	European Union
Eur J of Law & Ec	European Journal of Law and Economics

ff.	following pages/articles/sections/paragraphs
FF	French francs
Foro it.	Il Foro Italiano
Gaz Pal	Gazette du Palais (France)
GG	Grundgesetz (Basic Law, German Constitution)
GlUNF	Sammlung von zivilrechtlichen Entscheidungen (Collection of Civil Law Cases) founded by Glaser and Unger (since 1900) (Austria)
GmbHG	Gesetz betreffend die Gesellschaften mit beschränkter Haftung (German Limited Liability Companies Act)
Harv. LR	Harvard Law Review (USA)
HD	Högsta Domstola (Swedish Supreme Court)
HGB	Handelsgesetzbuch (German and Austrian Commercial Code)
HL	House of Lords
HR	Hoge Raad (Dutch Supreme Court)
ICLQ	International and Comparative Law Quarterly (United Kingdom)
IHR	Internationales Handelsrecht (Germany)
InsO	Insolvenzordnung (German Insolvency Act)
Int.Enc.Comp.L.	International Encyclopedia of Comparative Law
IPRax	Praxis des Internationalen Privat- und Verfahrensrechts (Germany)
I.R.	Informations rapides
JBl	Juristische Blätter (Austria)
JBusL	Journal of Business Law (United Kingdom)
JCL	Journal of Contract Law (Australia)
JCP	Juris-classeur périodique, La Semaine Juridique (France)
J L & Ec	Journal of Law and Economics (USA)
J L & Society	Journal of Law and Society (United Kingdom)
JLegStud	Journal of Legal Studies (USA)
J.O.	Journal Officiel
J.T.	Journal des Tribunaux (Belgium)
JuS	Juristische Schulung (Germany)
JW	Juristische Wochenschrift (Germany)
JZ	Juristenzeitung (Germany)
KB	Law Reports, King's Bench (1901–1952)
La. LR	Louisiana Law Review (USA)
Law Com.	Reports of the Law Commission for England and Wales
L.Ch.	Lord Chancellor
L.J.	Lord Justice
L.J.Ch.	Law Journal Reports, Chancery (1831–1949)
Lloyd's Rep.	Lloyd's List Law Reports
LM	Lindenmaier/Möhring, Nachschlagewerk des Bundesgerichtshofes (Collection of Cases of the German Federal Court)

LMCLQ	Lloyd's Maritime and Commercial Law Quarterly
LQR	Law Quarterly Review (United Kingdom)
L.R.Ch.App.	Law Reports, Chancery Appeal Cases (1865–1875)
L.R.Ex.	Law Reports, Exchequer (1865–1875)
LT	Law Times Reports (1859–1947)
LZ	Leipziger Zeitschrift für deutsches Recht (1906–1933)
Max Planck Enc.	J Basedow, KJ Hopt, and R Zimmermann (eds), *The Max Planck Encyclopedia of European Private Law* (2012)
MDR	Monatsschrift für deutsches Recht (Germany)
Mich. LR	Michigan Law Review (USA)
mn.	marginal note
Mod. LR	Modern Law Review (United Kingdom)
M.R.	Master of the Rolls
n.	Footnote or Annotation
no.	number
NedJur	Nederlandse Jurisprudentie (Netherlands)
New LJ	New Law Journal (United Kingdom)
NJA	Nytt Juridiskt Arkiv (Sweden)
NJW	Neue Juristische Wochenschrift (Germany)
NJW-RR	Neue Juristische Wochenschrift, Rechtsprechungs-Report (Germany)
Nw. ULR	Northwestern University Law Review (USA)
OGH	Oberster Gerichtshof (Austrian Supreme Court)
OGHZ	Oberster Gerichtshof für die Britische Zone (Supreme Court for the British Zone of Germany)
O.J.	Official Journal of the EEC, EC or EU
OJLS	Oxford Journal of Legal Studies (United Kingdom)
ÖJZ	Österreichische Juristenzeitung (Austria)
OLG	Oberlandesgericht (German Higher Regional Court)
OLGZ	Entscheidungen der Oberlandesgerichte in Zivilsachen (Decisions of the German Higher Regional Courts in Civil Matters)
OR	Obligationenrecht (Swiss Code of Obligations)
P.	Law Reports, Probate Division (since 1891)
Pas.	Pasicrisie belge (Belgium)
P.C.	Judicial Committee of the Privy Council (United Kingdom)
P.D.	Law Reports, Probate, Divorce and Admiralty Division (1875–1890) (United Kingdom)
PECL	Principles of European Contract Law
PICC	UNIDROIT Principles of International Commercial Contracts
Q.B.	Law Reports, Queen's Bench (1891–1900, since 1952)
Q.B.D.	Law Reports, Queen's Bench Division (1875–1890)
RabelsZ	Rabels Zeitschrift für ausländisches und internationales Privatrecht (Germany)

RDC	Revue des contrats (France)
Rep.Foro.it.	Repertorio Generale Annuale di Giurisprudenza del Foro Italiano (Italy)
Rép not Defrénois	Répertoire du Notariat Defrénois (France)
Req.	Cour de cassation, chambre de requêtes (France)
Rev crit jur belge	Revue critique de jurisprudence belge (Belgium)
Rev dr unif	Revue de droit uniforme (Italy)
Rev int dr comp	Revue internationale de droit comparé (France)
Rev trim civ	Revue trimestrielle de droit civil (France)
RG	Reichsgericht (German Imperial Court)
RGAT	Revue générale des assurances terrestres (France)
RGZ	Entscheidungen des Reichsgerichts in Zivilsachen (Decisions of the German Imperial Court in Civil Matters)
RL	Richtlinie (Directive)
Rn.	Randnote (marginal note)
Rome I Regulation	Regulation (EC) No. 593/2008 of the European Parliament and of the Council of 17 June 2008 on the Law Applicable to Contractual Obligations
Rome II Regulation	Regulation (EC) No. 864/2007 of the European Parliament and of the Council of 11 July 2007 on the Law Applicable to Non-Contractual Obligations
Rs.	Rechtssache (Case)
S.	Recueil Sirey (1791–1954, 1957–1964) (France)
s.	Section
S.Afr. LJ	South African Law Journal
Scand Stud L	Scandinavian Studies in Law
SJZ	Schweizerische Juristenzeitung (Switzerland)
Slg.	Sammlung der Rechtsprechung des Europäischen Gerichtshofs (Collection of Cases of the European Court of Justice)
Soc.	Cour de cassation, chambre sociale (France)
Stan. LR	Stanford Law Review (USA)
StGB	Strafgesetzbuch (German Criminal Code)
SZ	Entscheidungen des österreichischen Obersten Gerichtshofs in Zivil- und Justizverwaltungssachen (Decisions of the Austrian Supreme Court in Civil and Administrative Matters) (Austria)
TFEU	Treaty on the Functioning of the European Union
TLR	Times Law Reports (United Kingdom)
Trib.civ.	Tribunal civil (France)
Trib.gr.inst.	Tribunal de grande instance (France)
T.S.	Tribunal Supremo (Spain)
Tul. LR	Tulane Law Review (USA)
UCC	Uniform Commercial Code (USA)
U.Chi. LR	University of Chicago Law Review (USA)
UKSC	United Kingdom Supreme Court Reports
UNCITRAL	United Nations Commission on International Trade Law
UNIDROIT	International Institute for the Unification of Private Law

Uniform LR	Uniform Law Review (Italy)
U.Pa. LR	University of Pennsylvania Law Review (USA)
U.Tor. LR	University of Toronto Law Review (Canada)
Va. LR	Virginia Law Review (USA)
VersR	Versicherungsrecht (Germany)
VVG	Versicherungsvertragsgesetz (German Insurance Contracts Act)
Wisc. LR	Wisconsin Law Review (USA)
WLR	Weekly Law Reports (United Kingdom)
WM	Wertpapiermitteilungen (Germany)
Yale LJ	Yale Law Journal (USA)
ZBernJV	Zeitschrift des Bernischen Juristenvereins (Switzerland)
ZEuP	Zeitschrift für Europäisches Privatrecht (Germany)
ZfRvgl	Zeitschrift für Rechtsvergleichung (Austria)
ZHR	Zeitschrift für das gesamte Handelsrecht und Wirtschaftsrecht (Germany)
ZPO	Zivilprozessordnung (German Code of Civil Procedure)
ZvglRWiss	Zeitschrift für vergleichende Rechtswissenschaft (Germany)

1
Development of European Contract Law

A. Introduction	1
B. Contract Law and Economic Order	5
C. European Union Contract Law	8
D. A European Code of Contract Law?	11

A. Introduction

Today, all European countries have their own national contract law. Whether a valid contract has been concluded; whether it can be avoided due to mistake, misrepresentation, or duress; or whether one of the parties can demand payment of damages because the other party has not performed the contract or has not performed the contract correctly—all these issues are settled in France in accordance with French contract law, in Italy under Italian contract law, and in England pursuant to English contract law. Strictly speaking, there is no such thing as a European law of contract. The European Union has adopted a great many directives, with the result that some issues of contract law—particularly in the area of consumer law—are treated uniformly across all Member States.[1] Even these directives are not really fully effective until they are implemented by the individual Member States and incorporated into their national laws. Over twenty-five years ago, the European Parliament had already requested that 'a start be made on the necessary preparatory work on drawing up a European Code of Private Law' because it would only be possible to achieve a single market (as it was then called) by 'unifying major branches of private law'.[2] For some, this seemed like a Utopian dream. And indeed, we have still made no real progress towards having either a uniform European Civil Code or a harmonised European law of contract. Back in 1989, the goal of the European Parliament was genuine, even if many acknowledged that it might take a long time for the dream to be realised. It was pointed out at the time that the adoption of EU directives had thus far only managed to achieve harmonisation in a few individual areas. The laws of Member

---

[1] Therefore, the term 'European contract law' can also be used (in contrast to the way it is used in this book) when the term is meant to cover only those rules which are in force in all Member States of the European Union for the reason that they have a direct basis in European law, in particular in the Treaties on the European Union (now the Treaty on the Functioning of the European Union), in European regulations and directives, and in the general legal principles developed by the European Court of Justice. For detailed coverage of these topics, see K Riesenhuber, *EU-Vertragsrecht* (2013), and B Heiderhoff, *Europäisches Privatrecht* (4th edn, 2016).

[2] See the Resolution of the European Parliament of 26 May 1989 on action to bring into line the private law of the Member States (OJ C 158/89, 400). See also W Tilmann, 'Entschließung des Europäischen Parlaments über die Angleichung des Privatrechts der Mitgliedsstaaten' (1993) 1 *ZEuP* 613. The European Parliament has since repeated its demands several times.

States—including contract law—have become a colourful patchwork, where national laws overlap with harmonised European laws, and where boundaries are indistinct and based on different value choices. It was thought that these differences would disappear at a stroke with the creation of a harmonised European law of contract. Another reason why the intention of the European Parliament met with sympathy at the time was that it was in line with prevailing opinion in legal circles—namely that comparative law was charged with the important new task of 'Europeanising' laws, legal literature, and legal teaching in pursuit of the eventual creation of a harmonised system of European private law.

This set up a new challenge for the function of comparative law. The idea behind it has always been to contribute to the development of specific national laws by seeking comparisons with other jurisdictions, drawing conclusions, and proposing solutions in order to promote improved understanding of the national legal system, or to close gaps in its application. Another function has always been to identify the foundations considered essential to the harmonisation of a particular aspect of law.[3] In addition, comparative law has always involved a special pedagogic function. All these comparative law aims were important then, and remain so today.[4] But comparative law has now been given an extended function: developing a comparative basis on which to build a pan-European legal system. For some areas—not only for contract law, but also for tort law, collateral security law, company law, family law, and inheritance law—the aim is to demonstrate if (and for what reasons) there is a common basis across Europe, the extent of these acknowledged fundamentals, and whether developments are tending to converge or diverge.

It is clear today that business and politics operate in a European dimension, as demonstrated by the existence and success of the European Union. So there are good and practical reasons for the law to follow the consequences, and seek to identify a foundation on which to base European private law. But one should not forget that legal history has long regarded the matter of European private law as a legitimate and interesting subject of legal research. It is not as if the concept of European private law is a new idea. It is really a reawakening of something long forgotten—the rediscovery of that inner core of European law that existed under the influence of Roman law, Canon law, *ius commune, usus modernus*, natural justice, and legal thinking of the Enlightenment in all European countries until well into the eighteenth century. And, if you look closely, all this has not been lost even after the national civil law codes came into force.[5] In his captivating book *Europa und das römische Recht*, published in 1947, Paul

---

[3] An important example is the harmonisation of the law applicable to international contracts of sale. This area is now governed by the United Nations Convention on Contracts for the International Sale of Goods (CISG) that has been adopted in over 80 countries and would not have been possible without prior comparative work on the joint foundations of national laws on the sale of goods.
[4] For details on the aims of comparative law, see K Zweigert and H Kötz, *An Introduction to Comparative Law* (Tony Weir tr, 3rd edn, 1998) 13ff.
[5] On the importance for the development of European private law of the sources quoted in the text, see the contributions to the Max Planck Enc. (2012): R Zimmermann, 'Roman Law' (1487); A Thier, 'Canon Law' (133); N Jansen, 'Ius Commune' (1006); K Luig, 'Usus Modernus' (1755); J Liebrecht, 'Natural Law' (1189). On the relationship between comparative law and legal history, see also R Zimmermann, 'Das römisch-kanonische ius commune als Grundlage europäischer Rechtseinheit' [1992] JZ 8; R Zimmermann, 'Roman Law and the Harmonization of Private Law in Europe' in A Hartkamp et al.

Koschaker drew attention to the European character of private law, thus opening up a field of research where national borders should no longer play a role. In *Europäisches Privatrecht,* Helmut Coing provided a well-sourced overview of European private law, including the older *Gemeines Recht (ius commune)* in Volume I in 1985, and national legislation in Volume II in 1989.[6] In 1990, Reinhard Zimmermann published *The Law of Obligations, Roman Foundations of the Civilian Tradition,* the focus of which was not restricted to the Roman law of obligations. Zimmermann also follows the route taken by the Roman rules in the old and new *ius commune*, describes how these rules were taken up in the continental civil codes, and shows how German, French, and English jurisprudence have developed these rules up to the present day. The selection of subject matter and characterisation of concepts in this book are guided at every turn by the conviction that Roman law, Canon law, and *ius commune* 'provide the intellectual and doctrinal framework within which a new European legal unity may one day emerge'.[7] From here, it was but a small step to show the different ways in which comparative law could contribute towards setting up a unified European private law.[8]

An initial and—as it turned out—momentous step towards implementing this aim was when the Commission on European Contract Law began work in 1982, based on a private initiative by Professor Ole Lando from Denmark. The Commission comprised lawyers from every European jurisdiction, and it was tasked with drawing up a functional system of foundational rules for European contract law from the totality of basic rules making up national contract laws across Europe.[9] The findings of this Commission have since been published as the *Principles of European Contract Law* (PECL).[10] These Principles never had any force of law; and it is correct that they do not take account of the rules contained in many EU directives (that mostly came into force subsequently), particularly those intended to protect consumers. But this fact does not exclude the possibility that parties may conclude an agreement that allows for contractual disputes to be settled on the basis of the PECL.[11] The use of the PECL

(eds), *Towards a European Civil Code* (4th edn, 2011) 27; H Kötz, 'Vom Beitrag der Rechtsgeschichte zu den modernen Aufgaben der Rechtsvergleichung' in P Caroni and G Dilcher (eds), *Norm und Tradition, Welche Geschichtlichkeit für die Rechtsgeschichte?* (1998) 153; H Kötz, 'Was erwartet die Rechtsvergleichung von der Rechtsgeschichte?' [1992] *JZ* 20; A Flessner, 'Die Rechtsvergleichung als Kundin der Rechtsgeschichte' (1999) 7 *ZEuP* 513.

[6] See H Coing, 'Europäisierung der Rechtswissenschaft' [1990] *NJW* 937. The development of a European legal tradition based on joint sources, rules, and terms is also the subject of a book by HJ Berman, *Law and Revolution: The Formation of the Western Legal Tradition* (1983).

[7] R Zimmermann, *The Law of Obligations* (1990) X. On the importance of legal history for the development of European private law, see also J Liebrecht, 'Legal History' in Max Planck Enc. (2012) 1064 with numerous references.

[8] See H Kötz, *Gemeineuropäisches Zivilrecht*, in H Bernstein, U Drobnig, and H Kötz (eds), *Festschrift für Konrad Zweigert* (1981) 481.

[9] For a detailed description, see R Zimmermann, 'Principles of European Contract Law' in Max Planck Enc. (2012) 1325.

[10] O Lando and H Beale (eds), *Principles of European Contract Law Parts I* and *II* (2000); O Lando, E Clive, A Prüm, and R Zimmermann (eds), *Principles of European Contract Law Part III* (2003).

[11] See art. 1:101 (2) PECL. However, such a choice of law clause must only be observed by national courts where the applicable international private law allows the court to recognise reference to non-national law. This is usually inadmissible, particularly under art. 3 of Regulation (EC) No. 593/2008 on the law applicable to contractual obligations (Rome I). The situation is different in courts of arbitration. It should be noted that the PECL mainly contain discretionary law, and when confronted with mandatory

is also open to courts when the parties have concluded a contract to be governed by 'general principles of law', or by the *lex mercatoria* (merchant law) customary in commercial trading.[12] But the most important practical effect of the PECL lies elsewhere. They provide guidance for legislatures, courts, and jurisprudence as to the direction that the development, extension, and interpretation of national contract laws should take if one wishes to work towards the goal of legal unity in Europe. For this, there are already many examples.[13]

The PECL deal with European contract law. But they are not substantially different from the *Principles of International Commercial Contracts* (PICC), drawn up by the International Institute for the Unification of Private Law (UNIDROIT).[14] They are based on the contract law common to *all* countries, and are designed for use only in international commercial contracts.[15] Nevertheless, the two sets of rules end up with the same or similar solutions. This may be because of the dominant effect that European contract law has had on countries outside Europe, but may also be because—if one excludes the topic of consumer protection laws—the differences between general contract law and commercial contract law may not be as great as is sometimes assumed. The PECL and PICC are just some of the international sets of rules that will be considered in detail in this book. Others include the draft *Code of Contract Law* presented in 2002 by Guiseppe Gandolfi on behalf of the Academy of European Private Lawyers[16] and the *Draft Common Frame of Reference* (DCFR).[17]

---

national law, the national law will prevail and will be applied to the contract under international private law rules.

[12] See art. 1:101 (3) PECL.

[13] An outstanding example is the recent reform of French contract law which has been influenced to a major extent by the rules of the PECL and other European sources. See the detailed account by F Ancel, B Fauvarque-Cosson, and J Gest, *Aux sources de la réforme du droit des contrats* (2017). See also J Basedow (ed), *Europäische Vertragsrechtsvereinheitlichung und deutsches Recht* (2000); D Busch, E Hondius, H van Kooten, H Schelhaas, and W Schrama, *The PECL and Dutch Law: A Commentary* (, vol. I 2002, vol. II 2006); D Busch, 'The PECL before the Supreme Court of the Netherlands' (2008) 16 ZEuP 549; L Antoniolli and A Veneziano, *The PECL and Italian Law* (2005); C Vendrell Cervantes, 'The Application of the PECL by Spanish Courts' (2008) 16 ZEuP 534. See also A Hartkamp et al. (eds) (n 5): The contributions on contract law published in this volume also regard the PECL as a source of inspiration that should be taken into account in legislation, court decisions, and legal research as part of the Europeanisation of national laws.

[14] On this, see H Kronke, 'UNIDROIT' in Max Planck Enc. (2012) 1723.

[15] See UNIDROIT (ed), *UNIDROIT Principles of International Commercial Contracts* (2010). A comprehensive overview of the PICC rules can be found in S Vogenauer and J Kleinheisterkamp (eds), *Commentary on the UNIDROIT Principles of International Commercial Contracts* (2009). See also J Kleinheisterkamp, 'UNIDROIT Principles of International Commercial Contracts' in Max Planck Enc. (2012) 1727; R Zimmermann, 'Die Unidroit-Grundregeln der internationalen Handelsverträge in vergleichender Perspektive' (2005) 13 ZEuP 264; S Vogenauer, 'Die UNIDROIT Grundregeln der internationalen Handelsverträge 2010' (2013) 21 ZEuP 7.

[16] See Accademia dei Giurisprivatisti Europei (Coordinator G Gandolfi), *Code Européen des Contrats, Avant-projet* (2002), discussed by E Kramer, (2002) 66 RabelsZ 781. See also G Gandolfi, 'Der Vorentwurf eines Europäischen Vertragsgesetzbuches' (2002) 10 ZEuP 1; R Zimmermann, 'Der "Codice Gandolfi" als Modell eines einheitlichen Vertragsrechts für Europa?' in H-P Mansel, H Kronke, and T Pfeiffer (eds), *Festschrift für Erik Jayme* (vol. II 2004) 1401; and (with further evidence) K Siehr, 'Code Européen des Contrats (Avant-Projet)' in Max Planck Enc. (2012) 207.

[17] See below, pp. 10f.

Today, everybody is talking about the concept of European private law.[18] The influence of the Commission on European Contract Law has also spread to other areas of law, such as tort, enrichment, insurance contracts, trusts, family, and civil procedure.[19] Many new books being published use comparative law methods—not just in the field of contract law but also in other areas—in order to promote a European perspective. And there are journals that focus on the area of European private law.[20] Mention should also be made of the two-volume *Max Planck Encyclopedia of European Private Law* (2009), with its 400 individual entries, which follows the objective of 'proceeding from the historical and comparative foundations ... [to] analyze tendencies towards the international unification and European harmonization of the various fields of private law'.[21]

B. Contract Law and Economic Order

European contract law was the initial focus of comparative law research. This may be because from the outset the aim of the European Union had been to create a single market—an aim that, according to prevailing opinions, would not be possible without having a more or less uniform contract law regime across Europe. But that alone does not explain why so much research has concentrated on European contract law, and has resulted—at least in comparison with tort, unjust enrichment, and family law—in a sort of consensus being reached not only on fundamental principles, but also at a very detailed level. How can this be?

There is a close link between the economic order and contract law. Where questions concerning economic order are to be treated consistently, sooner or later a form of contract law will develop that is consistent with that economic order. In Europe, contract law remained in a fairly undeveloped state so long as the exchange of goods and services depended on personal status of family, tribe, profession, or rank into which a person was born, and which they would retain their whole life long. The vassal certainly owed services to his lord, the client to his patron, the serf to his landowner, and the apprentice to his master. Certain benefits were expected and provided in return for these services. Yet these entitlements and duties were based not on a contractual agreement, but on status relationships typical in the economic order of the society. The content of the exchanges was characterised by tradition, custom, and conventions. It was only when people began to realise the enormous benefits to be obtained from the division of labour that legal recognition of contracts really became necessary. People

---

[18] For a detailed view, see R Zimmermann, *Die Europäisierung des Privatrechts und die Rechtsvergleichung* (2006).

[19] See W Wurmnest, 'Common Core, Grundregeln, Kodifikationsentwürfe, Acquis-Grundsätze, Ansätze internationaler Wissenschaftlergruppen zur Privatrechtsvereinheitlichung in Europa' (2003) 11 ZEuP 714 and especially the overviews in Max Planck Enc. (2012): U Magnus, 'Principles of European Tort Law' (1325); S Meier, 'Unjustified Enrichment' (1742); H Heiss, 'Principles of European Insurance Contract Law' (1331); R Kulms, 'Trusts' (1697); W Pintens, 'Principles of European Family Law' (1329).

[20] For example, see the *Zeitschrift für Europäisches Privatrecht (ZEuP)*, *European Review of Private Law (ERPL)*, both of which have been published since 1993.

[21] Comments of the editors J Basedow, KJ Hopt, and R Zimmermann in 'Preface' to Max Planck Enc. (2012) VI.

who specialise—like the farmer in producing food, the trader in distributing goods, the tailor in making clothes, or the haulier, the moneylender, the construction worker, the teacher, the doctor, and others who provide specialist services—all must be able to exchange their products or services for money, and then use that money to procure the goods or services they need to live. They all need to make contracts. As the principle of the division of labour spreads through society, relationships between individuals cease to be a function of the status they were born to, and are constituted instead by the contracts they choose to make. As so succinctly summarised in a famous quotation by Sir Henry Maine, 'the movement of the progressive societies has hitherto been a movement from Status to Contract'.[22]

The bonds of feudalism, politics, and religion were loosened by the liberalism of the eighteenth and nineteenth centuries, for liberalism put the highest value on the autonomy of the individual. Everyone must be free to fashion the conditions of his life as he wished and to pursue his chosen goals, provided only that in doing so he did not infringe the similar freedoms of others. The state must accordingly respect this freedom by guaranteeing its citizens freedom of belief, expression, trade, and profession. The principle of freedom of contract follows from this: citizens must be free to decide whether or not to contract (i.e agree on an exchange of goods or services) and if so, on what terms.[23]

During the course of the nineteenth century, liberalism eventually took hold in all European countries, as did a form of contract law that largely fulfilled all the considerations required of it. Of course, there were—and continue to be—many limitations on freedom of contract. No party may invalidate a contract simply because he or she made a bad deal, where performance and consideration are not equal, or because the consideration (as is often stated in England) amounts only to a 'peppercorn'.[24] But the party will have a right to avoid a contract if the process by which the agreement was concluded with the counterparty is deficient to the extent that it would not be possible to regard the party's acceptance of the agreement as proper.[25] This would be the case,

---

[22] HS Maine, *Ancient Law* (11th edn, 1864) 165.

[23] See H Unberath, 'Freedom of Contract' in Max Planck Enc. (2012) 751. It is true that many are already sounding the death knell for freedom of contract. In their view, the concept of contract should be reformulated and turned into a legal relationship based on obligations of cooperation, solidarity, and fairness. For example, see Study Group on Social Justice in European Private Law (ed), 'Social Justice in European Law: A Manifesto' (2004) 10 *European Law Journal* 653. Other commentators have argued that contract law should aim for a proper distribution of wealth in society, and therefore support the poor against the wealthy, and the weak against the strong. See, for example, A Kronman, 'Contract Law and Distributive Justice' (1980) 89 *Yale LJ* 472; H Collins, 'Distributive Justice Through Contracts' (1992) 45 *Curr Leg Probl* 49. It is true that a person will certainly prosper if nature has endowed him or her with greater abilities and talents, the parents have provided him or her with more capital or a superior education, or Lady Luck has smiled on him or her more frequently. However, the adjustment of differences in income, wealth, and luck with standards of fairness and social justice is surely the role of the tax laws and the social services which taxes provide rather than the mission of contract law.

[24] On this, see GH Treitel, *The Law of Contract* (13th edn, by E Peel, 2011) no. 3-013ff, and with respect to 'Inäquivalenz von Leistung und Gegenleistung', 'iustum pretium', and 'laesio enormis', see chapter 7.B, pp. 110ff.

[25] With respect to the much-discussed difference between procedural and substantive deficiencies of contracts, see Unberath (n 23); M Trebilcock, *The Limits of Freedom of Contract* (1993); M Eisenberg, 'The Bargain Principle and Its Limits' (1982) 94 *Harv. LR* 323; J Gordley, 'Equality in Exchange' (1981) 69 *Cal. LR* 1587; P Atiyah, 'Contract and Fair Exchange' (1985) 35 *U.Tor. LR* 1; P Atiyah, 'Essays on Contract Law' (1988) 329.

for example, if a contracting party did not have the necessary capacity at the time the contract was concluded, or where there was misrepresentation or undue duress by the counterparty. Procedural problems can also arise if a party is talked by the counterparty into signing a contract while at the door of their residence, within the residence, at their place of work, while on the street, or on public transport. Particularly for those persons who are not really business-oriented, there is a danger that they will be disadvantaged by the element of surprise, and that they will be persuaded to conclude the contract without a sufficient consideration of the terms, or having an opportunity to compare prices. A process is also faulty if a party has only accepted disadvantageous contractual terms because, under the circumstances, it would have been too expensive to examine the contractual provision (usually a clause inserted by the counterparty into its standard terms and conditions), to negotiate for the provision to be amended, or to refuse to conclude the contract and to seek another provider.[26] The freedom of contract is also restricted in those areas where the legislature views certain classes of contractual parties (such as employees, tenants, or consumers) as requiring protection from the outset, and uses mandatory provisions to grant those parties rights that are non-negotiable. Finally, contracts can also be invalid if the parties unlawfully infringe the interests of third parties or the general public and have therefore offended common decency, or breached statutory provisions, *ordre public*, or public policy.

Nevertheless, it is proper that all European legal orders have adopted the principle of freedom of contract and only allow exceptions to this rule that are based on special reasons. There is a general rule that it is not wise

> to extend arbitrarily those rules which say that a given contract is void as being against public policy, because if there is one thing more than another which public policy requires, it is that men of full age and competent understanding shall have the utmost liberty of contracting and that their contracts, when entered into freely and voluntarily, shall be held sacred and shall be enforced by Courts of Justice.[27]

The driving force behind this development is that each person must have sufficient freedom not to have to justify their decisions either to the state or anyone else. One can also take the approach offered by utilitarianism and argue that the contract—as a freely concluded exchange of goods and services—has prevailed because in a world of scarce resources it allows people to optimise satisfaction of their needs. In fact, there are good reasons why contract has more to offer than a process whereby goods and services are distributed in accordance with fixed status relationships or—as in the socialist economic orders that have now largely disappeared—the stipulations of a state planning authority.[28]

---

[26] See chapter 8, pp. 131ff.
[27] Sir George Jessel MR in *Printing and Numerical Registering Co. v. Sampson* (1875) L.R. 19 Eq. 462, 465.
[28] The analysis of the welfare-enhancing effects of contract are an area of law and economics research, which has developed a special arsenal of terms and methods for this purpose. For an introduction into this area, see R Posner, *Economic Analysis of Law* (9th edn, 2014); R Cooter and T Ulen, *Law and Economics* (6th edn, 2012); R Craswell and A Schwartz, *Foundations of Contract Law* (1994); HB Schäfer and C Ott, *Lehrbuch der ökonomischen Analyse des Zivilrechts* (5th edn, 2012). See also R Kulms, 'Economic Analysis of European Private Law' in Max Planck Enc. (2012) 514.

From the wide acceptance of the principle of freedom of contract, there is a further consequence that has gone a long way towards establishing a uniform law of contract across all state boundaries. This arises from the fact that many rules of contract are dispositive—namely that they represent a sort of back-up framework that only comes into force as *règles supplétives*, implied terms, or default rules if the parties have failed to agree otherwise.[29] Thus, most European legal orders have developed a rule that a party is only entitled to avoid a contract if the other party has committed a 'fundamental breach' of the contract.[30] But this rule is dispositive: it does not apply if the contract makes other provisions. If there is agreement that a seller may cancel a contract if the purchase price is paid as little as one day after the agreed date for payment, provided the agreement about the payment deadline is valid and the deadline is not met, the seller may terminate the contract even though the late payment by the purchaser does not cause any material damage and the seller's 'true' reasons for desiring the cancellation of the contract are of an entirely different nature. Dispositive rules of law under Common Law systems are mostly developed as judge-made law. Under Continental legal orders, they are found in the civil codes—systematically ordered and differentiated by contract type. But as legislatures are unable to precisely formulate such rules, they are constantly refined and developed by judicial interpretation. What are the principles that should guide legislatures and judges in creating and developing dispositive law? Such rules should take account of typical interests, correspond to the 'hypothetical will' of the parties, and ought to be formulated in such a way as to reflect what the parties would have agreed—presuming that they would have negotiated with each other in good faith about the division of contractual risks, and that they would have agreed upon the optimal solution for both parties. Normally, the risk under consideration would be assumed by the party which is able to counter it at lower cost than the other party, to reduce the probability of its occurrence at lower cost, or to take precautions against the consequences of its occurrence—including by taking out insurance cover. This makes sense from an economic perspective or (for those that prefer a less dry approach) from a common-sense perspective—namely from considerations emanating from the interests of the parties and the facts themselves, not from the subtle distinctions of any national legal system. Thus, the search for the correct dispositive law will always be guided by the same test, namely by what reasonable and fair-minded parties would consider as appropriate in the light of the nature and purpose of their contract.[31]

C. European Union Contract Law

For around thirty years, EU law has exerted a considerable influence on contract laws in the individual Member States. Above all, this influence is derived from a long list of

---

[29] For further details, see chapter 6.E, pp. 100ff.   [30] See also chapter 13.D, pp. 224ff.
[31] For greater detail, see H Kötz, 'Dispositives Recht und ergänzende Vertragsauslegung' [2013] JuS 289 and (from a comparative law perspective) R Zimmermann, ' "Heard melodies are sweet, but those unheard are sweeter …": Condictio tacita, implied condition und die Fortbildung des europäischen Vertragsrechts' (1993) 193 *AcP* 121.

directives that are designed to ensure that the laws of Member States afford a substantially harmonised minimum level of consumer protection.[32] Some of these directives target particular types of consumer selling, such as door-to-door selling[33] and distance contract selling.[34] Other directives address a particular type of contract, such as for package tours,[35] timeshares,[36] consumer credit agreements,[37] and the sale of consumer goods.[38] The Directive of 5 April 1993 on Unfair Terms in Consumer Contracts falls into a special category: it allows judges to set aside standardised clauses in consumer contracts where they are regarded as 'unfair'.

The directives use different instruments in order to achieve their overall consumer protection goals. Sometimes they grant a limited right of cancellation.[39] Furthermore, businesses are often given duties to provide information that they must mostly fulfil before—but sometimes after—a contract has been concluded, so that consumers know—or at least have the opportunity to know—about the exact terms of the contract and how they can enforce certain rights granted.[40] Finally, certain rules governing the contractual distribution of risk must sometimes be made binding in favour of the consumer. This affects in particular rights applying to consumers as purchasers when they receive defective goods.

It is clear that these directives only address certain selected problems and thus have a 'fragmentary' or 'pointillist' character. They certainly make the contract laws of the Member States more uniform. But this uniformity has a limited scope as it does not include those rules of national jurisdictions, for example, that govern how a contract is concluded, interpreted, or avoided in case of mistake, deceit, or duress, or what a party's liability will be in the event of a breach of contract. National contract laws are not uniform even in the areas where directives apply. This may be due to Member States implementing the directives differently, or where their courts have interpreted the provisions in varying ways. In some cases, different national rules will continue

---

[32] This is apart from those areas of EU law that address particular fields of private law, such as competition law, company, and labour law, or international private law. Some directives address only business-to-business transactions—examples are the Council Directive of 18 December 1986 on the coordination of the laws of the Member States relating to self-employed commercial agents (86/653/EEC), and Directive 2000/35/EC of the European Parliament and of the Council of 29 June 2000 on combating late payment. We will also not be addressing those directives that prohibit discrimination against a person on the basis of gender, race, or ethnicity.

[33] See Council Directive of the European Parliament and of the Council of 20 December 1985 to protect the consumer in respect of contracts negotiated away from business premises (85/577/EEC). This Directive has now been repealed and integrated into Directive 2011/83/EU of 25 October 2011 on consumer rights.

[34] Directive 97/7/EC of the European Parliament and of the Council of 20 May 1997 on the protection of consumers with respect to distance contracts. This has also now been incorporated into Directive 2011/83/EU of 25 October 2011 on consumer rights.

[35] Council Directive 90/314/EEC of 13 June 1990 on package travel, package holidays, and package tours.

[36] Directive 2008/122/EC of the European Parliament and of the Council of 14 January 2009 on the protection of consumers in respect of certain aspects of timeshare, long-term holiday product, resale and exchange contracts.

[37] Directive 2008/48/EC of the European Parliament and of the Council of 23 April 2008 on credit agreements for consumers.

[38] Directive 1999/44/EC of the European Parliament and of the Council of 25 May 1999 on certain aspects of the sale of consumer goods and associated guarantees.

[39] For more on this, see chapter 11, pp. 191ff.

[40] See B Heiderhoff, 'Information Obligations (Consumer Contract)' in Max Planck Enc. (2012) 869.

to apply because the directives seek to ensure only a minimum level of protection and thus leave national law in force, provided that overall it protects the consumer as strongly (or even more strongly) than the directive.

For this reason, a number of attempts have been made to free existing consumer protections laws from their 'fragmentary' character, and to build up general rules to cover this area of law. Initially, a group of legal academics took on the task of summarising the *acquis communautaire* (the body of EU law in force), eliminating contradictions and disagreements, and then extending them so that they could constitute the basis for a European law on contract.[41] In 2003, the EU Commission presented an action plan in which it made proposals to take a further step in the direction of a common European contract law by developing a Common Frame of Reference that would take account not only of the existing *acquis communautaire*, but also of the *acquis commun*, that is the rules which the national laws of contract have in common and are presented in the PECL.[42] The preparation of the Common Frame of Reference was entrusted to a network of legal academics, some of whom had already been members of the working group on the *acquis communautaire*, while others came from the Study Group on a European Civil Code.[43] This Group sees itself as the successor to the Commission on European Contract Law. Under the chairmanship of C. von Bar, since 1999 this Group has taken on the comprehensive task of preparing European principles not just on contract law, but also of the entire law of obligations and certain aspects of property law. The result of this work is contained in the DCFR.[44]

It is clear that the EU Commission took a muted approach to the vast scope of the DCFR. Clearly, there is no current agenda to develop a European Civil Code, and the DCFR is only to be used as a 'source of inspiration' in the development of further EU rules.[45] The Commission issued a Proposal for a Regulation on a Common

---

[41] The results of the deliberations of this group were presented in 2007: see Research Group on the Existing EC Private Law (Acquis Group), *Principles of the Existing EC Contract Law (Acquis Principles), Part I* (2007). See also R Schulze, 'Die "Acquis-Grundregeln" und der Gemeinsame Referenzrahmen' (2007) 15 *ZEuP* 731; HC Grigoleit and L Tomasic, 'Acquis Principles' in Max Planck Enc. (2012) 10. A revised version of the *acquis* rules was published under the same name as Part II in 2010. The European Union then proposed an extensive directive on consumer rights drawn up on this basis. It was based on the principle of full harmonisation, and would have removed the right for states to retain a stronger level of protection than envisaged in the proposed directive. This restriction was unacceptable for many Member States. The result was a Directive dated 25 October 2011 on consumer rights that—applying the principle of full harmonisation—only merged the two directives on doorstep selling and distance contracts; furthermore, extensive information requirements were introduced for all consumer contracts in accordance with the principle of minimum harmonisation. For greater detail, see O Unger, 'Die Richtlinie über die Rechte der Verbraucher' (2012) 20 *ZEuP* 270.

[42] See Communication from the Commission to the European Parliament and the Council of 12 February 2003: 'A more coherent European contract law—An action plan' (COM 2003, 68).

[43] For detail, see M Schmidt-Kessel, 'Study Group on a European Civil Code' in Max Planck Enc. (2012) 1611.

[44] See C von Bar, E Clive, and H Schulte-Nölke (eds), *Principles, Definitions and Model Rules of European Private Law, Draft Common Frame of Reference (DCFR)*, Interim Outline Edition (2008). It includes rules on the general law of contract, the law governing contracts of sale, leasing, services and security agreements, the law governing torts, unjust enrichment and the management of another's affairs without his consent (*negotiorum gestio*), and also certain aspects of property law. The full version of the DCFR, including a detailed comparative analysis of the individual rules, was published in 2009 in six volumes under the same title. See R Zimmermann, 'Common Frame of Reference' in Max Planck Enc. (2012) 261.

[45] Communication of EU Council of 18 April 2004, published in (2008) 16 *ZEuP* 880.

European Sales Law (CESL) in 2011.[46] But this was withdrawn in 2014, mainly because many Member States (including France, Germany, Austria, the Netherlands, the United Kingdom, and Finland) regarded it as inappropriate. This is perhaps regrettable. The proposed CESL was intended to apply to cross-border transactions for the sale of goods, for the supply of digital content, and for related services. It was primarily aimed at consumer sales contracts, and applied to contracts between traders only if at least one of the parties was a small or medium-sized enterprise as defined in the proposed text. The essential point was that the Regulation was only supposed to be an optional instrument. It would have applied only if the parties had reached an express agreement to make the CESL applicable to their cross-border transaction. It would certainly have been most interesting to find out if the CESL would have been able to successfully compete against the national laws on which the parties might also have agreed under the applicable rules of international private law. Nevertheless, the CESL is interesting here for comparative purposes, as it includes not only rules on sale of goods, but also addresses rules that are of overall interest in contract law, such as rules about the conclusion and interpretation of contracts, about rescission in cases of mistake, deceit, or duress, about a fairness control of standardised contract conditions, and about the termination of the contract and liability of the party in breach. The CESL also includes the consumer protection elements of existing directives, which have also been partially improved and extended.

D. A European Code of Contract Law?

No one should bank upon the European Union drawing up a 'European Civil Code' or 'European Code on Contract' in the near future. Not only is there no clear competence at the European level, but there is also no political will in Member States that would be needed to create such a competence and pass the enabling legislative acts. This is not to say that matters are quiet on this front: many people are engaged in looking at the question whether further harmonisation or unification of contract law would be justified by sufficient practical requirements, and in which areas, on what basis, and by which procedure such a project might be realised.

When the PECL were published to great acclaim twenty years ago, many observers had the impression that it would not be long before a European Code on Contract would be enacted. The book edited by A Hartkamp in 1995 with the title *Towards a European Civil Code* was based on the idea that areas of European private law other than contract law would also allow for harmonised solutions and sooner or later for a codification of some sort or another.[47] This is also why the Study Group on a European Civil Code has been devoting its efforts to a comprehensive formulation of the principles of European private law since 1999, and which were presented to the public in the DCFR.

---

[46] COM 2011, 635.
[47] See A Hartkamp et al., (n 5). The opening essay by E Hondius, 'Towards a European Civil Code' gives an overview of the more than forty contributions to the volume, references the huge volume of literature on the subject, and comes to the conclusion that 'contract law is ready for codification' (13).

Of course, the topic attracts a lot of criticism.[48] Some argue that each country is so committed to its own legal traditions, values, and preconceptions that any attempt at harmonisation or unification of the written law would never work and is a mere chimera.[49] Some commentators also take the view that, even within the European Union, no country should be required to sacrifice its legal traditions on the altar of European legal harmonisation, not least when the sacrifices are based on considerations that do not really matter.[50] The EU Commission has put much emphasis on the argument that the advantage lies in saving transaction costs that arise for each party in cross-border business deals. These transaction costs are incurred by parties who—sometimes with the assistance of lawyers—seek certainty about the law of the different possible national jurisdictions, choose the cheapest jurisdiction from their own perspective, negotiate with their counterparty on the applicable jurisdiction, and—if all these costs are disproportionate—might even decide not to undertake the transaction at all.[51] It is also argued that concluding cross-border transactions is affected to a major extent by *other* factors, such as different tax regulations, different administrative requirements and differences of language, culture, customs, usages, and enforcement procedures. There is also the argument that many parties are not at all interested in the applicable law. They protect themselves *ex ante*, for example, by contracting only with parties with a good reputation or whose reliability they can assess through websites or on-line feedback mechanisms rating the quality of contract performance. If they are nevertheless disappointed, they will not be willing to take costly legal remedies made available by the applicable law. Even if the alleged transaction costs would actually arise, they would be far overshadowed by the cost of applying rules that would be uniform across

---

[48] For a comprehensive overview of the grounds for criticism (along with many references in the literature) see R Zimmermann, 'Codification, The Civilian Experience Reconsidered on the Eve of a Common European Sales Law' [2012] *ERCL* 367. See also JM Smits, 'Law Making in the European Union: On Globalization and Contract Law in Divergent Legal Cultures' (2007) 67 *La. LR* 1181; JM Smits, 'European Private Law: A Plea for a Spontaneous Legal Order' in D Curtin, JM Smits, A Klip, and J McCahery, *European Integration and Law* (2006) 55. On the objections put forward by English lawyers against further harmonisation or unification of European contract law, see for example E McKendrick, 'Harmonisation of European Contract Law: The State We Are In' in S Vogenauer and S Weatherill (eds), *The Harmonisation of European Contract Law* (2006) 5.

[49] In particular P Legrand, 'European Legal Systems Are Not Converging' (1996) 45 *ICLQ* 52; P Legrand, 'Against a European Civil Code' (1997) 60 *Mod. LR* 44. See also T Weir, 'Die Sprachen des Europäischen Rechts, Eine skeptische Betrachtung' (1995) 3 *ZEuP* 368. In particular, Legrand sees the differences between Civil Law and Common Law as unbridgeable. The contrary view is presented by R Zimmermann, 'Der europäische Charakter des englischen Rechts, Historische Verbindungen zwischen civil law und common law' (1993) 1 *ZEuP* 4; R Zimmermann, *Die Europäisierung des Privatrechts und die Rechtsvergleichung* (2006) 32ff.

[50] See G Cornu, 'Un Code civil n'est pas un instrument communautaire' [2002] D. 351; Y Lequette, 'Le Code européen est de retour' [2011] *RDC* 1028; T Genicon, 'Commission européenne et droit des contrats' [2011] *RDC* 1050. But there are also other viewpoints. See C Witz, 'Plaidoyer pour un Code européen des obligations' [2000] D. 79; B Fauvarque-Cosson, 'Faut-il un Code civil européen?' [2002] *Rev trim civ* 463.

[51] See the recitals for the Proposal for a Regulation on a Common European Sales Law (CESL, above, n 46): There is an extensive elaboration on the argument about transaction costs which concludes that '[d]ifferences in national contract laws therefore constitute barriers which prevent consumers and traders from reaping the benefits of the internal market. Those contract-law related barriers would be significantly reduced if contracts could be based on a single uniform set of contract law rules irrespective of where parties are established' (Recital no. 6).

Europe, but until now exist only on paper, are untested by the courts, and might be interpreted differently by them. It has also been noted that parties wanting to undertake the most important type of cross-border transaction—for the international sale of goods—can already choose to apply the CISG. Furthermore, regardless of the law applicable to a contract, pursuant to art. 6 of the Rome I Regulation a party can always rely on the mandatory consumer protection rules in force in the state where the party is domiciled.[52]

It is generally recognised that a measure to harmonise European law is not justified merely because there are differences between the laws in Member States. Any such measure to set aside differences must serve the purpose of improving the functioning of the single market.[53] It is sometimes asked whether the organs of the European Union take this restriction with sufficient seriousness, or if they just regard any legal difference as an unacceptable affront. In fact, it can be shown that many countries can have different legal orders where no one doubts the functioning of an internal market. The United States and Canada are prime examples: each of the fifty states in the United States and each of the eleven Canadian provinces have jurisdiction over their Civil Law, and thus over contract law. So contract law will be different in Louisiana and in Massachusetts, and will be different in Québec and in Ontario. There are also differences between English and Scottish contract law, but the United Kingdom has a perfectly functioning internal market. It is true that there is uniform law in all these countries to the extent that the federal legislature made use of the competence allotted to it under the constitution, or the individual states or provinces have seen fit to enact legislation based on a uniform model. But this only occurs where compelling reasons for certain uniform rules can be shown and sufficient political support can be mustered in the individual state—obviously more stringent conditions than appear to apply in Europe at present.[54] In fact, the United States can be seen as a gigantic laboratory for legal policy in which any state can move forward in any direction by legislation or judicial decision, and thus 'compete' with other states by setting an encouraging or

---

[52] However, consumer protection law varies from country to country, not least because EU directives normally only prescribe a minimum level of harmonisation. This leads to difficulties for those companies wishing to offer their goods or services across Europe under the same terms and conditions. Such difficulties could be avoided if the companies could agree with consumers that the CESL would be applicable: in such a case, the consumer protection as defined in the CESL would apply.

[53] See the judgment of the European Court of Justice on the Directive regulating the advertising of tobacco products: Case C-376/98, *Germany v. Parliament and Council*, Collection of cases decided by the ECJ 2000 I-8419 (mn. 84). The judgment refers to the competence rules under art. 95 Treaty of Rome, now replaced by art. 114 TFEU.

[54] For more details, see H Kötz, 'Contract Law in Europe and the United States: Legal Unification in the Civil Law and Common Law' (2012) 27 *Tulane European & Civil Law Forum* 1; R Hyland, 'American Private Legislatures and the Process Discussion' in A Hartkamp et al. (eds), (n 5) 71. The objection is sometimes raised that the laws of the individual American states are all based on the Common Law and therefore resemble each other much more than the laws of the Member States of the European Union. It is also said that all American lawyers speak the same language and that a strong unifying effect emanates from a common legal culture (such as uniform legal training in the law schools across the whole country). All that is correct, but raises the question of why no one in the United States is demanding a uniform contract law, or even a 'model contract law' that the individual states might or might not adopt. It could also be said that what is required in Europe should not be the premature enactment of legislation, but a harmonisation of 'legal culture', for example by a harmonisation across Europe of the training of lawyers and academic discussions.

horrifying example.⁵⁵ So there are good reasons why Europe might want to create harmonised European law in some areas, but to also allow national contract laws to remain applicable so that parties can decide which solutions should be winners in the regulatory competition between national and European legal systems.⁵⁶ This was also the path chosen for the Proposal for a Common European Sales Law.

Concerns can also be raised as regards the consumer protection rules laid down in the *acquis communautaire* and taken up in the DCFR and the Proposal for a Common European Sales Law. The general view seems to be that these rules might be supplemented in some places, tweaked here or there, and be freed of the odd inconsistency, but that they no longer stand in need of a fundamental revision and can therefore be paraded as an assured statement of European legal uniformity. But that is a fallacy.⁵⁷ There are, for example, good arguments for asserting that the *acquis communautaire* allows consumers a right of cancellation in cases where, in truth, convincing reasons are missing.⁵⁸ It is also doubtful whether the extensive duty to provide information that companies must comply with in consumer contracts is not too extensive. Naturally, there are contract clauses that judges deem to be unreasonable and may thus avoid. But the reasons for this are not—as so often stipulated in the *acquis communautaire*—that the consumer is the 'weaker party' and must at all costs be 'protected'. The real reason for the setting aside of such clauses is that the consumer has been in a situation where he had perfectly rational reasons not to consider the clause and was thus unable to make a reasonably considered decision about it.⁵⁹

We will repeatedly come back to such thoughts in the following chapters. The priority is to look at aspects of contract law in European countries, and to find out whether they allow us to derive general principles for a common European law of contract. This is the same aim set for the PECL and other international sets of rules, and so we will consider those rules too. There are good reasons why this text takes the national rules on contract law as its starting point. The old principle of the Enlightenment that all law should be based on legislative texts has long been laid to rest—and this also applies to European law. Law is also in the minds of the lawyers and academics, and it follows that a common European contract law will not come to life until, as Helmut Coing said many years ago, 'the lawyers in our countries find a way to create a common understanding, a mutual intellectual tradition that can do justice to the unified norms

---

⁵⁵ Regulatory competition is also the subject of intense discussion in Europe. See, for example, EM Kieninger, 'Competition between Legal Systems' in Max Planck Enc. (2012) 301. See also the critical discussion by S Vogenauer, 'Regulatory Competition through Choice of Contract Law and Choice of Forum in Europe: Theory and Evidence' (2013) 21 *ERPL* 13 (with further evidence).

⁵⁶ Each Member State would be free to amend their national law (by legislation or in the courts), to make adjustments for new needs or circumstances and thus to increase its attractiveness and improve its opportunities to succeed in the forum of regulatory competition. Nor should one forget that the national jurisdictions can react more quickly than the European Union, because amending a European legislative text presents an enormous challenge, not least requiring the involvement of the other Member States. Thus European rules are always in danger of becoming 'set in stone'.

⁵⁷ See in detail H Eidenmüller, F Faust, HC Grigoleit, N Jansen, G Wagner, and R Zimmermann, *Revision des Verbraucher-acquis* (2011); N Jansen, 'Revision des Acquis communautaire' (2012) 20 *ZEuP* 741.

⁵⁸ See chapter 11, pp. 191ff.   ⁵⁹ See chapter 8.C, pp. 136ff.

and ensure their equal application'.[60] Unfortunately, most law faculties in Europe continue to teach the national law of the country in which they are situated only. This is deeply to be regretted. Yet, for this very reason, it makes sense for this book to start from the position of national laws and on that basis to recommend an understanding of the European dimension of the issue. There are many areas that even the strictest prescriptions of a legislature cannot reach, for example where general abstract principles are proposed—such as the idea that contracting parties should act 'reasonably', follow the requirements of 'good faith', or disclose information wherever the other party regards it as useful, important, or material. Few will dissent from such general principles, and they may also seem clear and will often have been accepted in the civil codes of many national legal systems. On the other hand, such general principles are susceptible to widely differing interpretations—which depend on lawyers' traditional patterns of thought and frames of mind, on their working styles, methods of interpretation and value preferences, and on the different procedures traditionally applied by the courts in the various countries. Developing a feeling for such matters is not easy, but indicators can be found in the national legal orders. That is where we must start, because it is the national legal orders that develop the stuff from which European contract law is to be made.

---

[60] H Coing, 'Ius Commune, nationale Kodifikation und Internationale Abkommen: Drei historische Formen der Rechtsvereinheitlichung' in *Le nuove frontiere del diritto e il problema dell'unificazione, Atti del Congreso Internazionale di Bari* I (1979) 171, 192.

2

Negotiation and Formation of Contracts

A. The Consent of the Parties	17
B. The Offer	19
I. Definiteness of the offer	19
II. Intention to be bound	19
III. Effect of the offer	21
IV. Termination of the offer	21
1. Refusal or failure to accept an offer	21
2. Expiry of time for acceptance	22
3. Revocation of the offer	22
4. Death or incapacity	24
C. Acceptance	25
I. Declaration of acceptance	25
1. Acceptor's intention to be bound	25
2. Effectiveness of declaration of acceptance	25
II. Acceptance by conduct	26
1. Acceptance by commencing performance	26
2. Acceptance by silence	27
III. Qualified acceptance	29
IV. Delayed acceptance	31
D. Liability for Breaking Off Negotiations	32

A. The Consent of the Parties

At the very outset of their studies, law students are told that contracts need consent, and that consent is always manifested in two declarations: an *offer* by one party, matched by an *acceptance* by the other. In fact, it is by no means the case that contracts are always formed through the mechanism of offer and acceptance. Certainly, the requisite consent of the parties is manifested when an offer is accepted, but any other conduct of the parties suffices if it adequately reveals their intention to be bound to the contract. For a long time, there was no practical need to force consent into the structure of offer and acceptance because parties always made their contracts face to face. In Rome, for example, contractual obligations originally had to be made by *stipulatio*, for which both parties needed to be physically present. And even when this formality was dropped, contracts generally continued to be made in the presence of the parties. The Roman jurists therefore never came to think it necessary for consent to be expressed in two separate declarations of 'offer' and 'acceptance'.[1]

The need for this only arose after there was a reliable postal service, and contracting at a distance became possible and commonplace. When contracts are negotiated

---

[1] See R Zimmermann, *The Law of Obligations, Roman Foundations of the Civilian Tradition* (1990) 563f.

and concluded by correspondence between persons living at some distance from each other, their declarations are given sequentially, and it takes time for each of these declarations to reach its addressee. This raises several questions: how, when, and where is the consent of the parties achieved? When does an offer or acceptance become irrevocable? When does a revocation become effective?

In all modern legal systems, the rules on the formation of contracts by offer and acceptance essentially stem from the eighteenth century. They all give the impression that offer and acceptance is the *only* way a contract can come about,[2] but this is not correct. In many cases where a contract has unquestionably been formed, it is impossible, unrealistic, or arbitrary to regard the conduct of one party as an offer and that of the other as an acceptance. Take the case of a sale of land where the document is drafted by a notary and signed by the parties simultaneously: it would be hard to say that one of the parties is making an 'offer' to the other, and that the latter is declaring 'acceptance' of the offer. When a customer pays cash for a pack of cigarettes, it is quite clear that the parties are in agreement, but it is hardly helpful (except to budding lawyers) to analyse the proceedings into 'offer' and 'acceptance', and discuss whether it is the seller who makes the offer by handing over the cigarettes, or the buyer by putting the money on the counter. Another situation not easily accommodated in the procrustean bed of 'offer' and 'acceptance' is where agreement is reached only after a long period of negotiation, with offers and counteroffers going in both directions. It is difficult enough to decide precisely when the contract jelled, but the idea that contracts come about through offer and acceptance does nothing to facilitate the task.

Accordingly, when parties actually do express their agreement in two separate declarations that can be described as an offer, withdrawal of offer, counteroffer, acceptance, or revocation of acceptance, this is rather a special case; in practice, however, this special case is very important, so the following pages are concerned with it.

The rules of offer and acceptance have received a great deal of attention from comparative lawyers.[3] It has now been possible to unify such rules at an international level as regards the international sales of goods. The Vienna Convention on Contracts for the International Sale of Goods (CISG) regulates the 'Formation of the Contract' in arts. 14 to 24, and frequent reference will be made to the CISG in the following pages.

---

[2] For example, §§ 145ff. BGB; art. 3ff. OR; art. 6:217ff. BW; and art. 185ff. Greek Civil Code all speak only of the formation of contract by offer and acceptance. So does art. 1113 *Code civil*, which forms part of the new rules on offer and acceptance introduced in 2016. The situation is different under art. 2:211 PECL: 'A contract may be concluded either by the acceptance of an offer or by conduct of the parties that is sufficient to show agreement.' Similar also in art. 2:211 PECL. See also N Jansen and R Zimmermann, 'Vertragsschluss und Irrtum im europäischen Vertragsrecht' (2010) 210 *AcP* 196, 225 (n 154).

[3] R Schlesinger, *Formation of Contract, A Study of the Common Core of Legal Systems* (2 vols., 1968). See also the comparative law contributions from A von Mehren in *Int.Enc.Comp.L.* vol. VII/1 chapters 2–4; R Sacco, 'Formation of Contracts' in A Hartkamp et al. (eds), *Towards a European Civil Code* (4th edn, 2011) 483; J Schmidt, *Der Vertragsschluss, Ein Vergleich zwischen dem deutschen, französichen und englischen Recht* (2013).

B. The Offer

An offer must be such that if it is accepted, a contract is formed. It follows that an effective offer arises only if, as art. 14 CISG states, it is 'sufficiently definite' (see I below) and also 'indicates the intention of the offeror to be bound in case of acceptance' (see II below). Other points to consider are the time when the offer becomes effective (see III below) and the circumstances under which it expires (see IV below).

I. Definiteness of the offer[4]

Merely to inform another person that one is ready to negotiate or conclude a contract does not constitute an offer. An offer must be 'definite': it must specify the essentials of the proposed deal with sufficient precision that a valid contract will be formed if the addressee accepts it.[5] Thus, to be sufficiently definite, an offer to buy or sell must specify the thing and the price.[6] It will be sufficient, however, if the essentials of the contract can be rendered definite—where a reasonable person in the position of the offeree could tell from the context, in the light of relevant trade practice or the past dealings of the parties, what price, quantity, and quality of goods, or other essentials the offeror had in mind.

A contract of sale may even be valid although the price is neither stated nor inferable from the surrounding circumstances.[7] But this will be so only if it emerges from the negotiations as a whole that the parties have agreed that the contract is to be valid, notwithstanding that the price is to remain open for the time being. It is immaterial that at some stage in the dealings a proposal was made which fell short of being an 'offer' for want of a definite price. Consent is crucial for the conclusion of a contract, but it need not satisfy the requirements of 'offer' or 'acceptance'.[8]

II. Intention to be bound[9]

A contract only comes about if the parties intended to be contractually bound, and have manifested this intention in some perceptible manner. It follows that when a contract arises through offer and acceptance, the offer must make it clear that if it is

---

[4] See the extensive comparative materials in Schlesinger (n 3) 84ff, 431ff.

[5] So expressed, for example, in J Ghestin, *Traité de droit civil, La formation du contrat* (1993) no. 291ff; see also J Schmidt, *Négociation et conclusion de contrats* (1982) no. 72ff; See now art. 1114 *Code civil*: An offer must state 'les éléments essentiels du contrat envisagé'.

[6] See art. 14(1)(2) CISG; art. 2:201(1) PECL; art. 2.1.2 PICC.

[7] See art. 55 CISG. In such a case, 'the parties are considered, in the absence of any indication to the contrary, to have impliedly made reference to the price generally charged at the time of the conclusion of the contract for such goods sold under comparable circumstances in the trade concerned'. See also art. 1583 *Code civil*.

[8] See above, p. 18.—The apparent contradiction between art. 14 and art. 55 CISG is considered correctly and in detail by E Bucher, 'Preisvereinbarung als Voraussetzung der Vertragsgültigkeit beim Kauf' in *Mélanges Piotet* (1990) 371 and E Bucher (ed), *Wiener Kaufrecht* (1991) 53. See also P Schlechtriem and I Schwenzer, *Kommentar CISG* (5th edn, 2008) art. 14 mn. 19ff.

[9] Detailed comparative material may be found in Schlesinger (n 3) 77ff, 325ff, 645ff.

accepted, the offeror intends to be bound. In the absence of an intention to be bound, in law there is no offer at all, just an invitation for the recipient to make an offer, or say if he is ready to start bargaining (*invitatio ad offerendum*, invitation to treat, *offre de pourparlers*).

To distinguish an offer from an *invitatio offerendi* is easy enough if the proposal describes itself either as a 'binding offer' or else as *sans engagement, senza impegno, freibleibend*, without obligation, 'subject to agreement' or in other words to the same effect.[10] In the absence of any such indication, it depends on how the proposal would be understood by a reasonable person in the position of the addressee, in particular whether the addressee should have realised that the person making the proposal had a justified interest in reserving his position in the event of a positive response. This may be so, for instance, where the addressee knows that the proposal has been sent to a lot of other people simultaneously. In such a case, the proposal can hardly be an offer in the legal sense, since otherwise every addressee could make a contract by accepting, and the proponent would be liable in damages to all those it was unable to supply or satisfy. So where price lists and catalogues are distributed, or advertisements are mailed out in print or electronically—indeed whenever a proposal is sent to a large number of persons—it is generally held that there is no offer at all.[11]

This principle is subject to many exceptions. Courts in France hold that where someone has advertised goods for sale in a newspaper, a contract is formed with the first person to fulfil the conditions of the offer,[12] unless the buyer lacks particular attributes that it is reasonable for the advertiser to insist on, such as solvency or reliability.[13] In England, when manufacturers advertised in newspapers that they would pay £100 to any reader who contracted influenza after inhaling their allegedly prophylactic 'Carbolic Smoke Ball', this was held to be an offer.[14] When a tradesman displays

---

[10] A decision of the *Bundesgerichtshof* of 8 Mar. 1984, [1984] *NJW* 1885, is very instructive: the defendant had responded to the plaintiff's request by offering to supply an airplane at a stipulated rental 'without obligation and subject to availability'. In view of the particular circumstances of the case, the court held that the defendant's proposal was not simply an invitation to treat but an actual offer, admittedly subject to revocation. It was unnecessary to decide whether the offer was revocable even after acceptance since, even if it were, it needed to be revoked immediately after the acceptance was received, and the defendant had failed to do this. In the absence of a reservation such as the defendant here had made, an offer is in principle irrevocable in German law and in several other systems in Europe, but by no means all. See further below, pp. 22ff.

[11] See art. 14(2) CISG.

[12] Civ. 28 Nov. 1968, *JCP* 1969.II.15797; Civ. 13 June 1972, Bull.cass. 1972.III. no. 392. See also Ghestin (n 5) no. 297; Schmidt (n 5) no. 120ff.

[13] Dutch law starts from the principle that an offer to the public is binding in the same way as if it had been made to a particular person. Similarly, art. 1114 *Code civil* makes no distinction between offers made to a person '*déterminée ou indéterminée*'. An exception is made, however, where it appears from the circumstances that the personal qualities of the offeree are of interest to the offeror. In HR 10 April 1981, *NedJur* 1981, 532 the court held that an 'advertisement offering to sell a specific property at a certain price does, in principle, not qualify to be interpreted by potential offerees as anything else than an invitation to enter into negotiations, whereby matters such as the price, additional conditions of the purchase and the prospective buyer may be of importance.'

[14] *Carlill v. Carbolic Smoke Ball Co.* [1892] 2 QB 484; [1893] 1 QB 256. The manufacturers' intention to be bound was inferable from their statement in the advertisement that they had deposited £1,000 in a named bank 'showing our sincerity in the matter'. For an instructive and amusing article on this decision, giving full details of the case and the very interesting social and economic background, see AWB Simpson, 'Quackery and Contract Law, The Case of the Carbolic Smoke Ball' (1985) 14 *J Leg Stud* 345; AWB Simpson, *Leading Cases in the Common Law* (1995) 259ff.

goods in a shop window with a price tag attached, different positions are adopted. Generally, this is treated as a mere *invitatio ad offerendum*, but art. 7(3) OR provides that 'the display of goods marked with the price is normally to be seen as an offer'. Article 2:201(3) PECL goes further: it is presumed that there is an offer if a professional supplier in a public advertisement or a catalogue, or by a display of goods, makes an offer to sell or supply at that price. However, the offer is only valid until the stock of goods, or the supplier's capacity to supply the service, is exhausted. However, the professional supplier would then no longer have the opportunity to refuse to enter into a contract if the customer is regarded as insolvent or unreliable, or if for some other reason the supplier has good reasons not to wish to supply the customer.[15]

III. Effect of the offer

An offer takes effect as soon as its recipient could, by accepting the offer, conclude a contract. This moment occurs when the offer 'reaches' its addressee. An offer made verbally or by telephone reaches the addressee as soon as he hears it. An offer made by other means reaches the recipient when it enters his area of control and he can inform himself of it;[16] thus an offer made by post reaches the addressee when it is placed in his letterbox or post-office box, or is handed to someone he has authorised to receive it on his behalf.

There is general agreement that an offer is ineffective if notice of its withdrawal reaches the offeree before the offer or at the same time.[17]

IV. Termination of the offer

An offer ceases to be effective when it can no longer be accepted so as to produce a contract.

1. *Refusal or failure to accept an offer*—If an offer is rejected by the offeree, it expires immediately the rejection reaches the offeror,[18] and this is true even if the time fixed for acceptance is still running.

---

[15] See H Köhler, 'Das Verfahren des Vertragsschlusses' in J Basedow (ed), *Europäische Vertragsrechtsvereinheitlichung und deutsches Recht* (2000) 33, 36ff. See also GH Treitel, *The Law of Contract* (13th edn, by E Peel, 2011) no. 2-006ff; J Smits, *Contract Law, A Comparative Introduction* (2014) 44ff.

[16] See art. 15(1) 24 CISG; § 130 BGB; art. 3:37(3) BW; art. 167 Greek Civil Code; art. 224 Portuguese Civil Code; art. 61(1) Polish Civil Code. To like effect are art. 1.10(2) and (3), 2.1.3 (1) PICC; art. 1:303 PECL. See also in detail, M Hennemann, 'Zugang von Erklärungen um europäischen Vertragsrecht' (2013) 21 *ZEuP* 565.

[17] See art. 15(2) UN Sales Law; § 130(1)(2) BGB; art. 2.1.3 (2) PICC; art. 1115 *Code civil*; art. 3:37(5) BW; § 7 Swedish Contract Law; art. 230(2) Portuguese Civil Code; art. 61 sent. 2 Polish Civil Code. But see also art. 9(1) OR: an offer is considered to have been withdrawn if the addressee learns of the withdrawal before he learns of the offer itself, even though the withdrawal may have 'reached' him after the offer.

[18] See art. 17 CISG; art. 2.1.5 PICC; Treitel (n 15) no. 2-062; § 146 BGB; art. 187 Greek Civil Code; art. 6:221(2) BW; § 5 Swedish Contract Law; art. 33 CESL.

A verbal offer expires if not accepted immediately, or at any rate by the end of the discussion, unless the offeror has agreed that it may be accepted at a later time.[19]

2. *Expiry of time for acceptance*—An offer expires at the end of the period within which acceptance must take place.

The period in question may be set by the offeror, but if no such period is fixed, the offer expires after a 'reasonable' time.[20] What is reasonable depends on the interests of the parties. The offeror's interest is that the period be short: not only because freedom of action is limited while the offer remains open—for example, the offeror's ability to sell the goods to someone else—but also because, if the offer was to buy or sell at a fixed price, the offeror bears the risk of market fluctuation during the period of the offer. The offeree, on the other hand, has a comparable interest in the period being long: the longer the offer remains open, the more time the offeree has to consider whether or not to accept and to profit from movements of the market. Thus, in deciding how long a period is 'reasonable', one must consider not only the time it takes for the offer and acceptance to be transmitted by the means which the offeror has selected, but all the circumstances of the transaction. If the price of the goods or services is fluid, the offeree's time for reflection must be shortened in case the offeree is speculating at the expense of the offeror.

3. *Revocation of the offer*[21]—There is no general rule on whether an offer may be revoked by the offeror before it has expired by rejection or lapse of time.

Under English law, revocation is permitted in principle: an offer may be revoked at any time until it has been accepted. This is true even if the offeror undertook to keep it open for a given period of time.[22] This rule is said to follow from the Common Law doctrine of consideration, whereby in the absence of a formal deed a promisor is only bound if the other party provided or promised something in return (see chapter 4). Accordingly, for an offer to be irrevocable the offeror has to grant an 'option'—that is, make a contract for reward to keep it open (normally for a specified period). This is a cumbrous and expensive procedure, and it is often impractical to arrange an option or have a deed drawn up. Yet revocation of the offer within the period allowed for acceptance may lead to inequitable results if the offeree has already acted upon the offer, such as builders do when they submit a tender for a project on the basis of prices quoted in a subcontractor's offer. Even English commentators find it unsatisfactory that the offeror's stated intention to keep the offer open for a specified period does not bind the

---

[19] See art. 18(2)(3) CISG art. 2.1.7 sent. 2 PICC; § 147(1) BGB; § 862 sent. 2 ABGB; art. 5 OR; § 3(2) Swedish Contract Law.

[20] Article 18(2)(2) CISG; art. 2.1.7 sent. 1 PICC; *Ramsgate Victoria Hotel Co. v. Montefiore* (1866) LR 1 Ex. 109, and Treitel (n 15) no. 2-064f; art. 1117 *Code civil*; § 147(2) BGB; § 862 sent. 2 ABGB; art. 5 OR; art. 189 sent. 2 Greek Civil Code; art. 6:221(1) BW; § 3(1) Swedish Contract Law; art. 1326(2) *Codice civile*; art. 66(2)(2) Polish Civil Code; art. 211(2)(3) Hungarian Civil Code.

[21] For comparative law on the topic, see von Mehren (n 3) vol. VII chapter 9, 134ff.

[22] *Dickinson v. Dodds* (1876) 2 Ch.D. 463 (CA). The effect of stating a limit of time is to ensure that the offer lapses at the end of it, not that it may not be revoked earlier. See *Routledge v. Grant* (1828) 130 Eng.Rep. 920; *Byrne v. Leon van Tienhoven* (1880) 5 CPD 344: 'There is no doubt that an offer can be withdrawn before it is accepted, and it is immaterial whether the offer is expressed to be open for acceptance for a given time or not.' (Lindley LJ at p. 347). See also Treitel (n 15) no. 2-058.

offeror unless he has received consideration for an option contract. English law does consider the interests of the offeree in one respect. This is the mailbox rule, whereby acceptance by letter or telegram takes effect when the offeree posts the letter in the post box or hands the acceptance over at the Post Office, rather than at the later time when it reaches the offeror.[23] But while it is certainly true that the mailbox rule has the advantage of shortening the time within which an offer can be revoked—since revocation comes too late if it arrives after the offeree has posted his acceptance and thus formed the contract—it is far from obvious why an acceptance should be effective any earlier than an offer or any other declaration of intention (see above page 21).

In French law, an offer has rather more binding force. Under art. 1116(1) *Code civil*, an offer cannot be withdrawn before the expiry of a period the offeror himself fixed for acceptance or, though no time for acceptance was fixed, before the expiry of a '*délai raisonnable*'.[24] On the other hand, if the offer is withdrawn before the expiry of the period stated by the offeror or before the expiry of the *délai raisonnable*, a contract can no longer be formed by the offeree's acceptance. In that case, the offeree is only entitled to claim damages from the offeror under the law of tort, compensating him not for what he would have enjoyed had the contract come into being, but only for the harm suffered by his reliance on the offer remaining open.[25]

Offers have the greatest effect under German, Swiss, and Austrian law. As soon as the offer reaches the offeree, the offeror is 'bound' in the sense that revocation is impossible and ineffectual until the expiry of any period fixed in the offer or, if no period is fixed, then a reasonable period.[26] This binding effect can be excluded if the offeror describes the offer as *freibleibend*, or not binding. Such a formula allows the offeror to retain the freedom to revoke, and it may even be so construed as to allow revocation even after acceptance has reached him (and the contract is in principle already formed). The court may, however, hold that a 'non-binding offer' is not in law an offer at all, but only an invitation to treat.[27]

---

[23] *Adams* v. *Lindsell* (1818) 106 Eng.Rep. 250, considered in detail in Treitel (n 15) no. 2-027ff. and DM Evans, 'The Anglo-American Mailing Rule' (1966) 15 *ICLQ* 553. But see also *Entores* v. *Miles Far East Corp.* [1955] 2 QB 327 and *Brinkibon Ltd.* v. *Stahag Stahl* [1983] 2 AC 34: if acceptance is communicated by *telex*, the contract is made where the message arrives, not where it is sent.

[24] See Civ. 17 Dec. 1958, D. 1959.1.33 and Colmar, 4 Feb. 1936, D.H. 1936, 187: A supplier withdrew his offer after the offeree, in reliance on the offer, had put in a tender and had it accepted. The court held that an offer was binding 'dès lors qu'il résulte d'un accord exprès ou tacite, mais indiscutable, qu'elle a été formulée pour être maintenue pendant un délai déterminé'. In that case, however, no such agreement was established: when the offeror made the offer he did not know that the offeree was going to use it as the basis for a tender. In Italian law, the offeree has a claim for damages for the loss caused to him by the withdrawal of the offer if 'with no knowledge of the withdrawal of the offer he in good faith started to perform the contract' (art. 1328f. *Codice civile*).

[25] See art. 1116(2) and (3) *Code civil*.

[26] § 145 BGB; art. 3 and 5 OR; § 862 sent. 3 ABGB; art. 185f. Greek Civil Code; art. 230 Portuguese Civil Code. In the *ius commune*, the withdrawal of an offer was effective but gave the offeree a claim for damages, as in French law today—see Windscheid, *Lehrbuch des Pandektenrechts* vol. II (1865) 307. But the draftsmen of the BGB were of the opinion that 'commerce [requires] that business be done smoothly and quickly, whereas experience shows that damages claims lead to tricky lawsuits with uncertain results and have a chilling effect on trade'. See *Motive zu dem Entwurfe eines BGB* I, p. 166.

[27] See BGH 8 Mar. 1984 (n 10). See also art. 6:219 sent. 2 BW, according to which a 'non-binding' offer may be withdrawn even after acceptance, provided that this is done 'immediately' after the acceptance.

The three systems thus start out from very different viewpoints. In practice, however, the results may not be so very different—apart from the unacceptable English rule that the offeror may freely revoke an offer which he has undertaken, even in writing, to keep the offer open for a stated period. It does not make much actual difference whether one starts from the principle that an offer is binding, as in Germany, but that offers stated to be 'non-binding' are freely revocable, or from the principle adopted in France that offers are in principle revocable but that revocation may be sanctioned in damages if it frustrates the justified expectations of the other party. It was consequently possible to come to a sensible compromise when the uniform sales law was being drafted. Article 16(1) CISG starts from the position that offers are revocable, provided that revocation reaches the offeree before dispatch of the acceptance (as under the mailbox rule). But this does not apply, according to art. 16(2), if the offer 'indicates, whether by stating a fixed time for acceptance or otherwise, that it is irrevocable;[28] or ... if it was reasonable for the offeree to rely on the offer as being irrevocable and the offeree has acted in reliance on the offer'.[29]

4. *Death or incapacity*—May an offer still be accepted if the offeror dies after making it? Suppose it is the offeree who dies after the offer is sent off: may the heirs accept the offer and conclude the contract? The answers given in case of death will apply equally to cases of incapacitation.

Several legal systems accept that in principle an offer is acceptable despite intervening death or incapacity.[30] Other systems adopt the opposite viewpoint, whereby the offer lapses on the death or incapacity of either of the parties, unless there are special reasons for holding otherwise. In Italian law, an offer can be accepted after the death or incapacity of the offeror, but only if the offer expressly stated a time for acceptance, or either party was acting in the course of a business.[31] English law tends to hold that an offer may be accepted until the offeree learns of the death of the offeror.[32] Everyone agrees, however, that these rules are residual and that the answer really depends on the particular circumstances of the case—especially on whether the personal qualities of the party are relevant to the contract in question. This is clearly the case in contracts

---

[28] To like effect is art. 2.1.4(2)(a) PICC; art. 2:202(3)(a) and (b) PECL; art. 32(3) CESL. Note that the mere fact that a period for acceptance is fixed does not render an offer irrevocable: it must 'indicate' that the offer is irrevocable. This regrettably leaves it open for the offeror, especially one from a Common Law country, to argue that although the offeror fixed a time for acceptance, the offeree should have realised that this was only to let him know when the offer would lapse, and not to assure him that it was irrevocable. See, on this, Schlechtriem and Schwenzer (n 8) art. 16 mn. 9.

[29] Similar are art. 2.1.4(2)(b) PICC; art. 2:202(3)(c) PECL; art. 1328(1), 1329(1) *Codice civile*; and art. 6:219 BW.

[30] Thus § 862 sent. 4 ABGB; art. 6:222 BW; art. 188 Greek Civil Code. §§ 130(2) and 153 BGB so prescribe for the case of death or incapacity of the *offeror*, but commentators would apply the same rule to the case of the offeree: see J Busche in *Münchener Kommentar zum BGB* (7th edn, 2015) § 153 BGB mn. 7. The Portuguese Civil Code (art. 231(1)) and the Polish Civil Code (art. 62) provide likewise for the death or incapacity of the offeror, and art. 231(2) Portuguese Civil Code provides that the offer lapses when the *offeree* dies or becomes incapable.

[31] See art. 1329, 1330 *Codice civile*. In France, different viewpoints were taken by the courts and legal doctrine. Article 1117(2) *Code civil* now provides that an offer will lapse '*en cas d'incapacité ou de décès de son auteur*'.

[32] See Treitel (n 15) no. 2-067ff.

for personal services: an offer by an artist to paint a portrait for a specified sum can hardly be turned into a contract by acceptance if the artist—or his subject, for that matter—has died.

C. Acceptance

A contract is formed when an offer is accepted. Acceptance is generally effected by means of a declaration directed to the offeror (see I below), but it is often sufficient if the intention to accept is manifested by conduct, or even—exceptionally—by silence or inaction (see II below). In order to be effective, acceptance must in principle be made in good time and must match the offer without qualification. Sometimes, however, a contract may be formed even though the acceptance is qualified (see III below) or late (see IV below).

I. Declaration of acceptance

1. *Acceptor's intention to be bound*—A declaration only constitutes an acceptance if it expresses the acceptor's intention to be contractually bound on the exact terms contained in the offer. It is not enough if the offeree simply acknowledges receipt of the offer, or modifies its terms, or if it appears that while taking note of the offer he does not wish to commit until other conditions are fulfilled—for example, if the offeree were to receive a binding offer.

2. *Effectiveness of declaration of acceptance*—Now that technological developments have made instantaneous communication possible whatever the distance between the parties, the question of the precise moment when an acceptance becomes effective has lost much of its practical importance. If acceptance is sent by letter or telegram, however, it may matter whether it takes effect at the moment of dispatch or the moment of arrival. For one thing, only in the latter case can the acceptor withdraw acceptance by a revocation which reaches the offeror before, or simultaneously with, the acceptance. In addition, a contract can only be formed if the offer is still open when the acceptance takes effect, and when the acceptance arrives it may have been withdrawn or have lapsed through passage of time.

Most legal systems,[33] along with art. 18(2) and (24) CISG, hold that an acceptance (like an offer) becomes effective when it reaches the offeror—namely when it so enters his zone of control that he can inform himself of it.[34] It follows that, just like an offer, an acceptance may be withdrawn provided the withdrawal reaches the offeror no later

---

[33] See § 130 BGB; art. 1118(2) *Code civil*; art. 167, 192 Greek Civil Code; § 2, 3 Swedish Contract Law; art. 3:37(3) BW; art. 61 sent. 1 and art. 70(1) Polish Civil Code. So also art. 2.1.6(2) PICC; art. 2:105(1) PECL; art. 18(2) CISG. By contrast, art. 10(1) OR provides that the contract becomes effective when the declaration of acceptance is 'delivered for dispatch'. This comports poorly with art. 9(2), whereby a declaration of acceptance can be withdrawn by an 'overtaking' declaration with the result of retroactively undoing the contract which had become valid by art. 10(1).

[34] There is no inconsistency in holding that the dispatch of the acceptance determines the moment before which withdrawal of the offer must arrive in order to be effectual (as under art. 16(1) CISG), for

than the acceptance itself,[35] and also that the acceptance must reach the offeree before the expiry of the period fixed for acceptance.

It is true that under the mailbox rule the contract is formed when the written acceptance is dispatched by post or telegram.[36] But not much follows from this in English law, except that an offer can no longer be withdrawn once the acceptance has been posted.[37] It would be logical to hold that a posted acceptance cannot be withdrawn by a swifter communication, but there is no decision to that effect.[38] Whether an acceptance posted within the period allowed is effective if it arrives too late depends on the construction of the offer,[39] but generally if the offeror has specified a time within which acceptance must be made, that means that the acceptance must arrive within that period.

II. Acceptance by conduct

1. *Acceptance by commencing performance*—An offer can be accepted without any actual declaration to that effect. Unless the offeror insisted that acceptance be explicit and communicated, conduct on the part of the offeree that adequately evinces an intention to accept the offer may well be sufficient.[40]

This commonly occurs when the offeree embarks on performance of the proposed contract.[41] If a tradesman from whom a person has offered to buy goods dispatches them—or, not having them in stock, contracts to buy them from a third party or cashes the cheque which accompanied the offer—this may constitute acceptance. Similarly, if a person offers to sell goods to a customer, the latter may demonstrate acceptance by paying the price or crediting the seller's bank account. It is the same, to give two stock examples, when a hotelier reserves a room for a person who has written to book one, or when a person gets into a taxi plying for hire in the street.

In all such cases, there will only be a contract if it is clear that in the circumstances there is no need to communicate the acceptance to the offeror, as is the case when the offeror does not need or care to know that the contract has been concluded. This may be so not only when the offeror either expressly or impliedly waives the need for

---

the question when the contract is formed is quite different from the question when an offer becomes irrevocable.

[35] See art. 22, 24 CISG; § 130(1)(2) BGB; art. 1118(2) *Code civil*; art. 1328(2) *Codice civile*; art. 3:37(5) BW; § 7 Swedish Contract Law; art. 235(2) Portuguese Civil Code; art. 61 sent. 2 Polish Civil Code. But see art. 9(2) OR, whereby an acceptance can be withdrawn by a withdrawal of which the addressee becomes aware before learning of the acceptance, even though the withdrawal of the acceptance 'reaches' him after the acceptance.

[36] See text to n 23 above.   [37] So, too, art. 16(1) CISG.   [38] See Treitel (n 15) no. 2-029ff.

[39] See *Household Fire & Carriage Acc. Ins. Co.* v. *Grant* (1879) 41 LT 298, which confirms the mailbox rule but makes it clear that 'an offeror, if he chooses, may always make the formation of the contract which he proposes dependent upon the actual communication to himself of the acceptance' (at 304).

[40] See art. 18(3) CISG; art. 2.1.6 PICC; art. 2:204 PECL; § 151 BGB; § 864 ABGB; § 193 Greek Civil Code; art. 1327(1) *Codice civile*; art. 234 Portuguese Civil Code; art. 69 Polish Civil Code. See also Treitel (n 15) no. 2-015ff. Under art. 1113(2) *Code civil*, an acceptance (as well as an offer) might result not only from a '*déclaration*', but also from a '*comportement non équivoque de son auteur*'.

[41] Such conduct often consists of the offeree's adoption of a performance rendered to him, as when a person starts to use goods sent to him on offer, or otherwise deals with them as if he owned them.

communicated acceptance, such as when it asks the offeree to send the goods as soon as possible, but also when trade usage or past dealings between the parties indicates that they can dispense with communication of acceptance.

2. *Acceptance by silence*—It is a generally accepted principle that mere silence does not by itself amount to acceptance of an offer,[42] even if the offeror was bold enough to state in its offer that it does. Yet, in certain exceptional circumstances, silence on the part of the offeree may indeed constitute acceptance. Sometimes these circumstances are prescribed by statute. Thus art. L 112-2 of the French *Code des assurances* provides that if an insured sends the insurer a request by recorded delivery for an alteration or prolongation of an existing policy, the insurer is held to have accepted such offer unless it is expressly rejected within ten days of the offer being received.[43] The German Commercial Code (HGB) provides in § 362 that a merchant who is in the business of making arrangements for other people, such as a freight forwarder, warehouseman, or commission agent (*Kommissionär*), may be treated as accepting a request from a business client to effect such a contract if he fails to reply to it.[44]

In other cases, an existing contract or commercial relationship between the parties may be such as to indicate that silence in the face of an offer may be taken as acceptance. This is also the case if the offer was made at the silent party's particular instance, or in the course of contractual negotiations. If A says that he will reply within fourteen days if B makes him an offer to buy and proposes a price, a contract of sale at B's price will come about if A does nothing for the fortnight after receipt of B's offer. It was so held by the *Cour de cassation*.[45] Again, suppose that in the course of negotiation between merchants C makes a specific proposal to D; if D rejects this offer but makes a counteroffer to C *d'une manière qui suffisait à éveiller son attention*, C is bound if he makes no response.[46] In one case decided by the *Bundesgerichtshof*, the seller had stipulated a price of DM 4,850 for delivery in four months, with the proviso that the price might rise if the cost of wages or transport went up in the meantime. After the four months had elapsed, the seller wrote on 11 September that he was ready to deliver at a price of DM 6,845, but the buyer made no reply either to this or to a further communication. The seller claimed payment in

---

[42] So explicitly in art. 18(1)(2) CISG, art. 2:204(2) PECL; art. 2.1.6(1) PICC; art. 34(2) CESL. See also Treitel (n 15) no. 2-041 and art. 1120 *Code civil*: '*Le silence ne vaut pas acceptation, à moins qu'il n'en résulte autrement de la loi, les usages, des relations d'affaires ou de circonstances particulières*'.

[43] This does not apply to contracts of life assurance. A similar provision, applicable only to mandatory liability insurance for motor vehicles appears in § 5(3)(1) of the German Law on Mandatory Insurance (PflVerG).

[44] So also art. 395 OR if the offer relates to a transaction 'within his official duty or profession or which he had held himself out as undertaking'. See also Com. 9 Jan. 1956, Bull.cass. 1956.III. no. 17: A purchasing agent who failed to respond to an order for goods submitted by the plaintiff was held to the contract, formed on the basis of a usage of trade '*selon lequel le fait, pour un professionnel, de recevoir un avis confirmatif d'une commande et de ne pas y répondre télégraphiquement dans les 24 heures, équivaut à une ratification tacite de la commande*'.

[45] Civ. 12 Jan. 1988, Bull.cass. 1988.I. no. 8, n. J Mestre Rev trim civ 1988, 521.

[46] Com. 21 May 1951, Bull.cass. 1951.II. no. 168. Likewise Civ. 6 July 1966, Bull.cass. 1966.II. no. 737 (silence in response to confirmation of an order).

return for delivery, and won his case. The letter of 11 September contained an offer, which the buyer had accepted by silence:

> It is certainly the general rule that in commercial dealings silence is not to be treated as consent to an offer of a contract, but it must nevertheless be treated as consent if good faith and fair dealing require the offeree to reject the offer explicitly. Such rejection is especially required if the parties are already in a commercial relationship, when a contract is already on foot between them and particularly when, as here, the offeree should have realised that the offeror needed a speedy reply.[47]

It is different, however, when a contract between the parties already exists and new terms appear on an invoice or delivery note, such as is often sent along with the goods. This may well constitute an offer to modify the terms of the previous contract, but in this case silence on the part of the recipient is not held to constitute acceptance. While the terms of documents which initiate a contract are usually read with considerable care, so that consent can easily be inferred, this is not so true of documents tendered after the contract has been formed. Furthermore, invoices and delivery notes often go direct to a company's accounts department and not to the contracts department which decides on deals and their terms.[48] Even here, however, it may be different if the terms in question had previously figured in earlier dealings between the parties. Although they appear subsequently to the contract to which they relate, the addressee may have to express its dissent in order to avoid their effect.

One must distinguish the businessman's confirmatory note (*Bestätigungsschreiben*), which plays an important part in German decisions. When parties have been in negotiation and have either concluded a contract or are on the point of doing so, one party may send the other a confirmatory note summarising the heads of agreement, clarifying them, making them more specific, and perhaps amplifying them slightly. If the recipient doubts whether the document accurately reflects what was agreed, he must express his dissent forthwith, for if he remains silent he will be prevented from denying that the contract was made, or made on those terms.[49]

---

[47] BGH 4 Apr. 1951, BGHZ 1, 353, 355f. See also BGH 14 Feb. 1995, [1995] *NJW* 1281; BGH 2 Nov. 1995, [1996] *NJW* 919.

[48] See BG 25 Nov. 1986, BGE 112 II 500; Ghestin (n 5) no. 426ff; Schmidt (n 5) no. 202ff; H Mazeaud, L Mazeaud, J Mazeaud, F Chabas, *Leçons de droit civil, vol. III.1: Obligations, Théorie générale* (9th edn, 2006) no. 137, all with extensive references to the French cases. In England, any attempt to modify the terms of an existing contract by subsequent agreement is likely to prove abortive because such a subsequent agreement, like all other agreements, is invalid unless there is 'consideration'. Thus even if the recipient of the invoice in fact consented to the proposed modification of the contract, whether by silence or otherwise, the agreement would be valid only if the party benefiting from it (here the party sending the invoice) provided or promised something in return, which rarely happens. On the role of consideration in modifications of existing contracts, see below, pp. 63ff.

[49] This is the view taken in the German cases where the parties are merchants or conduct themselves as such in commerce. See BGH 24 Sept. 1952, BGHZ 7, 187; BGH 26 June 1963, BGHZ 40, 42; BGH 9 July 1970, BGHZ 54, 236; BGH 30 Jan. 1985, BGHZ 93, 338. See also BG 25 Sept. 1945, BGE 71 II 223 and BG 8 Feb. 1974, BGE 100 II 18. The Austrian courts are more conservative, and treat silence in response to a commercial confirmatory note as acceptance only if it is in line with prior negotiations, or if the recipient's essential interests are unaffected by any amplifications or modifications. See OGH 26 June 1974, [1975] JBl. 89 and OGH 16 June 1976, [1977] JBl. 593. The rule which Ghestin deduces from the French decisions is that '*en matière commerciale la réception sans réserve d'une lettre de confirmation vaut généralement acceptation*': Ghestin (n 5) no. 424f, but the cases on which he relies generally involved a 'qualified acceptance' (see below, p. 29). But see Req. 22 Mar. 1920, S.1920.1.208: a contract was concluded

A rule like this clearly makes it tempting for a party to include in his confirmatory note terms favourable to himself—deviating from or additional to those which were agreed—in the hope that they will remain unquestioned by the other party and so be incorporated into the contract. The *Bundesgericht* in Switzerland therefore holds that a note of confirmation only has these consequences 'if the person sending the note is honestly convinced that his confirmation note contains only what has in fact been already agreed verbally'.[50] However, it is not very easy for a court to see into the mind of man, so perhaps it would be better to apply a different restriction and hold that an uncontested note of confirmation does not have the usual effects if its terms differ so markedly from the terms agreed that the sender could not reasonably count on the recipient's agreement. On this view, if the confirmatory note contains an arbitration or penalty clause which was never mentioned in the negotiations, the recipient is not bound by that clause if it can show that its inclusion is not normal practice in that branch of commerce, and that it therefore had no reason to expect or suspect its insertion.[51]

III. Qualified acceptance

Acceptance must express unqualified concurrence with the offer. If the acceptance extends, limits, or amplifies the offer, no contract will result. Accordingly everyone agrees that in general such a 'qualified' acceptance is to be treated as rejecting the original offer and constituting a new offer—a counteroffer.[52]

But this is not necessarily so. If fifty units are offered for sale to a person who replies that he will buy eighty units, it is a matter of construction whether the buyer is accepting the offer of fifty units and asking for a further thirty, or whether he is rejecting the offer and will buy either eighty units or none at all. Furthermore, an offeree may make a counteroffer without intending to reject the original offer, such as where he reserves the option of returning to the original offer if the counteroffer is rejected.

Sometimes, the acceptance differs from the offer only in very minor respects. Here there is a risk that the offeror may keep quiet and then, if the contract proves unfavourable, deny its existence—saying that because the acceptance differed from the offer, it

---

by telephone and confirmed by one party's '*lettre nette et précise, écrite le jour même ... pour confirmer la conversation par téléphone*'. The silence of the other party was treated as acceptance, because commercial practice required dissent to be express. The German law rules concerning silence about a commercial confirmatory note are not included in the CISG, but are included under art. 2:210 PECL, provided that the negotiations between the parties have already resulted in a contract. See also art. 2.1.12 PICC: 'If a writing which is sent within a reasonable time after the conclusion of the contract and which purports to be a confirmation of the contract contains additional or different terms, such terms become part of the contract, unless they materially alter the contract or the recipient, without undue delay, objects to the discrepancy.' See Köhler (n 15) 48ff.

[50] BG 25 Sept. 1945 (n 49) 224. Similar is BGH 26 June 1963 (n 49), making the party sending the confirmation note answerable for the fraud of an assistant who conducted the negotiations and lied to him about their import.

[51] See BGH 24 Sept. 1952 (n 49) 192f. (arbitration clause); OGH 26 June 1974 (n 49) (penalty clause).

[52] Article 19(1) CISG; art. 38(1) CESL; § 150(2) BGB; art. 1118(3) *Code civil*; art. 191 sent. 2 Greek Civil Code; art. 1326(5) *Codice civile*; art. 6:225(1) BW; § 6(1) Swedish Contract Law; art. 233 Portuguese Civil Code; art. 68 Polish Civil Code. Likewise Com. 17 July 1967, Bull.cass. 1967.III. no. 299, n. J Chevallier [1968] *Rev trim civ* 707; OGH 2 July 1969, SZ 42 no. 103 (p. 323f.); Treitel (n 15) no. 2-018.

constituted a counteroffer which he rejects. That is why where the acceptance differs from the offer in an 'immaterial' point, art. 19(2) CISG, art. 38 CESL, art. 2:208 PECL, and art. 2.1.11(2) PICC stipulate that the contract will be concluded under the terms of the acceptance unless the offeror objects immediately. An 'immaterial' point can only be an amendment that does not result in a tangible disadvantage for the offeror, and which a reasonable person would assume to be acceptable to him.

If the acceptance differs 'materially' from the offer, and is therefore to be regarded as a counteroffer, a contract is formed only if this counteroffer is accepted in turn. Here again, the question arises under what circumstances silence can count as acceptance. The typical case is where goods or services are ordered at a given price, and in accepting the offer the supplier states in the confirmation note (*Auftragsbestätigung, lettre de confirmation* etc.) that its standard business terms apply. If the customer does not object, and proceeds with the contract by accepting the goods or services tendered, does this amount to an acceptance of that counteroffer? The general answer is that it does, if the parties are both businesses, and the standard business terms have become part of the contract in accordance with the general rules (see below, pages 134ff.).[53]

Particular difficulties arise when both parties stipulate that the contract is to be subject to their own standard business terms, and these two sets of terms differ. In such a case, art. 6:225(3) BW provides that the conditions of the offeror take precedence unless express objection has been taken to them in the acceptance, by what is called a 'defence clause' (*Abwehrklausel*). Such clauses are now so common that this hardly solves the problem. Application of the basic rules given above would mean that this 'battle of the forms' would be won by the party that fired the last shot—the one who insisted on its own terms of business just before the other party started to perform. This is unsatisfactory, not least because it generally favours the seller. Although it is usually the buyer who initiates the deal, perhaps including its standard terms in the offer to buy, the seller normally stipulates in the note of acceptance that its terms are to apply—with the result that if the buyer accepts the goods without objection, in law the seller's terms would apply. That is why courts in Germany have rejected the theory of the last word, and hold that any conflicting provisions between the parties' standard terms do not become part of the contract, and the resulting gap is filled by dispositive law.[54]

---

[53] See Civ. 6 May 1954, Bull.cass. 1954.II. no. 165; Com. 17 Oct. 1961, D. 1962, 106; Civ. 6 July 1966, Bull.cass. 1966.II. no. 737 and Ghestin (n 5) no. 424f; Treitel (n 15) no. 2-018; BGH 29 Sept. 1955, BGHZ 18, 212, 215: silence does not count as acceptance *per se*, but commencing performance will be regarded as acceptance.

[54] See BGH 26 Sept. 1973, BGHZ 61, 282, 287ff; OLG Cologne 19 Mar. 1980, [1980] *BB* 1237; BGH 20 Mar. 1985, [1985] *NJW* 1838, 1839; BGH 9 Jan. 2002, [2002] *NJW* 1651. This rule seems to have been accepted under art. 1119(2) *Code civil*, which says that in the case of a conflict between the parties' standard terms, '*les clauses incompatibles sont sans effet*'. See also art. 39 CISG; art. 2:209 PECL and art. 2.1.22 PICC: 'Where both parties use standard terms and reach agreement except on those terms, a contract is concluded on the basis of the agreed terms and of any standard terms which are common in substance unless one party clearly indicates in advance, or later and without undue delay informs the other party, that it does not intend to be bound by such a contract.' The English courts do follow the theory of the last word: *B.R.S. v. Arthur V. Crutchley* [1968] 1 WLR 811; *Butler Machine Tool Co. v. Ex-Cell-O Corp.* [1979] 1 WLR 401, and see Treitel (n 15) no. 2-019f. Although the problem is dealt with in the US by § 2-207 UCC (see EA Farnsworth, *On Contract* (1990) § 3.21), the drafters of the CISG were unable to agree on a solution to this difficult problem: see Schlechtriem and Schwenzer (n 8) art. 19 mn. 19ff. Among other

This seems a good solution. The theory of the last word should apply only if, in our example, the buyer who accepts the goods without demur really can be seen as consenting to the seller's standard terms of business. If the buyer has no alternative but to refuse the goods, summon a lawyer to ascertain the differences between its terms and those of the seller, and then start bargaining again, the buyer can hardly be said to be consenting, since the alternative is simply impractical. Indeed, it never actually happens because the cost to the buyer (what economists call 'transaction costs') would greatly exceed the modest advantage the buyer might achieve by wringing some minor concessions from the seller. For these reasons, acceptance of the goods by the buyer cannot be held to be an expression of will, so it does not constitute consent to the application of the seller's standard business terms. The gap must be filled by the rules which the parties would have agreed on if they had been able to negotiate without regard to cost in time and money—and those rules are the rules of dispositive law or the terms implied by construction of the contract.[55]

IV. Delayed acceptance

If acceptance of the offer is late, in principle no contract is concluded; the acceptance must take effect within the period set by the offeror, or whatever period is held to be reasonable in all the circumstances. There are, however, some exceptions to this rule.

For example, the offeror may inform the other party—either expressly or by conduct such as dispatch of the goods—that it is treating the late acceptance as timely. On the one hand, late acceptance (like qualified acceptance) constitutes a new offer, acceptable by the other party under the general rules given above (under I and II).[56] Alternatively, one could simply allow the original offeror to declare forthwith that the acceptance is timely and the contract is concluded.[57] The advantage of the latter construction is that the contract takes effect at the time the parties would naturally assume—namely from the arrival of the acceptance (admittedly late, but deemed to be in time), rather than on the arrival of the original offeror's declaration in response to the 'new' offer.

These rules would seem to be applicable however late the acceptance arrives. If it arrives very late, however, it may seem unfair that the offeror should have the option of bringing the contract into existence by declaring the late acceptance to be in time (which may be greatly to its advantage if market conditions have altered in the meanwhile). On the other hand, the risk of delay should always be borne by the party that can most easily avoid or reduce that risk. Here this is the offeree, who makes the

---

comparative treatments of the problem, see A von Mehren, 'The "Battle of the Forms": A Comparative View' (1990) 38 *Am J Comp L* 265; von Mehren (n 3) vol. VII chapter 9, 157ff; E Kramer, 'Battle of the Forms' in P Tercier et al. (eds), *Gauchs Welt, Festschrift Gauch* (2004) 493; G Rühl, 'The Battle of the Forms' (2003) 24 *U.Pa. J of Int'l Economic Law* 189. See also art. 2:209 PECL; art. 2.1.22 PICC; art. II.-4: 209 DCFR; art. 39 CESL.

[55] See below, pp. 100ff.
[56] Thus in § 150(1) BGB; art. 191 sent. 1 Greek Civil Code; § 4(1) Swedish Contract Law; and also art. 37(1) CESL.
[57] So in art. 21 CISG; art. 2:207(1) PECL; art. 2.1.9(1) PICC; art. 1326(3) *Codice civile*; art. 6:223(1) BW; art. 229(2) Portuguese Civil Code.

decision when and how to dispatch the acceptance. In other words, if a person dealing in goods in a notoriously fluctuating market chooses to contract by post at a fixed price, the offeree must bear the risk that if the acceptance letter is delayed, the offeror may nevertheless hold it to the contract.

A different question is presented if the offeror remains silent on receipt of the late acceptance. Generally, the answer must be that there is no contract: the offeror is entitled to treat the late acceptance as invalid, and is not bound to inform the other party of the fact. Nevertheless, there is one exceptional case in which it is agreed that the offeror is under a duty to respond, and is held to the contract if it fails to do so. If the offeror realises that although the acceptance was late in arriving it was dispatched in time, the offeror must forthwith inform the offeree that the acceptance arrived too late. If the offeror fails to do so, the acceptance is deemed to have arrived in time.[58]

German courts have gone a step further and imposed a duty to inform the offeree in cases where acceptance is delayed for other reasons, with silence counting as assent. Examples are: where the acceptance must arrive within a 'reasonable' period (because no exact period had been fixed by the offeror) and the offeree might not know exactly how long that period was; where the delay was slight; and where the offeree could not know that the offeror's position was going to change when the period expired.[59] In such exceptional cases, it would not be too much to expect a reasonable person to disabuse the other party of its reasonable belief that the contract has been formed, and a party failing to make the slight effort involved can hardly complain if it is treated as if the acceptance had arrived in time.

D. Liability for Breaking Off Negotiations

Negotiations also cost money and resources. The takeover company retains an accountant to value the target; the builder making a tender for a job spends a lot of time and trouble calculating its price; other cases may involve the costs of travel, obtaining information, taking legal advice, or preparing draft contracts. Ongoing negotiations may seem so certain to end up in a contract that, in reliance on that outcome, one of the parties rejects a favourable offer from someone else, terminates an existing contract, or enters into a new contract with a third party. If the negotiations collapse, those arrangements are rendered futile and expenses are wasted. Can compensation be claimed from the other party for this loss? Can a party go further and claim that, although the contract never came about, it should be treated as if it had and so claim the profit it would have made under that contract?[60]

---

[58] See art. 21(2) CISG; art. 2.1.9(2) PICC; art. 2:207 PECL; art. 37(2) CESL; § 149 BGB; § 862a sent. 2 ABGB; art. 5(3) OR; art. 190 Greek Civil Code; art. 6:223(2) BW; § 4(2) Swedish Contract Law; art. 229(1) Portuguese Civil Code; art. 67 Polish Civil Code.

[59] See RG 7 Oct. 1921, RGZ 103, 11, 13; BGH 31 Jan. 1951, LM § 150 BGB no. 1 (headnote c).

[60] See in general: JHM van Erp, 'The Pre-Contractual Stage' in A. Hartkamp et al. (eds), *Towards a European Civil Code* (4th edn, 2011) 493; von Mehren (n 3) vol. VII chapter 9, 112ff; N Cohen, 'Precontractual Duties and Good Faith in Contract Law' in J Beatson and D Friedmann (eds), *Good Faith and Fault in Contract Law* (1995) 25. One must consider not only claims for damages, but also claims for unjustified enrichment. If, during the negotiations and in anticipation of the contract, one party renders services to the other for which there is no legal basis, with the contract never being concluded, the

There is general agreement that parties incurring expense in the hope of a contract must in principle bear that expense themselves should the contract not be concluded. Any other result would be at odds with the principle of freedom of contract, which gives everyone the right to decide freely not only to make a contract, but also not to make one. This freedom would be seriously prejudiced if one could only break off negotiations at the price of making good the other party's expenditures.

On the other hand, persons engaged in negotiations owe each other certain duties, and breach may lead to sanctions. Even parties engaged in negotiation must behave reasonably and take some account of each other's interests. Everyone agrees that one must not deliberately deceive the other party: for example, it would be wrong to request an offer which will be expensive to prepare if one is already determined to reject it.[61] Other cases are trickier. What if a party gives the impression that the negotiations will lead to a contract when it knows (or should know) that this is unlikely, and that the other party will incur expense in the expectation of a successful conclusion? Given that one may in general break off negotiations without having to give any reason, what if the negotiations have been going on for a long time and the other party, counting on the contract, has incurred substantial expense? Must one then have a good reason for breaking off the negotiations?

The mutual duties of negotiators may be said to be based on different legal foundations. They may arise from a contractual agreement between the parties, either express or implied. Alternatively, one could say that they arise from the special relationship of trust which arises when parties start to negotiate and which obliges them to consider each other's interests—this is Rudolf von Jhering's doctrine of *culpa in contrahendo*, much used in this context in Germany and Switzerland. Finally, one could look to the law of tort, and say that a negotiator's liability for misconduct is based on breach of the general duty of care.[62] This is the path followed by courts in France and the UK in particular, although there are great differences. French law proceeds on the premise that the parties are free to decide whether or not to commence negotiations, how to proceed, and when to end negotiations. However, they must also proceed in good faith. If breaking off negotiations is held to breach this good faith requirement (see below, page 37), liability will be based on the general tort provisions of art. 1240 (formerly art.

---

recipient must restore what he has received *in specie* or else its equivalent in money (but not the contract price he was to pay). See *British Steel Corp. v. Cleveland Bridge and Engineering Co.* [1984] 1 All ER 504. So also if during the negotiations one party discloses to the other technical information of which the recipient subsequently makes profitable use, even in good faith; see *Seager v. Copydex* [1967] 1 WLR 923.

[61] For such a case, see BG 6 June 1951, BGE 77 II 135.

[62] Pursuant to § 311(2) no. 1 BGB, an 'obligation' can come into existence not only by way of contract but also by the 'commencement of contract negotiations'. This means that the negotiating parties must 'take account of the rights, legal interests and other interests of the other party' (§ 241(2) BGB) and, if they breach these obligations and can provide no exculpatory evidence, pursuant to § 280(1) BGB the other party may 'demand damages for the damage caused thereby'. This liability—often described as *culpa in contrahendo* liability—also applies in Switzerland and Austria. See H Honsell in *Basler Kommentar* (5th edn, 2014) art. 2 OR mn. 17; P Apathy and A Riedler in M Schwimann (ed), *AGBG-Praxiskommentar* (3rd edn, 2006) § 878 mn. 10ff. Also in Italy and Greece, where statutory provisions determine that during negotiations parties owe each other a duty of good faith: see art. 1337f. *Codice civile* and art. 197f. Greek Civil Code. For a historical development of *culpa in contrahendo*, see Zimmermann (n 1) 244f. and the evidence contained therein.

1382) *Code civil*.⁶³ English law takes a different approach. There is no general principle whereby parties must observe the principle of good faith and fair dealing during pre-contractual negotiations, disclose important information without being asked, or take any special account of the other party. There may be liability. It may be founded in a contract in which the parties have agreed to conduct the negotiations of the 'principal contract' with proper consideration of the other party's interests. A party may also have conducted the negotiations in a way that gives rise to liability in tort. If A has lied to B, B can claim damages for deceit; and if A gives B incorrect information, A can be held liable for misrepresentation,⁶⁴ or for negligence if the incorrect information constitutes a breach of the duty of care towards the negotiating partner.⁶⁵

We will deal first with contractual agreements made by the parties during the negotiations, prior to the conclusion of what we shall call the principal contract. The content and effect of such pre-contracts may be quite different from those of the principal contract. Where the parties are agreed on the main points of the principal contract, they may bind themselves by a pre-contract to conclude the principal contract. A party who then breaks off negotiations and refuses to proceed to the principal contract will accordingly be in breach of this pre-contract, entitling the innocent party to claim either that the principal contract be held to exist, or that it be awarded damages for the loss resulting from its non-occurrence. For this to happen, the parties need to have had the requisite intention to be bound, and the content of the pre-contract must be sufficiently specific, with the points remaining open being inessential and such that the court can supply them by means of implied terms or extensive interpretation.⁶⁶

A letter of intent or memorandum of understanding (*Grundsatzvereinbarung, accord de principe*) has rather less effect.⁶⁷ Such an agreement may have one or more of the following effects: limit the parties' freedom to break off negotiations, except on specified grounds; lay down that they are not to start negotiations with a third party, either with or without the knowledge of the other party; or provide that, if the negotiations fail, a party is to be indemnified for further preparatory expenses it may have incurred. Such an agreement will need to be interpreted in order to decide what the parties intended, and whether or not it is sufficiently precise to be enforced by the court.⁶⁸

---

⁶³ See art. 1116(3) *Code civil* and below, n 81. EU conflict of laws rules also deem liability for pre-contractual negotiations to be governed by tort law and therefore determine the applicable law under the rules of the EC Regulation on the Law Applicable to Non-Contractual Obligations. See art. 12 Rome II Regulation and art. 1(2)(i) of the Rome I Regulation.

⁶⁴ See pp. 163ff.

⁶⁵ For a comparative law treatment, see B Fauvarque-Cosson, 'Negotiation and Renegotiation: A French Perspective', and J Cartwright, 'Negotiation and Renegotiation: An English Perspective', both in J Cartwright, S Vogenauer, and S Whittaker (eds), *Reforming the French Law of Obligations* (2009) 33ff. and 51ff.

⁶⁶ On this, see the details on pp. 100ff.

⁶⁷ See M Fontaine, 'Les lettres d'intention dans la négociation des contrats internationaux' [1977] *Dr prat com int* 105; B Oppetit, 'L'engagement d'honneur' D.1979.Chron.107; M Lutter, *Der Letter of Intent* (1982); Ghestin (n 5) no. 343ff; J Schmidt, 'La période précontractuelle en droit français' (1990) 42 *Rev int dr comp* 545, 555ff; Treitel (n 15) no. 4-013; Farnsworth (n 54) § 3.26b; A Farnsworth, 'Negotiation of Contracts and Precontractual Liability: General Report' in *Kollision und Vereinheitlichung, Mélanges en honneur d'Alfred von Overbeck* (1990) 657.

⁶⁸ Similar questions arise in the case of 'letters of comfort' (*Patronatserklärungen*) given by a parent company to a party dealing with its subsidiary, or by a bank to someone doing business with a customer.

Where there is no express agreement, the circumstances may be such as to put a party under a duty to conduct the negotiations with proper consideration for the interests of the other party. In a case before the English Court of Appeal, a local authority granted a concession for the operation of pleasure flights from its aerodrome. It invited several flight operators, including the plaintiff, to submit anonymous tenders in a particular form by a given hour on a specified day. The plaintiff's tender was in fact submitted in time, but the defendants thought it was late and ignored it completely. The plaintiff's claim for damages succeeded: by arranging the tender process in the way they did, the defendants had contractually undertaken to consider every tender submitted in time.[69] A case decided by the *Bundesgerichtshof* is rather similar. The defendant held an architectural competition with a prize of DM 22,000. Here, too, the defendant's erroneous rejection of the plaintiff's entry as too late was held to be a breach of its contractual duty to conduct the competition fairly.[70] In another case, a German local authority invited tenders for the construction of an indoor swimming pool, although funding was not yet assured. The plaintiff, a Dutch builder, tendered for the job. When the time for considering the tenders arrived, finance was still not in place, so no tender was accepted. Months later, the local authority did obtain finance, but as it came from a programme to stimulate the local economy and could be used only for builders in the area, the plaintiff lost out. He claimed his expenses in preparing the tender, and the OLG Düsseldorf granted his claim—not on the ground of contract, but because by entering into negotiations a relationship of trust was established which obliged the defendant 'to make clear [to the plaintiff] that it lacked the necessary funds and that they might not be forthcoming within the stipulated time-frame'.[71]

A party guilty of culpable conduct during negotiations must put the other party in the position it would have enjoyed but for such conduct. This means that the culpable

---

Such letters of comfort undertake that it is the parent company's policy to support its subsidiary, or that the bank's customer has ample resources to fulfil the contract in question. Though this may not amount to a contract of guarantee in the strict sense, the question may arise whether the parent company or bank may not still be held liable if the subsidiary or customer was already insolvent at the time of their letter. See, for example, Com. 21 Dec. 1987, *JCP* 1988.II.21113, with conclusions by M Montanier; Com. 4 Oct. 1994, Bull.cass. 1994.IV. no. 276; Com. 15 Oct. 1996, D. 1997, 330; Com. 9 July 2002, D. 2002, 3332; *Kleinwort Benson Ltd.* v. *Malaysia Mining Corp.* [1988] 1 All ER 714; [1989] 1 All ER 785 (CA), and Treitel (n 15) no. 4-013; OLG Dusseldorf 26 Jan. 1989, [1989] *NJW-RR* 1116; BGH 30 Jan. 1992, [1922] *NJW* 2093.

[69] *Blackpool Aero Club* v. *Blackpool Borough Council* [1990] 3 All ER 25 (CA) and Treitel (n 15) no. 2-012, 4-021. See also *William Lacey (Hounslow)* v. *Davis* [1957] 1 WLR 932: In the expectation of being awarded the contract after being told that his tender was the lowest, the plaintiff builder produced further draft designs at the defendant's request. But the defendant sold the land to a third party, so the contract was never awarded. It was decided 'that the court should imply a condition or imply a promise that the defendant should pay a reasonable sum to the plaintiffs for the whole of these services which were rendered by them' (at p. 940).

[70] BGH 23 Sept. 1982, [1983] *NJW* 442. The relationship was held contractual under § 661 BGB, a competition of this kind being an *Auslobung* under § 657ff. BGB. However, the BGH held that the claim for damages could only be with respect to payment of the entire prize and that the architect thus had to show that he would have won. If the evidence could not be provided, he would receive nothing. That does not make sense. It would have been better to calculate the probability that the architect would have won the prize, and thus award him that percentage of the prize money corresponding to this probability. See H Kötz and HB Schäfer, *Judex oeconomicus* (2003) 266ff, and generally, see pp. 268ff below on the liability for the value of a missed opportunity.

[71] OLG Düsseldorf 27 Jan. 1976, [1977] *NJW* 1064, 1065.

party is liable for reliance damages (the negative, reliance interest) but not for performance damages (positive or expectation interest). This is reflected by art. 1112(2) *Code civil*, which provides that a party's '*faute commise dans les negotiations*' leads to its liability in damages, but not to a duty to compensate for '*la perte des avantages attendu du contrat non conclu*'. If the local authority in the above case had told the plaintiff the true facts, the court found that he could recover the expense of submitting a tender. Suppose, however, that the plaintiff would certainly have obtained the contract if the culpable party had not made the mistake. Even if only reliance interest is protected, the damages in this particular case will equal expectation damages. This was so in the important decision of the *Hoge Raad* in *Plas* v. *Valburg*.[72] The plaintiff's tender was the cheapest of all those submitted to the town of Valburg and well within the funds available. The only thing lacking was endorsement by the town council, which was thought to be a formality. However, a member of the council went to another builder and managed to obtain a lower tender from him, which the council then accepted. The *Hoge Raad* held that the conduct of the town council was contrary to the requirement of good faith and fair dealing. The negotiations had reached so advanced a stage, and the conclusion of the contract was apparently so imminent, that the builder was entitled to claim his expectation losses. So, too, the *Bundesgerichtshof* has held that a local authority which mismanaged a tender process and failed to consider the plaintiff's tender had to pay expectation losses if the plaintiff could prove that he would have been awarded the contract if the proceedings had been properly conducted.[73]

Misconduct during negotiations may arise in many other contexts. Credit arrangements are an example, and *Box* v. *Midland Bank* is typical.[74] The plaintiff wanted an overdraft from the defendant bank, and was informed by one of its officers that an overdraft would certainly be granted on certain conditions. The officer should have known that the chances of those conditions being met were slim, but did not tell the plaintiff, although he knew that the plaintiff would make arrangements on the assumption that the overdraft would be forthcoming. In another case, before the *Bundesgerichtshof* this time, the plaintiff was negotiating with the defendant bank for a $12 million confirmed letter of credit. Since it was urgently needed for the purchase of a cargo of kerosene, the plaintiff asked the appropriate officer of the bank if the letter of credit could be provided in time. Although the officer knew that this was far from certain, the plaintiff was told not to worry, and so did not look elsewhere for the facility.[75] Finally, a case from the Swiss *Bundesgericht*: the manager of a branch bank led a customer to believe that the negotiations would work out, although he knew that the head office might well refuse its approval, and that if he did not come clean the customer would make arrangements on the assumption that all would be well.[76]

---

[72] HR 18 June 1982, [1983] Ned.Jur. 723. On this, see JM von Dunné, 'The Prelude to the Contract, the Threshold of Tort: The Law on Precontractual Dealings in the Netherlands' in *Netherlands Reports to the XIIIth Congress of the International Academy of Comparative Law* (1991) 71. See also HR 23 Oct. 1987, [1988] *NedJur* 1017 and HR 31 May 1991, [1991] Ned.Jur. 647.
[73] BGH 25 Nov. 1992, BGHZ 120, 281.   [74] [1979] 2 Lloyd's Rep. 391.
[75] BGH 17 Oct. 1983, [1984] *NJW* 866.
[76] BG 6 Feb. 1979, BGE 105 II 75. See also BG 6 June 1951, BGE 77 II 135.

The defendant bank was held liable in damages in all three cases,[77] but not on identical legal grounds. In the German and Swiss cases, the conduct of the bank was seen as *culpa in contrahendo*—as a breach of the duty of care arising from the entry into contractual negotiations. The English court, on the other hand, based itself on the tort of negligence. This allows for the recovery of 'pure economic loss' due to a culpably erroneous representation given by a professional in the line of business if the representee was entitled to rely on its accuracy and took action on it to its detriment.[78] No difference in result seems to follow from the difference in legal analysis.

German and Austrian courts also accept the general rule that a person may end contractual negotiations 'at any time and for any reason—a change of heart, a change of circumstances, a better deal—or for no reason at all'.[79] This freedom to break off negotiations is, however, limited when A has led B to count on the conclusion of a contract, perhaps even indicating that a contract was as good as made, or has failed to apprise B of problems of which B was unaware but of which A was (or could more easily have been) aware. In such a situation, it is a breach of duty to break off negotiations and put forward either no reason at all, or only reasons which are irrelevant or factitious.[80] The French courts do likewise: if negotiations have very nearly reached a climax, and the plaintiff has incurred considerable expense in preparing for the contract, it is a breach of duty for the defendant to break off negotiations *'sans raison légitime, brutalement et unilatéralement'*.[81] Much depends on the precise circumstances of the case: whether a reasonable man in the place of the plaintiff would have counted on the conclusion of the contract; whether the defendant's conduct did and could be expected to contribute to such an assumption; and whether the arrangements made by the plaintiff were to the defendant's actual or possible knowledge substantial in extent, and such as a reasonable man would have made in the circumstances. Liability is determined on the basis that the cessation of negotiations took place under circumstances that appear to be 'brutal', 'abusive', or based on 'malicious' considerations. When French courts

---

[77] In BGH 17 Oct. 1983 (n 75), the seller resiled from the kerosene contract because the letter of credit was not forthcoming on time. The *Bundesgerichtshof* held that the customer could sue the bank for his lost profit provided he could prove that, if alerted in time, he could have obtained the facility from some other bank.

[78] The leading case in the House of Lords which inaugurated this extension of the tort of negligence is *Hedley Byrne & Co. v. Heller & Partners* [1964] AC 465.

[79] Farnsworth, *Mélanges von Overbeck* (n 67) 659.

[80] See, for example BGH 8 June 1978, BGHZ 71, 386, 395f; BGH 7 Feb. 1980, BGHZ 76, 343, 348f; BGH 29 March 1996, [1996] *NJW* 1884. Similarly in Austria, see OGH 6 July 1976, [1977] *JBl* 315; OGH 30 May 1979, [1980] *JBl* 33, and R Ostheim, 'Zur Haftung für culpa in contrahendo bei grundloser Ablehnung des Vertragsabschlusses' [1980] *JBl* 522 and 570. See also art. 2:301 PECL: 'A party is free to negotiate and is not liable for failure to reach an agreement. However, a party who negotiates or breaks off negotiations in bad faith is liable for the losses caused to the other party. It is bad faith, in particular, for a party to enter into or continue negotiations when intending not to reach an agreement with the other party.' See also art. 2.1.15 PICC; art. II.-3:301 DCFR.

[81] See Com. 6 Feb. 2007, Bull.cass. 2007.IV. no. 21 = [2007] D. 653, n. E Chevrier = [2007] Rev.trim.civ. 343, n J Mestre and B Fages. Article 1112 *Code civil* now provides that precontractual negotiations must conform with the requirements of good faith. A party in breach of these requirements will have to pay damages, which must not, however, compensate a party for *'la perte des avantages du contrat non conclu'*. See for example Com. 26 Nov. 2003, [2004] D. 869, n. A-S Dupré-Dallemagne = [2007] Rev.trim.civ. 343, n. J Mestre and B Fages. See also the decision of the Italian Court of Cassation, 12 March 1993, [1993] Foro it. I 956 (no. 2973).

do grant damages for a '*faute commise dans les négociations*', they do so on the basis of tort under art. 1240 (formerly art. 1382) *Code civil*, but the conclusions they reach do not seem any different from those in countries which operate with *culpa in contrahendo*. In any case, the *Cour de cassation* appears to assume that the injured party can only claim for the time and resources invested in the (curtailed) negotiations.[82]

English courts are less ready to impose liability in these cases. In *Walford* v. *Miles*,[83] the plaintiff and defendant had been negotiating over the sale of the plaintiff's business since January 1987, and they had reached an agreement in principle, though only 'subject to contract'—namely, conditional on a formal agreement being drawn up. The price would be £2 million, and the business was supposed to generate an income of £300,000 in the first year after the takeover. On 17 March 1987, the parties made a further agreement that the defendant should break off current negotiations with other interested parties, and consider no other offers.[84] When the defendant nevertheless sold his business to a third party a few days later, the plaintiff claimed damages on the basis that he had been deprived of buying for £2 million a business whose value he put at £3 million. The main line of his argument was that in the agreement of 17 March the defendant had undertaken 'to negotiate in good faith with the plaintiff', and by breaking off the negotiations he was in breach of this undertaking. The House of Lords dismissed the claim. A contractual 'duty to carry on negotiations in good faith' was inconsistent with the right of every party to stop negotiating, or threaten to do so whenever he thought right. Neither the other party nor a court could decide with sufficient assurance whether the reason for doing so was good enough.

> How is a vendor to know that he is entitled to withdraw from further negotiations? How is the court to police such an 'agreement'? A duty to negotiate in good faith is as unworkable in practice as it is inherently inconsistent with the position of a negotiating party. It is here that the uncertainty lies. In my judgment, while negotiations are in existence either party is entitled to withdraw from these negotiations, at any time and for any reason. There can thus be no obligation to continue to negotiate until there is a 'proper reason' to withdraw. Accordingly a bare agreement to negotiate has no legal content.[85]

These dogmatic generalities are unpersuasive. Continental courts have demonstrated that there are indeed practical and appropriate tests which enable them to distinguish proper from improper conduct in negotiations, and that the essential question is whether damages should be for the reliance or for the performance interest.

This particular claim would equally have been dismissed by a court in France or Germany. Judges in Germany would most likely have noted that the plaintiff here was not seeking compensation for expenses incurred in the belief that the contract would

---

[82] See, for example, Com. 26 Nov. 2003 (n 81); Civ. 28 June 2006, Bull.cass. 2006.III. no. 68 = [2006] D. 2963, n. D Mazeaud.

[83] [1992] 2 AC 128.

[84] This agreement was not invalid for want of consideration, since the plaintiff had been requested to provide a 'letter of comfort' (n 68) from his bank and had done so.

[85] Lord Ackner in *Walford* v. *Miles* (n 83) 138. The decision provoked a host of comment, mainly critical. See E McKendrick, *Contract Law* (8th edn, 2009) no. 4.1, and 12.10 and A Berg, 'Promises to Negotiate in Good Faith' (2003) 119 *LQR* 357. By contrast Treitel (n 15) no. 2-106.

be successfully concluded, but the benefit of the bargain—his performance interest. This is only granted exceptionally, where prior to the collapse of the negotiations the contract was confidently expected.[86] That was not the situation here, where all negotiations (including the agreement of 17 March) were 'subject to contract'—thereby expressing the intention of the parties *not* to be bound, even to a pre-contract. The French courts would perhaps have found that the defendant had good reason to break off the negotiations, and that therefore he had committed no *faute*. The defendant gave evidence that after 17 March he began to doubt whether the plaintiff's business methods would suit his workforce, and that if the staff were dismissed the guaranteed income of the business might not be reached. Furthermore, his advanced age and poor health made it doubtful whether he could fulfil the obligation he had undertaken to advise the purchaser for the year following the sale.

---

[86] See above, p. 36.

3

The Definiteness of the Contract

A. Introduction	41
B. Types of Case	42
I. Agreements to agree	43
II. Unilateral price-fixing	45

A. Introduction

An agreement cannot be contractual unless it is sufficiently 'definite'. Of course, contracts are very often incomplete in the sense that they do not cover every relevant point, or are so vague in their terms that their precise purpose is not ascertainable even by interpretation. Many a contract for the sale of goods says nothing about the time and place of delivery or the quality of the goods. But not all such agreements are invalid for want of 'definiteness'. Instead, terms designed by law for just this situation are read into the agreement in place of the missing stipulations—for example, that the goods are to be delivered 'within a reasonable time', or 'at the seller's place of business', and that they should have no 'concealed defects' which render them 'unfit for the purpose for which they are designed' (art. 1641 *Code civil*).[1] Often the missing stipulations are supplied by mercantile practice governing goods of that kind: when 100 tonnes of diesel oil are sold 'on normal conditions of payment', practice among oil traders indicates that the buyer must instruct a bank to open a letter of credit and thus to guarantee that the seller will be paid upon the production of a bill of lading or other documents representing the goods.[2] And if an importer of timber buys a quantity of softwood 'of fair specification', the customary business practices of timber merchants determine the limits of the specifications which the buyer may make.[3]

A contract does not lack definition merely because there is a problem with the modalities of conclusion of the contract. If the modalities of the principal obligation are missing, they will be supplied from previous dealings of the parties, the practices in that branch of commerce, or dispositive law (implied terms).[4] The same is generally true when the parties have not fully specified the principal obligation, for example, have said nothing about the price of the goods sold or simply agreed that it should be the 'normal' or 'fair' price. Frequently statutory provisions lay down how the price is to be fixed in such a case, with reference usually being made to the market price or the price generally charged by the seller or a 'reasonable' price.[5] The same rules also apply

---

[1] On this, see below, p. 367.
[2] See OLG Frankfurt 27 Apr. 1976, [1977] *NJW* 1015.
[3] *Hillas & Co.* v. *Arcos Ltd*. (1932) 147 LT 503.   [4] See pp. 100ff.
[5] See, for example, art. 7:4 BW; s. 8 Sale of Goods Act 1970; art. 1474 *Codice civile*; art. 212 OR; art. 883 Portuguese Civil Code. See also art. 6:104 PECL; art. 5.1.7(1) PICC; art. II.-9:104 DCFR. Article 55

to contracts of other types, such as contracts for services, or for other contracts where the parties have failed to precisely determine the price.[6]

All these rules can only be applied if it can be shown that the parties intended to be legally bound by their agreement. If the parties have said nothing about the scope of performance or the agreed price, this may be an indication that they did not intend to be bound, but such a conclusion will rarely be justified if the matter left open is merely collateral or ancillary. Thus, art. 2(1) OR assumes that 'where the parties have agreed on all the essential terms … the contract will be binding notwithstanding any reservation on secondary terms.' And § 155 BGB concerns cases where the parties have concluded a contract but have failed to recognise that they have 'in fact' not agreed on important points. The agreement actually made will apply provided it is to be assumed that the contract would have been entered into even without agreement on this point. The decisive question is always whether the parties *wanted* to be bound, despite the incompleteness or lack of definiteness. This intention is lacking if the circumstances show that even though the agreement was concluded, a party did not have an 'intention of creating legal relations', the intention '*de produire des effets juridiques*' or had acted without '*Rechtsbindungswillen*'.[7]

B. Types of Case

If a defendant asserts that the agreement being sued on is too incomplete or indefinite to be a valid contract, the judge must give a positive answer to two questions before holding for the plaintiff: did the parties *intend* to be contractually bound notwithstanding the incompleteness or indefiniteness of their agreement? And, secondly, can the judge, on the basis of what was agreed and the context in which it was agreed, complete the contract or render precise the point left indefinite?[8] In practice, these two questions are not always kept separate, either because only one is in issue in the case, or because both depend on the same considerations.[9] But it is useful to distinguish them, as the following discussion will show.

CISG states: 'Where a contract has been validly concluded but does not expressly or implicitly fix or make provision for determining the price, the parties are considered, in the absence of any indication to the contrary, to have impliedly made reference to the price generally charged at the time of the conclusion of the contract for such goods sold under comparable circumstances in the trade concerned.'

[6] See, for example, §§ 612, 632 BGB; arts. 1657, 1709, 1733, 1740 *Codice civile*; s. 15 Supply of Goods and Services Act 1982.

[7] For more, see pp. 66ff.

[8] See art. 2.1.14 PICC: If the parties have left a particular point to be resolved in future negotiations, and those negotiations fail, the contract may nevertheless be good if two conditions are satisfied: the parties must have *intended* to be bound, and further 'that there is an alternative means of rendering the term definite that is reasonable in the circumstances, having regard to the intention of the parties'.

[9] See *Scammell* v. *Ouston* [1941] AC 251, where the parties had agreed that part of the price for a lorry should be paid 'on hire purchase terms over a period of two years'. Lord Wright held the contract void because 'these words, considered however broadly and untechnically and with due regard to all the just implications, fail to evince any definite meaning on which the Court can safely act … But I think the other reason, which is that the parties never in intention nor even in appearance reached an agreement, is a still sounder reason against enforcing the claim' (at 268f.).

I. Agreements to agree

Quite often the parties deliberately leave a point to be covered by subsequent negotiation and agreement. If the goods are not to be delivered for twelve months, or the tenant is to take the house only in five years' time, it may be wise to leave the price or the rent to be fixed until delivery or entry, when the parties will know how the market or the currency has moved. The questions arise as to whether the parties actually want to be bound and, if so, what is to happen if they cannot reach agreement on the point left open. Both questions are usually answered in the affirmative, if they have nevertheless begun to perform. So, too, is the consideration that to hold the contract void removes the legal basis for their performances, which would then have to be restored, if possible, or their equivalent paid in money—something that the courts are reluctant to order, and with good reason. In *British Bank for Foreign Trade v. Novinex*,[10] the plaintiff had acted as middleman between the defendant and a third party, and the defendant promised 'an agreed commission' on future business done with the third party if the plaintiff would identify him. The plaintiff did so, and further business was transacted, but the defendant refused to pay. Without deciding what the situation would have been if the validity of the promise had been questioned *before* the defendant had disclosed the third party's identity, the court noted that here the promised service had been rendered and held the defendant's promise good for a 'reasonable commission', which it then fixed. The critical point was as follows:

> The principle to be deduced from the cases is that, if there is an essential term which has yet to be agreed and there is no express or implied provision for its solution, the result in point of law is that there is no binding contract. In seeing whether there is an implied provision for its solution, however, there is a difference between an arrangement which is wholly executory on both sides, and one which has been executed on one side or the other. In the ordinary way, if there is an arrangement to supply goods at a price 'to be agreed', or to perform services on terms 'to be agreed', then, although while the matter is still executory there may be no binding contract, nevertheless, if it is executed on one side, that is, if the one does his part without having come to an agreement as to the price or the terms, then the law will say that there is necessarily implied from the conduct of the parties a contract that, in default of agreement, a reasonable sum is to be paid. (at p. 158).

German courts take the same line. If a person joins a partnership and renders the agreed contribution in kind, the contract of partnership is valid notwithstanding that the parties deferred the question of how to value that contribution and could not subsequently come to an agreement.[11] If a person terminates a contract for the supply of electricity but continues to receive it, a new contract is formed even if the parties are still in dispute over the tariff. If they cannot agree, §§ 315, 316 BGB allow the supplier

---

[10] [1949] 1 All ER 155 (CA).
[11] BGH 23 Nov. 1959, [1960] *NJW* 430. See also BGH 24 Feb. 1983, [1983] *NJW* 1727; BGH 30 Sept. 1992, BGHZ 119, 283, 288 and J Busche in *Münchener Kommentar zum BGB* (7th edn, 2015) § 154 BGB mn. 6.

to fix the price unilaterally, leaving it to the customer to ask the court to determine whether the price is a 'fair valuation' and, if not, to fix what is fair.[12] The same is true when a house is sold along with its furnishings and handed over to the purchaser before any agreement is reached on the price for the furnishings. Here, too, the court held that in the circumstances the furnishings had indeed been sold for a 'reasonable' price, and since no such price had been agreed by the parties, the court itself set the price.[13]

It is more difficult if the validity of the contract is brought into question before either party has performed. Here, the courts tend to hold the agreement ineffective, especially if the point left open is one of particular importance to the parties, if agreement on it was only to be reached in the distant future, or if the court can find no basis for deciding what term to substitute for the one which is missing. The problem may arise where a lease for a certain period is to be continued thereafter 'at a rent to be agreed'. In a case before the *Bundesgerichtshof*, land had been leased for use as a cinema for a period of sixteen years, with a further possible extension—on terms to be decided, failing agreement between the parties, by an expert nominated by the chamber of commerce. The court held this agreement invalid because it did not include any precise or determinable factors to help the expert make his decision or the court control it under § 317 BGB.[14] By contrast, in *Brown* v. *Gould*[15] the English court upheld a contract whereby a tenant could call for the lease to be extended for a further twenty-one years 'at a rent to be fixed having regard to the market value of the premises at the time of exercising this option'. Here, unlike the German case, the parties had agreed on a method (though rather a vague one) for determining the rent payable. But more importantly, the parties had agreed that the period of extension was to be twenty-one years, whereas in the German case the expert was to determine not only the rent under the further lease but also its duration.

What if the lease grants the lessee an option to purchase? *Sudbrook Trading Estate Ltd.* v. *Eggleton*[16] is authority that a valid sale arises on the exercise of an option even if nothing is said about the price except that it be 'fair and reasonable'. The question was whether it made any difference that the price was to be fixed not by the parties themselves but by two experts, one nominated by each party, and, in the event they disagreed, by an umpire nominated by those experts. The House held that this made

---

[12] BGH 19 Jan. 1983, [1983] *NJW* 1777. It follows from §§ 315–19 BGB that where it is agreed that the price shall be fixed by one of the parties or a third party, in case of doubt it is to be fixed 'on a fair valuation', and if the court finds that this has not been done, it can fix such a price itself.
[13] OLG Hamm 24 Oct. 1975, [1976] *NJW* 1212.   [14] BGH 27 Jan. 1971, BGHZ 55, 248.
[15] [1971] 2 All ER 1505.
[16] [1982] 3 All ER 1 (HL). See also *Queensland Electricity Generating Board* v. *New Hope Collieries* [1989] 1 Lloyd's Rep. 205, 210: 'At the present day, in cases where the parties have agreed on an arbitration or valuation clause in wide enough terms, the Courts accord full weight to their manifest intention to create continuing legal relations. Arguments invoking alleged uncertainty, or alleged inadequacy in the machinery available to the Courts for making contractual rights effective, exert minimal attraction.'

no difference, since it was implicit in the agreement to nominate experts that a fair and reasonable price should be paid.

II. Unilateral price-fixing

Quite often parties to a contract for the sale of goods agree that the price should be set by the seller alone rather than by mutual agreement. This is especially common when the seller sells all its goods in accordance with a price list which it adjusts in the light of market changes and its own costs.[17] When a car is bought for future delivery, the price to be paid is generally the dealer's or manufacturer's list price at the date of delivery. The same is true when publicans or service station operators agree to take all their drinks or petrol for several years from a particular brewery or oil company, when a franchisee enters a comparable undertaking, or a subscriber contracts with a telecommunications company. Agreements like these, which restrain competition by binding the customer to take all goods or services from a single supplier, may be wholly or partially invalid for breach of competition law rules, or because they restrict the customer's economic independence and freedom of action too much or for too long.[18] Likewise, a clause in a consumer contract that unconditionally binds the consumer to pay whatever the list price may be on the day of delivery could be objectionable. German courts only uphold such agreements (*Tagespreisklauseln*) provided they give the consumer the right to withdraw from the contract if between contract and delivery the price rises much more than the cost of living.[19] In business-to-business contracts, such agreements are unobjectionable because 'experience shows that market forces prevent a single supplier insisting on prices which are too high in relation to the general market situation'. Also, unlike consumers, businessmen can be expected to resort to § 315 BGB and undertake the heavy burden of establishing that the price set by the seller is not in accordance with 'fair valuation'.[20]

French courts took a quite different approach to cases of this kind. The starting point was (and still is) that the validity of a contract depends, *inter alia*, on its having a sufficiently 'certain' content. This requirement is satisfied when a party promises something

---

[17] Credit institutions also reserve the right, when entering into long-term contracts, to change the rate of interest from time to time. In England and Germany, such agreements are unobjectionable; see *Lombard Tricity Finance* v. *Paton* [1989] 1 All ER 918 (CA) and BGH 14 Apr. 1992, BGHZ 118, 126.

[18] See chapter 7.C.

[19] See BGH 7 Oct. 1981, BGHZ 82, 21; BGH 1 Feb. 1984, BGHZ 90, 69. Accordingly, art. 3(3) of the EC Directive of 5 Apr. 1993 on Unfair Terms in Consumer Contracts (93/13/EEC) requires the courts of Member States to regard as unfair a term which allows the seller of goods or the supplier of a service to fix or raise the price without giving the consumer the right to cancel the contract if the price is 'too high' (Annex 1 (1)).

[20] BGH 27 Sept. 1984, BGHZ 92, 200, 204f. See also arts. 6:105 and 106 PECL; arts. II.-9:105 and 106 DCFR; arts. 31(2) and (3) CEC; arts. 74 and 75 CESL: Where the parties have agreed that the price or another contractual provision is to be determined by one of the parties or by a third party, if that price determination is 'grossly unreasonable', the judge can replace it with a 'reasonable price' or a 'reasonable contractual provision'. See also arts. 5.1.7(2) and (3) PICC, but only where it is the price that the party or the third party may determine.

which is '*déterminé ou déterminable*'.²¹ In the past, however, French courts took a very narrow-minded approach to the conditions under which a price was *déterminable*. They held that a price was not *déterminable* if it depended on some sort of future agreement between the parties, and certainly not if one party had a unilateral right to determine the price—for example, by a later change of its list price.²² The consequence was the invalidity of those long-term supply contracts for the supply of goods or services to publicans, service-station operators, franchisees, or telecommunications customers which reserved the right to charge the future list price. It was irrelevant whether this price was reasonable or in line with market prices—customers could claim invalidity of the contract even if they had no objection to the supplier's price or price strategy but wished to get out of the contract for other reasons. There was often a great deal of criticism about this approach by the courts. It was also pointed out that the approach was in stark contrast to the approach taken in other European legal systems and in other international sets of rules (see above n 19). Finally, the Court of Cassation gave in to the pressure. It heard a case whereby the telephone company GST Alcatel rented telephonic equipment to their customer, agreed to substitute new equipment on demand and if so, to charge for it '*sur la base du tarif en vigueur*'. The *Cour de cassation* decided that a price determined by the current tariff of the telephone company was a *prix déterminable*. The contract was therefore valid unless it was shown

> que la société GST-Alcatel eût abusé l'exclusivité qui lui était réservée pour majorer son tarif dans le but d'en tirer un profit illégitime, et ainsi méconnu son obligation d'exécuter le contrat de bonne foi.²³

This is indeed a '*revirement de jurisprudence spectaculaire*'.²⁴ There was no doubt that a new rule would have to be formulated in the course of the revision of the French law of obligations. Many proposals were made. The boldest suggestion was to require no more than a contractual agreement stating in clear language how the open point should be subsequently determined by one party or by a third party.²⁵ In comparison, the new rule in the *Code civil* appears rather half-hearted. Under art. 1164, in 'framework contracts'²⁶ one party may be given a unilateral right to determine the price; but

---

²¹ See now arts. 1128, 1163(2) *Code civil* (as recently amended).
²² See Req. 7. Jan. 1925, D.H. 1925, 57: A price is only determinable when it can be determined at the time it is charged '*en vertu des clauses du contrat par voie de relation avec des éléments qui ne dépendent plus de la volonté ni de l'une ni de l'autre partie*'. See Zimmermann 253ff. on the rules of Roman law regarding *pretium certum*.
²³ Com. 29 Nov. 1994, *JCP* 1995.II.22371, n. J Ghestin = [1995] D. 122, n. L Aynès. The Assemblée plénière of the *Cour de cassation* also fell into line; see Ass. plén. 1. Dez. 1995, D. 1996, 13, n. L Aynès = *JCP* 1996.II.22565, n. J Ghestin.
²⁴ See J Ghestin, *JCP* 1995.II.22371.
²⁵ This was the proposal for the reform of the French Code of Obligations made by a working group headed by F Terré. See F Terré (ed), *Pour une réforme du droit des contrats* (2009) art. 60(3).
²⁶ Under art. 1111 *Code civil* a 'framework contract' (*contrat cadré*) is a contract in which the parties have agreed on '*des caractéristiques générales de leurs relations contractuelles futures*'. It is strange that there is no corresponding rule covering contracts where one or both parties agree that performance is to be made in parts over a longer period of time ('*contrat à exécution successive*' pursuant to art. 1111-1(2) *Code civil*).

if the party has not acted in good faith in doing so, the counterparty may ask the judge to award damages or terminate the contract. A similar rule applies pursuant to art. 1165 if someone can demand performance of a service and the price is not determined in the contract: the party is allowed to determine the price itself, but is liable in damages '*en case d'abus dans la fixation du prix*'.[27]

---

[27] These rules still leave many questions unanswered that have been settled in many European legal orders and also in art. 6:104-108 PECL and in arts. 2.1.14 and 5.1.7 PICC: which rule should apply for contracts not covered by art. 1164f. *Code civil*? What is to happen if under the contract the determination of the price has been allocated to a third party? What if the point left open does not concern the price but another contractual term to be determined by one party or a third party? See in great detail J Kleinschmidt and D Gross, 'La réforme du droit des contrats: perspective allemande sur la balance délicate entre liberté contractuelle et pouvoirs du juge' [2015] *RDC* 674, 678ff.

4

Tests of Earnestness

A. Introduction	49
B. *Cause* as a Requirement for Validity?	51
C. Gifts	52
I. Formal requirements in continental law	53
II. The consideration doctrine in English law	53
III. Executed gifts	54
IV. The enforcement of informal promissory gifts	56
1. Pledges of contributions	56
2. Maintenance payments	57
3. Payment for services rendered	59
D. Other Gratuitous Transactions	60
I. Contracts of guarantee	61
II. Contracts for the use of property	61
III. Contracts for the management of affairs	62
IV. Offers to contract	63
V. Modification of contracts	63
E. The Intention to Enter a Legal Obligation	66
F. Summary	69

A. Introduction

All legal systems have to decide whether an agreement between the parties is sufficient to justify enforcement by allowing a party to claim performance or damages for non-performance. Certainly no such claim arises on a promise procured by deceit or duress, nor from an agreement which conflicts with legal rules or public policy. But is this enough? Should one not require evidence that the promisor seriously intended to undertake a legal obligation, or that there is some plausible objective motive for a reasonable person to incur a legal obligation? If the transaction is of a kind which people may enter with undue haste, should we not require that he make the promise in some solemn form, or some other indication that he was in earnest?

The problem did not really arise in early Roman or Common Law, when only certain identifiable promises were enforceable, for in those cases there could be little doubt that the promisor had really considered the legal obligation and seriously intended to undertake the obligation.

These enforceable promises under Roman Law included the strictly formal *stipulatio*, as well as informal promises to repay or return what had been handed over for some temporary purpose, such as monetary loans or the loan of a chattel. But most important in this connection are the 'consensual' contracts, which could give rise to an enforceable claim though there was neither form nor delivery, but only the parties' consent. Kaser said that consensual contracts were 'one of the greatest and most fruitful inventions of Roman law, outstripping the laws of Greece and Germany'.[1] But one must remember that only a limited number of agreements were so recognised—agreements such as sales, leases, contracts of employment and services, in which one party undertook to be bound in order to obtain counterperformance from the other. Other agreements were not actionable—*nuda pactio obligationem non parit*[2]—apart from the few pacts on which the praetor later allowed an action. Rome's legacy to medieval lawyers as regards actionable contracts was undeniably a very complex patchwork of particular claims.

The general principle that legal effect should be given to every seriously intended agreement to render or exchange performances was not fully recognised in the systems of continental Europe until the seventeenth century. The developing economy required no less. Even by the end of the Middle Ages, it is said, merchants already disregarded the Roman view that a *nudum pactum* was unenforceable.[3] This was consistent with canon law, which treated a promise as valid and its breach as morally reprehensible regardless of whether it figured on the list of enforceable types of contract. Aristotle's theory of virtue, mediated through Saint Thomas Aquinas and the late Spanish scholastics, provided further impetus in this direction.[4] The development was finally completed in the seventeenth century when the Dutch natural lawyers pronounced it as a general rule that the law will enforce every seriously intended contractual promise. This was soon accepted throughout continental Europe.

In early Common Law, one could sue on a contract only if there was an appropriate writ. The *writ of covenant* lay against a person whose promise was contained in a sealed deed, and the borrower of money could be sued for the promised repayment by the *writ of debt*. The general claim for damages for breach of contract emerged from the law of tort. At first, the *writ of trespass* was granted only where the defendant had damaged the plaintiff's person or property by force and against the King's peace. But later it lay where the defendant had undertaken (*assumpsit*) a public function: the doctor who harmed the patient instead of curing him, the blacksmith who shod the horse so badly that it died, or the ferryman who let the cargo sink instead of bringing it safely to shore could be sued for damages by the writ of *assumpsit*. This writ was gradually extended to cover all cases of misperformance of contractual undertakings and finally, about the middle of the sixteenth century, to cases where the plaintiff suffered harm—not because the contract was badly performed, but because it was not performed at all. In this way, the Common Law came to accept as a general principle that a party could claim damages whenever a duty undertaken by contract was not performed, or not performed properly.[5]

---

[1] Kaser, *Das römische Privatrecht* (2nd edn, 1971) 526.
[2] Ulpian, D.2.14.7.4. Later the formula was *ex nudo pacto non oritur actio*. But if a mere pact gave rise to no action, it could give rise to a defence. Thus a buyer could defend an action for the price by proving that the seller had agreed that payment of the price could be deferred (*pactum de non petendo*).
[3] On this and what follows, see R Zimmermann, *The Law of Obligations, Roman Foundations of the Civilian Tradition* (1990) 540ff; H Coing, *Europäisches Privatrecht*, vol. 1: *Älteres Gemeines Recht* (1985) I, 399f.
[4] See J Gordley, *The Philosophical Origins of Modern Contract Doctrine* (1991).
[5] This is very well presented by AWB Simpson, *A History of the Common Law of Contract, The Rise of the Action of Assumpsit* (1975) 199ff.

Contractual promises were then legally binding throughout Europe. But the question immediately arose as to whether this principle was too wide. Should an enforceable contractual obligation arise *every* time parties with capacity make an agreement untainted by mistake, deceit, or duress? No legal system so holds: they all accept that certain promises are valid or enforceable only if there is something *more* than the mere fact of consent. What is this 'something more'?

French law used the concept of *causa*, derived from Roman and canon law.[6] Certainly, *pacta sunt servanda* applies, but a pactum was not actionable if it was *nudum a causa*, as was the case when there was no reasonable or proper motive. Pothier's assertion that '[T]out engagement doit avoir une cause honnête'[7] led to the formula of art. 1131 of the *Code civil*: '*L'obligation sans cause, ou sur une fausse cause, ou sur une cause illicite, ne peut avoir aucun effet.*' As we shall see in a moment, this provision was abolished in the course of the recent reform of the French law of obligations.

English courts developed a comparable rule: the writ of *assumpsit* lay for damages for breach of contract only if the defendant's promise was for a reasonable motive, a 'consideration' which was 'good', 'sufficient', or 'adequate'.[8]

Many legal systems go further and require that in order to be valid and actionable certain contractual promises, however sensible and serious, must be drawn up in a particular *form*.[9] In other cases, courts ask whether the promise was really intended to be legally binding, whether there was an 'intention to create legal relations', or whether it was the promisor's intention 'that legal validity should attach to his conduct'.[10] The aim of all these techniques is the same, namely to distinguish binding and actionable promises from those which do not merit the protection of law. While their historical background is in part rather similar, they differ a good deal in legal profile and practical importance from one European country to another. We will now address these differences in detail.

B. *Cause* as a Requirement for Validity?

Before the recent reform of French contract law, art. 1131 of the *Code civil* provided that contracts were void if they had no *cause*, or a *cause* that was false or illicit. The Italian and Spanish civil codes have similar provisions.[11] The concept is quite unknown elsewhere in Europe, and consequently many foreign observers have seen *cause* as an important and even characteristic feature of French contract law, like the English doctrine of consideration, used to distinguish enforceable contracts from unenforceable agreements. This is far from being the case. In the heated debate conducted in France about whether or not the concept of *cause* should be

---

[6] On this, see Coing (n 3) 402f.
[7] *Traité des obligations* no. 42, reprinted in RJ Pothier, *Traites de droit civil et de jurisprudence française* vol. I (2nd edn, 1781).
[8] See the details in Simpson (n 5) 316ff. [9] See chapter 5.
[10] BGH 22 June 1956, BGHZ 21, 102, 106. For further details, see below, pp. 66ff.
[11] See art. 1325, 1343, 1418 *Codice civile*; art. 1261 Spanish Civil Code.

maintained as part of the reformed contract law,[12] it became fairly clear that *cause* means quite different things in different contexts, and that in many cases it is perfectly dispensable and contributes nothing to the proper resolution of the conflict of interests involved.

There is no plausible reason, for instance, why contracts should be void if their *cause* is prohibited by law or against public policy. In these cases, all legal systems hold the contract itself to be invalid, and it is not easy to see why the same result should depend on the illegality of the *cause* of the contract. In another group of cases, contracts have been struck down for *absence de cause* if one party was promised a counterperformance that was non-existent or lacking in any possible economic value.[13] In these cases, the contract may indeed be invalid, perhaps because they were procured by fraud, based on a shared mistake, or induced by one party's use of illegitimate or improper pressure.[14] These are the real reasons, rather than the absence of *cause*, which should be relevant to the solution of the cases.

The same approach also seems correct in the widely debated *Chronopost* decision.[15] In that case, a carrier had promised to deliver the other party's mail to its destination within a short period. When damages for breach of contract were claimed, the carrier's defence was that there was a clause in the contract under which its liability was limited to repayment of the price. The *Cour de cassation* held that the clause was void for *absence de cause*, since it released the carrier from an 'essential duty' under the contract. This result, while certainly acceptable, should now be based on the more plausible ground that the clause was invalid either because it deprived the carrier's *obligation essentielle* of its practical effect (art. 1170 *Code civil*, as amended), or because it created '*un déséquilibre significatif entre les droits et obligations des parties*' (art. 1171 *Code civil*, as amended).

C. Gifts

Promises are normally made in order to get something in return: *do ut des*. It is unusual for a person to promise to do something for no return at all, so the jurist immediately asks whether an act so altruistic can have been seriously enough intended or thought out with sufficient care to give rise to an obligation in law. Which indications of seriousness are required in order to transform a promise into a valid gift?

---

[12] The partisans of the *cause* include J Ghestin, *Cause de l'engagement et validité du contrat* (2006); J Rochfeld, 'A Future for "la cause"? Observations of a French Jurist' in J Cartwright, S Vogenauer, and S Whittaker (eds), *Reforming the French Law of Obligations* (2009) 73. For a contrary view, B Fauvarque-Cosson, 'La réforme du droit français des contrats: Perspective comparative' [2009] *RDC* 183, 198ff; R Sefton-Green, '*La cause* or the Length of the French Judiciary's Foot' in J Cartwright, S Vogenauer, and S Whittaker (eds), *Reforming the French Law of Obligations* (2009) 101.
[13] See Civ. 18 Apr. 1953, [1953] D. 403; Civ. 3 Nov. 1960, *JCP* 1960.II.11884; Civ. 4 May 1983, *JCP* 1983.IV.214; Civ. 3 July 1996, [1997] D. 499.
[14] Under the new art. 1143 of the *Code civil*, a contract is voidable for *violence* where one party, by abusing the other party's '*état de dépendance*', obtains from him a promise resulting in '*un avantage manifestement excessif*'. A party may also treat a contract as void if the counterperformance promised by the other party is '*illusoire ou dérisoire*' (art. 1169 *Code civil*).
[15] Com. 22 Oct. 1996, [1997] D. 121.

I. Formal requirements in continental law

In continental legal systems, gifts must normally, on pain of invalidity, be made in notarial form[16]—lest the donor be impulsive, thoughtless or naïve, or lured into promising the gift by flattery or a sob story. The involvement of a notary ensures not only that the donor's intention is clearly and unequivocally documented, but also that an expert will apprise the donor of all the legal implications. This is especially important on the Continent, where there is a close connection between gifts and legacies. For instance, if the donee is a relative of the donor, the gift may well amount to an anticipated legacy, such that the donee might have to account for it on claiming his rights of succession. Again, especially in Romanistic systems on the Continent, though not in the Common Law, close relatives have an inalienable mandatory right to inherit, and the law must therefore try to prevent the depletion of the estate by lifetime gifts that would frustrate the rights of close relatives.[17] The notary is required to give information about such matters.

The close connection between gifts *inter vivos* and transmission *mortis causa* perhaps also explains why on the Continent one speaks of a 'gift' only where a 'thing', a 'right', or 'asset' is gratuitously transferred,[18] or something is given by the donor 'that is his own'.[19] The rules on gifts consequently apply only where a person, without requesting any counterpart, promises to transfer land or a chattel, to make a payment, transfer a right, or release a debt. There is no gift when a person undertakes to render a gratuitous service, such as by providing information, giving advice, looking after someone's interests, guarding their property, or managing some other business for them.[20]

II. The consideration doctrine in English law

Matters lie differently in the Common Law. There the law of contract is dominated by the 'doctrine of consideration'—the principle that unless a promise is in the form of a 'deed',[21] it is binding and enforceable only if it is made in view of counterperformance of some sort by the promisee. Consideration is required not only for a promise to transfer a specific asset, but for a promise to provide a gratuitous service, such as providing information, transporting or storing goods, or completing another task. A person asserting a legal claim on a contract must therefore prove not only that the promise was actually made but also—unless the promise was made in the form of a deed—that the promise was given as the 'price' for the claimant incurring some detriment in law or giving up some benefit. In a contract of sale, the benefit and disadvantage are

---

[16] § 518 BGB; § 943 ABGB; art. 931 *Code civil*; art. 782 *Codice civile*; art. 498(1) Greek Civil Code. Sometimes notarial form is required only for gifts of land, with written form being sufficient for other gifts; art. 243 OR; arts. 632, 633 Spanish Civil Code; art. 497 Portuguese Civil Code.

[17] See art. 913ff. *Code civil*. On this and what follows, see JP Dawson, *Gifts and Promises, Continental and American Law Compared* (1980).

[18] See the wording of art. 894 *Code civil*; § 943 ABGB (*Sache*); art. 769 *Codice civile* (*diritto*); art. 498 Greek Civil Code (patrimonial object).

[19] § 516 BGB; art. 239 OR.   [20] For more on this, see below, pp. 60ff.

[21] On the form of the deed, see below, p. 77.

usually the same. So the promise given by a seller to deliver the goods is enforceable as it was given with respect to a *disadvantage* of the buyer (the promise to pay the purchase price) or with respect to a *benefit* (claim of the purchase price as against the buyer). It will also suffice if the promise is only given with respect to a disadvantage for the promisee. This would be the case, by way of example, if someone makes a promise to a bank to guarantee a credit paid to a third party: the promise is enforceable because, in granting the credit, the bank suffers a disadvantage even though there is no benefit for the promisor. We shall see later to what consequences this doctrine can lead—some of them are rather surprising. But the basic idea is clear: judicial enforcement of promises is justified only where the promise is given as a *quid pro quo*, in return for a counterperformance in which the promisor has an interest and which it wants from the promisee. If this is not the case, the promise is unenforceable. For the Common Law, it is not enough that the promisor has thought long and hard about the matter or is actuated by the highest motives, nor that there are strong moral grounds for regarding him as bound by his word. The Common Law also requires that the parties have struck a 'bargain', and that the promise whose enforcement is in question is part of that bargain: 'An Englishman is liable, not because he has made a promise, but because he has made a bargain.'[22]

Businessmen, not much in the habit of making gifts, will readily understand the reluctance of a legal system to enforce promises made out of pure generosity. Therefore, perhaps it is not by chance that the doctrine of consideration, which makes a principle out of such reluctance, should be at home in a country such as England, whose contract law has been said to have a 'commercial flavour',[23] a law designed for shopkeepers rather than peasants.[24]

But even continental systems recognise the basic idea underlying the doctrine of consideration as regards 'gifts' in the sense described above. In those systems, a person who has promised to pay money or to transfer goods or property without requesting any counterperformance can only be subjected to legal enforcement of the claim if he demonstrated his seriousness by observing a special formality. Notarised documents and deeds are different in important respects but the underlying principle is the same, even if its application leads to difficulties in practice.

III. Executed gifts

What if the donor, instead of promising to make a gift in the future, actually makes an outright gift right away—say by handing an asset or money over to the donee or by bank transfer, or by instructing his bank to hold his asset portfolio for the donee instead of himself? A person who is definitively disposing of an asset generally understands what he is doing, so there is no need to give time for reflection by requiring him to observe a formality. In many legal systems, therefore, the formality applies only to

---

[22] GS Cheshire, CHS Fifoot, and MP Furmston, *Law of Contract* (16th edn, 2012) 41.
[23] Ibid.
[24] See O Kahn-Freund, C Lévy and B Rudden, *A Source-book of French Law* (1979) 318: 'It certainly seems that the English law of contract was designed for a nation of shopkeepers. If that be so, the common lawyer might retort, then the French system was made for a race of peasants.'

promises of gifts[25] or to gifts 'without actual delivery'.[26] Likewise, only promises fall under the doctrine of consideration: if the promisor spontaneously performs his promise and actually hands over the promised item (with such form as may be required for the conveyance of property of that kind), there is a 'perfected gift', and the donor can no longer change his mind. It is true that art. 931 of the *Code civil* requires a notarial instrument for '*tous actes portant donation entre vifs*', but a '*don manuel*' is treated as perfectly effective even if it is quite informal. But it must be clear that the donor has definitively and irrevocably given up all power of disposition over the object in question during his life,[27] for if the donor intended to keep control over the asset until his death, it would be treated as a testamentary disposition requiring the appropriate form.

Once executed, a promised gift cannot be reclaimed on the ground that the promise was not made in the requisite form. Section 518(2) of the German Civil Code provides that lack of form 'is cured by performance of the promise'.[28] The doctrine of consideration leads to the same result, for the informal 'gift promise' is only unenforceable, not void, and so can serve the donee as a ground for retaining the gift. In France, the matter is less clear: art. 931-1(2) *Code civil* provides that voluntary performance cures the lack of form of a donative promise if the performance is by the *heirs* of the promisor. But the courts have held that, provided the donor was acting spontaneously and with donative intention in making the transfer, his handing over the thing pursuant to an informal promise can constitute a valid *don manuel*.[29]

Under certain circumstances, continental legal systems permit a donor to revoke a donative promise or reclaim a donation actually made, such as when 'the donee has demonstrated gross ingratitude towards the donor or one of his close relatives',[30] or if the execution of the gift leaves the donor unable to maintain himself or his family.[31]

---

[25] § 518 BGB; art. 243(1) OR.   [26] § 943 ABGB.

[27] See art. 894ff. *Code civil*. If a dispute arises about whether or not a '*don manuel*' has taken place, art. 1359ff. *Code civil* (formerly art. 1341ff.) apply (see below, pp. 78ff.). If the defence to a claim for possession is that the property was a gift, and the property was worth more than €1,500, the gift can only be proved by writing or witness testimony unless there is a '*commencement de preuve par écrit*' which renders it probable that the gift was made. The same is true if the recipient is an heir who wants to avoid bringing the property into account against his rights of succession, as required by art. 843 *Code civil*, and alleges that it was transferred by way of sale, not gift.

[28] § 518(2) BGB. Likewise art. 243(3) OR. 'If the promise to give has been fulfilled, the relationship is to be treated as a manual gift.' Article 498(2) of the Greek Civil Code is to the same effect.

[29] Dijon 26 Apr. 1932, [1932] D.H. 339.—Furthermore, the scope of art. 931 is significantly restricted by the fact that the courts in France regard a '*donation déguisée*' (dissimulated gift) as valid without any formality. Such a dissimulated gift occurs if the parties deliberately agree to clothe the gift in the guise of a sale, as by the 'seller' giving the 'buyer' a fictive receipt for the 'price' or where the price is visibly low, even as low as one franc (Civ. 29 May 1980, [1981] D.S. 273, n. I Najjar). Such decisions are clearly an evasion of art. 931, but are justified on the ground that the seriousness of the donor's intention to be bound is demonstrated by the trouble the parties have gone to in order to disguise the nature of their transaction. See G Thomas-Debenest, *Juris-classeur civil* art. 931 *Code civil* (Donations entre vifs, Fasc. A) no. 164: '*L'effort que le donateur doit accomplir pour dissimuler son intention libérale et masquer la donation sous l'apparence d'un contrat à titre onéreux atteste que l'opération a été mûrement réfléchie.*'

[30] § 530 BGB. See also § 948 ABGB; arts. 249(1) and (2), 250(1) OR; arts. 505, 506 Greek Civil Code; arts. 953, 955 *Code civil*; arts. 800, 801 *Codice civile*; art. 648 Spanish Civil Code; arts. 970, 974ff. Portuguese Civil Code.

[31] §§ 519, 528f. BGB; §§ 947, 954 ABGB; art. 250(2) and (3) OR. In Romanistic systems, a gift may be revoked if the childless donor becomes a parent; see art. 960ff. *Code civil*; art. 803 *Codice civile*; art. 644f. Spanish Civil Code; art. 508 Greek Civil Code.

There are no such rules in the Common Law, perhaps to spare the court the trouble of deciding whether the donor's need or the donee's ingratitude was sufficiently great.[32]

IV. The enforcement of informal promissory gifts

A donative promise not clothed in notarial form or a deed is invalid or unenforceable, even if the donee can prove that the donor had considered the promise with great concern and was really intent on assuming a legal obligation. After all, the formality is insisted upon precisely in order to avoid the uncertainties inherent in establishing and evaluating such evidence. But there are some difficult cases where it seems just and desirable to treat the promise as valid and actionable notwithstanding the lack of form. It may be that the purpose behind the promise was so thoroughly reasonable, meritorious, useful, or praiseworthy that the promisor (or the heirs) should not be able to get out of it just by pointing to the want of form. Again, the idea of protecting reliance may speak for enforceability. A person who has altered his arrangements and changed his position for the worse in the belief that the promise would be carried out deserves some protection, at any rate where the promisor should have realised that his promise was going to be taken seriously.

In such exceptional cases, courts almost always tend to hold the promisor to his promise, even in the absence of proper form. Admittedly, they hardly ever give the true reasons. An English judge will strive to find some kind of consideration, even if there is nothing between the parties that could be called a genuine 'bargain'. In Germany and France, the courts contrive through very close scrutiny to discover that the promise was not without reward (*unentgeltlich* or *à titre gratuit*), and that therefore no formality was required after all.

1. Pledges of contributions

Courts are quite ready to validate promises made for philanthropic or public purposes. French law offers many examples. When the city of Nancy opened a fund for the benefit of soldiers' families in 1914, M. Bailly pledged a contribution of one million francs. He then thought better of it, and denied that he was bound since his promise was not in notarial form. The court made him pay all the same: this was no gift, but a *contrat commutatif*. The city's 'counterperformance' consisting of advancing the money from its own funds and setting up an organisation for the purpose, as well as publicly lauding M. Bailly for his generosity '*de la façon la plus flatteuse*'.[33] In other cases where people had pledged contributions to a fund, the courts have held them liable on the ground that they were seeking some advantage, possibly impalpable, such as the cachet of being regarded as generous.[34] In Germany, a written undertaking to

---

[32] On this, see M Eisenberg, 'Donative Promises' (1991) 47 *U.Chi.LR* 1, 15f: 'Perhaps the civil-law style of adjudication is suited to wrestling with these kinds of inquiries, but they have held little appeal to common-law courts, which have traditionally been oriented toward inquiry into acts rather than personal characteristics.'

[33] Nancy 17 Mar.1920, D.P. 1920.2.65, upheld in Civ. 5 Feb. 1923, D.P. 1923.1.20.

[34] See, for example, Req. 14 Apr. 1863, D.P. 1863.1.402; Civ. 19 July 1894, D.P. 1895.1.125; Aix 30 Jan. 1882, D.P.1883.2.245, and the description by Dawson (n 17) 84ff.

contribute DM 50,000 to a cremation society for the construction of a crematorium was held valid. The reason given was that since the crematorium was to be built on city land, the society was really acting only as intermediary between the donor and the city, and not obtaining anything for itself.[35] But why should it matter whether it was to be the city or the society that eventually owned the crematorium? The decision is right, but is the true reason not the fact that the society had already begun the construction work in justifiable reliance on the subscriber's pledge of funds?

In English law, the actionability of a pledge of funds depends on whether the promisor induced the promisee to act in a particular manner, thus fulfilling the requirement of consideration. *Re Soames* is a case in point.[36] The sum of £3,000 was promised towards the building of a school by a person who made it clear that he wanted to help run the school and have a voice in what fees should be charged. The school was built and the promise enforced. If money is being raised for the construction of a chapel in a church, it helps if the subscriber expresses a wish to have the chapel named after him or a memorial stone placed in it in his honour;[37] otherwise, the church had better insist on a deed. Actually drawing up a deed is so simple that it is standard form in such cases,[38] so the doctrine of consideration does not really inhibit active philanthropy in England.

2. Maintenance payments

Deeds are not the standard form used when a person agrees to make maintenance payments to a relative, a cohabitee, or a separated spouse. Such promises are often made in writing, but to draw up a notarial document or call in a lawyer to prepare a deed in family matters is uncommon, to say the least. Are such promises nevertheless valid?

They are generally enforced if the promisor genuinely intended to bind himself and there were reasonable and laudable grounds for making the promise. So it is, for example, when a man separates from a woman by whom he had children but never married, and agrees to pay maintenance. The enforceability of such a promise in England certainly depends on whether the woman provided consideration, but *Ward v. Byham* shows how astute the judges can be in descrying these promises.[39] The father of an illegitimate child had promised the mother to pay sums towards the child's maintenance 'provided you can prove that [the child] is well looked after and happy'. The mother's legal claim on the promise succeeded. Although the mother was under a statutory duty to maintain the child, Lord Denning held that her performance of this

---

[35] RG 6 Feb. 1905, RGZ 62, 386.
[36] (1897) 13 TLR 439; and GH Treitel, *The Law of Contract* (13th edn, by E Peel, 2011) no. 3-011.
[37] See *Re Hudson* (1885) 54 L.J.Ch. 811; *Re Cory* (1912) 29 *TLR* 18.
[38] This is not so in the US, where most states have abolished the deed as a formality. The courts have long since discovered a way round the ensuing difficulty by holding that a promise is enforceable if the promisee acted in reliance on it, as the promisor did expect or should reasonably have expected ('promissory estoppel'). See § 90 *Restatement (Second) of Contracts*, and below, n 73. According to § 90(2), in the case of a 'charitable subscription' it is not actually necessary that the promisee should have taken action in reliance, only that the subscriber could have foreseen such action. See EA Farnsworth, *On Contract* (3 vols., 1990) § 2.19.
[39] [1956] 2 All ER 318 (CA).

duty was 'sufficient consideration',⁴⁰ while the other judges noted that the mother had promised to do more than merely maintain the child, namely to look after it properly and make it happy. In *Williams* v. *Williams*,⁴¹ a husband promised to pay maintenance to his wife although she had forfeited any right to it by leaving him for no good reason. His promise was held to be enforceable: the consideration consisted in her promise to be chaste, not to run up any debts on his account, and not to sue him for maintenance.⁴²

French and German courts find it easier to enforce such promises. In France, a father's promise to maintain an illegitimate child he has refused to recognise is seen as *l'accomplissement d'un devoir de conscience* or the *reconnaissance d'une dette naturelle*, rather than as a gift that requires formalisation.⁴³ In Germany, a transaction is only a gift if both parties regard it as gratuitous. This is not the case if 'the parties in their own minds regard the disposition as a return for something done or to be done by the promisee, whether or not it is of an economic nature'.⁴⁴ It was so held in a case where a father promised the mother to contribute to the upbringing of an illegitimate child, which she would continue to maintain.⁴⁵ The parties regard such a promise not as an act of pure altruism, but as the performance of a duty recognised by decent people, if not by the law. Likewise, a cavalry officer had to honour his promise to pay his long-standing mistress, a barmaid by whom he had three children, the sum of DM 15,000 if he married a woman of his own class, as he planned to do.⁴⁶ So too where a married man promised a 'dowry' of DM 3,000 if the promisee would marry the woman who was about to bear the promisor's child.⁴⁷ These last two cases raise the question of whether the promise was void for immorality, but the court was properly broad-minded and in both cases said that it was not. The courts also denied that these were gifts, for 'the promisor was not acting out of pure generosity and the promisee did not regard the promise as unearned'.⁴⁸

---

⁴⁰ This view is unorthodox. A counterperformance is not normally regarded as consideration if the promisee was already bound to render it either by law or by reason of an existing contract. See below, p. 63.
⁴¹ [1957] 1 All ER 305 (CA). But see also *Combe* v. *Combe* [1951] 1 All ER 767 (CA).
⁴² English law has another device when the promise is not to pay money but to transfer an interest in *land* and the requisite form has not been employed. The promisee who has taken steps in justifiable reliance on the promise can invoke the doctrine of 'proprietary estoppel' and demand specific performance of the promise or a fair sum of money in lieu. See below, pp. 86ff.
⁴³ Civ. 14 May 1862, D.P.1862.1.208; Civ. 15 Jan. 1873, D.P. 1873.1.180; Civ. 8 Dec. 1959, [1960] D. 241. Likewise Paris 25 Apr. 1932, [1932] Sem.Jur. 607 (a brother promised to pay a sum of money to his destitute sisters whom the father had bypassed by making a lifetime gift of all his property to the brother). See also BG 29 June 1927, BGE 53 II 198: Mr Stähelin gave an oral undertaking to the guardianship authority that he would look after his orphaned niece as his own and bring her up in his family. When the niece sued him some eight years later for having breached his duties as trustee of her property, he wanted to offset the expenditure on the ground that his promise was a gift promise requiring form. The *Bundesgericht* disagreed: 'It is enough that the disponent believes himself to be fulfilling a moral duty, as was certainly the case with Stähelin, even if such duty is not universally recognised. In such a case it cannot be said that the disponent had a donative intention, or that his promise, though unremunerated, constitutes a gift. His agreement to look after the plaintiff without charge therefore falls within the general principle that contracts require no special form, so that the oral agreement between Stähelin and the guardianship authority was valid' (pp. 199f.).
⁴⁴ RG 13 Nov. 1916, [1917] *JW* 103.   ⁴⁵ Ibid.; BGH 13 Apr. 1952, BGHZ 5, 302.
⁴⁶ RG 23 Feb. 1920, RGZ 98, 176. For a similar result, see Civ. 6 Oct. 1959, [1960] D. 515.
⁴⁷ RG 11 Jan. 1906, RGZ 62, 273.   ⁴⁸ Ibid. at 277.

Thomas v. Thomas is a most instructive case.[49] When John Thomas uttered a wish on his deathbed that his wife Eleanor should have his house, his executors agreed with Eleanor 'in consideration of such desire' that she should have the right to occupy the house for the rest of her life if she undertook to keep it in good order and pay £1 per year. One of the executors died, and the other contested the contract. Eleanor won the lawsuit. Consideration lay not in the executors' desire to respect the testator's wishes, highly praiseworthy though this was, but in Eleanor's promise to pay the yearly £1 and keep the house in good order. Eleanor's undertakings were manifestly and grossly inferior in value to the right to occupy the house, but that is irrelevant: consideration may well be sufficient even though it is 'inadequate' or even 'nominal'. The critical thing is whether the parties have expressed an earnest intention to form a binding contract, and this is the case not only when they have made a 'bargain' but also when they have intentionally made their agreement look like a bargain: 'The deliberate use of a nominal consideration can be regarded as a form to make a gratuitous promise binding.'[50]

3. Payment for services rendered

A promise to pay for services already rendered is unenforceable in English law: there is no consideration for it, since it prompts the promisee neither to undertake to render services in the future nor to actually render them. Accordingly, a tenant who spent his own money refurbishing landed property which was part of a descendant's estate found he was unable to enforce the beneficiaries' subsequent promise to pay him for what he had done.[51] The promise was regarded as a 'reward' from the heirs for carrying out the work, the works had already been carried out, and there can, therefore, be no consideration in return for the promise. This issue should not be pursued too vigorously when the promise is given after performance but there is still a close link between the two. In the case under discussion, had the tenant begun the improvements at the instance of the beneficiaries based on an understanding that some form of remuneration would be forthcoming, then there would have been sufficient *consideration* even if the consideration were not given until after the works had been completed.[52] A similar problem arises when an employer promises to give a retiring employee a bonus or pension. The promise is enforceable only if the employee provides some consideration, either by accepting some disadvantage at the employer's request or conferring some requested benefit on the employer, such as by agreeing to end a contract of employment early or undertaking not to compete with the employer thereafter.[53] The fact that such payment is really an extra reward for past services is

---

[49] (1842) 114 ER 330.

[50] Treitel (n 36) no. 3-014. Similar reasoning leads French lawyers to see a '*donation déguisée*' as a transaction meant in earnest; see above, n 29.

[51] *Re McArdle* [1951] Ch. 669—It is another question whether the beneficiaries should not be liable on a *quantum meruit* for the amount by which the improvements had unjustifiably enriched them.

[52] See *Re Casey's Patents* [1892] 1 Ch. 104 (CA); *Pao On v. Lau Yiu Long* [1980] AC 614 (PC); Treitel (n 36) no. 3-019ff.

[53] *Wyatt v. Kreglinger* [1933] 1 KB 793.

not enough to render the promise enforceable, however reasonable and earnest the employer's intention, for there cannot be said to be any 'bargain' unless the employee gives up something in return.

French and German courts do not need to go in for such reasoning. Certainly they must consider whether or not the promise is a gift, but if the circumstances show that the parties saw it as the performance of a duty rather than as a gift arising from pure generosity, then it is held not to be a gift at all. Here it is relevant what kind of services had been rendered, for how long, how they were remunerated, and how beneficial they were to their recipient. In one case, an annuity granted in writing by a man to his housekeeper had to be honoured by his heir after the court found that for many years she had been responsible for managing her master's properties during his frequent absences. The promise was thus not a 'donation' but the performance of an *obligation ordinaire*, and valid without notarial form.[54] German courts ask whether the promisor was just being magnanimous in his gratitude for services rendered, in which case there is a gift promise. 'But if the services rendered have given rise on the one side to a feeling of a real debt and on the other of a real claim, [and] the benefit is given and received as the acknowledgement of liability to pay for the services, then there is no shared sense that the benefit is gratuitous and it is not a gift.'[55]

D. Other Gratuitous Transactions

In continental systems, a transaction is only a gift when one person effects a transfer 'out of what is his', by paying a sum of money or transferring an asset or some other right. Every gift is a gratuitous transaction, but not all gratuitous transactions are gifts. Thus it is not a gift to let someone use your house for a time without payment, to grant him interest-free credit, provide him with information for nothing, or to do some other piece of business for him—even to guarantee a debt—without asking for anything in return. These actions may involve considerable economic loss and risk for the promisor, but they are not gifts, and so are not subject to the formal requirements that are used on the Continent to make sure the promisor's intentions were serious.

Under the Common Law, it is different. The doctrine of consideration renders *any* promise unenforceable unless the promisee is to render some counterperformance. It makes no difference whether what is promised is the house itself or just the right to live in the house: in both cases, without a deed the promisee acquires an enforceable claim only if he promises or actually does something in return at the request of the promisor. Much to the surprise of continental lawyers, therefore, because of the doctrine of consideration the Common Law finds it difficult—if not impossible—to enforce contracts of guarantee, contracts for gratuitous services, and many other agreements without a great deal of artificial reasoning.

---

[54] Civ. 3 Feb. 1846, D.P.1846.1.159. See also Civ. 21 Apr. 1959, Bull.cass. 1959.I. no. 205; Orleans 17 Jan. 1977, D.S.1977 I.R. 279; it is otherwise if the promise is seen as '*un acte de pure libéralité*'; see Req. 7 Jan. 1862, S.1862.1.599.

[55] RG 7 Feb. 1919, RGZ 94, 322; so also RG 22 Nov. 1909, RGZ 72, 188; BAG 19 June 1956, [1959] *NJW* 1746.

I. Contracts of guarantee

Since sureties must be protected from exploitation, all continental systems require their undertaking to be in a special form,[56] but if this is observed, the surety is legally bound. This is not the case in England. The Statute of Frauds of 1677 requires promises by sureties to be made in writing (s. 4) but, unless made by deed, even a written promise is enforceable by the creditor only if the guarantor has also provided some consideration.[57] If the loan whose repayment is being guaranteed is yet to be made, the consideration requirement is satisfied when the creditor agrees to make the loan or when he actually does so. But the case is more delicate when the loan has already been made but no surety has yet been given. Then one has to say that the consideration lies in the creditor undertaking, at the guarantor's express or implied request, to refrain from initiating or continuing proceedings against the debtor, to give him time to pay, to reduce the rate of interest, or actually to do any of these things. The consideration provided by the creditor in such cases does not benefit the guarantor personally. But this is immaterial, because the creditor suffers some detriment—even if it is economically insignificant—and that constitutes valid consideration. But is it really a counterperformance for the guarantor's acceptance of liability when the creditor agrees to give the debtor another month in which to pay? Is a guarantee a 'bargain' between the creditor and the guarantor? One may respectfully doubt it.

II. Contracts for the use of property

If A agrees to let B have the use of a property for nothing, no continental jurist would see this as a gift. The doctrine of consideration makes no distinction between this situation and a gift. This is plausible enough. If A has a car with six years of useful life left in it, the only difference between his giving it to B outright and his letting B use it free of charge for three years is the difference between the whole utility value of the car and half of it. Economists would treat both cases as gifts; lawyers—at any rate those on the Continent—would only regard the first as a gift.

The longer one lets another use one's property free of charge, the closer this action comes to being deemed a gift. In one case before the *Bundesgerichtshof*,[58] the owner of a house let someone have rooms in it 'for use as a residence without charge and for life'. The court admitted that 'the protective function of the requirement of formality which guards against hasty and unconsidered promises in the case of gifts appears appropriate also for contracts of loan', especially when the agreement is to last for the life of the beneficiary and the owner accordingly forgoes for all that time his ability to use the rooms himself or let them out for gain. Nevertheless, the court held the contract valid despite the lack of the notarial document required for an actual gift. In view of the fact that the very wording of § 598 BGB makes it clear that a 'contract of loan'—a contract by which someone agrees to let another use his property without charge—may

---

[56] For details, see below, pp. 80ff.
[57] On what follows, see J Chitty, *The Law of Contracts* vol. II (31st edn, by S Whittaker, 2012) no. 44-022ff.
[58] BGH 11 Dec. 1981, BGHZ 82, 354. Similar is BGH 20 June 1984, [1985] *NJW* 1553.

be validly created without the need for any form and regardless of its duration, one can hardly quibble.[59]

Both parties to a loan have contractual claims: the lender can sue if the car is returned damaged, and the borrower can sue if it was not roadworthy and caused an accident. English law also allows a claim in both these cases where there is negligence—but in tort, not for breach of contract. In consequence, if there is only economic harm—such as where the lender receives the car back later than expected, or the borrower has to hire a substitute car to replace the defective loaned vehicle and seeks reimbursement of the hire charges—there is no remedy in tort under English law. Whereas on the Continent, there may be a remedy in contract, though the lender's liability is mitigated: as a reward for his altruism, the lender only has to pay damages if he was guilty of malice or gross negligence, or deceitfully concealed the existence of the defect.[60]

III. Contracts for the management of affairs

Similar rules apply when a person undertakes to do another a favour, such as giving him information or advice, helping him get his property warehoused or transported, obtaining insurance for him, or acting as intermediary with a third party. No one on the Continent doubts that a perfectly informal agreement on such matters can constitute a valid contract,[61] with the result that the promisor can be made liable for breach if he causes loss to his contractor through negligence, generally without the beneficent mitigation of the standard of care enjoyed by the lender.[62]

Here, too, English law can often use the tort of negligence to reach the same conclusion. The defendant's fault need not always have caused physical harm to person or property, for damages under the tort of negligence may be available for merely economic harm if it is suffered in reliance on false or misleading statements made by the defendant in breach of a tortious 'duty of care'. Such a duty of care exists only where there is a 'special relationship of proximity' between the parties, such as arises in business contexts where the defendant has professional expertise in the subject-matter and ought reasonably to have realised that the plaintiff was one of those who might well rely on what he had said.[63] These are the very same factors a continental judge would consider in deciding whether a person who gave gratuitous information had undertaken a *contractual* obligation to do so with care, and is therefore liable when the information turns out to be incorrect.[64]

---

[59] Likewise arts. 1875, 1876 *Code civil*; art. 1803 *Codice civile*.
[60] See §§ 599, 600 BGB; art. 1891 *Code civil*; art. 1812 *Codice civile*.
[61] This is often laid down in the texts: see § 662 BGB; art. 394 OR; § 1004 ABGB; art. 1709 *Codice civile*; art. 1986 *Code civil*: 'Le mandat est gratuit, s'il n'y a convention contraire.'
[62] But see § 690 BGB: A person who has agreed gratuitously to look after the property of another must show only the standard of care 'which he normally shows in his own private affairs.'
[63] *Hedley Byrne v. Heller & Partners* [1964] AC 465; *Smith v. Eric S. Bush* [1990] 1 AC 831; *Caparo Industries v. Dickman* [1990] 2 AC 605.
[64] In *Hedley Byrne* (n 63), the defendant bank had given the plaintiff incorrect information about the creditworthiness of a third party. The bank was not liable in contract because it sought no consideration for its information, but it was held liable in tort. The problem thus solved was described by Lord Devlin as 'a by-product of the doctrine of consideration. If the respondents had made a nominal charge for the reference, the problem would not exist. If it were possible in English law to construct a contract without

IV. Offers to contract

Yet another consequence of the doctrine of consideration in English law is that a person who has made an offer to contract and declared his intention to be bound by his offer for a specified period may nevertheless revoke the offer at any time until it has been accepted. This is because the offeror's promise not to withdraw his offer within the stated period is only binding on him if it is clothed in a deed, or if the offeree promised or gave him something—however insignificant—in return.

Different rules apply on the Continent. Some systems are like English law in treating offers as revocable at any time, but are prepared under certain circumstances to award the offeree damages if the revocation causes him harm. In other systems, an offer is irrevocable, once the judge has checked that it really is an offer in the legal sense rather than just an invitation to treat (*invitatio ad offerendum*), and that the offeror has not reserved a right of revocation.[65]

V. Modification of contracts

Yet another kind of promise is invalidated by the doctrine of consideration. This is where a promise is made by A to B in return for something which B is already under an obligation to do: in agreeing to do what he is under a 'pre-existing duty' to do, B may be acknowledging or reinforcing his prior obligation, but he is creating no new obligation nor incurring any extra detriment which could count as consideration for A's promise.

Thus there can be no legal action to enforce a promise if the return for it is already due by law.[66] A publican who promises a thug 'protection money' for not trashing his premises need not pay, since the thug was already bound by law not to damage the property of others and has thus provided no valid consideration. It is, of course, plain that the publican need not pay, but surely the true reason is that otherwise the legal system would be encouraging extortion, with the courts acting as collecting agents for the extortionist. In other words, the promise is void as being contrary to public policy.[67] Likewise when a police authority or other state agency is promised money for doing its public duty. It is equally contrary to public policy to enforce such a promise, since public services should be available to those with a legal right to claim them, not just to those ready to pay for them. In any case, if the state wishes to charge for them, it should lay down the conditions by law. In all these cases, the doctrine of consideration is not just superfluous; it is actually harmful, for it makes it harder rather than easier to recognise the appropriate grounds for decision.

---

consideration ... the question would be, not whether on the facts of the case there was a special relationship [giving rise to a duty of care in tort], but whether on the facts of the case there was a contract.' (525.)

[65] On this, see above, p. 20.
[66] On such cases, see Treitel (n 36) no. 3-043ff. and *Ward v. Byham* (n 39) and n 38.
[67] See E Patterson, 'An Apology for Consideration' (1958) 58 *Col. LR* 929, 938: 'If D has promised not to murder C in exchange for C's promise to pay D $ 500, the transaction reeks of extortion and blackmail, and one need not have recourse to such a colorless doctrine as consideration.'

The rule also applies in a more important class of case, namely when an existing contract is modified or amplified by a subsequent agreement in favour of one or other of the parties. Take the case where a seller announces that the contractual goods are going to cost more to deliver than he expected, and in order to get the goods the buyer agrees to pay him a supplement. The doctrine of consideration entails that, after getting the goods, the buyer can refuse to pay the supplement, since the seller has done no more than he was already bound to do, namely to deliver the goods on time.

In some cases, there may well be good reasons for such a conclusion, but it is not certain that they existed in the much-cited case of *Stilk* v. *Myrick*.[68] After the desertion of an English merchant vessel by two of its crew in a Russian harbour, the captain—unable to enlist substitutes—promised the remaining sailors a bonus. Back in England, he refused to pay. The court dismissed the sailors' claim: they were bound to face all the perils of the sea as best they could, and those perils included the extra work due to the absence of the two sailors who had jumped ship. If one accepts that the sailors exacted the promised bonus by deliberately exploiting the captain's dilemma—possibly with an implied threat that otherwise they would follow the example of the deserters—the result is correct, for it is clear that a promise made under such circumstances is not actionable. But this conclusion has nothing to do with the doctrine of consideration, for the promise would be equally unenforceable if the sailors had offered some trivial 'counterpart', such as forgoing their contractual tea break or ration of rum. The true reason for the invalidity of the captain's promise is that it was procured by illegitimate duress.[69] Of course, it is open to businessmen to put pressure on their partner so as to extract favourable modifications of a contract—they need not wear kid gloves—but such threats must be legitimate in the circumstances. Such threats are not legitimate when used to take unfair advantage of a crisis the other party has got into, whether because of an unexpected turn of events or because in preparing for the contract the party has incurred great expense or liabilities which he can only recoup or mitigate by submitting or suing. Here continental lawyers use the concept of unlawful duress, and even in England it is agreed that where the rules of 'economic duress' are applicable, the doctrine of consideration is superfluous.[70]

The force of the doctrine of consideration is diminished by a further rule now known as 'promissory estoppel' that was first laid down in 1947 in a famous decision by Lord Denning.[71] Three years into a long lease of a block of flats, the outbreak of the War made it impossible for the tenant to sublet many of the flats, so the landlord

---

[68] (1809) 2 Camp 317, 170 Eng.Rep. 1168. But see the very different report of the case in 6 Esp. 129, 170 Eng.Rep. 851. Both reports are printed in HG Beale, WD Bishop, and MP Furmston, *Contract, Cases and Materials* (3rd edn, 1995) 105f.

[69] So held in *Harris* v. *Watson* (1791) Peake 102, 170 Eng.Rep. 94, where the captain, whose ship was in a storm, promised a bonus to the crew to spur them on to great efforts. Here too, the claim was dismissed—not for want of consideration, but, in the words of Lord Kenyon, because 'if this action was to be supported, it would materially affect the navigation of this kingdom ... for if sailors were in times of danger to insist on an extra charge on such a promise as this, they would in many cases suffer a ship to sink, unless the captain would pay any extravagant demand they might think proper to make'. Note how the case is presented in G Gilmore, *The Death of Contract* (1974) 22–8.

[70] See Treitel (n 36) no. 3-051 and below, pp. 185f.

[71] *Central London Property Trust* v. *High Trees House Ltd.* [1947] KB 130, following *Hughes* v. *Metropolitan Railway* (1877) 2 App.Cas. 439 (HL).

agreed to waive half the annual rent. Lord Denning held that the full rent was payable after 1945, since the reduction was intended to apply only while the flats were unlet owing to the War. But he left it in no doubt that had the landlord claimed the full rent while the War was on, his claim would have been dismissed. The fact that there was admittedly no consideration for his agreement to reduce the rent was irrelevant here, because this was a case 'in which a promise was made which was intended to create legal relations and which, to the knowledge of the person making the promise, was going to be acted on by the person to whom it was made, and which was in fact so acted on'.[72] The result is that a party who agrees to a contractual modification in favour of the other party must abide by the contract as so modified if he knew that the other party would adjust his affairs on the basis of that modification and it would be unfair, in view of such adjustment, to revert to the contract as originally agreed.[73]

The doctrine of consideration suffered a further blow, possibly a fatal one, in the decision of the Court of Appeal in *Williams* v. *Roffey Brothers & Nicholls (Contractors) Ltd*.[74] The plaintiff carpenter had contracted with the defendant to fit out twenty-seven flats, but got into financial difficulties after completing only nine of them. Concerned that the work be completed on time lest he have to pay a sizeable penalty to the owner, the defendant then offered the plaintiff an extra bonus of £575 for each flat he managed to fit out. The plaintiff proceeded to complete eight more flats, and then stopped work. The defendant was made to pay the bonus for the eight flats, as well as the agreed rate for all seventeen completed units. The crucial finding was that there was no duress or deceit on the plaintiff's part, with the second agreement being a well-considered proposal by the defendant in the reasonable interests of both parties. These are the same factors that a continental judge would look for in deciding on the validity of an agreed modification to an existing contract. The court in *Williams* v. *Roffey Bros.* did obeisance to the doctrine of consideration by noting that the defendant had secured a 'practical benefit' when agreeing to pay the plaintiff a bonus of £575 for each additional flat completed. As the plaintiff continued to work instead of throwing down his tools and waiting to be sued, the defendant thus secured a practical benefit of saving the cost of hiring another contractor in order to avoid incurring a contractual penalty with the owner. This reasoning is illuminating, showing the business reasons accepted as binding evidence of taking the contract seriously. That the reasons were held to amount to consideration is not a very convincing way of concealing the fact that, as a

---

[72] *High Trees* case (n 71) 134.

[73] The same rule applies where a party has unilaterally 'waived' a right, such as by agreeing to a later delivery date or a change in the method of payment or some lesser performance. See *W. J. Alan & Co.* v. *El Nasr Export and Import Co.* [1972] 2 All ER 127 (CA) and Treitel (n 36) no. 3-089ff; E McKendrick, *Contract Law* (8th edn, 2009) no. 5.24. In England, this rule can only be invoked by a party who is facing an action on the basis of the original contract, for no *claim* arises out of such modification. See *Combe* v. *Combe* (n 41). By contrast the 'doctrine of promissory estoppel' in the US has been expanded into a general contractual principle of protection of reliance. According to § 90 *Restatement (Second) of Contracts*: 'A promise which the promisor should reasonably expect to induce action or forbearance on the part of the promisee or a third party and which does induce such action or forbearance is binding if injustice can be avoided only by enforcement of the promise.' Details are given in Farnsworth (n 38) § 2.19.

[74] [1991] 1 QB 1 (CA).

test for the validity of contractual modifications, the doctrine of consideration really has no role left to play.[75]

E. The Intention to Enter a Legal Obligation

A valid contract must be made with the 'intention of creating legal relations'[76] or *'en vue de produire des effets juridiques'*;[77] in Germany it is said that the promisor must have intended 'that his conduct should have legal validity ... and the promisee [must have] accepted it on this understanding'.[78] If not, no binding legal obligation arises, even if it is an agreement that all decent people would honour, there being no mistake, deceit, or duress. The stock example is of the dinner guest who arrives at the appointed time only to find that his hosts have gone away: he cannot sue them for the wasted taxi fare.

Although 'intention' to create a legal obligation figures in all the formulae just given, a close look at the decisions shows that the courts impute to the 'intention' of the parties simply what is reasonable on other grounds. In the rare cases where the parties *explicitly* state that their agreement is to have no legal effect, their intention really does play a crucial role.[79] But generally they give no thought to whether or not their agreement is to have legal consequences, and when the court refers to the 'intention' of the parties, this is mostly a fiction. For example, on one occasion when the *Bundesgerichtshof* referred to the promisor's intention to be bound, it immediately added that it was not a question of his subjective intention, but rather of 'whether the recipient in all the circumstances would conclude from the conduct of the other party in the light of good faith and normal practice that such an intention existed'. Here one looks to objective factors such as the economic importance of the matter for the parties and the gravity of the consequences for either party if the other fails to perform properly or at all.[80]

---

[75] See McKendrick (n 73) no. 5.11-14; B Coote, 'Consideration and Variations: A Different Solution' (2004) 120 LQR 19. The same is true for an analogous group of cases, where a creditor accepts less than his due and waives the balance. According to *Foakes* v. *Beer* (1884) 9 App.Cas. 605, the creditor may still claim the balance because the debtor gave no consideration for the release. This rule is nowadays subject to considerable limitations. In the view of Treitel (n 36) no. 3-101, it should be replaced by the principle that such agreements are binding unless the debtor has taken unfair advantage of the creditor's difficulties (economic duress): 'The law would be more consistent, as well as more satisfactory in its practical operation, if it adopted the same approach [of *Williams* v. *Roffey Bros.*] to cases of part payment of a debt. Agreements of the kind here under discussion would then be binding unless they had been made under duress.' See also McKendrick (n 73) no. 5.15.
[76] Treitel (n 36) no. 4-001.
[77] J Ghestin, *Traité de droit civil, La formation du contrat* (1993) no. 10.
[78] BGH 22 June 1956 (n 10) 106.
[79] In *Rose & Frank Co.* v. *Crompton & Bros. Ltd.* [1925] AC 445, [1924] All ER 245 (CA), the parties contracted on the terms that 'this arrangement is not entered into ... as a formal or legal agreement ... but it is only a definite expression and record of the purpose and intention of the three parties concerned, to which they each honourably pledge themselves'. Analogous are cases where parties make their agreement 'subject to contract', or describe them simply as a 'letter of intent', an *'accord de principe'*, 'gentlemen's agreement', or 'comfort letter'. See above, p. 34.
[80] See BGH 22 June 1956 (n 10) 106, 107.

In the first place, one must ask if the parties were businessmen. If so, and performance is to be paid for, the 'intention to enter obligations' cannot reasonably be in doubt. It is otherwise if the parties have a close relationship, such as being married or related. The reason often given for refusing to enforce such agreements is that the parties did not 'intend' them to be enforceable, but the true reason is that the law is often too heavy-handed to deal with delicate and complicated family relationships. The son whose father reneges on his promise to pay him for mowing the lawn can pout, if he chooses, or refuse to eat or get bad grades at school, but he cannot go to court and sue for payment. There may be exceptions, of course. When a daughter who had cared for her father sued his heirs for payment and the court of appeal in Lyon dismissed her claim 'au motif que les soins donnés à un père par une fille vivant sous son toit ne sauraient donner lieu à un salaire', the *Cour de cassation* reversed and remanded the case for a finding whether or not a binding contract of employment had been made.[81]

In *Balfour* v. *Balfour*,[82] a colonial officer returning to Ceylon after a period of leave made a verbal promise to his wife, who had to remain in England on medical advice, to pay her the sum of £30 per month during the time they were to live apart. The marriage broke down, he stopped payment, and she sued. It was far from clear that she had given any consideration for his promise, but the critical point was that the parties had no intention that their agreement should have legal consequences. More crucially, it was said that such agreements:

> are outside the realm of contracts altogether. The common law does not regulate the form of agreements between spouses. Their promises are not sealed with seals and sealing wax. The consideration that really obtains for them is that natural love and affection which counts for so little in these cold courts ... In respect of these promises each house is a domain into which the king's writ does not seek to run.[83]

These considerations may be apt for spousal agreements whose breach is adequately sanctioned by the withholding of 'natural love and affection', but spouses quite often do business with each other—especially when marital accord has broken down, they are living apart, or a divorce is pending.[84] So, too, there may be a businesslike agreement between unmarried cohabitants wise enough to agree on the payments and transfers to be made if the relationship should collapse. If such an agreement is held invalid, it will not be because the parties had no intention of binding themselves but because substantively the contract is contrary to good morals or public policy.[85]

---

[81] Civ. 19 Mar. 1975, Bull.cass. 1975.I. no. 117 (third issue).
[82] [1919] 2 KB 571. See also *Jones* v. *Padavatton* [1969] 2 All ER 616 (CA).
[83] [1919] 2 KB 571, 579.   [84] See, for example, *Merritt* v. *Merritt* [1970] 2 All ER 760 (CA).
[85] See further chapter 7.A. In BGH 17 Apr. 1986, BGHZ 97, 372, an eighteen-year-old woman made a verbal promise to her partner (orally) to take the contraceptive pill, but she stopped taking it without telling him and a child was born. He claimed that this was a breach of contract and that he should be relieved of his duty to support the child. The court rejected his claim on the grounds that the woman's statement that she would take the pill 'could not be treated as given with an intention to be legally bound' (at p. 377). But the decision would surely be the same if the woman had sworn to high heaven that she would take the pill faithfully, or had put it in writing and even had it documented by a notary, since a woman cannot deprive herself by contract of the right to decide quite freely whether or not to have a child. Besides, as the *Bundesgerichtshof* noted (at 379f.), the child could suffer considerably if the mother had to release the father from his responsibility for its maintenance and bear the whole cost herself.

Many of the cases before continental courts which raise doubts about the parties' intention to enter legal relations involve promises by one of them to do something for the other for nothing, *'par complaisance'* or *'aus Gefälligkeit'*.[86] In England, the absence of consideration would usually put paid to any claim in contract. But although this route is not open to continental judges, they are perfectly familiar with the underlying idea and take it into account by checking whether, despite the lack of remuneration, there was a *'volonté d'assumer un engagement juridiquement obligatoire'*.[87] Thus, the *Cour de cassation* had to decide a case where an artist had handed a portfolio of pictures to a barman for safekeeping and it was lost. When the painter took legal action against the hotel, the court dismissed the claim since the portfolio had been accepted *'par pure complaisance'* and that there was consequently no valid contract of deposit.[88] When a firm allows a person to park on its premises as a favour, *'par simple tolérance'*, no *'contrat de dépôt ou de garde même tacite'* is formed.[89] Again it was simply a *'service bénévole'* for the employee of a Paris nightclub to agree to park a patron's car for him: there was no contract that the car would be kept safe.[90] On the other hand, a restaurant's contractual duties do not stop at providing edible meals: the courts hold that the contract includes looking after the customer's overcoat, so that if it is lost the restaurant is liable for breach of an *'obligation accessoire'*.[91]

If a group of people decide to club together to bet on a horse, and the one who was to place the bet puts it on the wrong horse by mistake or forgets all about it, can the others sue him if the fancied horse comes in first? English courts would most likely dismiss the claim on the ground that the person who promised to place the bet received no consideration for doing so. The *Bundesgerichtshof* would agree in the result, but not the reasoning. It would hold that the relative interests of the parties, properly evaluated, speak against the acceptance of a binding contract,[92] for otherwise the agent might be exposed on rare occasions to a crippling liability, whereas his mates could reasonably be expected to put up with the loss of the chance of winning, which is relatively improbable. But the decision would be different if the agreement was a business deal, and money was to be paid to have the bet placed or if ...

---

[86] See A Viandier, 'La complaisance' *JCP* 1980.I.2987 and D Willoweit, 'Die Rechtsprechung zum Gefälligkeitshandeln' [1986] *JuS* 96. It is doubtful whether there is a legally binding contract or just a non-binding promise if several persons agree to make a journey by car and divide the costs. Endless ink has been spilt in France on the question whether a passenger in a private car who suffers an accident has a *contractual* claim against the driver or a claim in tort. So when an accident has occurred in another country, jurisdiction is determined in accordance with the conflict of law rules governing tort (Civ. 6 April 1994, [1994] *Rev.trim.civ.* 866, n. P Jourdain). German law tends to hold that there is a contract (see BGH 20 Dec. 1966, [1967] *NJW* 558; BGH 14 Nov. 1991, [1992] *NJW* 498, 499). See also *Coward* v. *Motor Insurers' Bureau* [1963] 1 QB 259; *Albert* v. *Motor Insurers' Bureau* [1972] 2 AC 301. Compare A. Fötschl, *Hilfeleistungsabreden und contrat d'assistance* (2005).
[87] B Petit, *Juris-classeur civil* art. 1109 Code civil, Fasc. 2-1 no. 10.
[88] Com. 25 Sept. 1984, Bull.cass. 1984.IV. no. 242. The outcome in a case where the depositor was a guest at the hotel was different in RG 4 Dec. 1922, *LZ* 1923, 275.
[89] Civ. 29 Mar. 1978, Bull.cass. 1978.I. no. 126. So, too, OLG Cologne 5 Oct. 1971, [1972] OLGZ 213.
[90] Paris 14 Jan. 1988, *Gaz Pal* 1988.I.269.
[91] Paris 20 Mar. 1987, D.S.1987 I.R. 115; Civ. 13 Oct. 1987, Bull.cass. 1987.I. no. 262; Paris 3 Dec. 1987, D.S.1988 I.R. 28.
[92] BGH 16 May 1974, [1974] *NJW* 1705 (agreement to bet on specified numbers in a lottery). The BGH would have decided otherwise if the betting group had won but there was a dispute between the parties as to how the winnings should be split. See also *Simpkins* v. *Pays* [1955] 1 WLR 975.

several businessmen are speculating according to a plan and placing really large bets. In other cases, as here, it would not be consistent with the intentions of the parties to find a legal obligation, for which it would require an explicit agreement.[93]

It follows that a service which falls within the promisor's normal business activity will give rise to a contractual obligation, even if it is gratuitous or rendered 'as a favour', especially if the promisor should have realised how important it was to the promisee that the service be properly rendered. This was so in a case in which A, a carrier whose only available driver had suffered a fatal accident, needed to fulfil an urgent delivery and asked B, another carrier, for the loan of a substitute driver. The substitute was inexperienced and damaged A's vehicle. A's legal action against B for breach of contract was successful, despite B's defence that he had just been helping out in a difficulty and had acted 'only out of human sympathy and without any intention of entering a legal obligation'.[94] Nor, of course, can a bank which provides inaccurate information say that it should not be contractually liable because it was just 'doing a favour' and not charging for it:

> When a bank provides information the relationship between the inquirer and the bank impliedly acquires a contractual character or something very similar whenever the bank should realise that the inquirer regards the information as very important and will use it as the basis for important investment decisions.[95]

F. Summary

We have seen that while the consent of the parties is necessary for the formation of a binding contract between them, it is often not sufficient. What further requirements there may be, and when they are needed, are questions to which there is no uniform answer. The doctrine of consideration in the Common Law is a comprehensive and ambitious attempt to give such an answer, unlike anything in the continental systems, although the results in cases are often the same. From this, the English draw diverse conclusions. Some see the doctrine of consideration as a characteristic and indispensable feature of English contract law—the jewel in its crown, so to speak. However, critics of the doctrine note that since continental courts do very well without it, one could just as well also abandon the doctrine in England. Lord Wright, who frequently had occasion to apply Scots and South African law in the House of Lords and the Privy Council, once wrote:

> In these jurisdictions consideration has no place; nor has it a place in the laws of France, Italy, Spain, Germany, Switzerland and Japan. These are all civilized countries with a highly developed system of law; how then is it possible to regard the

---

[93] *Simpkins v. Pays* (n 92) at 1707.   [94] BGH 22 June 1956 (n 10).
[95] BGH 12 Feb. 1979, [1979] *NJW* 1595, 1597. Similar in BGH 4 Mar. 1987, BGHZ 100, 117, 118f: 'A binding contract may well arise between the client and the bank even though no payment is to be made.' In such a case, English courts would say that there was no liability in contract (because there is no consideration) but that there was liability in tort. See nn 63 and 64 above.

common law rule of consideration as axiomatic or as an inevitable element in any code of law?⁹⁶

He summed up his conclusions as follows:

> When I review in my mind the scattered threads of argument and illustration which I have set out in this article, I cannot resist the conclusion that the doctrine is a mere incumbrance. A scientific or logical theory of contract would in my opinion take as the test of contractual intention the answer to the overriding question whether there was a deliberate and serious intention, free from illegality, immorality, mistake, fraud or duress, to make a binding contract. That must be in each case a question of fact.⁹⁷

Another author has concluded that:

> English law would lose nothing if the doctrine of consideration were to be abolished ... The civil law systems have been able to develop a perfectly adequate law of contract without consideration. If the idea of the harmonization of laws, therefore, is to be taken seriously the doctrine of consideration must go. In its present form it makes no contribution to English law, it is alien to the civil law and it will serve no useful purpose in an enlarged area of European law.⁹⁸

These are hard words. But when one looks more closely, one sees that the scorn of English critics is directed not to the basic idea underlying the doctrine, but to the fact that in the course of time it has been put to uses and artifices at odds with its original mission.⁹⁹ There is thus little sympathy with the doctrine when it is used to question the validity of an agreement which modifies an existing contract in favour of one of the parties, or gives him the right to render a lesser performance than was originally agreed.¹⁰⁰ This has been described as 'that adjunct of the doctrine of consideration which has done most to give it a bad reputation'.¹⁰¹ The iron logic of the consideration doctrine is also held to lead to the conclusion that a businessman who unequivocally declares that his offer is to remain open for acceptance for a stated period may revoke it at any time before it is actually accepted. In England today, there is general agreement that these outposts of the doctrine should be quietly abandoned, since they can no longer be authoritatively defended. International sets of regulations also require no more for the conclusion, amendment, or revocation of a valid contract than a binding

---

⁹⁶ Lord Wright, 'Ought the Doctrine of Consideration to be Abolished from the Common Law?' (1936) 49 *Harv. LR* 1225, 1226.
⁹⁷ Ibid. at 1251.
⁹⁸ AG Chloros, 'The Doctrine of Consideration and the Reform of the Law of Contract, A Comparative Analysis' (1968) 17 *ICLQ* 137, 164f. See also for criticism, R Pound, 'Promise or Bargain' (1959) 33 *Tul. LR* 455, for the defence, Patterson (n 67); wryly for reform J Gordon, 'A Dialogue about the Doctrine of Consideration' (1990) 75 *Cornell LR* 987. In the opinion of P Atiyah, application of the doctrine of consideration generally turns on whether in the case at hand the court can find 'a sufficient reason' for holding someone to his promise; see P Atiyah, 'Consideration: A Restatement' in *Essays on Contract* 186 (1986). See also McKendrick (n 73) no. 5.29.
⁹⁹ This also emerges from the criticisms of Dawson (n 17) 207ff, and Gilmore (n 69) 21ff.
¹⁰⁰ See the text to nn. 68–75. Thus, art. 29(1) CISG provides, quite obviously to continental eyes: 'A contract may be modified or terminated by the mere agreement of the parties.'
¹⁰¹ Patterson (n 67).

'agreement' of the parties, and this 'without further qualification'—as can be seen by the clear departure from the doctrines of *cause* and consideration.[102]

The situation is different with regard to promises of gifts, namely promises whose performance would permanently diminish the estate of the promisor and increase that of the promisee. Both in England and on the Continent, such promises are valid only if they are in a particular prescribed form—a deed or a notarial document. Here European systems are in alignment, and for good reason: the formality provides cogent proof that the promisor really meant to be bound by his promise. Of course, some seriously considered promises will continue to be given verbally or in social or business correspondence, but it would make for undue uncertainty in the law if judges had to verify in each case whether or not the promisor's verbal or written declaration reflected a 'deliberate and serious intention'.

This leaves other gratuitous transactions. Here there is a deep and perhaps unbridgeable chasm between Common Law and Civil Law, for no English lawyer will accept that a person enters into a binding contract when he gratuitously agrees to let someone use his property, or give him information or help him out with a piece of business. But this dissension would only be a matter for regret if it made much difference in practice. But it is not clear that it does, for the continental courts can often hold that the promisor did not intend to enter legal relations[103] and the English courts can conjure up some consideration somehow. Furthermore, the claims that are actually brought in practice are not usually claims for enforcement, but claims for damages because the promise has been poorly executed. Here, where the continental systems offer a claim in contract, English law can quite often offer one in tort.[104]

---

[102] See art. 2:101 (1) PECL (in conjunction with art. 1:107 PECL); art. 3.1.2 PICC; art. II.-4:108 DCFR; art. 30 CESL.
[103] See text to nn 90ff. above.   [104] See text to nn 85f. above.

5
Formalities

A. Introduction	73
B. Reasons for Formal Requirements	75
C. Types of Formalities	76
D. Sanctions	78
I. Exclusion of oral evidence	78
II. Invalidity	80
1. Guarantees	80
2. Sales of land	83
III. Other sanctions	84
E. Enforcement of Contracts Lacking the Requisite Form	84

A. Introduction

All legal systems in Europe have rules that invalidate certain contracts if specified formalities are ignored. Such rules are commonly regarded as exceptional, the general principle being that no formalities are required. Indeed, this principle is explicit in most civil codes.[1] The French *Code civil* used to be silent on this point, but the recent reform of the law of obligations has led to the provision of art. 1172(2), under which contracts are void unless there was compliance with the '*formes déterminées par la loi*'.

Self-evident as it may seem to us today that contracts should not require any particular form, but be enforceable even if concluded by word of mouth, this has by no means always been accepted. Indeed, the further back into the past one goes, the more the validity of legal acts is found to depend on external formalities. To begin with, legal consequences ensued *only* from formalised conduct.[2] Older Roman law offers many instances. For example, in the *mancipatio*, which was essential for the acquisition of certain kinds of property, the transferee was required to grasp the item to be transferred and deliver himself of a specified form of words, all this being in the presence of the transferor, an independent *libripens* carrying scales, and five witnesses. The subjective intentions of the parties were irrelevant: the property was transferred by the formal act itself, even if this was not what the parties intended, such as where they were in error over the identity of the item.[3]

---

[1] Likewise § 883 ABGB; § 125 sent. 1 BGB; art. 11 OR; art. 158 Greek Civil Code; art. 1325 no. 4 *Codice civile*; art. 3:39 BW; art. 1278 Spanish Civil Code; art. 219 Portuguese Civil Code; art. 73 Polish Civil Code.

[2] For details, see R Zimmermann, *The Law of Obligations, Roman Foundations of the Civilian Tradition* (1990) 68ff, 82ff.

[3] The matter is well illustrated by the biblical story of Laban and Jacob. After Jacob had served Laban faithfully for seven years, Laban promised him the hand of his beautiful daughter Rachel in marriage.

As law matured and the economy developed, these archaic, cumbrous, and irksome formalities were progressively relaxed, replaced by simpler substitutes or abolished altogether. Whereas originally promises had to be made by formal *stipulatio* if they were to be binding, effect was later given to what were called the 'consensual contracts', where informal agreement was sufficient. The traditional forms were increasingly replaced by documents, often drawn up by scriveners, which might then have to be witnessed or registered with the authorities. The idea developed that formality was simply an *extra* requirement for the validity of the contract, over and above the consent of the parties, when there was some special reason for requiring it. One such reason was the prevention or dissuasion of fraud in litigation: as long as the rules of evidence were complex and juries easily misled, there was a risk that a plaintiff might allege that a contract had been made orally when it had not, forswear himself, or bring along corrupt witnesses. That is why in France as early as 1566, the *Ordonnance de Moulins* laid down that witnesses could not testify to the formation of contracts worth more than a hundred livres (art. 54, now art. 1341 *Code civil*). So, too, the purpose of the English Statute of Frauds in 1677, according to its Preamble, was 'the prevention of many fraudulent practices which are commonly endeavoured to be upheld by perjury and subornation of perjury'; it therefore provided that certain statements and contracts should be actionable only if they were made in writing.[4]

Such reasons no longer apply. Yet it would be a mistake to suppose that formalities are no longer important in modern systems—quite the contrary. New formal requirements are constantly being imposed everywhere, in the name of consumer protection, to such an extent that in France there has been much discussion of the *renaissance de formalisme*.[5] If lawyers still regard informality as the norm, they may perhaps be out of touch with current reality. Not only is form required for more and more contracts, but it remains an inveterate tendency of the man in the street to regard contracts as valid only if they are made in writing: 'A verbal contract isn't worth the paper it is written on.'[6] This is a perfectly understandable attitude, for really the only contracts which are still made orally are everyday transactions when the parties perform on the spot. In almost all other cases the parties sign a form, possibly with handwritten or typed additions. There are two reasons for this. First, firms need to have every transaction in writing because so many different departments are involved in checking the stock, in procuring, preparing, packing, and despatching the goods, and in keeping and crediting the customer's account. Secondly, firms want to do business on terms they

---

At the actual marriage ceremony, Laban deceitfully substituted her ugly sister Leah, heavily veiled. Jacob was understandably disappointed the morning after, but no one suggests that he thought to question the validity of the formally correct marriage ceremony, neither the Bible itself (Moses 1:29) nor Thomas Mann (*Joseph and his Brothers*, Book I (*The Adventures of Jacob*) ch 6).

[4] See E Rabel, 'The Statute of Frauds and Comparative Legal History' (1947) 63 *LQR* 174, criticised by AWB Simpson, *A History of the Common Law of Contract* (1975) 599ff.

[5] See J Ghestin, *Traité de droit civil, La formation du contrat* (1993) n 373 with references to the literature.

[6] This saying, attributed to Sam Goldwyn, is cited in HG Beale, WD Bishop, and MP Furmston, *Contract, Cases and Materials* (3rd edn, 1995) 139. See also GS Cheshire, CHS Fifoot, and MP Furmston, *Law of Contract* (16th edn, 2012) 288: 'It may well be that the most widely held misapprehension about English law is that a contract needs to be in writing and signed.'

themselves have worked out, and this can only be done if these terms are laid down in a prepared form and signed by the customer. Writing is consequently so dominant in business today that the law's insistence on it for an ever-increasing number of contracts in order to protect the consumer may not make much difference.

B. Reasons for Formal Requirements

It takes time and trouble to meet formal requirements—the text has to be drafted, properly recorded, and signed by the parties. The law therefore imposes such requirements only if there is some good reason for doing so.

One such reason has to do with *proof* and *evidence*. Parties whose agreement is purely verbal may easily find themselves in disagreement over what was agreed and when. If they put their undertakings and agreements in writing, such disputes are still possible, but they are much less likely.

Other formal requirements have the alternative or additional purpose of putting the parties on *notice*. Requiring a person who is about to embark on an important undertaking to go through a formality affords him a final chance to reflect on what he is doing. This is desirable not only when the transaction is an important one, but also when it is one-sided: a party giving something for nothing may need to be protected from impulsive generosity or exposure to unconsidered risks. This is why donative promises and guarantees are always subjected to formal requirements. The written-form requirement does not necessarily afford much time for reflection since it does not take long to draw up and sign a guarantee agreement, yet people—especially laymen—have the impression that when a pen is put in their hand they are entering the sphere of obligation, and this concentrates the mind on the question whether they really want to engage in a legally enforceable transaction.

Sometimes formalities are required in order to mark the *transition* from negotiation to contract. In circumstances where pre-contractual negotiations tend to be prolonged, the parties can easily disagree on whether the negotiations have reached the stage of agreement and legal obligation. But if the contract has to be in writing or notarised, the answer is clear. Parties know that nothing they say or write during the negotiations is binding in law and that they may break off the negotiations without liability; they also know that they should not rely on what the other party has said until it is put into the correct written form.

Modern legislation increasingly requires that a contract be put in writing when one of the parties to it needs special protection. Since these contracts are put in writing anyway, it may seem superfluous for the law to make it mandatory. In fact, the law is not so much concerned with the written form as such: it seeks to ensure that the party needing protection is provided with certain information before or at the time the contract is concluded. The primary purpose of this written-form requirement is to *provide information*. Thus a firm offering credit must provide the consumer with numerous data, precisely specified by law, in particular as to the 'effective' rate of interest.[7] Doorstep sales can indeed be agreed verbally without a written contract, but

---

[7] See art. 19 of the EC Directive on Consumer Credit 2000/48 of 23 April 2008 (OJ 2008 L 133/6).

the consumer must be given written details of his right to withdraw from the contract and the address where such withdrawal should be sent. France has been particularly zealous in requiring information,[8] sometimes in slightly dotty detail. Insurance contracts must not only be in writing, which is obvious enough, but policy terms must be '*en caractères apparents*' and certain terms enumerated by law must even be '*en caractères très apparents*'.[9] Such regulation is doubtless well intentioned, but it is doubtful whether it is effective.[10] A consumer in urgent need of money will hardly be deterred from accepting credit by the mass of information he has to be given, though it will prevent him saying afterwards that he did not know what he was letting himself in for. Good deeds overdone can be a bane. Man's ability to process information thrust on him is limited. The costs of such paternalistic legislation are sometimes underestimated. They comprise not only the cost of paper and printing, but also the legal uncertainty which results from the courts forever having to deal with the question of the sanctions to be applied—in particular whether the protected party can withdraw from the contract on the basis of a contravention of the duty to provide information, when he may have quite different reasons for wanting to get out of the obligation.

C. Types of Formalities

When contracts or other legal acts have to be made in a particular form, the form required nowadays is writing.[11] Usually the text must be embodied in a document signed by the grantor or the parties to the contract.[12] Sometimes the document has to be at least partly handwritten by the party issuing it: in some jurisdictions, a contract of guarantee is binding only if the guarantor puts in writing alongside his signature the maximum sum he is prepared to guarantee.[13] In other cases, certain items of information must be provided in writing.[14] Finally, there are several special written formalities.

---

[8] See the details in Ghestin (n 5) n 443; B Starck, H Roland, and L Boyer, *Droit civil, Obligations, Contrat et quasi-contrat, Régime général* (5th edn, 1995) n 197ff; F Terré, P Simler, and Y Lequette, *Droit civil, Les obligations* (11th edn, 2013) nn 139ff.

[9] Article L. 112-3, 112-4, 113-15 *Code des assurances*.

[10] See Starck, Roland, and Boyer (n 8) n 210: '*Il n'est pas sûr que ce fracas bureaucratique atteindra la protection tant recherchée... Quel esprit morbide s'aventurera dans la lecture attentive d'une telle masse de documents. Ce qui est certain, c'est qu'un contentieux ne manquera pas de naître de cette accumulation de précisions en pratique inaccessibles*'. See also the bitter critique by Terré, Simler, and Lequette (n 8) n 256.

[11] An unusual kind of form is sometimes produced in English law by the doctrine of consideration, whereby a promise is valid only if it is given with a view to some promise or performance by the promisee, the 'consideration'. Since consideration may be 'nominal', a valid option on a house is created if in return for a promise to keep the offer open the seller asks for £1, or even a peppercorn. This 'symbolic' consideration of no real value is a formality—one which makes clear to the offeror that a legally binding contract is in issue. See above, pp. 55, 58f.

[12] See § 126 BGB; arts. 13–15 OR; art. 160 Greek Civil Code; art. 1325 *Code civil*; art. 2702ff. *Codice civile*; art. 78 Polish Civil Code. In some cases, the written-form requirement is met when the document is signed not by the hand of the author but by a 'qualified electronic signature'. Member States of the European Union wishing to pass regulations permitting such electronic signature are bound by art. 9 of the EU Directive of 8 June 2000 on electronic transactions (OJL 178, p.1.). See also § 126a BGB; art. 1174ff. *Code civil*.

[13] Article 1376 *Code civil*, on which see below, pp. 80ff.

[14] Sometimes—particularly in consumer transactions—the information obligations imposed on the business are made less onerous in that the information must still be provided to the customer in written

One of these is the English 'deed'. Generally, under English law the requirement of writing is satisfied by 'some memorandum or note ... in writing and signed by the party to be charged therewith' (Statute of Frauds 1677, s. 4), but when anyone wants to make a valid promise for which he seeks no consideration, this must be delivered in the form of a deed. This is a signed, written document, which makes it clear that it is intended to be a deed, and a witness must attest the signature of the promisor. Until recently, the deed had to be sealed, but this formality had long become completely vacuous. The sealing requirement was satisfied, for example, if the document uttered by the person delivering it as his deed had the initials 'L.S.' (*loco sigilli*) or the word 'seal' printed on it, or if he (or his lawyer) affixed a circular red sticker with the relevant wording. It had long been realised that sealing was a superfluous requirement, even before Lord Wilberforce uttered his hope 'that we might have got rid of that mumbo-jumbo and aligned ourselves with most other civilized nations'.[15] Finally, Parliament gave way and in 1989 accepted the recommendation of the Law Commission: a deed must no longer be sealed.[16] Needless to say, the legal profession continues with its favoured practice: grants and contracts are still often made 'under seal'.

Another special form of the writing requirement, known only on the continent, is of extreme practical importance. This is the notarial document known as a '*notarielle Urkunde*'[17] or '*acte authentique*'.[18] The parties to the declaration or contract must sit before a notary—an independent legally trained professional with public functions—and make their declarations in his presence. The notary thereupon draws up a document and reads it out to them; if they approve, both they and the notary sign it. This proceeding undoubtedly takes both time and money, since the notary does not act for nothing, but it has considerable advantages. As a specialist in documentary transactions, the notary will see to it that the wording unambiguously reflects the intentions of the parties. Also, the fact that the parties have to seek an appointment with the notary for this particular purpose admirably meets the 'warning function' that also underlies many other cases where writing is required. Above all, the notary must try to ensure that the parties fully understand the legal effect of the business in question, that errors are removed and doubts cleared up, and that inexperienced or inexpert parties are not prejudiced. Lawyers in England, Ireland, and the Nordic countries, where it is unknown,[19] may find the notarial proceeding a little paternalistic, but no one on the continent would think of doing away with it, though one might perhaps adjust or restrict the number of transactions in which the notary's involvement is indispensable.

---

form but—as pursuant to § 126b BGB—a personal signature is not required. This means that, for example, such information may be sent by email.

[15] 315 HL Debs. c. 1213 (1970–71).   [16] Law of Property (Misc. Prov.) Act 1989, s. 1.

[17] See § 128 BGB and the German *Beurkundungsgesetz* of 28 Aug. 1969. In Austria, the term is *Notariatsakt* (eg in § 1278(2) ABGB), in Switzerland *öffentliche Urkunde* (art. 55 of the Final Title of the Swiss Civil Code).

[18] Article 1317 *Code civil*; art. 2699 *Codice civile*; art. 1216 Spanish Civil Code; art. 369 Portuguese Civil Code.

[19] A 'Public Notary' exists in England and a 'Notarius publicus' in the Nordic countries, but their principal task is to draw up documents required by foreign law which the parties wish to use abroad. See R Brooke, *Treatise on the Office and Practice of a Notary of England* (9th edn, 1985).

D. Sanctions

If a contract for which writing is required is made verbally, the law may treat it as void or 'unenforceable' (see II below), or else hold it valid, subject to some other sanction (see III below). First, however, we shall discuss the situation where the sanction applied is to restrict the ways in which the existence of the contract may be proved.

I. Exclusion of oral evidence

Article 1359(1) *Code civil* (formerly art. 1341) prescribes that all transactions worth more than €1,500 must be made in written or notarial form, or the evidence of witnesses will be inadmissible.[20] Many other provisions in the *Code civil* and elsewhere in the statute book require specified transactions to be made in writing. They are merely taken to refer to art. 1359, unless they specify that there must be a notarial document or that writing is required '*à peine de nullité*'.

The result is that if a claimant taking legal action on a contract whose existence is contested by the defendant cannot produce a contract, the judge must dismiss the claim because he cannot hear any witnesses. The rule does not apply when the defendant does not dispute the existence of the contract, or if the defendant has waived his rights under art. 1359. The rule is not mandatory, or '*d'ordre public*' as they say in France, and the court may not invoke the provision of its own accord. Indeed, the defendant may be held to have 'impliedly' waived his rights under art. 1359 if he raises no objection to the admission of the claimant's witnesses, or he asked them questions during their examination, or fails to contest their veracity.

One must not, however, suppose that every time the defendant contests the existence of a contract involving more than €1,500 it has to be proved by documentary evidence, for the rule of art. 1359 is subject to important limitations.

It does not apply, for instance, if the verbal contract in issue constituted a commercial transaction on the part of the defendant.[21] If a lender demands repayment of a loan that he asserts was made by verbal agreement, and the defendant disputes this, the court can hear the lender's witnesses if the defendant had borrowed the money in the course of his business. It makes no difference whether the lender carried out negotiations concerning the loan as a businessman or as a private citizen. Documentary evidence is therefore not required where the disputed contract either involves no more than €1,500, or constitutes a commercial transaction for the defendant or for both parties. It is clear that the legislature has acknowledged that both limitations make sense in economic terms. In the first instance, the expense of legal proceedings is not justified when the amount in dispute is relatively small. And in the second case, it

---

[20] In order to facilitate the adjustment of the monetary threshold in relation to inflation, art. 1359(1) provides that the threshold may be fixed by ordinance; it was last so fixed at €1,500 as at 1 January 2005. See also the monetary thresholds in art. 1341 Belgian Civil Code, art. 2721 *Codice civile*, art. 1280(2) Spanish Civil Code.

[21] Article 110-3 *Code de commerce*.

would gravely impede a businessman, whose time is money, if every contract he made in the course of his business had to be put in writing and signed by his customer.

There is a further important limitation on art. 1359: oral evidence is admissible if the plaintiff can offer a '*commencement de preuve par écrit*', that is, any document emanating from the defendant that is even partly probative and suggests a probability that the contract was indeed formed.[22] Such a document may have been signed by the defendant but may not satisfy other legal requirements—such as that there be as many originals as parties, or that a guarantor must have entered the limit of liability on the guarantee agreement in his own handwriting (art. 1326). If a lender seeking repayment of a loan can produce a letter from the borrower thanking him for the facility and rendering it probable in all the circumstances that the loan was made, then he can—notwithstanding art. 1359—introduce witnesses and any other evidence capable of persuading the court that the loan really was made. A *commencement de preuve par écrit* may also be assumed where a party called to court either does not appear at all, or gives such evasive answers to particular questions as to indicate that the verbal contract was actually made (art. 1362(2)).

Finally, pursuant to art. 1360 witness evidence is admissible where the contract was put into writing but the claimant, through no fault of his own, no longer has the document in his possession, or where it was a factual or moral impossibility for him to procure such a document. For example, in the case of a contract between spouses, parent and child, or employer and employee it may be tactless, rude, or counter-productive to demand that the contract be put in strict evidentiary form, and the *Code civil* is realistic enough to acknowledge this fact of life by admitting the evidence of witnesses in such cases.

In practice, therefore, little remains of the stark rule of art. 1359. One has the impression that French courts will always find a way of letting the claimant bring in witnesses if it is likely that a verbal agreement was reached. In Italy, indeed, the judge is expressly given discretion to admit or reject the evidence of witnesses. The *Codice civile* adopted the rule in art. 1359 *Code civil*, but added a rider that the judge may admit the evidence of witnesses if he thinks it reasonable 'in view of the nature of the parties, the nature of the contract and other circumstances' (art. 2721(2)).

Given that the original reasons for the rule of art. 1359 have long since disappeared, the question has been raised whether it should still be retained.[23] The only remaining justification is that it encourages people to put things in writing, but since the rule only applies in claims against private individuals, it is doubtful whether it actually provides any such incentive. Businesses always put their contracts with customers into writing anyway, as indeed do those private individuals who think that verbal contracts will otherwise lack validity. In any case, there would still be an incentive to put things in writing, even if art. 1359 were to be repealed. The testimony of witnesses would still be permitted in support of verbal agreements, but as such evidence can be unreliable in practice, it really makes sense to secure such contracts in writing.

---

[22] Articles 1361 and 1362 *Code civil*; likewise art. 2724 no. 1 *Codice civile*; art. 74(2) Polish Civil Code.
[23] See J Carbonnier, *Droit civil: Les obligations* (22nd edn, 2000) 187.

II. Invalidity

The situation is different when the requirement of form is designed to protect a party from undue haste in entering an important and risky transaction. Here, the party needing protection must be insulated from legal proceedings if the requisite form is not observed. This can be achieved in two quite different ways.

The way chosen by continental systems is to treat the contract as void: most codes contain a general provision that a 'legal act which lacks the form required by law is void'.[24] Article 1172(2) *Code civil* now provides that a contract lacking the form prescribed by law is '*nul, sauf possible régularisation*'.

English law took the other way. According to section 4 of the Statute of Frauds, 'no action shall be brought … whereby to charge the defendant … unless the agreement … or some memorandum … thereof shall be in writing and signed by the party to be charged therewith'. Lawyers have taken this to mean that the contract is not void, but simply 'unenforceable'. This actually makes very little difference in practice, since the only effect of holding the contract valid but unenforceable is that if it is actually performed, the performance rendered cannot be reclaimed.[25] Thus, a guarantor who pays up although his guarantee is not in writing cannot reclaim the payment in England, because it was made pursuant to a valid contract. Nor can he reclaim it in Germany, because although his promise is void, this nullity is said to 'be cured' by performance.[26] This concept of 'cure through performance' is used in many other contexts where a formality is required, and we now turn to the most important of these.

Transactions that include a formal requirement with a warning function include *gift promises* (see chapter 4.C). When such promises concern the gifting of a particular asset, they will only be valid under continental legal systems if a notary records the promise. Under the Common Law, the *doctrine of consideration* renders *all* promises unenforceable unless the recipient supplies or promises some consideration. However, this doctrine does not apply if the promise is given in the form of a *deed*.

1. Guarantees

Providing surety for another's debt—promising to pay a creditor if the debtor fails to meet his obligations—is a pre-eminently risky business. Not only do guarantors often overestimate the debtor's solvency and are overoptimistic believing that he will pay his creditor on time, but if the debtor is a spouse or member of the family, they are often under moral pressure applied or reinforced by the debtor himself. In order to ensure that the guarantor is aware of the risks and in earnest about what he is undertaking,

---

[24] § 125 BGB. Likewise art. 11(2) OR; art. 3:39 BW; art. 159(1) Greek Civil Code; art. 1325 no. 4 *Codice civile*; art. 220 Portuguese Civil Code; art. 73(1) Polish Civil Code.

[25] See GH Treitel, *The Law of Contract* (13th edn, by E Peel, 2011) no. 5-022.

[26] § 766 sent. 2 BGB. So also art. 849 sent. 2 Greek Civil Code; art. 7:859(2) BW. § 1432 ABGB provides that 'payments of a debt which is invalid only for want of formality' cannot be reclaimed. Swiss law is different, for in principle a guarantor who pays out on his guarantee in ignorance of its invalidity for want of form may sue for unjustified enrichment, though in some circumstances this may constitute an abuse of right. See BG 17 Oct. 1944, BGE 70 II 271; S Giovanoli in *Berner Kommentar* art. 493 OR mn. 12.

the guarantee is commonly required to be given in writing.[27] This needs amplification, for several reasons. First, the requirements as to form and substance may be severe or lax; secondly, the requirement may not be insisted on in the case of those who appear not to need any protection; and, finally, varying sanctions may be applied where the requirement has not been observed.

Most systems are content with a rule to the effect that the guarantee must be put in writing and signed by the guarantor himself.[28] The creditor's acceptance need not be in writing, but may be given verbally or deduced from his behaviour. The statement of essentials in the guarantee must be sufficiently clear: that the guarantor is standing in for the debt of another, who the creditor is, and the amount of the debt. The *Code civil* further requires that the upper limit of the guarantee be written into the document in the handwriting of the guarantor himself, both in words and figures ('*en chiffres et en toutes lettres*'—art. 1376).

In some legal systems, the requirements do not apply to classes of person with enough business experience not to need protection. Businessmen who give guarantees in the course of their business are exempted in France, Germany, and Austria.[29] But there are no special rules covering businesses in Switzerland and the Netherlands, where the rule turns on whether or not the guarantor is an individual or a legal person. In the Netherlands, written form is required only of individuals acting outside the course of any business or profession (art. 7:857 BW). Indeed, a verbal guarantee of a company's debts incurred in the 'normal course of business' may be given by a board member or managing director of a listed company or a limited liability company, but only where the majority of shares in the company are held by the board members or the managers. In Switzerland, a guarantee given by an individual must be notarised (art. 493 OR), unless the sum involved is 2,000 Swiss francs or less, in which case simple written form suffices. In this case, the guarantor must write the liability limit into the document by hand. While this may be in figures alone, words are generally added since this helps to identify the handwriting.

Such provisions are doubtless well intentioned, but it is not clear that they meet their purpose, for it may be disputed whether or not a guarantor is a 'businessman' in the technical sense, or whether or not he was acting as an individual in the course of a business or profession. Furthermore, there are some businessmen who need protection, just as there are private individuals with first-rate business acumen. There is thus much to be said for the clear English solution, whereby *all* guarantees of another's debt must be made in writing. It is true that the written-form requirement may be a slight burden in the odd case of inter-bank guarantees and in a few other branches of business. But these are the very cases where the parties will treat

---

[27] Some systems merely require that the guarantor 'expressly' state his intention to stand surety: see art. 1937 *Codice civile*; art. 1827 Spanish Civil Code. This means that the surety must have expressed himself in clear and unmistakable terms, not that he need have put his intention in writing, though the creditor would be well advised to insist on a written form, since otherwise he runs the risk of not being allowed to bring witnesses to prove it. See also the text below at pp. 114ff. on the question of whether a guarantee, even if laid down in the required form, may not be invalid on other grounds.

[28] Statute of Frauds, s. 4; § 766 BGB; art. 849 sent. 1 Greek Civil Code; art. 7:859(1) BW.

[29] France: art. 109 *Code de commerce*; Germany and Austria: § 350 HGB. See also the different solution of art. 439f Spanish Commercial Code.

a guarantee as binding even if it is purely verbal: a bank would ruin its commercial reputation if it tried to avoid liability under a guarantee just because it was not made in writing. One might, however, consider adding the requirement that the written guarantee should state the limit of the guarantor's liability.[30] This would admittedly involve the creditor in having to work out what that sum was—taking interest and associated costs into account—but in comparison with the advantage to the guarantor of having a clear idea of the extent of its exposure, this is a relatively trivial burden.

If a guarantee is not given in the proper form, it is void or 'unenforceable' and the creditor's claim must be dismissed. The position of the French courts is less clear. The main reason for this is that art. 1376 was originally simply a rule of evidence: the requirement that the limit of liability be handwritten by the guarantor '*en chiffres et en toutes lettres*' was to inhibit forgery. Now that the courts have turned it into a provision protective of the guarantor, guarantees ought always to be held void if the requirements of art. 1376 are not satisfied, but the *Cour de cassation* has not taken this step. Certainly it will hold the guarantee void if the debt is for a fixed amount and this is not stated in the guarantor's handwriting, or is stated in figures only and not in words as well.[31] But where the debt is not fixed, as in the case of a running account with a bank, the court is satisfied if it appears from the guarantee '*de façon explicite et non équivoque*' that the guarantor was aware of the nature and extent of his undertaking. In these cases, the lack of the requirements of art. 1376 does not lead to the invalidity of the guarantee, but only makes its proof more difficult. Everything depends on the circumstances, with the court taking into account not only the wording of the guarantee but also the extent of the guarantor's experience in business, his relationship with the debtor, and his knowledge or means of knowledge of the risk he was running.[32] Thus it makes a great difference whether the person who has given surety to a bank for the debtor's running account is the managing director of a company he controls[33] or a wife guaranteeing her husband's overdraft.[34] A guarantee that fails to meet the requirements of art. 1376 may nevertheless be regarded as a '*commencement de preuve par écrit*', so that the court may hear witnesses as to whether the defendant was sufficiently aware of the risk he was undertaking in giving the guarantee.[35] Rules such as these give the courts considerable leeway, but it is another question whether they manage to strike the right balance between justice in the individual case and legal certainty.

---

[30] As in art. 493(1) OR and art. 1938 *Codice civile* (as amended by the Bank Contract Law of 17 Feb. 1992, no. 154).
[31] Com. 29 Oct. 1991, *JCP* 1992.II.21874, n. D Legeais.
[32] Civ. 22 Feb. 1984, *JCP* 1985.II.20442, n. M Storck; Civ. 28 Oct. 1991, *JCP* 1992.II.21874, n. D Legeais; Com. 18 Feb. 1992, *JCP* 1992.IV.1147.
[33] Com. 26 Nov. 1990, *JCP* 1991.II.21701, n. D Legeais; Com. 25 May 1993, *JCP* 1993.IV.1853.
[34] Civ. 10 Mar. 1992, Bull.cass. 1992.I. no. 77.
[35] Com. 26 June 1990, Bull.cass. 1990.IV. nos. 188 and 189; Civ. 15 Oct. 1991, *JCP* 1992.II.21923, n. P Simler; Civ. 20 Oct. 1992, *JCP* 1992.IV.3083; Com. 16 March 2002, *JCP* 2002.592, n. D Legeais. A different solution applies where the guarantee was given by a consumer.

2. Sales of land

It is not easy to say exactly why many legal systems have special formal requirements for sales of land. While it is true that such sales often involve large sums of money, so do sales of equities, ships, airplanes, and other very valuable chattels. However, the sale or purchase of a house is the most important transaction a person of modest means ever enters into, and then only a few times in a lifetime. This suggests that the special formality for land transactions may be a sensible kind of consumer protection, especially given the aggressive salesmanship characteristic of property companies and realtors. It is also true that in most countries the only way a buyer can obtain an impregnable title is by having ownership entered in the public register, and for this purpose the owner needs a document, since the registrar will hardly act on a mere report of a verbal sale. It is also desirable to have a legal expert involved in drafting such documents, so that they are clear and unambiguous. This is done on the Continent by requiring notarisation,[36] though written form is all that is required in Italy,[37] as in England where 'a contract for the sale or other disposition of an interest in land can only be made in writing'.[38]

In France, by contrast, a verbal contract for the sale of land is valid in the sense that the buyer acquires title to the land without the need for any separate conveyance.[39] It is true that witnesses cannot be adduced to prove that the contract was entered into (art. 1359), but this does not apply if there is a '*commencement de preuve par écrit*', such as a letter in which the seller informs the notary of the transaction and asks him to draw up the document. Indeed, if the seller dies after sending off such a letter, so that no notarial act is ever drawn up, the court can find that the contract was formed if it is sure that the parties were already at one regarding the object of the sale and the price.[40]

This applies only between the parties themselves. If the seller resells or mortgages the property, the first buyer will prevail only if his title is registered, and such registration is possible only if there is a notarial act of sale. It follows that the buyer of land who wishes his title to be good against the world must have the sale notarised: '*Cela impose pratiquement de passer les ventes immobilières par acte notarié*'.[41]

---

[36] § 311(b) sent. 1 BGB; art. 216(1) OR; art. 875 Portuguese Civil Code.
[37] Article 1350 nos. 1–8 *Codice civile*.
[38] Law of Property (Misc. Prov.) Act 1989, s. 2(1). Note that in England and Germany a distinction is drawn between the contract of sale and the transaction whereby, in execution of that contract, the ownership in the land is conveyed to the buyer. This conveyance (*Auflassung* in Germany) in its turn requires a certain form, in England a deed (Law of Property Act 1925, s. 52(1)), in Germany a notarial act (§ 925 BGB).
[39] Articles 1196, 1583 *Code civil*. This leads to the surprising conclusion that a verbal contract for the sale of land is valid whereas one for a toothbrush, if effected on the doorstep, is void (see below, pp. 192f.). A notarial act is, however, required in France where the purchase of the land includes a house yet to be built (*Code de la construction et de l'habitation*, art. L 261-11). Verbal contracts for the sale of land may also be valid in Austria: see § 883 ABGB and OGH 15 Sept. 1970, [1971] *JBl* 305.
[40] Civ. 1 Apr. 1971, *JCP* 1972.II.16998, n. J Ghestin; Civ. 27 Nov. 1990, [1992] D. Somm. 195, n. G Paisant.
[41] Carbonnier (n 23) 173. Meanwhile, this has been explicitly laid down in art. 1198(2) *Code civil*: If two parties claim to have acquired the same land or interest in land from the same person, priority will be given to the acquirer who has the first '*publié son titre d'acquisition passé en la forme authentique au fichier immobilier*' provided that the acquisition was in good faith.

III. Other sanctions

In many cases, it is not always sensible to hold a declaration or type of contract void or unenforceable, or exclude the evidence of witnesses, just because the requisite formality was lacking. For example, if the law requires a party to provide certain information in writing because the other party needs special protection, it would not serve the interests of the protected party to treat the whole contract as void just because the information was not provided. The legislature must therefore fashion some other sanction that both encourages the provision of the required information and protects the interests of the weaker party. Some examples may make this clearer.

Examples may be found in the European legislation on consumer contracts. Such contracts must not only be made in writing, but the professional party must also comply with detailed pre-contractual information duties which it is hoped—perhaps somewhat optimistically—would restore the balance of power between the parties. Such duties exist for doorstop sales, distance selling, timeshares, package travel, and consumer credit agreements.[42] In these cases, the consumer is also given a mandatory right to withdraw from the contract with a period of fourteen days.

Most directives on consumer contracts leave it to the Member States to decide what sanctions to apply when there is a contravention of the duty to inform, and the different national systems offer a wide variety of solutions. Take the case of a bank that grants the consumer a loan without informing him of the effective rate of interest. In France, the bank will be prevented from claiming any interest—in effect rendering the loan interest-free.[43] In Germany, the creditor may only claim the statutory interest of 4 per cent per annum, provided that the consumer received the loan.[44] In the Netherlands, non-compliance with the duty to provide information is regarded as an unfair commercial practice.[45] In England, the bank can do nothing without a court order, and the court may make such order as it thinks reasonable under the circumstances.[46] Two conclusions may be drawn. On the one hand, it is interesting—although perhaps disappointing—to see how the varying national legal traditions have led to different practical results. On the other hand, it is equally interesting—and perhaps equally disappointing—that despite the huge effort invested in the directives, a uniform level playing field for European business has not yet been achieved.

E. Enforcement of Contracts Lacking the Requisite Form

We have seen that statutory provisions often lay down that when the agreement of the parties must be made in a particular form, the contract is invalid in the absence of such form, regardless of whether in the particular case the legislature's aim in prescribing the formality has been met in other ways. For example, if a guarantee is not

---

[42] See, for example, the staggering variety of information to be provided by a creditor wishing to conclude a credit agreement with a consumer: Art. 10 of the Directive on Credit Agreements with Consumers (n 7).
[43] Article L 311-48 *Code de la consommation*.   [44] § 494 BGB.   [45] Article 7:60(3) BW.
[46] Consumer Credit Act 1974, ss. 60, 61, 65, 127.

in the proper form, the guarantor is not liable even if the creditor can prove that before giving it the guarantor had independent advice and ample time for reflection.

Yet sometimes the rigorous application of this principle leads to unacceptable results. 'While it is important not to undermine the general rule that the formalities should be observed, it is equally important that the law should not be so inflexible as to cause unacceptable hardship in cases of non-compliance.'[47] Here too, the question is how to reconcile the need for legal certainty and the desire for justice in the individual case.

The problem generally arises in cases where a person has promised to transfer land, either gratuitously or in return for consideration, without observing the prescribed form. Under what circumstances can the promisee nevertheless claim performance? In Germany, Switzerland, and England, there are many decisions on the issue. But not in France. We have already seen the reason for this, namely that in France, given sufficient agreement and intention to create legal relations, verbal contracts for the sale of land are valid *inter partes*.[48] If the seller contests the matter, the buyer can adduce witnesses if there is a '*commencement de preuve par écrit*'—some document which renders his allegations plausible (arts. 1359, 1361). Such a document can often be produced. Even this is not necessary in the common case where a man has entered into a verbal contract for the sale of land to his cohabitee or son, and it was '*moralement impossible*' for them to insist on having it put in writing or notarised (art. 1360).

It is different in countries where a special form is required before an obligation to transfer land arises. In Germany and Switzerland, this form is a notarial act. In England, a deed is required if the transfer is a gift; otherwise the transfer must be made in writing.

In Germany, a seller cannot invoke the want of form if he fraudulently caused the innocent buyer to suppose that the transaction was valid, with the intention of revoking it if prices increased.[49] Such cases are rather rare. Much more common are cases where both parties were aware of the invalidity of the contract, or mistakenly supposed it valid, or failed to apply their minds to the question at all. Here, too, the contract may be upheld if certain conditions are fulfilled. In Germany, this happens 'if, given the relationship of the parties and all the circumstances of the case, it would be inconsistent with good faith to allow contractual claims to founder on a formal defect'.[50] This formula contains no indication of how it is to be applied, but it does make it clear that the courts lay great stress on the conduct of the parties and their relationship to each other, and ask themselves whether it would be inequitable, disloyal, or faithless for a party to renege on his promise just because of a mere formality.

---

[47] Law Commission, *Formalities for Contracts for Sale etc. of Land* (Law Com. no. 164, 1987) 17, para. 5.1.

[48] See above, p. 83. In France, a verbal promise of a *gift* of land is void (art. 931 *Code civil*), but if the promisor has allowed the promisee to live on the land and by his conduct has '*volontairement créé de faux espoirs dans l'esprit de celui-ci*', he is guilty of a tort and consequently liable in damages under art. 1382ff. (now art. 1240ff.). See Aix 11 Jan. 1983, D.S.1985, 169, n. G Légier.

[49] RG 4 Oct. 1919, RGZ 96, 313, 315; BGH 3 Dec. 1958, BGHZ 12, 6. In England, damages could be claimed in the tort of deceit, but not the property, unless the facts gave rise to a 'proprietary estoppel', to be discussed below.

[50] Constant holdings; see, for example, BGH 3 Dec. 1958, BGHZ 12, 6, 10.

In this context, the English courts have developed the concept of *proprietary estoppel*. This doctrine bars a promisor from relying on the invalidity of a promise to transfer an interest in land if the promisee has made arrangements on the basis of its validity such that to treat the contract as invalid would be inconsistent with the principle that justifiable reliance is to be protected.[51]

It is generally accepted that a promisee deserves no protection if he relies on the promise in circumstances where no reasonable person would have done so. This is the case where the promisee knew quite well that the promise was invalid, but trusted to its being kept because the promisor had pledged his word as a gentleman[52] or otherwise indicated that he would consider himself bound despite the invalidity.[53] It is the same when there is an 'agreement in principle', even in writing, and one party, in the confident and by no means unreasonable belief that a definitive agreement will be reached, goes into possession of the property, reconstructs it to suit his needs, and installs his workforce. Where an agreement in principle is expressly 'subject to contract', each party takes the risk of losing his expenditure if the contract fails to eventuate.[54] So, too, where a purchaser sued to enforce a formally defective contract for the sale of the house he had lived in for fourteen years, keeping it in good condition and paying all the instalments of the price. His claim was dismissed because the court found that he was 'not entirely convinced' of the seller's readiness to transfer the house and knew that in paying the instalments of the price he was running 'a certain risk'.[55]

In *Pascoe v. Turner*,[56] the parties had been living together for eight years in the plaintiff's house. The plaintiff then told the defendant that she could regard the house as hers. Three years later, however, after he had established a relationship with another woman and left the house, he tried to regain possession. The court dismissed his claim for possession and granted the defendant's counterclaim that the house be transferred into her name. The crucial finding here was that—with her partner's acquiescence—the defendant had spent a considerable part of her savings on modernising the house, in reliance on what her partner had told her. German courts also lay stress on whether the promisee arranged his affairs and changed his position for the worse on the basis of the other party's representations. If a son gives up his career plans and labours for years under his father's eye improving the farm which the father has promised to transfer to him in due course, the father cannot then make the farm over to his

---

[51] Treitel (n 25) no. 3-119ff. See also K Gray and SF Gray, *Elements of Land Law* (3rd edn, 2001) 756. The doctrine applies 'where the owner of an estate in land has expressly or impliedly given some formal assurance respecting present or future rights in that land.' In that case, the doctrine 'restrains that person from any unconscientious withdrawal of his representation if the person to whom it was made has meanwhile relied upon it to his or her own disadvantage.'

[52] RG 21 May 1927, RGZ 117, 121.   [53] BGH 21 Mar. 1969, [1969] *NJW* 1167, n. D Reinecke.

[54] *Attorney General of Hong Kong v. Humphreys Estate Ltd.* [1987] 2 All ER 387 (PC); *Cobbe v. Yeoman's Row Management Ltd.* [2008] 1 WLR 1752. Similarly, BGH 25 Feb. 1966, BGHZ 45, 179 where the verbal statements were in general terms and no assurance was given.

[55] BGH 22 June 1973, [1973] *NJW* 1455. It is another question whether in such cases the promisee may not be able to claim damages or restitution of the promisor's unjustified enrichment.

[56] [1979] 2 All ER 945. See also *Inwards v. Baker* [1965] 2 QB 29, *Crabb v. Arun District Council* [1976] Ch. 179; and *Greasley v. Cooke* [1980] 1 WLR 1306.

daughter, saying that his promise to the son was merely verbal, and therefore void.[57] The decision is the same in cases where one party incurs considerable expense with the encouragement, consent, or knowledge of the other during negotiations for a contract that later fails, or pursuant to a contract that is formally defective.[58]

Decisions in Switzerland are in a similar vein. The courts may treat it as a 'manifest abuse of right' (art. 2(2) ZGB) to invoke the lack of form, especially if the contract has been wholly or substantially performed by both parties.[59] No explicit reference is made to the question of detrimental reliance on the validity of the contract, but in fact such reliance is usually present in cases where both parties performed some time previously. This was the case in a decision of 1967.[60] The parties had contracted to buy and sell a piece of agricultural land, and the buyer promptly leased it back to the seller. The proper formality was not observed, and nine years later the buyer claimed his money back on the ground that the contract of sale was void. The court dismissed his claim: the buyer had paid the price, was entered as owner in the land register,[61] and had claimed and received rent from the seller who throughout this period had been tending the property as tenant.

In Germany, too, we find decisions where reliance by the promisee is not taken into consideration, and the question is whether in the circumstances of the case it is conscientious or abusive for the promisor to rely on the defect in form. One instance is the case where in 1943 the defendant company had leased numerous allotments on its estate and undertaken in each lease, which was in writing but not notarised, to transfer the title in five years if the allotment-holder had fulfilled all the terms of the lease. In 1952, one of the allotment holders sued for the title to the plot he had been renting. The facts do not disclose whether the lessee had spent money on improving the plot in reliance on the lessor's promise, or lost out on the chance of buying another plot of land. But his claim was allowed because the lessor, who 'with all the prestige of its social position', had been dealing with persons unfamiliar with business or law and had induced them to believe that their legal position was secure. In these circumstances, it was contrary to good faith for the lessor to 'create and maintain the possibility of keeping the contract in limbo for years with freedom to execute it or to claim it as void as it chose'.[62]

By contrast, for English courts the critical point is whether the promisee made deleterious arrangements—namely, changed their position—in consequence of relying

---

[57] BGH 16 Feb. 1954, BGHZ 12, 286. Likewise BGH 5 Feb. 1957, BGHZ 23, 249 according to which 'the most important fact is whether the promisee gave up something of value in reliance on the promisor's assurance, especially if he has given up a secure livelihood for himself and his family' (at 263).

[58] BGH 30 Oct. 1961, [1962] WM 9; BGH 16 Apr. 1962, [1962] WM 786.

[59] See BG 1 Nov. 1966, BGE 92 II 323; BG 21 Mar. 1967, BGE 93 II 97; BG 14 Mar. 1978, BGE 104 II 99; BG 25 Mar. 1986, BGE 112 II 107; BG 24 Sept. 1986, BGE 112 II 330. This rule, which applies when the parties knew of the formal defect when they executed the contract, may be extended to the case where they erroneously supposed the contract valid.

[60] BG 21 Mar. 1967 (n 59).

[61] Under German law, the formal defect would have been 'cured' by such entry (§ 311(b) sent. 2 BGB), provided that the conveyance itself was valid despite the formal defect in the sale and that the buyer had by registration obtained a title good against the world.

[62] BGH 18 Feb. 1955, BGHZ 16, 334, 338. See also BGH 27 Oct. 1967, BGHZ 48, 396 and BGH 29 March 1996, [1996] NJW 1884.

on the promise: 'The promisee must have relied on the promise or representation to his detriment.'[63] Thus there are no grounds for proprietary estoppel if the promisor can show that the promisee would have done what he did in any case, for example because it was in his economic interests[64] or he thought it to be his duty, given his close family ties with the promisor. It must also be shown that the action taken by the promisee in reliance on the promise made his position so much worse that it would be unfair to treat the promisor's conduct as not binding. Quite often cases involve the promisee having built a house on the promised land, or refurbished or modernised the promised house. But it may be enough that the promisee gave up his previous dwelling or career prospects in order to be of service to the promisor or his family.[65]

If the preconditions of proprietary estoppel are fulfilled, the judge has the discretion to decide on which remedy should be granted. Everything turns on the individual facts of the case. Often a claim for specific performance is granted, giving title to the promised property[66] or creating a right to live in the property for life without charge.[67] In other cases, for example when the promisee has already given up the property or where the value of the property far outstrips his detriment, the promisee may only be granted a sum of money. Again, the amount granted will depend on the individual circumstances. The judge can make a decision on the basis of loss to the promisee, whether in cash or kind, or on the gain to the promisor in being able to sell at current prices a piece of land built on or otherwise improved by the promisee.[68]

German judges have a similar discretion. If the contract is held valid despite the formal defect, a claim for performance must be allowed. But if the contract is held to be invalid, this certainly does not mean that the promisee goes away empty-handed. The promisee may have a claim in unjustified enrichment, as there is no legal basis for anything he has done for the promisor in pursuance of the invalid contract (§ 812 BGB). In addition, the courts may grant the promisee a claim for damages based on *culpa in contrahendo*. This does not happen often, for if a party who broke off negotiations had to indemnify the other party, this would frustrate the very purpose of the formal requirement—namely to preserve the parties' freedom of decision until the contract is notarised.[69] Even so, there is a duty to provide one's partner during the negotiations with such information about the risks of the transaction, as a reasonable man similarly situated would do. It may also be a breach of this duty if a person with legal and business experience assures the other party, who has no such experience, that the contract will certainly come about and tenders a document that he himself has drafted, knowing that the other party will suppose that a mere signature will secure his rights, and when he perhaps encourages him to arrange his affairs in that expectation.[70] In such a case, it is also possible to uphold the contract and grant the promisee an action

---

[63] Treitel (n 25) no. 3-128; Gray and Gray (n 51) 793ff.
[64] See *Taylors Fashions Ltd.* v. *Liverpool Victoria Trustees Co.* [1982] QB 133.
[65] See *Grant* v. *Edwards* [1986] Ch. 638 and the detailed treatment by Gray and Gray (n 51) 796ff.
[66] As in *Pascoe* v. *Turner* (n 56). [67] As in *Inwards* v. *Baker* and *Greasley* v. *Cooke* (n 56).
[68] For details, see Gray and Gray (n 51) 807ff; Treitel (n 25) no. 3-138ff.
[69] See above, p. 75 and BGH 18 Oct. 1974, [1975] *NJW* 43; BGH 8 Oct. 1982, [1982] *WM* 1436.
[70] BGH 29 Jan. 1965, [1965] *NJW* 812; BGH 16 Feb. 1965, [1965] *WM* 674; BGH 19 Apr. 1967, [1967] *WM* 798.

for enforcement. It is for the judge to decide what is fair in all the circumstances. A claim for damages will likely be enough if a large housing enterprise agrees in writing to transfer a piece of land and then assures the inexperienced purchaser that all is in order.[71] But an award of damages may be inadequate—and an order of specific performance more appropriate—where the buyer was advanced in years, regarded the promised house as his final home, and put all his savings into the purchase price, especially if he would have to hunt for another house and perhaps die before finding another property.[72]

Although courts in Germany and England may well come to similar conclusions on this difficult question, one should realise that the differences are significant, and perhaps characteristic. The main difference is that in England the courts rigorously insist on 'detrimental reliance', whereas the German courts are ready to treat it as unconscionable for a party to use the ground of the formal invalidity of his promise to back out of a deal which he has presented to a naïve contractor as entirely free from risk. English judges are less sensitive on this point. In *Taylors Fashions*,[73] both plaintiff and defendant had supposed for many years that the former had an option to renew a lease and that the option did not need to be registered. On discovering that the option was invalid for want of registration, the defendant claimed the premises. Lord Oliver clearly disapproved of the defendant's posture as

> not one which impresses itself upon one immediately as overburdened with merit, and the first impression is not significantly improved by closer examination of the background. But if they are right in law and if there is no equity which assists the plaintiffs, it is not part of a judge's function to seek to impose upon a party to litigation his own idiosyncratic code of commercial morality.[74]

---

[71] BGH 29 Jan. 1965 (n 70).   [72] BGH 21 Apr. 1972, [1972] *NJW* 1189.   [73] Above, n 64.
[74] Ibid. at 135.

6
Interpretation of Contracts

A. Introduction	91
B. Intention and Expression: the Two Theories	91
C. Objective Interpretation	93
D. Maxims of Interpretation	98
E. Forms of Constructive Interpretation	100
I. Implication of terms by default rules	102
II. Constructive interpretation	103
III. Collateral duties	106

A. Introduction

Words are not always understood as intended. The meaning of a verbal statement depends essentially on what the parties speaking and listening think it means, but since what people think depends on their personal knowledge, experience, preferences, concerns, and interests, a statement often means different things to the speaker and the listener. Literature and many other humanities often have to engage with the fact that readers of a given text (a poem, a novel, or a philosophical treatise) may understand it in ways unintended by the author, or that readers at different times and places may interpret the same text in different ways. Lawyers must also tackle this issue, but face the extra difficulty that their texts—be they *statutes* affecting everyone or *contracts* engendering rights and duties for the parties alone—create a binding order from which legal consequences may flow. Thus lawyers must seek to give the text a single meaning, one which will be the same for all those affected. The process of educing such a meaning is called construction, *interpretation*, or *Auslegung*.[1]

B. Intention and Expression: the Two Theories

Interpretation is required if contracting parties agree on what they said or wrote, but differ as to what it means. There are two possible, but contrary, starting points. The

---

[1] See C-W Canaris and HC Grigoleit, 'Interpretation of Contracts' in A Hartkamp et al. (eds), *Towards a European Civil Code* (4th edn, 2011) 587; S Ferreri, 'The Interpretation of Contracts from a European Perspective' in R Schulze (ed), *Informationspflichten und Vertragsschluss im Acquis communautaire* (2003) 117; N Kornet, *Contract Interpretation and Gap Filling* (2006); JH Herbots, 'Interpretation of Contracts' in JM Smits (ed), *Elgar Encyclopedia of Comparative Law* (2006) 325; S Vogenauer, 'Interpretation of Contract' in *Max Planck Enc.* 973; S Vogenauer, 'Interpretation of Contracts: Concluding Comparative Observations' in A Burrows and E Peel (eds), *Contract Terms* (2007) 123; R Zimmermann, 'Die Auslegung von Verträgen: Textstufen transnationaler Modellregelungen' in T Lobinger (ed), *Festschrift für E Picker* (2010) 1353.

first is that precedence is given to the *intention* of the parties, which is consistent with the principle of party autonomy that legal obligations arise from, and are justified by, the free will of the individual. As Savigny said, 'We must regard the intention as the only important and effective thing, even if, being internal and invisible, we need some sign by which to recognise it.'[2] The other view gives precedence to that sign, the external fact of the *expression*, because social and commercial interaction requires that reliance be protected, and reliance is placed on what others actually say, not on what they meant to say.

Even in ancient Roman law, interpretation hovered between these two poles. Originally, when specific procedures or particular words or phrases were required in order to create legal obligations, interpretation turned on the external phenomena, since obviously the legal effect resulted from the actions, words, or phrases and not from the intentions of the person doing or saying them: *cum in verbis nulla ambiguitas est, non debet admitti voluntatis quaestio*.[3] Gradually, however, intention began to take on greater importance, and another maxim of interpretation was adopted: *In conventionibus contrahentium voluntatem potius quam verba spectari placuit*.[4] In the later Empire, under the influence of Greek moral philosophy and Christian doctrines of virtue, interpretation which hewed to the external phenomena increasingly lost ground until it was not so much the *verba* as the *voluntas* that counted. This 'subjective' method of interpretation held sway in the sixth century AD when, on Justinian's orders, excerpts from the classical jurists were collected as the basis of the intended codification of Roman law. Scholars believe that many of the texts so preserved were 'interpolated' or altered so as to reflect the newer—and supposedly more progressive— 'subjective' doctrine.[5]

This tension between more subjective and more objective interpretations—the 'intention theory' and the 'expression theory', as they came to be called—runs through the whole of European legal history. Subjective interpretation dominated legal literature until the late nineteenth century, though whether it was equally dominant in practice is less certain. It figures in the French *Code civil* (art. 1156: *On doit dans les conventions rechercher quelle a été la commune intention des parties contractantes, plutôt que de s'arrêter au sens littéral des termes*), and most of the European civil codes have followed suit: § 133 BGB, for example, provides that in interpreting an expression of intention 'it is necessary to ascertain the true intention rather than adhering to the literal meaning of the declaration'. However, these provisions are often complemented by another rule which looks more to the 'objective' meaning of the expression, and a discrepancy ensues which it falls to the judge to resolve in the individual case. Thus, alongside § 133 BGB we find § 157, which provides that contracts are to be interpreted 'as required by good faith, taking customary practice into consideration'. The Austrian ABGB even puts both canons of interpretation into a single provision, § 914: while 'one is not to cleave to the literal sense of the expression, but to ascertain the intention

---

[2] FC von Savigny, *System des heutigen römischen Rechts* (1840) iii, 258.   [3] Paul, D.32.25.1.
[4] Papinian, D.50.16.219.
[5] The position is very clearly set out in R Zimmermann, *The Law of Obligations, Roman Foundations of the Civilian Tradition* (1990) 621ff.

of the parties', nevertheless the contract is 'to be understood compatibly with decent business practice'.

If parties choose to use words in a distinctive sense, different from their usual meaning, everyone agrees that it is their intention rather than their expression that counts: *falsa demonstratio non nocet*.[6] Thus, if buyer and seller both use the word *Haakjöringsköd* to signify 'whale meat' when it properly denotes 'shark meat', the contract is for whale meat, and if the seller tenders shark meat the buyer can claim damages for non-performance.[7] The same applies to contracts for the sale of land that specify the wrong plot of land.[8] Here the Common Law respects the intention of the parties, but not on the basis of an interpretation of the contract. If what appears in the document differs from what the parties agreed on, 'rectification' of the written contract may be sought if a party can show a 'continuing common intention'—*consensus ad idem*.[9] The same also applies if the true intention of one party differs from the wording of the contract, and the other party has recognised this 'unilateral mistake' by the other party but still concludes the contract.[10] The same solution can be found in art. 8 CISG, where interpretation of a party's statements, including any statements made for the purposes of concluding the contract, should be made according to that party's intention 'where the other party knew or could not have been unaware what that intent was'. The approach in art. 5:101 PECL is the same: contracts are to be interpreted 'according to the common intention of the parties even if this differs from the literal meaning of the words'. This also applies even if only one party gives the wording of the contract a particular meaning, provided that it can be shown that 'at the time of the conclusion of the contract the other party could not have been unaware of the first party's intention'.[11]

C. Objective Interpretation

Cases where the contracting parties were really in agreement but expressed themselves in an inaccurate or muddled manner do not often come before the courts, because in such cases both parties normally do what they intended. Disputes are much more common when the parties attach different meanings to the agreed form of words, with the difference of opinion arising either at the time of the negotiations (where the parties did not realise that the difference of opinion existed or hoped that it would not matter) or later, when something occurs which makes them reflect on the proper scope of their apparent agreement. How should such disputes be resolved?

In cases like this, it is clearly futile to look for the 'common intention' of the parties, at any rate if by that we mean an actual historical fact. Nor can one simply adopt

---

[6] This is laid down expressly in art. 1281(2) Spanish Civil Code and art. 236(2) Portuguese Civil Code.
[7] RG 8 June 1920, RGZ 99, 147.   [8] BGH 25 Mar. 1983, BGHZ 87, 150.
[9] See *Craddock v. Hunt* [1923] 2 Ch. 136 (CA) and generally on rectification, see GH Treitel, *The Law of Contract* (13th edn, by E Peel, 2011) no. 8-059ff.
[10] See Treitel (n 9) no. 8-067ff. Also under German law: see, for example, BGH 20 Nov. 1992, [1993] *NJW-RR* 373.
[11] As in art. 5:101 PECL. Also art. 4.2(1) PICC; art. 34(2) CEC; art. II-8:101(2) DCFR; art. 58(2) CESL. Also BGH 20 Nov. 1992, [1993] *NJW-RR* 373.

the meaning that one or other of the parties gave to the words used, either then or later. What counts is rather the meaning that would be given to the words by a reasonable person, supposing him to be in the situation of the addressee and to understand the words used in the context of all the other relevant circumstances of which he could have been aware. This is generally agreed, and it is the formula used in the UN Convention on Contracts for the International Sale of Goods. In art. 8(1) statements made by a party 'are to be interpreted according to his intent where the other party knew or could not have been unaware what that intent was'. If, as usually happens, this provides no solution, statements are to be interpreted 'according to the understanding that a reasonable person of the same kind as the other party would have had in the same circumstances' (art. 8(2)). In making this determination, 'due consideration is to be given to all relevant circumstances of the case including the negotiations, any practices which the parties have established between themselves, usages and any subsequent conduct of the parties' (art. 8(3)).

Thus, if a businessman in the export business gives a 'demand guarantee' of the price payable for exported goods, he must pay immediately upon demand by the seller, for that is how the phrase is understood in foreign trade. The guarantor can raise defences to the claim only in a subsequent action for restitution, even if he did not realise the technical meaning of the clause. But a guarantee given in respect of an everyday loan by the borrower's wife who has no business experience will be construed as a simple guarantee, subject to all the defences the borrower himself could raise. The guarantor would regard her promise as a simple guarantee and so, in all the circumstances, would the reasonable lender.[12]

Rules like this are recognised everywhere, often in statutory form. Regard must be had to 'good commercial practice', 'the mandates of good faith',[13] and 'well-regarded business usage'[14] International rules also contain long descriptions of such circumstances to be taken into account in interpretation of contracts, most of which are similar in form. These include: the nature and purpose of the contract; the interpretation of the parties with respect to previous contracts they have concluded; the pre-contractual negotiations between the parties; and also their behaviour after the contract has been concluded, where such behaviour throws light on the issue in dispute.[15]

English law has long reflected the view that the interpretation of a written contract turns on the meaning that a reasonable person would give to the same terms and conditions as the contract under consideration: 'Interpretation is the ascertainment of the meaning which the document would convey to a reasonable person having all the background knowledge which would reasonably have been available to the parties in the situation in which they were at the same of the contract.'[16] As well as the 'background' that a reasonable person must take into account in order to interpret a contract correctly, other aspects include the purpose that the parties attach to the transaction, the actual circumstances under which the contract was concluded,

---

[12] BGH 12 Mar. 1992, [1992] *NJW* 1446. [13] § 157 BGB; art. 1366 *Codice civile*.
[14] § 914 ABGB. [15] See art. 5:102 PECL; art. 4.3 PICC; art. II.-8:102(1) DCFR; art. 59 CESL.
[16] *Investors Compensation Scheme Ltd. v. West Bromwich Building Society* [1998] 1 WLR 896, 912-3 (Lord Hoffmann).

customary business practices, and 'absolutely anything which would have affected the way in which the language of the document would have been understood by a reasonable man'.[17] One could draw the conclusion that English law also takes account of all 'relevant circumstances' in interpreting a contract, such as those set out in art. 8(3) CISG and (in even greater detail) in art. 5:102 PECL. But that is not the case. As Lord Hoffmann clarified in a later decision by the House of Lords, 'absolutely anything' does not include evidence from pre-contractual negotiations between the parties being used to interpret the contract.[18] This is based on the idea that statements made by parties in negotiations often carry one-sided expectations, are only meant to be subject to contract, and will later be replaced by the mandatory wording of the contract itself. This is undoubtedly correct, but must not lead to the position that pre-contractual negotiations are completely excluded as a means of interpreting the contract. Instead, it should mean that judges must regard their evidentiary value with the necessary reservation.[19]

What if the interpretation of a written contract on the basis of the rules stated here leads to a particular result, but one party claims that another agreement was reached prior to or upon conclusion of the contract that gives the contract another meaning that the (correct) interpretation of the contract as it stands? Can that party support the claim with documents or witnesses? Must the court examine these documents or hear the witnesses? Continental legal systems would allow such examination of hearings, even if it is difficult to dispute the presumption that the written contract is complete and correct. In France, hearing witnesses may already be precluded by art. 1359 (formerly art. 1341) *Code civil*.[20] Under the Common Law, it is presumed that legal certainty in business transactions is paramount so 'that parties who have reduced a contract to writing [are] bound by that writing and that writing alone'. Thus the *parol evidence rule* states that a written contract cannot normally be contradicted by evidence of a prior contract. Admittedly, the Common Law recognises that the parol evidence rule is not always just, and has been held to be inapplicable in so many cases that the Law Commission has recommended abolition of the principle. Today, it is 'highly

---

[17] Lord Hoffmann in *Investors Compensation Scheme* (n 16) 913.
[18] *Chartbrook Ltd.* v. *Persimmon Houses Ltd.* [2009] 3 WLR 267. Reliance on post-contractual behaviour of the parties is also not allowed for the purposes of interpretation. Justification for this rule was given in *Whitworth Street Estates Ltd.* v. *James Miller & Partners* [1970] AC 583 on the basis that, if a different decision were made, 'one might have the result that a contract meant one thing the day it was signed, but by reason of subsequent events meant something different a month or a year later' (Lord Reid at p. 603). Similarly in *L. Schuler* v. *Wickman Machine Tool Sales Ltd.* [1974] AC 235. But contrast art. 5:102(b) PECL; art. 4.3(c) PICC; art. 59(b) CESL; and art. 8(3) CISG. German law also takes a different approach. See, for example, BGH 7 Dec. 2006, [2007] *NJW-RR* 529, where there is correct clarification that assertions concerning post-contractual behaviour of a party may only be decisive for the purposes of interpretation if it turns out that the mutual intention of the parties was already in that direction *when the contract was concluded*.
[19] See also E McKendrick, 'The Interpretation of Contracts: Lord Hoffmann's Restatement' in S Worthington (ed), *Commercial Law and Commercial Practice* (2003) 139, 155f. See also H Kötz, 'Vorvertragliche Verhandlungen und ihre Bedeutung für die Vertragsauslegung' (2013) 21 *ZEuP* 777. Furthermore, Lord Hoffmann raised the fear that litigation costs before courts and arbitration tribunals would increase significantly if pre-contractual negotiations could be taken into account in interpretation; on this, see also Kötz, ibid., 783ff.
[20] See pp. 78f.

unlikely that the parol evidence rule will preclude a party from leading evidence on terms which were intended to be part of the contract'.[21]

These rules are not inconsistent with the assertion in many legal systems, and also in art. 5:101 PECL, that the aim is to find the 'common intention' of the parties. In France, courts and academics agree in saying that interpretation seeks the *commune intention des parties contractantes*. This is also the starting point in art. 1188(1) *Code civil* (as recently amended). However, when in fact no such common intention can be found, art. 1188(2) now expressly provides that the contract is to be interpreted '*selon le sens que lui donnerait une personne raisonnable placée dans la même situation*'. Some help may also be given by art. 1194 *Code civil*, under which a contractor must not only do what has been expressly undertaken, but also what is required in contracts of that type by '*l'équité, l'usage et la loi*'. In practice, of course, a judge will hardly ever be able to discern any real historical intention of the parties, and will inevitably have regard to 'objective' considerations—to ask how, in the light of all the circumstances, a reasonable person would and should normally understand what was stated. This is so even if the court may sometimes say, perhaps with tongue in cheek, that its interpretation is based on nothing else but the *commune intention des parties contractantes*.

If it is not possible to determine a common intention of the parties, which is normally the case, interpretation of the contract turns on the meaning that 'reasonable persons of the same kind as the parties would give to it in the same circumstances' (art. 5:101 PECL), not only if the contract term could be interpreted in more than one way but also when its meaning seems 'clear and unequivocal'. It is true that some older judicial decisions refuse to consider an alternative interpretation 'if the wording of the document is entirely clear and unequivocal and there is no doubt about the sense of the wording as stated'.[22] The *Cour de cassation* also refuses to review the construction of a contract, treating it as a matter of fact to be decided by lower courts. But where there is a '*clause claire et précise*', the *Cour de cassation* will quash decisions of lower courts which have given it any meaning other than its objective one, even on the ground of a supposed common intention of the parties.[23] This has now been laid down in the new provision of art. 1192 *Code civil*, under which *clauses claires et précises* must not be distorted by interpretation. However, the question of whether or not a clause is really 'clear' turns not only on the wording, but also on the purpose of the contract and the circumstances under which it was concluded. Thus the *clause claire et précise* rule only clarifies that the *Cour de cassation* is entitled to overturn a decision if it determines that there has been a particularly grave mistaken interpretation.[24] Nevertheless, the

---

[21] See McKendrick (n 19) 185. See also Treitel (n 9) no. 6:012ff; Vogenauer (n 1) 135ff. The international sets of rules do not contain provisions equivalent to the parol evidence rule. The situation is different if the written contract contains a *Parteivereinbarung* or merger clause that expressly states that the contract is 'complete'. In such circumstances, evidence of additional verbal or written agreements or statements may only be used in support of interpretation of the written contract, but not as proof of an amendment of supplementary agreement. See in detail art. 2:105 PECL; art. 2.1.17 PICC; art. II.-4:104 DCFR; art. 72 CESL and O Meyer, 'Die privatautonome Abbedingung der vorvertraglichen Abreden' (2008) 72 *RabelsZ* 562.
[22] RG 28 Oct. 1911, [1912] *JW* 69; also RG 8 Nov. 1918, [1919] *JW* 102, 103.
[23] Civ. 15 Apr. 1872, D.P. 1872.1.176; Civ. 14 Dez. 1942, D. 1944.112, n. P Lerebours-Pigeonnière.
[24] See F Terré, P Simler, and Y Lequette, *Droit civil, Les obligations* (11th edn, 2013) no. 459; Vogenauer (n 1) 132ff.

rule remains that construction of a written contract is to be determined on the basis of the wording of the document. German law has developed a formula that recognises a 'presumption that the written document is complete and correct' if 'the wording and content of the written document express a specific business content, taking into account customary business practices'. This presumption is, however, rebuttable. Anyone arguing to their own advantage that the contract indicates a different content may rely on 'means of interpretation external to the document' by providing evidence (and this is not easy from a practical standpoint) that exceptionally the parties intended a different meaning than recorded in their contract.[25] Newer English cases also follow this line, that the wording chosen in the formal document should be given its common meaning, based on the

> common sense proposition that we do not easily accept that people have made linguistic mistakes, particularly in formal documents. On the other hand, if one would nevertheless conclude from the background that something must have gone wrong with the language, the law does not require judges to attribute to the parties an intention which they plainly could not have had.[26]

To sum up: in days gone by, and more on the Continent than in England, the conflict in the interpretation of contracts between the 'intention theory' and the 'expression theory' may have had some significance, but it hardly matters at all today. Admittedly, a contract does not come about if the parties did not intend to bind themselves, but an intention has to be expressed and intimated to the other party, or it has no effect at all. Every statement is thus an act of social communication for which the person making it must take responsibility, in the realisation that the other party will rely on what *he* takes the statement to mean, and will accept the apparent offer and proceed to carry out the contract or make other arrangements on that basis. That is why anyone making a statement must reckon with the meaning which, in all the circumstances of the case, would be accorded to it by a reasonable man in the position of the addressee. One starts with the meaning that the words would have in everyday speech, and then asks whether there were any special circumstances which would suggest to the reasonable man that the statement was meant in an unusual sense. If the parties are both in the same line of business, they must reasonably expect their statements to be understood as they normally are in that commercial context. This is especially important when the terms to be interpreted are standard terms used in numerous other contracts or standardised documents such as bills of lading, or bills, or promissory notes which may get into the hands of third parties. Reasonable reliance on such documents should not be frustrated by interpretation.

---

[25] See, for example, BGH 31 May 1995, [1995] *NJW* 3258; BGH 5 Feb. 1999, [1999] *NJW* 1702; BGH 11 Sept. 2000, [2001] *NJW* 144; BGH 7 Feb. 2002, BGHZ 150, 32, 37ff. Swiss law takes the same approach: see BG 5 July 2001, BGE 127 III 444, 445.

[26] Lord Hoffmann in *Investors Compensation Scheme* (n 16) 913. This case concerned a contractual provision that, contrary to its clear wording, was interpreted in such a way to accommodate the reasonable intention of the parties. Similarly in *Mannai Investment Co. v. Eagle Star Life Assurance Co.* [1997] AC 749: Here the notice of termination from a tenant, which would have been invalid based on its exact wording, was interpreted in such a way that a reasonable person would have interpreted the position of the landlord and was thus found to be valid. See also Treitel (n 9) no. 6-011.

It occasionally happens that a clause is utterly ambiguous in the sense that, despite best efforts at interpretation, no single meaning can be given to it, since a reasonable man would find either of two meanings equally plausible. If such a clause relates to an essential point of the transaction, the contract fails for want of agreement. This situation is rare. Take the case where the price of goods is agreed in 'francs'. Even if the buyer was thinking in French francs while the seller had Swiss francs in mind, it will normally be possible to establish whether—in the light of all the relevant circumstances (place of contracting, or location of bank where payment to be made)—a reasonable person would regard the contract as being for French or Swiss francs. But the English case of *Raffles v. Wichelhaus*[27] may be a true instance of lack of agreement. The plaintiff had sold the defendant 125 bales of cotton 'to arrive ex *Peerless* from Bombay', and tendered cotton which arrived in Liverpool in December on a vessel of that name. The defendant refused to accept the goods, and when the seller claimed damages, offered witness evidence that he had in mind a quite different vessel—also called *Peerless*—which had sailed from Bombay earlier and arrived in Liverpool in October. The court held that this would be a good defence and would have allowed the witness evidence. The case never came to trial on the actual facts, but if one accepts that in the light of the evidence the reasonable observer would have been unable to determine which of the vessels the parties had agreed on, it would be right to hold that no contract had come about.[28]

D. Maxims of Interpretation

All legal systems provide judges with maxims or rules of thumb to help them interpret contracts. But they are not really of much practical use, as they generally only say what the judge's common sense would tell him anyway. That is why the draftsmen of the German Civil Code declined to include any such 'rules of reason without any positive legal content': it was not part of the legislature's task 'to teach the judges practical logic'.[29] Yet in some civil codes, one finds many such maxims of construction, all of which were known to ancient Roman law and to the *ius commune*.[30] We are told, for example, that one should prefer a reading of a clause which gives it some effect rather than none.[31] If a clause is ambiguous, one is to adopt the meaning which is more

---

[27] 159 Eng.Rep. 375 (1864). On this case, see AWB Simpson, 'Contracts for Cotton to Arrive: The Case of the Two Ships *Peerless*' (1989) 11 *Cardozo LR* 287, and AWB Simpson, *Leading Cases in the Common Law* (1995) 135, where he gives full details of the legal and factual background.
[28] See GS Cheshire, CHS Fifoot, and MP Furmston, *Law of Contract* (16th edn, 2012) 317f; Treitel (n 9) no. 8-042. It is different if a consensus can be established under general rules of interpretation and the question arises whether one party can void the contract on the basis of a mistake. See below, pp. 180ff.
[29] B Mugdan (ed), *Materialien zum BGB* I (1899) i, 436. [30] See Zimmermann (n 5) 637f.
[31] Article 1191 *Code civil*; art. 1367 *Codice civile*; art. 1284 Spanish Civil Code; Ulpian, D. 45.1.80: '*Quotiens in stipulationibus ambigua oratio est, commodissimum est id accipi quo res, qua de agitur, in tuto sit.*' English law is to the same effect: see *Langston v. Langston* 6 Eng.Rep. 1128, 1147 (1834), per Lord Brougham: 'There are two modes of reading an instrument: where the one destroys and the other preserves, it is the rule of law, and of equity, … that you should lean towards the construction which preserves, than towards that which destroys. *Ut res magis valeat quam pereat* is a rule of common law and common sense.' Similarly, art. 5:106 PECL; art. II.-8:106 DCFR; art. 40 CEC; art. 63 CESL.

convenient to the real matter of the contract[32] or the sense which would be attributed to it in the place where the contract was drawn up.[33] Where an expression is indefinite, its scope should be narrowed so as to cover only what the parties really intended,[34] and individual clauses must be construed in the light of the contract as a whole,[35] and so on. In actuality, such maxims—which Carbonnier describes as constituting a 'primer for simpletons' (*guide-âne*)[36]—play little part in court practice. Indeed, the *Cour de cassation* decided at an early stage that it would not quash a decision just because the lower court had ignored one of these rules.[37] One rather has the impression that judges only cite those maxims of interpretation which support a conclusion already reached on quite different grounds.[38] It therefore seems logical that the elaborate maxims of interpretation of the earlier version of the *Code civil* received short shrift in the recent reform.[39]

The rules of interpretation so far discussed are designed to elicit the meaning which a reasonable man would accord to a contract term whose meaning is unclear. Other rules have a different function. They represent a legal value judgement and seek to promote the meaning most consonant with that value judgement. Thus the *Code civil* provides that in case of doubt words in an individually negotiated contract—in a '*contrat de gré à gré*'—should be construed against the creditor and in favour of the debtor (art. 1190) and that a contract of sale should be construed against the seller and in favour of the buyer (art. 1602(2)). These rules may reflect the widespread, but inaccurate, belief that creditors and sellers are always rich and powerful, and that debtors and buyers are always weak and poor and in need of protection. To that extent they are unpersuasive, but they make good sense where the creditor or seller actually drafted the clause in issue. So it was in ancient Rome, where these rules were first adopted.[40] It may also be the case today that sellers and creditors draft the terms of contracts more often than buyers or debtors, but there are many instances where it is otherwise. Nowadays, the rule is reduced to its proper scope: an unclear contract term is to be construed against the party who did the drafting and could have done it better. It is right that the risk of ambiguity in a contract clause should be borne by the party who could more cheaply

---

[32] Article 1369 *Codice civile*; art. 1286 Spanish Civil Code; Julian, D. 50.17.67: '*Quotiens idem sermo duas sententias exprimit, ea potissimum excipiatur, quae rei gerendae aptior sit.*'

[33] Article 1368 *Codice civile*; Ulpian, D. 50.17.34: '*Semper in stipulationibus et in ceteris contractibus id sequimur ... quod in regione in qua actum est frequentatur.*'

[34] Article 1364 *Codice civile*; art. 1283 Spanish Civil Code.

[35] Article 1363 *Codice civile*; art. 1285 Spanish Civil Code. To the same effect is *Chamber Colliery Co. v. Twyerould* [1915] 1 Ch. 268, 272, per Lord Watson. See also art. 5:105 PECL; art. 4.4 PICC; art. 60 CESL.

[36] J Carbonnier, *Droit civil: Les obligations* (22nd edn, 2000) no. 68.

[37] See, for example, Com. 19 Jan. 1981, Bull.cass. 1981.I no. 34.

[38] See R Megarry, 'Book Review' (1945) 61 *LQR* 102: 'The cynical truth about interpretation in England seems to be that the Bench has been provided with some dozens of "principles" from which a judicious selection can be made to achieve substantial justice in each individual case. From time to time, all the relevant principles point in the same direction and leave the Court no choice. But in most of the cases susceptible of any real dispute, the function of counsel is merely to provide sufficient material for the Court to perform its task of selection.'

[39] Compare the old arts. 1158–1163 with what the *Code civil* now has to say on the interpretation of contracts in arts. 1188–1192.

[40] For the details, see Zimmermann (n 5) 639ff.

avoid it, and that is usually the party who selected or drafted the clause rather than the party to whom it was presented.

This *contra proferentem* rule for ambiguous clauses can only be applied when it is clear that a party formulated the clause in question, or played a major role in its formulation. This is obvious enough when general conditions of business are used. The Council Directive on Unfair Terms in Consumer Contracts states that where there is doubt about the meaning of general terms and conditions, 'the interpretation most favourable to the consumer shall prevail'.[41] In some legal systems, the *contra preferentem* rule is used not only for the protection of consumers, but of any party,[42] and sometimes it is even used in cases where the unclear clause does not form part of a standard contract, but has been individually negotiated. The international sets of rules that have been drafted also take different positions on this. Article 4.6 PICC says the *contra proferentem* rule should apply to *all* unclear clauses, but art. 5:103 PECL says it should apply only to terms that are 'not individually negotiated'.[43] However, both proposals state that it is preferred that terms should be interpreted against the party that drafted or supplied the term.

These ambiguity rules, like all canons of interpretation, presuppose that the meaning of the clause in question is indeed unclear. But it must be noted that, in their eagerness to protect the consumer from unfair standard form terms, the courts have proved remarkably clever at discovering or divining 'ambiguities' in such clauses. This was especially true when the courts had no statutory power to strike down clauses unfairly prejudicial to the customer. Now that such provisions have been enacted in most European countries, there is no need to use ambiguity rules in order to do indirectly what is better done directly by controlling the substance of general terms of business in an open manner.[44]

E. Forms of Constructive Interpretation

Interpretation or construction of a contract is not limited just to ascertaining the meaning of what the parties actually said. While the contract is being performed, a problem may arise for which the parties have provided no solution—either because they did not foresee the problem at all, or foresaw it and failed to deal with it. There is an omission in the contract, but how can that be? Sometimes, when concluding a contract parties think only about the main promises they make to each other, and

---

[41] Article 5 sent. 2 EU Directive 93/13/EEC of 5 April 1993 (OJ L 95 p. 29). See also art. L. 133-2 *Code de la consommation*; art. 6:238 (2) BW; § 915 ABGB. This rule applies in Germany even if the general terms and conditions have been agreed between businesses and it is a business that is trying to rely on the rule. See § 305c(2), 310 BGB and below, pp. 136ff.

[42] See now art. 1190 *Code civil*, which provides that doubts over the terms of a standardised contract are to be resolved '*contre celui qui l'a proposé*'. See also art. 1370 *Codice civile* and art. 1288 Spanish Civil Code. Under English law, the *contra preferentem* rule only applies where the aim of the unclear contractual clause is to waive liability. See Treitel (n 9) no. 7-1014ff. But case law in other countries also predominantly deals with such clauses.

[43] On this, see Zimmermann (n 1) 1360ff.

[44] The *Hoge Raad* was explicit on this in HR 1 July 1977, [1978] *NedJur* 125 and HR 28 Sept. 1989, [1990] *NedJur* 583. See also below, pp. 134ff.

cover only the essential issues. In other cases, they say nothing on the conditions that constitute a breach of contract and the practical consequences that ensue. Such omissions are not due to stupidity or idleness of the parties, but that negotiations over the omitted points do not seem worth the effort, are too difficult or expensive, or would have derailed the contract negotiations. It may also be that the parties wish to portray themselves as effective in the pre-contractual phase and do not want to address the issue of what will happen if things go wrong. Particularly in the case of long-term contracts—such as employment contracts, shareholder agreements, or multi-year supply agreements—the parties lack sufficient will to consider all the ways in which a contract might go wrong and to account for such contingencies in the contract. The reason behind most contractual omissions is an economic consideration. Contractual negotiations cause an expense (transaction cost) that is out of proportion to the benefit achieved. If the probability of a particular risk occurring is 1:100, and in this case the party suffers a cost of 500, it would not make sense to invest more than 5 in contractual negotiations to transfer the risk to the other party. Therefore, it is no coincidence in practice that relatively 'complete' contracts are only drawn up where the expense is justified. This is the case, for example, when both parties have a lot of money riding on the contract, or when one of the parties concludes many contracts of the same type—even if the single contracts are for only a small economic amount—so that the expense of drafting lengthy and detailed contracts (usually in the form of general terms and conditions) is justified. Of course, there is no such thing as a 'complete' contract. Experience shows that even if the parties and their lawyers have taken great care to draft the contract, there will still be omissions that need to be filled by a judge. Sometimes, in this case the judge will apply the default rules that the legislature or case law hold in reserve in the absence of an agreement by the parties. If there are no such rules, or if they cannot be applied, continental legal systems correct the omission by applying 'constructive interpretation'. In England, the contract is supplemented with an 'implied term', which—in accordance with the traditional English approach—has nothing at all to do with the general rules of interpretation. However, recent case law seems to indicate that 'implication of a term' is really nothing more than correct interpretation of the contract.[45]

The sets of international rules are unanimous that the contractual omission should be filled by informal agreement, to be determined by the judge taking into account the intention of the parties, the nature and purpose of the contract, the customary practices of the parties, commercial practices, and good faith. The corresponding provisions can usually be found in the sections governing 'content' of the contract, not its

---

[45] See Lord Hoffmann in *Attorney General of Belize v. Belize Telecom Ltd.* [2009] 1 WLR 1988 (PC): 'It follows that in every case in which it is said that some provision ought to be implied in an instrument, the question for the court is whether such provision would spell out in express words what the instrument, read against the relevant background, would reasonably be understood to mean' (Nr. 21). Also Lord Hoffmann, 'The Intolerable Wrestle with Words and Meanings' (1997) 114 *S.Afr. LJ* 656, 662: 'In fact, of course, the implication of a term into a contract is an exercise in interpretation like any other. It may seem odd to speak of interpretation when, by definition, the term has not been expressed in words, but the only difference is that when we imply a term, we are engaged in interpreting the meaning of the contract as a whole.'

interpretation, thus following the traditional English approach that allows judges to supplement the content of a contract with an implied term.[46]

I. Implication of terms by default rules

In this situation, the continental judge looks first to the civil and commercial codes and any special laws, since for most current types of contract they contain rules designed to be applied by the court 'in default' of a contractual agreement by the parties. In France, these statutory rules, along with the glosses added by the courts, are called *règles supplétives*, in Germany *dispositives Recht*.[47] Thus, when parties to a sale in France have said nothing about the seller's liability for latent defects, the courts apply not only art. 1645 *Code civil*—which renders the seller who knows of the defect liable for all consequential loss due to it—but also the judge-made rule, which imputes such knowledge to all commercial distributors such as manufacturers, wholesalers, and retailers.

The aim of these suppletive or dispositive rules lain down by the legislature and developed by the courts is not only to accommodate the typical interests of the parties in a just manner, but also to save the parties the expense of prolonged negotiation by offering them appropriate 'default rules'.

Although continental legal systems offer a fairly complete set of dispositive rules for the most important types of contract, there is an issue that the Common Law fails to address: this is whether the parties can also conclude *other* contracts and, if they have done so, how the applicable dispositive rules are to be determined. It goes without saying that the principle of freedom of contract allows the parties to conclude other contracts. So in a contract between hotelier and guest, for example, the court may apply the dispositive rules on lease if the guest is unhappy with the condition of his hotel room, those on sale if he is given a bad meal, and those on deposit if his luggage is stolen after being accepted for safe keeping.[48]

In England, too, gaps in contractual agreements are made good by recourse to general rules—'terms implied in law'—which apply unless the parties have provided otherwise and depend on the type of contract in issue. The Sale of Goods Act 1979 and the Supply of Goods and Services Act 1982 contain rules which, as applied in

---

[46] See art. 6:102 PECL; art. 32(1) CEC; art. 68 CESL. The rule in PICC tries to accommodate both approaches. See art. 4.8 (interpretation) and art. 5.1.2 (supplementing contract with an 'implied term'). Even if the systematic ordering of the question has little relevance, the best solution would be to regard rectification of an omission as a specific problem of contractual interpretation to be taken into account by the judge to the same extent as other applicable general principles of interpretation. See also Zimmermann (n 1) 1364f.

[47] See, for example, H Mazeaud, L Mazeaud, J Mazeaud, and F Chabas, *Leçons de droit civil, vol. III.1: Obligations, Théorie générale* (9th edn, 2006) no. 347f; D Medicus, *Allgemeiner Teil des Bürgerlichen Gesetzbuchs* (9th edn, 2006) mn. 338ff; R Bork, *Allgemeiner Teil des Bürgerlichen Gesetzbuchs* (4th edn, 2016) mn. 532ff. It is to be noted that while dispositive law generally yields to any contrary provision adopted by the parties, this is not invariably so. Many legal systems show a tendency to treat agreements in the form of general conditions of business as invalid if they purport to strip away from the customer the protection afforded to him by dispositive rules. See also below, pp. 140ff.

[48] On such *contrats innomés*, see Mazeaud and Chabas (n 47) no. 111f; on *typengemischte Verträge* see K Larenz and C-W Canaris, *Lehrbuch des Schuldrechts, vol. 2: Besonderer Teil (Part 2)* (13th edn, 1994) § 63; on 'mixed contracts', see art. II.-1:108 DCFR.

the cases, perform the same role for contracts of sale and services as the corresponding suppletive rules in the continental civil codes. *Statutory* provisions of this kind are not, however, very common, and in their absence English judges apply rules they themselves have developed in relation to the major types of contract, such as govern contracts of sale, carriage, and insurance. If an architect contracts to provide plans for a building that must meet certain requirements and guarantees, but there is no express term as to quality, the courts hold that it is an 'implied term in fact' that the work must meet those requirements, and the architect must pay damages even if not personally responsible for the building not meeting those requirements.[49] The same is true for other contracts of work and labour, as where a publicity firm was to advertise its client's wares by flying low over towns towing a streamer bearing the slogan 'Eat Batchelor's Peas'. The firm chose to fly on Armistice Day when the crowds in the main square were observing a period of silence and contemplation. The public were scandalised, and the client was allowed to terminate the agreement:

> There must be implied in that contract a term that the flying under the contract would be carried out with reasonable skill and reasonable care, having regard to the object of the contract, and, in whatever precise words the implied obligation is expressed, it must be, I think, certainly wide enough to exclude flying in a way which would bring the advertisers into hatred and contempt.[50]

Likewise, a person who hired out a motorboat was liable under the 'implied term that the vessel hired shall be as fit for the purpose as reasonable care and skill can make it'.[51] And when the lifts and staircase lights in a fifteen-storey tower block were constantly out of order because the landlord failed to maintain them properly, the landlord was in breach of an implied term 'to take reasonable care to maintain the common parts of the building in a state of reasonable repair'.[52] An employer is bound to ensure that its employees' place of work is such that they are exposed to no unnecessary risk to their health, even if the contract says nothing about it,[53] but the employer is not bound to take out insurance to cover employees against any tortious liability they may incur towards third parties whom they cause injury while at work.[54]

II. Constructive interpretation

'Terms implied in law' and dispositive statutory rules are usually framed in such general terms as to be applicable, failing contrary provision, to all contracts of a particular type. But they are not of much use where the parties have left open a particular point which calls for a made-to-measure solution. Suppose that two doctors agree to exchange practices and one of them, not caring for the new place of work, wants to

---

[49] *Greaves & Co. Ltd.* v. *Baynham Meikle & Partners* [1975] 3 All ER 99.
[50] *Aerial Advertising Co.* v. *Batchelor's Peas Ltd.* [1938] 2 All ER 788, 792, per Atkinson J.
[51] *Reed* v. *Dean* [1949] 1 KB 188, 193.   [52] *Liverpool City Council* v. *Irwin* [1977] AC 239.
[53] *Matthews* v. *Kuwait Bechtel Corp.* [1959] 2 QB 57.
[54] *Lister* v. *Romford Ice & Cold Storage Co.* [1957] AC 555. By contrast, a term will be implied into a contract for driving lessons that the instructor has insurance covering the learner driver's liability: see *British School of Motoring* v. *Simms* [1971] 1 All ER 317.

return to the previous base only nine months later. Would this be allowed, or can a term be implied disallowing such return in case the doctor's old patients flock back to him at the expense of the other doctor? Again, in *The Moorcock*[55] the plaintiff was to unload his ship at the defendant's jetty on the Thames; when the tide went out, the ship naturally settled, and was holed because the riverbed was uneven. Could it be said that the defendant was contractually bound to warn the plaintiff if he knew that the bed of the river was uneven at that point, or tell him if he did not? In neither of these two cases did there appear to be any dispositive rules or terms implied by law which could be used to fill in the gaps.

In such cases, English judges ask whether the incomplete contract can be filled by a 'term implied in fact'.[56] This is only done when the term to be implied is so obvious that if a disinterested observer had drawn the parties' attention to its omission, they would unhesitatingly have agreed to its inclusion.[57] A test often applied is whether such an addition is necessary 'to give the transaction such business efficacy as the parties must have intended'.[58] It was so held in *The Moorcock*, since the defendant had much better access than the plaintiff to information about the condition of the riverbed adjacent to his mooring:

> The owners of the jetty, or their servants, were there at high tide and low tide, and with little trouble they could satisfy themselves, in case of doubt, as to whether the berth was reasonably safe. The ship's owner, on the other hand, had not the means of verifying the state of the jetty.[59]

Judges in Germany would ask if the gap in the contract can be filled by constructive interpretation (*ergänzende Vertragsauslegung*), and frequently use the following formula: 'Where the parties have omitted to say something' the judge must 'discover and take into account what, in the light of the whole purpose of the contract, they would have said if they had regulated the point in question, acting pursuant to the requirements of good faith and sound business practice'.[60] In the case of the doctors who exchanged practices, the *Bundesgerichtshof* used this form of words and held that neither party was free to return to the immediate vicinity of his previous practice for a period of two to three years.[61] Contracts for the sale of a business are often constructively interpreted so as to impose on the seller an obligation not to start up another business in competition with the buyer so as to prejudice the goodwill of the business.[62] Thanks to constructive interpretation, a person who had taken a lease of one of the two shops in a building could prevent the owner from letting the other to a person

---

[55] (1889) 14 PD 64.
[56] See Treitel (n 9) no. 6-029ff; McKendrick (n 19) no. 9.8; *Scally v. Southern Health and Social Services Board* [1992] 1 AC 294, 306f.
[57] See *Shirlaw v. Southern Foundries Ltd.* [1939] 2 KB 206, 227.
[58] *Luxor (Eastbourne) Ltd. v. Cooper* [1941] AC 108, 137, per Lord Wright.
[59] *The Moorcock* (n 55) at 69, per Lord Bowen.
[60] BGH 18 Dec. 1954, BGHZ 16, 71, 76. See also BGH 22 Apr. 1953, BGHZ 9, 273, 278; BGH 29 Apr. 1987, BGHZ 84, 1, 7. Swiss and Austrian courts decide likewise: see BG 23 Apr. 1981, BGE 107 II 144, 149; BG 13 Oct. 1981, BGE 107 II 411, 414; OGH 1 Feb. 1972, [1973] *JBl* 309; OGH 31 May 1983, [1983] *JBl* 592.
[61] BGH 18 Dec. 1954 (previous note) at p. 81.   [62] RG 31 May 1925, RGZ 117, 176.

in the same line of trade.⁶³ Gaps in partnership agreements are also often filled in this manner.⁶⁴

French courts actually decide in much the same way, even though they often invoke the rule that the gap is to be filled by the *commune intention des parties contractantes*. For example, it has been held—'*par une interprétation rendu nécessaire par l'ambiguïté de la convention sur ce point*'—that a radio station which had commissioned a play, accepted the manuscript, and paid the playwright a commission without objection was not only entitled, but actually obliged, to produce and broadcast the play, and was liable in damages for refusing to do so.⁶⁵ The *Cour de cassation* decides likewise in cases where a contract becomes incomplete because an agreed provision subsequently proves unworkable. For example, if the indexation which the parties to a long-term contract have selected to determine future fluctuations in the price payable proves to be inoperative because the stipulated index does not exist, or ceases publication, or fails to obtain the requisite authorisation, the courts look for the closest possible clause which will work or obtain authorisation, and fill the gap in this way.⁶⁶

Whether such constructive interpretation is really 'interpretation' at all—or whether the judge is not simply fixing on a rule which provides a just and appropriate solution to the dispute—is a point on which views may differ. Usually it is impossible, as well as unnecessary, to draw a clear distinction. Certainly the judge must not reach a conclusion at variance with what the parties have actually agreed, nor read a clause into the contract just because it appears reasonable to do so. Similarly, a judge may not try to save a party from its nonchalance, negligence, or predilection for risk-taking by inserting—at the expense of the other party—a clause which the party would have been well advised to include, but did not. The function of the judge, according to the apt phrase of Ripert-Boulanger, is 'to make the contract speak' rather than to speak himself.⁶⁷ If a contract does not include agreement about the allocation of a particular risk, the judge must fill the gap with a provision that the parties would be presumed to have agreed if they had negotiated the allocation of the risk and had agreed on the most advantageous—and thus most efficient—solution for each party. In this sense it would be possible to speak of the 'hypothetical will of the parties'. Normally, the burden of the risk should be allocated to the party for whom the costs of averting the risk are lowest, who can reduce the probability of the risk occurring at a lower cost

---

⁶³ RG 2 Feb. 1931, RGZ 131, 274.

⁶⁴ See, for example, BGH 23 Nov. 1978, [1979] *NJW* 1705; BGH 28 Jun. 1982, [1982] *NJW* 2816. Constructive interpretation may be used if the available statutory dispositive rules do not match the probable intention of the parties. For the relationship between constructive interpretation and dispositive rules, see Bork (n 47) mn. 534ff.

⁶⁵ Civ. 2 Apr. 1974, Bull.cass. 1974.I. no. 109.

⁶⁶ Civ. 15 Feb. 1972, D.1973, 417, n. J Ghestin; Com. 7 Jan. 1975, JCP 1975.II.18167, n. J Ghestin; Civ. 9 Nov. 1981, Bull.cass. 1981.I. no. 332; Civ. 18 July 1985, Bull.cass. 1985.III. no. 113. This has now been laid down expressly in art. 1167 *Code civil* (as amended). To the same effect are BGH 25 Jan. 1967, [1967] *NJW* 830; BGH 30 Oct. 1974, BGHZ 63, 132, 136.

⁶⁷ G Ripert and J Boulanger, *Droit Civil* vol. II (1957) no. 470: '*l'art de faire parler le contrat*'.

than the other party, or who can best insure against the consequences of the risk—including by taking out insurance.[68]

III. Collateral duties

So far we have been considering cases where the parties have omitted to deal with some particular aspect of their *principal* duties. Somewhat different are cases where they have failed to regulate their *collateral* duties, such as the duty, as the contract proceeds, to take care of the other party's life or health, to look after the other party's property carefully, or inform or warn about possible hazards. In cases like this, German law rarely seeks to find a gap in the contract to be settled by means of constructive interpretation. Since judges in Germany feel obliged to refer to a statutory text, they often invoke § 242 BGB, which requires them—when deciding what is due from the party rendering performance—to apply the same standard as they apply under § 157 BGB when interpreting a contract, namely the standard of good faith and proper commercial practice. Both sections are often cited in tandem, and writers agree that it is neither possible nor necessary to distinguish their respective fields of operation.[69] The French courts may now rely on art. 1194, which provides that a contractor must do not only what he has expressly promised to do, but also what is required by '*l'équité, l'usage ou la loi*'.

Such legislative provisions being at best hortatory, with no specific applicable content, the rules on the implication of collateral contractual duties not expressly regulated by the parties are entirely judge-made. In France, this development can be dated back to 21 November 1911, when the *Cour de cassation* decided for the first time that a carrier was obliged not only to carry the passenger to the agreed destination but also, as part of the contract, to see that he arrived at his destination safe and sound.[70] So if the passenger is injured in an accident during the journey, the carrier may be liable for breach of his contractual *obligation de sécurité*. There is no need to show that the carrier was at fault; indeed, the carrier can avoid liability only by proving that the accident was due to a *cause étrangère*, such as an incident unconnected with the carriage or perhaps the fault of the passenger.[71] This contractual obligation is stricter than tortious liability, which reveals why the French courts have found such a contractual *obligation de sécurité* not only in contracts of carriage, but in practically all types of contract whereby one party's person or property is brought into an area of danger under the control of the other party, who can be expected to offer such protection as the circumstances indicate.[72] The French courts have stuck to their position, although

---

[68] The same considerations arise with the issue of whether or not standard terms and conditions are 'reasonable' and thus valid, or if an 'extraordinary' risk has been realised which the parties had not considered upon conclusion of the contract and had thus not taken into account (see pp. 140ff.).
[69] See, for example, D Medicus and W Lorenz, *Schuldrecht* vol. I (19th edn, 2010) § 16 II 1.
[70] Civ. 21 Nov. 1911, D. 1913.1.249, n. L Sarrut.
[71] This is true only when the *obligation de sécurité* is an *obligation de résultat*, as it is in the case of carriage. On the distinction between *obligations de résultat* and *obligations de moyens*, see below, pp. 248ff.
[72] See the impressive presentation in G Viney, *Les obligations, Responsabilité: conditions* (1982) no. 499ff.

the law of tort has subsequently developed in such a way as to weaken the original reason for treating *obligations de sécurité* as contractual.[73]

In German law, too, a plaintiff can in many respects do better by suing in contract rather than tort now that the courts have adopted wide contractual duties of care for the person and property of the other party.[74] They have done this in order to effect a reasonable allocation of risks, without purporting to base it on any actual or hypothetical will of the parties to this effect.[75]

A similar development has taken place as regards contractual duties to inform, advise, or warn (*obligations de renseignement et de conseil*). Some contracts have the provision of information as their very core, as where an expert is to report on the authenticity of a picture, the value of a plot of land, or the prospects of success in litigation, but we are concerned here with cases in which the debtor's principal obligation is something else, such as to deliver goods, see to a particular piece of business, afford a credit facility, or take out insurance cover. Such a person may also be placed under an obligation to advise the other party and give him all the relevant information he possesses or ought to possess, information to which he has easier access, usually because of his expert knowledge, and which the other party needs. Article 1129-1 *Code civil* now provides a general statutory basis for a party's mandatory duty to provide information on all facts that have a 'direct' and 'necessary' link with the subject matter of the contract or the characteristics of the parties and are on that ground 'important' for the other party. For example, even if the thing sold is perfectly good, a seller must give the buyer such information as he needs to be able to use it safely, to install it correctly, and to maintain it properly.[76]

Under English law, too, contractors are often bound to take reasonable care to avoid causing damage to their partner. But this duty is seldom seen as a contractual duty based on an implied term. In *The Moorcock*,[77] the defendant was held liable for breach of contract in not warning the plaintiff of the unevenness of the riverbed. In general, however, the duty is not held to arise out of the contract: the English courts prefer to deal with these cases under the law of tort, principally the tort of 'negligence'.

This is possible in Germany as well: a buyer who suffers personal injury through being insufficiently informed of how to use the item purchased can base a claim for damages not only on the collateral duty (of information) in the sale contract, but also on the general duty in tort to avoid causing harm.[78] However, if the only damage suffered by the defendant consists of mere pecuniary loss (*reine Vermögensschaden*), only the contractual claim is possible, since in principle pure economic loss is not

---

[73] See also Viney (n 72) no. 501.

[74] Germany has indeed gone further than France in two respects. First, German courts allow contractual claims for damages when the damage is caused by breach of duty during the stage of negotiations, where France would allow only a claim in tort. Secondly, German courts accept that contractual duties of care may be owed not only to the other contracting party but also to third parties. On this last point, see below, pp. 325ff.

[75] See also Viney (n 72) no. 515.

[76] See, for example, Com. 5 Feb. 1973, *JCP* 1974.II.17791; Com. 16 Oct. 1973, *JCP* 1974.II.17846, n. P Malinvaud; Civ. 9 Dec. 1975, *JCP* 1977.II.18588, n. P Malinvaud; BGH 5 Apr. 1967, BGHZ 47, 312; BGH 19 Feb. 1975, BGHZ 64, 46.

[77] Above, n 55. [78] BGH 19 Feb. 1975 (n 76) 49.

compensable under § 823(1) BGB. On this point, the situation in France is different again. No claim in tort arises in these cases, not because art. 1240 ff. (formerly art. 1382 ff.) *Code civil* would not apply, but because the doctrine of *non-cumul* prevents a tortious claim from arising where there is a breach of a contractual obligation, here the *obligation de sécurité, de renseignement ou de conseil.*

From all this, we can draw two conclusions. The question whether or not there is a collateral contractual duty in a given case depends not on the actual or supposed will of the parties but, as in the law of tort, on whether the imposition of such a duty is justified as a reasonable allocation of the risks. Secondly, whether the defendant's liability arises in contract (*ex contracto*) or tort (*ex delicto*) is a question of technique rather than substance. What matters is whether, in the relevant jurisdiction, it is easier for the judge to reach the desired result by taking the contractual or the tortious path. If both paths are open, the classification is not that important. Thus in *Lister* v. *Romford Ice*, when the parties differed on the question whether the employee's duty to take care of his employer's property arose from an 'implied duty' or under the law of tort, Lord Radcliffe regarded the question as purely academic:

> Since, in any event, the duty in question is one which exists by imputation or implication of law and not by virtue of any express negotiation between the parties, I should be inclined to say that there is no real distinction between the two possible sources of obligation.[79]

---

[79] See n 54 at 587.

7
Unfair, Illegal, and Immoral Contracts

A. Introduction	109
B. Inequality between Performance and Counterperformance	110
C. Undue Restraints on Personal or Economic Freedom	117
I. Basics	117
II. Long-term contractual relationships	118
III. Non-compete agreements	119
IV. Partial invalidity	121
D. Breach of the Law	122
E. Restitution of Benefits Conferred	125

A. Introduction

When parties to an agreement have thought about the matter, seriously intend to bind themselves, and are unaffected by mistake, deceit, or duress, the contract is normally binding. But if the agreement is that A is to pay B for giving perjured evidence on his behalf, neither party would be able to claim either for performance or for damages for non-performance. However committed a legal system may be to the principle of freedom of contract, it is bound to deny enforcement to a contract which conflicts with the law or good morals or offends 'public policy' or is *contraire aux bonnes moeurs ou à l'ordre public*.

Legislative provisions in this area are necessarily rather vague.[1] Some continental civil codes do no more than distinguish between contracts which are illegal and those which are immoral,[2] to which the Dutch Civil Code adds contracts in breach of public order.[3] The French *Code civil* used to deal with the present problem in relation to the concept of *cause*. This was abandoned in the course of the recent reform of French contract law,[4] and arts. 1128 and 1162 now simply provide that a contract must have '*un contenu licite*' and must not derogate from '*l'ordre public*'.[5]

The codal texts on contracts which conflict with good morals, public order, or legal prescriptions are all what German lawyers call 'general clauses', which need to be fleshed out by reference to court decisions. That is why commentators who try to put

---

[1] See A von Mehren in *Int.Enc.Comp.L.* vol. VII ch 1, 37ff.
[2] See §§ 134, 138 BGB; § 879 ABGB; art. 20(1) OR; arts. 174, 178 Greek Civil Code. It is noteworthy that Swiss law draws a distinction between contracts which are illegal or immoral (art. 20 OR) and those which are in breach of art. 27(2) Civil Code, which provides that 'no one may alienate his liberty or restrict it to a degree inconsistent with law or morals'. On this distinction, see the details in E Bucher, *Berner Kommentar* vol. I part II/2 (1993) art. 27 ZGB mn. 92 and 162ff.
[3] Article 3:40(1) and (2) BW. [4] See above, pp. 51f.
[5] As to contracts that are illegal or immoral, the Dutch and Portuguese Civil Codes have also abandoned the link with *cause*: see art. 3:40(1) and (2) BW, art. 280 Portuguese Civil Code.

the cases into some sort of order invariably add that the categories they adopt are neither exhaustive nor mutually exclusive.

Contracts which until quite recently were regarded as offensive may now be perfectly acceptable. This is especially the case with respect to contracts where it is uncertain if they contravene generally accepted principles of family life or sexual morals. Contracts whereby a party in an unmarried partnership could promise to pay the other a certain sum of money if the partnership were to end would previously have been unthinkable. Similarly, contracts concerning payment of a sum of money or maintenance between a married man and a woman to whom he was not married. Today, such contracts are held to be valid if the judge can determine that the promise was based on laudable motives, namely with the aim of securing the maintenance of the other partner after the end of a long-term relationship, or as an expression of gratitude to that partner for support or care provided.[6]

A comparison of different legal orders shows that the very same contract can be treated as invalid in some jurisdictions as a breach of statutory provisions, but in others as invalid because provisions contravene (unwritten) rules on good morals or public policy. For these specified reasons, a contract can sometimes be found to be 'void' or 'invalid', while it is described as 'unenforceable' in other legal systems. Often a contract will be deemed void by one legal order, whereas the very same contract will be treated elsewhere as valid, but under certain circumstances one party will be able to challenge or cancel obligations arising from the contract because of an allegation of fraud or duress. Both solutions can be found in the PECL. Pursuant to art. 4:109(1), a party may avoid a contract if the other party knowingly exploits the weak position of the other, thereby benefiting from an unfair or excessive advantage. On the other hand, pursuant to art. 15:101 a contract is 'of no effect' if it is 'contrary to principles recognised as fundamental in the laws of the Member States of the European Union', and under art. 15:102 PECL also where a contract infringes a mandatory applicable rule of law.[7]

Here we shall deal with circumstances where there is an evident inequality between performance and counterperformance, and it is thus doubtful whether the contract is void for that reason alone or due to other additional reasons. Secondly, we will look at cases where validity turns on whether the contract improperly restricts personal or economic liberties. Finally, special problems can arise where the formation or execution of a contract infringes some statutory provision.

B. Inequality between Performance and Counterperformance

The question of whether a balance between performance and counterperformance can determine the validity of a contract has been the subject of debate in Europe for many

---

[6] See, for example, Civ. 22 Oct. 1980, Bull.cass. 1980.I. no. 269; Civ 11 Feb. 1986, Bull.cass. 1986.I. no. 21; BGH 31 Mar. 1970, BGHZ 53, 369; BGH 12 Jan. 1984, [1984] *NJW* 2150: BG 17 Jan. 1983, BGE 109 II 15. See also the case law discussed in GH Treitel, *The Law of Contract* (13th edn, by E Peel, 2011) no. 11-040.

[7] See H MacQueen, 'Illegality and Immorality in Contracts' in A Hartkamp et al. (eds), *Towards a European Civil Code* (4th edn, 2011) 555.

centuries. Classical Roman law had no such requirement, and recognised the validity of a contract of sale whatever the relationship between the price and the true value of the goods. It was only in the later Roman period, according to the *Corpus Iuris*,[8] that an ordinance was promulgated—there is some doubt whether it dates from the third or only the sixth century AD—which gave the seller of land the right to resile from the contract if the price agreed was less than half its true value. Socio-political considerations were clearly behind this innovation: peasants impoverished by the Emperor's brutal taxing policies were to be protected from selling their fields for a song to city capitalists eager to safeguard their wealth from inflation.[9]

It was not until the Middle Ages that the idea that all contracts must show a balance between performance and counterperformance was fully accepted. Thomas Aquinas and other fathers of the Church maintained that the two sides of a contract must be balanced, and that to pay less than a fair price or *iustum pretium* was a sin. What was ordained by Christian morality was seen by natural lawyers as standing to reason: a contract could be avoided for *laesio enormis*. Unfortunately, the principle of equivalence proved rather difficult to apply in practice. Could the buyer prevent the avoidance of the contract by paying a supplement? Was it only the seller of land who could avoid the deal by invoking *laesio enormis*, or could the seller of goods do so too? Did the buyer have a comparable right if the price was too high? What about contracts of lease and employment? Above all, how was the 'just price' to be ascertained?

The civil codes of the early nineteenth century differed in the extent to which they adopted the doctrine of *laesio enormis*. The Austrian ABGB went furthest: under § 934, either party may resile from a contract if the value of his performance exceeds that of the other's by more than half (*Verkürzung über die Hälfte*). This right is not available to a party dealing as a business,[10] nor to a seller who was fully aware of the value of the property, and, for example, sold it cheap to a friend (*Freundschaftspreis*), nor to a buyer who said when he was buying the property that he was paying 'an exceptional price out of particular predilection for it' (§ 935).

The French *Code civil* is more hesitant. According to art. 1168, the general principle is that a contract is valid despite the inequality of performance and counterperformance. However, the law may provide otherwise. It does so in art. 1674 ff: if the price paid for land is less than seven-twelfths of its true value at the time of the contract, the seller has two years in which to avoid the sale. Rescission is excluded if it appears from the context that the sale was an 'aleatory transaction', or that it was really intended as a gift to the buyer. The buyer can forestall rescission by offering to pay the difference between the agreed price and 90 per cent of the current market value—but can keep the other 10 per cent so as not to be entirely deprived of the

---

[8] C. 4.44.2.
[9] On this, and what follows, see R Zimmermann, *The Law of Obligations, Roman Foundations of the Civilian Tradition* (1990) 259ff. with references to the extensive literature on the history of *laesio enormis*. See also von Mehren (n 1) vol. VII ch 1, 83ff.
[10] § 351a Austrian Commercial Code.

benefit of the bargain (art. 1681). The practical application of this article has not been trouble-free.[11]

Such rules do not figure in more recent civil codes: they were rather out of place in an economy increasingly dominated by liberalism. In an acquisitive bourgeois society founded on freedom of contract, establishment, and competition, it was an article of faith that people were sufficiently businesslike and judicious to look after themselves. Thus, any rule that allowed the judge to avoid a contract because of substantial inequality was paternalistic and prejudicial to legal certainty. The drafters of the BGB accordingly believed right up till the last moment that they need do no more than include a general clause to the effect that contracts were void if they conflicted with the law or with good morals (§ 138(1) BGB). In the end, however, the sense prevailed that unequal contracts are suspect and unjust, and a second element was added. Thus § 138(2) BGB combines the tests of 'procedural' and 'substantive' fairness, and renders a contract void if (a) performance and counterperformance are 'clearly disproportionate', and (b) one of the parties exacted the contract 'through exploiting the predicament, inexperience, lack of judgement or significant indecisiveness' of the other party.

Most other civil codes in Europe have adopted this solution.[12] The Italian *Codice civile* alone adheres to a mathematical formula: the disadvantaged party, which can rescind only if it entered the contract out of a *stato di bisogno*, must show that what it gave was worth twice as much as what it was to receive (art. 1448).[13] By contrast, the Dutch Civil Code makes no reference to any imbalance between performance and counterperformance, but allows a contract to be avoided for 'abuse of the situation' if the other party improperly induced the claimant to enter the contract when the other party was or should have been aware of the claimant's predicament, dependency, inexperience, fecklessness, or naivety (art. 3:44(4)).[14]

International sets of rules require a party to have secured an 'excessive benefit' or a 'grossly unfair advantage' and that—similar to § 138(2) BGB—the disadvantaged party was in economic distress, had urgent needs, lacked bargaining skill, or was in some other specific predicament that the other party knew or ought to have known about, and took advantage of.[15] German law is moving more towards the position that merely a 'gross disparity' (*grobes Missverhältnis*) between performance and counterperformance suffices for the invalidity of the contract. In effect, this signals a reawakening of the old doctrine of *laesio enormis*. With respect to contracts of sale, such a gross disparity has indeed been found if a good is sold for less than half or more than double its market value. In such a case, even if there is no exploitation of predicament

---

[11] See the details in J Ghestin, *Traité de droit civil, La formation du contrat* (1993) no. 555ff; B Starck, H Roland, and L Boyer, *Droit civil, Obligations, Contrat et quasi-contrat, Régime général* (5th edn, 1995) nn 806ff.

[12] § 879(2) no. 4 ABGB; art. 21 OR; art. 179 Greek Civil Code; § 31 Nordic Contract Law; art. 282 Portuguese Civil Code. See also art. 388 Polish Civil Code.

[13] See It. Cass. 28 June 1994, republished in part in *ZEuP* 1997, 475 with note by C Becker.

[14] See *Hoge Raad* 29 May 1964, [1965] *NedJur* 104: A vendor, whose age-related inexperience was taken advantage of, may rescind a contract for the sale of real property even if the agreed price was reasonable.

[15] See art. 4: 109 PECL; art. 3.2.7 PICC; art. II.-7:207 DCFR; art. 30(3) CEC; art. 51 CESL. There is agreement that a contract concluded under such circumstances is not void per se, but can be voided or challenged by the disadvantaged party.

pursuant to the requirements of § 138(2) BGB, the disadvantaged party can still assert that the contract is void pursuant to § 138(1). It is true that the advantaged party must have acted 'with reprehensible attitude', but such an attitude can be assumed even if the advantaged party had no knowledge of the gross disparity.[16]

The French *Code civil* contains no rule comparable to § 138(2) BGB, but the courts reach much the same results in practice by allowing the advantaged party to impugn the contract on the ground of '*violence*'. Under art. 1143 *Code civil*, it is to be considered as a case of *violence* if one party exploits the '*état de dépendance dans lequel se trouve l'autre partie*'—by reason of that party's old age, ill health, youthful inexperience, or some other weakness—and in this way obtains an advantage from that party which is '*manifestement excessif*'. Where the price agreed is so derisory that the deal can be described as *un véritable scandale* or a *prix dérisoire*, the courts may be able to help the disadvantaged party by holding the contract void on the ground that the price is '*illusoire ou dérisoire*' (art. 1169 *Code civil*).[17]

English law also lacks a general principle that would allow a party to escape from an obviously disadvantageous contract entered into owing to a crisis or other transactional handicap of which the other party has taken advantage. Instead, it has a scattering of rules which—under various preconditions—give the weaker party protection analogous to that provided in continental systems. Thus a party may sometimes invoke *economic duress* if it was in a situation of particular difficulty when it entered the prejudicial deal, such as where the party only agreed to a disadvantageous modification of a contract because the other party had threatened to breach the contract otherwise and, under the circumstances, such threat is deemed unconscionable (see chapter 10).[18]

Some older decisions, dating back to the eighteenth century, allowed a party to rescind a disposition when the party's inexperience or perplexity had led it to part with valuable property for a trivial sum, or mortgage it on leonine terms. Typical was the case where a young man of good family, but no income of his own, sold his rights of succession for a trivial amount in order to cover his living expenses or meet his gambling debts. Such grounds for holding a contract invalid can, at a pinch, be found in a modern context, as in *Cresswell* v. *Potter*,[19] where a telephone operator on the brink of divorce was naïve enough to give up her share in joint property in return for her husband's promise to release her from further liability under the mortgage.

---

[16] See BGH 19 Jan. 2001, BGHZ 146, 298; BGH 19 July 2002, [2002] *NJW* 3165; BGH 29 June 2007, [2007] *NJW* 2841. The assumption that they have acted with a 'reprehensible attitude' can be refuted by the advantaged party if it can be shown that the parties had relied on an (erroneous) expert report. For criticism of this, see T Finkenauer, 'Zur Renaissance des *laesio enormis* beim Kaufvertrag' in *Festschrift H.P. Westermann* (2008) 183; R Bork, *Allgemeiner Teil des Bürgerlichen Gesetzbuchs* (4th edn, 2016) mn. 1193, 1199.

[17] In some cases of this type, the contract has been held invalid for *dol*. See, for example, Civ. 20 April 1966, Bull.cass. 1966.I. no. 224; Civ. 23 Jan. 1969, Bull.cass. 1969.I. no. 21; Civ. 30 May 2000, Bull.cass. 2000.I. no. 69; Civ. 3 April 2002, Bull.cass. 2002.I. no. 108.

[18] See Req. 12 Jan. 1931, *Gaz Pal* 1931.1.441; Paris 22 Mar. 1952, *Gaz Pal* 1952.2.102. Occasionally, the courts have allowed the disadvantaged party to attack the contract on the ground of *erreur*; see Ghestin (n 11) nos. 513, 579, 586, 588.

[19] [1978] 1 WLR 255; and compare *Backhouse* v. *Backhouse* [1978] 1 All ER 1158, 1165f.

The important English institution of *undue influence* gives grounds for avoiding a contract where a party can show that, although there was no duress, the contract was concluded following undue pressure or on the basis of false information provided by the other party. Such proof is not required if there is a relationship of special trust on the basis of which one party could expect the other party to give loyal and complete advice. The courts have found such a relationship of special trust, for example, in the relationship between child and parent, ward and guardian, patient and doctor, penitent and confessor, and client and lawyer or other professional adviser. When under a contract made between parties to such a relationship a benefit has been conferred by the reliant party which 'calls for an explanation' or 'is not readily explicable by the relationship of the parties', the presumption is that it results from 'undue influence'.[20] In general, no such relationship of special trust exists between spouses. However, the courts try to help in a different way. Take the most obvious example, where a wife has given a bank a guarantee to cover her husband's business liabilities, or for the same reasons she has given the bank a charge against a property which she owns or co-owns. There is a presumption that the transaction—if it 'calls for an explanation' or evidently does not reflect the interests of the woman—came about due to the undue influence of her husband. This presumption is rebuttable by the bank, which must then show that it took reasonable steps to ensure that the decision was made freely by the wife. In practice, this means that the bank must explain to the wife that it will only undertake the transaction after she has provided a written statement from a lawyer documenting that, in the absence of her husband, she had been fully informed about the possible consequences of the pending transaction.[21]

There is debate as to whether the English legal rule set out above can be turned into a general principle: A contract would always be void when it resulted in a grave disadvantage for one party, which had only agreed to the contract because its bargaining power was substantially less than that of the other party. This was the view taken by Lord Denning in *Lloyd's Bank Ltd. v. Bundy*.[22] In this case, a customer who wanted an extension of credit told the bank that his father, who owned a small farm, would provide security. An official of the bank called upon the father in the company of the son, and without giving any further information about the son's financial situation or any opportunity to obtain independent advice, procured the father to take out a charge against his farm, which was virtually his only asset. When the bank sought possession of the farm, the Court of Appeal rejected its claim. Two of the judges based this

---

[20] See Treitel (n 6) no. 10-013ff. In continental systems, one often finds texts which seek to guard against such conflicts of interest. Thus parents and guardians, as statutory agents, are like all other agents prohibited from entering *Insichgeschäfte*, ie transactions in which they act as both agent and beneficiary. On this, see below, pp. 303f. See also arts. 907, 909 *Code civil*, whereby contracts and testamentary dispositions made during a fatal illness are void if made in favour of an attendant doctor or priest. Transactions are also void if made by a resident in a residential home for senior citizens in favour of the personnel: see arts. L.331-4 and L.443-6 French *Code de l'action sociale et des familles*; BGH 9 Feb. 1990, BGHZ 110, 235; BayObLG 28 June 1991, [1992] *NJW* 55. See in detail, AP Bell, 'Abuse of a Relationship: Undue Influence in English and French Law' (2007) 15 *ERPL* 555.
[21] *Royal Bank of Scotland v. Etridge (No. 2)* [2001] 4 All ER 449; see also *Barclays Bank v. O'Brien* [1994] 1 AC 180 and Treitel (n 6) no. 10-013ff.
[22] [1975] QB 326 (CA).

on undue influence, since the father had been a customer of the bank for very many years and the circumstances were such that he could expect it to give him full information and advice. But the third judge, Lord Denning, adduced a general principle of law in support of the same conclusion. After recounting all the various ways in which English law had protected the weaker party from disadvantageous contracts, he said:

> Gathering all together, I would suggest that through all these instances there runs a single thread. They rest on inequality of bargaining power. By virtue of it, the English law gives relief to one who, without independent advice, enters into a contract on terms which are very unfair or transfers property for a consideration which is grossly inadequate, when his bargaining power is grievously impaired by reason of his own needs or desires, or by his own ignorance or infirmity, coupled with undue influences or pressures brought to bear on him by or for the benefit of the other.[23]

Not everyone in England agrees that it would be desirable to replace the traditional rules by any such general principle: the House of Lords has cold-shouldered the proposal,[24] but many writers have endorsed it.[25]

In France, too, there have been cases where a person has agreed to answer for the debts of a member of the family without really considering or understanding the liability. In one instance before the Paris Cour d'Appel, a seventy-three-year-old widow *'de situation très modeste, sans instruction particulière ni connaissance des affaires'* had given a bank a guarantee of the debts of her son-in-law, whose speculations in land were to prove disastrous. When he owed the bank 1.4 million francs, it sued the widow. She could not possibly pay, and the court—having found that there was *'une disproportion frappante entre la pauvreté des ressources de veuve Silly et l'énormité du cautionnement souscrit par elle'* and that owing to her inexperience in law and in business she had no idea what she was letting herself in for—concluded that her guarantee could be avoided for error as to its content.[26] Today, such cases are usually covered by art. L. 341-4 *Code de la consommation*: if a 'natural person' has taken on an obligation by way of guarantee that is *'manifestement disproportionné à ses biens et revenues'*, the

---

[23] Ibid at 339.
[24] See *National Westminster Bank v. Morgan* [1985] 1 All ER 821, 830 (per Lord Scarman). In this decision, Lord Scarman doubted 'whether there is any need in the modern law to erect a general principle of relief against inequality of bargaining power. Parliament has undertaken the task—and it is essentially a legislative task—of enacting such restrictions upon freedom of contract as are in its judgment necessary to relief against [such] mischief.' Such laws are enacted where there is a need, for example, to protect consumers against disadvantage from credit agreements (see Consumer Credit Act 1974, s. 140 A and B) or from unfair contract terms (see Unfair Contract Terms Act 1977; Unfair Terms in Consumer Contracts Regulations 1999; and below, pp. 140ff.).
[25] See, for example, H Beale, 'Inequality of Bargaining Power' [1986] *OJLS* 123; S Thal, 'The Inequality of Bargaining Power Doctrine' [1988] *OJLS* 17; S Smith, 'In Defence of Substantive Fairness' (1996) 112 *LQR* 138; E McKendrick, *Contract Law* (8th edn, 2009) no. 17.4 and 7; contra Treitel (n 6) no. 10-046. In other Common Law jurisdictions, such as Canada and Australia, the development is clearly in this direction, and in the US § 2-302 UCC provides that a court may refuse to enforce a contract or clause in a contract which it finds 'unconscionable'; Restatement (Second) of Contracts § 208 is to the same effect.
[26] Paris 18 Jan. 1978, JCP 1980.II.19318, n. P Simler. See also the decision of the court of Bordeaux 6 Dec. 1977, ibid.: guarantees of a notary's debts given by his wife and parents-in-law were void for *'défaut de cause et erreur substantielle'* where they had had no conception of the extent of his liability. See also Civ. 25 May 1964, D.P. 1964, 626 and HR 1 Jun. 1990, [1991] *NedJur* 3293. In cases of this type, the contract may also be void on the ground of *violence* (art. 1143 *Code civil*).

bank cannot enforce the guarantee where the person is not aware of the extent of the liabilities.[27]

In such cases, German courts invoke § 138 BGB. Subsection (2) of this provision, as mentioned above, is admittedly inapplicable since it is impossible for performance and counterperformance to be 'clearly disproportionate' in the case of a guarantee, where there is no counterperformance at all. Instead, one looks to subsection (1) and asks if the guarantee is morally offensive. Usually it is not, since even adults whose experience of business is slight are bound to know that there are considerable risks in giving a guarantee.[28] It may be otherwise when a bank obtains a guarantee from one of the debtor's relatives, such as a spouse, fiancée, parent, or child. The guarantee is valid in such a case where it is also beneficial to the guarantor—an example would be where the guarantor would be co-owner of a property to be purchased with the credit for which the guarantee is being given. But where there is no such benefit, § 138(1) BGB renders the guarantee void if the relative is thereby 'greatly overstretched'. Such is the case, for example, if it is likely that the creditor will not even be able to meet regular interest payments for the loan. In such a case, there is a practically irrefutable presumption that the relative took on the guarantee because of an 'emotional bond' to the debtor and that these circumstances have been used by the creditor to its advantage in an objectionable manner.[29] One argument against this approach by the courts is that it only speaks to guarantors without assets, and not guarantors who have some assets and thus will not be 'greatly overstretched' by their liability. Above all, the crucial issue should be whether or not the guarantor has exercised the freedom of choice in a responsible manner. Of course, there will be considerable doubt if the guarantor assuming the liability is related to the debtor. But it would be preferable if the courts followed the English approach. They would then start from the view that in these cases there is a presumption that the guarantee has come about because of undue influence from the debtor. But they would also recognise that the creditor can rebut this presumption by showing, firstly, that it informed the family member about the need to be advised by an independent lawyer and, secondly, that it took on the guarantee only after a lawyer's written statement of such advice has been submitted. In such a case, the creditor may assume considered and independent decision-making on the part of the guarantor.[30]

---

[27] See also § 25d of the Austrian Consumer Protection Law: under this, the judge may 'reduce or even waive in its entirety' the liabilities of a consumer arising from a guarantee (or from another form of intercession) if 'under all the circumstances the liability is out of all proportion to the financial abilities' of the consumer. The circumstances that the judge can take into account include the benefit flowing to the consumer from the performance of the creditor and 'the imprudence, predicament, inexperience, agitation or dependence of the intercessionary to the debtor when the liability was assumed'.

[28] The guarantor must also issue the guarantee in writing (see above, chapter 5.B), and if undertaken as a consumer as part of a doorstep contract, such guarantee may also be subsequently recalled (see below, chapter 11.B.I).

[29] See, for example, BGH 18 Sept. 1997, BGHZ 136, 350; BGH 14 Nov. 2000, BGHZ 146, 37; BGH 14 May 2002, BGHZ 151,34; BGH 14 Oct. 2003, BGHZ 156, 302; BGH 25 Jan. 2005, [2005] *NJW* 971 (settled case law).

[30] For a historical legal and comparative history of the issue, see also N Jansen, 'Seriositätskontrollen existentiell belastender Versprechen' in R Zimmermann (ed), *Störungen der Willensbildung bei Vertragsschluß* (2007) 125. Also G Wagner, 'Materialisierung des Schuldrechts unter dem Einfluß von

There is also great debate about whether a contract that offends 'good morals' or contravenes *ordre public* is always void per se, or whether a judge may modify, reduce, or reform the contract, thus maintaining its validity with a modified content.[31] What is the position, for example, if a party insists on an unconscionably high or low price, or accepts a guarantee that 'greatly overstretches' the debtor? Can the judge reduce or raise the purchase price to a reasonable level, or so restrict the scope of the guarantee that the guarantor can meet the resulting liabilities with available means? The answer is clearly no if the party is known to have blatantly exceeded the boundaries of what was legally legitimate. In such cases, the total invalidity of the contract (also) has another deterrent effect: all parties must weigh up the risk of the contract being invalid and thus be discouraged from concluding such contracts. This aim would not be served if the judge were to be free to amend the contract, as then 'the worst-case scenario for a party disadvantaging the other party in an immoral manner would be for the court to impose a reasonable and conscionable solution.'[32] However, there have been cases where deterrence played no part, such as where a party had a good reason to seek the advantageous contract and held the agreement to be valid because the boundaries of legitimacy were unclear. Such cases could provide good grounds for arguing that the contract should be revised instead of quashed, at least if rules of constructive interpretation indicate that the parties would have agreed on a certain 'reformed' version of the contract if they had recognised that the contract was invalid.

C. Undue Restraints on Personal or Economic Freedom

I. Basics

A society based on the principles of individual rights and freedom of trade is bound to discountenance contracts that unduly restrict another's personal or economic

---

Verfassungsrecht und Europarecht—Was bleibt von der Vertragsfreiheit?' in K Blaurock and B Hager (eds), *Obligationenrecht im 21. Jahrhundert* (2010) 13, 30ff.

[31] This problem also arises where a contract includes provisions by which there is an 'excessive' restriction on a party's freedom of contract, an 'excessive' disadvantaging of the party's legal status, or an 'excessive' contravention of statutory provisions designed to protect the party's position. The overriding question is whether the impact of the 'excess' may be reduced in order to maintain the validity of the contract. On this, see pp. 121, 143. The matter is different if the party relying on the invalidity of the contract states a willingness to accept the contract if the terms are amended to its advantage. International rules allow for contractual amendment in such cases. See art. 4:109(2) PECL: a party can avoid a contract if its weakness has been exploited by the other party, thereby giving that party an unfair or excess benefit. Upon the request of the disadvantaged party, the judge may 'if it is appropriate adapt the contract in order to bring it into accordance with what might have been agreed had the requirements of good faith and fair dealing been followed.' Similarly, art. 3.2.7(2) and (3) PICC; art. II.-7: 207(2) and (3) DCFR. Those legal orders that recognise *laesio enormis* permit the perpetuation of the contract, provided that the advantaged party is prepared to allow its own performance to be adapted so that there is a balance with the performance of the other party. See art. 1450 *Codice civile*; art. 1674 *Code civil*; § 947 ABGB. Pursuant to art. 3:54(2) BW, at the request of one party, instead of declaring a contract to be void due to exploitation of the circumstances, the judge may adapt the contract so as to balance out the disadvantage. See, in the same sense, BG 26 June 1997, BGE 123 III 292 and the comparative note by P Pichonnaz (1999) 7 *ZEuP* 140.

[32] BGH 21 March 1977, BGHZ 68, 204, 207; BGH 14 Nov. 2000, BGHZ 146, 37, 47f; BGH 17 Oct. 2008, [2009] *NJW* 1135.

freedom. Thus, if a borrower promises a lender not to move house or change jobs without the lender's written permission, nor to take out further loans or dispose of any of his property, the borrower is not bound by his promise.[33] Equally invalid is a transaction whereby a person transfers so much of his property to another as virtually to deprive himself of the capacity and ability to make any future dispositions.[34]

While the principal concern in such cases is the public interest in the citizen's freedom of trade, profession, and artistic activity, there is also an element of protecting the economically weaker or inexperienced party from disadvantageous agreements. This can be seen in *Schroeder Music Publishing Co. v. Macaulay*.[35] The plaintiff songwriter assigned to the defendant publisher the copyright in all the songs he might compose in the following ten years, all for the sum of £50. The House of Lords held this contract void as being in 'undue restraint of trade', as it improperly restricted the plaintiff's freedom of artistic expression. Relevant considerations were that the defendant was not obliged to publish any of the plaintiff's songs, and that whereas the publisher could terminate the contract at any time, the songwriter could not. Most material, however, was the consideration that the plaintiff, who was only twenty-one years old and still struggling for artistic recognition, clearly had less bargaining power than the defendant.[36] Restriction of artistic freedom was also involved in a case before the *Bundesgerichtshof* in 1956,[37] in which an author had promised to offer the defendant publisher all his future works for possible publication. Although the plaintiff had the right to go elsewhere if the defendant declined to publish or offered less favourable terms, the *Bundesgerichtshof* held that the author's contract involved a 'one-sided burden that constrained his economic and personal freedom to an unacceptable extent'. This was because even if the relationship of mutual trust collapsed, the author would still be bound to offer his works to the defendant, and it would seriously restrict his freedom to deal with other publishers if the defendant could pick out the best works and insist on publishing them himself.

II. Long-term contractual relationships

In some situations, the return on one party's capital investment depends on the other remaining bound to the contract for a considerable time. Typical of such contracts is where the operator of a petrol station or public house agrees for an oil company or brewery to be the exclusive supplier of oil or beer for a period of several years.

---

[33] *Horwood v. Millar's Timber & Trading Co.* [1917] 3 KB 305.

[34] See BGH 9 Nov. 1955, BGHZ 19, 12: here a contract was invalidated whereby a building contractor assigned his future fee to a bank which had already, through superior economic power, taken a transfer of the rest of the debtor's estate and thereby 'removed all ability to make independent economic or mercantile decisions' (p. 18). On assignment of all future fees, see below, pp. 341ff.

[35] [1974] 3 All ER 616 (CA). See also BG 23 May 1978, BGE 104 II 108, 116ff, where a very similar contract was held void for conflicting with art. 27(2) Swiss Civil Code (n 2).

[36] See especially the speech of Lord Diplock at pp. 623f. The decision is criticised by M Trebilcock, 'An Economic Approach of the Doctrine of Unconscionability' in B Reiter and J Swan (eds), *Studies in Contract Law* (1980) 379, 396f. He particularly stresses that music publishers would be discouraged from concluding further such contracts, thus potentially depriving young songwriters of an opportunity to earn a living. A suitable comprise might have been to hold such contracts valid, but limit their duration.

[37] BGH 14 Dec. 1956, BGHZ 22, 347, 354.

Here a different approach may be taken: to invalidate such long-term arrangements would disadvantage operators of petrol stations and public houses, since they have very little capital themselves and need the companies to provide them with stock or loans for investment. Even in such cases, however, the obligation must not be of undue duration. The House of Lords accepted a period of five years for a solus agreement between a petrol station and an oil company, but regarded twenty-one years as too long.[38] The *Bundesgerichtshof* accepted five years without question, and would be prepared to endorse longer periods.[39] By contrast, where a petrol station operator had terminated the solus agreement after twenty-five years, the oil company was not allowed to insist on a clause whereby it had an option to continue the agreement on the terms offered to the operator by another supplier: to enforce such a clause 'would limit the petrol station operator's economic independence and freedom to trade in an unacceptable manner'.[40] There may be another reason for the invalidity of such contracts: they may constitute an unacceptable restraint on competition in conflict with the competition rules of national or European law (arts. 81ff. of the Treaty of Rome, now arts. 101ff. TFEU).

III. Non-compete agreements

An undertaking not to compete with the other party could, if held valid, involve an unacceptable restriction of economic freedom. Such non-compete agreements often figure in contracts of employment, since employers are afraid that employees may leave to join a competitor, or set up a business of their own, and then make contact with the employer's customers or exploit the special skills or information they gained in their previous job. On the other hand, a non-compete agreement may have a serious impact on an employee's ability to work—often their only source of income. The employer's greater bargaining power also means that agreements often favour the employer's interests at the expense of the employee. Accordingly, employment law upholds such non-compete agreements only in special circumstances, and they are often laid down by statute or in collective bargaining agreements. Thus, art. 2125 of the Italian *Codice civile* provides that a non-compete agreement is only valid if it is made in writing, is restricted in scope, duration, and locality, with the further condition that the employee must be paid something extra for agreeing to it.[41] Courts in France and England have evolved somewhat similar rules.[42]

---

[38] *Esso Petroleum Co. v. Harper's Garage (Stourport) Ltd.* [1968] AC 269.
[39] See BGH 9 June 1969, BGHZ 52, 171, 176. Twenty years is accepted by the courts as the outside limit for contracts for the exclusive supply of beer. But everything depends on the circumstances of the particular case—for example, whether the obligation extends to the whole or only part of the publican's requirements for drinks, whether a minimum order is required, and how much the brewery has invested. See BGH 14 Jun. 1972, [1972] *NJW* 1459; BGH 17 Jan. 1979, [1979] *NJW* 865; BG 21 June 1988, BGE 114 II 159; OGH 13 Oct. 1983, SZ 56 no. 144; OGH 21 Mar. 1991, [1992] *JBl* 517.
[40] BGH 31 Mar. 1982, BGHZ 83, 313, 319.
[41] The non-compete agreement must not exceed three years, or five years in the case of senior management. See the comparable rules for employees in §§ 74ff. HGB, arts. 340ff. OR, art. 2125 *Codice civile* (for employees), § 90a HGB, art. 418d OR, art. 1751 bis *Codice civile* (for commercial representatives).
[42] See Treitel (n 6) no. 11-056ff.

When a business is sold, it is very common for the seller to promise not to enter into competition with the buyer. Such a covenant benefits the seller as well as the buyer, for the buyer will pay more for the business in confidence that the seller will not compete, solicit former customers, or try to profit from special familiarity with sources and outlets. This consideration identifies the viewpoint from which the validity of such a clause must be judged: it should not limit the seller's freedom to compete beyond what is needed to maintain the value of the business being sold and its goodwill (clientele, sources of supply, distributors, and so on).[43] It follows that a clause which prohibits competition without limit in space or time can only be upheld under very exceptional circumstances.

Such an exceptional case occurred in *Nordenfelt v. Maxim Nordenfelt*.[44] Here the seller of an arms and munitions factory covenanted not to engage in a similar activity anywhere in the world for a period of twenty-five years. This restraint was upheld because the seller's business connections were worldwide: 'He had upon his books almost every monarch and almost every State of note in the habitable globe.' The buyer thus had a reasonable interest in preventing the seller engaging in such business anywhere in the world. In general, however, limitations in terms of time, space, and type of activity are essential. In another case, the managing director of a business had promised on leaving it not to establish or engage or participate in any similar business within twenty-five kilometres for a period of ten years. The *Bundesgerichtshof* held that the period of the restraint was excessive, since any advantage the director could have drawn from his previous business relationships would have evaporated long before, and the firm would suffer no more from his engaging in competition then than it would if a total newcomer entered the market.[45]

Similar rules apply when a professional such as an attorney, accountant, or consultant engineer agrees not to compete for a period after leaving a partnership. The *Bundesgerichtshof* upheld a promise by an accountant that for two years he would not make contact with any firms he had advised in the three years prior to his departure.[46] Yet agreements which inhibit competition generally, rather than just addressing business with previous clients, are treated more severely. Thus the *Cour de cassation* released a consultant engineer from his undertaking not to give advice in his specialist field anywhere in the world for a period of five years, the engineer then being forty-five years old and at an age when '*il n'est plus temps pour lui de se reconvertir utilement*

---

[43] Here one must also consider the compatibility of the clause with national or European competition law. See BGH 3 Nov. 1981, [1982] *NJW* 2000: here the non-compete clause in the sale of a business was unobjectionable under § 138 BGB, but possibly in conflict with § 1 Act against Restraints of Competition (GWB).

[44] [1894] AC 535.

[45] BGH 13 March 1979, [1979] *NJW* 1605. The decision in Com. 19 Jan. 1981, D.S. 1982.I.R.204, n. Y Serra, is apparently much more generous: it upheld a contractual restraint on competition by the seller of a grocery business who had promised not to compete for twenty years within twenty kilometres of the business sold.

[46] BGH 26 March 1984, BGHZ 91, 1, 6ff; see also BGH 9 May 1968, [1968] *NJW* 1717. To like effect is *Bridge v. Deacons* [1984] AC 705 (PC): a solicitor can validly covenant that for five years after leaving the partnership he will not accept retainers from clients he had advised during his last three years in the partnership. See also Soc. 12 June 1986, D.S. 1987.Somm. 264, n. Y Serra: covenant valid whereby a lawyer engaged by a *conseil juridique* promises for three years not to advise prior clients.

dans une autre branche d'activité, notamment dans celle d'un ingénieur conseil.[47] A *fortiori*, the seller of a legal practice cannot validly bind himself never to compete anywhere at all.[48]

IV. Partial invalidity

A restraint on competition which is greater than is permissible—namely too wide in scope, duration, or geographical area—generally does not invalidate the whole contract, but is the clause itself void in its entirety or can it be reduced to an acceptable level? In *Mason v. Provident Clothing & Supply Co. Ltd.*,[49] an employee had promised that after leaving employment he would not compete with the company for a period of three years 'within 25 miles of London'. The House of Lords considered this geographical restriction to be too wide, but as the defendant had set up in business in the very same part of London in which he had been employed, it was argued that the prohibition, even if reduced to cover the district where the employee had worked, would still entitle an injunction. The House of Lords rejected the argument:

> It would in my opinion be *pessimi exempli* if, when an employer had exacted a covenant deliberately framed in unreasonably wide terms, the Courts were to come to his assistance and, by applying their ingenuity and knowledge of the law, carve out of this void covenant the maximum of what he might validly have required.... The hardship imposed by the exaction of unreasonable covenants by employers would be greatly increased if they could continue the practice with the expectation that, having exposed the servant to the anxiety and expense of litigation, the Court would in the end enable them to obtain everything which they could have obtained by acting reasonably.[50]

In many cases, however, courts have held otherwise. The *Bundesgerichtshof* once had a case in which a publican refused to honour an exclusive supply contract with a brewery after it had been running for ten years. The contract purported to bind him for twenty-four years, and though the court held this void for immorality, it reduced the period to sixteen years and made the publican pay the agreed penalty of 15 per cent of the estimated throughput of beer for each of the remaining six years.[51] English courts also have occasionally reduced restrictive covenants to a permissible level.[52]

---

[47] Paris 7 Feb. 1980, *JCP* 1981.II.19669, n. O Edwards.
[48] BGH 28 Apr. 1986, [1986] *NJW* 2944.   [49] [1913] AC 724.
[50] Lord Moulton, ibid., at 754f. So, and for the same reasons, BGH 28 Apr. 1986 (n 48); BGH 15 Mar. 1989, [1989] *NJW-RR* 800. Contrast OLG Zweibrücken 21 Sept. 1989, [1990] *NJW-RR* 482, where the parties had expressly agreed that if their clause were invalid it should be replaced by one 'which approximated to it as closely as possible in economic effect': the court reduced a covenant without limit of time to one for five years and upheld the claim.
[51] BGH 16–17 Sept. 1974, [1974] *NJW* 2089. See also BG 5 Oct. 1965, BGE 91 II 372; BG 27 July 1970, BGE 96 II 139; and BG 21 June 1988 (n 39): in the last case, a clause for the exclusive supply of beer 'in perpetuity' was reduced to twenty years, on the ground that that was the period the parties would have agreed on 'had they been conscious of the invalidity of perpetual contracts'. However, the contract will be struck down *in toto* if, in addition to containing an unduly long restriction on competition, it also has other substantive flaws, such as standard terms conflicting with the applicable law; see, for example, BGH 27 Feb. 1985, [1985] *NJW* 2693, 2695.
[52] See, for example, *Goldsoll v. Goldman* [1915] 1 Ch. 292 (CA); *T. Lucas & Co. v. Mitchell* [1974] Ch. 129; *Attwood v. Lamont* [1920] 3 KB 571; as well as Treitel (n 6) no. 11-158ff. See also BGH 26 March

The picture in France is similar. An employee who had promised not to work for a competitor in the same field during the ten years following his departure, a manifestly excessive period, nevertheless took a position with a competitor in the same city on the very day he left the plaintiff's employment. He was held liable, for *'une clause de non-concurrence ... ne doit être annulée que dans la mesure où elle porte atteinte à la liberté du travail en raison de son étendue dans le temps et dans l'espace et quant à la nature de l'activité de l'intéressé'.*[53]

The question of whether a restrictive covenant can be reduced to an acceptable level in this way is often said to depend on whether the objectionable part can be 'severed' without affecting the balance of performance and counterperformance envisaged by the parties when they made the contract. Sometimes it is argued that the judge should not take the place of the parties to force a 'new' contract on them. But the principal consideration must be whether the policy underlying the prohibition of undue restrictions on economic activity is better advanced by reducing the clause in question or striking it out altogether. Thus, if a party has exacted a manifestly excessive non-compete agreement without making any real attempt to render the restriction reasonable, there is much to be said for quashing the clause, for to hold otherwise might run counter to the deterrent aim of the policy.

D. Breach of the Law

In order to carry through their economic social and legal policies, all modern welfare states enact laws prohibiting certain types of conduct or permitting them only subject to an official licence or consent. If a contract is formed or executed in breach of such rules or regulations, is it valid or void?

The matter is put beyond doubt if the statute itself declares the contract void. Thus § 1 of the German Act against Restraints of Competition (GWB) states that contracts between undertakings are void if they are apt to 'have as their object or effect the prevention, restriction or distortion of competition'. Likewise, if a law forbids an insurance company, unless appropriately authorised, to 'carry on ... insurance business', defined as 'the business of effecting and carrying out contracts of insurance', a policy issued by a company with no such authorisation is void and any claim will be denied. This is hard on the insured if he had no reason to doubt the validity of the policy, but the court has no choice in the matter. It can hardly order the insurer to pay the insured sum, for that would be to require it to 'carry out' the contract and do what the legislature has expressly forbidden it to do.[54]

1984 (n 46) 6f. Here the court *upheld* a clause insofar as it restrained the defendant from contacting the plaintiff's customers but *struck it down* to the extent it restrained him from general competition. Swiss decisions are to the same effect, see BG 5 Oct. 1965, BGE 91 II 372 (temporal and geographical restraints on a travelling salesman).

[53] Soc. 21 Oct. 1960, *JCP* 1960.II.11886; Soc. 1 Dec. 1982, Bull.cass. 1982.V. no. 668; Soc. 25 Jan. 1984, Bull.cass. 1984.V. no. 31. See also Ghestin (n 11) no. 915.

[54] *Bedford Insurance Co. v. Instituto de Resseguros do Brasil* [1985] QB 966; *Phoenix General Insurance Co. v. Halvanon Insurance Co. Ltd.* [1988] QB 216.

More often statutes do not allude to the question whether contracts formed in breach of their provisions are valid or not; they simply provide that the infringer shall be punished, have its licence withdrawn, or suffer some other sanction. Here the judge must construe the statute in order to discover whether its unexpressed intention was that contracts formed in breach of it should be void. Thus § 134 BGB provides that contracts which infringe a statute are void 'unless the statute leads to a different conclusion'.[55]

If the statutory prohibition is directed at both parties and both of them have breached its terms in forming the contract, one must generally conclude that the contract is invalid.[56] For example, if a law provides that both parties to a sale of goods of a certain type must have a licence, the contract of sale is void if the seller is the only party to have one. Indeed, even if the buyer had fraudulently represented that he had a licence, he may defend a claim for damages for non-acceptance on the ground that the contract is void, 'however shabby it may appear to be'.[57] In Germany, where the Clandestine Employment Act[58] seeks to combat operations on the black economy by making it an offence both for the unregistered person to render a service and for the customer to pay for it, the courts infer that if both parties are deliberately flouting the law, their contract is void, and neither performance nor damages for non-performance can be claimed by either party.[59]

But often only one of the parties is breaking the law by entering the contract. Here the question is whether the aim of the law can be achieved by simply applying the sanctions expressly laid down in it, or whether in addition the contract should be invalidated:

Where a statute merely prohibits one party from entering into a contract ... it does not follow that the contract itself is impliedly prohibited so as to render it illegal and void. Whether or not the statute has this effect depends on considerations of public policy in the light of the mischief which the statute is designed to prevent, its

---

[55] Likewise art. 3:40(2) BW.
[56] The conclusion will be the same where only one party was in breach, but the other knew of it. For example, if a haulage firm supplies for the carriage of a heavy load a vehicle that by law may not be used for that purpose, the cargo-owner who knew of this has no contractual claim for damage to the cargo. See *Ashmore Benson Pease & Co. Ltd.* v. *A. V. Dawson Ltd.* [1973] 2 All ER 856.
[57] *Re Mahmoud and Ispahani* [1921] 2 KB 716 (CA): 'If an act is prohibited by statute for the public benefit, the Court must enforce the prohibition, even though the person breaking the law relies on his own illegality' (at 729). It is a different question whether the seller in such a case may claim damages from the buyer for deceit, or whether the buyer can claim his money back if it has already been paid. The Court of Appeal was not concerned with these questions, since the seller's claim had been the subject of arbitration, and the only question put by the arbitrator to the court was whether or not the contract was valid.
[58] *Gesetz zur Bekämpfung der Schwarzarbeit* of 31 May 1974 (BGBl. 1974 I 1252, as amended BGBl. 1982 I 110). Compare the French rules against *travail dissimulé*: art. L 8221-1ff *Code du travail*. The main aim of such laws is to put an end to the activities of craftsmen who fail to register and thus escape official control, pay no taxes and social security charges, do not respect the laws about accident prevention, and take on foreign employees without permission—all of which enables them to underbid firms which are properly registered.
[59] BGH 23 Sept. 1982, BGHZ 85, 39. Here again it is another question whether performance rendered pursuant to the void contract can be reclaimed or, if not, its value. See below, pp. 125ff.

language, scope and purpose, the consequences for the innocent party, and any other relevant consideration.[60]

If, for example, court officials (*huissiers*) are forbidden to engage in remunerated activity outside of their employment, it is doubtful whether they may claim the agreed commission from a person for whom they illicitly negotiate a deal. The law is certainly designed to deter *huissiers* from such activities and it would clearly serve this aim if their claim were denied. On the other hand, the aim of the law might be achieved by applying disciplinary sanctions in proportion to the offence and the gain to be made from the forbidden transaction. If one also accepts that the principal purpose of the law is to preserve the '*dignité professionnelle*' of the *huissier* rather than to protect the client from obtaining an undeserved bonus by not paying for the service, one can understand why the *Cour de cassation* upheld the contract and allowed the *huissier* to claim his commission.[61] The decision is the same where a transaction is carried out by an unlicensed freight forwarder[62] or real estate broker,[63] or if an accountant illicitly acts as a broker for profit,[64] or a haulage firm carries goods belonging to a customer in a vehicle licensed only to carry its own.[65] In another case, a contract for the construction of a dwelling was upheld although the builder was unregistered but this fact was not known to the customer. Admittedly, the customer could not demand that the unregistered builder complete the job that he had partly performed, but could claim that the unregistered builder have it completed by a properly registered builder, or else claim for the cost of retaining a registered builder to complete the job.[66]

It is clearly open to a court to hold that, in view of the meaning and purpose of the enactment, a contract must be held void even if only one of the parties broke the law in entering or executing it. Thus, where an architect illegally promised to pay the plaintiff for introducing a client, the plaintiff's claim for the fee was dismissed although he had broken no law.[67] This is so particularly when the law infringed by one party was intended for the protection of the other. For example, if only banks may lawfully conduct leasing business, a customer may disregard a leasing contract made with a firm of

---

[60] *Phoenix General Insurance Co.* (n 54) per Kerr LJ at 176. To the same effect is BGH 23 Oct. 1980, BGHZ 78, 263, 265. Such a flexible solution can also be found in art. 15:102 PECL. The most important consideration is whether the effects of the infringement upon the contract are expressly prescribed by the mandatory rule. Where the mandatory rule does not expressly prescribe the effects, the contract may be declared to have full effect, to have some effect, to have no effect, or to be subject to modification. This turns in particular on the purpose of the rule which has been infringed, whether the party claiming invalidity belongs to the category of persons for whose protection the rule exists, and any sanction that may be imposed against the infringer under the rule infringed. A similar approach is taken under art. 3.3.1(3) PICC; art. II. -7:302(3) DC FR.

[61] Civ. 15 Feb. 1961, Bull.cass. 1961.I. no105; Civ. 21 Oct. 1968, D.S. 1969, 81.

[62] Com. 11 May 1976, *JCP* 1976.II.18452, n. R Rodière (freight forwarder obtains a valid lien, arising out of the contract, on the goods of the principal).

[63] BGH 23 Oct. 1980, BGHZ 78, 269 (the agent may claim the commission).

[64] BGH 23 Oct. 1980, BGHZ 78, 263 (tax adviser can claim the agreed fee).

[65] *Archbolds (Freightage) Ltd. v. Spanglett Ltd.* [1961] 1 QB 374 (CA): the carrier could not defend a claim for the value of the goods which had been stolen by arguing that the contract of carriage was void, but could he have claimed the agreed sum for the carriage if they had been duly delivered? *St John Shipping Corp. v. Joseph Rank* [1957] 1 QB 267 held that he could: the carrier's claim for freight was granted although the captain had committed an offence by overloading the vessel.

[66] BGH 19 Jan. 1984, BGHZ 89, 369.   [67] Amiens 9 Feb. 1976, *JCP* 1977.IV.45.

any other kind because the law is designed to protect '*non seulement l'intérêt général et celui des établissements de crédit, mais aussi celui des crédit-preneurs*'.[68] By contrast, a building society empowered by law to accept only first mortgages was able to enforce a second mortgage, since the aim of the law was to protect the society and its members, not its debtors.[69]

E. Restitution of Benefits Conferred

Neither party to a void contract can demand performance from the other, nor can damages be claimed for non-performance. It is another question, however, whether any benefits conferred in pursuance of the void contract may be reclaimed, and the question is especially delicate when both parties were actuated by an immoral purpose. The Roman jurists discussed many such cases. No claim could be brought by a person who bribed a judge[70] or gave hush money to a person who caught him *in flagrante delicto*[71] or paid for immoral services:[72] 'I replied that no restitutionary claim lay for money paid when both payer and recipient had an immoral purpose, and that where the parties were equally guilty the possessor should prevail.'[73]

This venerable rule has managed to survive—in many countries it is enacted law,[74] while in others it is applied by the courts[75]—but in modern conditions its application is becoming increasingly difficult.

---

[68] Com. 19 Nov. 1991, n. J Mestre in (1992) 91 *Rev trim civ* 381. Different is Civ. 13 Oct. 1982, Bull.cass. 1982.I. no. 286: here the defendant obtained a perfectly normal loan of FF 600,000 from the plaintiff which was not lawfully entitled to give credit of this kind, not being registered as a bank. The *Cour de cassation* held that the plaintiff's breach of the law '*ne portant atteinte qu'à l'intérêt général et à celui de la profession du banquier ... n'est pas de nature à entraîner la nullité du contrat de prêt*'.
[69] *Nash v. Halifax Building Society* [1979] 2 All ER 19.   [70] Paul D. 12,5,3.
[71] Ulpian D. 12,5,4 pr.   [72] Ulpian D. 12,5,4,3.
[73] Papinian D. 12,7,5 pr. For historical details and a comparative view, see Zimmermann (n 9) 863ff.
[74] See § 817 sent. 2 BGB; art. 66 OR; § 1174 ABGB; art. 2035 *Codice civile*. Dutch law is different: benefits conferred pursuant to an invalid contract may in principle be reclaimed even if the nullity results from infringement of the law or morals. But under art. 6:211 BW a court may reject the claim in restitution if decency and fairness so require. On this, see HR 28 June 1991, [1992] *Ned Jur* 787. This solution has the merit of allowing the judge to weigh openly the reasons for and against the claim for restitution. A similar flexibility has been proposed in England: in *Tinsley* v. *Milligan* [1992] Ch. 310 (CA), [1993] 3 All ER 65 (HL) two parties who had both contributed to the purchase of a house on the basis that it should belong to them in equal parts registered it in the name of the plaintiff alone in order that the defendant could dissimulate her wealth and so claim higher social security benefits. When the parties fell out, the plaintiff sought possession of the house which was in her name alone, and the defendant counterclaimed for an order that the house be sold and that half of the proceeds be paid to her. Both the Court of Appeal and the House of Lords allowed the counterclaim, though with dissents in each instance, even though the counterclaimant had used the transaction in an attempt to defraud the social security authorities and secure herself an illegal benefit. In the Court of Appeal, Nichols LJ applied what he called the 'public conscience test': 'The court must weigh, or balance, the adverse consequences of granting relief against the adverse consequences of refusing relief. The ultimate decision calls for a value judgment ... Balancing these considerations I have no doubt that, far from it being an affront to the public conscience to grant relief in this case, it would be an affront to the public conscience not to do so. Right-thinking people would not consider that condemnation of the parties' fraudulent activities ought to have the consequence of permitting the plaintiff to retain the defendant's half-share of this house. That would be to visit on the defendant a disproportionate penalty, in the circumstances as they are now' (at 319–21). The House of Lords reached the same conclusion, but decisively rejected the 'public conscience' test. For further details, see McKendrick (n 25) no. 15.18.
[75] French courts are rather given to using the formula *nemo auditur propriam turpitudinem allegans*, which is rather wider and prompts commentators to ask whether it may not apply to claims for a

As long as cases involved parties who had flouted basic moral precepts or conspired to do something punishable by law it seemed reasonable enough to deny restitution 'als Strafe für die Betätigung verwerflicher Gesinnung' (punishment for putting disgraceful intentions into action)[76] or to justify its denial as protecting the dignity of the court: 'No court will lend its aid to a man who founds his cause of action upon an immoral or illegal act.'[77] In Germany also, it was said that restitution must be denied 'in order to protect the state from abusive invocation of its jurisdiction by deliberate criminals'[78] and Larombière wrote that in these cases 'la Justice se voile dans un mouvement d'indignation et de dégoût'.[79]

But such rhetorical flourishes no longer carry much weight now that most cases involve infringement of provisions of a rather technical and administrative nature, designed to implement the state's social or economic policies. Indeed often one, or even both, of the parties may have been unaware at the time of the contract that any infringement was involved. As we have seen, an infraction does not necessarily make the contract void in such cases (above, pages 122ff.), but if it does, and claims for performance or damages for non-performance are therefore excluded, it may not be necessary to go further and exclude claims for the restoration of what has been rendered. In both cases, the solution should depend on the purpose behind the law infringed, but even if its purpose requires the contract to be avoided, the question remains whether it is better served by allowing the recipient to keep what has been received, or allowing the performer to reclaim it. The same is true when the contract is invalid by reason of an offence against good morals or public policy rather than infringement of the law. Here too, the judge must not only consider the actual consequences in this case of a decision either way, but also ask quite openly whether the denial of the restitutionary claim will advance the public interest in dissuading citizens from entering into such contracts.[80]

Have the courts developed rules and standards to assist them in the inquiry as to whether the public interests to be protected tip more in favour of allowing or of

---

declaration that the contract is void or to claims in delict. See P le Tourneau, Juris-classeur civil art. 1131 à 1133 (Règle 'nemo auditur') no. 34ff.

[76] The courts in Germany often use this phrase. See, for example, RG 8 Nov. 1922, RGZ 105, 270, 271 and BGH 31 Jan. 1963, BGHZ 39, 87, 91. The idea of punishment is clearly inappropriate, since for one thing the 'punishment'—the denial of restitution—can be entirely out of proportion to the seriousness of the infraction and because furthermore the 'punishment' leads to the enrichment of the complicitous defendant who can retain what was transferred even when his conduct was much more deplorable and therefore more deserving of 'punishment' than the claimant's. It would be more logical to allow the state to claim the benefit transferred and so deny it to both parties; this was done in the Prussian ALR (1794), § 172f. I 16 and in art. 411f. Polish Civil Code.

[77] *Holman v. Johnson* (1775) 1 Cowp. 341, 98 Eng.Rep. 1120, per Lord Mansfield.

[78] Supreme Court for the British Zone 10 Dec. 1950, OGHZ 4, 57, 60.

[79] *Théorie et pratique des obligations* (2nd edn, 1885) i, 333, cited by Ghestin (n 11) no. 931.

[80] Thus Treitel (n 6) no. 11-127: the 'general rule' is that benefits rendered in performance of an illegal contract cannot be reclaimed, but 'It would be better if the law did not adopt a "general rule" but asked in relation to each type of illegality whether it was recovery or non-recovery that was the more likely to promote the purpose of the invalidating rule.' The same approach is taken by art. 15:104 PECL whereby restitution of services performed under a contract turns on whether or not this is justified on the grounds on which the validity of the contract itself depends. Similarly also art. 3.3.2.(2) PICC.

rejecting the restitutionary claim? One such rule is surely that restitution should be allowed if the defendant is the person primarily responsible for the illegality or immorality, and the claimant is relatively innocent or in need of protection. In England, the saying is that the claim for restitution should only be denied when the parties are '*in pari delicto*'. If the defendant deceived the claimant into believing the contract licit, or took advantage of the claimant's predicament, inexperience, or fecklessness, or the claimant belonged to a class which it was the purpose of the rule infringed to protect, then the parties are not '*in pari delicto*' and restitution should be allowed. The French courts operate very largely on the principle that restitution should be denied only in cases of '*égale culpabilité*', and should be granted to a claimant '*paraît moins coupable que l'autre*'.[81] Nor is this principle unknown to the German courts. Applying § 817 sentence 2 BGB, they deny restitution only when the claimant's conduct in rendering performance was deliberately and consciously illegal or immoral, but not, for example, when the claimant made a forbidden payment because of a crisis and 'by reason of this difficulty unwillingly acceded to the demands of the economically superior' defendant.[82]

All courts therefore allow tenants to reclaim premiums illegally demanded by a landlord for granting a lease.[83] Likewise, a buyer can reclaim instalments when the minimum down-payment required by the law was not made, and this is so even if the buyer paid them '*en pleine connaissance de cause*', knowing the law quite as well as the seller. Here the law was passed to protect the buyer, and this aim would be frustrated if buyers were barred from reclaiming any payments made under the void contract.[84] Naturally, the buyer must restore what had been received from the seller, insofar as the buyer is still in possession. This point was overlooked by the Swiss *Bundesgericht* in a case where a loan made by a bank was illegal (under a law in force at that time) because a prior loan to the customer was still outstanding. After holding the second loan invalid for breach of the law, the *Bundesgericht* denied the bank's claim for the

---

[81] See C Larroumet, *Droit civil, vol. III: Les obligations, Le contrat, Effets* (6th edn, 2007) no. 581. There is special need for the differentiation in accord with the degree of culpability in cases where the reasons for the invalidity of the contract are not known to one party, which is therefore 'innocent'. In such circumstances, both the 'innocent' and the 'non-innocent' party may assert the contract to be invalid (see Civ. 7 Oct. 1998, D. 1998, 563 = JCP 1998.II.10202, n. MH Maleville = JCP 1999.I.114, n. C *Jamin*). If it is the non-innocent party that asserts the claim for restitution, such claim may be denied on the basis of the rule '*nemo auditur*'; in addition, the party may also be liable for other damages under the law of tort.

[82] RG 24 Oct. 1919, RGZ 97, 82, 84. The claimant was accordingly allowed to reclaim the part of the price which was illegal. So too BGH 23 Nov. 1959, LM § 817 BGB no. 12, where a merchant could reclaim the interest paid on a loan void for immorality. Admittedly, he himself had acted immorally in paying the excessive interest, since as a merchant he must have known that his conduct would accelerate his financial collapse and prejudice his other creditors, but he had displayed no 'deplorable attitude' since it was only his economic difficulties which led him to enter the contract. Compare BG 21 Nov. 1950, BGE 76 II 346, 369ff: a criminal who has paid hush money can reclaim it despite art. 66 OR if he paid only in response to blackmail: it is an abuse of right under art. 2 Swiss Civil Code to invoke art. 66 OR in order to refuse repayment of hush money.

[83] RG 10 Jan. 1930, RGZ 127, 276, 279; *Gray* v. *Southouse* [1949] 2 All ER 1019; *Kiriri Cotton Co.* v. *Dewani* [1960] AC 192 (PC).

[84] See Com. 11 May 1976, Bull.cass. 1976.IV. no. 162.

return of the capital paid out.[85] This decision went too far. The financial sanctions on the bank for breach of the law were already stringent, and it was quite unnecessary to deny its claim to restitution and give the customer an undeserved bonus. Furthermore, the purpose of the law was to cool the economy rather than to protect the borrower, and leaving the borrower with the money had just the opposite effect.

French commentators often note that while restitution is denied in the case of *immoral* contracts, it is generally allowed where the contract is merely *illegal*.[86] Although it is not always easy to distinguish a *contrat immoral* from a *contrat seulement illicite*, there is a grain of truth in this. When the legislature enacts 'technical' prohibitions to control and regulate the economy, its purpose is often enough met by refusing to enforce the contract which infringes them, thereby rendering immaterial any requirements for performance or payment of damages. There is no need to refuse restitution to a party who has paid more than the lawful rent or price, or paid money to somebody to carry out a transaction which is unauthorised or in breach of exchange control regulations.[87] Nevertheless, it all comes back to the purpose of the prohibition and the circumstances of the particular case. Factors in favour of allowing the restitutionary claim are that the defendant has abused the claimant's trust, or that the claimant was unaware that exchange control regulations were being breached[88] or that the law infringed was of a purely technical nature—namely, not one of those laws which 'by reason of their intrinsic meaning or long duration must have entered the general consciousness so that their familiarity may be presumed'.[89] However, the Swiss *Bundesgericht* once refused a claim for the return of money paid illegally for a supply of gold: 'Morally displeasing' though it was that the defendant should be able to keep the money, deterrence from illicit transactions could only be achieved by refusing to hear any claim a participant might make.[90] But the situation may not always be so. While a contract for black market services is void if both parties were aware of its illegality,[91] deterrence may be sufficiently achieved by holding that the agreed remuneration cannot be claimed by the performer, who may in any case be punished and made to pay back taxes. On the other hand, the purpose of the

---

[85] BG 21 Dec. 1976, BGE 102 II 401, 411f. The decision has been severely criticised. It would have been better to allow the bank to recover the money lent under the second loan, at least after the agreed period. German courts decide in this way when a loan has been made on terms which are usurious and accordingly immoral. The effect of § 817 sent. 2 BGB is that the bank cannot claim interest for the period of the loan, but can recover the capital at the end of the agreed period. The leading case is RG 30 June 1939, RGZ 161, 52, 57ff. and subsequent decisions.

[86] See, for example, Starck, Roland, and Boyer (n 11) no. 937ff; J Carbonnier, *Droit civil: Les obligations* (22nd edn, 2000) no. 49. This is explicit in Aix 28 Mar. 1945, Gaz.Pal. 1945.2.12; Colmar 4 Jan. 1961, Gaz. Pal. 1961.1.304. The commentators all agree, however, that this is simply a rule of thumb.

[87] Civ. 18 June 1969, *JCP* 1969.II.16131, n. P.L.; see also Angers 2 Apr. 1952, JCP 1952.II.6953.

[88] *Shelley* v. *Paddock* [1980] 1 All ER 1009 (CA). It is different if both parties know that the proposed transaction infringes exchange control regulations: see *Bigos* v. *Bousted* [1951] 1 All ER 92.

[89] RG 16 May 1919, RGZ 95, 347, 349.

[90] The *Bundesgericht* allows an exception only when the claimant was deceived by the defendant. See the decision to this effect of 27 Jan. 1948, BGE 74 II 23. See also OLG Hamm 22 May 1986, [1986] *NJW* 2440: a person who runs a bar without the proper licence, and pays money to the defendant to ensure that the true licence-holder keeps quiet, cannot reclaim the money unless the defendant has taken advantage of the economic plight or inexperience of the plaintiff so that, as the English judges might say, the parties are not '*in pari delicto*'.

[91] See text to n 59 above.

law is not met if the customer can keep the benefit of the services rendered without paying anything to the black market service provider. The customer should pay the objective value of those services, which will be rather less than the contract price in view of the fact that the customer has no come-back should the services prove defective.[92]

In English law, a restitutionary claim may be allowed if the transaction was not fully executed. This 'locus poenitentiae', as it is called, gives the claimant an incentive to back out of the objectionable transaction. The rule is not easy to apply in practice, for it is not clear how far the transaction must remain unexecuted, or whether it is enough that it remained unexecuted not because the claimant thought better of it, but because the defendant was no longer minded to perform or was prevented from doing so by external circumstances.[93]

Other English decisions hold that restitution should be granted if the claimant can formulate his claim without mentioning the forbidden transaction. For example, if the claimant has pledged, hired out, or deposited property which he owns, or has sold goods with reservation of title, the claimant can claim on the basis that the property is his and that the defendant has sold or used it without his consent; then it is the defendant who has to raise the point that the goods were handed over pursuant to a forbidden transaction. The courts here tend to give judgment for the claimant, who is simply relying on ownership and therefore appears to be 'innocent'.[94] French courts do much the same when they grant immediate possession to a landlord who has let premises for use as a brothel,[95] as do the German courts in holding that a claim for possession by an owner cannot be defeated by § 817 sentence 2 BGB.[96] Yet in such cases the decision should depend not on whether or not the claimant can assert ownership, but rather on whether granting or rejecting the claim for restitution better advances the purpose of the law infringed or the public interest in the repression of immoral dealings. To this extent it is irrelevant whether the plaintiff's illicit conduct took the form of letting an asset or lending money, or whether or not ownership in the asset illicitly sold passed to the buyer. The true reason behind the general practice of preventing the lessee of a brothel from defeating the landlord's claim for possession on the ground that both parties were guilty of immoral conduct is not that the landlord can rely on his ownership but because, as the *Bundesgerichtshof* correctly holds, if this defence were upheld the lessee could continue to use the premises for a purpose discountenanced by the law, and the result would be a 'legalisation of the brothel business'.[97]

---

[92] See BGH 31 May 1990, BGHZ 111, 308, 312ff.   [93] See Treitel (n 6) no. 11-136ff.
[94] See *Bowmakers Ltd. v. Barnet Instruments* [1945] KB 65, and on it Treitel (n 6) no. 11-139ff.
[95] See for example Paris 16 Mar. 1926, S. 1926.2.76; Nancy 8 June 1934, D.P.1935.2.33, n. Voirin.
[96] Thus when an owner has delivered property of his to the defendant in circumstances of illegality or immorality, he can claim damages if the defendant damages the thing or, if he uses it, the objective value of such use. See BGH 14 June 1951, [1951] *NJW* 643; BGH 8 Jan. 1975, BGHZ 63, 365, 368f.
[97] BGH 20 May 1964, BGHZ 41, 341, 343ff. The decision could hardly be different when demand is made for immediate repayment of a *loan* to set up a brothel. Here there is no question of the lender relying on his ownership, but the claim must be granted because otherwise the defendant could use the money to run the brothel without even having to pay interest on it.

8
The Control of Unfair Contract Terms

A. Introduction	131
B. Judicial Control	134
C. Legislative Options	136
I. Unfair contract terms in contracts between businesses	136
II. Standard terms and individually negotiated terms	139
III. When is a contract term unfair?	140
IV. Partial invalidation of terms	143
D. Preventive Control	145
I. Criminal sanctions	145
II. Group actions	146
III. Administrative controls	147

A. Introduction

There can be various reasons why a contract is invalid in its entirety: it may contravene *form requirements* (chapter 5) or *good morals* or *ordre public* (chapter 7). It may also be that one of the parties made a relevant *mistake* upon concluding the contract (chapter 9), or the party may have been maliciously deceived or put under illegal *duress* by the other party and is thus entitled to avoid the contract (chapter 10). Here one might also include the case where, under certain circumstances, a party may be allowed to *revoke* the contract retrospectively without giving any reason (chapter 11). This must be distinguished from circumstances where the overall validity of the contract is not in doubt, but one party wishes to overturn one clause, because it does not form part of the contract; because it is 'inappropriate', 'unreasonable', or 'improper'; because it contravenes 'good faith' or in some other way 'grossly disadvantages' the party. If, by way of example, goods are not delivered or are delivered late or in a defective condition, buyers will often discover that they have agreed to a contract term that excludes or restricts their right to claim damages, to demand replacement or betterment of goods that are defective, or to withdraw from the contract. To invalidate the whole contract would mean that the buyer would have to return the goods, which might be contrary to his wishes. Instead, the buyer might want to hold the seller to the contract but have the exemption clause struck down so that it no longer stands in the way of any claims under the rest of the contract. The same problem may be presented by other clauses disadvantageous to the buyer, such as those which prohibit set-off, or give the seller the right to withdraw from the contract whenever and for any reason, to raise the price after the contract is formed, to deliver goods other than those contracted for, or to exact a penalty for non-acceptance.

Such clauses may occasionally be the well-considered result of discussion between the parties, but usually they are drafted unilaterally by one party and incorporated in the contract without any negotiation over their possible amendment. Such pre-formulated terms are often used by a party not just for one contract with a particular customer—the intention is usually to use the clause as the basis for all such contracts of a similar nature. Such 'general conditions' or 'standard terms of business' (*clauses prérédigées*) can be found, for example, on the back of a cloakroom, bus, or parking ticket; displayed in a launderette; or lurking among a host of other clauses in an elaborate document. Though drafted by one party, they are binding on the other if the other party knew or could have known of them, and either expressly or impliedly agreed to their application.

Standard terms are a product of the industrial revolution of the nineteenth century: as the production of goods and services was standardised, so were the terms of business on which such goods and services were supplied. Standard terms contribute to the rationalisation and development of mass transactions, for they save companies and their customers the cost and trouble of negotiating the terms of each contract individually, or of going to court to have the contract construed and amplified. Standard terms therefore make it easier to forecast the cost of doing business, simplify its procedures, and thus contribute to keeping costs and prices low.

But there is another side to the picture. Rationalising contracts is not the company's only aim in drafting terms of business; they are also used to shift as many risks as possible on to the other party. Of course, one can only speak of shifting risks in this sense if one knows what the distribution of risks would otherwise be. This can often be inferred from the default rules laid down by statute or judicial decision, and implied into contracts in the absence of any contrary term. Such rules are designed to produce a reasonable accommodation of the interests of both parties, whereas the company will be concerned only with its own. Accordingly, if the default rules are substituted by terms that protect the drafting party, these will be felt by the other party to be 'unfair'.

There is now general agreement that the law and courts must set limits to the validity of these clauses, but it is not so clear how to justify such control. It is not enough that the customer accept a disadvantageous clause without objection. The critical question is *why* the customer habitually accepts such prejudicial clauses without demur. The reason generally given is 'unequal bargaining power' between the parties: faced with the economic superiority of the company, the customer has no alternative but to submit to the standard terms. Sometimes the company has a monopoly position, and thus sees no need to negotiate over the content of its contracts. Even in a competitive environment, competitors often use very similar standard terms of business. Commentators often point to the psychological and intellectual superiority of the entrepreneur who knows so much more about law and business than his customers that they will think it futile to protest against disadvantageous terms. In an influential and much-cited article in 1943, Friedrich Kessler wrote: '[S]tandard contracts in particular could ... become effective instruments in the hands of powerful industrial and commercial overlords enabling them to impose a new feudal order of their own making upon a vast horde of vassals.'[1] This idea that general terms of business must

---

[1] F Kessler, 'Contracts of Adhesion—Some Thoughts About Freedom of Contract' (1943) 43 *Col.LR* 629, 640.

be controlled in order to protect the weak and inexperienced against the powerful and knowledgeable has really come to dominate discussions of legal policy. After this argument became the battle-cry of the consumer protection movement, most countries in Europe have passed laws since the 1970s based more or less on the view that as consumers are the 'weaker' of the contracting parties, they must be protected against contract terms forced upon them by companies abusing their economic superiority. The Council Directive of 5 April 1993 on unfair terms in consumer contracts is based on the concept that the justification for control of standard terms is to correct the 'abuse of power' between companies and 'consumers'.[2]

Yet it is far from clear that this is the nub of the matter. Certainly a customer will occasionally refrain from objecting to an unfavourable term because he thinks it futile to negotiate over it in view of the other party's superiority in economic or other respects, but this is not the normal case. Even in areas of commerce where competition is so lively that there can be no question of economic superiority, quite experienced contractors accept such terms without demur. Businesses do not haggle over the standard terms proffered by carriers, warehousemen, credit institutions, security firms, or credit information agencies. In such cases, the customer 'submits' to the proffered terms of business because it is not worth investing the time and money involved in getting the terms modified or seeking out other firms whose terms are less unfavourable in some respect or other. A private person or even a businessman who parks his car in a garage or buys a computer or arranges for his goods to be carried accepts the terms on offer without discussion—not because they are forced on him by a 'powerful industrial or commercial overlord' but because the cost of negotiating, obtaining the necessary information, or tracking down a more favourable offer would be out of all proportion to the advantage to be gained. The company exploits this fact by saddling the customer with the risks of the deal on the assumption that, for the reasons given, the customer will neither object nor go elsewhere. But the fact that the customer agrees to the conditions does not make it incompatible with the principle of freedom of contract for the law to control such terms, since it is only when both parties had a fair chance of influencing the content of contracts that the principle requires them to be respected. In the situations under consideration, the customer has no such opportunity—not because of the superiority of the company in economic or other respects, but because of the prohibitively high transaction costs of utilising any such opportunity.[3] We shall return to this point later.

---

[2] See Recital 9 to this Directive of 5 April 1993 (93/13/EEC, OJ 1993 L 95/29).

[3] See M Trebilcock and D Dewees, 'Judicial Control of Standard Form Contracts' in A Burrows and C Veljanovski (eds), *The Economic Approach to Law* (1981) 93; M Adams, 'Ökonomische Analyse des Gesetzes zur Regelung des Rechts der AGB' in H Neumann (ed), *Ansprüche, Eigentums- und Verfügungsrechte*, Schriften des Vereins für Socialpolitik (1983) 655; P Behrens, *Die ökonomischen Grundlagen des Rechts* (1986) 155ff, 170–2; M Eisenberg, 'The Limits of Cognition and the Limits of Contract' (1955) 47 *Stan.LR* 211, 243; HB Schäfer and C Ott, *Lehrbuch der ökonomischen Analyse des Zivilrechts* (5th edn, 2012) 552ff; H Kötz, 'Der Schutzzweck der AGB-Kontrolle' [2003] *JuS* 209; G Wagner, 'Zwingendes Vertragsrecht' in H Eidenmüller, F Faust, HC Grigoleit, N Jansen, G Wagner, and R Zimmermann (eds), *Revision des Verbraucher-acquis* (2011) 1, 31ff; P Leyens and HB Schäfer, 'Inhaltskontrolle allgemeiner Geschäftsbedingungen' (2010) 210 *AcP* 771; L Leuschner, 'AGB-Kontrolle im unternehmerischen Verkehr' [2010] *JZ* 875, all with further details.

B. Judicial Control

The courts have gradually developed general rules which enable them to give some protection against unfair terms. The first question they put is whether the term has really become part of the contract. This can always be questioned if the customer entered the contract without having had any real chance of ascertaining its terms. It can be assumed that in agreeing to a contract, the customer is not agreeing to terms which are almost illegible in a printed document, barely visible in the shop, or stuck on the back of a cloakroom ticket which the customer receives only after handing over his coat. A holidaymaker injured when a deckchair on the beach collapsed under him was not bound by a clause purporting to exclude any claim for personal injury printed on the back of the ticket he was given when he hired the chair.[4] English courts have decided that the more unusual or prejudicial a clause is, the greater the care the contractor must take to bring it to the attention of the customer.[5] This does not define exactly how bold the print must be or how large the type or whether they should add a scarlet arrow or make the customer sign the clause, but in any case the customer must always be given notice of the clause before the contract is formed. A notice displayed in a hotel room exempting a hotelier from liability for loss of valuables is not binding on the guest, since the contract is formed when the guest is handed the room key at the reception desk.[6] It is the same when one puts money in the machine at the entrance to a parking garage and the ticket spewed out has an exemption clause printed on the back.[7]

The question whether standard terms have been incorporated in the contract is covered by statute in many countries. The Italian *Codice civile*—the first code in the world to have special rules for *condizioni generali di contratto*—provides in art. 1341 that they form part of the contract only if the customer knew of them at the time of the contract, or would have known of them had he been properly alert. It adds that certain particularly suspect types of clause, listed in art. 1341(2), must be specifically approved in writing by the customer.[8] Recent legislation has favoured more flexible rules which dispense with the time-consuming and often impractical formality of special endorsement. In fact, § 305(2) BGB provides that standard business terms only become part of the contract if the supplier referred to them at the time of contracting and 'enabled the other party to take proper account of their content'. Even when this condition is met, the judge may still deem terms not to form part of the contract if they are in the circumstances 'so unusual' that the other party 'need not expect to encounter them'.[9]

---

[4] See *Chapelton v. Barry UDC* [1940] 1 KB 532. Further examples are given in GH Treitel, *The Law of Contract* (13 edn, by E Peel, 2011) no. 7-003ff.

[5] See *Interfoto Library Ltd. v. Stiletto Ltd.* [1989] 1 QB 433 (CA), where the opinion of Bingham LJ is well worth reading, not least for its comparative discussion.

[6] *Olley v. Marlborough Court Ltd.* [1949] 1 KB 532; to the same effect Lyons 12 June 1950, D. 1951 Somm. 2. More French decisions can be found in J Calais-Auloy and H Temple, *Droit de la consommation* (8th edn, 2010) 162ff.

[7] See *Thornton v. Shoe Lane Parking Ltd.* [1971] 2 QB 163.

[8] See it. Cass 23 May 1994, no. 5024, commented by EM Kieninger in [1996] 4 ZEuP 468.

[9] § 305c(1) BGB; § 864a ABGB. On inclusion of standard terms in contracts, see the comparative treatment by F Ranieri, *Europäisches Obligationenrecht* (3rd edn, 2009) 333ff. The CISG does not contain a

Another technique which judges have adopted for controlling such terms is to first hold that the clause in question is unclear or ambiguous, and then—on the principle that exemption clauses must be narrowly construed or that ambiguous expressions must be interpreted against the party who drafted them (*contra proferentem*)—read it in an artificial and unexpected manner favourable to the customer.[10] Innumerable decisions have employed this technique.[11] One objection is that judges only construe the clause so artificially because they regard it as substantially unfair *ab initio* and wish to protect the consumer without openly invalidating the clause and apparently infringing the principle of freedom of contract. A further objection is that the benefit is very short-lived, since the companies just have their lawyers draft other clauses to the same effect but clear enough to withstand hostile interpretation.[12]

Only in a few countries have the courts had the nerve, in the absence of a legislative mandate, to go beyond these techniques of 'covert control of the substance' and invalidate clauses which unduly and unreasonably prejudice the customer. This has been done in cases where companies guilty of fraud or gross negligence[13] have sought to hide behind an exemption clause. But it was the German courts that first assumed the power of 'open control' over *all* pre-formulated contract terms.[14] For this they cited § 242 BGB, a general clause which simply provides that parties are to perform their contractual obligations 'according to the requirements of good faith in relation to good business practice'. Its invocation was therefore merely a gesture. In reality this was pure judge-made law, a very praiseworthy achievement without parallel for many years in any other country.[15]

Meanwhile, laws have come into force in all European countries that allow courts, under certain circumstances, to invalidate unfair contract terms.[16] But there are great differences between these laws, which have not all been set aside by the coming

---

provision governing inclusion of standard terms, but the courts come to the same conclusion via another route. See BGH 31 Oct. 2001, [2002] *NJW* 370 and, Ranieri ibid., 357ff.

[10] See above, p. 99.

[11] For the English cases, the judgment of Lord Denning in *George Mitchell (Chesterhall) Ltd. v. Finney Lock Seeds* [1983] QB 284, 297 is well worth reading; see also Treitel (n 4) no. 7-014ff. Likewise art. 1370 *Codice civile*; § 305c (2) BGB; art. 11 Portuguese Law no. 446-85 of 25 Oct. 1985; and art. 5 sent. 2 of the European Directive on Unfair Terms in Consumer Contracts (n 2): 'Where there is doubt about the meaning of a term, the interpretation most favourable to the consumer shall prevail.'

[12] The point had already been made by K Llewellyn in his review of 'The Standardization of Commercial Contracts in English and Continental Law' by O Prausnitz, (1938) 52 *Harv. LR* 700, 702f.

[13] See art. 1229 *Codice civile*; art. 100 OR. The French courts so held where the defendant is guilty of *faute lourde équivalente au dol*; see Ass.plén. 30 Jun. 1998, *JCP* 1998.II.10146, n. P Delebeque. See now art. 1171 *Code civil* and below, p. 138.

[14] The groundbreaking decision was BGH 29 Oct. 1956, BGHZ 22, 90.

[15] But see HR 19 May 1967, [1967] *NedJur* 261, n. GJ Scholten.

[16] One notable exception is Switzerland. Swiss law does not allow a party to escape liability on the basis of an exclusion clause if it intentionally causes damage to the counterparty or is grossly negligent (art. 100(1) OR and see above, n 13). Courts also hold that a standard contract term is invalid if it is so 'unusual' that the disadvantaged party had no plausible reason to expect anything like it. See, for example, BG 6 Dec. 1983, BGE 109 II 452; BG 5 Aug. 1993, BGE 119 II 443; BG 28 Jan. 2009, BGE 135 II 225. Article 8 of the Swiss Law Against Unfair Competition (as amended in 2011) now provides that it is an unfair trade practice for a firm to include in a contract with a consumer a standard term which is 'contrary to the requirements of good faith' and causes 'a significant imbalance in the parties' rights and obligations'. It remains to be seen what the practical consequences of this rule will be. See EA Kramer, T Probst, and R Perrig, *Schweizerisches Recht der AGB* (2016).

into force of the Council Directive of 5 April 1993 on unfair terms in consumer contracts.[17] The Directive required the Member States to enact provisions allowing judges to declare a contractual clause invalid 'if, contrary to the requirement of good faith, it causes a significant imbalance in the parties' rights and obligations arising under the contract, to the detriment of the consumer' (art. 3(1)). But, as its name indicates, the Directive is limited to 'consumer contracts'. It applies only when the contract is concluded between a 'seller or supplier' and a 'natural person' who is 'acting for purposes which are outside his trade, business or profession' (art. 2b). Furthermore, the Directive only applies to contractual terms that have 'not been individually negotiated' but have been 'drafted in advance' with the consequence that 'the consumer has therefore not been able to influence the substance of the term' (art. 3(1) and (2)). Finally, provided that they are stated in plain intelligible language, clauses shall not be regarded as unfair where they concern the 'main subject matter of the contract' or 'the adequacy of the price and remuneration' (see art. 4(2)). In addition to these issues, some Member States take account of other approaches, without being in conflict with the Directive. In particular, they may adopt or retain more stringent provisions than the Directive in order to 'ensure a maximum degree of protection for the consumer' (art. 8). Not least, Member States could be active in areas falling outside the scope of the Directive, particularly with respect to allowing control of contracts that are not classed as consumer contracts but as business-to-business contracts.

C. Legislative Options

Legislatures that wish to give the courts power to control the terms of contracts have several options available.

I. Unfair contract terms in contracts between businesses

It must first be decided whether protection is to be afforded only to consumers or also to firms acting in the course of business. Legislatures in different European countries have adopted different positions on this question.

Many European legislatures also allow for the control of contractual terms in business-to-business contracts. Here too, the approach is not uniform. The Scandinavian countries have passed consumer protection laws that now take account of the provisions of the Directive. In addition, s. 36 of the Scandinavian Contracts Act allows in general terms a contract clause to be adjusted or set aside if the judge holds

---

[17] The Directive of 5 April 1993 (93/13/EEC, OJ 1993 L 95/29) has now been transposed into national law by all EU Member States, but in different ways. Some countries have enacted the Directive in their civil codes, including the Netherlands and Germany (after the modernisation of the law of obligations). Other countries have passed special consumer protection acts to enact the provisions of the Directive, including France (*Code de la consommation*) and Italy (*Codice del consumo*). In England, the Directive was transferred word for word into the Unfair Terms in Consumer Contracts Regulations 1994 (see also Statutory Instruments 1999/2083), but the question remains how these Regulations apply in the context of the longstanding Unfair Contract Terms Act 1977. An overview of the different forms of implementation of the Directive can be found in J Basedow in *Münchener Kommentar zum BGB* (6th edn, 2012) before § 305 BGB mn. 22–49.

it to be 'unfair'. Subsection 2 requires the judge to pay particular interest to the extent to which the party must be protected, especially if that party is a consumer or there are other reasons for its 'inferior position'. But there is nothing to prevent a judge from considering a business-to-business contractual clause. German law has long taken the same view. During the discussions thirty years ago surrounding a first legislative draft, it was argued that judicial control over standard terms should only be allowed with respect to consumers. This view was soon abandoned, mainly because it was demonstrated that the courts had already held standard terms to be invalid—even without statutory backing—that overwhelmingly concerned business-to-business contracts. Countries such as Austria, the Netherlands, some Baltic states, and Portugal also draw no basic distinction between consumer contracts and business-to-business contracts.[18] The English Unfair Contract Terms Act 1977 does not have a general clause, only provisions that address the valid boundaries of agreements where parties try to exclude or limit their liability. Of these provisions, some apply only to parties relying on them 'as against a person dealing as consumer'.[19] Other provisions in the Act do not have this restriction. Pursuant to s. 2, an agreement is always invalid if a party seeks to restrict its liability for death or personal injury resulting from negligence. Where a party seeks to exclude or restrict liability for other loss or damage, such a clause is only valid—even between businesses—if it is 'reasonable'. It is the judge who decides what is reasonable, depending on the particular circumstances of the case. This may include:

> the respective bargaining power of the parties, whether the exclusion clause was freely negotiated, the extent to which the parties were legally advised, the availability of insurance, the availability of an alternative source of supply to the innocent party and the extent to which the party seeking to rely on the exclusion clause sought to explain its effect to the other party.[20]

In fact there are no convincing reasons why judges should only be able to examine contractual terms where the disadvantaged party is dealing as a consumer.

The real justification for mandatory provisions governing the control over contractual terms is not that the weak must be protected from the mighty, but that there is no negotiation over many standard terms because the high transaction costs involved would not make economic sense for the affected party.[21] The rule that no one does anything when it is not worth it applies to rational persons whether they are a consumer or a trader. Of course, persons acting in the course of a business will more often be in

---

[18] However, business contractors in the Netherlands cannot rely on the general clause in art. 6:233 BW if they have more than fifty employees or as a commercial company are required to publish an annual report (art. 6:235 BW). Even in these circumstances, such a clause may still be held invalid on the basis of the general principle that the behaviour of the parties must be in accordance with the principles of 'good faith and fair dealing' (arts. 6:2 and 6:248 BW).

[19] See ss. 6 und 7 Unfair Contract Terms Act 1977. Pursuant to s. 12, a party to a contract deals as a 'consumer' if 'he neither makes the contract in the course of a business nor holds himself out as doing so; and the other party does make the contract in the course of a business.'

[20] E McKendrick, *Contract Law* (8th edn, 2009) no. 11.14. See also the case law set out there that underlies the findings summarised in this citation.

[21] See above, p. 133 and pp. 140ff.

a situation where it does pay to negotiate over contract terms than will a consumer. But that is no reason to exclude business-to-business contracts per se from any form of control over their standard terms. Article 4:110 PECL takes this approach: terms which have not been individually negotiated may be avoided by a judge if the contract has been made between businesses and even if the contract is between two private parties. French law has recently taken the same step.[22] In the course of the reform of French contract law, the *Code civil* now makes a distinction in art. 1110 between a '*contrat de gré à gré*' whose terms are freely negotiated by the parties, and a '*contrat d'adhésion*' whose general conditions have been laid down in advance by one party and were therefore not subject to negotiations. As to *contrats d'adhésion*, art. 1171 provides that any clause which creates 'a significant imbalance in the parties' rights and obligations' may be struck down by the court. This rule applies to all *contrats d'adhésion*, even if both parties are companies acting in the course of a business.

If the content control were to be extended to business-to-business contracts, one must expect that more flexible criteria would have to be applied in this area in order to take account of the peculiarities of business dealings. German courts have been said to be too rigorous in their control of standard terms in business-to-business contracts. They assume indeed that a term is 'negotiated' only where the business parties have actually changed the term during the course of the negotiations.[23] They also hold that the rules of § 308 and § 309 BGB invalidating certain terms in consumer contracts are also applied, more or less automatically, to contracts between businesses.[24] There can be no complaint about this when the contract between traders is for low-value goods or services, such as parking a company car in a public garage, commissioning a credit report about the financial position of a customer, buying foodstuffs for the company canteen, or hiring another company to transport or store their goods. But matters are different when the transaction has a considerable financial impact on the parties and it makes sense to closely analyse (perhaps with specialist legal support) a

---

[22] A law passed in 2008 had already allowed a court to hold a commercial party liable in damages if it had submitted its commercial contract partner to an obligation '*créant un déséquilibre significatif*'. See art. L. 442-5(1) *Code de commerce*.

[23] If the contract term has not been changed, but is adopted in the contract in the form proposed by its 'provider', it is regarded as 'negotiated' only where the provider made it reasonably clear that he would be willing to modify the term, and this was known to the customer. See BGH 3 Nov. 1999, BGHZ 143, 103, 111f; BGH 17 Feb. 2010, BGHZ 184, 259.

[24] See BGH 18 Mar. 1984, BGHZ 90, 273, 278; BGH 19 Sept. 2007, BGHZ 174, 1. Practising lawyers have therefore asserted that it is not rare, and therefore recommended for future transactions, that in order to exclude the strict content control under German law, business parties should agree to make their contracts subject to Swiss law (see above, n 17). The same argument has also been made with respect to English law. In s. 27 Unfair Contract Terms Act 1977, there is an express provision that the application of the Act is excluded where the parties have agreed on English law as the law governing their contract. The same applies with respect to s. 26, if the parties have concluded an 'international supply contract'. Dutch law is similar: Pursuant to art. 6:247 BW, provisions concerning content control of standard terms do not apply if the parties are both traders, have their registered office in the Netherlands, and have agreed that their contract should be subject to Dutch law. See EM Kieninger, 'ABG-Kontrolle von grenzüberschreitenden Geschäften im unternehmerischen Verkehr' in P Jung et al. (eds), *Einheit und Vielfalt im Unternehmensrecht, Festschrift für U Blaurock* (2013) 177. It has even been suggested that there is a sort of regulatory competition between the jurisdictions to attract international business to their courts in order to allow the parties, under certain circumstances, to ensure that content control is excluded with respect to their standard terms. See H Eidenmüller, 'Recht als Produkt' [2009] *JZ* 641, 645.

contract provided by the other party and to negotiate about content of terms and the allocation of risks. This would be so, for example, where the parties have agreed on a contract for the sale of a business, a construction agreement for an industrial facility, a long-term loan agreement, or a large-volume contract for the delivery of products. However, there is debate in Germany about whether this is best achieved by means of new legislative provisions, and how any solution would do justice to the principle of legal certainty. One proposal is to recognise as valid a negotiated express agreement by traders under which any court control of standard terms would be excluded. This would probably go too far.[25] It would be more acceptable for contract terms, whether or not amended by the parties, to always be deemed as 'negotiated' (and therefore not subject to judicial content control) if the traders have 'negotiated on terms in a manner appropriate to the subject matter of the contract and the circumstances of its conclusion'.[26] The Law Commission for England and Scotland has proposed that there should be no judicial content control for contracts between traders if the value of the transaction exceeds £500,000;[27] other commentators suggest a transaction value of at least €500,000 or €1 million.[28]

II. Standard terms and individually negotiated terms

Another question is whether judicial control should extend to all terms of consumer contracts, or only to those which were *pre-formulated* by one party (for all of its future transactions of the same kind, or just for the one specific contract) and *not negotiated* with the other party. Many legal orders refuse to acknowledge such a restriction. This is the case in Scandinavian jurisdictions;[29] French and Belgian law also permit content control for consumer contracts even if the contract term in question has been individually negotiated.[30] German and Dutch law take a different approach.[31] In Germany

---

[25] See N Jansen in H Eidenmüller et al. (eds), *Revision des Verbraucher-acquis* (2011) 87; H Eidenmüller, N Jansen, EM Kieninger, G Wagner, and R Zimmermann, 'Der Vorschlag für eine Verordnung über ein gemeinsames Europäisches Kaufrecht' [2012] *JZ* 275, 280. This would mean that a trader could then exclude content control of his standard terms even for low-value transactions, which would on this ground be accepted by the other trader without demur.

[26] See the solution under German proposed by KP Berger, 'Für eine Reform des AGB-Rechts im unternehmerischen Geschäftsverkehr' [2010] *NJW* 465, 467ff. Similarly T Miethaner, 'AGB oder Individualvereinbarung' [2010] *NJW* 3121.

[27] See The Law Commission and the Scottish Law Commission, *Unfair Terms in Contracts*, Reports No. 292 and No. 199 (2005) pp. 55ff. It follows that small companies with fewer than nine employees should be treated as consumers if the value of the transaction is less than £500,000 in total. See McKendrick (n 20) no. 11.16.

[28] For further detail, see Leyens and Schäfer (n 3) 793ff; Leuschner (n 3) 882ff; W Müller, C Griebeler, and J Pfeil, 'Für eine maßvolle Kontrolle von AGB im unternehmerischen Verkehr' [2009] *BB* 2658; Kieninger (n 24); Miethaner (n 26).

[29] See above, pp. 136f. with respect to s. 36 Scandinavian Contracts Act.

[30] See art. L. 13-1(3) *Code de la consommation*: with respect to consumer contracts, the control competence of the judge extends to all contract terms 'quels que soient leur forme ou leur support'. See also § 6 Austrian Consumer Code: most of the clauses described in (1) are invalid even if they are 'individually' negotiated. The general clause in § 879(3) ABGB applies only to contract terms contained in 'standard terms or printed contract forms'.

[31] See § 307 BGB, art. 6:231 BW. Also under art. 4:110 PECL and art. 83(1) and 86 (1) CESL content control is only permissible when it concerns a contract term 'which has not been individually negotiated'.

in particular, the restriction of content control to standard terms is seen as important. When the proposed Unfair Terms Directive—which sought to make all contract terms subject to judicial control—was published in 1990, it attracted great wails of protest, and one would have thought that the Council had sounded the death knell for the market economy.[32] In response to these hefty protests, the Directive was reduced to cover only contract terms that had *not* been 'individually negotiated'.

That this issue had launched such a swarm of emotions would have been understandable if there was a fear that courts, if also allowed to consider 'negotiated' contract terms, would run headlong towards open control of equivalence of performance and counterperformance. But there are no grounds for such mistrust. It is self-evident that a judge cannot invalidate a clause just because it makes the relationship between price and performance seem 'inappropriate'. This follows for consumer contracts from art. 4(2) of the Unfair Contract Terms Directive.[33] In practical terms, therefore, we are only talking about control of contractual collateral agreements. In consumer transactions, they can be unfair or inappropriate even if they are negotiated, but this will be rare. There is also no question that contract terms are invalid if they are prohibited by specific laws designed to protect consumers as borrowers, holidaymakers, or buyers, and it does not matter whether they have been pre-formulated or individually negotiated. A rule that requires only pre-formulated clauses to be subject to judicial control could also create legal uncertainty as it is often doubtful whether or not the clause that the customer wishes to challenge for invalidity can be shown to have been individually negotiated. Therefore, with respect to consumer contracts, little harm would be done if content control were extended to all contract terms.[34]

III. When is a contract term unfair?

Sometimes the law can be so specific in identifying what terms are unfair that there can hardly be any doubt whether a particular term is valid or not. But often it has to use rather vague concepts, such as saying that a term is invalid if it grants the company an 'unreasonably high' claim for damages, or a right to resile from the contract

---

[32] See HE Brandner and P Ulmer, 'Die EG-Richtlinie über mißbräuchliche Klauseln in Verbraucherverträgen' [1991] *BB* 701, 704.

[33] See above, p. 136 and the rules by which art. 4(2) of the Directive has been transposed into national legal orders. See § 879(3) ABGB; art. L. 132-1(7) *Code de la consommation*; art. 6:231 BW; no. 6(2) Unfair Terms in Consumer Contracts Regulations 1999. In the Scandinavian countries, the general clause of § 36 Contract Act does not include such a restriction. That the judges would then have been price commissioners has not previously been reported. However, it is correct that there is dispute about the correct interpretation of art. 4(2) of the Directive (and the national transposition rules); national courts also often fail to recognise that any disputes should be referred to the Court of Justice of the European Union for a ruling. See *Office of Fair Trading v. Abbey National plc and others* [2010] 1 All ER 667: in this case, the English Supreme Court accepted that standard terms of British banks, whereby customers whose accounts were overdrawn had to pay certain fees, were *not* subject to judicial content control because the terms related to the 'main purpose of the contract', namely the price that the customer had to pay the bank for services. The Court of Appeal had reached a different decision on the convincing ground that the specified clauses were not 'part of the essential bargain' but just 'ancillary terms' and therefore subject to judicial control. See H Kötz, 'Schranken der Inhaltskotrolle bei den AGB der Banken' (2012) 20 ZEuP 332. Also HR 19 Sept. 1997, [1998] *NedJur* no. 6.

[34] See Jansen (n 25) 90 and (critical) Wagner (n 3) 32ff.

'without adequate reason', or binds the other party to the contract for 'an unreasonably long period'. These formulae give judges some discretion—more so if they also had to apply a 'general clause' and examine whether 'contrary to the requirement of good faith' a term 'causes a significant imbalance in the parties' rights and obligations arising under the contract'[35] or produces *un déséquilibre manifeste entre les droits et obligations des parties*,[36] or 'unfairly prejudices' the other party,[37] or to his disadvantage 'so limits essential rights or duties arising from the nature of the contract as to impair the achievement of its purpose'.[38] Even the English Unfair Contract Terms Act 1977 could do no better than deploy the uncertain criterion of 'reasonableness'.

Such formulae seem to have no objective meaning. Are they simply an appeal to the judge's sense of justice and sound common sense? Are there any concrete rules to tell us whether a contract condition is 'unfair', 'inappropriate', or 'unreasonable'? The following consideration may help. Let us recall that a contract term is to be regarded as invalid if the party prejudiced by it had no real chance of affecting its substance. The absence of such opportunity is generally not due to the superior economic power or bargaining strength of the company the customer is dealing with, but to the fact that the transaction costs of checking the conditions and comparing them with those offered by others and making counterproposals in further negotiations would exceed any possible advantage the customer might gain. Such behaviour on the part of customers is thoroughly rational, but may be exploited by the entrepreneur. The conditions should accordingly be treated as 'unfair' or 'unreasonable' if they are disadvantageous in comparison with the terms that would have been agreed if the parties had been able to negotiate them in a world without transaction costs.[39]

In such a world, risks would be allocated to the party that could avoid them at the least cost. For example, if the buyer can take protective measures against certain risks should the goods prove defective, and it would cost the buyer less than the seller to install a foolproof system of quality control, then the buyer would accept the risks and offer a price that took account of the cost of prevention. This would be a better arrangement for both parties than if the seller took the risk and increased the price

---

[35] Article 3(1) EC Directive of 5 Apr. 1993 (n 2). Whether or not these requirements (after transposition into national law) are met in the individual case must be decided by the *national courts* as the case turns on an evaluation of the particular circumstances of the case. See EuGH 1 Apr. 2004, Rs. C-237/02—*Freiburger Kommunalbauten*, Slg. 2004, I-3403 = (2005) 13 *ZEuP* 418. It is debated whether national courts have an obligation under such circumstances to refer the case to the European Court of Justice. See W Wurmnest in *Münchener Kommentar zum BGB* (6th edn, 2012) § 307 mn. 29f.
[36] Article 31, Belgian Law of 14 July 1991.   [37] Article 6:233 BW.
[38] § 307 (2) no. 2 BGB.
[39] See Wurmnest (n 35) § 307, mn. 39 and Basedow (n 17) before § 307 mn. 4–6. See also H Kötz, *Vertragsrecht* (2nd edn, 2012) mn. 272ff. A similar approach was taken by the European Court of Justice in *Mohamed Aziz* v. *Caixa d'Estalvis de Catalunya, Tarragona i Manresa* (Case C-415/11 of 14 March 2013, [2013] *Common Market Law Reports* No. 5, p. 89). It was held that a term would not cause 'a significant imbalance' in the parties' rights and obligations and would therefore be 'fair' under art. 3 of the EC Directive on Unfair Terms if the supplier 'dealing fairly and equitably with the consumer, could reasonably assume that the consumer would have agreed to such a term in individual negotiations' (see mn. H 17). Non-negotiated terms should therefore be upheld as 'fair' if reasonable parties would have reached the same result in hypothetical negotiations, taking into account their costs and benefits. This test was also applied in *ParkingEye Ltd.* v. *Beavis* [2015] UKSC 67, where the Supreme Court held (by a majority) that a clause imposing a charge of £85 on a person parking in a car park when he overstayed the two-hour parking limit was 'fair' (mn. 108f, 209ff, 308ff.).

to take account of his own higher expenditure. This would not, of course, apply if no appropriate preventative action were possible, or possible only at disproportionate cost in relation to the risk to be avoided.[40] In such a case, reasonable parties would allocate the risk to the party that could more cheaply guard against the possible harm, and in particular insure against such risk more cheaply.

The *Bundesgerichtshof* was therefore right to invalidate a clause whereby a domestic fuel supplier sought to exclude all liability for overflow if the customer had ordered more oil than his tank could hold.[41] This clause transferred to the customer a risk that the fuel supplier itself could bear at lesser cost. Filling oil tanks was its daily business, and the supplier could select appropriate staff, equip them with suitable devices for checking the capacity of tanks, and train them in their use, all at much less cost per transaction than the individual customer if, knowing nothing of the business, the customer had to guard against the malfunctioning of his tank gauge in the annual event of replenishment. In another case, the decision was different. A shipowner claimed compensation for the damage done to his ship by a fire carelessly started by employees of the defendant ship-repairer. Here the *Bundesgerichtshof* upheld the protective clause in the ship-repairer's general conditions of business because the shipowner's crew, who remained on board ship during the repairs, was just as well placed as the ship-repairer's employees to take proper precautions against the risk of fire. Furthermore, the harm in question was of a type which shipowners themselves invariably insure against.[42]

In the English case of *Photo Production Ltd. v. Securicor Transport Ltd.*,[43] a nightwatchman employed by the defendant security firm set a fire in the plaintiff's factory, and when he let it get out of control the factory was burnt to a cinder. The contract contained an exclusion clause whereby the defendant firm was not to be liable for any harm due to the carelessness of its employees, provided it had exercised proper care in their selection and supervision. The plaintiff's claim was dismissed. In Lord Diplock's view:

> this apportionment of the risk of the factory being damaged or destroyed by the injurious act of an employee of Securicor while carrying out a visit to the factory is one which reasonable businessmen in the position of Securicor and the factory owners might well think was the most economical ... The risk that a servant of Securicor would damage or destroy the factory or steal goods from it, despite the exercise of all reasonable diligence by Securicor to prevent it, is what in the context of maritime law would be called a 'misfortune risk'—something which reasonable diligence of neither party can prevent. Either party can insure against it. It is generally more economical for the person by whom the loss will be directly sustained to do so rather than that it should be covered by the other party by liability insurance.[44]

---

[40] This would be so if the cost of prevention was 100 even if the harm to be avoided was as great as 1,000, supposing that the chance of its occurrence in the absence of preventative measures was only 1 in 50.
[41] BGH 24 Feb. 1971, [1971] *NJW* 1036.   [42] BGH 3 Mar. 1988, BGHZ 103, 316.
[43] [1980] AC 827.
[44] *Photo Production Ltd. v. Securicor Transport Ltd.* [1980] AC 827, 851. Compare BGH 19 Sept. 1960, BGHZ 33, 216: a security firm which was guarding a ship had limited its liability in respect of damage to it to the ridiculously low figure of DM 300, but this clause was upheld since there was first-party insurance in place and the harm arose 'from imprudence and omissions of the part of employees of the kind

This explains why an exemption or limitation clause in a contract for the carriage of goods by sea is *valid* if the damage to the cargo is due to the conduct of the crew *during the voyage,* but *invalid* if it is due to the *initial* unseaworthiness of the vessel before loading began.[45] In both cases, the damage would be covered by the insurance normally taken out by cargo-owners, but the distinction is that in the first case the carrier is no better placed to guard against the damage. But in the second case the carrier can guard against damage more cheaply: while it is not possible to control the captain and crew of the vessel during the voyage so as to prevent navigational or other mistakes causing damage to the cargo,[46] the carrier can easily (or at any rate more easily than the cargo-owner) check that the vessel is fit to receive the cargo—for example, whether its refrigeration equipment is adequate for a cargo of bananas, or whether its portholes are strong enough to withstand the sea spray which might rust the iron in the holds.

The same approach can be adopted towards exclusion clauses in contracts of sale. In *George Mitchell (Chesterhall) Ltd. v. Finney Lock Seeds Ltd.,*[47] the seed which a farmer bought from the defendant for £200 turned out to be wholly unsuitable, and his harvest was a total loss. When the farmer claimed damages of £61,500, the seller pointed to a clause which limited its liability to the return of the price of the seed. The House of Lords invalidated the clause as not being 'reasonable', with due note being taken of considerations of damage prevention and insurability. The farmer could not discover the unsuitability of the seed, whereas the supplier (and its own supplier, a sister company) not only could have done so, but had carelessly failed to do so. Furthermore, while it was virtually impossible for the farmer to obtain insurance against crop failure, it was quite normal for seed merchants to have cover against liability.[48]

IV. Partial invalidation of terms

If a clause in a contract is invalid, the rest of the contract remains in force. This is because the rules as to the invalidity of unfair contract terms are designed to protect the party they prejudice, and this aim would be thwarted if a trader could treat the whole contract as void, force the consumer into making restitution, and thus transfer the risks to the customer. It is for this reason that the invalidity of a single clause will not lead to the invalidity of the whole contract.[49] This does not answer the question

---

which cannot be avoided even in a well-run business'. It would have been different if the defendant 'had failed, by reason of poor management and organisation, to meet the general prerequisites of its duty to guard' (at 222).

[45] Contrast BGH 2 July 1973, [1973] *NJW* 2107 with BGH 25 June 1973, [1973] *NJW* 1878 and BGH 8 Dec. 1975, BGHZ 65, 364. These cases are examined in greater detail in H Kötz, 'Unfair Exemption Clauses, An Economic Analysis' (1987) 72 *Svensk Juristtidning* 473.

[46] The risk of such mistakes is what Lord Diplock (*Photo Production Ltd. v. Securicor Transport Ltd*, n 44) calls a 'misfortune risk', namely a risk which the shipowner cannot effectively or at reasonable cost exclude through careful selection of his crew or organisation of his business, and therefore should be borne by the party which can more cheaply *insure* against it.

[47] [1983] 2 AC 803.

[48] See the judgment of the Court of Appeal in [1983] QB 284, 302, 307, 313f. See also the considerations concerning the 'reasonableness' test in *Philipps Products Ltd. v. Hyland and Hamstead Plant Hire Co. Ltd.* [1987] 2 All ER 620.

[49] This is the case with consumer contracts: art. 6(1) of the Unfair Terms in Consumer Contracts Directive. But the same rule should also apply to business-to-business contracts: see, for example, §

of whether another clause should replace the invalid clause, and what the content of such a clause should be. Sometimes, it is sufficient for the clause to be ignored, such as is the case when agreement for a contractual penalty is invalid. If the legal system has a relevant rule (*dispositives Recht, règle supplétive*, terms implied by law) which it would imply into the contract, that rule will be substituted for the invalid clause.[50] For example, if a clause prohibiting the buyer from setting off any claim against the seller's demand for the price is held invalid, the buyer will be allowed a set-off subject to the normal preconditions. If there is no relevant legal rule, it must be possible for the judge to replace the invalid provision with a provision based on constructive interpretation.[51]

Often a clause goes only slightly beyond what could validly have been stipulated. In such a case, can it be held valid to the extent it is unobjectionable? Where the invalid part can realistically be severed, the valid part should surely be upheld. The *Bundesgerichtshof* so holds,[52] but the English Court of Appeal held otherwise in *Stewart Gill Ltd. v. Horatio Myers & Co.*[53] The buyer here withheld part of the purchase price on the ground that the goods delivered did not conform with the contract, and that he therefore had a counterclaim. The seller invoked a clause of the contract which forbade the buyer to withhold any part of the purchase price whether the goods were defective or 'for any other reason'. The Court of Appeal regarded this clause as 'unreasonable' since, taken literally, it would prevent the buyer from withholding payment of the price even if the seller were guilty of deceit or owed him money under some other contract. Given such a clause, according to the court, it would not do 'to put a blue pencil through the most offensive parts and say that what is left is reasonable'[54] so they avoided it *in toto*. But surely it would have been quite easy and sensible to sever the specific case mentioned in the clause, namely breach of contract by the seller, from 'any other reason' for which there might imaginably be a right of retention. The question should have been whether the exclusion of the right of retention was 'reasonable' *in this case*, and it might well have been so held, seeing that this was a contract between two businesses.

Sometimes, however, it is not really possible to separate the acceptable from the unacceptable parts of the clause. Here, the German courts hold the entire clause invalid:[55] the judge is not allowed to reduce the scope of a clause which is invalid as

306(1) BGB. Article 4:106 PECL also allows the contract as a whole to remain valid if one clause is invalid, unless this would be 'unreasonable' under the circumstances. Similarly, art. 79(2) CESL.

[50] See § 306(2) BGB. A similar approach is taken by those jurisdictions where an invalid clause is not just ignored, but 'adapted' by the judge: see § 36(1) of the Scandinavian Contract Law.

[51] See pp. 100ff.

[52] See, for example, BGH 18 Nov. 1988, BGHZ 106, 19, 25f; BGH 18 Apr. 1989, BGHZ 107, 185, 190f. See also Basedow (n 17) § 306 BGB mn. 17f.

[53] [1992] 2 All ER 257; contrast the decision of the BGH 18 Apr. 1989 (n 52).

[54] Per Stuart-Smith LJ in *Stewart Gill Ltd.* (n 53) 263.

[55] BGH 17 May 1982, BGHZ 84, 109, 114ff; BGH 24 Sept. 1985, BGHZ 96, 18, 25ff. These cases are based on the rule that a '*geltungserhaltende Reduktion*' (validating reduction) is inadmissible. For criticism of this view, see Basedow (n 17) § 306 BGB, mn. 12ff. However, the European Court of Justice seems to have held in *Banco Español de Crédito SA v. Joaquin Calderón Camino* (14 June 2012, Case C-618/10) that the Directive (n 17) forbids the courts of Member States from modifying an unfair term in a consumer contract by revising its content and upholding the clause in its modified form. For comments on these

it stands and hold it valid as so reduced. Otherwise companies would be tempted to include clauses which were obviously unacceptable: most of their customers would be taken in by the wording, and those who went to court would be worse off with a judgment upholding the clause in part than if the clause had never been in the contract at all.[56]

D. Preventive Control

It is undeniably good that laws and courts allow people to contest the validity of unfair clauses in their contracts, but this does not by itself prevent the use of such clauses in the first place, which is surely the underlying aim.

The rules so far mentioned are futile unless they are invoked during negotiations or in a legal application by the party they are supposed to protect. Yet often such actions make no sense and may even be counterproductive. The disadvantaged party has to unearth the relevant rules (or hire a lawyer to do so), enter into negotiations with the counterparty, and even go to court, all of which involves time and trouble disproportionate to the harm involved. It is more sensible and practical simply to submit to the clause without protest, even if it is clearly invalid. Companies are perfectly aware of this, and are consequently tempted to employ terms they know to be invalid in the hope that most of their customers will just accept them. Should one of the customers prove difficult and start legal action, the company can simply buy that customer off by acceding to the demands, but still continue to use the offensive clause in contracts with other customers. Even if the customer manages to get a court to declare the clause invalid, there is nothing to stop the company from continuing to use the clause in contracts with other customers where the advantages outweigh the disadvantages.

It follows that if companies are to be stopped from using improper clauses, it is not enough to allow the individual customer to complain. Other sanctions are necessary for the law to guide contractors in the desired direction. Here there are several possibilities.

I. Criminal sanctions

Criminal sanctions tend to be imposed only where a person has exacted a grossly disproportionate return from a party by consciously exploiting his or her difficulties. Thus § 291 of the German Criminal Code (StGB) imposes a penalty on a person who exploits the predicament of another and extracts a counterperformance which is 'in striking disproportion' to the value of the service, particularly with respect to residential leases and credit arrangements. By contrast, mere breaches of consumer

---

decisions, see P Rott [2012] *ERCL* 470; P Schlosser [2012] *IPrax* 507; W Hau [2012] *JZ* 964; E Hondius (2016) 24 *ERPL* 457, 466ff.

[56] A similar problem arises where a contract is in part offensive to good morals or contrary to law. See pp. 121f.

protection laws are rarely criminalised in Germany, unlike in France where 'le droit pénal occupe ... une place importante dans le droit de la consommation'.[57]

The efficacy of criminal sanctions in this area is certainly open to question, since the offender must first be caught and convicted and then the sanction must be severe enough to offset the advantages to be gained by committing the offence. This rarely happens, because the prosecuting authorities are short of resources and 'the penalties imposed by the courts for criminal offences might still leave the trader with a net profit out of his illegal activities'.[58]

II. Group actions

Better results can be expected if consumer groups are given the right to take legal action. German legislation to this effect[59] has since been followed in many other countries.[60] Furthermore, the Unfair Contract Terms in Consumer Contracts Directive requires Member States to introduce rules which permit consumer associations to 'take action ... before the courts or before competent administrative bodies for a decision as to whether contractual terms ... are unfair, so that they can apply appropriate and effective means to prevent the continued use of such terms' (art. 7(2)).

This gives consumer associations and some others the means of obtaining an injunction against a company to stop it using particular terms which the court finds unacceptable. Such an injunction is apt to be effective because the recalcitrant defendant has to pay a fine to the state or, as in France, an *astreinte* to the complainant. It is true that other companies are not bound by such an injunction and may continue to use a similar clause. But this is rather unwise, since consumer associations make sure that decisions in their favour are published in the daily and specialist press, and they may even be recorded in a public register to which everyone has access.

Group actions would be even more effective if damages could be claimed, but only France allows for this. The courts there have held that if a firm's conduct harms '*l'intérêt collectif des consommateurs*', the judge has a free hand in deciding on the damages payable[61]—often, admittedly, only one *franc symbolique*. However, the damage caused to *individuals* by the use of the improper clause can only be asserted by that individual. In practice, this is unlikely to happen; such legal actions make no economic sense for the individual as the level of damage is usually too low, and the interests of the company in the dismissal of his action are too high. Nevertheless, the European Union is considering whether it would make sense to allow consumer

---

[57] Calais-Auloy and Temple (n 6) no. 18.
[58] G Borrie, *The Development of Consumer Law and Policy* (1984) 71.
[59] See the Injunctions Act (*Gesetz über Unterlassungsklagen bei Verbraucherrechts- und anderen Verstößen*) of 27 Aug. 2002.
[60] See art. 421-6 *Code de la consommation*; art. 6:240ff. BW; §§ 28ff. Austrian Consumer Protection Act.
[61] See Grenoble, 13 July 1991, *JCP* 1992.II.21819, n. G Paisant; and Civ. 1 Feb. 2005, *JCP* 2005.II.10057, n. G Paisant.

groups to launch 'group actions' (similar to the class actions permitted in the United States).[62]

Opinions vary as to the efficacy of group actions. In Germany, consumer associations obtain hundreds of injunctions per year, and in many more cases the mere threat of action is enough to dissuade the company from continuing to use the clause in question. Furthermore, groups have quite frequently pursued cases all the way up to the *Bundesgerichtshof*, and brought sizeable companies or branches of commerce to their knees in a blaze of publicity. Even so, critics claim that since unfair contract terms seem to be as prevalent as ever, group actions have clearly not been as successful as was hoped.

III. Administrative controls

The reason consumer associations do not strike as hard as they might is that their financial resources are usually very limited. Accordingly, it has often been suggested that the state should set up administrative bodies with ample powers to check the conduct of companies in the market. Sweden did this in 1971 by creating a special authority under the Consumer Ombudsman charged with seeing that companies operating in the market conduct themselves in accordance with 'good commercial standards'. If the authority finds that a company is marketing unreasonably dangerous goods, or using deceptive advertising, or engaging in unfair competitive practices, or—to come to our point—using unfair contract terms, it can seek to stop such behaviour by negotiation with the company or with the professional organisation to which the company belongs. This is the bulk of the authority's activity, but if negotiation fails to produce the desired result, the Ombudsman may seek an injunction from the 'market court', constituted for this very purpose.[63]

In the United Kingdom, the Office of Fair Trading (set up by the Fair Trading Act 1973) has power to check market practices which improperly affect the interests of consumers,[64] and the war against unfair contract terms is only one small part of its activities. The Office may indeed go to court in order to obtain an injunction, but in practice negotiation with the companies in question has proved much more effective. In consequence of such negotiations, important groups of producers and suppliers of certain goods and services (motor cars, furniture, package holidays) have accepted voluntary Codes of Practice as regards their dealings with consumers. In other countries, too, industry-wide agreements between consumer groups and groups of suppliers have helped to make conditions of business fairer, but there is still much to be said for having a state authority with adequate powers since a group energetic enough to

---

[62] See (with further evidence) H Koch and J Zekoll, 'Europäisierung der Sammelklage mit Hindernissen' (2010) 18 *ZEuP* 107 and S Madaus, 'Keine Effektivität einer europäischen class action ohne "amerikanische Verhältnisse" bei deren Finanzierung' (2012) 20 *ZEuP* 99.

[63] See JN Ebersohl, *Vertragsfreiheit und Verbraucherschutz in der schwedischen Gesetzgebung* (2003).

[64] For further details, see Borrie (n 58); Treitel (n 4) no. 7-118; S Whittaker, in *Chitty on Contracts* (31st edn, 2012) no. 15-149ff.

fight for the interests of consumers cannot always be found.[65] The Netherlands has struck out on yet another path. A governmental commission may be set up under art. 6:214 BW to draft 'standard contracts' for particular areas of commerce, and once such a 'standard contract' has been approved by the government and officially published, it will apply, just like a law, to all individual contracts in the field, unless the parties agree otherwise.

---

[65] The essential difficulty in organising a consumer group is that the expense to each member of creating and running such a group outweighs the advantages he might hope to obtain by joining it. Furthermore, since people may benefit from the group's activity without actually belonging to it, there will be many 'free riders'.

9

Mistake

A. Introduction	149
B. Avoidance for Mistake	151
I. There must be a contract	151
II. Avoidance and liability	152
1. Claims by buyer for non-conforming goods	152
2. Other claims for non-performance	154
C. Preconditions of Avoidance for Mistake	155
I. Historical background	155
II. Mistakes as to the qualities of the thing or person	156
1. General	156
2. Causality	158
3. Mistaken motive	159
4. Mistake as to the value of the thing	161
5. Risk in transactions	162
6. Negligent mistakes	162
7. Offer to make good the consequences of a mistake	163
III. Mistakes caused by the other party	163
IV. Recognisable mistakes	165
V. Shared mistakes	166
VI. A European law on mistake?	167
1. Primacy of the contract	168
2. 'Special reasons' for allowing avoidance	169
D. Effecting Avoidance for Mistake	171

A. Introduction

Quite often the assumptions and expectations entertained by a contractor on making the contract turn out to be unfounded. If so, can a party claim not to be bound because he entered the contract under a mistake? In general, the answer must be 'no'. If I buy a brewery in the expectation of a long hot summer, I cannot avoid the purchase because the weather turns out badly, demand for beer is sluggish, and brewing shares plummet. Sometimes, however, the answer must be different. So the question is how to draw the line between mistakes that count, and those which are immaterial.

Everyone agrees that one is not bound when the mistake is due to the other party's deception (see below chapter 11). But we shall attend first to cases which are not so simple—cases where good reasons can be given both for allowing and for refusing to allow the contract to be avoided, depending on which point of view one adopts.[1]

---

[1] See the comprehensive comparative law treatment by E Kramer, *Der Irrtum bei Vertragsschluss* (1998).

Take the case that a picture thought to be by an unknown later turns out to be the work of a famous artist, and worth twenty or even a hundred times the price it was sold for. Should the seller be able to claim back the painting because of his mistake in selling it so cheaply? What if the seller failed to consult an expert on the provenance of the painting, as a reasonable man would have done? Is it relevant if either of the parties was a connoisseur who could have identified the painting more easily than the other party? What if the buyer was an art dealer and assured the seller, who had no special expertise, that he believed the painting to be the work of an artist of no account? The art dealer's belief was an honestly held opinion, although objectively incorrect, but had persuaded the seller to go through with the sale. What if a landlord lets a dwelling at a low rent because he erroneously supposes that it is subject to rent control, or if a builder agrees to dig foundations and unexpectedly strikes rock, which raises the cost very considerably?

It should be obvious that in such cases there can be no simple test to determine when the mistaken party can withdraw from the contract and when not, but a legal system can start out from either of two opposite positions. One is based on the 'intention theory', according to which contractual obligations are enforceable only because the obligor intended to bind himself. On this view, it is essential that the party's intentions are genuine and not vitiated by a mistake (or indeed by deceit or duress). If it is, this 'defect in intention' enables the mistaken party to claim that the contract is invalid, or, as we shall say from now on, to 'avoid' it.

The weakness of this approach is that it does not pay enough heed to the interests of the other party. Those interests are the primary concern of the opposite approach, that a person who makes a statement as part of a business transaction must take the risk of being wrong in his appraisal of the circumstances. The party may certainly try to get the other party to agree that the contract should only be valid if the suppositions are in fact correct but, in the absence of such agreement, the party is bound by its statement. There would be serious disruption to commercial security if a party could question the validity of the contract just because he had made a mistake. On this view, therefore, a party should only be allowed to avoid a contract for mistake under very exceptional circumstances—namely when there are special grounds for holding that the other party's reliance on the statement's validity does not deserve protection.

On the Continent, the older civil codes—up to and including the German Civil Code of 1900—clung to the former approach, and commentators developed a whole general doctrine of defects of intention (*Willensmangel, vice de consentement, vizio del consenso*), whereby the intention of a promisor can be vitiated by a mistake as well as by deceit or duress. The promisor's intention is then ineffective to bring about a valid contract. As art. 1130 *Code civil* pithily states, '*l'erreur, le dol et la volence vicient le consentement*'.

The Common Law is quite different. Until the nineteenth century, the notion that a contract might be invalidated by mistake was hardly recognised at all. Certainly, a contract could then—as now—be avoided by a party who entered into the transaction in justified reliance on a *misrepresentation* or false statement made by the other party during the negotiations. But here the emphasis was not so much on the mistake caused as on the *causing* of the mistake by the misrepresentation, regardless of whether the misrepresentation was intentional or made in good faith. In other cases, English courts were able to construe a contract as containing an *implied condition* that vital matters were as supposed.[2] But the Common Law never allowed general rules for the avoidance of contracts for mistake, and did not share the concern of continental lawyers that the intention of the promisor should not be vitiated. The Common Law was more interested in protecting the party that had reasonably relied on the promisor's intention being what it seemed in the circumstances—a reflection of English contract law's characteristic predilection for the needs of commerce which has led to the observation that, unlike continental law, it was a law for shopkeepers rather than peasants.[3]

In the late nineteenth century, when they were more familiar with Roman law and much impressed by Pothier's contributions to the topic,[4] the English courts started to accept that in certain circumstances a mistake may indeed invalidate a contract. But many commentators still doubt whether these continental ideas, so recently imported, sit very well with the Common Law's propensity for protecting commercial reliance.[5]

B. Avoidance for Mistake

I. There must be a contract

A contract has to be in existence before it can be avoided for mistake. The point is worth making because a mistake may actually prevent a contract coming into existence in the first place. This does not happen very often.[6] Even when the offer is understood by the offeree in a sense different from that intended by the offeror, and each party is consequently mistaken as to the meaning attributed to it by the other, a contract nevertheless comes into being. Contract formation does not depend on whether the subjective intentions of the parties coincided when making their promises: a true '*consensus ad idem*' or 'meeting of the minds' is not required. The question is whether from an objective standpoint—that is, in the view of a third party aware of the surrounding circumstances—the promises could be correctly interpreted as congruent.

---

[2] See *Couturier* v. *Hastie* (1856) [1843–60] All ER 280. A cargo of wheat became overheated *en route* from Salonica to London, and had to be sold in Tunis. The parties in London were unaware of this and contracted for the sale of part of the cargo, which in fact no longer existed. The seller's claim for the price was dismissed, not because the buyer could rely on his mistake or because the contract was impossible of performance (see text below, to nn 88ff.) but because on its proper construction the contract was subject to the condition that the goods existed: 'The whole question turns upon the construction of the contract ... Looking to the contract itself alone it appears to me clearly that what the parties contemplated, those who bought and those who sold, was that there was an existing something to be sold and bought' (per Lord Cranworth, at 682). On the connection between avoidance for mistake and contractual construction, see also AWB Simpson, 'Innovation in Nineteenth Century Contract Law' (1975) 91 *LQR* 247, 268f.

[3] See above, chapter 4 at n 24.

[4] See, for example, Blackburn J in *Kennedy* v. *Panama, New Zealand and Australian Royal Mail Co.* (1867) LR 2 QB 580, 588, and further references in R Zimmermann, *The Law of Obligations, Roman Foundations of the Civilian Tradition* (1990) 618ff.

[5] The rules on the invalidation of contracts for mistake have been described as an 'unhappy piece of innovation' (Simpson, n 2, at 268) and as 'hopelessly confused—a confusion which could have been avoided if English law had resisted the meddlesome transplants of Victorian contract lawyers' (H Collins, 'Methods and Aims of Comparative Contract Law' (1991) 11 *OJLS* 396, 398).

[6] On the following, see above, pp. 97f.

Only after concluding that a contract came into existence can one can proceed to ask whether it should be avoided for mistake. Only when interpretation fails to elicit an unambiguous meaning—that is, when the reasonable bystander would conclude that the parties had more than one meaning in mind—will there be no contract to avoid.[7]

II. Avoidance and liability

If a party fails to fulfil a contract, or fails to fulfil it properly, the other party may claim for breach of contract. But if a claim for breach of contract is not possible or barred by a term in the contract itself or by lapse of time, can a party achieve the same result and get around the bar by avoiding the contract for mistake?

1. Claims by buyer for non-conforming goods

If the buyer of a gold ring receives a gilt ring instead, the buyer can sue for breach of contract, resile from the contract, and claim back the price on returning the ring. Alternatively, the buyer can claim his money back on the basis that he mistakenly believed at the time that the ring was gold, and should be able to avoid the contract.

The buyer will normally bring a claim for breach of contract, needing only to prove that the seller had not delivered the ring as promised, and had delivered non-conforming goods. This is an easier task for the buyer, who need only prove that non-conforming goods were delivered, rather than proving the more difficult task concerning his mental state at the time of the contract and establishing that he was mistaken as to the quality of the ring. Yet if the prescriptive period for the claim for damages for breach of contract had already expired—and a claim for avoidance for mistake was still possible—the buyer would readily resort to the latter claim, despite the heavier burden of proof. The same would be true if the buyer had failed to give the seller due notice of the defect, or if there were a clause in the contract which excluded the seller's liability. Should the buyer be allowed to avoid the contract for mistake in such cases?[8]

Where the item is sold 'as is' or there is an effective contractual exclusion of liability, the answer must be in the negative—for in agreeing to such a term, if valid, the buyer must be taken to have waived the right to avoid for mistake.[9] The answer should also be negative where the buyer has omitted to give due notice of the defect, or has allowed the period of prescription for the claim for breach of contract to expire.[10] There is good

---

[7] Some commentators in France are of opinion that a mistake may be so serious as to prevent a contract arising, speaking of 'erreur-obstacle' as opposed to 'erreur-vice de consentement'. They would include under the former the case where a person appears to be buying a thing when he is really accepting it as a gift: see F Terré, P Simler, and Y Lequette, Droit civil, Les obligations (11th edn, 2013) no. 210ff. The courts have only rarely followed this view, and most authors are right to reject it; for example, J Ghestin, Traité de droit civil, La formation du contrat (1993) no. 495; C Larroumet, Droit civil, vol. III: Les obligations, Le contrat, Effets (6th edn, 2007) nos. 321 and 346.

[8] For a comparative treatment of this question, see F Ranieri, Europäisches Obligationenrecht (3rd edn, 2009) 953ff.

[9] See also the text below to n 56.

[10] Expressly in art. 917 Portuguese Civil Code. Article 7:23 BW is also understood in the same sense: the buyer who does not notify the defective nature of the goods within the prescribed period 'can no longer

reason for making the liability of the seller for delivering non-conforming goods subject to his receiving timely notice and to his being subject to legal action within the appropriate period; and there is no good reason to relieve the buyer of the requirements of giving notice and taking legal action in time just because, as later transpires, he was mistaken in assuming that the seller would perform properly and that the goods would be as agreed.

Thus courts in Germany and Italy exclude *a limine* any claim to avoid a sale for mistake as to the existence of a certain quality in the goods in cases where the absence of that quality constitutes a defect for which the buyer had a claim for breach of contract.[11] A recent decision by the English Court of Appeal made it clear that the purchaser of land cannot avoid the sale on the ground of mistake when the terms of the contract put the risk of that particular defect on him.[12] In France, the buyer is allowed to avoid the sale on the ground of mistake, but on several occasions the *Cour de cassation* insisted that the claim for avoidance be made '*dans un bref délai*', namely within the same period allowed for claims for '*vice caché*' under art. 1648 *Code civil*.[13] However, the position taken by French courts is bewildering. In some cases, the *Cour de cassation* has allowed a claim for mistake even though the buyers of defective used cars had failed to make the claim within the *bref délai* period in which they should have lodged their claims.[14] The court then altered its position again, and after expiry of the *bref délai* no longer allowed buyers to avoid the contract for mistake (though the contract could be avoided for deceit).[15] The Swiss Federal Court has also allowed a buyer to invoke a mistake as to the qualities of the goods even though the contractual claim was out of time under art. 210 OR, since 'technology and the mass contract have altered the significance and function of simple contracts of sale so that the buyer needs more protection against poor service than before'.[16] This reasoning is perhaps ill-adapted to the facts of the case, which involved the purchase of an expensive painting—hardly a 'mass contract', nor one in which the protection of the buyer should have been especially dear to the heart of the legal system. But that is not the

---

rely on the fact that the goods do not conform with the contract'. See also art. 3.2.4 PICC: 'A party is not entitled to avoid the contract on the ground of mistake if the circumstances on which that party relies afford, or could have afforded, a remedy for non-performance.' But see also art. 4:119 PECL, art. II.-7:216 DCFR; art. 57 CESL.

[11] BGH 14 Dec. 1960, BGHZ 34, 32 (standing case law); Cass. 14 Oct. 1960, no. 2732, [1960] Foro it. 1914. By contrast, it has been held that the buyer may avoid for mistake if the goods were as promised but lacked some other quality which the buyer mistakenly expected; see BGH 26 Oct. 1978, [1979] *NJW* 160; BGH 9 Oct. 1980, BGHZ 78, 216, 218. This is dubious. If the seller delivers goods which possess the qualities expressly guaranteed and are fit 'for the use foreseen in the contract' (§ 459 BGB), the seller has done all that is required of him. The risk that in such a case the goods do not meet the buyer's expectations should be borne by the buyer, since he knew what he expected and could and should have made it a term of the contract.

[12] *William Sindall Plc v. Cambridgeshire CC* [1994] 1 WLR 1016, 1034f. (Hoffmann LJ).

[13] Civ. 19 July 1960, Bull.cass. 1960.I. no. 408; Civ. 11 Feb. 1981, *JCP* 1982.II.19758, n. J Ghestin.

[14] Civ. 18 May 1988, D. 1989, 450; Civ. 28 June 1988, Bull.cass. 1989.I. no. 268.

[15] Civ. 14 May 1996, D. 1998, 305, n. F Jault-Seseke; see Terré, Simler, and Lequette (n 7) no. 255 and Ranieri (n 8) 356ff.

[16] BG 7 June 1988, BGE 114 II 131, 138 (standing case law). Commentators in Switzerland are on the whole opposed to this development: see n. H Merz [1990] *ZBJV* 255. Austrian courts also allow the buyer to avoid the contract for mistake as to the qualities of the goods even if he could sue on the contract: see OGH 26 Apr. 1966, [1966] *ÖJZ* 461; OGH 30 Apr. 1975, SZ 48 no. 56; OGH 13 Jan. 1982, SZ 55 no. 2.

only objection: if the period within which the buyer must object is thought to be too short, the problem should be solved at source—namely in the law of sale of goods, rather than by calling on the rules of avoidance for mistake.

The question also arises when buyer and seller are in different states and the UN Sales Law (CISG) applies. The remedies of the buyer when the goods delivered are substandard are laid down in art. 45 ff, but could the buyer alternatively try to get his money back by avoiding the contract? The answer generally given is negative, since the rules of the UN Sales Law as to the rights of the buyer when the goods are defective are regarded as a *lex specialis*, which excludes more general rules.[17]

2. Other claims for non-performance

There are other situations in which the rules as to breach of contract should have priority over the rules of avoidance for mistake. One example is where the seller has been unable to provide a clear title to the goods sold, either because he does not own them or because they are restricted by the rights of a third party. Since the buyer's claim for such a breach includes the right to resile from the contract, he cannot instead seek to avoid it on the ground that he erroneously believed the seller to be the owner. The same must be true of the lease of a dwelling or a contract for work when what is provided is not what the contract specified.

The same question may also arise where the contract purports to transfer the risk of what happened onto the claimant. In an English decision,[18] the claimant entered into a sale and leaseback agreement with a customer who wanted to raise financing of around £1 million, and the defendant guaranteed that the customer would perform all his obligations. It later transpired that the customer was a rogue, and that the four engineering machines which had been sold and leased back had never existed. On being sued on the guarantee, the defendant argued first that, on its proper construction, the contract was conditioned on the existence of the machines; and, secondly, that it was void for mistake. Steyn J held that the critical matter was what the defendant had undertaken in the contract:

> Logically, before one can turn to the rules as to mistake … one must first determine whether the contract itself, by express or implied condition precedent or otherwise, provides who bears the risk of the relevant mistake. It is at this hurdle that many pleas of mistake will either fail or prove to have been unnecessary. Only if the contract is silent on the point is there scope for invoking mistake.[19]

---

[17] See I Schwenzer in P Schlechtriem and I Schwenzer (eds), *Kommentar zum einheitlichen UN-Kaufrecht* (6th edn, 2013) art. 39 mn. 30; P Schlechtriem and U Schroeter, *Internationales UN-Kaufrecht* (6th edn, 2016) mn. 169ff; P Huber, 'UN-Kaufrecht und Irrtumsanfechtung' (1994) 2 *ZEuP* 585. It is supported by the following consideration. The UN Sales Law does not unify the rules regarding avoidance for mistake, so such rules would, according to the conflict rules of the court hearing the dispute, have to be taken from the state whose law is applicable to the sales contract. This would be to frustrate the UN Sales Law's aim to unify the rules applicable to international sales, and to do so on an important point.

[18] *Associated Japanese Bank (International) Ltd. v. Crédit du Nord S.A.* [1988] 3 All ER 902.

[19] Ibid. at 912.

In the case itself, the judge concluded that the risk of the non-existence of the subject matter of the lease was on the plaintiff and not undertaken by the defendant in his guarantee. The claim was therefore dismissed. The judge also held that the contract was void for mistake, but this was a secondary ground and although his remarks are well worth reading, they are really only *obiter dicta*.

Similar arguments were raised in the much-discussed case of *McRae v. Commonwealth Disposals Commission*.[20] The defendant sold a wrecked oil tanker to the plaintiff, who was a salvage merchant. The wreck was described as 'lying on Jourmand Reef approximately 100 miles north of Samarai'. In fact there was no such wreck. Unimpressed by the defendant's argument that the contract was void by reason of the parties' common mistake as to the existence of the tanker, the court held that the contract was valid and that the defendant must compensate the plaintiff for the expense of fitting out the salvage expedition. The court found that the defendant had impliedly warranted the existence of the wreck at the designated spot and, furthermore, it could not rely on a mistake that was its own fault.

C. Preconditions of Avoidance for Mistake

I. Historical background

Historically, the first distinction drawn between material and immaterial mistakes turned on the subject matter of the mistake. It emerged from cases in which the Roman jurists held that there was no valid contract because the parties had failed to agree on essential points—such as where there was no real agreement on the identity of the land being sold because the seller had one plot in mind and the buyer another. Later it came to be said that the contract was void for *error in corpore*. If a person borrowed money from A, supposing him to be B, there was an *error in persona* and no contract of loan came about. The term *error in negotio* was given to the case where a person was mistaken as to the nature of the transaction, the recipient believing, for example, that money deposited with him was intended as a loan. Finally, there was *error in substantia*, where the parties were agreed on the identity of the thing being sold, but the buyer believed the ring to be gold or the barrel to contain wine, whereas in reality the ring was silver and there was oil in the barrel. It was accepted that the contract was void if the thing sold was entirely different in its nature from what the buyer supposed, but the jurists disagreed over whether this was equally true where the buyer received not an *aliud* but a *peius*, where the ring was gilt rather than gold, or the wine was sour.[21]

These categories, which were designed to identify which mistakes are 'essential' enough to justify avoidance, were inherited from Roman law and ventilated for centuries thereafter. They still figure, out of pious deference to tradition, in many current civil codes. Thus, under the Swiss Law of Obligations art. 24(1) no. 1 and 2, a mistake is 'essential' if 'the mistaken party intended to enter a type of contract other than the one he agreed to' (*error in negotio*), or if 'the intention of the mistaken party was

---

[20] (1951) 84 CLR 377, a decision of the High Court of Australia, based on English law.
[21] See Zimmermann (n 4) 587ff, and on *error in substantia* 592ff.

directed to a thing or person different from that of his promise' (*error in corpore* and *error in persona*).²² The natural lawyers were already dubious about the merits of these traditional categories of error, and tried to find a general formula.²³ One distinction they drew was between the intention which the contractor sought to express, and the expression actually given—a distinction which laid the basis for the view, unacknowledged by Roman law, that the interests of the other party could be taken into account and some protection afforded to the reliance on what was expressed. The natural lawyers differed as to the consequences to be drawn from this distinction in particular cases. Yet one already finds among them the idea that the contractor should have the contract with the mistaken party avoided only in special circumstances, indeed only where the contractor's reliance on the promise of the mistaken party deserves no protection. They also suggested that the contractor should be helped out with a claim for damages against the mistaken party. Finally, they developed the idea that a mistake did not render the contract void automatically: the party suffering from the mistake had to take steps to avoid the contract.

II. Mistakes as to the qualities of the thing or person

Although the traditional Roman categorisation is of no practical help in distinguishing those errors which are significant from those which are not, continental legal systems were so much under its spell that provisions relating to *error in substantia* and *error in persona* can be found in most civil codes, and have been interpreted by the courts in such a way that, even today, they cover the great majority of cases of mistake.

1. General

Under the old art. 1110 *Code civil*, a mistake was significant if it related to '*la substance même de la chose*'. Finding this phrasing too narrow, the French courts soon departed from it, and for a long time now have held mistakes as to '*qualités substantielles de la chose*' sufficient. This approach was accepted, and indeed broadened, by art. 1132 and art. 1133, which were adopted during the course of the recent reform of French contract law. Under art. 1132, a contract may be avoided if the mistake bears on the 'essential qualities' of what was promised in the contract or of the person of the other contracting party. These provisions now take the position adopted by other codes in rather similar language. Under § 119(2) BGB, avoidance is possible for an 'error as to qualities of the person or thing as are customarily regarded as essential', and § 871 ABGB allows it for an 'error relating to the principal thing or an essential feature of it'.²⁴ Accordingly, the mistaken buyer can avoid a contract for the purchase of a building plot which cannot be built on²⁵ or which is smaller than promised.²⁶ Other

---

²² See also art. 1428 *Codice civile*; art. 142 Greek Civil Code; art. 1266 Spanish Civil Code; art. 251 Portuguese Civil Code.
²³ See Zimmermann (n 4) 612ff.
²⁴ See the rules on error as to qualities in art. 142 Greek Civil Code; art. 1429 no. 2 *Codice civile*; art. 1266(1) Spanish Civil Code.
²⁵ Civ. 2 Mar. 1964, Bull.cass, 1964.I. no. 122; BG 7 July 1970, BGE 96 II 101, 103.
²⁶ OGH 2 Nov. 1955, *JBl* 1956, 365; Civ. 15 Dec. 1981, D.S.1982.I.R.164.

decisions allow avoidance of the purchase of a painting that is not by the attributed artist,[27] of artificial pearls sold as natural,[28] and of the controlling interest in a company which contrary to the buyer's expectations is no longer operational.[29]

In all these cases, it was the buyer who made the mistake.[30] But the seller also may invoke a mistake as to the qualities of the thing, such as when a painting is sold at a low price but is later shown to be by an old master.[31] Furthermore, an heir who disclaimed an inheritance in the erroneous belief that it would then fall to a particular

---

[27] See Civ. 16 Dec. 1964, Bull.cass. 1964.I. no. 575; Civ. 20 Oct. 1970, JCP 1971.II.16916, n. J Ghestin; BG 7 June 1988 (n 16).

[28] Req. 5 Nov. 1929, S.1930.1.180.

[29] Com. 7 Feb. 1995, D. 1996, 50, n. J Blasselle. See in detail Terré, Simler, and Lequette (n 7) no. 216 with many other examples from French courts.

[30] And so would be able to avoid the contract by proving that the seller was in breach of contract by supplying goods lacking the stipulated qualities. On the view represented here, this would be the *only* ground for avoidance. See above, pp. 152ff.

[31] See RG 22 Feb. 1929, RGZ 124, 115, 120; BGH 8 June 1988, [1988] *NJW* 2597; Civ. 24 Jan. 1979, Bull. cass. 1979.I. no. 34, as well as the decisions in the famous 'Poussin affair', reproduced with commentary in H Capitant, *Les grands arrêts de la jurisprudence civile* (12th edn, by F Terré and Y Lequette, 2008) II 30ff, especially Civ. 22 Feb. 1978, D. 1978, 601, n. P Malinvaud and Civ. 13 Dec. 1983, D. 1984, 340, n. J-L Aubert. See also Civ. 17 Sept. 2003, Bull.cass. 2003.I. no. 183: A painting that was described in the sale catalogue as 'from the school of Nicolas Poussin', was sold in 1985 for 1.6 million French Francs. Nine years later, after publication of a study into Poussin's work, the seller concluded (and this was supported by an expert valuation) that the painting was by Poussin himself and was worth 45–60 million French Francs. The seller's claim for avoidance of the contract of sale was upheld. It is extremely doubtful that the seller, whose mistake was as to the real value of the painting, should have been allowed to avoid the contract just on this basis. Such grounds are denied by H Fleischer, 'Zum Verkäuferirrtum über werterhöhende Eigenschaften im Spiegel der Rechtsprechung' in R Zimmermann (ed), *Störungen der Willensbildung bei Vertragsschluss* (2007) 35. Particularly with respect to contracts of sale for objects where provenance or age are not entirely certain, it is often assumed that this constitutes a 'risk transaction' with no right to avoid the contract for mistake either for the seller (if the object turns out to be worth more than thought) or for the buyer (if the object is worth less than thought); on this, see p. 162. It is particularly absurd to allow the seller to avoid the contract when the true value of the asset was revealed as a result of efforts by the *buyer*. In such circumstances, the avoidance of the contract is detrimental to those *'qui savent découvrir des pièces de qualité, là ou les autres n'ont rien decelé; c'est décourager l'effort intellectuel et le goût'* (Terré, Simler, and Lequette (n 7) no. 218). See the well-known 'cantharus' decision by the *Hoge Raad* (19 June 1959 [1960] *NedJur* no. 59): the Dutch court refused to allow the seller to avoid a contract for the sale of a metal beaker found in 1943 during dredging operations in the Meuse and sold by the finder to a relative. Two experts consulted by the relative's heiress reported that, while it was made out of solid silver, it had no particular historical or artistic merit. One of the experts, a goldsmith with interests in art history, bought it from the heiress for 125 guilders. The expert became obsessed with the origins of the drinking vessel and engaged in time-consuming and exhaustive research which established, to the satisfaction of other experts, that the cup was a cantharus from the second century AD and of inestimable value. The heiress sought its return, but her claim was rejected; the court could find no fraud or fault in the buyer, and held that the preconditions of a claim based on mistake were not present. The result is surely right. There is a general public interest in learning the provenance of items which may have great artistic value, and if buyers of such objects had to return the item if their researches proved fruitful, there would be no incentive to invest in the ascertainment of such origins. For a similar reason, a French court—while permitting the seller of a painting to reclaim it—indicated that the buyer was entitled to claim his expenses in verifying the provenance of the painting on the basis that in doing so he had been acting as the seller's *negotiorum gestor*; however, the court should really have dismissed the action, since it is not enough to give the buyer a claim for his expenses. The actual decision (Trib.gr.inst. Paris, 6 Mar. 1985) is unpublished, but commented by Ghestin (n 7) no. 641. See also Civ. 25 May 1992, JCP 1992.IV.2129: A painting attributed to Fragonard which a man had bought for 55,000 French Francs turned out, after restoration, to be authentic, and the buyer sold it to the Louvre for 5.15 million French Francs. The seller was allowed

third party was allowed to disavow his disclaimer,[32] and an insured was allowed to resuscitate a policy which he had cancelled on 15 October, with effect from 1 October, unaware until many months later that on 9 October he had suffered a loss which the policy would have covered.[33]

These examples may suggest that a contract may be avoided for any mistake, unless it is really trivial, but this is not the case. The ability to avoid a contract for mistake as to qualities has been restricted, and the courts have developed rules that give some protection to the interests of the other party. To this we now turn.

2. Causality

It is generally agreed that a contract may only be avoided if the mistake was '*le motif principal et déterminant*' of the party in making his promise,[34] or that the mistaken party would 'not have entered the contract had he known the facts and understood the situation' (§ 119(2) BGB).[35] This restriction is necessary, for otherwise a person could invoke a mistake that was not really crucial in order to avoid a contract which he had other reasons for regretting.

One must therefore ask whether a reasonable man 'free from idiosyncrasy, caprice and folly'[36] and knowing the true facts would have entered into the contract. A person who buys a Delacroix cannot avoid the contract just because he supposed it had once hung in the artist's bedroom.[37] Nor can the buyer of a racing car rely on a mistake as to the power of its engine if, though it was slightly more powerful than agreed, the car could still be entered for races.[38] The decision was different in a case where a person sold a picture he thought was by Duveneck when it was actually by Leibl, a Munich artist: the attribution made no difference in value, but the seller, also from Munich, was allowed to resile because his particular predilection for a painting by a fellow-citizen was quite understandable.[39]

---

to avoid for mistake, subject to a claim by the buyer for 1.5 million French Francs as his expenses, on the basis of unjustified enrichment (!).

[32] Civ. 15 June 1960, *JCP* 1961.II.12274; compare OLG Hamm, 27 Nov. 1965, [1966] *NJW* 1080.
[33] Civ. 25 Feb. 1986, Bull.cass. 1986.I. no. 40.
[34] Req. 17 June 1946, Gaz.Pal. 1946.2.204; see also Ghestin (n 7) 498; B Starck, H Roland, and L Boyer, *Droit civil, Obligations, Contrat et quasi-contrat, Régime général* (5th edn, 1995) no. 416f; and full details in G Vivien, 'De l'erreur déterminante et substantielle' (1992) 91 *Rev trim civ* 305, all with references to the cases.
[35] To similar effect art. 6:228 BW. Similarly art. 4:103(1)(b) PECL and art. 3.2.2 PICC. Also, pursuant to art. 48(1)(a) CESL, the right of a party to avoid a contract for mistake depends on the party who 'but for the mistake, would not have concluded the contract or would have done so only on fundamentally different contract terms and the other party knew or could be expected to have known this'. See S Martens, 'Die Regelung der Willensmängel im Vorschlag für eine VO über ein gemeinsames Europäisches Kaufrecht' (2011) 211 *AcP* 845, 854f; D Looschelders, 'Das allgemeine Vertragsrecht des CESL' (2012) 212 *AcP* 581, 618ff, both with further evidence.
[36] RG 22 Dec. 1905, RGZ 62, 201, 206. [37] See Trib.civ. Seine 8 Dec. 1950, D. 1951, 50.
[38] Civ. 3 Oct. 1979, D.S. 1980, 28. [39] BGH 8 June 1988 (n 31) 2599.

3. Mistaken motive

In several continental jurisdictions, commentators and even statutes state that contracts may not be avoided for mere 'error of motive'.[40] This principle can be traced back to Savigny. He held that the stage at which a party formed his intention to enter a contract must be distinguished from the stage at which he expressed it. A mistake in the earlier stage was an error in motive and legally insignificant, whereas a mistake in expressing an intention formed without error entitled one to avoid the contract.[41]

The only place one finds any echo of Savigny's doctrine in the German Civil Code is § 119(1) BGB.[42] The difficulty is that the mistakes which are most important in practice, that is, mistakes as to the essential attributes of thing or person (§ 119(2) BGB), usually affect the intention itself rather than the expression subsequently given to it, and should therefore be regarded as 'mistakes in motive'. Nevertheless, Savigny's principle that motivational errors should be disregarded is basically sound in policy. The 'motives' which induce a party to form a contract—the expectations, suppositions, aims, or plans that he hopes to achieve by the contract—are either unknown to the other party or of no concern to them. It would be disastrous if the validity of a contract could be questioned just because a party had unrealistic expectations, or made inappropriate assumptions. A person who buys a wedding present cannot avoid the purchase if the wedding is cancelled, nor can an official who takes out a lease in the confident expectation of a certain posting back out of the lease when he is posted elsewhere. If an owner insures his property on the assumption that the premiums will cover the risk of damage and that a beneficial owner will pay or reimburse the premium, he cannot avoid the policy if this assumption proves mistaken for *'les motifs vrais ou erronés qui peuvent inciter une partie à conclure une opération à titre onéreux ... sont sans influence sur la validité de l'opération'*.[43] A contract for the supply of advertising materials cannot be avoided because the campaign is less successful than the customer hoped;[44] and a contract of sale for property cannot be avoided for mistake if the buyer discovers that the renovation costs cannot be offset against income taxes and generate a tax advantage.[45]

---

[40] See art. 24 (2) OR; § 901 sent. 2 ABGB; art. 143 Greek Civil Code. Article 1135 *Code civil* now provides that *'l'erreur sur un simple motif'* which is extraneous to the essential qualities of what is owed under the contract does not affect its validity unless the parties have expressly agreed that the correctness of the mistaken party's assumptions is a 'decisive element of their consent'.

[41] On this doctrine, see the essay by K Luig, 'Savignys Irrtumslehre' (1979) 8 Ius commune 36 and W Flume, *Allgemeiner Teil des Bürgerlichen Rechts* vol. II (2nd edn, 1975) § 22, 2.

[42] Under § 119(1) BGB, a promise that the promisor 'had no intention whatsoever of making' can be avoided, for example when the promisor failed to express himself correctly in speech or writing (mistake as to form of expression). Avoidance is also permitted under this subsection to one who, without making any such error in speech or writing, meant what he said in a sense different from that reasonably understood by the other party (mistake as to content). In both cases one can say that there is a mismatch between intention and expression in the sense set out by Savigny, and that avoidance is therefore justified. The distinction between the two kinds of mistakes under § 119(1) BGB will not be further discussed here, since it is not very important in practice and is quite unknown in other legal systems; furthermore they too are subject to the restrictions on avoidance for mistake. See also art. 4:104 PECL; art. 3.2.3 PICC; art. 48(3) CESL; also criticism by Martens (n 35) 857f.

[43] Civ. 3 Aug. 1942, D.A. 1943, 18.   [44] Civ. 16 May 1939, S. 1939.1.260.

[45] Civ. 13 Feb. 2001, Bull.cass. 2001.I. no. 31. This also applies if the seller knew of the buyer's intentions, but not if the parties had made realisation of the tax advantage a part of the contract: *'L'absence*

It is different if the obligation is conditional on the *bien-fondé* of a promisor's hopes and expectations. Such a condition may be explicit, but it may also be inferred when the contract is construed in context.[46] A contract may therefore be avoided for mistake if the disappointed party's expectations were not merely unilateral but '*sont entrés dans le champ contractuel*', to quote a formula often used in France. In respect of errors over qualities, this means that if one party entered a contract on the assumption that the object of the contract (or the person with whom the contract was to be made) had certain qualities and the assumption proves false, the contract can be avoided for mistake only when the object or person 'is not as the contract supposes'[47] or, to follow Ghestin, when the missing feature was a '*qualité convenue*'.[48] This is another rule which has now been adopted in statutory form. Article 1133(1) *Code civil* provides that the qualities of a party's performance are 'essential' only when they were expressly or impliedly 'agreed' and taken into consideration on contracting.

Thus, a person who discovers that his builder is not registered and is operating in the black economy cannot in general avoid the building contract for mistake as to the quality of the person. It would be different if the person had indicated during the negotiations, without demur from the builder, that he regarded the matter as important:

> If the concept of mistakes as to qualities is not to produce an intolerable degree of legal uncertainty, no quality of the person is to be treated as essential [in the sense of § 119(2) BGB] unless the party has perceptibly indicated in some matter that it is to be the basis of the contract, even if not necessarily part of his promise.[49]

In a case before the *Cour de cassation*, a managing director of a limited liability company who had guaranteed the company's debts was sued by one of the company's creditors on debts incurred after he had left office. The court held that while it was one of the '*motifs déterminants*' for the director giving the guarantee that he supposed it applied only to debts arising while he was director, this assumption had not been '*introduit dans le champ contractuel*' and avoidance was not possible.[50]

---

de satisfaction du motif considéré ... ne pouvait entraîner l'annulation du contrat faute d'une stipulation expresse qui aurait fait entrer ce motif dans le champ contractuel en l'érigeant en condition de ce contrat.

[46] See above, pp. 100ff.

[47] See Flume (n 41) 477f, followed by most writers in Germany; see the cases cited below, n 49.

[48] See Ghestin (n 7) no. 526: '*L'erreur ne justifie l'annulation du contrat que lorsqu'elle s'analyse en un désaccord entre l'objet réel et sa définition contractuelle. Il faut qu'elle porte sur une qualité expressément ou tacitement convenue.*' See also Ghestin's notes to Com. 20 Oct. 1970, *JCP* 1971.II.16916 and to Com. 4 July 1973, D. 1974, 538. See also P Malinvaud, 'De l'erreur sur la substance': D. 1972. Chron. 215, 216; Vivien (n 34) 332f; Terré, Simler, and Lequette (n 7) no. 217.

[49] BGH 22 Sept. 1983, BGHZ 88, 240, 246. Similar is BGH 18 Dec. 1954, BGHZ 16, 54, 57f. (on mistakes as to the qualities of a thing).

[50] Com. 6 Dec. 1988, D.S.1988, 185, n. L Aynès. Compare Paris 15 Nov. 1990, D. 1991, Somm. 160: the seller of a statue could not avoid the sale either because the exact provenance of the statue was not a *qualité convenue* or because it was the seller's own fault that he had not investigated its provenance before making the sale. In that case, the error, being due to his fault, did not entitle him to avoid (on this, see below, pp. 162ff.).

4. Mistake as to the value of the thing

It is generally agreed that a contract cannot be avoided just because a party made a mistake as to the value of its subject matter, as opposed to a mistake as to qualities of the thing which affect its value.[51] Article 1136 *Code civil* now says expressly that a contract cannot be avoided for a mere '*erreur sur la valeur*' based on one party's '*appréciation économique inexacte*'. This is often justified on the basis that the price of goods and services is not fixed, but fluctuates according to supply and demand. If a buyer offers to pay a price well above the going rate, the seller may properly attribute this not to a mistake but to a difference of view regarding the market. The better reason, however, is that both parties must bear the risk of undervaluing or overvaluing what they are to give or get under the contract, and must abide by the contract even though it later appears that they paid too little or too much. Otherwise, business confidence would be ruined. The *Bundesgerichtshof* was right to hold that a doctor could not avoid the purchase of an expensive piece of equipment which did not meet his needs even though it answered the contractual description. The reason given was that the value of a thing, including its 'economic utility', was not an essential quality in the sense of § 119(2) BGB,[52] but the better reason is that typically it is the buyer that takes the risk of making a mistake as to 'economic utility'.

Those concerned with fair apportionment of risk may well doubt the wisdom of the distinction between an error as to value as such and an error as to qualities (which determine the value). Should it matter whether a person who buys shares overvalues them by mistake, or erroneously supposes that they will give a controlling interest in the company?[53]

Given that the buyer of an apartment block cannot avoid the contract just because of a mistake about its value, should it make any difference that a buyer erroneously supposed that a highway or underground station was to be built nearby? Surely it should not depend on whether his mistake was as to the value of the house or some attribute such as its traffic links, nor indeed on whether such attribute was 'objectively essential' or a '*qualité substantielle*'. The true issue is whether the mistake in question—as in this case—fell within the buyer's sphere of risk. Only the buyer can know his intentions in buying the building, so it is up to the buyer to ascertain whether the circumstances on which the expectations depend are present or likely to arise. If it takes too much time or trouble to obtain such information, or it is very difficult, impossible or too expensive, then the buyer must elicit appropriate guarantees from the seller or see to it that the issues figure in the contract as '*qualités convenues*'. If the buyer fails to do so, he must put up with the consequences.

---

[51] BGH 18 Dec. 1954 (n 49) 57; BGH 14 Dec. 1960 (n 11) 41; and Ghestin (n 7) no. 512.
[52] BGH 18 Dec. 1954 (n 49).
[53] See Com. 26 Mar. 1974, Bull.cass. 1974.IV. no. 108 and Ghestin (n 7) no. 512 and J Mestre in (1987) 86 *Rev trim civ* 741ff; Terré, Simler, and Lequette (n 7) no. 220.

5. Risk in transactions

If, as is often the case, a transaction exposes a party to particular risks, it should be obvious that the party cannot evade them by seeking to avoid the contract for mistake: *'L'aléa chasse l'erreur'*[54] or, as is now provided by art. 1133(3) *Code civil*, *'l'acceptation d'un aléa sur une qualité de la prestation exclut l'erreur relative à cette qualité'*. Such a risk may be allocated by an express term: if the seller has stipulated that he is not to be liable for defects in quality, and the goods are in fact defective, the buyer can no more avoid the contract on the ground that he was mistaken in supposing the goods free from defect than he can sue for breach of contract.[55] So, too, where the allocation of risk emerges from the circumstances—for example, when a person has guaranteed another's debts: neither the guarantor[56] nor anyone else offering security[57] can escape liability by arguing that he erroneously overestimated the solvency of the debtor. Transactions in the art world often put the risk of inauthenticity on the buyer.[58] The Dutch Civil Code explicitly excludes avoidance for error in the case of risk transactions: according to art. 3:228(2) BW, there is no right to avoid for a mistake which 'according to the nature of the contract, the view of businessmen or the circumstances of the case is the responsibility of the mistaken party'.

6. Negligent mistakes

It is not open to parties to avoid a contract for mistake if they could and should already have ascertained the truth of the situation. Someone who purchases hunting rights, and then finds there is less game in the area than expected must abide by the contract if he could have reconnoitred the land and checked the state of the game beforehand.[59] Several reasons can be given for this. One could say that in all the circumstances of the case (for example, because the parties agreed on a low price) the abundance of game

---

[54] Mestre (n 53) 743. See also Ghestin (n 7) no. 529f; Larroumet (n 7) no. 345 (n 138*bis*); Terré, Simler, and Lequette (n 7) no. 217.

[55] See BG 13 July 1965, BGE 91 II 275, 279 (in such a case it is inconsistent with good faith to seek avoidance); Com. 4 Dec. 1979, Bull.cass. 1979.IV. no. 324 (avoidance permitted only because the exclusion of liability was not included in the contract); BGH 15 Jan. 1975, BGHZ 63, 369, 377 (buyer of an inauthentic painting cannot avoid for mistake where the contract contains an exclusion clause because 'this would render almost worthless the allocation of risk' envisaged by the exclusion clause).

[56] Civ. 11 Feb. 1986, Bull.cass. 1986.I. no. 22; see also BGH 2 Dec. 1964, [1965] *NJW* 438: the unexpected insolvency of the debtor owing to unforeseeable circumstances does not afford the guarantor a claim that the 'foundation of the transaction' has collapsed, and this must involve that he has no claim for avoidance on the ground of mistake. It is quite another question whether a guarantee may be avoided on the ground that the creditor did not perform a duty to inform the guarantor about the financial situation of the debtor. See below, chapter 10 n 39.

[57] BG 16 July 1982, BGE 108 II 410, 412.

[58] See, for example, Civ. 24 Mar. 1987, D. 1987, 489, n. J Aubert (painting sold not as 'by Fragonard' but 'attributed to Fragonard'); Civ. 31 Mar. 1987, Bull.cass. 1987.I. no. 115 (statue from Tang dynasty sold as 'greatly restored'). On these two decisions see Mestre (n 53). Contracts for sale concluded at flea markets and antiquarian dealers can be a risk transaction for both parties. If, for example, old sheet music has been sold, the seller cannot avoid the contract for mistake if it turns out that the sheet music may have been Mozart's, nor can the buyer avoid the contract if the sheet music turns out to be a modern fake and thus worthless. See AG Coburg 24 April 1992, [1993] *NJW* 93.

[59] Amiens 30 Nov. 1954, D.H. 1955, 420. So also Req. 21 Jan. 1935, S. 1935, 179 (decorator cannot avoid the contract on finding that the surface to be painted is larger than he expected).

expected by the huntsman was not an underlying assumption of the contract—not a '*qualité convenue*' of the land—so that this was a mere error in motive (see above, pages 159f.). Or in the absence of a contractual term as regards the state of the game one could say that a contract about hunting rights is an 'aleatory transaction', a speculation which excludes any right to avoid it (see above, page 162). But one could also say that avoidance is excluded because the mistake in question was the mistaken party's own fault. This is the line taken by courts in France, Belgium, and Spain.[60] They ask whether the mistaken party could and should reasonably have ascertained the truth of the situation before entering into the contract. The greater the person's expertise and experience, the readier the courts will be to find fault, or to be more forbearing and apt to treat the mistake as excusable in a person unfamiliar with transactions of that type, or incapable for other reasons of obtaining the requisite information.[61]

According to art. 26 OR, a party 'whose mistake is attributable to his own negligence' must compensate the other party for the harm which non-performance causes,[62] and the *Bundesgericht* infers from this that while the fault of the mistaken party renders liability in damages, it does not bar avoidance.[63] A similar view is taken in Germany, since § 119 BGB does not expressly state that fault on the part of the mistaken party excludes avoidance.[64] This should not, however, be accepted uncritically, since in answering the question whether the mistake is a mere mistake in motive or falls within the mistaken party's sphere of risk, the German judge can deploy the same considerations which move the courts in France to hold that the mistaken party was at fault.

7. *Offer to make good the consequences of a mistake*

It is generally agreed that avoidance is excluded if the other party, on being informed of the mistake, forthwith agrees to treat the contract as valid on the terms that would have been agreed but for the mistake.[65] The rule is not very important in practice.

III. Mistakes caused by the other party

If A makes a statement during negotiations which he knows to be untrue, and B is thus led to make a mistake, B can avoid the contract on the ground of deceit (see chapter 11), but the contract may also be avoided even if A actually believed what he

---

[60] Under art. 1132 *Code civil*, a party may avoid a contract only if his mistake is 'excusable'. See also Civ. 29 June 1959, Bull.cass. 1959.I. no. 320; Civ. 2 Mar. 1964, Bull.cass. 1964.I. no. 122; Civ. 9 Oct. 1969, Bull. cass. 1969.III. no. 634; Cass.belge 6 Jan. 1944, Pas. 1944.I.133; T.S. 14 June 1943, [1943] Aranzadi no. 719; T.S. 16 Dec. 1953, [1953] Aranzadi no. 3514.

[61] See Ghestin (n 7) no. 523; Starck, Roland, and Boyer (n 34) no. 418ff, both with references to the cases.

[62] This is not so where the other party was aware of the mistake, or would have been aware of it had he taken care. In Greece (art. 145(3) Civil Code) and Germany (§ 122 BGB), the mistaken party is liable in damages regardless of fault.

[63] BG 13 July 1965, BGE 91 II 275, 280.   [64] RG 22 Dec. 1905, RGZ 66, 201, 205.

[65] See art. 25(2) OR; art. 1432 *Codice civile*; art. 6:230 BW; art. 144 Greek Civil Code; art. 248 Portuguese Civil Code; also art. 4:105 PECL; art. 3.2.10 PICC; art. II.-7:203 DCFR. Commentators in Germany also support this view: see Flume (n 41) 421f; C Armbrüster in *Münchener Kommentar zum BGB* (6th edn, 2012) § 119 BGB mn. 141.

said. Even if A had no intention to deceive, he has still *caused* B to make a mistake, whether by negligence or in perfect innocence, and therefore cannot expect to have his reliance on the validity of the contract protected.

Often the erroneous statement becomes a term of the contract. An inaccurate statement by a seller about the quality of the goods may well constitute a contractual guarantee that the goods have the stated quality; if so, the buyer may claim for breach of contract. But even if the erroneous statement has no contractual force, the person who made it can hardly complain if the person he misled seeks to avoid the contract. In such cases, English law allows the addressee of the erroneous statement to avoid the contract for *misrepresentation*, and in certain cases to claim damages as well. Though continental systems focus on the mistake caused by the misstatement, the same idea appears in many of them, for they allow the mistaken party to avoid the contract if his mistake 'was caused by the other party' (§ 871 ABGB) or was 'due to a statement of the other party to the contract' (art. 6:228a BW).[66]

The English law reports offer a particularly rich harvest of cases. 'Misrepresentations' are false verbal or written statements made prior to the contract, or even conduct equivalent to statements, such as a wink, nod, or gesture. Mere expressions of opinion do not suffice, nor statements about the law, nor normal business puffery that reasonable men would not take at face value. When a vendor asserted that land was currently let to 'a most desirable tenant', the truth being that the tenant was several months in arrears with the rent,[67] this was a misrepresentation, though not when the vendor encouragingly opined that agricultural land was 'fertile and improvable'.[68] Whether or not a statement that land could support 2,000 sheep constitutes a misrepresentation depends on the circumstances: it will not do so if, as the buyer knew, the vendor never raised sheep there and a reasonable man would therefore take his statement to be a mere expression of opinion.[69] A misrepresentation which helps to induce the mistaken party to enter the contract, as intended by the misrepresentor, renders the latter liable in damages unless he can prove that he was not at fault, that he honestly and without negligence believed in the truth of what he said.[70] But even if the misrepresentation

---

[66] See too art. 84(1) Polish Civil Code. In France and Germany, the courts do not recognise the idea of 'caused mistake', but in fact a mistake which satisfies the requirements of art. 1132f. *Code civil* or § 119(2) BGB will often have been caused by the other party, even if this is not emphasised. See, for example, Req. 19 Jan. 1925, S. 1925.1.101. Sometimes, where the mistake has been caused by negligence the mistaken party may have a claim for damages even if he cannot avoid the contract—the result will be much the same, the claim being based on art. 1240 (formerly art. 1382) *Code civil* or, in Germany, *culpa in contrahendo*. In BGH 31 Jan. 1962, [1962] *NJW* 1196, the seller of a machine measured the place where the buyer planned to install it and asserted—erroneously, as it turned out—that the machine could be accommodated there. This assertion hardly qualified as a contractual guarantee of a feature of the machine. But because during the negotiations the seller had given carelessly false advice to the buyer, and thereby broken a duty incumbent upon him, the seller was liable in damages. The seller was also bound to release the buyer from the contract, which he would not have entered into but for the false advice. See also RG 4 Dec. 1920, RGZ 101, 51: the price at which the plaintiff bought shares from the defendant was stated by the defendant to be the current price, which was in fact lower. A lower court had granted the plaintiff's claim for damages, since he had been given carelessly false information by the defendant; but the Reichsgericht found that a mistake under § 119(2) BGB had been established. For a detailed treatment, see D Henrich, 'Die unbewußte Irreführung' (1963) 162 *AcP* 88, 92ff.
[67] *Smith* v. *Land and House Property Corp.* (1884) 28 Ch.D. 7.
[68] *Dimmock* v. *Hallett* (1866) LR 2 Ch.App. 21. [69] *Bissett* v. *Wilkinson* [1927] AC 177.
[70] Misrepresentation Act 1967, s. 2(1).

is perfectly innocent, the mistaken party can rescind the contract. This would be too severe a sanction if holding the mistaken party bound would cause him little hardship, and releasing him would cause considerable loss to the other party. In such a case the court can—if it seems reasonable in the circumstances to do so—hold the mistaken party to the contract and allow him damages in lieu of rescission.[71]

It is an important question whether mere silence can amount to a *misrepresentation* or serve as the 'cause' of a mistake. It does so only when there is a duty to volunteer information, to disclose certain facts or particular matters without being asked. A person who remains silent in breach of such a duty cannot only be held to have 'caused' the partner's mistake, but to have done so deceitfully and thus rendering liability for damages. The question of duties of disclosure will accordingly be dealt with in detail below in chapter 10.A.II.

IV. Recognisable mistakes

Many systems accept that if a party knew or could have known that the other party entered the contract pursuant to a mistake, it does not deserve any protection for his reliance on its validity. Thus art. 1428 *Codice civil* requires not only that a mistake be 'essential' but also 'recognisable' by the other party. This requirement is satisfied if, given the nature of the contract, the situation in which it was formed, and the position of the parties, a person taking reasonable care should have been aware that an error was being made (art. 1431). So, too, § 871 ABGB states that avoidance is possible for an essential mistake if 'in the circumstances it must have been obvious' to the other party.[72] Even in systems that lack the concept of 'recognisable mistake', one can find occasional decisions that refer to it. Thus, in determining whether a mistake is 'essential', the Swiss *Bundesgericht* considers 'whether in the light of general experience or the facts of the case as proved the plaintiff could have realised that the defendant put particular weight on the fact he misunderstood, that is, that the defendant would not have contracted but for his error'.[73]

The rule must, however, be limited. For example, if the seller becomes aware during the negotiations of the buyer's plans regarding the property, one cannot grant the buyer the right to avoid the contract just because the seller knew of circumstances which would frustrate such plans. Nor can the buyer that offers a high price for goods on the supposition that demand is going to exceed supply avoid the contract just because the better-informed seller knew that supply would soon increase and prices drop because the harvest was expected to be good, or freight rates were about to sink. It is true that in both these cases avoidance could be barred on the grounds that the risk was on the buyer that the goods might prove less valuable than thought (above, pages 161f.), or that mere errors as to value are to be disregarded (above, pages 159f.). So if one is going to make the outcome turn on whether or not the other party could have

---

[71] Misrepresentation Act 1967, s. 2(2). For details, see GH Treitel, *The Law of Contract* (13th edn, by E Peel, 2011) no. 361ff.
[72] Similar provisions may be found in § 32(1) Swedish Contract Law; art. 6:228b BW; art. 247 Portuguese Civil Code; art. 84(1) Polish Civil Code.
[73] BG 10 Feb. 1987, BGE 113 II 25, 27f.

known of the mistake, one must add the further requirement that it was a party's duty to correct the error and he was in breach of it.[74] Here again we see that there is a close connection between the question whether a contract may be avoided for mistake, and the question of whether the mistake was due to a breach by the other party of a duty to provide information or, as here, to correct misapprehension. The matter will be discussed further below from page 175 ff.

V. Shared mistakes

Many legal systems have a special category of 'common mistake' covering circumstances where both parties made the same mistake when concluding the contract. Thus art. 6:228c BW allows a claim for avoidance 'if at the time of the contract the other party proceeded on the same mistaken assumption' and must have known that, if correctly informed, the claimant would not have entered the contract. The effect of art. 24(1) no. 4 OR is similar: it permits avoidance if the mistake concerns a matter such that 'the mistaken party would in good faith regard it as the basis of the contract'. The courts treat a mistake as 'basic' if it concerns 'an assumption which for both parties necessarily and objectively constituted an imperative precondition of contracting, whether they were conscious of this or not'.[75] Common error is not dealt with in the BGB, but the courts fill the gap by applying the rules of 'collapse of the basis of the transaction' in cases where in making the contract both parties were mistaken as to an essential fact.[76] Common mistake is one of the few kinds of mistake for which English law permits avoidance, provided that it is of 'fundamental character'. This is the case when it is based on a circumstance that both parties 'must necessarily have accepted in their minds as an essential and integral element of the subject matter'.[77] In other words, the common mistake must 'render the subject matter of the contract essentially and radically different from the subject matter which the parties believed to exist'.[78] This requirement is rarely deemed to be met, particularly when the common mistake concerns the characteristics of the goods or the performance that one

---

[74] This is made clear in art. 6:228b BW. In OGH 19 Oct. 1978, SZ 51 no. 144, this requirement was met: the seller mistakenly quoted a price which was much less than a hundredth of the going price for such goods. Not only was this a mistake which 'must have been obvious' to the buyer (§ 871 ABGB), but also one that the buyer was bound, by the standards of fair business practice, to disclose. Compare also OGH 7 Dec. 1966, [1967] *JBl* 426, n. P Bydlinski.

[75] BG 10 Feb. 1987 (n 73) 27; likewise BG 25 Oct. 1983, BGE 109 II 319, 322.

[76] See, for example, BGH 13 Nov. 1975, [1976] *NJW* 565 (common mistake in a transfer contract as to the football player's entitlement to play); BGH 25 Sept. 1986, [1987] *NJW* 890 (common mistake as to a third party's right of pre-emption); BGH 6 Dec. 1989, [1990] *NJW* 567 (common mistake as to the possible throughput of a pub). But § 313(2) BGB now expressly states that the provisions governing the collapse of the basis of the transaction pursuant to § 313(1) BGB also apply if there is a common mistake of the parties, namely if 'material conceptions that have become the basis of the contract are found to be incorrect'. The reference to § 313(1) BGB means that a party disadvantaged by such a common mistake cannot place reliance on a collapse of the basis of the transaction if—'taking account of all the circumstances of the specific case, in particular the contractual or statutory distribution of risk'—the party should be held to the contract (see also p. 283). Otherwise the party can request an 'amendment of the contract' or, if it is not possible or reasonable, the party may revoke the contract. An amendment of the contract where there is common mistake is also permitted under art. 4:105 (3) PECL and art. II.-7:203 (3) DCFR.

[77] Lord Thankerton in *Bell v. Lever Brothers Ltd.* [1932] AC 161, 235.

[78] Lord Steyn in *Associated Japanese Bank (International) Ltd. v. Crédit du Nord S.A.* (n 18) 912f.

party was promised under the contract. By way of example, there is no 'fundamental' common mistake if the parties believe that a painting sold was by a particular artist,[79] that the natural product being sold contained no additives,[80] or that the car being sold was built in 1948 (instead of 1939).[81] A similar result was reached in a case where the defendant salvage company undertook to organise a salvage operation for a ship stranded in the South Indian Ocean. The defendant concluded a contract with the owner of the 'Great Peace', which was near to the apparent location of the ship in trouble. The contract was to hire the 'Great Peace' for five days—against payment of at least $82,500—so it could change course as soon as possible, sail towards the stricken ship, and take that ship's crew on board should the ship sink. At the time of the contract, both parties incorrectly believed that the 'Great Peace' was only about thirty-five miles away from the stricken vessel and that the 'Great Peace' could reach the vessel within a few hours. It quickly became apparent that the ships were actually about 415 miles apart. The defendant then hired another ship and declared the original contract with the owners of the 'Great Peace' to be invalid due to common mistake about the exact location of the stricken vessel. The Court of Appeal was of a different opinion: the mistake was not fundamental, the contract was valid, and the claimant shipowners were awarded the agreed minimum payment.[82]

Clearly, the conditions under which contracts can be avoided in the interesting cases set out here are always described in similar terms, regardless of whether the conditions are referred to as a 'basic error', a 'collapse of the basis of the transaction', or a 'common mistake'. However, one must admit that when applying these approaches at a practical level, the courts often come to very different conclusions.

VI. A European law on mistake?

The different viewpoints adopted in Europe for deciding whether or not a contract can be avoided for mistake are, as we have seen, varied and confusing.[83] We have also seen that such viewpoints are in large measure interchangeable. If the judge is of the opinion

---

[79] *Leaf v. International Galleries* [1950] 2 KB 86. See also Lord Atkin in *Bell v. Lever Brothers* (n 77) 224: 'A buys a picture from B; both A and B believe it to be the work of an old master and a high price is paid. It turns out to be a modern copy. A has no remedy in the absence of representation or warranty.'

[80] *Harrison and Jones v. Burton and Lancaster* [1953] 1 QB 646.

[81] *Oscar Chess Ltd. v. Williams* [1957] 1 WLR 370.

[82] *Great Peace Shipping Ltd. v. Tsavliris Salvage (International) Ltd.* [2003] QB 679. The decisions of English courts are not always uniform. For greater detail about common mistake, see Treitel (n 71) no. 8-002ff; E McKendrick, *Contract Law* (8th edn, 2009) no. 14.2.

[83] It must be noted that the overview given here is far from complete. For example, in Austrian law avoidance is allowed if the mistake 'is declared in good time' (§ 871 ABGB). 'In good time' means that the other party must have been notified of the mistake before he has taken any detrimental action on the basis that the contract is valid. See, for example, OGH 20 May 1953, SZ no. 129. But it is not clear why the other party should be protected only if he can prove that he took detrimental action in reliance. See E Kramer, 'Die Gültigkeit der Verträge nach den UNIDROIT-Principles of International Commercial Contracts' (1999) 7 *ZEuP* 209, 217f. and 'Bausteine für einen "Common Frame of Reference" des europäischen Irrtumsrechts' (2007) 15 *ZEuP* 247, 256. It is a different question whether—if avoidance is permissible but it would prove arduous to undo the contract by reason of the steps taken in reliance—one should not give the court power to uphold the contract or part of it and grant the mistaken party damages in lieu. This is done by art. 3:53(2) BW. A similar idea underlies the rule in s. 2(2) Misrepresentation Act 1967 (see above, n 71).

that a contract must be upheld despite the claimant's mistake, the judge can find that the mistake was the claimant's own fault, that it was a mere mistake in motive or a mistake as to the value of the thing, or the judge can construe that contract so as to put the risk of the error on the claimant. What method the judge chooses to adopt depends on the traditions and conventions of the legal system, and often on his own juridical taste.

Even so, one can detect a few common threads in the development of a European law on mistake, which explains why the proposals for avoiding contracts as stated in the various international sets of rules seems to follow a common train of thought.[84]

1. Primacy of the contract

The first thing to note is that there are many cases when one or other of the parties is mistaken, but the rules on avoiding a contract for mistake cannot be applied. Such is the case where it appears that the parties have come to an agreement, but their statements could be interpreted by a reasonable person in more than one way. Here the parties have merely misunderstood each other; there is no need to avoid a contract for mistake, as there is no agreement between the parties (and therefore no contract).[85] More often, a contract has been concluded, but it is clear that there is no question of avoiding the contract for mistake. If the goods delivered to the buyer do not comply with contractual specifications as to amount, identity, or characteristics, or the buyer is not given clear title to the goods, or the goods are simply not delivered, the buyer could claim a mistaken belief that the seller would fulfil the contract as specified. Here the buyer has a claim for breach of contract and there is no reason why it should be able to assert a claim that the contract should be avoided for mistake.[86] Instead the general principle is that before examining the rules governing the avoidance of a contract for mistake, a judge 'must first determine whether the contract itself ... provides who bears the risk of the relevant mistake'.[87] So if a volume of goods has been sold that did not exist at the time of the contract, although the parties did not know this, some legal orders will have a statutory provision that invalidates the contract under such circumstances.[88] But these provisions are mostly not regarded as binding, so that interpretation of the contract may result in the seller being found to have guaranteed

---

[84] See art. 4:103 PECL; art. 3.2.2 PICC; art. 151 CEC; art. II.-7:201 DCFR; art. 48 CESL. See also Kramer (1999) 7 ZEuP 209 (n 83); M Wolf, 'Willensmängel und sonstige Beeinträchtigungen der Entscheidungsfreiheit in einem europäischen Vertragsrecht' in J Basedow (ed), *Europäische Vertragsrechtsvereinheitlichung und deutsches Recht* (2000) 85; Kramer (2007) 15 ZEuP 247 (n 83); R Sefton-Green (ed), *Mistake, Fraud and Precontractual Duties to Inform in European Contract Law* (2005); N Jansen and R Zimmermann, 'Vertragsschluß und Irrtum im europäischen Vertragsrecht' (2010) 210 *AcP* 196, 229ff; Martens (n 35) 854ff.

[85] See above, p. 98. [86] See above, p. 152. [87] *Lord Steyn* (nn 18, 19).

[88] See, for example, s. 6 Sale of Goods Act 1979; art. 20 OR; § 878 ABGB; art. 1346 *Codice civile*. But the situation is different under art. 6:74 BW; see also art. 4:102 PECL and art: 3.1.3 PICC. The earlier provision under § 306 BGB, which held such a contract to be invalid, has now been replaced by § 311a BGB, which deems the contract to be valid. The buyer can no longer claim performance of the contract, but can claim damages, unless the seller can show that he was not aware of the non-existence of the goods at the time of the contract and was 'also not responsible for his lack of awareness'. See H Kötz, *Vertragsrecht* (2nd edn, 2012) mn. 788f, 1107f.

the availability of the goods or, in other words, had taken on the risk of the goods not being available. It is clear that in such circumstances the seller should not be able to invalidate the contract by claiming that at the time of the contract both parties had been commonly mistaken as to the existence of the goods. These considerations must also apply where the mistake of the parties does not turn on the question of whether the seller is in a position to deliver the contractual goods. So if a landlord and tenant mistakenly think that a rented apartment is not subject to rent control, or when a guarantee is given and the parties erroneously assume that the debtor transferred title in goods to the creditor as security for a loan,[89] then the parties share a common mistake. But that does not mean that the contract can be avoided by a party that subsequently discovers the contract to be disadvantageous after the common mistake has been revealed. The more important consideration is who carries the risk of the mistake in due consideration of the contractual provisions and all the circumstances of the case. If it is the claimant—perhaps because it would have been in a better position than the other party to uncover the relevant information at the time the contract was concluded—then the claimant will be bound to the contract. The same also applies if the risk of mistake was the same for both parties, or could only be allocated to the defendant. If the contract makes some reference to risk allocation—and this often does not emerge until the contact is interpreted or construed by the court—there is no question of the contract being avoided for mistake. This approach is well recognised with respect to speculative or aleatory transactions.[90] But every contract is about the allocation of risk to a certain extent; thus any contract, if analysed with sufficient vigour, can reveal information as to whether certain incorrect assumptions or expectations that motivated a party are for that party's benefit and, therefore, provide no grounds for avoidance of the contract for mistake.[91] Finally, it is often the case that a party is mistaken, but does not claim avoidance of the contract on that basis or on that basis alone. Such parties' first line of attack may be that the other party caused the mistake by breaching their *duty to provide information* and that they are thus liable to reimburse the resulting *damages*. This is the case where during negotiations the other party *intentionally* made a statement that was incorrect or incomplete, thereby *deceiving* the counterparty.[92] But a party must also pay damages, either for breach of contract or in tort, if the incorrect or incomplete information was given *negligently*, or if the party said nothing, thus breaching their duty to provide information.[93]

2. 'Special reasons' for allowing avoidance

If avoidance of a contract is not excluded *ab initio*, one must ask under what conditions avoidance may be allowed.

---

[89] So was the case in *Associated Japanese Bank (International) Ltd. v. Crédit du Nord* (n 18).
[90] See above, p. 162.
[91] See also arts. 6:101 and 102 PECL: these provisions specify the conditions under which an express clause or construed interpretation of the parties' intention 'is to be treated as a contractual obligation'. If the conditions are met, the party that has not performed its obligations is liable for breach of contract, but cannot escape liability by seeking to avoid the contract for mistake.
[92] See below, pp. 173ff.   [93] See below, pp. 175ff.

It is clear that the venerable categories of mistake into error *in persona, in substantia, in negotio,* and so on are of no assistance here. Nor is it enough to ask whether the error relates to a '*qualité essentielle*' or to a quality of person or thing 'regarded in commerce as essential'. Such formulae have little ascertainable or serviceable intrinsic content. Instead, they conceal the fact that it is the interest of the other party which determines whether avoidance should be permitted, and that the question is when, and under what conditions, a party must put up with the contract being undone and his commercial plans coming to nothing.

English law has always adopted the position that this is only acceptable in exceptional circumstances, but Austrian law goes some way towards it: § 871 ABGB was drafted under the influence of natural lawyers, who were much concerned with the protection of commerce. More recent civil codes have also taken up this position, notably the *Codice civile* and the Dutch Civil Code. In Germany and France the codes were unduly imprecise, so it fell to the courts to take proper account of the interests of commerce and the need to protect reliance.

Generally, each contract must be applied as agreed between the parties, even if they made a mistake. The disadvantageous consequences must generally fall on the party that has made the mistake. Exceptions to this basic principle must be allowed, but they cannot depend on the psychological conditions under which the mistake was made, whether it bears on a motive, concerns the quality or value of the contractual object, or is related to the current position, future developments or other factual or legal assumptions. A party can only avoid a contract for mistake when there are exceptional reasons why the counterparty's reliance on the validity of the contract deserves no protection. All international sets of rules follow this premise. What are those exceptional reasons that justify avoidance of the contract?

Firstly, the mistake must not be based on an ancillary term: it must concern a point that is so important that a reasonable person in full knowledge of the facts would not have concluded the contract without that term or under substantially different conditions.[94] If this condition is met, a party may avoid the contract for mistake if the counterparty had *induced* the mistake—for example, when the counterparty made an incorrect or incomplete statement (perhaps innocently), thereby causing the party to make a mistake. Under such circumstances, the counterparty must tolerate the party avoiding the contract for mistake on this basis.[95] A party can also induce the mistake of the counterparty by failing to say something, but only if under the circumstances that party has a *duty to inform* the counterparty.[96] Avoidance of the contract is also permissible if the party did not induce the mistake, but is not deserving of protection because it had *recognised* the mistake by the other party or *should reasonably have recognised* the mistake and did not inform the other party, even though fair business practice would have required that they do so.[97] Finally, avoidance will be permitted if

---

[94] See art. 3.2.2(1) PICC; art. 4:103(1)(b) PECL; art. II.-7:201(1)(a) DCFR; art. 48 (1)(a) CESL.

[95] Article 4:103(1)(a)(i) PECL; art. 3.2.2(1)(a) PICC; art. II.-7:201(1)(b)(i) DCFR; art. 48(1)(b)(i) CESL.

[96] Article II.-7:203(1)(b)(iii) DCFR and art. 48(1)(b)(ii) CESL expressly state that the avoidance of the contract is also permissible if the counterparty 'caused the contract to be concluded in mistake by failing to comply with a pre-contractual information duty'. See below, p. 175.

[97] Article 4:103(1)(a)(ii) PECL; art. 3.2.2(1)(a) PICC; art. II-7:201(1)(b)(ii) DCFR; art. 48(1)(b)(iii) CESL.

both parties made the same mistake upon conclusion of the contract and there is thus a *common mistake*.[98]

There is no need to check whether these conditions have been met if there are grounds for excluding avoidance of the contract for mistake from the outset. One such reason would be that the mistake was 'inexcusable',[99] namely that the party relying on the mistake 'was grossly negligent in committing the error'.[100] The other rule is more practically important: avoidance is not possible if the contract (sometimes on the basis of construction of the contract) shows that the risk of the mistake was only allocated to one party. This party cannot avoid the contract for mistake, as it would thereby be avoiding the disadvantage that it carried as a result of risk allocation in the contract.[101]

It is certainly reassuring that there is a general consensus in the various international sets of rules governing avoidance of a contract for mistake. But one should not make the mistake of assuming that in applying these rules European courts all come to the same result. It is unfortunate, but unavoidable, that legislatures (including the European legislature) have no option here but to restrict themselves to rather general and imprecise formulations. Whether under certain circumstances a risk is allocated to one party or the other, whether a party has a duty to inform and must thus provide the counterparty with certain information without being asked, or whether there is a need to inform the counterparty after a mistake has been recognised: these are all questions posed by legislatures, but answered only by judges. And judges answer such questions on the basis of values that, as the above examples show, vary from country to country and are often dependent on which types of cases typically land in front of the courts, and the sort of parties that courts typically need to take into account.

D. Effecting Avoidance for Mistake

The right to avoid a contract for mistake is effected by the mistaken party indicating that it does not want to be bound by the contract because of the mistake—with such indication being given either by express notification or by conduct from which it is clearly inferable. Romanistic systems have a tendency to require that the mistaken party assert the right to avoid the contract by means of a claim in court, or by a defence in enforcement proceedings.[102] There is no good reason for this. If the other party thinks avoidance justified, it can agree to dissolve the contract quite informally; if not, it may sue for specific performance or claim damages for breach and leave it

---

[98] Article 4:103(1)(a)(iii) PECL; art. 3.2.2(1)(a) PICC; art. II-7:201(1)(b)(iv) DCFR; art. 48(1)(b)(iv) CESL. Pursuant to art. 3.2.2(1)(b) PICC, avoidance for mistake should always be permitted as long as the other party has not at the time of avoidance reasonably acted in reliance on the contract (also § 871 ABGB). See above, n 84.

[99] Article 4:103(2)(a) PECL; art. II.-7:201(2)(a) DCFR.

[100] Article 3.2.2(2)(a) PICC. Critically Kramer (2007) 15 *ZEuP* 258f (n 83). Also art. 48 CESL contains no such rule.

[101] Article 4:103(2)(b) PECL; art. 3.2.2(2)(b) PICC; art. II.-7:201(2)(b) DCFR; art. 48 (2) CESL: The allocation of risk in the contract is particularly important where one party seeks avoidance of the contract on the ground of common mistake. See p. 166.

[102] See art. 1441f. *Codice civile*; art. 1301 Spanish Civil Code.

to the mistaken party to establish in court that his mistake allows avoidance of the contract.

There are major differences regarding the time within which notification, claim, or defence must be made. Time runs from the moment at which the mistaken party discovers the error that entitles avoidance of the contract; sometimes, this period begins earlier, namely when the mistaken party *could* have known of the mistake. On grounds of legal certainty, some legal systems specify a particular period of time, such as one year (art. 31 OR), three years (art. 3:52c BW), or five years (art. 1304 *Code civil*).[103] However, depending on the type of transaction there may be differing interests requiring the contract to be finally valid after expiry of a certain time. For example, avoiding a contract for goods with rapidly fluctuating prices or that must be resold within a short time must take place within a shorter timeframe than avoiding a contract for the sale of land. Furthermore, if the time for avoidance is fixed, there is the risk that the mistaken party may speculate at the expense of the other party by waiting to see whether the market moves to his advantage or disadvantage before he decides to avoid. A flexible solution is thus desirable. These disadvantages do not arise in German law, where § 121 BGB requires avoidance to be declared 'without culpable delay': in practice, this means that the mistaken party is granted a deadline that seems reasonable when also taking into account the interest of the other party. The solutions offered in the international sets of rules take the same line: when the mistaken party has recognised the mistake or could have done so, avoidance of the contract should be declared 'within a reasonable time'.[104]

---

[103] Romanistic systems tend to allow the mistaken party to rely on the mistake without any time limit, provided it is used to *defend* the claims under the contract; see art. 1442(4) *Codice civile*; art. 287 II Portuguese Civil Code; Larroumet (n 7) no. 569 with further French cases.

[104] See art. 4:113(1) PECL, art. 3.2.12 PICC; art. II.-7:210 DCFR. But under art. 52(2) CESL the mistaken party may avoid the contract six months after having become aware of the mistake. That is in stark contrast to § 121 BGB, but appears sensible because under art. 48 CESL avoidance of a contract for mistake is only granted (differently than under German law) if the special reasons stated above apply. It then appears—as Martens correctly states (n 36) 880—'justified to subject this party to a longer period of uncertainty about a possible avoidance of the contract than under German law which also allows avoidance for purely internal and even self-inflicted mistakes'.

10

Deceit and Duress

A. Deceit	173
I. Elements	173
II. Non-disclosure as deceit	175
1. Duties to inform in general	175
2. Attribution of duties to inform	177
3. Negligent breach of duties to inform	179
4. 'Duties of disclosure' in English law	180
III. Deceit by third party	182
IV. Claims for damages	184
B. Duress	185
I. Duress and exploitation	185
II. Elements of duress	185
III. Duress by third party	188

A. Deceit

I. Elements

Deceit is like mistake in that anyone deceived into entering a contract does so under a mistake; the difference is that in deceit the mistake is consciously caused by the other party. Thus deceit may be seen as a special case of 'caused mistake'.[1] This is so in English law, which has a special category for mistakes caused by misrepresentation, and distinguishes between innocent or negligent misrepresentation, and those that are made with knowledge of their falsity. In the latter case, one speaks in England of fraudulent misrepresentation, in France and other Romanistic countries of *dol* or *dolo*, in Germany and Switzerland of *arglistige* or *absichtliche Täuschung*, in Austria of *List*, and in the Netherlands of *bedrog*.

A person who has contracted under a mistake would be well advised to base the claim for avoidance not just on mistake but also on deceit, if possible, for then he can obtain damages as well.[2] Sometimes, indeed, avoidance may be allowed for deceit when mistake alone would not suffice, as where the mistake is as to motive or not 'essential'.[3] Sometimes, the period allowed for avoidance is longer for deceit than for

---

[1] See above, pp. 163ff.   [2] See below, pp. 184ff.
[3] This is express in art. 1139 *Code civil* (as recently amended) under which a contract is void for *dol* even though the mistake bears only on the value of the subject matter of the contract or is merely a 'simple motif'. See also art. 28(1) OR; art. 86 Polish Civil Code; Com. 19 Dec. 1961, D. 1962, 240; Civ. 13 Feb. 1967, Bull.cass. 1967.I. no. 58; BG 22 June 1982, BGE 108 II 102, 107; OGH 3 Feb. 1932, SZ 14 no. 18; RG 22 Nov. 1912, RGZ 81, 13, 16; HR 27 Jan. 1950, [1950] *NedJur* no. 559.

mistake. Finally, a contractual term excluding avoidance for mistake does not apply to mistakes due to deceit, since one cannot contract out of liability for fraud. Thus, if a second-hand-car salesman has effectively excluded liability for defects, the buyer cannot avoid the purchase for error as to its qualities,[4] but may be able to do so if he can prove that the salesman lied about the car.

Proof of deceit is not always easy, for it must be established that the representor knew either that what he said was false, or that it might well not be true.[5] Thus it is deceitful to make a statement at random, like a salesman optimistically asserting that a car he has not even examined has only a few scratches,[6] but a person who honestly believes in the truth of what he says is not guilty of deceit, however unreasonable his belief.[7]

The deceit must furthermore be fraudulent (*arglistig*) (§ 123 BGB) or intentional (*absichtlich*) (art. 28 OR), namely undertaken with the aim of inducing the other party to contract. It is not a requirement that the representor intend to harm the other party or realise that harm is likely, though this is often the case. If one asks why a person deceived into buying a thing can avoid the contract even if the thing was worth the price, as the seller knew, and no harm was meant, the reason is that the rules permitting avoidance for deceit are designed to ensure that buyers can make up their mind without being misinformed, rather than to save them from harm.[8]

A person may avoid a contract for deceit only if it induced him to enter the contract, not if he would have entered the contract on the same terms anyway—as is the case if he knows that the other party is lying or would have contracted even if fully informed (*omnimodo facturus*).[9]

Some Romanistic systems suggest that the party deceived can avoid the contract only if he would not have contracted *at all* had he been correctly informed: if he would have contracted, though only on better terms, the case is one of *dolus incidens* and he can only claim damages.[10] The result is that if the judge thinks that the buyer would

---

[4] See above, pp. 151f.
[5] See *Derry v. Peek* (1889) 14 App.Cas. 337, 374: 'Fraud is proved when it is shown that a false representation has been made knowingly without belief in its truth, or recklessly, careless whether it be true or false.'
[6] BGH 18 Mar. 1981, [1981] *NJW* 1441; BGH 8 May 1980, [1980] *NJW* 2460.
[7] In such a case, however, the other party has a claim for damages which, like a claim for avoidance, may result in having the contract undone. See below, pp. 179ff.
[8] See OGH 2 Sept. 1980, SZ 51 no. 52. Also J Ghestin, *Traité de droit civil, La formation du contrat* (1993) no. 561; H Kötz, *Vertragsrecht* (2nd edn, 2012) mn. 338, all with further references.
[9] Such cases are rare. Suppose that the seller of a house states that the lift is in good order when he knows that it is not: the buyer may resile even if he was going to demolish the house anyway. It is true that he is indifferent as to the condition of the lift, but had he not been deceived as to its condition, he would normally have insisted on a lower price, and this is enough to justify avoidance for deceit.
[10] This was based on the wording of the former art. 1116 *Code civil*, whereby the right to avoid arose only if the deceptive practices were such '*qu'il est évident que, sans ces manœuvres, l'autre partie n'aurait pas contracté*'. Likewise art. 1440 *Codice civile*; art. 1270(2) Spanish Civil Code. Some French cases (Civ. 22 June 2005, Bull.cass. 2005.III. no. 137) and commentators (F Terré, P Simler, and Y Lequette, *Droit civil, Les obligations* (11th edn, 2013) no. 238) were opposed to the doctrine of *dolus incidens*. The new art. 1137(1) *Code civil* seems to have abandoned it by providing that there is *dol* if a party managed '*d'obtenir le consentement de l'autre par des manœuvres ou des mensonges*'. The Swiss *Bundesgericht* rejected the doctrine in a long and careful opinion on 4 May 1938, BGE 64 II 144, but has subsequently accepted it on occasion: '*Lorsque la rescision du contrat paraît choquante dans un cas où le dol n'a été qu'incident, le juge peut la refuser et se borner à réduire les prestations du lésé dans la mesure où celui-ci aurait conclu*

still have bought the goods, though at a lower price, had he known the truth and not been deceived about their qualities, damages may be awarded but the contract is not avoided. Quite often the buyer may indeed be content to keep the goods and get damages, but should the buyer not be allowed to avoid the contract if he chooses?

Since statements by a seller as to the value of the goods should not be taken at face value, there is no deceit if a buyer allows himself to be misled by laudatory puffery that no reasonable man would have taken literally.[11] However, if the seller makes specific assertions of fact, the buyer misled by them can avoid the contract even if he could easily have ascertained the truth for himself and so could be said to be negligent.[12]

Generally, no one doubts that there is deceit if a party intentionally makes an incorrect statement in order to induce the other party to contract. But there are exceptional cases where a party is not allowed to avoid a contract though he was told a lie by the other side. This may be the case where a party has a legally protected interest that certain characteristics or qualities about his person should *not* be essential to the decision by the counterparty as to whether to enter into the contract. A woman applying for a job does not have a duty to disclose to the employer that she is pregnant, if she is not asked; but if she is asked, such a question is not allowed and the woman may lie if the employer would interpret a refusal to answer as an affirmation of the question.[13] This must also apply if the legislature—in implementing various EU Directives[14]—seeks to avoid discrimination against a person on the basis of characteristics or qualities based on race, ethnic origin, gender, religion, age, or disability.

II. Non-disclosure as deceit

1. Duties to inform in general

Although several of the Romanistic civil codes suggest that trickery of some sort is required—*manœuvres*,[15] *raggiri*,[16] *maquinaciones insidiosas*[17]—everyone accepts that a simple lie will suffice. Indeed, even silence may constitute deceit. A person who deliberately keeps quiet about facts that he knew, or should have known, were of particular importance to the other party to the negotiations may be guilty of deceit, but only if he was under a duty to proffer such information.[18]

---

le contrat s'il n'avait pas été trompé' (BG 7 June 1955, BGE 81 II 213, 219; see also BG 25 Sept. 1973, BGE 99 II 308).

[11] See Ghestin (n 8) no. 564; Terré, Simler, and Lequette (n 10) no. 232; and on English law, see above, p. 164. According to art. 3:44(3) BW, 'general commendations' are not in themselves to be taken as deceptive.

[12] Redgrave v. Hurd (1881) 20 Ch.D. 1 (CA); BGH 28 Apr. 1971, [1971] *NJW* 1795, 1798; OGH 10 Mar. 1954, SZ 27 no. 63 (150f.); BG 8 June 1906, BGH 32 II 337, 350. Courts in France admittedly hold that one cannot avoid for a mistake which is negligent (above, pp. 162f.), but if the mistake is induced by the *dol* of the other party, it is treated by art. 1139 *Code civil* as '*toujours excusable*'.

[13] See BAG 15 Oct. 1992, [1993] *NJW* 1154; Soc. 2 Feb. 1994, Bull.cass. 1994.V. no. 38 and in detail G Wagner, 'Lügen im Vertragsrecht' in R Zimmermann (ed), *Störungen der Willensbildung bei Vertragsschluß* (2007) 59ff.

[14] For detail, see K Riesenhuber, *EU-Vertragsrecht* (2013) § 6. [15] Article 1137(1) *Code civil*.

[16] Article 1439 *Codice civile*.

[17] Article 1269 Spanish Civil Code; so also art. 253 Portuguese Civil Code.

[18] This is made explicit in the new art. 1137(2) *Code civil* under which *dol* is equally established where a party intentionally conceals information he knows to have a '*caractère déterminant*' for the other party.

Pre-contractual duties of disclosure are sometimes derived from special statutory rules. Anyone wishing to take out an insurance contract must during the pre-contractual negotiations disclose to the insurer all known risk factors which are relevant to the insurer's decision to conclude the contract with the agreed content.[19] Numerous EU Directives have also ensured in recent years that Member States have been required to impose pre-contractual duties on companies to disclose information in consumer contracts. These duties are extraordinarily detailed, sometimes to a quite ridiculous level.[20] In general, it is the courts that must decide whether or not a duty to disclose exists in the individual case. Statutes imposing duties of information tend to be couched in very broad and general terms. Pursuant to art. 3:44 III BW, there is deceit if during pre-contractual negotiations a party remains silent about pertinent circumstances 'which the silent party was under a duty to communicate', but there is nothing on when such a duty exists. Article 1112-1 *Code civil* (as recently amended) attempts to be more specific. It imposes a mandatory duty to disclose all information which is of 'decisive importance' for the other party's consent but only where it was 'legitimate' for the other party to ignore the information or to trust in the silent party's duty of disclosure. Non-compliance with the duty of information may not only lead to the silent party's liability in damages but also to the invalidity of the contract on the ground of the silent party's *dol*.[21]

The *Bundesgerichtshof* tells us that in principle there is a duty 'to inform the other party of matters which could frustrate the other's purpose in entering the contract and which are therefore of vital importance to him, to the extent that he could expect to be so informed according to good business practice'.[22] In Switzerland, the *Bundesgericht* finds an intentional deceit '*dans le silence gardé sur des faits que la bonne foi commerciale exigeait de signaler*'.[23]

The international sets of rules provide some helpful suggestions. They clarify that there is deceit if a party remains silent about information that it should have disclosed 'in accordance with good faith and fair dealing'. In order to substantiate this general

---

[19] See § 19 German Insurance Contract Act (VersVG); art. L 113-8 French Insurance Code.

[20] Such duties to disclose information apply not only to distance selling and consumer credit contracts, but also—as stated in art. 5 of the Directive on Consumer Rights of 25 October 2011 (O.J. 2011 L 304/64)—for *all* consumer contracts: traders must provide consumers with the main characteristics of the goods or services, the trader's address and telephone number, the total price, the arrangements for payment, delivery and performance, and many other details. One is somewhat relieved to find that there is no duty to provide information where it is 'already apparent from the context' or where the consumer contract involves 'day-to-day transactions and which are performed immediately at the time of their conclusion' (art. 5 (3) Consumer Rights Directive). The same provisions can be found in art. 20 CESL; art. 49(1) also states that a trader commits fraud if it induces the consumer to conclude the contract by fraudulent non-disclosure of any pre-contractual information that the trader is required to disclose, as stated in great detail in arts. 13–28 CESL. See Riesenhuber (n 14) § 7 mn. 16ff. and (more or less critical) B Heiderhoff, 'Information Obligations (Consumer Contracts)' in *Max Planck Enc.* (2012) 869; HC Grigoleit, 'Die Aufklärungspflichten des acquis' in H Eidenmüller, F Faust, HC Grigoleit, N Jansen, G Wagner, and R Zimmermann (eds), *Revision des Verbraucher-acquis* (2011) 223, 229ff; Terré, Simler, and Lequette (n 10) no. 261f. See also below, n 26.

[21] Article 1112-1(6) *Code civil*. See also art. 1137(2) *Code civil* (n 18).

[22] BGH 2 Mar. 1979, [1979] *NJW* 2243; BGH 27 Feb. 1974, [1974] *NJW* 849, 851. To like effect is OGH 12 Dec. 1981, [1982] *JBl* 450.

[23] BG 13 May 1931, BGE 57 II 276, 280. Compare also RG 15 Nov. 1911, RGZ 77, 309, 314: 'Silence may constitute fraud where good faith calls for speech.'

formulation, specific circumstances have been set out under which the judge should look at this question. A party is more likely to be given a duty to disclose information if that party has a greater understanding about the information in question (in comparison with the other party), and if the cost of finding out that information is lower (in comparison with the other party). Other relevant considerations are whether the other party might reasonably have been able to find out the information for itself, and how important that information is for the other party.[24] The following shows how these points, and others, have already been taken up by the courts.

2. Attribution of duties to inform

In relation to remunerated transactions, the Reichsgericht said in 1925 that

> as to sales in particular the duty to inform must not be unduly extended. The general view of business is that buyer and seller, given their conflicting interests, cannot expect each other to offer information about market factors relevant to the determination of the price, especially not whether prices are likely to rise or fall; on such matters they must consult disinterested third parties.[25]

Indeed, in a competitive economy the law must encourage people to inform themselves about the qualities, serviceability, and saleability of goods and services. This incentive would be weakened if a party who had acquired such information through training, experience, or research were bound to supply this information to the other party and thus sacrifice any informational advantage.[26] If a firm goes to great expense to discover that there is probably oil underneath a given tract of land, it need not inform the owners of its discovery on approaching them with a view to purchase. Nor need an art expert who scours the market for bargains tell the owners what their treasures are really worth.[27] A similar situation existed in the famous case given by Cicero: hearing of a famine in Rhodes, an Egyptian merchant sailed there with a cargo

---

[24] See art. 4:107(3) PECL; art. II.-7:105(3) DCFR; art. 49(3) CESL.

[25] RG 7 July 1925, RGZ 111, 233, 234f. Likewise OGH 15 July 1981, [1982] JBl. 86, 87.

[26] See AT Kronman, 'Mistake, Disclosure, Information and the Law of Contract' (1978) 7 *J Leg Stud* 1; P Legrand, 'Precontractual Disclosure and Information: English and French Law Compared' (1986) 6 *OJLS* 322; B Nicholas, 'The Precontractual Obligation to Disclose Information' in D Harris and D Tallon (eds), *Contract Law Today, Anglo-French Comparisons* (1989) 166; S Waddams, 'Precontractual Duties of Disclosure' (1991) 19 *Can. BJ* 349; H Kötz, 'Precontractual Duties of Disclosure from a Comparative and Economic Perspective' (2000) 9 *Eur J of Law & Ec* 5; M Fabre-Magnan, 'Duties of Disclosure and French Contract Law' in J Beatson and D Friedman (eds), *Good Faith and Fault in Contract Law* (1995) 99; B Rudden, 'Le juste et l'inefficace, Pour un non-devoir de renseignements' [1985] *Rev trim civ* 91. A devastating critique of the modern tendency to impose information duties is O Ben-Shahar and C Schneider, 'The Failure of Mandated Disclosure' (2011) 159 *U.Pa. LR* 647.

[27] In the *Poussin* case (see above, p. 157), the seller who had sold a painting for a song that later turned out to be by Poussin was admittedly allowed to avoid the sale for mistake. The buyer was the *Musée du Louvre*, whose experts had presumably kept an eye on the Paris art auctions and doubtless exercised the state's right of pre-emption because they had a hunch about the painting's authenticity. The decision has rightly been criticised on the ground that it discourages collectors who can tell the excellent from the average: 'Sanctionner une telle aptitude est sanctionner en même temps ceux qui ont le plus de goût, de flair ou de l'oeil, bref tous ceux qui font progresser l'histoire de l'art.' (J Chatelain in (1982) 102 *Rép not Defrénois* 681, 682f.) *A fortiori* avoidance should be barred when it is only *after* the purchase that the buyer manages to discover the true value of the object purchased (see above, p. 157).

of wheat and sold it at a vast price, without divulging that *en route* he had sighted other vessels similarly bound which would surely cause the price to fall. Cicero thought the merchant should have disclosed this fact,[28] but this is questionable, for we should not rob merchants of the incentive to help the victims of famine in the best way, namely by getting food as fast as possible to the place where it is most needed. Then there was a case in the *Bundesgerichtshof*, where a businessman assigned the broadcasting rights in an American television series reserved to himself a right to 50 per cent of the proceeds of any sub-licence that the assignee might grant. He later released this right against payment of $10,000, and then sought to avoid the release on the ground that the assignee had failed to tell him that there was increased interest in the shows and that it had already received an offer of DM 8.3 million for a sub-licence. Both lower courts held that the company was under no duty of disclosure in the circumstances and dismissed the businessman's claim, but the *Bundesgerichtshof* reversed on the ground that there had been a long-standing and close business relationship between the parties, indeed even a personal connection.[29] This decision is dubious. The claimant was a professional licensing agent, he had himself proposed the deal (which was clearly speculative), and he could easily have discovered the change in the market for himself. The close business and personal relationship between the parties is surely immaterial: tradesmen know full well where friendship stops and business begins.[30]

There is accordingly no duty to proffer information that is the product of one's own efforts in evaluating market conditions or ascertaining the attributes of property that enhance its value. But it is different if the party with superior information acquired it just by chance, happened upon it by serendipity without any real investment, or was able to come by it very much more cheaply than the other party. Thus there is an obligation on manufacturers and distributors, who either know or can easily find out about the special properties of the things they deal in, to inform the buyer about the goods—all the more so if the buyer would be put to great expense to obtain the same information by himself.[31]

This is why used-car salesmen are generally regarded as bound to volunteer information about faults in the vehicle; as an non-professional, the customer could only discover such information at considerably greater expense, and the information is clearly material to the customer's decision as whether or not to buy.[32] The seller of land

---

[28] Cicero, *De officiis* 3.50 and 57. Hugo Grotius, however, thought the merchant had acted with permissible cunning (*licita sollertia*), see *De iure belli ac pacis libri tres* (1625) II 12.9.2.

[29] BGH 31 Jan. 1979, LM § 123 BGB no. 52.

[30] It would be different, as is universally recognised, if there was a fiduciary relationship between the parties such that one party could count on the other to disclose all relevant information. Such a relationship exists between parties to a trust, partnership, employment, or agency relationship. On German law, see C Armbrüster in *Münchener Kommentar zum BGB* (6th edn, 2012) § 123 BGB mn. 32; on French law, see Ghestin (n 8) no. 657ff; on English law, see below, p. 180.

[31] If such parties were to bargain over whether the seller should provide the information and charge extra, or remain silent and charge less, they would choose the first alternative, which is better for both of them. Of course parties do not in fact bargain over the matter, since it would cost too much, but if this amounts to a gap in the parties' agreement, the legal system should adopt a rule which fills the omission as the parties themselves would have filled it if they had in fact bargained over the matter.

[32] See, for example, Civ. 19 June 1985, Bull.cass. 1985.I. no. 201 (it is fraudulent of a used-car salesman not to tell a private customer that a four-year-old car has an eleven-year-old reconditioned engine); OGH 5 Sept. 1973, SZ 46 no. 84 (a dealer 'causes' a mistake by the buyer of an apparently decent used car if he omits to say that the chassis is rusty and 'really a wreck'); BGH 3 Mar. 1982, [1982] *NJW* 1386 (the

also must make spontaneous disclosure of matters which he must know are material to the buyer and would cost the buyer a lot to discover, such as the suitability of the terrain for building or features of the house the seller has learned about simply through living in the building. If, for example, the seller knows that the business intended by the buyer needs a water supply or a chimney erected, the seller must reveal the fact that there is no connection to the water mains[33] or that building a chimney would not be allowed.[34] Equally, the seller must disclose that a house apparently solidly constructed of brick is in fact timber-framed,[35] or that dry rot had affected the roof area and, though treated, might recur.[36] If the seller tells the buyer that the planning authority has given permission for construction, the seller must also reveal that the decision is under appeal.[37] If a building is sold as 'residential and business premises', the seller must tell the buyer that while the authorities had indeed approved the use of part of the building for residential purposes, this permission had been withdrawn.[38] But there is no duty on the seller to inform the buyer of matters which the buyer can learn just as easily as himself: in selling a café, the seller need not mention that another café is about to be opened next door if the buyer could see the building operations for himself, and find out as easily as the seller what kind of business was to be opened there.[39]

3. Negligent breach of duties to inform

A party who has failed to inform the other party when he was under a duty to do so is guilty of deceit only if he was aware of the facts he should have disclosed, and knew that his silence would lead the other party into an error which would induce or contribute to conclusion of the contract. In many jurisdictions, however, a merely negligent breach of a duty to inform may entitle the other party to avoid the contract and claim damages. In one case before the *Cour de cassation*, the owner of a plot of land for which the authorities had granted building permission divided it into three plots, one of which was bought by the plaintiff who proposed to build a house on it. It then

---

salesman must spontaneously inform the buyer that although the car is a relatively recent model, it had been involved in a serious accident requiring extensive repairs). Courts often justify such decisions by saying that the buyer 'should have been able to rely' on the expertise of the seller, which hardly squares with the fact that used-car salesmen are widely regarded as rather untrustworthy. The true reason for protecting the buyer is not that he 'trusts' the seller, but because it would not be sensible to make the buyer bear the consequences of an error which the seller could correct at very *little* cost, and the buyer could only correct with *a great deal* of expense.

[33] Civ. 7 May 1974, Bull.cass. 1974.III. no. 186. [34] BGH 16 Oct. 1987, [1988] *NJW-RR* 394.
[35] OGH 20 Apr. 1955, SZ 28 no. 103. [36] BGH 23 Feb. 1989, [1989] *NJW-RR* 972.
[37] Civ. 25 Feb. 1987, Bull.cass. 1987.III. no. 36. [38] BGH 16 June 1988, [1988] *NJW-RR* 1290.
[39] Versailles 21 May 1986, D.S. 1986, 560, n. M Jeantin. But see Civ. 27 Mar. 1991, Bull.cass. 1991. III. no. 108 and the remarks of J Mestre in (1992) 91 *Rev trim dr civ* 81: When a seller sought to avoid his sale of land to the local commune on the ground that it had failed to inform him that it had already initiated a change in the development plan, the *Cour de cassation* held that it was wrong in law for the lower court to ignore this fact. But could the seller himself not have found out about the proposed alteration and the consequent increase in the value of his land? Equally worthy of criticism is a decision of the same court which allowed a guarantor to resile from his guarantee on the ground that the bank was guilty of *dol par réticence* in not volunteering the information '*que la situation du débiteur est irrémédiablement compromise ou à tout le moins lourdement obérée*'. (Civ. 10 May 1989, Bull.cass. 1989.I. no. 187). To the same effect, however, is HR 1 June 1990, [1991] *NedJur* 759.

appeared that the authorities had not consented to the division of the plot, and that the building permission covered only the whole plot and not just the parcel bought by the plaintiff. The buyer succeeded in having the contract avoided, although there was no finding that the seller had known of the lack of building permission: the buyer was a private citizen and the seller, as a property company with specialist knowledge, was under a duty to give him precise information.[40] Here a professional seller's negligent breach of the duty to give information was treated as fraud. But occasionally the French courts have gone even further and, without asking whether the breach amounts to fraud, hold that mere silence in breach of duty automatically gives rise to a liability in damages (and thus also to the avoidance of the contract).[41]

One can see the same thing happening in Germany, Switzerland, and Austria, where it has long been accepted that in principle each party to the negotiations is bound to consider the interests of the other, and must, depending on the circumstances, furnish appropriate information and advice. Culpable breach of this duty leads to liability in damages for *culpa in contrahendo*.[42] This does not fit easily with the wording of § 123 BGB, § 870 ABGB, and art. 28 OR, which are obviously based on the idea that a contract can be avoided for non-disclosure only when silence amounts to deceit. Nevertheless the courts in Germany have always held that a contractor

> who has been badly advised and misled by the fault of his partner may, even if the preconditions of avoidance for fraud are not present, bring an action for damages based on fault in the formation of the contract and claim release from its legal consequences.[43]

4. 'Duties of disclosure' in English law

English law does not accept that there is any general duty of disclosure in pre-contractual negotiations.[44] Exceptions may be found in a few dispersed factual situations, but they are not yet recognised as resting on any general principle. The traditional viewpoint, smacking of robust Victorian individualism, is that each party

---

[40] Civ. 3 Feb. 1981, D. 1984, 457, n. J Ghestin. See also Com. 13 Oct. 1980, D.S. 1981.I.R.309, n. J Ghestin.

[41] See now art. 1112-1 and art. 1137(2) *Code civil* (n 18 and n 21). See also Civ. 28 May 2008, Bull.cass. 2008.I. no. 154: a seller had negligently failed to inform the buyer of an apartment that the view out over greenery would be impacted by a planned building on a neighbouring plot. The *Cour de cassation* held that the buyer could demand damages because the behaviour of the seller '*s'analysait aussi en un manquement de l'obligation précontractuelle d'information*'. See the comment by D Looschelders [2009] 17 *ZEuP* 800.

[42] Liability for damages has long been accepted by the German courts, and now also has statutory support from §§ 311(2), 276, 280 BGB. See, for example, Kötz (n 8) mn. 359ff. Similar—at least by result—is Austrian and Swiss law. See, for example, RH Weber in *Berner Kommentar* vol. VI (2000) art. 97 OR mn. 88ff; P Rummel in *Kommentar zum ABGB* (3rd edn, 2000) before § 918 ABGB mn. 14ff.

[43] BGH 2 Apr. 1969, [1969] *NJW* 1625, 1626; see also BGH 26 Sept. 1997, [1998] *NJW* 302; BGH 6 April 2001, [2001] *NJW* 2875. The courts find this solution attractive, because by holding that the defendant negligently breached a duty of information they can, without exposing him to the ignominy of being found fraudulent, make him liable in damages and so release the claimant from the contract.

[44] On what follows, see Nicholas (n 26); Legrand (n 26) 323ff; P Atiyah, *An Introduction to the Law of Contract* (6th edn, by SA Smith, 2005) 241ff; Waddams (n 26); GH Treitel, *The Law of Contract* (13th edn, by Edwin Peel, 2011) no. 9-123ff; E McKendrick, *Contract Law* (8th edn, 2009) no. 12.1–7.

must equip itself with such information as it needs for decision-making, and cannot look to the other party to volunteer such information, even if the latter was aware of the other party's mistake and could easily have put him right.[45]

But any statement actually made in negotiations must be accurate, and the statement is inaccurate if it is misleading through being incomplete. A seller who says quite truly that the house on offer is currently let to a tenant for an annual rent of £950 will be guilty of misrepresentation if he omits to add that the tenant is insolvent or has just given notice to terminate the lease.[46] Further, if a statement made during the negotiations was true when made, but later becomes false to the knowledge of the person who made it, he must correct it.[47] Extensive duties of disclosure attach also to contracts of insurance, partnership, employment, and other 'contracts *uberrimae fidei*', and also to contracts to which, as a result of a 'fiduciary relationship' between the parties, the rules on undue influence apply—such as contracts between trustee and beneficiary, guardian and ward, parent and child, lawyer and client, doctor and patient, or principal and agent.[48]

Despite these instances, one has the impression that English law, unlike continental systems, is reluctant to admit pre-contractual duties of disclosure. This is sometimes criticised by commentators. It is said that it works for transactions between persons experienced in business affairs, but can sometimes lead to unfortunate consequences for contracts between private parties.[49] The vendor of land must tell the truth when asked by the buyer about defects; but the vendor may also choose to remain silent that there is woodworm in the rafters, the utility pipes are defective, or that construction of a new bypass is about to start close to the property. But the difference is perhaps not as great as it first appears. Continental courts also do not require a seller to disclose deficiencies that are obvious, or can be discovered equally well by both parties.[50] In some of the above cases, by contrast, the English courts would grant a buyer damages.[51] But

---

[45] See *Smith* v. *Hughes* (1871) LR 6 QB 597, holding that a buyer who supposed that the goods had a certain quality is bound by the contract even if the seller knew that he was wrong and failed to correct him 'for, whatever may be the case in a court of morals, there is no legal obligation on the vendor to inform the purchaser that he is under a mistake, not induced by the act of the vendor' (at 606f. per Blackburn J).

[46] See *Dimmock* v. *Hallett* (1866) 2 Ch.App. 21. Had the seller kept entirely quiet, the answer would presumably be different, even if he knew that the buyer supposed the tenant to be solvent or that the lease was still in force.

[47] See *With* v. *O'Flanagan* [1936] Ch. 575; *Davis* v. *London & Provincial Marine Ins. Co.* (1878) 8 Ch.D. 469. But see also *Wales* v. *Wadham* [1977] 1 WLR 199.

[48] See also pp. 114, 303.

[49] See, for example, Atiyah (n 44) 243; McKendrick (n 44) no. 12.1ff. One must keep in mind that legislation on contracts for the supply of goods and services makes the supplier impliedly liable for breach of contract should the goods or services turn out to be unsatisfactory or unfit for the buyer's stated purpose. See, for example, Sale of Goods Act 1979, s. 14; Supply of Goods and Services Act 1982, s. 13 and similar legislation in continental countries. In these cases, there is no need for the buyer to rely on the seller's breach of a duty of information. He will simply avail himself of his remedies for breach of contract.

[50] See, for example, BGH 13 July 1988, [1989] *NJW* 763: The principle is that 'the party who concludes a contract must ... ascertain to his own satisfaction whether or not there is an advantage for him. The other party may rely on this, and need not refer to circumstances that he might assume he would be asked about if they were considered to be important.'

[51] So in the case detailed under n 38 above, for *misrepresentation*, in the cases detailed under n 39 and n 41 for breach of the (express or silent) affirmation that the house sold was a 'residential house' or that the parcel of land sold 'could be built on'. In other cases, there may be a claim for damages for the tort of negligence, as where a person puts a thing into circulation without taking care to specify how it can safely be used.

in transactions between private parties, a pre-contractual duty to disclose information should be supported with regard to defects known to the seller that are latent, or for other reasons can only be uncovered by the buyer at very considerable expense. Thus there are sound reasons in these cases for an economically correct allocation of risk. As to contracts made between businessmen in an ordinary commercial context, however, the situation is different. An English judge once commented that the rule that there is no obligation to speak within the context of negotiations

> is one of the foundations of our law of contract ... There are countless cases in which one party to a contract has in the course of negotiations failed to disclose a fact known to him which the other party would have regarded as highly material, if it had been revealed. However, ordinarily in the absence of misrepresentation, our law leaves that other party without a remedy.[52]

III. Deceit by third party

What if the deceit is practised not by the other party to the contract, but by someone else? Here, too, the misled party's intention has been influenced by a deceit and has thus been 'defective' in its conclusion. But when the other party to the contract was not involved in the deceit, that other party has an interest in its being upheld, and this interest is regarded as primary. So the contract cannot be avoided. The misled party may have suffered a loss because of the contract, but must look to the third party who deceived him in order to recover that loss.

Most European codes therefore provide that deceit committed by a 'third party' does not entitle the party misled to avoid the contract.[53] 'Third party' here does not include any representative, agent, assistant, or other person entrusted with conducting negotiations on behalf of the other party. A principal who allows negotiations to be conducted on his behalf by someone else must accept that the intermediary's fraud will be treated as his own.[54] It is irrelevant whether or not the principal was aware of the intermediary's deceit, or whether or not the intermediary was deviating from the principal's instructions.[55] In England, too, deceit practised by an agent acting for his principal during negotiations is treated as being the deceit of the principal.[56]

---

[52] *Banque Financière* v. *Westgate Insurance Co.* [1989] 2 All ER 952 (per Justice Slade at 1010).
[53] See § 123 BGB; art. 28(2) OR; § 875 ABGB; art. 3:44(5) BW; art. 147 Greek Civil Code; art. 1439(2) *Codice civile*; art. 254(2) Portuguese Civil Code; art. 86(2) Polish Civil Code; and see also § 30(1) Swedish Contract Law.
[54] Under art. 1138(1) *Code civil* a contract may be avoided for *dol* even if it originates from the other party's representative, a person who manages his affairs, his employee, or from a person standing surety for him.
[55] OGH 28 June 1967, [1968] *JBl* 365; OGH 15 Oct. 1970, [1971] *JBl* 304; BGH 8 Feb. 1956, BGHZ 20, 36, 39f; BG 10 Feb. 1937, BGE 63 II 77; BG 7 June 1955, BGE 81 II 213, 217; Com. 27 Nov. 1972, Bull.cass. 1972.IV. no. 308; Civ. 2 Nov. 1954, Gaz.Pal. 1955.1.74. See also art. 4:111(1) PECL; art. II.-7:208(1) DCFR: a party must stand by the behaviour of a third party as if it were its own behaviour if it is 'responsible' for the behaviour of the third party, or if the third party carried out the deceit on the other party with its approval. Similarly art. 3.2.8(1) PICC.
[56] 'Every person who authorizes another to act for him in the making of any contract, undertakes for the absence of fraud in that person in the execution of the authority given, as much as he undertakes for its absence in himself when he makes the contract.' (*Weir* v. *Bell* (1878) 3 Ex.D. 238, 245 per Bramwell

It follows from the general principle that a person who gives a guarantee to a bank or other creditor cannot avoid liability under it by showing that he was deceived by the principal debtor. The debtor is a 'third party', even if he was told by the bank to conduct the negotiations with the guarantor and equipped with a form for the guarantor to sign.[57]

A person who buys goods on credit and borrows money to pay for them cannot avoid liability under the loan on proving that the seller deceived him into making the purchase.[58] The sale and the loan are independent contracts, and deceit leading to one does not justify avoiding the other. It is different, however, where the two contracts are closely linked, such as when seller and bank had a prior agreement that the seller might make the necessary arrangements for the customer to finance the sale by taking out the loan. As early as 1956, the *Bundesgerichtshof* held that in such a case the customer could avoid the contract of loan even if it was the seller who deceived him into entering the sale contract.[59] Since then, most European countries have adopted statutes on consumer credit that contain rules to this effect.[60]

It remains true that one is not entitled to avoid a contract, except perhaps a gift,[61] on the ground of deceit practised by an extraneous third party. It is different where the other party was aware of the third party's deceit, and now wants to take advantage of the transaction. Most codes say this expressly.[62] The same must be true of a contractor who did not actually know of the third party's deceit, but must in the circumstances have suspected it and could easily have ascertained the truth of the matter.[63] Thus, when a bank knows that a customer who wants a loan for his business will ask his wife to accept liability and agree to a mortgage on a property she owns, it must realise that the husband may well dissimulate or downplay the risks of the transaction, or induce the wife to assume them 'by kicks or kisses'. Here

---

LJ). Compare also *Briess v. Woolley* [1954] AC 333, 348; *London County Freehold v. Berkeley Property Co.* [1936] 2 All ER 1039; *Kingsnorth Trust v. Bell* [1986] 1 All ER 423. See also *Barclays Bank v. O'Brien* [1994] 1 AC 180 (HL).

[57] Civ. 26 Jan. 1977, Bull.cass. 1977.I. no. 52; Civ. 28 June 1978, Bull.cass. 1978.I. no. 246; BGH 5 Apr. 1965, [1965] *WM* 473. But see OGH 29 Apr. 1971, SZ 44 no. 59: by authorising the debtor to conduct the negotiations with the guarantor, the bank constituted him 'a person of trust' *vis-à-vis* the guarantor, who was exceptionally allowed to avoid the contract when the debtor deceived him.

[58] So stated in terms by Com. 14 Dec. 1977, Bull.cass. 1977.IV. no. 293.

[59] BGH 8 Feb. 1956, BGHZ 20, 36 and constantly thereafter.

[60] See, for example, § 359 BGB; art. L. 311-20ff. *Code de la consommation*. See also Consumer Credit Act 1974, s. 56: if a supplier who is in relations with a bank negotiates with a customer over a sale which is to be financed by the bank, the seller is held to be negotiating 'in the capacity of agent of the creditor', from which it follows that deceit on the part of the seller as agent renders the bank liable as principal (see above, n 56). Similar rules have since come into force in all Member States of the European Union; see art. 15(2) of the EC Directive of 23 April 2008 on Consumer Credit Contracts (O.J. EC 2008 L 133/66).

[61] In France, a gratuitous promise induced by the fraud of a third party may be avoided, see Ghestin (n 8) no. 573 (*ad fin.*). So, too, art. 86(2) Polish Civil Code.

[62] See the texts listed above, n 53. Also art. 4:111(1) PECL; art. II.-7:208(1) DCFR: a party must stand for the behaviour of a third party for which it was 'responsible' or who with a party's assent is involved in the making of a contract. Similarly, art. 3.2.8 (1) PICC.

[63] See the texts listed above, n 53. However, the deceived party must be allowed to avoid the contract if the other party was not aware of (and should not be aware of) the deceitful behaviour of the third party, but 'has not acted in reliance on the contract'.

English courts hold that the bank has 'constructive notice' of such deception, and grant the wife a defence to the bank's claim. How can the bank avoid this? The English courts require the bank to inform the wife prior to the contract that she should seek independent legal advice in the absence of her husband, and that the bank concluded the contract only after having received written confirmation from a lawyer that the wife has been properly informed of the nature and extent of the risks of the transaction.[64]

IV. Claims for damages

The primary concern of a person who has entered a disadvantageous contract as a result of deceit or erroneous or inadequate information will be to escape from liability. Sometimes, however, it may not be enough to simply avoid the contract. The person may have taken steps in reliance on its validity which cannot easily be undone at no cost, or may have forgone the chance of making another contract on better terms than those now available. Can that person demand damages for such loss? Most jurisdictions think it can, even in cases where the other party did not 'deceive' the innocent party in the strong sense of the word, but was merely negligent in providing incorrect or incomplete information or in breaching a duty to provide correct information. There is less agreement on the legal basis of this claim for damages. In France, a misrepresentation made in pre-contractual negotiations is treated as a delict, and the claim is based on art. 1240 f. (formerly 1382 f.) *Code civil*. In England, too, such claims are laid in tort: deceit if the misrepresentation is deliberate, negligence or under the Misrepresentation Act 1967 if it is not. In Germany, one may claim in delict under § 826 BGB, but in practice claimants prefer to base their claim on the defendant's breach, whether intentional or negligent, of the pre-contractual duty to inform: the rules of *culpa in contrahendo* which then apply are akin to those for breach of contract.[65]

This is consistent with the international sets of rules allowing the deceived party a claim for damages if the other party knew of the deceit, or should have known;[66] the same claim also applies if the party is induced into concluding a contract by the counterparty's negligent mistake. If the contract is avoided for deceit (or negligent mistake), the aim of the damages is 'to put the avoiding party as nearly as possible into the same position as if it had not concluded the contract'. If the contract is not avoided, because the avoidance time limit has passed, or because the deceived party or party suffering from the mistake wishes to confirm the contract, the claim for damages will be based on balancing out the disadvantage caused by the deceit or mistake.[67]

---

[64] See above, pp. 114ff. and art. 4:111(2) PECL; art. II.7:208(2) DCFR; art. 3.2.8(2) PICC.
[65] See above, n 42.   [66] Article 4:117 PECL; art. 3.2.16 PICC; art. II.-7:214 DCFR.
[67] See art. 4:117(2) PECL and art. II.-7:214(2) DCFR.

B. Duress

I. Duress and exploitation

In all continental systems, duress figures along with error and deceit as factors that vitiate intention. A person subjected to *Drohung*,[68] well-grounded fear,[69] *violence*,[70] intimidación,[71] or *coacçao moral*[72] which put him in a predicament where he rightly feared 'that he or someone close to him was threatened with an imminent and serious danger to life and limb, honour or property'[73] may seek release from a contract he entered into in order to avert that danger.

English law says that such a contract is voidable for duress, but nowadays duress of an economic nature (economic duress) can also lead to invalidity. Such a case would be if a party threatened economic disadvantages against the counterparty, but is not justified in making such threats, and the counterparty only concluded the contract in order to avoid the disadvantages. Closely related to this (and they are often difficult to tell apart) are the rules on undue influence, whereby a party can avoid a disadvantageous contract if it can show that it was concluded due to 'undue influence' from the other party. Such undue influence will be assumed mostly in cases where there is a special relationship of trust between the parties, thus invoking the presumption that the party abused the position of trust.[74]

II. Elements of duress

Often a person is not really free to decide whether or not to enter a contract, but rather faces a choice of evils, between the evil of accepting the offer or the evil of declining it. It is not duress for the offeror to highlight the disadvantages of refusing the offer; this constitutes a mere warning about the consequences. It is a threat if the offeror highlights disadvantages that he can influence should the party decline the offer, but such threats are also permitted until they cross the bounds of legitimacy and become duress. Legislative texts try to mark these limits by providing that a contract cannot be avoided simply for duress, but that the party applying the pressure must have acted 'unlawfully'.[75] This shows that it is not quite accurate to consider duress as vitiating intention, as if it were some defect which falsified, violated, or affected the will of the person pressurised. After all, the person under pressure knows exactly what he intends to do: if a gun is held to someone's head, he will hand over his wallet and will

---

[68] See § 123 BGB; art. 3:44(2) BW; §§ 28 and 29 Swedish Contract Law; arts. 150, 151 Greek Civil Code; art. 87 Polish Civil Code.
[69] Article 29(1) OR; see also § 870 ABGB.
[70] Article 1140 *Code civil*; art. 1434 *Codice civile*; art. 1267 Spanish Civil Code.
[71] Article 1267 Spanish Civil Code.   [72] Article 255 Portuguese Civil Code.
[73] Article 30(1) OR. There are similar descriptions in art. 1140 *Code civil*; arts. 1435, 1436 *Codice civile*; art. 151 Greek Civil Code; art. 1267(2) Spanish Civil Code.
[74] See above, p. 114.
[75] See § 123 BGB; art. 29(1) OR; § 870 ABGB; art. 3:44(2) BW; art. 150 Greek Civil Code; art. 255(1) Portuguese Civil Code.

intend to do so. If the pressurised party is allowed to avoid the contract, although he entered it quite deliberately and in full awareness of the situation, it must be because the legal system discountenances the conduct of the person whose threats engineered the situation.[76] For example, if the buyer places an order only because the seller threatens to otherwise stop deliveries under earlier contracts, we must ask whether anything in the situation permits us to describe the seller's conduct as improper, as could be the case if he were unlawfully abusing a dominant position in the market.[77]

It is clearly illegitimate to threaten the other party with anything that is unlawful, regardless of motive. For example, if someone threatens to beat or kill the other party,[78] to impound his goods,[79] or get him put behind bars by making a perjured statement.[80] The case is more difficult when what is threatened is not unlawful in itself. One instance is where the person making the threat has a right to do so—for example, to bring a legal claim, initiate a prosecution, protest a negotiable instrument for non-payment, or terminate a contract. Under art. 1438 *Codice civile*, to constitute duress such a threat must be designed to procure an 'unjustified' advantage or, as art. 30(2) OR puts it, be one which is 'excessive'.[81] In France, the *Cour de cassation* insists on 'abusive' conduct; this is satisfied when court process is *détourné de son but* or used for other than its proper purposes, or where its aim is to obtain an advantage which is quite disproportionate or unrelated to the original obligation of the party threatened.[82] Also someone who threatens to use a means that he or she is entitled to take is also acting improperly if the use of such means requires the threatened person to do something that is prohibited. A person who knows that another has committed a crime is perfectly entitled to make a criminal complaint, but it is abusive to demand hush money as the price of not doing so.[83]

---

[76] See the convincing arguments to this effect in P Atiyah, 'Economic Duress and the "Overborne Will"' (1982) 98 *LQR* 197.

[77] The unlawfulness of such conduct normally arises from the rules of competition law; in Germany, see §§ 20 GWB, in France arts. 420-2, 442-6 *Code de commerce*.

[78] *Barton v. Armstrong* [1976] AC 104.   [79] *Maskell v. Horner* [1915] 3 KB 106 (CA).

[80] If a union threatens to strand a ship by calling the seamen out on strike unless the shipowner pays a certain sum to their social fund, any payment made may be reclaimed as paid under duress, unless the union was engaged in a lawful industrial dispute. See *Universe Tankships v. International Transport Workers' Federation* [1983] 1 AC 366 and *Dimskal Shipping Co. v. International Transport Workers' Federation* [1991] 4 All ER 871.

[81] See also art. 255(3) Portuguese Civil Code, whereby a threat to exercise a right in a 'normal' manner does not amount to *coacçao moral*.

[82] Civ. 17 Jan. 1984, Bull.cass. 1984.III. no. 13; see also the first instance decision of Paris 8 July 1982, D.S. 1983, 473, n. D Landraud. Article 1141 *Code civil* now provides that the threat of legal action is lawful, but may exceptionally constitute *violence* if such action 'est détournée de son but ou lorsqu'elle est invoquée ou exercée pour obtenir un avantage manifestement excessif'. This also includes cases where a captain accepts payment of an exorbitant sum to a salvage company to rescue his distressed ship. Can the shipowner then avoid the salvage contract and refuse to pay because the contract was concluded under 'economic duress'? Such a draconian decision could only be justified if it would prevent salvage companies from demanding overly high salvage fees. But the correct solution must surely be to reduce the salvage fee so as to give the salvage companies sufficient incentive to continue providing their economically desirable services. See Civ. 27. Apr. 1887, D.P. 1888.1.263; *The Port Caledonia* [1903] P. 184: RE Cooper, 'Between a Rock and a Hard Place: Illegitimate Pressure in Commercial Negotiations' [1997] 71 *Austr. LJ* 686 and the provisions passed by national jurisdictions in light of the International Convention on Salvage of 28 April 1989. For details, see TN Trümper, 'Salvage' in *Max Planck Enc.* (2012) 1517.

[83] BG 21 Nov. 1950, BGE 76 II 346, 368f. This approach is set out in art. 4:108 PECL, art. 3.2.6 PICC, art. II.-7:206 DCFR, which state that something is a threat when it is a disadvantageous conduct that is

A person may threaten to submit a criminal complaint or institute civil proceedings if he has suffered damage from the party and simply wants swifter or fuller compensation, but even here what is demanded must not be disproportionate to the original obligation but approximately equal in value. Thus, if a debtor agrees to sell his creditor a piece of land in order to ward off a threat of court proceedings, he cannot undo the deal if the price is fair.[84] But annulment is possible if at the notary's office the creditor suddenly insists that the neighbouring plot also be included in the sale, or he will ruin the debtor within the week by protesting a bill of exchange.[85] The matter is particularly tricky when a threat to bring proceedings against a suspect is used to exact a benefit from his spouse or other relative. The *Bundesgerichtshof* has treated such a threat as permissible if the wife was at all implicated in the husband's crime or profited from it in some way or other,[86] but otherwise the wife could avoid the transaction, whether for duress[87] or, in England, for undue influence.[88]

It quite often happens that a party to an existing contract wants it modified, and backs up his wish with an implication that otherwise he will not perform at all. Of course, the party threatened can refuse the proposed modification and sue for damages for breach of contract if the threat is carried out, but this is often impracticable and too much to expect. If an employee is told that unless he agrees to a prejudicial modification of the terms of his employment he will forfeit his wages, one can hardly expect him to stand firm, sue for the wages withheld, and live off his savings in the meantime. The employee will normally give in to the employer's pressure and agree to the modification. If so, he should be able to avoid his agreement on the grounds of duress.[89] In one case, an importer of four carloads of eggs was faced with a demand for an extra payment for the last two carloads, backed by a threat that otherwise the two already *en route* would be diverted. The buyer submitted under protest to the seller's demand, since he would have had to sue him in a foreign court, and the buyer was allowed to avoid his agreement and refuse to pay the agreed supplement.[90]

From this, one can draw the general conclusion that a threat is generally not allowed if A demands that B amend an existing contract and threatens that if B does not agree to the change, then he will not perform the original contract. Here A is threatening a

---

permissible per se, but is 'wrongful' to use as a means to obtain the conclusion of the contract under the circumstances. See also S Martens, 'Duress' in *Max Planck Enc.* (2012) 505.

[84] Civ. 17 Jan. 1984 (n 82).   [85] BGH 25 June 1965, LM § 123 BGB no. 32.
[86] BGH 23 Sept. 1957, BGHZ 25, 217; see also BGH 20 Nov. 1972, [1973] *WM* 36; BGH 16 Mar. 1973, [1973] *WM* 574.
[87] OLG Karlsruhe 11 Jan. 1991, [1992] VersR 703. If there is no threat, the contract may also be invalid for being contrary to public policy pursuant to § 138(1) BGB. But this requires that a party intentionally abused the particular predicament of the counterparty and that the party's behaviour under the circumstances appeared to be 'objectionable'. See BGH 7 June 1988, [1988] *NJW* 2599 and above, p. 116. It has been held in France that there can also be an unlawful threat if a party seeks to exploit the 'economic inferiority' of the other party and thereby secures a disproportionate advantage. See Civ. 30 May 2000, D. 2000, 879, n. JP Chazal = [2000] *Rev.trim.civ.* 827, n. J Mestre and BF Fages, and the critical observations by Terré, Simler, and Lequette (n 10) no. 248. The matter now seems to have been decided by the new art. 1143 *Code civil: violence* includes a case in which a party, by abusing the other side's '*état de dépendance*', extracts from him '*un avantage manifestement excessif*'.
[88] *Kaufman v. Gerson* [1904] 1 KB 591; *Mutual Finance Ltd. v. John Wetton & Sons* [1937] 2 KB 389; and Treitel (n 44) no. 10-009.
[89] Thus Soc. 30 Oct. 1973, Bull.cass. 1973.V. no. 541.   [90] BG 6 Oct. 1906, BGE 32 II 641.

breach of contract, which is a type of behaviour that is not permitted, and thus renders the threat wrongful. But there is doubt as to whether this approach is always correct. Should it not turn on whether or not the threatened party had sufficient time to carefully weigh up the options, and whether or not the threatened party gave up without a fight or only agreed to the change under protest? Should the threatened party lose the right to avoid the amendment to the contract when it had a 'reasonable alternative', namely could have rejected the amendment demands and made clear to the threatening party that damages would be demanded if he carried out the threat and failed to perform under the contract?[91] Should importance not also be placed on whether or not the amendment demanded appears reasonable perhaps because it corrected an obvious imbalance in the original contract, or remedies an omission in a reasonable manner? Identifying the difference between a (permitted) warning and a (prohibited) threat can also be difficult. So if a building construction company 'threatens' that it is in financial difficulties, and despite its best efforts may not be in a position to fulfil a construction contract, it could be that the principal will agree to pay a supplement on top of the existing contract price. Can the principal who is subsequently sued for non-payment of the supplement defend the claim by stating that the contract to pay the supplement was agreed under the influence of duress? This question must be answered in the negative.[92] The disadvantaged party must also distance itself from the forced contract amendment as soon as possible. A case decided in England in 1978[93] involved a contract for the construction of a tanker at a fixed price in US dollars. When the value of the dollar fell by 10 per cent, the shipbuilder demanded an increase of 10 per cent for the remaining instalments, and threatened not to deliver the tanker unless this was agreed. The shipowner was well aware that the demand was unjustified, but agreed since it had already chartered the tanker to an oil company, and wanted to avoid the trouble and uncertainty of litigation. The court regarded the conduct of the shipbuilder as wrong, and would have ordered the return of the supplement on the grounds of economic duress but for its finding that the shipowner had acquiesced by doing nothing for eight months after the crisis had been ended by the delivery of the tanker.

III. Duress by third party

Where the threats are made not by the other party or his agent or representative but by a third party, the question whether avoidance is possible is the same as in cases of

---

[91] In fact, the rules listed above in n 83 state that a threat, even if 'wrongful', does not entitle avoidance of the contract if the threatened party had 'a reasonable alternative' that it did not take and thus just accepted the amendment to the contract.

[92] See, but only for the result, *Williams* v. *Roffey Brothers* [1991] I QB 1. See McKendrick (n 44) no. 17.2. He correctly notes that it would be different if the building construction company had only landed the contract in the first place because it had intentionally bid a very low price, and was now trying to achieve a reasonable price for the job. In these cases, English courts often ask in addition whether the amendment is invalid because the disadvantaged party received no consideration from the other party. See pp. 63ff.

[93] *North Ocean Shipping Co.* v. *Hyundai Construction Co.* [1978] 3 All ER 1170. See also *Pao On* v. *Lau Yiu Long* [1980] AC 614 (PC); *Atlas Express* v. *Kafco* [1989] 1 All ER 641; *Dimskal Shipping Co.* v. *International Transport Workers' Federation* (n 80); *The Evia Luck (No. 2)* [1992] 2 AC 152, 166.

deceit. It does not seem to be very important in practice, but all the continental codes deal with it, though in different ways. Some systems draw no distinction between deceit and duress on this point, and accordingly allow avoidance for duress only when the other party knew or should have known of the duress practised by the third party.[94] German law and the Romanistic systems regard the contractor's will as more strongly vitiated by duress than by deceit, so allow avoidance even as against a party in good faith.[95] Other legal systems do likewise only if the duress was of a particularly brutal kind, such as a threat of bodily injury or some other very serious and imminent harm.[96] Swiss law is different again: avoidance is possible even against a party who could not have been aware of the third party's duress, but in such a case, if equity so requires, the claimant may have to indemnify the contractor for reliance damage.[97]

---

[94] See § 875 ABGB; art. 3:44(5) BW. English law is to the same effect. Thus if a debtor pressures his parents into granting a charge over their property to a bank, or fraudulently exploits their gullibility, the parents cannot avoid the charge against the bank on the ground of undue influence unless the debtor was acting as agent for the bank, or the bank knew or should have known of his misconduct. See *Avon Finance Co. v. Bridger* [1985] 2 All ER 281; *Coldunell v. Gallon* [1986] QB 1184; and *Barclays Bank v. O'Brien* [1994] 1 AC 180 and above, n 64. The same approach is followed in art. 4:111(2) PECL; art. 3.2.8(2) PICC; art. II.-7:208(2) DCFR. However, the innocent party is allowed to avoid the contract for duress even though the other party neither knew nor ought to have known of the third party threat, provided that avoidance is claimed by the innocent party at a time when the other party had not yet acted in reliance on the contract.
[95] See § 123 BGB; art. 1142 *Code civil*; art. 1434 *Codice civile*; art. 1268 Spanish Civil Code.
[96] See arts. 28 and 29 Swedish Contract Law, and art. 256 Portuguese Civil Code.
[97] Article 29(2) OR. Article 153 Greek Civil Code is to the same effect.

11
Rights of Withdrawal

A. Introduction	191
B. Basis and Reasons for Withdrawal	192
I. Doorstep selling	192
II. Loan agreements, timeshare contracts	193
III. Distance-selling contracts	194
C. Consequences of Withdrawal	195

A. Introduction

Mandatory statutory provisions give rights for one party to withdraw from certain types of contract within a specified period without having to give a reason for the withdrawal. Such a right of withdrawal is permitted even if the counterparty has properly performed its obligations under the contract, or there is no doubt that it intends to perform its future obligations in full. The right of withdrawal is intended to give the party a 'cooling-off period' to come to a decision about whether it really intends to be bound by the contract. The withdrawal may perhaps be desired because of a feeling that the counterparty had exerted psychological or other pressures to force conclusion of the contract, or even because, after reconsidering the matter at leisure in the absence of the counterparty, the party has now recognised a disadvantage and no longer wishes to continue with the contract. One special case is where someone has bought goods by telephone, email, or order card on the basis of a description in a catalogue or prospectus. If after delivery these goods turn out to be defective, if the buyer does not like them, or for some other reason does not want to continue with the contract, he or she is also allowed to exercise a right of withdrawal.

Rights of withdrawal have a long history in European legal systems. They were initially introduced for contracts of sale where the buyer agreed to pay for the goods in instalments, and subsequently for all contracts concluded by parties in their private residence, at their place of work, or while on a promotional excursion. Since the 1980s, initiatives to create rights of withdrawal have moved over to the European Community, which has enacted numerous corresponding directives to implement its consumer protection programme.[1] However, this does not mean that there is legal

---

[1] For a detailed and comprehensive overview, see P Mankowski, 'Right of Withdrawal' in *Max Planck Enc.* (2012) 1476; H Eidenmüller, 'Widerrufsrechte' in H Eidenmüller, F Faust, HC Grigoleit, N Jansen, G Wagner, and R Zimmermann (eds), *Revision des Verbraucher-acquis* (2011) 109; G Wagner, 'Zwingendes Vertragsrecht' (ibid.) 1, 21ff. See also K Kroll-Ludwigs, 'Die Zukunft des verbraucherschützenden Widerrufrechts in Europa' (2010) 18 *ZEuP* 509: it is suggested that the consumer's right of withdrawal should be done away with entirely, and instead replaced by protection on the basis of extensive duties for traders to provide information.

harmony in these areas. In some cases, the European directives introduce rights for consumers to withdraw from certain types of contracts, but detailed specification of the terms and consequences is left up to national legal systems. The national legal systems also have the discretion to introduce stronger legal protection for consumers than is envisaged in the directives themselves, and they can also introduce rights of withdrawal for types of contracts not covered by the directives. So in the Netherlands, where pursuant to art. 7:2 BW the buyer of a piece of land can revoke a contract to buy land within three days of signing the paperwork. In Germany, anyone (whether or not a consumer) may withdraw from an insurance contract within the fourteen days after he or she was provided with the statutory information required, received the insurance contract, and was advised of the right of withdrawal: § 8 Insurance Contracts Act (*Versicherungsvertragsgesetz*). In France, the list of contracts that can be revoked by a mandatory statutory right of withdrawal is very long.[2]

B. Basis and Reasons for Withdrawal

A mandatory right of withdrawal allows a party to retrospectively revoke a binding contract without any particular reason. This is a clear infringement of the principle of freedom of contract. Therefore, one should examine the types of contract for which such a mandatory right of withdrawal is granted, and question whether the rights are justified in these cases.

I. Doorstep selling

A right of withdrawal for consumers concluding a contract by way of doorstep selling was originally created by the Council Directive of 20 December 1985.[3] Consumers could withdraw from contracts concluded at their home or at their place of work, unless the visit by the trader or representative to the home or place of work was at the express request of the consumer for the purpose of contractual negotiations. Another revocable type of contract is a contract signed by a consumer during an excursion arranged by the trader—for example, during a promotional excursion organised by the trader, or other sorts of recreational events. In fact, there are good grounds for having a mandatory right of withdrawal for such contracts. But they are not founded on the 'weakness' of the consumer's position, nor on the idea that consumers are in an inferior economic or intellectual position *vis-à-vis* the trader, and also not on the assumption that consumers will often be talked into accepting poor quality goods for an inflated price. The real justification is that in such a situation consumers cannot

---

[2] See the overview in F Terré, P Simler, and Y Lequette, *Droit civil, Les obligations* (11th edn, 2013) no. 263. The text also mentions the many other cases where French law steps in to protect the 'weak' contractual party with a 'waiting period' within which he or she is forbidden to accept an offer; any acceptance made before the expiry of the 'waiting period' will have no effect.

[3] Council Directive 85/577/EEC of 20 December 1985 (O.J. 1985 L 372/31). For transposition into national law, see § 312 BGB; arts. L 121-21ff. *Code de la consommation*, § 3 Austrian Consumer Code; Consumer Protection (Cancellation of Contracts Concluded away from Business Premises) Order 1987 (Statutory Instruments 1987/2112).

make a responsible and considered decision about the transaction—because they are unprepared for the contract negotiations, are taken by surprise, are unable to compare the price or quality of goods with products offered by other traders, and perhaps even just agreed to the contract because they thought that was the only way to get rid of the person pressing them to buy.

The Directive on Consumer Rights of 25 October 2011[4] now gives a right of withdrawal to a consumer that concludes an 'off-premises contract' with a trader outside his business premises. It may be that consumers are as similarly surprised or overwhelmed by concluding an off-premises contract as they would be if the contract were concluded in their home or place or work.[5] However, it makes no sense that the Directive also gives consumers a right of withdrawal even when they have *invited* the trader to negotiations away from the trader's premises.[6] Such is the case, for example, when someone is unable to visit the trader's premises for reasons of ill health, and expressly asks the trader to visit him or her at home. It is fairly certain that the consumer cannot be said to be 'surprised' or 'overwhelmed' by such a visit. It could be that the visit of the trader or its agent may not exclude the consumer being misled, hoodwinked, threatened, or put under psychological pressure, but such circumstances could also arise if the negotiations were taking place on the trader's premises. In such cases, one must turn to the general rules that allow for contracts to be avoided for mistake, deceit, or duress. But a general right for consumers to withdraw from *all* contracts does not exist or, as is to be feared, does not exist *yet*.[7]

II. Loan agreements, timeshare contracts

Consumers also have the right of withdrawal from loan agreements and timeshare contracts.[8] The reason given is that such contracts are legally complex transactions that can have a considerable adverse impact on consumers over a long period. Of course, there are many other types of contract that can have a similar long-term impact, but where consumers have no right of withdrawal. It should be asked why the fourteen-day period for reconsideration before the deadline for withdrawal would allow consumers to come to a considered opinion if they had already failed to reach such conclusions in the time *prior* to the contract, when they had all the time in the world. On the other

---

[4] Directive 2011/83/EU of 25 October 2011 (O.J. 2011 L 304/64).
[5] Under German law, investors buying share certificates in an investment company at a place 'other than the company's normal place of business' already have a right of withdrawal (see § 23 *Gesetz über Kapitalanlagegesellschaften* of 9 Sept. 1988).
[6] See art. 2(8) of the Directive. See also art. 40 CESL in conjunction with the definition of an 'off-premises contract' in art. 2(9) of the draft CESL Regulation.
[7] Also Eidenmüller (n 1) 141ff; O Unger, 'Die Richtlinie über die Rechte der Verbraucher: Eine systematische Einführung' (2012) 20 *ZEuP* 270, 279. Also disputable is the corresponding rule in the CESL (n 6); on this, see B Zöchling-Jud, 'Acquis- Revision, CESL und Verbraucherrichtlinie' (2012) 212 *AcP* 550, 566.
[8] See art. 14 Directive 2008/48/EU on Consumer Credit of 23 April 2008 (O.J. 2008 L 133/79); art. 6 Directive 2008/122/EU on Protection of Consumers in Respect of Certain Aspects of Timeshare Agreements of 14 January 2009 (O.J. 2009 L 33/10). The latter Directive extended consumer protection to matters including contracts for long-term holiday products. See in detail B Haar, 'Consumer Credit (Regulatory Principles)' in *Max Planck Enc.* (2012) 365; A Staudinger, 'Timeshare Contracts' in *Max Planck Enc.* (2012) 1660.

hand, it might be that consumers are very often misled by the traders' staff to underestimate the risks with respect to these kinds of contracts, and for *this* reason it makes sense for the consumer to be given time to subsequently reconsider the transaction in the absence of the seller.[9] It should also be taken into account that the right of withdrawal is rarely exercised for these types of contracts, that the costs incurred are not substantial, and that it is not particularly difficult for a trader to adapt to the circumstance that the contract will not be finally valid until fourteen days after the signing. It is a different matter, however, that the right of withdrawal remains intact so long as the trader has not expressly informed the consumer of its existence. In addition, in order to avoid legal disadvantages, he must have given the consumer the mandatory information required by law prior to signing the contract—such information being comprehensive and in the form stipulated by law. The information required is indeed so extensive and complicated, and it is so difficult to separate out the important from the unimportant information, that there is doubt as to whether this exceeds the competence of consumers to process such information properly.[10]

III. Distance-selling contracts

The right of withdrawal has another meaning with respect to *distance-selling contracts*.[11] Such contracts only come into being when distance communications (such as telephone, email, Internet) are used—where the consumer and trader never meet personally prior to the contract being concluded, and the consumer does not have the opportunity to examine and check the goods, as would be the case if buying in a shop. Traders offering their goods for sale by distance selling are well aware that such distribution networks can only be successful if customers have a right to return the product if they are unhappy. So there are good reasons why traders would *voluntarily* grant a right of withdrawal from such contracts. Nevertheless, the Directive governing distance-selling contracts gives consumers a mandatory fourteen-day right of withdrawal that starts after receipt of the goods. In addition, extensive information about the goods must be provided to the consumer before the contract is concluded.[12] It is doubtful whether this makes sense, because consumers will make their decisions about the continuation of the contract on the basis of the examination of the delivered goods, and will have no reason to invest time and resources in reading information about the goods and call off the deal before delivery. Doubts have even been raised about whether a right of withdrawal is justified for all types of distance-selling contracts. Empirical studies carried out in Germany show that the right of withdrawal is exercised in around a third of distance-selling contracts—and in more than half

---

[9] See Eidenmüller (n 1) 147ff.
[10] On the much-discussed problem of 'information overload', see HC Grigoleit, 'Die Aufklärungspflichten des *acquis*' in H Eidenmüller, F Faust, HC Grigoleit, N Jansen, G Wagner, and R Zimmermann (eds), *Revision des Verbraucher-acquis* (2011) 223, 247ff. (with further evidence). For a radical critique of rules imposing information duties, see O Ben-Shahar and C Schneider, 'The Failure of Mandated Disclosure' (2011) 159 *U.Pa. LR* 647.
[11] See G Rühl, 'Distance Contracts' in *Max Planck Enc.* (2012) 489.
[12] See art. 9 of the Directive (n 4) on the right of withdrawal and art. 6 on the detailed information requirements.

of the cases where the product being purchased is women's clothing.[13] The costs for the trader in processing such transactions and the often considerable value loss of the returned goods means that prices increase and therefore fall on *all* customers—including those who have not made use of the right of withdrawal and have not (as does happen) made the exercise of that right a pet issue. It has therefore been suggested that the mandatory rule should remain, but that traders should be given the option of offering to sell the goods to consumers at a higher price *with* the right of withdrawal, or at a lower price *without* it.[14] The Directive (and art. 40 CESL) did not adopt such a solution. This is indeed plausible, since it would give customers an incentive for 'opportunistic behaviour': they could order the goods at the higher price with a right of withdrawal, and then return them (even though they want to buy). After reimbursement of the higher price, they could order the same goods a second time—but at the lower price and without a right to withdraw.

C. Consequences of Withdrawal

Once the right of withdrawal is exercised, parties are no longer required to perform the contract, and they may demand restoration of the performance already carried out under the contract. With respect to distance selling and off-premises contracts, this is governed in detail by arts. 12–15 of the Directive of 25 October 2011.[15] Consumers must return goods already delivered and traders must return payments received 'without undue delay and in any event not later than 14 days' from the date when the consumer exercised the right to withdraw and the trader has been informed of this withdrawal. The trader has a right to hold back reimbursement of payments received, but only until such time as the returned goods are returned to or collected by the trader, or until the consumer has supplied evidence of having returned the goods. Pursuant to art. 13(1) of the Directive, the trader must reimburse all payments received from the consumer, including 'costs of delivery' that have been paid by the consumer.[16] On the other hand, a trader may impose the costs of return postage on the consumer without reference to the value of the items being sent back; if this were not so, that would herald the downfall of the very last incentive for the consumer to make a careful check on the goods. However, this requires the trader to have informed the consumer prior to the conclusion of the contract that he will have to bear the costs of

---

[13] See in detail Eidenmüller (n 1) 120ff.
[14] See Eidenmüller (n 1) 133ff; Unger (n 7) 29f, disputed by Zöchling-Jud (n 7) 565f.
[15] Above, n 4. See also arts. 44–46 CESL. On the rules in the Directive, see in detail Unger (n 7). For a comprehensive treatment that also takes account of the rules in the DCFR, PECL, and PICC, see R Zimmermann, 'Rückabwicklung nach Widerruf' in H Eidenmüller, F Faust, HC Grigoleit, N Jansen, G Wagner, and R Zimmermann (n 1) 167ff. If the withdrawn contract is a *loan agreement* the consumer must pay the monies loaned back to the lender within thirty days of sending the declaration of withdrawal and also reimburse any interest as specified in the contract that may have accrued between the loan being paid out to the consumer and being paid back to the lender.
[16] See also (on the previous Directive Concerning Distance-Selling Contracts, n 3) ECJ 15 April 2010, Rs. C-511/08 (*Heine v. Verbraucherzentrale NRW*), Slg. 2010, 3047 = [2010] *NJW* 1941 and BGH 7 July 2010, [2010] *NJW* 1651.

return postage should the right of withdrawal be exercised. If the trader fails to give this information, he will have to bear the cost of the return postage.[17]

Great practical importance is attached to the question of whether the consumer, after exercising the right of withdrawal, should reimburse the trader for any loss in value caused by the goods being returned to the trader. Pursuant to art. 14(2) of the Directive, consumers are not liable for any diminished value of the goods provided that they handled them as they would have done in a shop. They are only liable for any diminished value of the goods to the extent to which this is due to a handling different from that necessary 'to establish the nature, characteristics and functioning of the goods'. The consumer is also not liable if the trader failed to provide notice of the right of withdrawal in the required form.[18]

---

[17] Pursuant to art. 14(1) para. 3 of the Directive, these rules should also apply to off-premises contracts. In this case, the trader is required to collect the goods from the consumer's address (and thus to save him the cost of return passage) only where 'by their nature, the goods cannot normally be returned by post'. This restriction makes little sense, because with an 'off-premises contract' consumers are always surprised by the contract and should *in no way* be made to bear the cost of returning the goods. See Zimmermann (n 15) 191.

[18] A differentiation must be made between the loss from the diminished value of the goods and the profit that would have been generated by the consumer's use of the goods up until the time of withdrawal from the contract. So if, exceptionally, the consumer is required to reimburse the diminished value, one may ask whether he or she should not also pay an amount of money corresponding to the value of the benefit taken from the use of the goods up until the withdrawal from the contract. The Directive is silent on this issue. See Unger (n 7) 294 and Zimmermann (n 15) 186ff. See also Unger (n 7) 296ff. on the question of whether the consumer, after having benefited from the trader's *services* until the time of withdrawal, must not reimburse him for their value.

12
Claims for Performance

A. Introduction	197
B. Solutions of National Legal Systems	198
I. Continental law	198
II. Common law	202
C. Harmonised Rules in Europe	205
I. Claims for performance	205
1. Impossibility of performance	206
2. Unreasonably high cost	207
3. Personal performance	208
4. Concluding a substitute transaction	209
5. Timely claim for performance	209
II. Claims for supplementary performance	210
D. The Efficient Breach of Contract	212

A. Introduction

A person who enters a contract expects the other party to do as he promised. But what if he is disappointed, such as where the seller of goods fails to deliver goods or to deliver them in time? What can a client do if the building contractor fails to start agreed construction works, or leaves the site before work is complete? First of all, the innocent party (often called the creditor) will usually insist upon compliance with the contract and demand that the defaulting party (often called the debtor) does what it has contractually agreed to do. In doing so, the creditor is asserting a claim for performance by asking the judge to issue judgment to the effect that the defendant must deliver the goods sold, or start or continue with the agreed construction work.

However, assertion of such a legal claim in many cases does not suit the purpose of the creditor. It may be in his interest to waive the claim for performance, and instead reach out for other legal remedies available against the debtor if the contract has not been carried out, or only carried out in part. Such is the case, for example, if a seller has not delivered the goods to the buyer in time and the market price for the goods has now fallen. Here, it would be foolish for the buyer to insist upon performance of the contract, because if the delivery were to be repeated, the buyer would have to pay a price higher than the current market value. Instead, the buyer will try to terminate the contract with the seller (see chapter 13) and seek to get the same goods from another supplier at a lower price. But what if the price has increased? In this case, the buyer can assert the claim for performance and demand damages from the seller for losses caused by the delay in delivery. But often, even in this case, the buyer is best advised to terminate the contract with the seller. Its claim for performance is lost, but it no longer needs to pay the agreed purchase price to the seller. It can procure the goods from a third party and demand the difference in price from the original seller as damages for non-performance (see chapter 14).

In many cases, however, the claim for performance is extremely important for the creditor. This is obvious where the claim is for the payment of money.[1] But there are other situations in which the claimant has no interest in other legal remedies that might be available. Here the question arises as to if, and under which circumstances, a judgment requiring performance can be obtained, and how to ensure that it is respected.

B. Solutions of National Legal Systems

I. Continental law

All continental legal systems in Europe today observe the principle that each party to a contract has the right to have that contract fulfilled, and that the courts can also enforce such claims. The principle is not quite as self-evident as it may appear. If debtors do not perform, creditors cannot just take matters into their own hands. A buyer cannot just take the goods sold from the seller against his will; at the end of a tenancy, a landlord cannot just remove the tenant from the apartment by force; and a creditor cannot force performance from a debtor by threatening violence or other prohibited pressure. Instead, the creditor must turn to the courts, and any court judgment can only be enforced against the debtor in a state-regulated process. For a long time, it was indeed doubtful whether courts could issue such a judgment to enforce performance *in natura*, or whether creditors should merely be entitled to damages. Traditional Roman law started from the presumption that the court's judgment could only deal with the payment of money (*omnis condemnatio pecuniaria*). But more and more exceptions to this rule emerged over time, particularly where the debtor owed the creditor a particular thing, such as a seller owing delivery, or a renter or borrower having promised to return an item.[2] However, if the debtor had agreed to do something, or to refrain from doing something, the tendency was to just award the creditor damages—perhaps because in such cases the promised performance could not be precisely described in the judgment, or because as a free person the debtor could not be forced by the state to do something against his will.

A similar train of thought underlies the former provisions of the French *Code civil*, although they were not without contradiction. Article 1142 appeared to restrict the creditor to a claim for damages if the debtor had agreed to an '*obligation de faire ou de ne pas faire*'. On the other hand, art. 1184(2) specified that a creditor who has not received what he was promised in a mutual contract can not only demand termination

---

[1] A claim for performance concerning the payment of money is universally recognised, even if it is sometimes made dependent on certain additional requirements. See, for example, art. 9:101 PECL; art. 7.2.1 PICC; art. III.-3:301 DCFR; and (on payment claim by the seller) art. 62 CISG; art. 123 CESL. See in detail A Flessner, 'Der Geld-Erfüllungsanspruch im europäischen Vertragsrecht auf den Stufen zum Gemeinsamen Referenzrahmen' in *Festschrift für Eugen Bucher* (2009) 145ff.

[2] For a detailed historical overview, see R Zimmermann, *The Law of Obligations, Roman Foundations of the Civilian Tradition* (1990) 771ff.

of the contract and damages, but also has the option to force the debtor to perform the contract, where such performance is possible. The French courts have settled this contradiction in favour of art. 1184 in that they have affirmed the principle that the creditor always has a claim for performance.[3] This starting point is also adopted by art. 1221 now in force: a debtor in default of performance can always be required by the creditor to perform the obligations under the contract, unless this is impossible, or there is a *disproportion manifeste* between the cost of performance for the debtor and the interests of the creditor in insisting on performance.

Similar rules apply in other continental legal orders in Europe. Sometimes they are laid down in statutory form,[4] and sometimes such provisions are regarded as self-evident. So § 241(1) BGB merely states that an obligation (in this case arising from a contract) entitles a creditor 'to claim performance from the debtor'. It also means that performance of the obligations under the contract can be pursued in the courts, and the creditor can secure a judgment to enforce the claim. The type of contractual obligation is not relevant. So if other legal remedies are unavailable or unattractive, legal action can be taken by a buyer to demand delivery of the purchased item, by a seller to demand that a buyer accepts ordered goods, by a landlord to get an apartment back from a tenant, or by a client to make sure that work is carried out. A seller can also insist that a buyer stops selling purchased goods to a third party in contravention of a contractual arrangement. There is also general acceptance that there can be no claim for performance if it is 'impossible' for the debtor to perform the contractual obligation (see § 275(1) BGB, art. 1221 *Code civil*). So if the buyer has been sold a particular boat, used car, or painting, it will be impossible for the seller to perform its obligations if, before being handed over to the buyer, the object is destroyed or stolen by an unknown third party. Here, the buyer has a right to terminate the contract, and to demand damages if the seller is somehow contractually liable for the destruction or theft.

A judgment ordering the debtor to perform is not of much use to the creditor unless the legal system provides the means to make it effective. The question of whether and how such a judgment may be enforced depends on the law of civil procedure of the country whose courts have issued the judgment. These rules may vary widely, even if one assumes that the substantive law on the availability of claims for performance were harmonised across Europe.

---

[3] On the former approach, see F Terré, P Simler, and Y Lequette, *Droit civil, Les obligations* (11th edn, 2013) no. 1108ff; P Malaurie, L Aynès, and P Stoffel-Munck, *Les obliations* (6th edn, 2013) no. 1129ff. The courts have sometimes gone a long way with claims for performance, such as in cases where a contractor has not built a house or swimming pool as contracted. Here, without making too much fuss, the courts allowed the claim by the clients for construction of a completely new house or swimming pool (Civ. 11 May 2005, Bull.cass. 2005.III. no. 103, and below, n 34; Civ. 17 Jan. 1984, [1984] *Rev trim civ* 711). On the reform debate, see YM Laithier, 'La prétendue primauté de l'exécution en nature' [2005] *RDC* 161; YM Laithier, 'The Enforcement of Contractual Obligations' in J Cartwright, S Vogenauer, and S Whittaker, *Reforming the French Law of Obligations* (2009) 123.

[4] See, for example, §§ 918, 919 ABGB, art. 3:296(1) BW, art. 1453(1) *Codice civile*. Under the Scandinavian legislation on the sale of goods, buyers can also claim performance *in natura* from the seller.

Civil procedure rules often make enforcement so difficult and time-consuming that creditors have good reason to seek other legal remedies that would help them to reach their objectives more quickly. For example, if a buyer's claim for performance concerns the delivery of a purchased asset, under German law judgment can only be given against the seller if the purchased asset can be described in sufficient detail for the item to be easily identified and removed by a court-appointed bailiff from amongst the debtor's other chattels (see §§ 883–886 ZPO). That is not difficult if the debtor must hand over a particular piece of property or a specified item. It might also be possible where the seller has set aside the agreed number of items for the buyer, and the buyer knows where those items are located. But it is impossible if the seller does not yet have the items in his possession because he must first procure them from a third party. If the claim on which the creditor has obtained judgment is that the debtor should take some positive action other than the handing over of property, and if that action could be equally well performed by someone else, the only available method of execution is for the creditor, on the authority of the court granted at his request, to have the act performed by a third party at the expense of the debtor (§ 887 ZPO). Obviously, the creditor can achieve the same objective much more cheaply and quickly by ignoring the claim for performance, terminating the contract, appointing a third party to take the action, and demanding reimbursement of the extra costs from the debtor by way of damages for non-performance of the contract. A judgment for performance would be even less useful for the creditor when it refers to action that can only be taken by the debtor himself. In this case, the method of execution is to punish the unwilling debtor with a fine or imprisonment (§ 888(1) ZPO). Even that applies only if the action 'depends exclusively on the will of the debtor'. If that is not the case—for example, because the action to be performed by the debtor does not only depend on his will, but also on his artistic inspiration or scientific talent—no method of enforcement is available. A publisher may certainly obtain a judgment against an author ordering him to deliver a promised manuscript. This judgment, however, is an empty threat because there are no means to enforce it, and the publisher must content himself with a claim for damages (§ 893 ZPO). Nor is it possible to have enforcement of a judgment requiring the debtor to perform services (§ 888(3) ZPO). The situation is different if the judgment requires the debtor to give a contractually agreed declaration: the declaration is deemed given as soon as the judgment has attained legal force (§ 894 ZPO). And if the judgment requires the debtor to cease and desist from actions, the courts can threaten coercive fines to be enforced if the order is violated (§ 890 ZPO). These fines are paid to the state.

French law has a special way of enforcing judgments for performance. For a long time, the courts have taken the approach of threatening an unwilling debtor with a fine, which must be paid to the creditor (*astreinte*).[5] The court normally sets the debtor a deadline for performance of the obligations, and imposes a fine for every day after

---

[5] The *astreinte* is now covered by statutory provisions. See art. 33ff. of Law no. 91-650 of 9 July 1991. Article 33(1) states that '*tout juge peut, même d'office, ordonner une astreinte pour assurer l'excécution de sa décision*'. A comprehensive overview of the *astreinte* can be found in O Remien, *Rechtsverwirklichung durch Zwangsgeld: Vergleich, Vereinheitlichung, Kollisionsrecht* (1992) 33ff.

that deadline where the obligation has not been performed. If the obligation is not performed, or is not performed until after the deadline, upon application of the creditor the court can fix the amount that the debtor must pay to the creditor. The amount of damages caused to the creditor by the failure to perform or by late performance is irrelevant. Instead the determining factors are to what extent the debtor can be held responsible for the lack of performance, the financial position of the debtor, and whether it had justified reasons that made it difficult to perform the obligation in time. If the debtor can show that performance was hindered by a *cause étrangère* or *force majeure*, no *astreinte* may be issued.[6]

There may be no judgment for performance or threat of an *astreinte* if it is impossible for the debtor to perform, or if performance has a 'personal' character, namely where the debtor must contribute some special artistic or scientific talent or inspiration. Otherwise, the *astreinte* is widely used to implement performance claims—such as where a managing director of a company is required to submit accounts,[7] an employer is required to provide an employment reference,[8] or a landlord is required to install an electricity connection in an apartment.[9] The courts have also imposed an *astreinte* where it would have been possible for the creditor to secure performance by the state-regulated process of enforcement—namely with the assistance of the bailiff—in instances such as forcing a debtor to hand over a particular motor vehicle,[10] or making a tenant vacate an apartment.[11] An *astreinte* is also seen as permissible where a neighbour has been ordered to tear down a boundary wall[12] or a construction company to hand over an apartment,[13] even though in these cases the creditor could also have asked the court for an order to have the debtor's action carried out by a third party at the cost of the debtor. Monetary debts are usually enforced with the assets of the debtor being seized, auctioned off, and the proceeds being handed over to the creditor. But even in such cases the *Cour de cassation* thought it possible to threaten the debtor with an *astreinte* for non-payment at least where the creditor had no other effective means to implement his monetary claim.[14]

The *astreinte* is a statutory and evidently widely used means to implement claims for performance, but still it often raises objections in France. One problem in particular is that the *astreinte* is intended to break the debtor's resistance towards respecting the performance judgment, and while it depends on the reproachability of the debtor's conduct and its financial position, it still flows into the private assets of the creditor. In addition, the *astreinte* does not affect the creditor's claim for damages. Thus it seems possible for a creditor, after receiving the penalty payment stipulated in the *astreinte*, to abandon the claim for performance and instead demand damages from the debtor for breach of contract. In other European countries, there are rules that are similar to

---

[6] See art. 36 of the Law in n 5. On *cause étrangère* and *force majeure*, see pp. 248ff.
[7] Civ. 5 July 1933, D.H. 1933, 425. [8] Soc. 29 June 1966, Bull. 1966.IV. no. 641.
[9] Civ. 17 March 1965, Bull. 1965.I. no. 195. [10] Com. 12 Dec. 1966, Bull. 1966.III. no. 478.
[11] Com. 15 Nov. 1967, Bull. 1967.III. no. 369. [12] Civ. 7 April 1965, Bull. 1965.I. no. 262.
[13] Civ. 12 February 1964, Bull. 1964.I. no. 82.
[14] See Com. 17 April 1956, *JCP* 1956, 9330, n. P Vellieux in a case where the creditor had a monetary claim against the City of Marseille.

the French model, such as in Belgium, Luxembourg, and the Netherlands.[15] Article 7.2.4 PICC also states that 'Where the court orders a party to perform, it may also direct that this party pay a penalty if it does not comply with the order.'[16]

II. Common law

In contrast to continental legal systems, the Common Law starts from the principle that it is only in exceptional cases that the creditor who has not received performance can force the debtor to perform its promise. The Common Law does assume in principle that the creditor acquires a 'primary right' upon concluding the contract that the debtor will perform its contractual promise *in natura*.[17] But when one asks what the creditor can do in practical terms if the debtor has not performed the contract, or has not performed it correctly, it is no longer the 'primary right' that matters, but only whether the special conditions are satisfied under which the remedy of specific performance is available to the creditor. This question is answered in the affirmative when the claim is based on payment of a sum of money. But the situation is different when the creditor requires delivery or acceptance of goods sold, construction of a building, performance of agreed services, or another sort of action or forbearance. The creditor has a claim for damages for breach of contract if the necessary conditions are met, but there is no general claim for performance. The renowned American judge Oliver Wendell Holmes said that 'the only universal consequence of a legally binding promise is that the law makes the promisor pay damages if the promised event does not come to pass.'[18]

This principle applies with only a few important exceptions. Claims based on the defendant's breach of contract have their historical roots in the law of tort, which explains why the sole remedy is damages.[19] But in practice, equity courts soon developed rules allowing the creditor to demand performance *in natura* by granting an 'order for specific performance', or an 'injunction' when the debtor would be required to refrain from doing something. But such remedies were only available as an exception—namely only if the equity court was satisfied in the case in question that the general claim for damages was 'inadequate' and failed to take sufficient account of the interest of the creditor. This remains the basis of the Common Law. It is still stressed that the judge has the 'discretion' to exceptionally allow the creditor a claim for performance if damages would be inadequate. But this discretion has

---

[15] See, for example, art. 611a ff. of the Netherlands Code of Civil Procedure and the comments by Remien (n 5) 41*ff*.

[16] Of course, the drafters of PICC were aware that this rule would often be opposed to the enforcement provisions of the applicable national law. Therefore, art. 7.2.4(2) states that a penalty shall only be payable to the aggrieved party 'unless mandatory provisions of the law of the forum provide otherwise'. See also H Schelhaas in S Vogenauer (ed), *Commentary on the PICC* (2nd edn, 2015) art. 7.2.4.

[17] This circumstance is stressed in particular by H Unberath, *Die Vertragsverletzung* (2007) 211ff. and MP Weller, *Die Vertragstreue* (2009) 118ff, 392ff. They would thus consider it mistaken that the CISG (art. 45f, 61f.), the PECL (art. 8:101, 9:102), and even this book focus on the concept of 'remedies'.

[18] OW Holmes, *The Common Law* (1881) 301. See also OW Holmes, 'The Path of the Law' (1896) 10 Harv. LR. 457, 462: 'The duty to keep a contract at common law means a prediction that you must pay damages if you do not keep it—and nothing else.'

[19] See above, p.50 and in detail in Zimmermann (n 2) 776ff.

long since developed into fixed rules that allow some degree of certainty about when a court will allow a creditor's application for an order for specific performance or an injunction.

Damages would be inadequate, for example, if the buyer would be unable to buy equivalent goods or services instead of those promised under the contract. Such is the case where someone has bought a parcel of land. The buyer's interest in this land cannot easily be compensated for by money, because it is impossible to buy land from somebody else with exactly the same attributes that would put the buyer in the same position as if it had acquired the land promised in the contract. The same applies when a claimant has contracted to buy a particular asset that is unique or especially rare, whose value is difficult to assess, or where the claimant has a particular intangible interest in its delivery. So where the claimant has bought an heirloom, a particular yacht, a rare tobacco tin, or a particular horse that it had selected especially, or perhaps already ridden, the buyer can demand *specific performance* of the claim if the seller does not meet its obligations under the contract.[20] The situation is different for generic goods. If they are not delivered when promised, and the risk has not yet been passed to the buyer, it cannot demand specific performance even if the goods are still available on the market. In such circumstances, the Common Law takes the view that it would be a waste of time and money to allow the buyer to demand specific performance and force the seller to perform the contract *in natura*. Instead, it would be perfectly sufficient to allow buyers damages for breach of contract, thus putting them in a position to take matters into their own hands and acquire the goods from another provider (substitute transaction).[21] The same approach is followed where a debtor has failed to deliver the agreed work or services, but the creditor would have no problem to have the contract performed by a third party. Such is usually the case for contracts with building contractors when performance of the promised work can also be carried out by another contractor.[22]

Specific performance cannot be granted when performance turns on special personal characteristics of the debtor. If, for example, the debtor is an employer who has improperly terminated the contract, the employee may ask the employer to continue with the contract, provided that the necessary trust between the parties still exists.[23] In the reverse situation, the debtor promised to provide personal services to the creditor.

---

[20] Under s. 52 of the Sale of Goods Act 1979, the court may at the instance of the purchaser of 'specific or ascertained goods' issue judgment 'that the contract shall be performed specifically'.

[21] See *Sky Petroleum Ltd.* v. *VIP Petroleum Ltd.* [1974] 1 WLR 576: The claimant bought a large volume of fuel for its petrol stations from the defendant on the basis of a long-term contract. After a rapid rise in the price of fuel, the defendant ceased deliveries for no specific reason. Here the court allowed the claimant's request for an order for specific performance because petrol had become so exceptionally scarce that he had no other source of supply.

[22] But see *Wolverhampton Corp.* v. *Emmons* [1901] 1 KB 515. At 524f, there is a description of the exceptional conditions under which a building contractor may be forced to perform the construction contract itself.

[23] See *Powell* v. *Brent London Borough Council* [1987] Industrial Relations LR 466. See also BAG 10 November 1955, [1956] *NJW* 359. Under employment laws, an improper termination of an employment contract by an employer can also result in the employer being forced to continue the employment contract. See Employment Protection (Consolidation) Act 1972, and the German Employment Protection Act (*Kündigungsschutzgesetz*) 1969.

In this case, specific performance will be denied. An actress who had undertaken to be available to the plaintiff for film work for a year cannot be forced to perform the contract by way of an order for specific performance. One reason given for this is that otherwise the defendant would be forced into a kind of involuntary servitude; another is that services performed under such coercion would probably be of doubtful quality. A third reason is that it would be extremely difficult for the court to determine whether the services so performed were in accordance with the contract. For these reasons, the court refused specific performance, but helped the plaintiff by issuing an injunction forbidding the defendant to work for other film companies for the duration of the contract.[24] One consideration, however, was that the plaintiff's claim for damages, being difficult to calculate, was not 'adequate', and that the injunction, even if forbidding the actress from taking on other film work in this period, must not debar her from all activity whatsoever, since otherwise she would be indirectly forced to perform the contract for the plaintiff.

Another argument against an order for specific performance is that it would be difficult for the court to check if the debtor against whom the order was granted had actually performed in line with the contract. Such difficulties could arise if the contract covers a long period, and if it fails to specifically set out the performance of the debtor in a clear and unambiguous manner. This could result in an ongoing dispute between the parties (which the court would have to decide on) as to whether the debtor has performed as required under the contract, and thus whether or not the debtor has fulfilled the order of specific performance. The situation is illustrated by a decision by the House of Lords from 1998.[25] The defendant lessee had concluded a long-term lease agreement to operate a supermarket during normal business hours in a shopping centre built by the claimant. After the lessee discovered that the supermarket operations at this location were not profitable, it ended the lease and offered damages to the lessor in order to 'buy' out the remainder of the lease. The lessor did not agree, and applied to the court for an order of specific performance requiring the defendant to operate a supermarket at the location for the remainder of the lease—a further nine years. The Court of Appeal allowed the application, but the House of Lords overturned this decision:

> From a wider perspective, it cannot be in the public interest for the courts to require someone to carry on business at a loss if there is any plausible alternative by which the other party can be given compensation. It is not only a waste of resources but yokes the parties together in a continuing hostile relationship. The order for specific performance prolongs the battle. If the defendant is ordered to run a business, its conduct becomes the subject of a flow of complaints, solicitors' letters and affidavits. This is wasteful for both parties and the legal system. An award of damages, on the other hand, brings the litigation to an end. The defendant pays damages, the forensic

---

[24] *Warner Brothers Pictures Inc. v. Nelson* [1937] 1 KB 209. See also *Page One Records v. Bitton* [1968] 1 WLR 157 and, in greater detail, GH Treitel, *The Law of Contract* (13th edn, by E Peel, 2011) no. 21-055.

[25] *Co-operative Insurance Society Ltd. v. Argyll Stores (Holdings) Ltd.* [1998] AC 1. See also *Ryan v. Mutual Tontine Westminster Chambers Ass.* [1893] 1 Ch. 116; *Giles Co. v. Morris* [1972] 1 WLR 307.

link between them is severed, they go their separate ways and the wounds of conflict can heal.²⁶

If the court issues an order for specific performance or injunction, the Common Law regards it as contempt of court if the debtor does not do as the court orders. This does not apply if the creditor has a claim to a parcel of land or a particular asset: such a judgment can be enforced by the court authorising a court bailiff to take possession of the land, buildings, or chattels. In all other cases, the debtor must expect the court to issue a coercive penalty or imprisonment for contempt of court. The degree of punishment is at the discretion of the court, and can have a drastic scope. Perhaps this also explains why English judges are reluctant to issue orders for specific performance.²⁷

C. Harmonised Rules in Europe

I. Claims for performance

Claims for performance are generally regarded as permissible in continental legal systems, but not under the Common Law. The first solution is supported by the idea that each contractual party should have a legal and not just a moral duty to fulfil a contract: *pacta sunt servanda*. The general principle of contractual fidelity favours the approach that where there is a breach of contract, the parties should stick to it and give a fair chance to a solution being found on its basis. By contrast, the Common Law tends to take the approach that things should be cleared up as quickly as possible after a breach of contract has occurred—thus favouring the approach whereby the disadvantaged party has a right to withdraw from the contract and claim damages. Only this approach allows the parties in dispute to avoid being bound into an unsatisfactory relationship against their will, and possibly over a long period of time. If judgments for performance were permitted, they would have to be monitored by the courts and, if the debtor failed to comply, they would have to intervene with sanctions. There would also be a danger of the party complying with the contract being able to claim *more* than just damages, and the Common Law regards this as another convincing argument.²⁸

---

²⁶ *Lord Hoffmann* in *Co-operative Insurance Society* (n 25) 15–16. Under German law, the lessor would have been able to secure a judgment for performance. But it is doubtful whether this would make sense, because there is uncertainty about whether such an order could be enforced. Pursuant to § 888(1) ZPO, a debtor failing to perform can only be threatened with a coercive penalty if the action can only be carried out by him or her (and not by a third party) and also where that action 'depends exclusively on the will of the debtor' (see above, p. 200). Both conditions were found to be lacking in a case where the judgment for performance would have required a lessee to operate a food business in the lessor's premises (OLG Hamm 10 Oct. 1972, [1973] *NJW* 1135). The only remedy remaining for the lessor was a claim for damages.
²⁷ See also *Lord Hoffmann* (n 25): 'The quasi-criminal procedure of punishment for contempt ... is a powerful weapon; so powerful in fact, as often to be unsuitable as an instrument for adjudication upon the disputes which may arise over whether a business is being run in accordance with the terms of a court's order.'
²⁸ If the order for specific performance is expensive to comply with, the debtor has an incentive to offer the creditor a price to make him give up his claim for performance *in natura*. This price would have to be higher than the damages actually suffered by the creditor. He would then be in the same position as

This conflict is also not solved by the United Nations Convention on Contracts for the International Sale of Goods (CISG), although it generally allows claims for performance. A seller can require the buyer to accept the goods, and a buyer can demand delivery, and if the goods do not meet the specifications of the contract, thus constituting a material breach of the contract, the seller or buyer can demand repair or delivery of substitute goods (arts. 46(2) and (3), 62 CISG). But the CISG is promising more than it can deliver. Pursuant to art. 28, a court may refuse a judgment for performance 'unless the court would do so under its own law in respect of similar contracts of sale not governed by this Convention'. In practice, this means that judges in a country where the Common Law applies would be able to turn down the request for specific performance although a French court would, under the same circumstances, be required to grant such an order.

A solution edges closer if one sets aside the general considerations for and against a claim for performance and instead concentrates on the issue of the conditions under which European legal orders actually allow or turn down claims for performance. Thirty years ago, Guenther Treitel already found that the gap between the Common Law and continental legal orders

> is not as great as might appear. On the one hand specific enforceability in civil law countries is subject to important exceptions; in particular, most of them observe the principle that obligations to render personal services cannot, in the last resort, be specifically enforced; orders for enforced performance of other obligations are sometimes more difficult to enforce than in common law countries; and, perhaps most important of all, an aggrieved contracting party will often prefer to claim compensation in money, as that is generally a quicker and to that extent a better remedy. On the other hand, some of the restrictions on specific performance are beginning to disappear in common law countries, as their historical foundations are eroded. This is not to say that there are no differences at all between civil and common law systems, but they are less considerable than the starting theories of the two approaches might suggest.[29]

The PICC and PECL developed a convincing compromise on this basis. Claims for performance are generally allowed, in contrast to the approach of the Common Law. But such claims are excluded when they would not be allowed under Civil Law jurisdictions, or where they are allowed but no forms of execution are made available, or where they have no practical benefit for creditors because enforcement is too arduous or where creditors could reach the same result more quickly using other available legal remedies—particularly damages.

1. Impossibility of performance

A claim for performance is excluded if it is factually or legally impossible for the debtor to perform the contract.[30] So if a painting that has been sold is destroyed, or a

---

if *liquidated damages* or a *penalty* had been agreed upon (see below, p. 275). Why should he be given this advantage if no such agreement has been made?

[29] GH Treitel, *Remedies for Breach of Contract, A Comparative Account* (1988) 71.
[30] Article 9:102(2)(a) PECL; art. 7.2.2(a) PICC; art. III.-3:302(3)(a) DCFR.

leased ship is seized by the state, a judgment can no longer be used to require the seller to hand over the painting or the lessor to deliver the ship. The same applies if a seller agrees to deliver Nigerian peanuts from the 2012 harvest, but the Nigerian government bans exports of this crop, thus making it legally impossible for the seller to perform the contract. This rule is recognised by legal systems everywhere.[31] In practice, one would be hard-pressed to find a judge who would be prepared to order a debtor to do something where it is clear that performance is not possible. Whether a creditor would be able to demand damages from a debtor under such circumstances is another question.

2. Unreasonably high cost

A claim for performance is also excluded if performance would result in an unreasonably high cost for the debtor.[32] What level of cost is 'unreasonably high' is a matter for the judge to decide on the basis of the particular circumstances. The judge must examine whether the expenses that would be incurred by the debtor in performing the contract would be 'grossly disproportionate' to the interests of the creditor in having the contract performed. The question arises often in cases where the creditor is not asking for performance in the strict sense but—because the debtor had performed the contract badly—is asking for *supplementary performance*. Thus the creditor is requesting a judgment ordering the debtor to rectify deficient performance or to deliver a replacement product.[33] A good example is provided by a much-discussed English case where a building contractor had agreed to build a swimming pool for the sum of £17,800. The pool turned out not to be 2.29m deep, as contracted, but only 2.06m. The court said that the pool was usable and increased the value of the property as it would have done had it had the contracted depth. The client did not ask for the pool to be replaced with a new pool that was free of deficiencies. Such a claim for specific performance is excluded under English law, since payment of damages is regarded as 'adequate' compensation. Other legal orders would have also declined to order the contractor to replace the pool, as the cost of doing so would have been disproportionate to the client's benefit.[34] Instead, the client claimed *damages* in the amount of the cost of

---

[31] See, for example, § 275(1) BGB; art. 1221 *Code civil*; art. 1463 *Codice civile*; art. 3:236 BW; art. 119(1) OR § 1447 ABGB. If the goods sold have a generic characteristic and the seller has contracted to supply a certain amount and quality, performance by the seller will only become impossible (and only then can the claim for performance by the buyer be excluded) if the class of goods is destroyed, seized by the state, or covered by an export ban, and it is impossible to procure any goods of the class covered by the contract. Note that a buyer cannot secure a judgment for performance if those goods have already been allocated to him by the seller as contractually stipulated, but are subsequently lost, stolen, damaged, or have otherwise gone astray—and in particular if they have been handed over to a carrier for delivery. In this case, the 'risk' has already been transferred to the buyer (see art. 66ff. CISG; art. IV.A.-5:101ff. DCFR). This means that the buyer, although he or she has not yet received the goods, must pay the purchase price.

[32] Article 9:102(2)(b) PECL; art. 7.2.2 (b) PICC; art. III.-3:302(3)(b) DCFR. See also art. 110(3)(b) CESL. Performance cannot be required of the seller where 'the burden or expense of performance would be disproportionate to the benefit that the buyer would obtain.'

[33] See below, pp. 210ff.

[34] See, for example, § 275(2) BGB, and also §§ 439(3), 635(3) BGB: sellers and contractors may refuse to provide supplementary performance 'if this cure is possible only at disproportionate expense'. The new art. 1221 *Code civil* also denies the creditor a claim for performance if a cost-benefit analysis shows that

constructing a new pool, which was £21,500. The Court of Appeal awarded the client this amount. But the House of Lords held that the damage suffered by the client was merely the loss of certain amenities, and that the sum of £2,500 awarded by the judge at first instance amounted to appropriate compensation.[35]

There can be other reasons why specific performance of the contract would be a disproportionate burden for the debtor, thus rendering a judgment for specific performance improper. In an English case, somebody had bought a house and asked the seller to convey it to him. Although an order for specific performance is usually granted in such circumstances, it was denied in this case because in the four years which had passed since the conclusion of the contract (this being the fault of neither party) the seller had become seriously ill, was depending on the assistance of a neighbour, and thus wished to stay in the house he had sold.[36] The court saw these circumstances as a particular case of 'hardship'. In fact, cases where the debtor seeks to counter a claim for specific performance with the argument that performance would involve an 'unreasonably high cost' are difficult to differentiate from other cases where not just an order for specific performance but also damages are opposed on the ground that circumstances had 'changed materially' since the contract had been concluded, that the 'basis of conclusion of the contract' no longer applied, or that fulfilling the contract would create a particular 'hardship'.[37]

3. Personal performance

Similarly widely recognised is the rule that a claim for performance is excluded if the debtor is required to provide services or work of a personal character, or where there is a personal relationship between the parties.[38] French and English courts have developed similar principles. In Germany, § 275(3) BGB states that a debtor can refuse performance—and thus exclude a judgment for specific performance—if performance must be rendered 'in person' and such performance 'cannot be reasonably required of the debtor when the interests of the parties are weighed against each other'.[39]

---

performance *in natura* would obviously be uneconomic. The situation used to be different. See Civ. 11 May 2005, Bull.cass. 2005.III. no. 103: The client asserted that a house constructed by a building company was 33cm lower than stipulated in the contract, and the client was demanding that the house be torn down and rebuilt. The appeal court rejected the claim, but was overturned by the *Cour de cassation*. For a critical view, see n. D Mazeaud [2006] *RDC* 323 and n. B Fauvarque-Cosson [2006] *RDC* 529.

[35] *Ruxley Electronics and Construction Ltd.* v. *Forsyth* [1996] AC 344.

[36] *Patel* v. *Ali* [1984] Ch. 283 (CA). Under German law, such an application by the buyer would also have been denied pursuant to § 275(2) BGB. Even if the claim had been allowed and an order for specific performance had been issued, a court would have been able to prevent execution of the order on the ground that this would entail a hardship for the defendant which 'would, under the special circumstances of the case, be in conflict with good morals'. (§ 765a ZPO).

[37] See art. 6:111 PECL; art. 6.2.2 PICC and also Schelhaas (n 16) art. 7.2.2 PICC mn. 30f. A claim for performance is also excluded if the debtor can show that performance is hindered by circumstances beyond his control (see art. 79 CISG; art. 8:108 PECL; art. 7.1.7 PICC; and below, pp. 255, 288f.).

[38] Article 9:102(2)(c) PECL; also see art. 7.2.2(d) PICC; art. III.-3:302(3)(c) DCFR.

[39] Note that a creditor will have no interest in a judgment for specific performance if the *execution* of such a judgment is ruled out under German procedural law (see above, p. 200).

4. Concluding a substitute transaction

Creditors also may not assert a claim for specific performance if the contract can be performed by a third party and, under such circumstances, a reasonable person in the same situation would have obtained the performance from another source.[40] This rule is based on the same approach taken by the Common Law. It deviates from the approach taken in Civil Law jurisdictions, but even here creditors do not bother to claim performance from a debtor that is unwilling or unable to perform.[41] Generally, the cheapest solution for the creditor is to terminate the transaction and demand damages from the debtor for non-performance. To deny a claim for specific performance in these cases is a sacrifice in the eyes of continental legal systems. But it is a sacrifice that should, for practical reasons, not be given too much weight. Yet this instance of exclusion of a claim for specific performance has a rather important practical consequence. If the seller fails to deliver the goods on time, or refuses to deliver the goods, the buyer must claim damages from the seller on the basis of the substitute transaction that was concluded (or could have been concluded) with a third party *immediately* after discovery that the original contract will not be performed. The buyer cannot first hide behind the claim for performance and not move on to claim damages until a later stage when the price of the goods has increased and the actual basis for the damages against the (original) seller is much higher.

5. Timely claim for performance

If the grounds for exclusion of non-performance stated above do not apply, there is uncertainty for the debtor as to whether the creditor will make a claim for performance, or claim damages instead. In order to shorten this period of uncertainty, art. 9:102(3) PECL provides that the creditor will lose the right to specific performance if it 'fails to seek [specific performance] within a reasonable time after it has, or ought to have, become aware of the non-performance'.[42]

---

[40] Article 9:102(2)(d) PECL; art. 7.2.2(c) PICC. On the other hand, the DCFR (art. III.-3:302(5)) and the CESL (arts. 110(3), 163(1), 164) allow a buyer to require performance from a seller even if performance could be obtained from another source. However, this might be very risky for the buyer. If obtaining performance from another source would have been reasonable and would not have caused considerable costs or effort, but the buyer failed to do so and insisted on performance by the seller, then it runs the risk when later seeking damages for non-performance of only being able to recover the difference between the contract price and the price payable under the substitute transaction if it had been concluded immediately. So if the debtor is a seller who failed to deliver goods on time, or indeed at all, the buyer would be well advised (especially if prices are rising) to conclude a substitute transaction immediately and to immediately require payment of damages. That is also the practical solution provided by the Common Law, which has also been adopted by the provisions of the PECL and PICC stated above.

[41] A judgment for specific performance is often an unattractive option for a creditor because enforcement is either excluded or difficult, or only results in the creditor being authorised by the court to obtain performance from a third party, with the substitute transaction being at the cost of the debtor (see above, p. 200).

[42] See also art. 7.2.2(e) PICC; art. III.-3:302(4) DCFR; and § 376(1) HGB.

II. Claims for supplementary performance

A special form of a claim for performance is when the aggrieved party claims supplementary performance of the contract. Such is the case where the counterparty has made an attempt to fulfil the contract but performance is deficient because it is not in conformity with the contractual stipulations. Is the aggrieved party (the creditor) entitled in such a case to claim supplementary performance by requiring the debtor to repair defective goods, deliver missing parts, deliver replacement goods, or in some other way cure the defect? May the creditor only withdraw from the contract or demand damages for non-performance if it has previously made an unsuccessful claim for supplementary performance? Should the other party, having performed below par, be given a right to meet performance obligations by way of faultless supplementary performance, thereby preventing the aggrieved party from immediately triggering a right of withdrawal or asserting a claim for damages for non-performance? For contracts of sale and contracts for work, these questions primarily arise when the seller has delivered goods or a contractor has provided services that are not as stipulated in the contract.

Claims for supplementary performance remained unknown in continental legal systems so long as they were still oriented on the model of Roman law. Trading on the markets in ancient Rome was mainly for slaves, animals, and foodstuffs—goods that buyers could examine personally before buying and whose hidden defects could not be made good at a later stage. This is why buyers under Roman law—and also under the law applicable in Germany until 2002—were not able to claim supplementary performance when the goods were not in conformity with the agreement, but could only terminate the contract, demand a rebate in the purchase price, and in certain cases ask for damages. This rule had ceased to make sense in modern times where there is frequent trading of mass-produced goods which cannot be examined by buyers before the contract was concluded, and where defective goods can be repaired by sellers at low cost. That the outdated rules remained on the statute books is due to the beneficent circumstance that these rules were dispositive—namely they could be replaced by contractual agreement. In practice, commercial sellers moved headlong towards the position, normally stipulated within their standard terms and conditions, that buyers should ask for supplementary performance if products were deficient, and should only be able to turn to other legal remedies such as termination or damages if supplementary performance was impossible, had been denied by the seller, or had failed to remedy the problem.

In the meantime, this development has led to substantial changes in the statutory rules governing sale of goods. At an international level, the CISG has played an important role. Where goods are deficient, both buyer and seller are entitled to ask for or offer supplementary performance. Article 46(2) CISG gives the *buyer* a right to require the delivery of a replacement only where delivery of deficient goods was a 'fundamental breach of contract'. This requirement is met only rarely, especially if the defect can subsequently be repaired. In such cases, pursuant to art. 46(3) CISG the buyer may require the seller to remedy the lack of conformity by *repair* unless such repair is 'unreasonable' for the seller—for example, if it is disproportionately expensive. However, what if the buyer has placed special emphasis on the conformity of the goods and has given the seller a reasonable time for repair along with a reminder that timely repair is essential? In that case it will normally be seen as a 'fundamental breach of contract' if the seller does not comply within the deadline set or if the repair turns out to be inadequate. The buyer may then terminate the contract.[43] What about the seller's position? Pursuant to art. 48 CISG, it is also entitled to cure any defects in the goods it supplied, provided that this can be done 'without causing the buyer unreasonable inconvenience'. If the seller has told the buyer that it is prepared to remedy the defect within a stated deadline, the buyer can demand damages for the *delay* in performance but cannot terminate the contract before expiry of the deadline.

It is not only the PECL and PICC that follow the CISG model.[44] The CESL is based on the same approach, but only where the buyer is not a consumer. If he is a consumer, the EC Directive on the Sale of Consumer Goods applies. It gives buyers who have received defective goods the right to demand supplementary performance from the seller by choosing either repair of the defect or delivery of substitute goods.[45] Both must take place 'within a reasonable period', 'without significant inconvenience to the consumer' and 'free of charge'.[46] However, pursuant to art. 3(3) of the Directive the seller may refuse supplementary performance in the form chosen by the buyer if that form is impossible or would involve disproportionately high costs for the seller.[47] The buyer may only withdraw from the contract or reduce the purchase price if the seller has refused both forms of supplementary performance, or if the form of supplementary performance chosen by the buyer has not been successful or is unacceptable.

---

[43] See P Schlechtriem and U Schroeter, *Internationales UN-Kaufrecht* (6th edn, 2016) mn. 328ff, 465, 483.

[44] Article 9:102 PECL and art. 7.2.3 PICC state that if performance is imperfect, the creditor—usually a buyer—has a claim for performance unless such claim is excluded for the reasons stated above or if the claim is made too late (see above, p. 207). However, the buyer—in contrast to the buyer under art. 46(2) CISG—can demand the delivery of a replacement even if there is no 'fundamental breach of contract' by the seller. On the other hand, the seller is under certain conditions entitled to offer the buyer 'a new and conforming tender' of the goods and to set a deadline within which the buyer is precluded from seeking other legal remedies (see art. 8:104–106 PECL; art. 7.1.4–5 PICC).

[45] Article 3 Directive 1999/44/EC of 25 May 1999 (O.J. 1999 L 171 at p. 13). The Directive has been implemented in England by the Sale of Goods Act 1979, s. 48A and B, which has brought English law much closer to the Civil Law, if only for consumer sales. Prior to the Directive, the consumer had to have the defective goods repaired at his own cost, and then claim back the money from the seller by way of damages. Another possibility was to terminate the contract, buy flawless goods elsewhere, and claim damages. Now the consumer can claim specific performance by asking the seller to bring the goods into conformity with the contract by repair or replacement. In Germany, the new rules of §§ 439, 475(1) BGB apply also to commercial buyers, but do so only as default rules. Diverging agreements will normally not be individually negotiated, but form part of the seller's standard terms of business and must therefore comply with the tests developed to check their validity (see above, pp. 140ff.).

[46] The term 'free of charge' has been interpreted by the ECJ as meaning that if the seller has remedied the lack of conformity by replacement, the buyer is not liable to pay for any use he made of the replaced item in the period prior to the replacement, even though that period may have been quite long and the buyer may have derived a considerable advantage from the use (see Case C-404/06, 17 April 2008, Slg. 2008 I-2685 = [2008] *NJW* 1433). See also art. 112(2) CESL.

[47] This rule has also been interpreted by the ECJ to favour consumers. If the defective goods have been built into the buyer's house, and supplementary performance can only take place by delivery of a

D. The Efficient Breach of Contract

When legal rules are examined from an economic perspective, the focus is on whether they contribute to the efficient allocation of resources. In other words: do they provide incentives to motivate individuals to act not only for their own benefit but also for the overall good? Viewed from this perspective, claims for performance should raise red flags for economists. They might ask: why should a party be obliged to perform or provide supplementary performance when this involves costs that are higher than if the party just had to pay damages? Would it not be a more efficient rule if the party breaching the contract were to pay damages, but would not be bound to perform or provide supplementary performance, thus giving that party the possibility to utilise the resources that would remain after damages had been paid out?[48] Such a solution may be contested from a legal ethical perspective. Even if damages were paid in full, the debtor would have an incentive to intentionally withdraw from a binding contract simply because a cost-benefit analysis appears to give a private benefit. As the Common Law takes a more restrained approach to the claim for performance, it appears to favour the 'efficient breach of contract' more than continental legal systems. But whether this is really the case is best assessed when one takes a closer look at certain types of case.

The idea of an 'efficient breach of contract' is often raised with respect to contracts of sale where the seller has contracted to deliver goods to a buyer, but receives a higher offer for the goods from a third party after conclusion of the contract. If the seller accepts the third-party offer, and tells the original buyer that it is no longer prepared to honour the contract and will instead pay damages, this would represent an 'efficient' breach of contract if the price paid by the third party was high enough for the seller to retain a surplus after paying damages to the original buyer. However, this calculation only works if the damages paid by the seller to the original buyer cover all of the disadvantages from not receiving the delivery. However, this is not the case when the contract is for the sale of a house or another interest in land or for a singular asset in which the buyer has a peculiar interest, since it would in both instances be impossible to conclude a 'covering transaction' for an equivalent replacement asset. This is why in such cases the Common Law grants the buyer a claim for specific performance and then makes sure the seller performs the contract *in natura*.[49] It is true that even in these cases specific performance may be

---

replacement, the seller must also bear the costs for de-installing the defective goods and installing the replacement goods. The seller may not even refuse replacement delivery if such costs are disproportionate. See Case C-65/09, 16 June 2011, Slg. 2011 I- 5257 = [2011] *NJW* 2269.

[48] See HB Schäfer and C Ott, *Lehrbuch der ökonomischen Analyse des Zivilrechts* (5th edn, 2012) 504ff; D Friedman, 'The Efficient Breach Fallacy' (1989) 18 *J Leg Stud* 1; T Ulen, 'The Efficiency of Specific Performance' (1984) 83 *Mich. LR* 341; RJ Scalise, 'Why No "Efficient Breach" in the Civil Law?: A Comparative Assessment of the Doctrine of Efficient Breach of Contract' (2007) 55 *Am J Comp L* 721. See also U Huber, *Leistungsstörungen* vol. I (1999) 49ff; Neufang, *Erfüllungszwang als 'remedy' bei Nichterfüllung* (1998) 366ff; H Kötz, *Vertragsrecht* (2nd edn, 2012) mn. 774ff.

[49] It should be noted that a seller, even when faced with a judgment to deliver the purchased asset, will not always be deterred from taking the 'efficient breach of contract' route. It may be that the seller will 'buy' the judgment performance issued in the buyer's favour for a price that is higher than the damages

unavailable if the asset is no longer in the seller's possession because it has already been delivered to a third party. The seller might then argue that specific performance is impossible, or that its cost would be disproportionately high as it would have to repurchase the asset from the third party. Even in these circumstances, however, the seller's interest in an efficient breach of contract can be thwarted in other ways. Some legal systems give the buyer an option to hold the seller liable for the full amount it received from the third party.[50] Sometimes, it will be hard for the seller to find a third party willing to buy the goods at the higher price. If the third party not only knows about the seller's breach of contract, but is also encouraging it and might even have promised to indemnify the seller for any damages to be paid to the original buyer, this can constitute a tort by the third party that in itself requires the third party to pay damages to the buyer.[51] Nor is there an incentive for an efficient breach of contract if the sale is for fungible items that the seller can obtain in the same quality from another source. In this case, a third party will only offer the seller a higher price for such goods if the market price has risen since the original contract. But the damages payable to the buyer by the seller will also rise accordingly, as these are calculated on the basis of the substitute transaction that the buyer would have to conclude at the higher market price. Selling fungible goods to a third party at a higher price makes no economic sense for the seller, because the damages it will have to pay to the buyer will rise correspondingly.

The situation is different for *contracts of work*, where an efficient breach of contract is permitted everywhere. An example would be where a building contractor has secured a contract to erect a building, but the client then decides that it no longer wishes to go ahead with the contract because another contractor would be prepared to take on the contract for a lower price. In such cases, the client is allowed to cancel the contract without giving reasons, even if the building contractor has already started work. However, the price of cancelling the contract is that the client has to pay the agreed price, less any amount that the building contractor has saved by the premature termination of the contract, or has acquired by redeploying its resources.[52] In practical terms, this means no more than the client having to pay damages. In the reverse situation, a building contractor may realise after concluding the contract that it would be advantageous to terminate the contract because it could deploy its resources more profitably elsewhere for a price in excess of the damages it would have to pay to the disappointed client. Here the building contractor has no right of termination, and it may

---

that would have to be paid to the buyer, but less than the price that a third party would pay him for the goods. See above, n 28.

[50] See § 285 BGB.

[51] In such a case, the third party would be liable under German law pursuant to § 826 BGB for 'incitement to breach of contract', under English law for the 'tort of procuring a breach of contract', and under French law in accordance with art. 1240 (formerly art. 1382) *Code civil*, because of a 'faute' in his behaviour. See for details Scalise (n 48) 756ff; V Palmer, 'A Comparative Study (From a Common Law Perspective) of the French Action for Wrongful Interference with Contract' (1992) 40 *Am J Comp L* 297.

[52] See § 649 BGB; art. 324 OR; § 1168 ABGB; art. 7A:1647 BW; art. 377 OR; art. 700 Greek Civil Code; art. 644 Polish Civil Code. Other legal systems take the same approach, by requiring a client after cancellation of a contract to pay damages to the contractor. See, for example, art. 1794 *Code civil*; art. 1671 *Codice civile*.

well be that the client will be granted a judgment for specific performance. But such a judgment makes no sense for the client, perhaps because enforcement is excluded (for example, where the contract requires artistic or scientific input), and perhaps because enforcement will only result in the client being authorised by the court to have the work carried out by a third party at the cost of the defendant building contractor, which means in substance that the client will only receive damages. Parties must also pay damages for *contracts for services* if they do not accept or provide the promised service, thus breaching the contract. There is no fear that a judgment for specific performance will be granted. So where a client has concluded a contract for services with a lawyer, a patient with a doctor, or a schoolchild with the operator of a boarding school, a judgment to perform the promised service will mostly fail on the fact that the service has a personal character or turns on a relationship of trust between the parties. Even if an order for specific performance can be granted, the execution of this order is often excluded or is impractical for the creditor. The reverse situation is no different, where a party wishes to provide the service but the other party does not want to accept: here no order of specific performance can force the other party to accept the service. Instead, it must pay the agreed price (with certain deductions)—in effect, pay damages.[53]

How can it be that for contracts of work and for services the contractor is allowed to take the path of the 'efficient breach of contract', whilst the same process is denied (or at least made much more difficult) for sellers in contracts for the sale of land and specified assets? For these particular contracts of sale, one can assume that when the contract is concluded, the seller still owns the object of sale, but is now acting as a sort of 'trustee' on behalf of the buyer. It must therefore deliver the object or, if delivery is no longer possible, hand over to the buyer any advantage secured from utilising the contractual object elsewhere. In a contract of work, the situation is different. A building contractor must deliver the work as promised, but remains in control of arranging the deployment of its staff and machinery and organising its business operations; it is entitled to profit from any advantages secured from another more profitable deployment of its resources. The client is reimbursed for any harm caused and will be placed in the same position as if there had been no breach of contract. If, on the other hand, a seller of certain individual contractual objects is seen as a 'trustee' for the buyer, it cannot just offer damages and walk away from the contract. The claim for damages here would be regarded as 'inadequate', because a 'covering' transaction as a basis for calculation of the damages is normally not feasible, and the damage suffered by the buyer is often of an immaterial nature and cannot be fully compensated for by money. But if the price that the seller would have to pay in damages for breach of contract were too low, the breach of contract would no longer be 'efficient'. So, from an economic perspective, a legal system is doing the right thing if it tries to prevent this from happening by granting a remedy for specific performance.

---

[53] See § 615 BGB; §§ 1155 ABGB; art. 324 OR; art. 7 A:1638 d BW; art. 2227 *Codice civile*.

13

Termination of Contracts

A.	Introduction	215
B.	Interests of the Parties	216
C.	Solutions	218
	I. French law	219
	II. English law	220
	III. German law	223
D.	Requirements	224
	I. Basic requirements	224
	II. Impossibility of performance	226
	III. Anticipatory non-performance	228
	IV. Delayed performance	229
	V. Incomplete performance	231
	VI. Defective performance	233
E.	Restitution	237

A. Introduction

Every party to a contract trusts that the counterparty will perform the contract as promised. If this does not happen, the question arises as to how the innocent party—sometimes referred to as the 'creditor'—can react to this circumstance. One way is to insist on the contract being performed. So if the counterparty—sometimes referred to as the debtor—is a seller who has not delivered the contractual goods, or not delivered them on time, or at the agreed location or in the agreed packaging or not as stipulated in the contract, then the buyer can stand by the contract of sale and assert a claim for performance (see chapter 12). He or she can therefore insist on delivery of the contractual goods and give the seller an additional deadline by which it must comply. If the delivered goods were faulty, the buyer can demand repair of the defect or delivery of fault-free replacement goods.[1] If the seller takes the initiative and demands payment of the purchase price, the buyer can assert a right of retention by refusing to pay so long as the seller fails to meet its obligations, namely before it delivers the contractual goods as promised in the contract.[2] The buyer also has the option of asserting

---

[1] This is referred to as supplementary performance; see above, p. 210.
[2] The party that in a reciprocal (synallagmatic) contract asserts a 'defence of unperformed contract', is only stating that it is refusing to perform its own obligations, and not that its obligations have been terminated. Practically, the situation is often that a party *initially* asserts this defence, and then later (if the contract remains unperformed) terminates the contract in order to cancel out its own obligations. On the 'exceptio non adimpleti contractus', see for example § 320 BGB; §§ 1052, 1062 ABGB; art. 6:262 BW; art. 374 Greek Civil Code; art. 1460(1) *Codice civile*; art. 428 Portuguese Civil Code. Some legal systems incorporate this defence for contracts of sale in a statutory provision (see s. 28 Sale of Goods Act 1979; art. 1612, 1653 *Code civil*). This solution has been accepted by the courts whenever the contract shows that the parties' reciprocal obligations are to be performed hand in hand; see GH Treitel, *The Law of*

a claim for performance as well as claiming damages for harm caused by the seller in not delivering the goods as contractually stipulated, or for some other breach of a contractual term.

So long as the creditor insists on contractual performance in this manner, it must also expect to complete its own obligations under the contract if the debtor performs as required. This could be a problem, such as when the creditor has contracted for the supply or delivery of goods but the price for the same goods or services has fallen in the meantime. Under such circumstances, the creditor has an evident interest in cancelling its own obligations to pay the contract price, in order to be free to conclude the transaction at a better price with another party. This is the question to be addressed below: under which conditions is the creditor entitled to terminate the contract, thereby cancelling out the requirement for either party to perform their obligations under the contract? If the contract is terminated, a further question arises as to how the parties can claim back what they have already rendered.[3]

The text below refers to 'termination' of the contract, but we could also use terms such as rescission, revocation, distancing from the contract,[4] or withdrawing from the contract.[5] German law refers to *Rücktritt* and *Kündigung*, French law to *résolution* and *résiliation*, Italian law to *risoluzione* and *recesso*, and Dutch law refers to *ontbinding*, or dissolving the contract. English law uses a range of terms, but in recent times 'termination' has become more prevalent[6] and has also been adopted by the international sets of rules. Whichever term is used is a matter of taste, but all of these terms basically mean the same: the main consequence of the termination of the contract is that neither party will have any further obligations to perform in the future. In many cases, the innocent party has not only an interest in terminating the contract, but also in claiming damages for breach of contract. Both remedies can be cumulated.[7] They must nonetheless be distinguished, and the innocent party's claim for damages will be discussed separately in chapter 14.

B. Interests of the Parties

The question of whether a contractual party can terminate the contract as indicated is not easy to decide. On the one hand, a party confronted by a breach of contract may have a strong interest in liquidating the contract for this reason, thus giving it a free hand to contract with a third party if that seems advantageous. However, the counterparty may have an equally strong interest in ensuring that the contract continues.

Contract (13th edn, by E Peel, 2011) no. 17-013ff; F Terré, P Simler, and Y Lequette, *Droit civil, Les obligations* (11th edn, 2013) no. 630ff. See also art. 58 CISG and art. 9:201 PECL; art. 7.1.3 PICC; art. III.-3:401 DCFR; art. 133 CESL.

[3] See E below (pp. 237ff.).

[4] See P Schlechtriem, 'Abstandnahme vom Vertrag' in J Basedow (ed), *Europäische Vertragsrechtsvereinheitlichung und deutsches Recht* (2000) 159.

[5] See A Flessner, 'Befreiung vom Vertrag wegen Nichterfüllung' (1997) 5 *ZEuP* 255.

[6] See in particular the section on 'termination' in GH Treitel, *Remedies for Breach of Contract, A Comparative Account* (1988) pp. 239ff.

[7] This is sometimes stated explicitly. See, for example, § 325 BGB; § 921 ABGB; art. 1217 *Code civil*; art. 45(2) CISG; art. 8:102 PECL; art. 7.4.1 PICC.

The conflict of interest here is clear if one considers a contract by which the creditor has agreed to pay the seller for the delivery of goods, the building company to build a house, or the lessor to lease business premises or a ship. What can the creditor do if the debtor fails to meet its obligations, or fails to meet them in full? A debtor may be unable to deliver the goods sold because it is forbidden to do so by law, or delivery may be impossible for some other reason. It could also be that the seller's own contractor has failed to deliver the goods, and so the seller is unable to deliver them in turn to the creditor. Or strikes by its staff may mean that the building company is only able to finish a construction job with some delay, or there may be transport problems or other reasons that prevent the debtor from delivering purchased goods on time. What can be done if the debtor delivers on time, but the goods do not meet the contractual stipulations? What if a debtor, in breach of its contractual obligations, fails to repair at its own cost defects in a building that it has rented out, or fails to repair damage to the engines on a ship it has chartered out? And what if the debtor has delivered the first instalment of goods on time, but then breaches the contract by delivering the same goods to a competitor of the creditor, perhaps even at a lower price?

In these sorts of cases, the creditor is often best advised to stand by the contract and require performance from the debtor. If the goods have not been delivered on time, the creditor can also insist on delivery even if it is not on time when it finally arrives. If the goods or service are defective, the creditor is entitled, and often even obliged (at least at first), to assert a claim for *supplementary performance*—to demand that the debtor take further steps to repair the defect in the goods or services, or deliver a defect-free replacement. The creditor may also keep the faulty goods or services, and demand that the debtor agree a discount on the price. Finally, even if the creditor wishes to demand performance or supplementary performance of the contract, nothing prevents it from demanding damages from the debtor for the harm suffered as a result of the debtor not fulfilling the contract, or not fulfilling the contract correctly.

It is another question that is in the foreground of the following considerations: under which conditions is the creditor entitled to *terminate* the contract if the debtor has not met its contractual obligations, or not met them in full? The creditor may wish to take this course of action because it no longer trusts the debtor, or does not want to spend a long time in dispute on when and how the other party's breach of contract might be cured or remedied in some other way. Another reason may be that the price promised by the debtor to perform its obligations has fallen after the contract was concluded, and the creditor could now secure the goods or service from a third party at a lower cost. The same applies if the price has since increased and a seller wishes to get out of the original contract—perhaps because the buyer breached it by a failure to prepay a part of the price—so as to be able to sell the goods to another buyer at the higher market price. There is indeed always a possibility that the creditor finds out later that it did a poor deal, and now avails itself of the debtor's breach—be it ever so insignificant or negligible—to bring the contract to an end and thus rid itself of a bargain that was bad in the first place. On the other hand, one must also consider the interests of the debtor. It is clear that after the termination of the contract, the debtor loses the profit it would have made had the contract been performed. Another loss can result if the debtor has already started to perform its contractual obligations. It may have prepared the building site, hired subcontractors, ordered raw materials, or even partially produced the goods to be delivered. The costs incurred in this way would be lost if the creditor were entitled to terminate the contract. It is true that the debtor is responsible for the breach: after all, it did not want to live up to what was promised in the agreement. In many cases, however, the debtor would be much relieved if it could get away with paying damages rather than face the grim fact that the creditor, by terminating the contract, destroyed the basis on which the parties had so far been dealing with each other.

This is why the parties have good reasons to make special agreements on how the risk of termination is to be divided. Such agreements may make it easier for the innocent party to terminate the contract, such as where a buyer is allowed to immediately terminate if a specified delivery date is not met. Such agreements can also make termination more difficult—for example, if termination is expressly excluded and the debtor is required to pay the creditor damages for any harm caused by non-performance or poor performance of the contract. The parties can also agree that avoidance should only be permissible if the debtor's breach has particularly grave consequences, or if the creditor has set the debtor a deadline for supplementary performance of the contract, and this deadline has expired. Such agreements are often made, but if no such agreement is reached the gap may be filled by 'dispositive rules' that set out the general rules for termination. But what form should such rules take?

C. Solutions

It might seem obvious that a creditor must be able to cancel a contract if the promised performance does not happen, or if the debtor breaches the contractual terms in some other way. But general rules on the right to terminate a contract did not develop in most European legal systems until very late, and they did not exist in Roman law. Contracts of sale could include an agreement entitling the seller to declare the contract ended if the buyer failed to pay at the time specified in the contract.[8] There are also signs that Roman law allowed the party being sued for performance to rely on a defence—later called an *exceptio non adimpleti contractus*—by refusing performance if the plaintiff himself had failed to perform.[9] This rule was also adopted in Canon law and given a broader basis. Since every breach of a promise was considered to be sinful, and therefore morally reprehensible, the conclusion was reached not only that in principle all contractual agreements were valid,[10] but also that anyone breaching a promise could not require fidelity to the contract from the other party: *fidem frangenti fides non est servanda*. The natural law theorists clad the same principle in another form. They assumed that in reciprocal contracts each party was promising to fulfil its obligations only 'on condition' that the other party would also fulfil its obligations. Furthermore, in such cases the innocent party should not merely be given a defence

---

[8] On this *lex commissoria* agreement, see R Zimmermann, *The Law of Obligations, Roman Foundations of the Civilian Tradition* (1990) pp. 737f.

[9] See in detail and with references to the extensive historical literature Zimmermann (n 8) 800ff; see also R Zimmermann, 'Heard Melodies are Sweet, but those Unheard are Sweeter ...' (1993) 193 *AcP* 121, 160ff.

[10] See above, p. 50.

if sued for performance by the party in breach, but should be allowed to go one step further and bring the whole contract to an end.

I. French law

Until recently, French law also followed this approach. Art. 1184(1) *Code civil* stated that each reciprocal contract was subject to the condition precedent of timely fulfilment of the contract by the other party.[11] If that party failed to fulfil the contract, pursuant to art. 1184(2) the counterparty could choose either to assert a claim for performance, or to instead terminate the contract and assert a claim for damages. Art. 1184(3) went on to say, however, that the decision about the termination of the contract could only be made by the judge, who could determine that the contract would only come to an end if the debtor failed to perform within a period set by the court.

It is obvious that the principle of *judicial termination* of contracts brings disadvantages in the course of ordinary commercial practice. If this principle is taken seriously—and there is a presumption that until a termination judgment is issued by the court a party would remain fully bound by its contractual obligations—this would mean that a seller would not be able to re-sell goods elsewhere until after a termination judgment had been handed down, nor would a buyer be able to obtain replacement goods from another supplier. French law has avoided this by recognising a long list of 'exceptions' that permit the innocent party to effect unilateral termination of the contract. This is the case if the contract contains an agreement allowing such a unilateral termination. The same assumption is made, even without such an agreement, if the contract (such as a tenancy agreement or employment contract) is for an indeterminate period or envisages performance in instalments. The same also applies for agency contracts, such as the provision of information and advice, the storage of goods, the distribution and marketing of the client's goods, or the management of its affairs. Here either party can unilaterally declare the contract to be at an end if they have a justified reason to have lost trust in the reliability or competence of the other party.[12] Above all, in a judgment dated 13 October 1998, the *Cour de cassation* decided that unilateral termination of a contract is permitted if the counterparty has committed a severe breach of its obligations.[13] What constitutes such a severe breach depends on the circumstances, but the criteria will usually be met if the creditor has set the debtor a deadline for performance after the original due date, and the subsequent deadline has also not been observed. It is

---

[11] See art. 1184(1): '[L]a condition résolutoire est toujours sous-entendue.' For the historical development of this formulation, see Terré, Simler, and Lequette (n 2) no. 644.
[12] See in detail Terré, Simler, and Lequette (n 2) no. 478ff; P Malaurie, L Aynès, and P Stoffel-Munck, *Les obliations* (6th edn, 2013) no. 881. In such cases, one speaks not of *résolution*, but of *résiliation* of the contract, with the consequence that the contract is only cancelled for the future. See also below, pp. 238f.
[13] '*La gravité du comportement d'une partie à un contrat peut justifier que l'autre partie y mette fin de façon unilatérale à ses risques et périls.*' See Civ. 13 Oct. 1998, D. 1999, 198, n. C Jamin = *JCP* 1999.II.10133, n. N Rzepecki. Also Civ. 20 Feb. 2001, D. 2001, 1568, n. C Jamin = [2001] *Rev trim civ* 363, n. J Mestre and BF Fages. See also Terré, Simler, and Lequette (n 2) no. 660; Malaurie, Aynès, and Stoffel-Munck (n 12) no. 891; M Storck, Juris Classeur civil art. 1184 Fasc. 10 (2007) no. 68, all citing French cases decided before the recent reform of French contract law.

correct that courts always warn creditors that they are acting '*à ses risques et périls*' if they effect unilateral avoidance. But that merely underlines what is self-evident—namely that the debtor can always have recourse to the court to assert that the unilateral avoidance was unjustified. If the debtor is successful in the application, the creditor has also committed a breach of contract by terminating the contract without justified reason, and must pay damages.

This prepared the ground for the recent revision of the law on contractual termination. Firstly, arts. 1224 and 1225 state that the parties can agree that a contract is to be avoided if a party fails to meet certain obligations (*clause résolutoire*).[14] Even if no such agreement is reached, the creditor may unilaterally terminate the contract (without recourse to a court), but only if the non-performance is '*suffisament grave*' and the creditor has given the debtor a reasonable period for supplementary performance and has warned it '*expressément*' that the contract will be terminated if this deadline is not complied with (arts. 1224, 1225 *Code civil*). The *Code civil* does not say what non-performance is *suffisament grave*. It did adopt the formulation used by the French courts by which a creditor unilaterally terminating a contract is acting '*à ses risques et périls*'—namely running the risk that a judge will at some later point refuse to recognise the termination as valid. In that case, the contract would still be in force, and the judge could order the defendant to perform the contract, perhaps within a certain period (art. 1228 *Code civil*). It remains open whether a creditor, by terminating the contract without sufficient reasons, commits a breach of contract and is therefore liable to pay damages.

II. English law

English law starts from the general principle that the innocent party may terminate a contract if the other party's breach is sufficiently important: there must be a 'substantial failure of performance'. However, this is only a rule of thumb that is subject to many exceptions.

In order to distinguish between 'substantial' and other breaches, English case law relies on the difference between 'warranties' and 'conditions'. Any contractual promise carries either an 'express warranty' or an 'implied warranty'. If a party does not comply with such a promise, the innocent party may claim damages for breach of contract, but remains otherwise bound by it. A party is only entitled to escape from the contract altogether where the promise breached by the other party constitutes a 'condition'.

That English law refers here to a condition, as did French law under the former art. 1184 *Code civil*, is no accident. English law also used to regard fulfilment of an important contractual promise as a 'condition' for the counterparty's duty to perform. Unless the innocent party had expressly agreed to perform in advance, it was therefore entitled to refuse performance so long as the other party had not made or tendered its own performance. This line of thought was later strengthened so that,

---

[14] Unless otherwise agreed, this only applies if the creditor has put the debtor in default by a warning notice in which express reference was made to the termination agreement (art. 1225).

upon breach of a condition, the innocent party could treat its obligation as having come to an end. It was entitled to terminate the contract and to claim damages under certain circumstances—this time for non-performance of the (now terminated) contract.[15]

How can one distinguish between a warranty and a condition?[16] If the contract clearly labels a contractual term as a condition, this is generally accepted as such by the courts, even if the disadvantages suffered by the innocent party do not appear under the circumstances to be particularly onerous.[17] The situation was different in *Schuler AG v. Wickman Machine Tool Sales Ltd.*[18] A sole distributor had undertaken to visit six named companies at least once a week to solicit orders, but failed to meet this requirement. Although the contract stated that this term was a condition, the claimant was denied a right to terminate the contract because the court felt that the parties cannot have strictly meant the clause to be a condition: If this were the case, even a minor breach regarding one single visit would have had drastic consequences. If there is no express agreement that a clause is a condition, it depends on whether the breach leads to a 'substantial failure of performance' or (as is often said) 'goes to the very root of the matter'. In this respect, the gravity of the consequences that the innocent party would face if the breach were to occur is generally important. A clause is unlikely to be accepted as a condition if a breach would cause only minimal harm, or where damages might be sufficient to reasonably compensate the innocent party.

On the other hand, there are cases in which courts have been fairly relentless in treating contractual promises as conditions. The courts have taken this position particularly in cases in which business firms have agreed on a specific period of time in which promises were to be performed, or declarations were to be made. In *Bunge Corp. v. Tradax SA*,[19] a buyer of 15,000 tonnes of soya had to provide a ship at some port on the US Gulf Coast and to inform the seller at least fifteen days before the boarding date of the readiness of the ship so that the seller could select the port and deliver the soya in time. The buyer gave less than fifteen days' notice. The seller then immediately terminated the contract, and the court held that it was entitled to do so. In business-to-business transactions, the principle is that 'time is of the essence'. The agreement of a fifteen-day notice period was thus a condition, and the seller was entitled to terminate the contract regardless of whether or not it would have been able to select the loading port and transport the soya within less than fifteen days. Nor did the court consider whether this would have resulted in extra costs for the seller, and how high those costs might have been. The case would certainly not have been decided any differently if the soya price had risen after the contract was

---

[15] For detail, see Zimmermann (n 9) 153ff. The use of the term 'condition' in French and English law is regarded as resulting from a close historical link between the natural lawyers and the *ius commune* on the one hand and the Common Law on the other; both legal traditions are, in the words of Zimmermann, 'cut from the same cloth in the area of contract law at least' (169).

[16] See the extensive discussion in Treitel (n 2) no. 18-039ff; E McKendrick, *Contract Law* (8th edn, 2009) no. 10.1ff, 19.6ff. and (comparatively) Treitel (n 6) pp. 259ff. and Flessner (n 5) 266ff.

[17] See, for example, *Lombard North Central plc v. Butterworth* [1987] QB 527.

[18] [1974] AC 235.   [19] [1981] 1 WLR 711 (HL).

concluded, and the 'real' motivation for the seller's termination of the contract was to have the chance of selling the soya to another buyer at a higher price. One might say that it is in some cases unfair to allow a party to terminate the contract and turn its back on an unfavourable agreement. However, this must—in the opinion of the court—be tolerated.[20]

Sometimes it is the legislature that raises certain (express or implied) terms to the status of a condition, especially where a seller has delivered goods that are not in conformity with contractual stipulations, not suitable to attain the aim of the contract, or for other reasons do not have the qualities required to be deemed 'satisfactory'. Sections 12-15 of the Sale of Goods Act 1979 state that in these circumstances the seller has breached an implied term, and these implied terms are expressly deemed to be conditions.[21] However, pursuant to s. 15(A) a buyer may not terminate the contract if the defect in the delivered goods is 'slight', and must console itself only with damages.[22]

What about the situation where neither the agreement between the parties nor the case law or statutes classify a contractual promise as either a condition or warranty? Such promises, which are usually called 'intermediate terms' or 'innominate terms', can carry consequences if breached, and these consequences can be so severe that the innocent party will basically no longer receive what was promised in the contract. Here too the party can demand termination of the contract, as was settled in a landmark case from 1962.[23] The claimant shipowner had chartered out a ship for two years to the defendants, and the ship was already unseaworthy at delivery because of its old engines. Because of this, during its first voyage from Liverpool to Osaka the ship's engines were under repair for three weeks, and for a further fifteen weeks after arrival in Osaka. The charterers then purported to terminate the charter. It was important to note that the charter price for ships of the same type had fallen in the meantime, and that the charterers would then probably have been able to secure a ship of the same type for a lower rate. The shipowner argued that although it may have breached the contract by delivering an unseaworthy ship, this did not entitle the charterers to terminate the charterparty. For this reason, the shipowners alleged that the termination in itself constituted a breach of contract, and that the charterers owed it damages for non-performance of the contract. The Court of Appeal followed this viewpoint. The shipowner had breached its obligation to provide a seaworthy ship, and on this basis might owe the charterers damages as stipulated in the contract. But this breach by the shipowner was, under the circumstances, not as severe as to allow the charterers a termination of the contract in its entirety. By terminating the contract without sufficient reason, they were in breach themselves and were therefore liable in damages to the shipowner.

---

[20] See the impressive considerations of *Lord Wilberforce* in *Bunge* ibid. 715, and also Treitel (n 2) no. 18-042 and 18-050; McKendrick (n 16) no. 10.4.

[21] See ss. 11(3), 13(1A), and 14(6) Sale of Goods Act 1977.

[22] This does not apply if the buyer is a consumer (see below, pp. 236f.). See the criticism of s. 15(A) Sale of Goods Act 1977 in Treitel (n 2) no. 18-053f.

[23] *Hong Kong Fir Shipping Co. Ltd.* v. *Kawasaki Kishen Kaisha Ltd.* [1962] 2 QB 26.

III. German law

Under German law, termination of a reciprocal contract is called *Rücktritt*.[24] It is permissible if a debtor fails to perform on time or in line with the contract and the creditor has also 'specified, without result, a reasonable period for performance or cure' (§ 323(1) BGB). This *Nachfrist* model is also used by other legal orders as the starting point for statutory provisions governing termination of a contract.[25] English law has no such requirement, although it is recognised that it may in some cases be important for the right to terminate if the creditor can show not only that the debtor did not perform or performed badly, but also failed to perform within a reasonable period set by the creditor.

German law has numerous important cases where the setting of a *Nachfrist* is unnecessary and where a contract can be terminated with immediate effect. This is so where the performance of the debtor is 'impossible' in accordance with § 275 BGB.[26] So if the painting sold has been destroyed, or the goods are no longer available, the buyer not only loses its claim for performance *in natura*, but can also relieve itself from the duty to pay the price by immediately terminating the contract without having to set a deadline, as it would be pointless under these circumstances (§ 326(5) BGB).

More important are the cases that permit immediate termination as specified in § 323(2) BGB (and in art. 108 OR). A creditor need not set a *Nachfrist* for performance if the debtor 'seriously and definitively refuses performance' after it is due.[27] Nor is a *Nachfrist* required if the debtor has not performed its obligations by the agreed due date, or within the agreed period, and it appears from the contract that the creditor's interest in timely performance is 'essential'. This is meant to cover cases where, after interpretation by the court, the contract will 'stand or fall' on the punctuality of the debtor's performance. This will apply, for example, where the date of performance is described as '*fix*' or '*fest*', or that the debtor must perform 'without any additional period' or 'no later than agreed'. Thus it may appear from the contract that the goods are to be used in a particular way—such as to be sold in the upcoming bathing season, to be shown at a particular trade fair, or to be loaded onto a ship with a specified departure time. Here, when the goods are not delivered on time the buyer will be able to terminate the contract without any need to set a *Nachfrist* if it is clear that the

---

[24] The term 'Kündigung' is used when someone wishes to withdraw from a contract creating a *Dauerschuldverhältnis*, or continuing obligation, such as a rental contract, a contract for services, a partnership agreement, or an open-ended agency agreement. The conditions under which such a contract can be terminated are often stipulated by agreement between the parties; but where there is no such agreement or the agreement is invalid, it can be governed by statutory provisions. They allow for *außerordentliche Kündigung* (extraordinary termination) when there is a *wichtiger Grund* (good reason). If no such rules have been agreed, the mandatory provision under § 314 BGB applies: it allows for termination of a contract for continuing obligations *aus wichtigem Grund* (for a good reason).

[25] See art. 107 OR; § 918 ABGB; art. 383 Greek Civil Code; art. 808 Portuguese Civil Code. See also arts. 6:265 and 6:82 BW and art. 1454 *Codice civile*, both with the further condition that the deadline must be given in writing, and under Italian law it must be at least fifteen days. See Flessner (n 5) 271f.

[26] See chapter 12.C (above, pp. 300ff.).

[27] See, for example, BGH 25 Feb. 1971, [1971] *NJW* 798. If the debtor says or indicates *before* performance is due that it will not or cannot perform its obligations, it is 'obvious' that the requirements for immediate termination will be met, and there is no need to set a *Nachfrist*. See § 323(4) BGB and below, p. 228.

intended use of the goods is no longer possible if they are delivered later. There may also be other reasons (such as for goods where the price can change from day to day) where—as they say in England—'time is of the essence'.

Finally, immediate termination of a contract is also permitted when justified by 'special circumstances' (§ 323(2) no. 3 BGB). The courts have held that this condition is met if the debtor has not performed at all, or not in line with the contract and this circumstance alone leads to the conclusion that the creditor is no longer interested in a supplementary performance and must thus be allowed to terminate the contract forthwith. It is, of course, not sufficient that the market price has meanwhile fallen, and it is for this reason alone that the buyer is now interested in an immediate termination of the contract. This is, after all, a risk that the buyer would have had to bear if the seller had delivered the goods on time. On the other hand, 'special circumstances' are held to exist when the buyer resold the goods to a third party and that party terminated the contract because of the buyer's failure to deliver goods which it had not received in time from the seller. Similarly, a building contractor that has not received the promised goods or services from a subcontractor on time can terminate the contract without setting a *Nachfrist* if, as a consequence, the building contractor's own client did not receive performance from it on time and has thus terminated the contract.[28]

When one summarises all these examples of immediate termination, it appears that the common denominator is that the non-performance or poor performance of the contract carries a disadvantage for the innocent party that is so detrimental that it 'substantially deprives that party of its expectations under the contract'. That is exactly the definition of a 'fundamental breach of contract' that art. 25 CISG states to be the most important condition for an immediate termination of the contract. Thus one can conclude that the requirements for immediately terminating a contract for non-performance or poor performance are in German law not much different from those set out in the CISG.

D. Requirements

I. Basic requirements

In comparative legal literature, there is no longer much debate about the basic requirements needed for an immediate termination of the contract. It was important for this consensus that the matter was looked at in great depth when the CISG was being drawn up, and that the solution of the CISG seems to work very well. It is true that the CISG only applies to contracts for the sale of goods and that the sellers and buyers of those goods must be business firms located in different countries. Even so, the CISG solution has been influential during the reform of national contract laws, including the modernisation of the law of obligations in Germany in 2002. In addition, the CISG

---

[28] See, for example, RG 26 May 1922, RGZ 104, 373, 375; BGH 25 Feb. 1971 (n 27); BGH 10 Mar. 1998, [1998] *NJW-RR* 1489, 1491 and W Ernst in *Münchener Kommentar zum BGB* (6th edn, 2012) § 323 mn. 122ff, and in particular U Huber, *Leistungsstörungen* vol. II (1999) §§ 48 II 2, 49 III 1. The cases stated and explained by Huber refer to the now-repealed provision of § 326(2) BGB, but still apply today as § 323(2) no. 3 BGB contains a very similar provision.

has now been ratified by eighty countries, including almost all Member States of the European Union, and has been applied by courts and arbitration panels in countless cases.[29]

The consensus referred to previously concerns three important points. Firstly, in a reciprocal contract the creditor has the option of whether or not to terminate the contract. It is for the creditor to make the decision—and not the court, as originally required by art. 1184(1) *Code civil*—though a court can still subsequently examine whether or not the termination by the creditor was justified. Secondly, the termination of the contract by the creditor is only justified if the breach by the debtor is sufficiently grave: 'The most important single principle used to control the remedy of termination ... is that the remedy is only available if the default attains a certain minimum degree of seriousness.'[30] For these reasons, termination usually requires the breach to be 'significant' or 'fundamental'. Thirdly, there is recognition—particularly if the breach is not 'significant' or the creditor has doubts about its significance—that termination of the contract by the creditor can be justified if the debtor has failed to perform or perform successfully on time, the creditor has set a reasonable additional period for performance, and the debtor has failed to perform within this additional period.

It cannot be denied that these three points are rather vague. It remains to be seen if and how far they can be substantiated depending on the type of breach committed by the debtor. Particularly questionable is how the term 'significant breach of contract' is to be defined. One can rely on the consequences of the breach, particularly how great the disadvantages are which the creditor has already suffered or might suffer in the future. One can also rely on the importance that the debtor's breach has in light of what the creditor has promised in the contract. Art. 25 CISG chooses a formulation that tries to take account of both approaches. Whether or not there is a 'significant breach of contract' depends on the one hand on the disadvantages suffered by the creditor, and on the other hand whether these disadvantages mean that the creditor would be deprived of what it would have expected 'under the contract'.[31]

One important case of non-performance is where the performance is definitely impossible for the debtor (see II below). Another case is where the debtor declares before the due date for performance that it does not wish to meet its obligations (see III

---

[29] There is now a great deal of literature about the CISG. For an introduction, see P Schlechtriem and U Schroeter, *Internationales UN-Kaufrecht* (6th edn, 2016).
[30] Treitel (n 6) p. 259; see also Flessner (n 5) 266ff.
[31] However, there is no 'fundamental breach' under art. 25 CISG if its consequences are unforeseeable for a reasonable person in the position of the debtor. See in detail Schlechtriem and Schroeter (n 29) mn. 317ff; G Lubbe, 'Fundamental Breach under the CISG: A Source of Fundamentally Divergent Results' (2004) 68 *RabelsZ* 444. The international sets of rules follow the CISG in that they only permit termination if the debtor's breach is 'fundamental'. See art. 9:301(1) PECL; art. 7.3.1(1) PICC; art. III.-3:502(1) DCFR; art. 114, 134 CESL. On the other hand, some rules try to define what constitutes a 'fundamental breach of contract' more closely than the CISG, or state criteria to be taken into account by a judge when considering this question. According to the definition in art. 8:103 PECL, a breach is 'fundamental' if 'strict compliance with the obligation is of the essence of the contract', if the breach 'essentially deprives the aggrieved party of what it was entitled to expect from the contract', or if the debtor's breach was intentional and the innocent party fears that the debtor will no longer fulfil the contract. Similarly art. III.-3:502(2) DCFR and art. 87(2) CESL. Article 7.3.1(2) PICC lists no fewer than six points to be taken into account by a judge when considering whether the breach is fundamental.

below). Then there is the case where the debtor does not perform by the due date, and is thus in default, but it is still possible for it to perform, or the creditor believes this to be the case (see IV below). The other two cases are 'incomplete' and 'defective' performance (see V and VI below).

II. Impossibility of performance

It is impossible for a debtor to perform where performance is permanently impossible for factual or legal reasons. Such is the case if a seller has sold a particular ship, but cannot deliver because the ship has sunk, has been seized by the state, stolen by someone, or sold and handed over to a third party. If a contract is for the sale of goods of a certain kind rather than for a particular thing, delivery will only be impossible if the entire genus to which the goods belong has been destroyed or is no longer available anywhere. In these cases, it is evident that the buyer (or any other creditor) must be able to free itself of its duty to pay the price (or provide some other counterperformance). Why should a buyer have to pay for goods, a tenant for rent, or a client for services if the counterparty cannot perform as promised? In such cases, the core expectations of the innocent party are so affected that there will always be a 'fundamental breach of contract'. This party must therefore be able to terminate the contract without going through the useless ceremony of setting a *Nachfrist*.[32]

It follows that the creditor's right to terminate does not depend on whether the breach by the debtor was negligent or intentional, or whether the creditor is liable for other reasons. Take the case where the impossibility is based on reasons for which the debtor is not responsible—such as where there is '*force majeure*' or a '*cas fortuit*',[33] or because they reflect an impediment that according to art. 79 CISG is 'beyond his control',[34] or because 'the basis of the transaction no longer exists' or there is 'frustration of contract': While it is true in these cases that the debtor is not liable for damages,[35] it is also true that the creditor may terminate the contract, and it has sometimes

---

[32] Termination of a contract must be distinguished from its *validity*. Despite its termination, a contract remains in place as a basis for the innocent party's claim for damages. Some legal systems still have the older rule, whereby contracts are void when they concern performance that was impossible per se (see art. 20(1) OR; § 878 ABGB; art. 1346 *Codice civile*). But art. 4:102 PECL takes a different approach: 'A contract is not invalid merely because at the time it was concluded performance of the obligation assumed was impossible.' See also art. II.-7:102 DCFR and § 311a(1) BGB: contracts are valid even if the performance promised by the debtor is impossible from the outset; while such contracts can be terminated by the creditor immediately, they may still serve as a basis for the recovery of damages for breach.

[33] See standing French case law Civ. 2 June 1982, Bull.cass. 1982.I. no. 205 = [1983] *Rev trim civ* 1340, n. F Chabas. Under the former art. 1184 *Code civil*, a court can terminate a contract for non-performance 'même si cette inexécution n'est pas fautive et quel que soit le motif qui a empêché cette partie de remplir ses engagements, alors même que cet empêchement résulterait du fait d'un tiers ou de la force majeure'.

[34] Article 79(5) CISG states expressly that the debtor would in this case not be liable to pay damages, but that the creditor would still be able to exercise other rights, in particular the right to terminate the contract. See also art. 8:101(2) PECL: if the debtor for some reason is not responsible for the non-performance as stated in art. 8:108, the creditor can no longer claim performance or damages, but may terminate the contract. See also art. 7.1.7 PICC; arts. III.-3:101(2) and 3:104 DCFR.

[35] This is why exonerating reasons will only be discussed in the section on damages (chapter 14).

been proposed that the contract should in these cases be 'automatically' regarded as terminated.[36]

In principle, the right to terminate the contract does not, therefore, turn on whether the debtor is liable for the breach for whatever reason. Of course, in some cases a fundamental breach of contract will more likely be assumed if the debtor does not entirely refuse performance (more on that shortly), but its actions nonetheless indicate that it is taking its obligations lightly and is not making much effort, and this gives the creditor reason to believe that the obligations are unlikely to be performed. Pursuant to art. 8:103(c) PECL, there is 'fundamental non-performance' if the non-performance by the debtor is intentional and the creditor has 'reason to believe that it cannot rely on the other party's future performance'.[37] In this case, the creditor is also entitled to immediately terminate the contract even if no harm, or only minimal harm, has so far been caused by the debtor's actions.

No termination is possible if the creditor itself was responsible for the debtor's failure to perform the contract. If, for example, a debtor has not commenced building work by the agreed time, or has failed to deliver the agreed goods, this may be because of conduct by the creditor that is contrary to the terms of the contract. A creditor may have denied the debtor access to the building site, or failed to issue instructions required under the contract which the debtor needed to select the correct building materials, pack the goods correctly, or send them to the correct address. In such cases, the creditor is not only precluded from terminating the contract—it must also pay damages to the debtor because of its own breach.[38]

Furthermore, there is no right to terminate the contract if there are special reasons why the creditor itself bears the risk that the performance owed to it but not yet delivered has been destroyed, damaged, or stolen, and it has thus become impossible for the debtor to perform its obligations. Many legal systems find one reason for transferring such risk to the creditor in a situation in which the creditor was offered the agreed performance by the debtor, but did not accept it for some reason and was therefore in 'default in acceptance': in this situation, it is the creditor's risk that after default in acceptance performance became impossible due to no fault of the debtor. While the debtor is unable to perform the contract, it nonetheless has a claim for the counterperformance owed by the creditor. In such a case, if the debtor is a seller, it can demand the price from the buyer even though no goods were delivered, and it is evident that the buyer cannot, by purporting to terminate the contract, free itself from

---

[36] The creditor need not give a notice of termination if, pursuant to § 313 BGB, the 'basis of the contract disappeared' or the contract is deemed to be 'frustrated'; see Treitel (n 2) no. 19-090ff. See also art. 9:304 (4) PECL: if the debtor is permanently unable to perform because of an impediment for which it is not liable under art. 8:103 PECL, then 'the contract is terminated automatically and without notice at the time the impediment arises'. See also art. III.-3:104(4) DCFR.

[37] See art. 7.3.1 (2c) PICC; art. III.-3:502(2b) DCFR; art. 87(2b) CESL. See also Treitel (n 2) no. 18-034f. and below, pp. 233ff.

[38] See art. 8:101(3) PECL; art. 7.1.2 PICC; art. III.-3:101(3) DCFR. Article 80 CISG also states that a party cannot 'rely' on non-performance (ie not terminate the contract) if the 'failure was caused by [its] act or omission'. Many national legal orders take the same approach. See, for example, §§ 323(5), 326(2) BGB; art. 6:266(1) BW; Civ. 21 Oct. 1964, Bull.cass. 1964.I. no. 463; Civ. 25 May 1976, Bull.cass. 1976. III. no. 229.

the duty to pay the price.³⁹ Another important reason for the risk to pass to the creditor can be seen in contracts for sale where the seller agrees to send the goods to the buyer. Here, the risk of non-performance for reasons for which neither party is liable passes to the buyer 'when the goods are handed over to the first carrier for transmission to the buyer in accordance with the contract of sale'.⁴⁰ So the buyer must still pay the purchase price if the goods are destroyed or damaged during transportation, and the contract may not be terminated by the buyer on the grounds that the goods were damaged or not delivered at all.⁴¹

III. Anticipatory non-performance

The creditor is also entitled to terminate the contract if the debtor seriously and clearly states before performance is due that it has no intention of performing its obligations and thus will not meet a fundamental obligation under the contract. The debtor may plead as an excuse that it regards the contract as invalid, or that it considers that it too has a right to terminate the contract due to an apparent breach by the creditor. In such cases, the creditor can have good reason to hold the debtor to the contract despite the refusal to perform, and to demand performance. However, the creditor can also accept the refusal to perform as it is intended. In this case, it is in the same position as if the debtor's performance is impossible, and it can therefore terminate the contract without setting a *Nachfrist*,⁴² and perhaps also claim damages for non-performance.

---

³⁹ Rules transferring the risk to the creditor after a 'default of acceptance' can be found, for example, in §§ 323(6), 326(2), 293ff. BGB; art. 1257ff. *Code civil*; art. 1206ff. *Codice civile*; § 1419 ABGB; art. 815 Portuguese Civil Code; art. 381(2) Greek Civil Code; see also Flessner (n 5) 299f. In the CISG, the same result is reached in that the seller retains the claim for payment of the price (and the buyer's right to terminate the contract is thus excluded) 'from the time when the goods are placed at [the buyer's] disposal and [it] commits a breach of contract by failing to take delivery'. See art. 69(1) CISG. See similar rules in art. IV.A.-5:201 DCFR; arts. 140, 142(3), 144 CESL.

⁴⁰ See art. 67(1) sent. 1 CISG, and also art. IV.A.-5:202 DCFR and art. 145 CESL. Similar rules can also be found in national legal rules. See, for example, § 447 BGB; art. 185(2) OR. Under French law, as between the parties, ownership passes to the buyer upon the conclusion of the contract of sale, and if goods of a certain kind have been sold, ownership passes at the time the goods were sufficiently 'individualised'. It follows that after the conclusion of the contract, the buyer bears the risk that the goods were damaged or destroyed by accident. See Terré, Simler, and Lequette (n 2) no. 669 and art. 1196 *Code civil*. In English law, this risk generally passes to the buyer only after it acquired ownership in the goods. But exceptions are made if the seller hands over the goods to a carrier for transportation to the buyer. See L Merrett, 'Sale of Goods' in *J Chitty on Contracts* vol. II (32nd edn, 2015) no. 44-187ff. The situation is different if the buyer is a *consumer*. In this case, it is always the seller's risk if the goods were destroyed or damaged during carriage. This does not apply where the consumer, without following any recommendations made by the seller, arranged for the carriage of the goods. See art. 20 of EU Directive 2011/83/EU on Consumer Rights of 25 October 2011 (O.J. 2011 L 304/64). The same rule can be found in art. 142(4) CESL.

⁴¹ The situation for contracts for work is similar. In principle, it is the contractor who bears the risk of building work being lost, destroyed, or damaged before handover. So if a half-finished house is destroyed by fire, the contractor must start work anew. If the contractor refuses, although the building work may still be carried out, this would be a breach entitling the client to terminate the contract. The situation is different if the client was liable for the fire—for example, if the fire was caused by the client or its agents, if the client had stored highly flammable materials on the site, or if the client had not followed its own fire-protection measures at the site. For details, see Flessner (n 5) 301f.

⁴² See § 323(2) no. 1, 323(4) BGB and the commentary (that refers to earlier versions of the law, but is still applicable) in Huber (n 28) §§ 51–53. See also art. 108 no. 1 OR; BG 15 May 1984, BGE 110 II 141, 143f; art. 6:83(c) BW; OGH 19 April 1967, SZ 40 Nr. 53; OGH 21 Dec. 1987, SZ 60 Nr. 287 (p. 784); art. 385

IV. Delayed performance

In the cases looked at so far, performance is not carried out because it is impossible or because it is clear prior to the time of performance that the contract will not be performed. A more common situation is where there is no performance by the agreed date but the creditor neither knows why nor whether and at what time the debtor may be able to perform. Under what conditions can the creditor then terminate the contract?

Sometimes, merely missing the agreed date for performance can entitle the creditor to immediately terminate the contract, but only where it has a special interest in the timeliness of performance. That is why the CISG and the international sets of rules give the creditor a right to immediate termination only if the debtor's failure to perform on time amounts to a 'fundamental breach'.[43] This is also the basic approach of English law.[44] German law has no concept of a fundamental breach. Under the *Nachfrist* system, termination is allowed only when performance has not been made within the time allotted in the contract and the debtor failed to perform within a reasonable period set for this purpose by the creditor. But there are many special cases in which the setting of a *Nachfrist* is not required.[45] If one were prepared to see a 'fundamental breach' in these special cases, there would be no great practical difference between German law and the CISG solution. French law also allows immediate termination if the parties have agreed on a *clause résolutoire* (art. 1225 Code civil).

Nevertheless, one cannot deny that the willingness of national courts to allow immediate termination may vary greatly. In France, the creditor can incorporate this right into the contract, but nothing can stop the debtor from subsequently asking a court to declare the termination unjustified—perhaps by asserting that the contractual agreement relied on by the creditor was insufficiently specific, that any doubt as to its validity must be interpreted to the creditor's disadvantage or that, as it was formulated as a standard term, it is in conflict with consumer protection provisions.[46] To a certain extent, this is in contrast to the relentlessness by which English courts regard late performance as a fundamental breach, at least if the contract has been concluded by commercial parties of a similar bargaining strength, as in *Union Eagle Ltd. v. Golden Achievement Ltd.*[47] In a provision stated in the contract as being 'of the

---

Greek Civil Code. On French law, see S Whittaker, 'How Does French Law Deal with Anticipatory Breaches of Contract?' (1996) 45 *ICLQ* 662. Article 72(1) CISG allows for termination of the contract if it is 'clear' prior to the date of performance that the other party will not meet its obligations. See also art. 9:304 PECL; art. 7.3.4 PICC; art. III.-3:504 DCFR; art. 116, 136 CESL. In England, this is called 'anticipatory breach of contract'; for detail, see Treitel (n 2) no. 17-073ff; McKendrick (n 16) no. 19.9.

[43] See art. 49(Ia), 64(Ia) CISG and the international sets of rules set out in n 31.
[44] See above, section C.II (= pp. 220ff.).
[45] See above, section C.III (= pp. 223ff.).
[46] See Terré, Simler, and Lequette (n 2) no. 662 and the impressive overview of the restricted validity given by courts to '*clauses résolutoires*' in Storck (n 13) Fasc. 20 no. 7ff. See also BGH 17 Jan. 1990, BGHZ 110, 88: a winery bought one million aluminium capsules to close its bottles that turned out to be unusable due to an undisputed hidden defect. The winery cancelled the contract and demanded damages, relying on its standard terms and conditions which stated that its claims would expire only three years after delivery, that the agreed delivery date was a fixed date, and that termination of the contract was therefore permitted without an additional period for performance (*Nachfrist*). Although both parties were businesses, the court dismissed the claim as it regarded the standard terms and conditions as 'surprising' and 'unreasonable', and therefore as invalid.
[47] [1997] AC 514 (PC).

essence of the agreement', the buyer of a flat had agreed to pay the remaining purchase price by 5 p.m. on 30 September 1991. When the money was offered ten minutes late, the seller refused to accept it and terminated the contract immediately. The buyer held this to be 'unconscionable', and demanded performance of the contract. Its claim was dismissed:

> The principle that equity will restrain the enforcement of legal rights when it would be unconscionable to insist upon them has attractive breadth. But the reasons why the courts have rejected such generalisations are founded not merely upon authority ... but also upon practical considerations of business. These are, in summary, that in many forms of transaction it is of great importance that if something happens for which the contract has made express provision, the parties should know with certainty that the term of the contract will be enforced. The existence of an undefined discretion to refuse to enforce the contract on the ground that this would be 'unconscionable' is sufficient to create uncertainty.[48]

What remains are cases where the special conditions for immediate termination are not present, or seem so uncertain that the creditor does not want to take the risk of immediate termination. The risk is that, at a later stage, the court might find no sufficient reasons for such termination, so that the termination itself would be a breach and the creditor would be liable for damages resulting from the fact that it terminated the contract for no good reason, refused performance, and rejected the debtor's offer to perform.

In this situation, the CISG gives the creditor an option similar to the *Nachfrist* system under German law. If the creditor is a buyer that has not received goods on time, pursuant to art. 47 it can set 'an additional period of time of reasonable length for performance by the seller of his obligations'. Before the expiry of this period, the buyer may not terminate the contract, but its right to claim damages from the seller for the delay remains unaffected. Whether or not the period set by the buyer is reasonable depends on the circumstances, such as the type of performance, the reasons preventing the seller from performing on time, and the weight of the buyer's interest in securing performance as soon as possible. If the additional period is too short, the normal assumption is that the buyer will not be able to assert its rights until after expiry of a longer 'reasonable' period.[49] But some sort of deadline must be set; merely insisting that the seller should perform 'as soon as possible' is not enough. It must also be made clear to the seller that there will be legal consequences if performance is not effected by expiry of the deadline. Also permitted, though not necessary, is a declaration by the

---

[48] Per *Lord Hoffmann* ibid. 519. On the reasons underlying the different approach of the courts in Civil Law and Common Law jurisdictions, see the commentary by H Beale, 'Remedies: Termination' in A Hartkamp et al., *Towards a European Civil Code* (2nd edn, 1998) 348ff.

[49] This is the position of German case law. See, for example, RG 16 Dec. 1903, RGZ 56, 231, 234f; BGH 12 Aug. 2009, [2009] *NJW* 3153 and in detail Huber (n 28) § 43 I 5. In Switzerland, if the period is too short the court may only replace it by a period of 'reasonable' length if the debtor has attacked the period as being too short. If the debtor does not do so, the period set by the creditor is binding. See BG 30 Jan. 1979, BGE 105 II 28, 34; BG 24 Sept. 1990, BGE 116 II 436, 440f. The situation is different under art. 47 CISG; Schlechtriem and Schroeter (n 29) mn. 471: a buyer that has set a deadline that is too short must set a new reasonable period, and termination of the contract by the buyer is possible only after unsuccessful expiry of the new period.

buyer that, if performance is not forthcoming within the *Nachfrist*, the contract will be deemed as 'automatically' terminated (ie without further declaration by the buyer.)

If there is no performance before expiry of the deadline, the creditor who is a buyer can avoid the contract pursuant to art. 49(1)(b) CISG.[50] This is a sensible balancing of the interests of both parties. The debtor receives one last opportunity to avert termination of the contract by performing before expiry of the new deadline. The creditor must await the end of the deadline, but achieves certainty about its right of termination and can avoid the risk set out above. Even if the debtor complies with the additional deadline, the creditor can still demand damages for harm caused by performance not being made by the agreed due date.

This solution is followed not only by German law, but other national legal systems as well.[51] Even creditors who can rely on a contractually agreed right of termination are reminded that they are best advised in many cases to play it safe, set a reasonable period for performance, and terminate only when this period has expired and performance has not been forthcoming.[52] In English law, too, it is recognised that the creditor may set an additional period in cases where the contractual time stipulation 'is not of the essence of the agreement': 'If the time stipulated is reasonable and the guilty party has failed to comply when it expires, the injured party is entitled to terminate.'[53]

V. Incomplete performance

One special case for non-performance is where the debtor has partially performed but failed to complete the rest. There is no part performance where the debtor is required to perform in parts, but these parts are agreed to be 'indivisible'. In these cases, if the debtor fails to perform part of the contract, it is the contract as a whole which has not been performed, and it follows that only termination of the whole contract is possible. If, for example, the creditor is a publican who has bought a property from its brewery and has also undertaken to buy its beer from it, then the purchase of the property and the supply of beer may be regarded as indivisible. The consequence would be that if the beer is substandard, the publican can only avoid the contract as a whole and would also have to give the property back if the contract were to be terminated.[54] The situation is different if performance by the debtor can be divided into instalments, such as where a seller contracts to supply 500,000 roof tiles and delivers some but not all of

---

[50] If the creditor is a buyer, the same applies pursuant to art. 64(1b) CISG. This solution is also found in arts. 9:301(2) and 8:106(3) PECL; arts. 7.3.1(3) and 7.1.5 PICC; art. III.-3:503 DCFR; art. 115, 135 CESL.
[51] See above, n 25.   [52] On this, see Storck (n 13) Fasc. 20 no. 10ff.
[53] Treitel (n 2) no. 18-095 with further details.
[54] See RG 16 Nov. 1907, RGZ 67, 101 and Huber (n 28) § 45 I 2 c. See also Civ. 13 Jan. 1987, Bull.cass. 1987.I. no. 11 = JCP 1987.II.20860: a driving school promised to prepare its clients for their driving tests and, if they failed to pass, to continue to provide tuition until they passed. After the driving school refused to continue lessons for a client, he terminated the contract and demanded payment of the entire amount he had paid to the school. The *Cour de cassation* approved the claim, because the parties 'ont voulu faire une convention indivisible', and not an agreement '*fractionnée en une série de contrats*'. See also Terré, Simler, and Lequette (n 2) no. 655.

the goods. In this case, the buyer may exercise its right of termination only in relation to the part the seller failed to perform.

Even in such a case, the creditor can have an interest in terminating the contract as a whole. This is a radical step that will be of interest if the creditor is a buyer who prepaid the full price and wants it back even though there has been part performance. Avoidance of the contract as a whole is in this case only permitted if, as stated in art. 51(2) CISG, the 'failure to make delivery completely or in conformity with the contract amounts to a fundamental breach of the contract'.[55]

Such is the case if the part performance is of no use to the creditor, and it is not possible or reasonable for it to secure performance of the remainder from a third party and demand the additional cost as damages. The same approach is taken by § 323(5) sent. 1 BGB, whereby, if the debtor has only performed in part, the creditor 'may revoke the whole contract only if he has no interest in part performance'.[56] The creditor will have no such interest if the part performance already received does not meet the purpose it had in mind when the contract was concluded. This would be so in the case described above where the buyer wanted to re-tile his roof, provided that the amount of tiles delivered is insufficient to complete the job and other tiles cannot be obtained elsewhere in the same quality, or it would be unreasonable to do so. The buyer can also terminate the contract as a whole if the seller delivers a car but not the car registration papers, or where the buyer of IT equipment has been delivered the hardware but the seller has not delivered the necessary software that has been customised for the buyer.[57]

English law imposes even stricter limitations on termination of the contract as a whole. Suppose a buyer paid the full price in advance, but received only a part of what it was promised by the seller. In this case, it may only terminate the whole contract and recover the price if there was a 'total failure of consideration'. The general rule is that if the seller performed in part, the buyer is limited to a claim for damages. This rule is controversial. It does not seem to apply where the contract and the circumstances show that the part performed by the seller can easily be apportioned to a part of the prepaid price; in this case the unearned remainder of the price can be demanded after partial termination of the contract.[58]

In many similar cases, the question can arise as to whether the creditor has a right of *partial termination*: can it retain the received part and pay for it, and then terminate the rest of the contract and be relieved of its remaining obligations? The first

---

[55] See also art. 9:302 sent. 2 PECL: the creditor can only terminate the contract as a whole 'if the non-performance is fundamental to the contract as a whole'. See also art. III.-3:506(3) DCFR; arts. 117(3), 137(3) CESL.

[56] See also § 920 sent. 2 ABGB. Similarly art. 6:265 BW: where the debtor has in some way breached the contract, the creditor may terminate all or part of the contract unless this is not justified due to the particular nature of the breach or its insignificant consequences. Under art. 1464 *Codice civile*, when performance is 'partially impossible' for the debtor the creditor can usually terminate the contract as a whole unless it has a 'significant interest' in part performance.

[57] See BGH 7 March 1990, [1990] *NJW* 3011. The same result is reached if the delivery of car and car papers or of the IT equipment and software are regarded as indivisible. In this case, the delivery only of the car or only of the IT equipment is not part performance, but non-performance of the whole contract. For this reason, the buyer would be entitled to terminate the contract as a whole.

[58] For details, see Treitel (n 2) no. 22-004.

requirement for such a partial termination is that the non-performance of the missing part amounts to a 'fundamental breach': see arts. 51(1), 49 CISG. But that is not sufficient, since with partial termination the contract remains partially in force. Care must be taken to ensure that the parties are not left with a rump contract that is quite different from the original contract. Thus partial termination can only be considered if both the performance of the creditor and that of the debtor can be easily divided. This is lacking where the parties' promises were intended to form an indivisible 'unit'; in that case, only a termination of the contract as a whole will be possible. The counter-performance of the creditor is usually divisible, at least when it consists of payment of money. Even then, it can be difficult to work out the amount payable by the creditor for the part performance already made. If, in the case mentioned above, the buyer had received half of the roof tiles, but it wished to cancel the rest of the contract, this would be also dependent on the ability to calculate a fractional price that plausibly takes into account any discount that the creditor had been given for the full order.[59]

Similar rules apply if the debtor must complete the overall contractual performance in instalments, or if the overall performance has not been determined in the contract, but the debtor promised to provide part performances called up by the creditor over a fixed period of time. With these 'multiple delivery contracts', the question arises as to what the consequences are if the debtor fails to provide an instalment. Pursuant to art. 73 CISG, if the creditor is a buyer it can usually terminate the contract only to the extent to which the seller's past performance is in breach of contract and that breach is 'fundamental'. By contrast, the buyer can 'declare the contract terminated for the future' if the seller has not performed its duty to provide an instalment and this gives the buyer good grounds to believe that the seller will not deliver future instalments in accordance with the contract. Exceptionally, the buyer can even terminate the contract 'in respect of deliveries already made' if past and future instalments are so interdependent that the buyer cannot use previous deliveries for the purpose intended.[60]

VI. Defective performance

The debtor will also be in breach of the contract if performance is defective, that is not in conformity with what the debtor promised in the (correctly interpreted) contract. This includes in particular the delivery of a defective product. But defective performance can also take many other forms: examples are where a seller breaches an obligation to use the buyer's trademark only on goods described in the contract, and not on other goods; or where a seller passes on business secrets of the buyer that it became aware of during performance of the contract; or where a buyer breaches its contractual obligations by selling the purchased goods at a lower price than agreed, or with a heavy discount in a budget shop.

---

[59] See art. 9:302 sent. 1 PECL: a partial termination of the contract is only possible if the contract can be performed by the debtor 'in separate parts' (its performance is not deemed to be indivisible), and if the counterperformance by the creditor 'can be apportioned'. See also art. III.-3:506 (1) and (2) DCFR; arts. 117(1), 137(1) CESL.

[60] On art. 73 CISG, see Schlechtriem and Schroeter (n 29) mn. 622ff. and (with similar arguments) Flessner (n 5) 294ff.

In these cases, it will usually be the end of the matter that the innocent party claims damages for breach of contract from the counterparty. But sometimes it may wish to terminate the contract as a whole, to get back what was already provided under the contract, and perhaps to demand damages for breach of contract. This is only possible if the breach is 'significant' or leads to a 'substantial failure of performance', or is so severe it would be 'unreasonable for the contract to continue'.[61] Whether the debtor breached a 'fundamental' or an 'ancillary' obligation is not relevant, because this difference would only lead to the judge upgrading any obligation to a 'fundamental' obligation if termination is regarded as permissible, and to an ancillary obligation if a different view had been taken. It is also irrelevant whether the debtor committed the breach deliberately or for other reasons. This does not exclude the probability that a fundamental breach of contract becomes ever more likely when the behaviour of the debtor indicates that it no longer has any intention of performing its obligations under the contract.[62] So if a seller, in breach of its contractual obligations, has attached the buyer's trademark to its own goods and displayed these at a trade fair, this can constitute a fundamental breach of contract within the meaning of art. 25 CISG, and will entitle the buyer to immediately terminate the contract.[63] In an English case, an advertiser had agreed to provide advertising for the claimant's canned vegetables by towing a banner behind its aircraft with the text 'Eat Batchelors Peas'. To the horror and annoyance of all parties, the aircraft flew over a town's marketplace just as several thousand people had gathered to hold a minute's silence to mark Armistice Day. The court viewed this breach as so 'disastrous' that it allowed the claimant to cancel the whole contract and reject any subsequent performance.[64]

The most important instance of defective performance is when the seller delivers goods that do not have the required contractual characteristics. In many continental legal systems, there used to be (and in some cases still are) special rules that entitle the buyer to terminate the contract or immediately reduce the price payable. These rules are based on the model of Roman law, and made sense so long as goods were traded by the parties personally, with the goods present. This allowed the parties to check the characteristics of the goods, and sellers were not able to subsequently repair defects in those goods. These rules are no longer timely, because goods are increasingly mass produced, the buyer can no longer examine them before purchase, the defects can often be repaired or cured in some other way, and replacements can be

---

[61] §§ 324, 241(2) BGB allow for immediate termination if the debtor breached the contract by not taking into account the 'rights, legal interests and other interests of the creditor' and it would under the circumstances be 'unconscionable' for the creditor to be held to the contract. So if a seller's driver has damaged the buyer's premises while delivering goods or offended its staff, this can justify termination of the contract as a whole.

[62] More about German law in H Kötz, *Vertragsrecht* (2nd edn, 2012) mn. 922f; on English law, see Treitel (n 2) no. 18-034; on French law, see Terré, Simler, and Lequette (n 2) no. 652, 660.

[63] See OLG Frankfurt 17 Sept. 1991, [1992] *NJW* 633 and Schlechtriem and Schroeter (n 29) mn. 325ff.

[64] *Aerial Advertising Co. v. Batchelors Peas Ltd.* [1938] 2 All ER 788 and Treitel (n 2) no. 18-036. See also Com. 11 Dec. 1990, Bull.cass. 1990.IV. no. 316 = [1991] *Rev.trim.civ.* 526, n. J Mestre: a security company had promised to guard the plaintiff's property. When one of its guards had stolen something on the secured premises, the plaintiff was permitted to terminate the whole contract and to refuse to pay the agreed price even though the company had also used reliable guards and thus partially performed the contract.

delivered by the seller which are in conformity with the contract.[65] Some countries, such as France, have slowly adapted their laws to the new requirements. In Germany and the Netherlands, the old rules have now been replaced by provisions that make it difficult to terminate a contract because of a defect in the goods. The Common Law and the international sets of rules regard delivery of defective goods or defective service as a normal breach of contract; termination of the contract is only permitted if the general requirements are met.

How strict these requirements are with respect to contracts for sale is seen, for example, in the CISG. Pursuant to art. 49(1)(a), the buyer can only avoid the contract if the defect amounts to a 'fundamental breach of contract'.[66] This condition is met if the express agreement in the contract shows that the buyer had an unconditional interest in certain characteristics being present in the goods. If there is no such agreement, it depends on the circumstances as to whether an assumption of a fundamental breach is justified. It will not be so if the buyer's interests are sufficiently protected by the other remedies available if defective goods have been delivered. This includes the buyer's right to accept the defective goods and reduce the purchase price.[67] If the seller made an offer to repair the defect or deliver a replacement at its own cost, within a reasonable period and without any obvious disadvantages for the buyer, then there is no fundamental breach if the buyer can be expected under the circumstances to accept such a remedy.[68] It should also be remembered that even if buyers cannot terminate the contract and remain bound to it, their interests are often sufficiently protected by their remedy of claiming damages for delay as well as for any other harm caused by the seller's breach. For this reason, the *Bundesgerichtshof* denied a buyer a right to terminate a contract, even though the delivered goods neither conformed with the contractual quality nor with the agreed place of origin. The buyer could reduce the purchase price or sell the goods for a lower price elsewhere and demand damages from the seller. Nor did the contract clearly state that compliance with the agreed qualities was of 'fundamental importance' for the buyer.[69] Termination of the contract is therefore seen by the CISG as a last resort, not least because it leads to a reversal of the transaction and would involve especially high costs and risks with respect to cross-border deals. With a bit of effort, one can also recognise a tendency in national legal systems to limit termination of contracts. In particular, this right is denied to buyers if the delivered goods are not as stated in the contract, but this is not regarded as decisive because the defect is insignificant or the seller's breach 'does not go to

---

[65] See above, p. 210.

[66] The international sets of rules also regard a performance not in line with the contract as a breach, but give the aggrieved party a right to terminate the contract only if the breach is 'significant' or 'fundamental'. See above, n 30.

[67] Article 50 CISG; also art. 9:401 PECL; art. III.-3:601 DCFR; art. 120 CESL. The reduction of the price is in substance a partial termination of the contract because, on the one hand, the buyer pays only a part of the price and, on the other hand, the seller is partially freed from its obligations to deliver goods in conformity with the contract.

[68] Article 48 CISG. See also art. 8:104 PECL; art. 7.1.4 PICC; art. III.-3:201-204 DCFR; art. 109 CESL.

[69] BGH 3 Apr. 1996, BGHZ 132, 290. See also OLG Düsseldorf 9 July 2010, [2011] IHR 120; Appellate Court Basel-Stadt 22 Aug. 2003, [2005] IHR 2005, 117; BG 18 May 2009, [2010] IHR 27; OGH 22 Nov. 2011, [2012] IHR 114 and Schlechtriem and Schroeter (n 29) mn. 328ff.

the root of the contract'. In one English case, the seller had undertaken to deliver around 3,300 tonnes of citrus pulp pellets to be used by the buyer as animal feed and to be shipped by the seller 'in good condition'. The goods were found to be partially defective upon arrival in Rotterdam, and the buyer refused to accept them and demanded reimbursement of the prepayment of around £100,000. The goods were then auctioned off at the order of a Dutch court, and purchased by none other than the buyer, who had to pay a knock-down price of only £30,000 and then used them for animal feed as originally planned. The Court of Appeal held that the undertaking to ship the goods 'in good condition' was not a 'condition' in the technical sense but was to be regarded as an 'intermediate term'. The court thus held that the termination was not justified, because in this particular case the delivery of defective goods did not go 'to the root of the contract'.[70]

The same approach is taken by statutory provisions that deny a buyer termination of the contract if the goods are not as contractually stipulated, but where the breach 'is so slight, that it would be unreasonable for the [buyer] to reject [the goods]'.[71] Also § 323(5) sent. 2 BGB provides that the creditor's right of termination is excluded if the debtor has not performed in line with the contract, but the breach is 'trivial'.[72]

It is also the case that many legal orders only allow termination of a contract if the creditor has set the debtor a reasonable deadline for supplementary performance and this deadline has expired without rectification of the problem. It is correct that such a deadline is not necessary in some cases.[73] It is also correct that the supplementary performance—whether by means of repairing the non-contractual performance or replacement with properly functioning goods—may be impossible for the debtor, or the debtor may refuse performance. In these cases, there is no need to set an additional deadline, and the contract may therefore be terminated immediately.[74] But these are exceptions. On the whole, a buyer cannot terminate a contract until it has given the seller an opportunity to rectify the defective delivery by repairing the defect or providing a replacement within a reasonable period.[75]

All these rules are dispositive, meaning that they can be agreed or amended between the parties, even though agreements in the form of standard terms and conditions

---

[70] *Cehave N.V. v. Bremer Handelsgesellschaft m.b.H. (The Hansa Nord)* [1975] 3 WLR 447. See above, n 23 and Treitel (n 2) no. 18-049ff.

[71] S. 15(A) Sale of Goods Act 1979, and s. 5(A) Supply of Goods and Services Act 1982. Both provisions were introduced by the Sale and Supply of Goods Act 1994. See criticism in Treitel (n 2) no. 18-054.

[72] If the goods are defective, the question of whether or not the seller's breach is trivial normally depends on the 'balancing of the costs of remedying the defect against the purchase price'. See BGH 29 June 2011, [2011] *NJW* 2872, 2873. See also OGH 24 May 2005, [2005] *JBl* 720 and n. W Faber, 'Zur "geringfügigen Vertragswidrigkeit" nach Art 3 Abs. 6 der Verbrauchsgüterkauf-Richtlinie 1999/44/EG' (2006) 14 *ZEuP* 67.

[73] See text above to nn 25ff.   [74] See, for example, §§ 439, 440 BGB and Kötz (n 62) mn. 952ff.

[75] The question is handled differently under the CISG, unless the delivery of goods that do not conform with the contract is *in itself* a fundamental breach of the contract. If it is not, the buyer cannot demand delivery of defect-free replacement goods (art. 46(2)), but can only ask the defect to be remedied within a deadline set for this purpose (art. 46(3), 47). Even if the seller does not comply with this deadline, the buyer cannot just terminate the contract. Pursuant to art. 49(1)(b), termination of the contract is only allowed if the buyer receives no goods at all, and not just if the delivered goods are defective. So the buyer remains tied to the contract, and must seek a remedy in damages or in the right to reduce the purchase price. See for details Schlechtriem and Schroeter (n 29) mn. 336.

must comply with the special rules governing their validity. Stricter rules apply to contracts for the sale of moveable goods if the buyer is acting as a consumer. Under art. 3 of EU Directive 1999/44/EU of 25 May 1999, all Member States are required to introduce binding provisions entitling consumers to demand that sellers bring the goods into conformity with the contract free of charge and within a reasonable period—at the consumer's choice either by repair or replacement of the defective goods. The consumer may reduce the price or terminate the contract only under certain conditions, in particular where the seller rejected both ways to remedy the defect as 'impossible' or 'disproportionately expensive', or where the seller's attempt to remedy the defect turned out to be a failure.[76]

E. Restitution

If the debtor has not performed its obligations under the contract, or not performed them properly, the creditor has two options: it can either stand by the contract and demand that the debtor perform (if this is possible), or claim damages for the harm caused by the failure to perform. In some cases, however, the creditor can terminate the contract and demand damages from the debtor for non-performance.[77] If the creditor is entitled to terminate the contract, and has informed the debtor in good time that it does exercise this right and therefore regards the contract as terminated, then the parties are both no longer under any obligation to perform it. If performance has already been made, the question is when and how each party must restore what it received.

In principle, the aim of the restitution is to restore the *status quo* that existed before the contract was made. Such restitution is needed not only where the contract has been terminated, but also if it has failed for other reasons—such as where a party can show that the contract is illegal or immoral, or where it has been avoided because of mistake, deceit, or duress. This is why many legal systems have developed rules for the restoration of benefits received which turn on the respective reason for the contract being terminated.[78] In addition, EU directives have required legal systems in the Member States to adopt special rules on restitution that only apply when a consumer is withdrawing from the contract[79] or terminating it due to delivery of defective goods.[80]

---

[76] See above, pp. 210f.
[77] On this option for the creditor, see the comparative law considerations discussed by Flessner (n 5) 302ff. and Treitel (n 6) pp. 177ff.
[78] The PECL also has different rules governing restitution. Article 4:115 will apply if the contract is invalid because of mistake, deceit, or duress, or because a party has secured an 'excessive benefit' or 'unfair advantage'. If the contract is illegal or immoral, art. 15:104 will apply; and art. 9:305 applies if the contract has been terminated by a party. By contrast, the PICC has only one restitution rule. Nonetheless, some differences exist depending on whether a contract is avoided for a general reason (art. 3.2.15), whether it is invalid as infringing a mandatory rule (art. 3.3.1), or because it has been terminated (art. 7.3.6). However, the rules applicable in these cases are largely identical. See R Zimmermann, 'Restitutio in integrum: Die Rückabwicklung fehlgeschlagener Verträge nach den PECL, den PICC und dem Avant-projet eines Code Européen des Contrats' in *Festschrift für E Kramer* (2004) 737; R Zimmermann, 'The Unwinding of Failed Contracts in the UNIDROIT Principles 2010' [2011] *Uniform LRev* 572; S Vogenauer, 'Die UNIDROIT Grundregeln über internationale Handelsverträge 2010' (2013) 11 *ZEuP* 7, 33–8.
[79] See above, chapter 11.C (pp. 195f.).   [80] See above, chapter 13.D.VI (= pp. 233ff.).

There has been much discussion about whether or not the same rules should apply regardless of the reasons why the contract 'failed'.[81] Here, we address only the basic principles of restitution following termination of such contracts.

There is broad agreement that after termination the parties' duty to perform the contract comes to an end. However, termination does not have a retroactive effect.[82] Previous performance of the parties does not lose its 'legal basis' with the termination (art. 6:271 BW). The parties are required to return 'performances received and emoluments taken' (§ 346(1) BGB), but these obligations are based on the contract. The practical consequence is that in case of the buyer's insolvency, the seller's claim for the recovery of the goods competes with the claims of other creditors. This is why sellers often seek to agree on a retention-of-title clause, under which the ownership of the goods remains with them until such time as the buyer pays.

Yet French law used to take a different approach to this point. If the contract is terminated, and one party is relieved of its obligations, a 'condition' was deemed to apply that the parties had made the validity of the contract dependent on its timely fulfilment by the other party. This had the consequence that the terminated contract 'est considéré comme n'ayant jamais être conclu; il est anéanti rétroactivement'.[83] This principle could not be upheld in full by French law. In particular, those contractual provisions that the parties intended to apply in the event of a termination remained in force. Examples of such clauses could be agreements covering the extent of restitution, provisions nominating a particular court to have jurisdiction, clauses setting out a contractual penalty, provisions binding the parties to confidentiality, or non-compete clauses.[84] Restitution also failed where the contract can be split and an assumption can be made that the termination affects only the future part of the contract that has not yet been performed.[85] The same applied to a contract 'à exécution successive ou échelonnée'[86] or if the contract is for an indeterminate period—such as a rental contract, an employment contract, or a distributor agreement: if such contracts have been correctly performed by the parties in part or for some time, and termination is subsequent, French law refers to a 'résiliation' that is only effective *pro futuro* and has no

---

[81] The idea finds approval in the recent comparative study by S Meier, 'Die Rückabwicklung gescheiterter Verträge: Neue europäische Entwicklungen' (2016) 80 *RabelsZ* 851, 857ff. (with copious references).

[82] See § 346 BGB; art. 6:271 BW; art. 9:308 PECL.

[83] See Terré, Simler, and Lequette (n 2) no. 653. This rule leads, for example, to significant practical problems if a buyer has already transferred title to the delivered goods to a third party and the contract is not terminated until after this time. As part of the retroactive effect, this is then regarded as if the buyer was not the owner, with the consequence that the third party is only deemed to acquire ownership when the acquisition was in good faith. See Terré, Simler, and Lequette (n 2) no. 656; Malaurie, Aynès, and Stoffel-Munck (n 12) no. 880; Storck (n 13) Fasc. 10 no. 85ff. Italian law is different: pursuant to art. 1458 *Codice civile*, the termination of the contract has retroactive effect (subsection 1), but this does not affect 'rights acquired by third parties' (subsection 2).

[84] See Terré, Simler, and Lequette (n 2) no. 653. Meanwhile, art. 1230 expressly provides that a termination of the contract 'n'affecte ni les clauses relatives au règlement des différends, ni celles déstinées à produire effet même en cas de résolution, telles les clauses de confidentialité ou de non-concurrence.' To the same effect are art. 9:305(2) PECL; art. 7.3.5(2) PICC.

[85] See above, n 54.

[86] Terré, Simler, and Lequette (n 2) no. 655; Storck (n 13) Fasc. 10 no. 54, 80ff. See also art. 1458(1) *Codice civile*.

retroactive effect.[87] The issue is now governed by the new provision of art. 1229 *Code civil*, which states that the time when the contract is terminated depends primarily on the contractual arrangements. If there is no such agreement, termination takes effect either at the date of receipt by the debtor of the creditor's notice of termination, or at the date fixed by the judge. The details of the restitution are governed by the special provisions of arts. 1352–1352-9 *Code civil*.

It is sometimes difficult to say what it is that each party must return. The matter is simple where at the time of termination the performance provided by each party is still available in its original condition. In this case, each party may claim restitution of whatever it has supplied under the contract, provided that such party concurrently makes restitution of whatever it has received under the contract.[88] More difficult are cases in which a house was painted, goods were carried, or other services were provided. What about contracts of sale where the buyer has received the goods but cannot return them in their original condition because they have been destroyed or damaged while in its possession, or they have been used, processed, or sold to a third party? Should the right of termination be excluded in such cases? What must be given back if termination is permitted?

In the CISG, the buyer's right of termination is *excluded* pursuant to art. 82(1) 'if it is impossible for him to make restitution of the goods substantially in the condition in which he received them'. In this case, the buyer must rely on its claim for damages. However, art. 82(2) allows the buyer to terminate the contract in important cases, such as where the impossibility to return the goods in their original condition 'is not due to [the buyer's] act or omission'. The meaning of this is not quite clear. Of course, the buyer retains the right to terminate the contract if through no fault of its own the goods are destroyed or damaged by a conflagration, a flood, or an earthquake: similarly, where the goods are defective and it is this defect that caused the destruction of or damage to the goods. On the other hand, the buyer's right of termination is excluded if the goods have been destroyed by water damage, and liability for this can be attributed to the buyer because it stored the goods in a flood-prone storage depot. This need not be due to any negligence of the buyer. Nonetheless, the risk of loss can be allotted to it as forming part of its 'sphere of responsibility'.[89] Pursuant to art. 82(2c) CISG, the buyer can also terminate the contract where it cannot return the goods because they had been sold to a third party or were consumed or transformed 'in the normal course of business'. Here, the buyer can terminate the contract and demand return of the purchase price if it has already been paid, but must reimburse the seller for 'all benefits which [it] has derived from the goods' whether from their sale, use or processing (art. 84 CISG).

Most national legal systems and the international sets of rules take a different approach. They give the buyer a right of termination even if the received goods can no

---

[87] Terré, Simler, and Lequette (n 2) no. 479, 655; Malaurie, Aynès, and Stoffel-Munck (n 12) no. 881. In Italy, the term is '*recesso*', in Germany it is '*Kündigung eines Dauerschuldverhältnisses*'. See above, n 24 and Flessner (n 5) 293ff, 313; Treitel (n 6) no. 179ff.

[88] See § 346(1) BGB; art. 6:271 BW; and now art. 1230 *Code civil*. See also art. 7.3.6(1) PICC; art. III.-3:511(1) DCFR; art. 81(2) CISG.

[89] See Schlechtriem and Schroeter (n 29) mn. 767f.

longer be returned to the seller. However, the buyer must reimburse the seller for the value of the goods[90] and—if the buyer used the goods in the time between delivery and return—for the value of any benefits derived from their use.[91] The value must also be reimbursed if it is before the termination of the contract that the buyer has used or processed the goods or sold them to a third party. By contrast, the buyer need not reimburse this value if the seller is somehow responsible for the destruction of or damage to the goods.[92] This must also apply if the goods have been destroyed or damaged in a way for which the buyer is not responsible, or bears only minimal responsibility.[93]

---

[90] Article 7.3.6(2) PICC states that if restitution of the received performance in kind is not possible (or not practicable, as it is too expensive), 'an allowance has to be made in money whenever reasonable'. This allowance should normally be determined in accordance with the value of the performance. See in detail Zimmermann (n 78) [2011] *Uniform L.Rev.* 572ff; Meier (n 81) 877. A similar, but much more precise, rule on replacement value can be found in § 346(2) nos. 2 and 3 BGB, and in arts. III.-3:511(4) and 3:513 DCFR.

[91] See, for example, § 346(2) BGB; art. 6:272 BW; art. 1352-3 *Code civil*; art. 9:309 PECL.

[92] Pursuant to art. 7.3.6(3) PICC, the party required to make restitution does not need to pay compensation if the impossibility of making restitution in kind 'is attributable to the other party'. See the corresponding rules in § 346(3) no. 2 BGB; art. 1492(2) *Codice civile* and art. III.-3:513 (3) DCFR.

[93] See, for example, § 346(3) no. 3 BGB. According to art. 1352-1 *Code civil*, a buyer must also reimburse the value of the goods to the extent that they have lost value through 'dégradations et détériorations'. However, this does not apply if the buyer acted in good faith and the reasons for the loss in value are not the buyer's fault. But suppose the goods were destroyed or damaged without the buyer's fault, namely by an act of God or *force majeure*: should the buyer not even in this case be accountable for the value of the loss? Since the buyer had possession of the goods, and could have insured them, it would also be reasonable to let the buyer bear the risk of accidental destruction or damage.

14

Damages

A. Non-Performance of the Contract	242
B. Attribution	244
I. Fault principle	244
II. *Obligations de moyens* and *obligations de résultat*	248
III. Breach of contract	252
IV. International rules	254
C. Link Between Non-Performance and Damage	257
I. Liability for remote damage	257
II. Contributory responsibility of the creditor	261
D. Nature and Extent of Damages	264
I. Liability for expectation interest	264
II. Calculating damages for non-performance of contracts of sale	266
III. Liability for lost profits and lost expectations	268
IV. Liability for disgorgement of profits	270
V. Liability for intangible loss	271
VI. Agreements on limitation of damages	275

If a party (debtor or obligor) does not perform its obligations under a contract, or does not perform them properly, the other party (creditor or obligee) can demand performance of the obligations due. The claim is for *performance* or—if the performance has been defective—for *supplementary performance*. Under some circumstances, a creditor can also ask for a court judgment that orders the debtor to perform or provide supplementary performance (chapter 12). But there may be circumstances where the creditor is not, or is no longer, interested in securing performance. It may then investigate whether the debtor has committed such a serious breach of the contractual terms that the contract can be *terminated* (chapter 13). The creditor can also ask for *damages*, either by insisting on performance of the contract and simultaneously asking for damages for the harm caused by the debtor performing late or having breached contractual obligations in some other way. But a claim for damages may also arise if the contract has been terminated. The termination ends the claim for performance, but the creditor can claim damages for non-performance of the contract or—as German law says—ask for *Schadensersatz statt der Leistung*.[1]

---

[1] General opinion is that the claim for damages competes with other 'remedies' available to the innocent party. Articles 45(2) and 64(2) CISG state that buyers and sellers do not lose their claim for damages because they seek to pursue 'other remedies'. See also art. 8:102 sent. 2 PECL which states that 'a party is not deprived of its right to damages by exercising its right to any other remedy'. There is often an express rule that a party can claim damages if it has terminated a contract. See § 325 BGB: 'The right to demand damages in the case of a reciprocal contract is not excluded by termination.' See also § 921 ABGB: 'The termination of the contract has no effect on the claim for damages caused by culpable non-performance.' See also art. 7.3.5 PICC: 'Termination does not preclude a claim for damages for non-performance.' See also art. 1217 *Code civil*.

There is little debate about the most important conditions needed for the innocent party to claim damages. *Firstly*, the debtor must not have performed its obligations under the contract, or performed them badly, or in some other way breached its contractual obligations (see section A). *Secondly*, the non-performance must be 'attributable' to the debtor, in that it must be responsible or answerable to the creditor (see section B). *Thirdly*, there must be a legally relevant connection or link between the non-performance of the contract and the harm for which damages are sought (see section C). *Fourthly*, there can be doubt as to whether the harm is compensable and how it can be calculated (see section D). It will become clear that it is not always possible to keep these issues separate. We will also see that the available legal rules are largely 'default' rules and will therefore often be replaced by the parties' other arrangements. Examples of this would be where parties define liability, effectively exclude or limit it, or agree in advance to a fixed level of liability.

A. Non-Performance of the Contract

According to the international sets of rules, a party is only obliged to pay damages if the harm is caused by the non-performance of the contract, which is understood to mean that the party has not fulfilled its obligations under the contract, or not performed them correctly. It does not matter whether the debtor can be blamed for the non-performance, nor is it relevant whether the party performed late, whether the goods failed to have the characteristics agreed in the contract, or whether there was any other 'failure to co-operate in order to give full effect to the contract'.[2] French law uses the term '*inexécution de l'obligation contractuelle*' in the same sense.[3] In Germany, an obligation to pay damages depends upon a party having breached a *Pflicht aus dem Schuldverhältnis*; here the *Schuldverhältnis* arises from the parties' contract.[4] Article 74 CISG also states that damages can be claimed for a breach of contract 'suffered by the other party as a consequence of the breach'. In practice, it makes little difference whether the non-performance of the contract or the breach of obligations is taken as the starting point. The normal usage of the term 'breach of contract' includes an understanding that the actions of the party in default are somehow blameworthy, objectionable, or subject to disapproval. But that is not the legal meaning of the term. A breach of contract really means nothing more than the more neutral and less pejorative term 'non-performance'. The legal meaning is that the actions of a party are less than what was promised in the contract. If someone fails to go to work because he

---

[2] Pursuant to art. 9:501(1) PECL, a party must compensate the other for losses caused by its 'non-performance', a term which is defined more closely in art. 1:301(4) PECL. See also arts. 7.4.1 and 7.1.1 PICC; arts. III.-3:701 and III.-1:101(3) DCFR; arts. 159(1) and 87(1) CESL.

[3] See only F Terré, P Simler, and Y Lequette, *Droit civil, Les obligations* (11th edn, 2013) no. 570. Even after the reform of the law of obligations in France, the *Code civil* still provides that damages may be claimed '*soit à raison de l'inexécution de l'obligation, soit à raison du retard dans l'execution*' (art. 1231-1).

[4] § 280(1) BGB. Pursuant to art. 97(1) OR, the obligation of a party to pay damages depends on 'an obligation not being performed, or not being performed properly'; and under art. 6:74 BW it depends on whether there is a '*tekortkoming in de nakoming van een verbintenis*'.

or she is ill, no one will object, but there is still a breach or a non-performance of the employment contract. The situation is no different if a party does not perform a promised obligation because it is impossible, or not reasonable because performance would involve disproportionately high costs. The innocent party cannot then demand performance (see chapter 12.C.I), but it can terminate the contract (see chapter 13.D.II). It can also demand damages unless the other party can show why the non-performance or the breach is not 'attributable' to it.[5]

Many legal systems start from the premise that the creditor cannot claim damages until it has reminded the debtor of the maturity of its claim and has thereby put the debtor in 'default'. In addition, if the creditor wishes to terminate the contract and demand damages for non-performance, it must sometimes have set a specific period for performance (*Nachfrist*) and warned the debtor that it will have to pay damages if performance is not effected before expiry of the period.[6] Sometimes the default by the debtor (*mora debitoris*) has been celebrated as evidence of a 'humane' contract law.[7] This is to be doubted, as in many cases it is recognised that neither a warning nor a supplementary deadline are necessary—such as if the debtor declares that it does not intend to perform, or if performance has become impossible for the debtor. A specific warning or setting of a deadline is also not necessary if the debtor has failed to meet a deadline stated in the contract (*dies interpellat pro homine*) or if, as stated in § 286(2) no. 4 BGB, no special warning is required because 'for special reasons, weighing the interests of both parties, the immediate commencement of default is justified'. For these reasons, one should not wonder that the Common Law and the international sets of rules do not insist on the setting of an additional deadline as a prerequisite for termination of the contract. They permit termination only if there is a fundamental breach or fundamental non-performance. In these cases, setting an additional deadline is usually not necessary.[8] This applies in particular if the creditor bases termination of the contract on the debtor not having performed by the time the parties agreed was important to the contract, in accordance with the principle that 'time is of the essence'. It has been held in English cases that if time is not of the essence under a contract, the creditor is entitled to do what common-sense suggests, namely to advise the debtor that performance must be completed by a certain date: 'If the time stipulated is reasonable and the guilty party has failed to comply when it expires, the injured party is entitled to terminate.'[9]

---

[5] See below, pp. 244ff.
[6] See art. 1231 *Code civil*; art. 1729ff. *Codice civil*; art. 6:81-83 BW; art. 102f. OR. Under German law, a distinction is drawn between whether the creditor is standing by the contract and only demanding damages for 'delayed performance', or whether the creditor is declaring the contract to be at an end and asking for damages instead of performance. In the first case, it is sufficient when the debtor fails to perform after having been put in default (§§ 280(2), 286 BGB). In the latter case, the creditor must give the debtor a reasonable supplementary deadline for performance. The creditor can usually only demand damages instead of performance if the *Nachfrist* expires without performance (§§ 280(1), 281 BGB).
[7] See E Bucher, 'Mora früher und heute' in *Mélanges en l'honneur de Bruno Schmidlin* (1998) 407.
[8] See above, pp. 226ff.
[9] GH Treitel, *The Law of Contract* (13th edn, by E Peel, 2011) no. 18-095.

B. Attribution

If the debtor has not performed its obligations under the contract, or not performed them correctly, this does not by itself lead to a liability to compensate the creditor for the resulting harm. The debtor is only liable to pay damages to the creditor if the non-performance of the contract can somehow be 'attributed' to it, either because it is to blame for the non-performance, or because it agreed to assume the risk of non-performance, or because it cannot excuse itself by proof that the non-performance was unavoidable or caused by *force majeure*. Termination is possible where the debtor fails to perform or has breached another significant contract term.[10] But if the creditor claims damages, it seeks payment of compensation so as to be put into the position it would have been in had performance been carried out properly. In this case, mere non-performance is not sufficient—it must somehow be attributable to the debtor if it is to be held liable.

On this ground, liability for damages depends under Civil Law on two separate questions: did the debtor perform its contractual obligations? And, if not, can the non-performance be attributed to the debtor? This distinction is unknown in the Common Law. There are cases, however, in which this distinction makes little sense even in the Civil Law—for example, where a debtor failed to provide the agreed services. Take the case where a doctor offers to treat a patient, a lawyer to represent the client's interests, or a bank to advise its customer on buying securities. If a claim for damages is made against the doctor, lawyer, or bank, it is not so easy to determine if they have failed to perform their contractual obligations and, if they have, to determine whether or not the non-performance can be attributed to them. Liability depends in reality on one single question: did the doctor, lawyer, or bank official do what would under the agreement be expected from a reasonable person acting in the same circumstances? If not, the debtor will be liable in damages, and there will be little room for the question whether or not the non-performance can on some ground be 'attributed' to the debtor, perhaps because the breach was caused by its failure to exercise reasonable care.[11]

I. Fault principle

In Civil Law, most legal systems still differentiate (at least implicitly) between non-performance and attribution, and the main reason why a debtor may have non-performance of the contract attributed to it can be that the debtor was to *blame* for

---

[10] See above, chapter 13.D.II = pp. 226ff.
[11] See GH Treitel, *Remedies for Breach of Contract* (1988) s. 8: it states that in Common Law 'the requirement of fault is discussed (if at all) ... in order to determine whether there is a breach ... In Civil Law systems, however, the question of fault is more commonly discussed under the heading of the legal effects of a failure in performance'. So under the Common Law fault merely plays a role at most in deciding whether or not there is a breach of contract. If it does, then it is clear that the creditor can demand damages. In Civil Law, however, non-performance of the contract turns solely on whether or not there is a difference between performance of the debtor required under the contract and what is actually delivered. Fault is not discussed until the question is raised as to whether or not the creditor can claim damages. See also H Kötz, *Vertragsrecht* (2nd edn, 2012) mn. 1079.

the non-performance. There is a presumption that the debtor's non-performance is based on some sort of fault. So a debtor wishing to avoid liability for damages must in German law rebut the presumption of fault by proof that the non-performance was caused neither intentionally nor negligently. A debtor would be seen as negligent pursuant to § 276(2) BGB if it 'fails to exercise reasonable care', namely acts in a different manner than would be expected of a reasonable party in the same circumstances in proper performance of the contract. According to § 278 BGB, it makes no difference if responsibility for the fault lies with the debtor personally or agents, so long as the agents—in most cases employees, but in some cases also independent contractors—have been brought in by the debtor for the purpose of performing its contractual obligations. The debtor is also liable for damages under Swiss law, unless it can prove that neither it nor its agents can be held responsible for the fault (art. 97(1), 101 OR). The situation is the same under art. 6:74–76 BW: a party must pay damages for non-performance that can be attributed to that party—namely where there is fault, including fault of other persons of whom the debtor availed itself in the performance of its obligations. However, non-performance can also be attributed to the party by way of statutory provisions, contractual agreement, or 'commonly accepted opinion' (art. 6:75 BW).

All legal systems that take the fault principle as their starting point also admit many exceptions. A debtor will often have to pay damages in circumstances where neither it nor its agents bear any blame for non-performance. One exception is where the debtor does not perform because it does not have the money—a party must ensure that it has the necessary funds available to perform a contract.[12] The party must not only be able to pay the agreed price, wages, or rent at the specified time. Strict liability will also apply where the debtor owes some other type of performance but fails to perform because it does not have the money and cannot get a loan from its bank. Anyone not delivering goods or providing building services promptly because they do not have the money to purchase goods or supplies from third parties, or because they cannot hire the required crane, will be liable to pay compensation for the resulting harm. Not having the money to do so will be no excuse, and it makes no difference whether the lack of money is based on the debtor's fault or not.

Statutory provisions sometimes render fault irrelevant for the debtor's liability, or make the debtor liable only when the non-performance is due to circumstances that it would not have been able to avoid even by taking great care. So if the harm caused to a lessee is due to a defect that was already present at the time of the lease, and the leased object was thus not suitable for the contractual purpose, the lessor must pay damages even though it cannot in any way be blamed for not having kept the leased object free of defects (§ 536a BGB). A carrier hired to transport goods must pay its client compensation for harm suffered if the goods are lost or damaged during transit, or if they are not delivered on time. The carrier can only exceptionally avoid this liability if it can show that the non-performance could not have been avoided even by the exercise of

---

[12] For a comparative perspective, see Treitel (n 11) s. 17.

'greatest care' and even that care could not have prevented the damages suffered by the client as a consequence of the carrier's non-performance (§ 426 HGB).[13]

Another important exception to the fault principle is where it follows from the wording of the contract or its correct interpretation that the debtor will be strictly liable. Under art. 6:75 BW, liability for non-performance is attributed to the debtor even where it is not to blame for the non-performance, provided that stricter liability can be based on a contractual provision or what is called 'commonly accepted opinion' (*in het verkeer geldende opvattingen*). Section 276 BGB also fully recognises the fault principle, but adds that other conclusions may be reached from the contract and its interpretation 'including but not limited to the giving of a guarantee or the assumption of a procurement risk'. Commercial practice generally holds that a procurement risk is assumed where someone has sold goods of a type specified in the contract and which are to be delivered to the buyer in a volume (number, weight, or other measure) as stipulated in the contract. In such cases, the seller is responsible for having a sufficient amount of the goods at the required time in order to deliver to the buyer. If the seller does not have enough of the goods, and the buyer demands compensation for delay or (after termination of the contract) for non-performance, the seller can only escape liability by showing that no goods of this type were available. Contracts of sale will often clearly define the type of goods that the seller must deliver. For example, it may be agreed by the parties that the goods must come from a specific source or be manufactured by a particular supplier. In that case, the seller will not be liable if the specific source is exhausted or the specific producer ceased business and the goods of the agreed type are no longer available. If a wine producer sold its own wine to a hotel but cannot deliver because its vines have been invaded by pests, or because its production facilities have burned down, it will not be liable unless it, or its agents, were responsible for the pest infestation or the fire. In other cases, the contract may say that the seller shall not be liable if the non-performance is caused by an act of God (*höhere Gewalt, force majeure*), war, natural catastrophes, strikes, or crop failures. Sometimes the contract may provide that the seller shall not be liable if its own supplier failed to make a correct and timely delivery of the goods sold to the buyer.[14] All this is to be distinguished from the case where the seller can still deliver but can exceptionally rely on being freed from contractual responsibilities due to frustration of the purpose of the contract.[15]

The fault principle also does not apply if the correctly interpreted contract shows that a party has taken on a *guarantee*, namely by undertaking that a particular risk will not occur and thus prevent the proper performance of the contract. A party may

---

[13] By contrast, there are also cases where legislation provides that the debtor shall only be liable where the non-performance was due to intentional or grossly negligent behaviour. The debtor receives this lenient approach if, for example, it had acted unselfishly when concluding the contract and thus deserves mitigation of liability. Pursuant to art. 99 OR, the debtor is 'generally liable for any fault' but the scope of liability can be 'judged more leniently where the obligor does not stand to gain from the transaction'. See also §§ 521, 599 BGB: a donor or a lender who makes an item available to its contractual partner at no charge is only liable for intent and gross negligence (see also art. 248(1) OR).

[14] For interpretation of such a *Selbstbelieferungsklausel*, see BGH 6 Mar. 1968, BGHZ 49, 388; BGH 14 Nov. 1984, BGHZ 92, 396; BGH 22 Mar. 1995, [1995] *NJW* 1959.

[15] See below, chapter 15 = pp. 279ff, and the comparative treatment in Treitel (n 11) s. 18.

guarantee, for example, that it has the necessary abilities, knowledge, and facilities required for performance of the contract; that it is the owner of the goods sold; that delivery of the goods sold requires no official permit or that such a permit will be provided; or that it does not yet have possession of the goods sold, but can procure the goods from a third party and deliver to them on time. If any of these risks occur and there is no performance, the debtor must pay damages without being able to avoid liability by being able to prove that it was not to blame. Whether or not such a guarantee has been given turns on the wording in the contract. If no clear agreement has been reached, the intention of the parties must be determined by interpretation of the contract, taking into account commercial practice, general customs, and the surrounding circumstances.

A special practical importance attaches to the question of whether the seller has guaranteed the *qualities* of the goods sold—namely whether it has guaranteed that the goods will have certain qualities and characteristics, or be free from certain defects. Generally, the condition of the goods will be described in the contract; but if no specific agreement has been made, construction of the contract will determine the characteristics that the goods must have in order to make them suitable for the contractual purpose, or for ordinary usage. In legal systems that follow the fault principle, this alone does not constitute a quality guarantee.[16] In German law, for example, it is required that the seller must also have undertaken 'in a contractually binding manner to assume the risk that the goods will have a particular agreed characteristic, and has thereby made it clear that he or she is prepared to be responsible for all consequences of this characteristic not being present'.[17] Such a guarantee can arise from an interpretation of the contract, but this usually requires that the seller has a particular knowledge and experience and is aware of the fact that the buyer will rely on the presence of the agreed quality of the goods, is itself unable to check their conformity at reasonable cost (such as by quality controls), and cannot protect itself against the risks resulting from any hidden defect (such as using insurance).

If there is no quality guarantee, the seller can defend itself against the buyer's claim for damages by proving that it bears no responsibility for the defect in the goods. The same applies if a service provider has delivered a defective work product. But in many cases it is difficult in practical terms to provide this exculpatory evidence, particularly when the seller or service provider has itself produced or provided the defective goods. Here the rule of thumb is: someone who works carefully does not make mistakes, and someone who produces defective products does not work carefully.[18] In such cases, the dispute is normally about which characteristics the goods or the service should have under the contract. Once this has been determined, and it is clear that the seller

---

[16] This does not exclude the possibility that the buyer can, under certain conditions, *terminate the contract* on account of the defective goods either in full or (if it demands a reduction in the price) in part. See chapter 13 n 68 = p. 235.

[17] BGH 29 Nov. 2006, BGHZ 170, 86, 92 (standing case law).

[18] See also (though with a more reserved formulation) BGH 25 Jan. 1989, [1989] *NJW-RR* 559, 560: If the seller itself is the producer of the goods, 'it seems reasonable to assume that the delivery of defective goods was based on negligence, perhaps because … they were not designed by the seller so as to be in conformity with the agreed purpose for which the goods were to be used'.

or service provider has not met this standard, the exculpatory evidence is often a *probatio diabolica* for them. The situation is different where the seller is a *trader* that has received defective goods from its supplier, or when a building contractor has installed windows in a house it is building for its customer, and those windows procured from a supplier turn out to be defective. Here German law makes a differentiation: if, under the circumstances, the seller or service provider was required to examine the delivered goods before sale or installation, exculpatory evidence would be permissible, but difficult to provide, as it must show that the defect would not have been discoverable under such examination. By contrast, exculpatory evidence will often succeed where there is no duty of examination, perhaps because the seller or service provider does not have the necessary specialist expertise or equipment, or because such an examination would destroy the goods or render them unsellable.[19] It is very doubtful, however, whether it is correct for the German courts to allow exculpatory evidence in these cases. It is the seller or service provider that sought out the manufacturer as a business partner, and they, rather than the buyer, should therefore be responsible for conducting the dispute with the manufacturer and bear the attendant performance and solvency risks. It will be shown that the approach of the German courts is not mirrored in other jurisdictions.

A different approach is taken in the Netherlands. The *Hoge Raad* heard a case in which the buyer, a rose-grower, received delivery of a defective herbicide that the seller had obtained in packaged form from its supplier, a chemical factory. The seller had to pay damages to the rose-grower, even though it did not and could not recognise the defect. But the non-performance of the contract could be 'attributed' to the seller pursuant to art. 6:75 BW, not because it was to blame, but because under '*in het verkeer geldende opvattingen*' it was the seller who had to carry the risk of defects.[20]

II. *Obligations de moyens* and *obligations de résultat*

French courts have developed a special solution to the question of whether the debtor must pay damages in case of non-performance. It is not clear from the *Code civil*.

---

[19] A buyer that purchased the defective goods as a *consumer* will have a mandatory right to demand *supplementary performance* or *reduction of the purchase price*, and under certain conditions may also terminate the contract (art. 3 EU Directive of 25 May 1999 on Consumer Contracts, and above, p. 237). But national contract laws remain applicable with respect to the buyer's *claim for damages* (see § 485(3) BGB). So where a buyer received a delivery of defective parquet blocks that the seller had acquired from a producer, the seller was not liable to pay damages to the buyer because 'the trader could not recognise the defect in the goods in their packaged state', and 'any blame attached to the manufacturer can not be attributed to the seller pursuant to § 278 BGB ... because the manufacturer is not an agent of the seller' (BGH 15 July 2008, BGHZ 177, 224, 235, and above, p. 245). For a critical view, see U Schroeter, 'Untersuchungspflicht und Vertretenmüssen des Händlers bei Lieferung sachmangelhafter Ware' [2010] JZ 495. In his opinion, the manufacturer should always be held to be the trader's agent. Accordingly, if the manufacturer was negligent in producing the goods, its negligence must be attributed to the trader and seller pursuant to § 278 BGB. German courts have so far rejected this view unless special reasons can be shown. It has been held, for example, that where the seller needs to show the buyer how to use the goods properly and supplies it with instructions prepared by the manufacturer that have substantial deficiencies, the seller was (exceptionally) held liable pursuant to § 278 BGB for the manufacturer's faults. See BGH 5 April 1967, BGHZ 47, 312, 316.

[20] HR 27 April 2001, [2002] *NedJur* 1461 (Nr. 213).

Pursuant to art. 1231-1, the debtor must pay damages if it has not performed, or not performed in time. But this does not apply if the debtor can show that the failure to perform or late performance is due to *force majeure*, or in other words (as is now specified in art. 1218 *Code civil*) that the debtor has been prevented from fulfilling the contract by circumstances that lie outside its control, were not reasonably foreseeable by the debtor when the contract was concluded, and could not be averted by reasonable measures.

However, the debtor will only need to fall back on *force majeure* if it has assumed an *obligation de résultat*, namely where the contract shows that the debtor agreed to attain a certain result. The situation is different if the contract shows that the debtor has merely agreed an *obligation de moyens*, meaning that it has merely promised to take all necessary measures that a reasonable person in the same situation would undertake to achieve the purpose of the contract. In such cases, the creditor must prove that the debtor breached an *obligation de moyens* by failing to take the care to be expected from a reasonable person. Sometimes the courts also refer to an *obligation de moyens renforcée*: there is a presumption in this case of the debtor's fault, which it can rebut by proof that it did act in accordance with the generally required care. No difference is made in both cases between the debtor's personal fault and the fault committed by an agent brought in by the debtor to help with the performance of the contract.

The difference between an *obligation de résultat* and an *obligation de moyens*[21] is sometimes difficult, but often quite clear. Where a seller undertakes to deliver goods specified in a contract to a buyer on time, it promises a certain result. This is an *obligation de résultat*, and if the promised result does not materialise, the seller can only escape liability under the strict conditions of art. 1218 *Code civil*. So when a certain volume of oats from the 1914 harvest was sold, but not delivered because the military authorities had seized the harvest, the seller could still be liable to pay damages. Confiscation is generally seen as *force majeure*, but the situation was different in this case because the seller missed an opportunity to deliver the goods to the buyer before the confiscation took place.[22] If production, transportation, or delivery is hindered or delayed by a strike, the more general and unforeseeable the strike is under the circumstances, the more likely this is to be generally regarded as a case of *force majeure* now described in some detail in art. 1218 *Code civil*.[23] So in cases where goods of a certain type described in the contract were sold but not delivered, or not delivered on

---

[21] This difference is also discussed by commentators and courts in other European countries, particularly Italy. Under art. 1218 *Codice civile*, a debtor who does not perform the contract, or performs late, must pay damages unless it can prove that the non-performance is due to an '*impossibilità della prestazione derivante da causa a lui non imputabile*'. This provision is largely similar to the rule in art. 1218 *Code civil*. On the other hand, art. 1176 *Codice civile* refers to the debtor only having to show the due care of a '*buon padre di famiglia*'. With respect to the sometimes difficult question of whether the stricter or milder liability applies in a particular case, the approach of the French courts also plays an important role in Italy. See more in F Ranieri, *Europäisches Obligationenrecht* (3rd edn, 2009) 594ff, 636ff; M Pellegrino, 'Subjektive oder objektive Vertragshaftung?' (1997) 5 *ZEuP* 41, 44ff. (both with extensive evidence).

[22] Civ. 16 Mai 1922, D. 1922.I.131. See also Civ. 19 June 1923, D.P. 1923.I.94; Req. 28 Nov. 1934, S. 1935.I.105. For a comparative view, see Treitel (n 11) s. 18.

[23] See, for example, Ch. mixte 4 Feb. 1983, Bull.cass. 1983 no. 1 and 2; Civ. 7 March 1966, D. 1966 Somm. 82; Com. 24 Nov. 1953, *JCP* 1954.II.8302, n. J Radouant; Com. 6 March 1985, Bull.cass. 1985. IV. no. 90; Civ. 6 Oct. 1973, *JCP* 1993.II.22154, n. P Waquet.

time, French courts basically come to the same result as in Germany, though German courts would have to say that the seller had assumed the procurement risk.

The situation is the same for a work contract, provided the contractor has promised its client that it will not only *try* to achieve the desired result (it would then be a contract for services) but to actually promise that the result will be achieved. Article 1792 *Code civil* expressly states that building contractors and architects must pay damages caused to clients by faulty building or planning services, unless they can avert liability by showing a *cause étrangère* or *force majeure*.[24] There is strict liability also where a seller has delivered goods that have a hidden defect. The seller will have breached the *garantie des vices cachés* applicable under the sales provisions of art. 1641 ff. *Code civil*. It is true that the seller is liable only for reimbursement of the purchase price and any costs accruing to the buyer, and that it is only liable to pay full damages if it *knew* about the defect (art. 1645f.). But French courts have consistently found that a professional seller of commercial goods is deemed to know that such a defect existed. So commercial traders are liable to pay damages in full without the court having to look into the issue of negligence; this strict liability applies even if the contract purports to exclude or limit liability for hidden defects.[25]

Damages can also be demanded by someone who, during performance of a contract, uses the rooms and facilities controlled by the other party and thereby suffers some harm. As such harm usually takes the form of bodily harm or property damage, it seems reasonable to raise the issue of whether the basis of the claim might not be in tort. French law has consistently taken the view that an injured party that has a contractual arrangement with the other party may not assert a claim in tort, but should be restricted to seeking a remedy in contract.[26] In the above cases, these claims for non-performance are based on a contractual *obligation de sécurité*, which may be either an *obligation de résultat* or an *obligation de moyens*. A company that concludes a transportation contract for a train must bring its clients safely to their destination on the basis of an *obligation de sécurité de résultat*. Consequently, if a traveller gets hurt during the journey, the company will only escape liability if it can prove that the harm was

---

[24] The case law is not clear for other work contracts. See Terré, Simler, and Lequette (n 3) no. 590. So if a trader has promised to clean an item of clothing, it will be liable for breach of an *obligation de résultat* if the item gets lost while it is being cleaned and cannot be found. However, if the cleaning is faulty and the clothing is damaged, there is an assumption that the trader must have been negligent, but the assumption is rebuttable. See Civ. 20 Dec. 1993, Bull.cass. 1993.I. no. 376; Versailles 28 Oct. 1983, *Gaz Pal* 1984.2. Somm. 354.

[25] See Civ. 30 Oct. 1978 and Com. 6 Nov. 1978, *JCP* 1979.II.19178, n. J Ghestin. In addition, anyone, whether or not a buyer, who has suffered bodily harm or damage to other goods as a consequence of a defective product, may claim damages from its manufacturer. Under certain conditions damages may also be sought from anyone acting 'like a manufacturer', who has imported the defective product or brought it to market. This 'product liability' (which is independent of contractual claims) was introduced by Directive 85/374/EEC of 25 July 1985 and transposed into French law by art. 1245ff. *Code civil*. See in general F Bruder, 'Product Liability' in *Max Planck Enc.* (2012) 1200.

[26] This principle of '*non-cumul des responsabilités contractuelle et délictuelle*' is a peculiarity of French law; see Terré, Simler, and Lequette (n 3) no. 875f. English law takes a different approach: see *Henderson v. Merrett Syndicates Ltd.* [1994] 3 All ER 506, 523ff. German law also takes a different view; see BGH 24 May 1976, BGHZ 66, 315 and G Wagner in *Münchener Kommentar zum BGB* (6th edn, 2013) before § 823 BGB mn. 68ff. For a comparative perspective, see T Weir in *Int.Enc.Comp.L.* vol. XI ch 12, 47ff.

due to *force majeure*.²⁷ More difficult cases concern circumstances where the injured party enjoys a certain independence and freedom of movement while using the premises. If a fairground owner lets a visitor drive a dodgem car at a fairground, it will be liable for the breach of an *obligation de résultat* if the dodgem car is defective and the visitor suffers harm.²⁸ But there is only an *obligation de moyens* if the visitor suffered harm before or after the ride in the dodgem car, for example because he or she tripped over a step while entering the fairground ride.²⁹ There is an *obligation de moyens* if a hotel or restaurant owner needs to make sure that its rooms or staircases are safe for customers,³⁰ or if a swimming pool operator needs to make sure the pool is safe.³¹

There is only liability from an *obligation de moyens* from someone who offers to look after the interests of another party—for example, where a lawyer, notary, or tax advisor looks after the legal or tax interests of their client; where an expert draws up a report for a client; where an architect monitors a building project to make sure construction is proceeding properly; or where someone is to give information, collect receivables from a third party, or look after the securities of another party. Similarly, a doctor who promises medical services to a patient is only liable with respect to an *obligation de moyens*, but even here one can observe a trend towards strengthening the liability of the doctor. There is an assumption in favour of the patient that the doctor may not have correctly warned him or her about the dangers of a treatment, and it is up to the doctor to prove otherwise.³² An even stricter *obligation de sécurité de résultat* applies to a hospital if a patient catches an unrelated infection; the hospital can only escape liability by showing *force majeure*.³³ There is also strict liability for the breach of an *obligation de résultat* if a doctor treats the patient by giving or prescribing something which is not in perfect condition or actually harmful to the patient's health, such as faulty dentures, incorrect medication, or a defective blood product.³⁴

---

[27] This applies only if the traveller suffers the harm only after he or she has begun to enter the train and before disembarkation is complete. If the harm suffered takes place before or after these times—perhaps because the traveller slips on an icy station platform and falls onto the tracks—the claim will then be made in tort. See, for example, Civ. 7 March 1989, Bull.cass. 1989.I. no. 118 = D. 1989, 1, n. P Malaurie; Civ. 13 March 2008, JCP 2008.II.10085. The train operator must also pay damages if the traveller suffers bodily harm and property theft during a robbery on the journey. The operator cannot rely on *force majeure*, because robberies are foreseeable, and the operator can ensure a certain deterrent effect by '*la présence de contrôleurs en nombre suffisant parcourant les wagons de façon régulière*' (Civ. 3 July 2002, D. 2002, 2631). There is also strict liability if the harm suffered by the traveller results from loss of luggage (Civ. 26 Sept. 2006, JCP 2006.II.10206).

[28] The result is the same under German law: the entrepreneur has leased the dodgem car to its customer and is on this ground considered by § 536a BGB to have given a guarantee that the car was safe at the time the contract was concluded. See BGH 21 Feb. 1962, [1962] NJW 908.

[29] Civ. 30 Oct. 1968, D. 1969, 650; Civ. 28 April 1969, JCP 1970.II.16166, n. A Rabut. See also Civ. 11 March 1986, JCP 1986.IV.186 (cable car); Civ. 4 Nov. 1992, D. 1994, 45, n. P Brun (tow lift).

[30] Civ. 7 Feb. 1966, D. 1966, 314; Civ. 22 May 1991, Bull.cass. 1991.I. no. 163. Here too there is doubt whether the hotel or restaurant owner has an *obligation de moyens renforcée*. In that case, there would be a presumption of liability, which can only be avoided by providing evidence to the contrary. If a hotel or restaurant owner has delivered bad food, it will be liable for an *obligation de résultat*; see Poitiers 16 Dec. 1970, JCP 1972.II.17127, n. G Mémétau.

[31] Civ. 20 Oct. 1971, Bull.cass. 1971.I. no. 227.

[32] Civ. 25 Feb. 1997, JCP 1997.I.4025, n. G Viney. On medical liability for doctors, see in detail Terré, Simler, and Lequette (n 3) no. 1004ff.

[33] Civ. 18. Feb. 2009, Bull.cass. 2009.I. no. 37.

[34] Civ. 15 Nov. 1988, Bull.cass. 1988.I. no. 319; Civ. 9 Nov. 1999, JCP 2000.II.10251, n. P Brun; Civ. 7 Nov. 2000, Bull.cass. 2000.I. no. 279 = JCP 2001.I.340, n. G Viney. The situation is different, however, if

III. Breach of contract

In contrast to the continental legal systems, the Common Law basically regards the contract as a guaranteed promise. If the debtor has not done what was promised in the contract, it must pay damages for breach. This liability is strict, because it does not generally turn on whether responsibility, in particular some form of fault or negligence, can be laid at the door of the debtor or his or her employees, agents, or subcontractors. As we will see, the Common Law also has many cases where a debtor has to pay damages if it did not exercise due care. However, if the debtor exercised due care, it will not be liable in damages—not because the breach is excused, but because there is no breach in the first place since the debtor did all it was required to do under the (correctly interpreted) contract.[35]

The strict liability under a breach of contract in England is often traced back to the case of *Paradine* v. *Jane*.[36] The plaintiff landlord's claim was not for damages for breach of contract, but for performance of the contract, namely payment of the backlog of rent due on a property. The lessee countered that he had been unable to use the property during the lease, as it had been occupied by armed rebels. The defence was rejected: 'When the party by his own contract creates a duty or charge upon himself, he is bound to make it good, notwithstanding any accident by inevitable necessity, because he might have provided against it by his contract'. It follows that the lessee would not have had to pay damages if the contract had had a term providing that the rent would not be due if the property were to be overrun by armed third parties, thus transferring that risk to the lessor. It is indeed quite common today that contracts have express terms under which the debtor need not perform if a specific obstacle arises—such as strikes, war, natural catastrophes, or non-delivery of the goods by the seller's own supplier. Relief from liability can arise not only from express agreements, but also from construction of the contract. This approach was used in *Taylor* v. *Caldwell*. The plaintiff had hired a music hall from the defendant in order to hold four concerts on consecutive days, but the hall accidentally burned down before the first concert. The plaintiff's claim for the damages arising from the cancellation of the concerts was denied, not because the lessor could not be blamed for the destruction of the hall, but because the properly constructed contract had an implied term that 'in contracts in which the performance depends on the continued existence of a given person or thing a condition is implied that the impossibility arising from the perishing of the person or thing shall excuse the performance'.[37] The basis of this decision has gradually been developed into a doctrine of frustration, which is discussed in greater detail in chapter 15: parties will be freed from their obligations under the contract, thus extinguishing liability for breach of contract, if after conclusion of the contract an

---

a surgeon operates using latex gloves and these cause a massive allergic reaction in the patient. As the gloves were not faulty, and the surgeon's conduct was not culpable, the patient's claim was denied (Civ. 22 Nov. 2007, *JCP* 2008.II.10069, n. I Corpart). In such cases, a party can under certain circumstances claim damages from the *public purse*. See the *Loi Kouchner* of 4 March 2002 (L. 1142-1 *Code de la santé publique*).

[35] See text above to n 11.   [36] (1647) 82 Eng.Rep. 897.   [37] (1863) 122 Eng.Rep. 309, 314.

unforeseen change in circumstances (for which neither party bears the risk) makes performance impossible, or very much more difficult than planned.

Such cases arise only rarely. The general rule is that a debtor is strictly liable when it has contractually agreed to do something, but fails to do so.[38] The rule applies not only when the debtor cannot pay a promised amount of money, but also if the contract promises to provide or process goods—for example, where a seller is to deliver goods, a building contractor to erect a building, a shipowner to deliver a ship, or a landlord to rent out a house. Unless otherwise agreed, all must make sure that the promised performance is made on time and in the form promised in the contract. If the seller has failed to deliver fifty tons of soy beans or other generic goods as promised, it must pay damages in Germany or France even if it is not to blame—in Germany because it is assumed that the seller will carry the procurement risk, and in France because is the seller has assumed an *obligation de résultat* and can only escape paying damages in the rare case that it can prove *force majeure*. In England, this result is derived already from the basic rule: only the properly interpreted contract ascertains which specific risks the seller has assumed, and which it has not. If there is no other clause in the contract, it is no defence for the seller to say that there was no shipping space available to get the goods to their agreed destination or that it was let down by its own supplier.[39] A person buying milk who becomes ill because the milk is contaminated with bacteria can still claim damages if the seller can show that it would not have been able to recognise the contamination even if it had taken the greatest care with the product.[40] A building contractor must also pay damages if it has used products during the construction that have been delivered by a supplier in a defective condition. The contractor will be unable to escape liability even if it can prove that it was blameless and the supplier was extremely reliable, or that the defect of the delivered goods was not discovered despite a careful check, or could not have been revealed even if such a check had been made.[41]

The situation is different if a professional such as a doctor, lawyer, accountant, or investment advisor promises a service. What they are promising in the contract is not to achieve a specific result. They are merely promising to act on behalf of their client in

---

[38] 'It is axiomatic that, in relation to claims for damages for breach of contract, it is, in general, immaterial why the defendant failed to fulfil his obligation, and certainly no defence to plead that he had done his best' (*Lord Edmund Davies* in *Raineri* v. *Miles* [1981] AC 1050, 1086). 'It does not matter whether the failure to fulfil the contract by the seller is because he is indifferent or wilfully negligent or just unfortunate. It does not matter what the reason is. What matters is the fact of performance. Has he performed or not?' (*Sellers J.* in *Nicolene Ltd.* v. *Simmonds* [1952] 2 Lloyd's Rep. 419, 425). Similarly *Lord Greene MR* in a case about the liability of a laundry: 'The laundry company undertakes not to exercise due care in laundering the customer's goods, but to launder them, and if it fails to launder them it is no use saying "I did my best. I exercised due care and took reasonable precautions, and I am very sorry if as a result the linen is not properly laundered"' (*Alderslade* v. *Hendon Laundry* [1945] 1 All ER 244, 246 [CA]). However, this decision also states that if the clothing cannot be returned because it is *lost*, the laundry company is not liable if it can prove that it had carried out its duty to watch over the clothing with the necessary customary care.

[39] See Treitel (n 9) no. 17-064, and, for a comparative view, Treitel (n 11) p. 18.

[40] *Frost* v. *Aylesbury Dairy Co. Ltd.* [1905] 1 KB 608; *Daniels* v. *White & Son* [1938] 4 All ER 258. See Treitel (n 9) no. 17-065 and, for a comparative perspective, Treitel (n 11) s. 19. French law comes to the same conclusion (see above, n 25). German law takes a different approach if the seller is not the manufacturer of the defective goods, but is just acting as a trader (see above, n 19).

[41] *G.H. Myers* v. *Brent Cross Service Co.* [1934] 1 KB 46; *Young & Marten Ltd.* v. *McManus Childs Ltd.* [1969] 1 AC 454. See Treitel (n 9) no. 17-065 and, for a comparative perspective, Treitel (n 11) s. 19.

the manner to be expected of a reasonable doctor, lawyer, accountant, or investment advisor in the same circumstances. So if an expert drafts a report about the value of a property, there is no non-performance (and thus no breach of contract) if the expert merely delivers an incorrect report, but only if the expert fails to exercise the due care expected of a professional expert in that field.[42] In England, s. 13 of the Supply of Goods and Services Act 1982 states that where a supplier offering a service is acting in the course of a business, 'there is an implied term that the supplier will carry out the service with reasonable care and skill'. Of course, the Act makes clear that this is only a default rule, and that the parties may (expressly or impliedly) agree a stricter liability of the debtor. So, for example, an architect's services are subject to differing levels of liability: there is strict liability if the architect's planning is defective, but if he or she has only assumed a duty to supervise the activities of the building contractor, (including its duty to inspect the materials delivered by third parties) the architect will be liable in damages only if he or she failed to exercise due professional care in performing their job.[43] If dentures are faulty, a dentist cannot avoid liability by claiming that he or she has only done their best,[44] and two further cases show vivid debate about how to interpret the agreement of a doctor to sterilise a patient: is the doctor promising to take due care in providing a service, or promising that the service will be successful—namely rendering the patient infertile?[45]

IV. International rules

We have seen that the national legal systems take different approaches to these fascinating questions. Not one of them accepts a uniform solution that is based solely on the fault principle or on the principle of guarantee liability: all adopt a mixed approach. Some legal orders (German law in particular) allow the debtor to show that it acted neither deliberately nor negligently, and is thus not responsible for the non-performance. This fault principle finds 'its clearest and most explicit expression'[46] in § 276 BGB. However, as we have seen, it is subject to severe restrictions. Liability appears to be stronger in France, at least in those common cases where the debtor has an *obligation de résultat* to fulfil, and thus can only avoid liability by showing that non-performance is due to *force majeure*, ie based on circumstances that were outside its control and which a reasonable person could neither have foreseen nor averted by appropriate measures. The Common Law starts from the guarantee principle, but admits that there are contracts requiring the debtor only to exercise the care of a reasonable person in like circumstances. In that case, if such care is demonstrated, then there is no non-performance and no breach of contract.

---

[42] See *South Australia Asset Management Corp. v. York Montague* [1997] AC 191 (HL). But even if the expert is found liable, the amount of damages payable is uncertain. On this, see below, nn 65f.
[43] *Greaves & Co. v. Baynham Meikle & Partners* [1975] 3 All ER 99, 103. See also Treitel (n 9) no. 17-068 and, for a comparative perspective, Treitel (n 11) s. 25ff.
[44] *Samuels v. Davis* [1943] 1 KB 526.
[45] *Thake v. Maurice* [1986] QB 644; *Eyre v. Measday* [1986] 1 All ER 488.
[46] Treitel (n 11) s. 9.

Despite differing starting points, similar cases in different jurisdictions nevertheless often come to a similar result. Thus Treitel correctly noted that in considering the approaches taken by the Common Law and Civil Law 'the practical differences between the two types of systems are much less significant than their apparently conflicting theories might suggest'.[47] This is certainly one reason why it was possible for the drafters of the international sets of rules to propose a uniform solution.

This solution is based on the principle that the debtor must pay compensation for the harm caused to the creditor by the non-performance of the contract.[48] The question of what constitutes non-performance depends solely on what the debtor promised to the creditor in the contract. If the debtor has promised to achieve a specific result, there will be non-performance if the result has not been achieved at all, is not in accordance with the contract, has not been achieved at the agreed date, or in some other way falls short of what had been promised. But the contract can also show that the debtor only promised to do that what is expected of a reasonable person of the same kind in the same circumstances.[49] In both cases, the debtor will be liable in damages if it has not performed what was required by the contract. The debtor can only avoid liability in the exceptional case where it can show that the non-performance was based on an impediment beyond its control, and where this could not reasonably be expected to have been considered upon conclusion of the contract, nor was avoidable or manageable.[50]

Thus the international sets of rules have settled on a solution that allows the defaulting debtor to exclude liability for damages only under the strictest of circumstances. This follows the line set by art. 79 CISG, which (although restricted to international contracts of sale) settles the issue of relief for the debtor in the same manner. Under this rule, there can only be no liability to pay damages if the debtor (usually the seller) can prove that the non-performance of its contractual obligations is based on an impediment that is 'beyond his control'. So if a seller has failed to perform its obligations because it does not have the money to do so and it cannot raise the money from a bank, this may well be an impediment, but it is not 'beyond [the seller's] control'. This requirement is fulfilled by impediments that are external, namely not dependent on any defects of the debtor's own circle of business activity. The debtor will thus be unable to escape liability if the non-performance of its obligations is due to a lack of available financial resources, a lack of the professional abilities required to avoid an impediment to performance, or failures by the debtor or a third-party

---

[47] Treitel (n 11) s. 8. See also P Schlechtriem, 'Rechtsvereinheitlichung in Europa und Schuldrechtsreform in Deutschland' (1993) 1 *ZEuP* 217, 228ff.

[48] Article 9:501(1) PECL; art. 7.4.1 PICC; art. III.-3:701(1) DCFR; art. 159 (1) CESL.

[49] Article 5.1.4(1) PICC states that a party can have a duty 'to achieve a specific result'; the second paragraph of this section differentiates where only a 'duty of best efforts in the performance of an activity' is required. These rules are based on the difference in French law between *obligations de résultat* and *obligations de moyens*. This difference is not recognised in the PECL. But art. 6:102 PECL states that the 'implied terms' in a contract must also be taken into account. And, depending on the circumstances in the case, these may be important for the question of whether the debtor has assumed a 'duty to achieve a specific result' or a 'duty to use reasonable efforts'. The difference may be decided by the same criteria as stated in art. 5.1.5 PICC.

[50] See also art. 8:108 PECL; art. 7.1.7 PICC; art. III.-3:104 DCFR; art. 88 CESL. See also chapter 15 below.

contractor it has entrusted with performance. It makes no difference whether or not the debtor, its agents, or a third party asked to perform the contractual duties can be blamed or in some other way held 'answerable', 'accountable', or 'responsible' for the non-performance. From this, the *Bundesgerichtshof* has concluded that under art. 79 CISG (differently than under German law) the seller must also pay damages if it has merely acted as a trader who bought the defective goods from a manufacturer and delivered them to the buyer in the original packaging. Nor does it make any difference that the reason for the defects lies solely in the manufacturer's sphere.[51] Unless otherwise agreed, the debtor will also be liable if non-performance is caused by other impediments in its 'control', if it has not received the goods from its own supplier, or has not received the materials it needs to perform the contract. But it can be outside the seller's 'control' if its premises have burned down or flooded, and the seller has taken all possible steps required to avoid the fire or protect against flooding. 'External' impediments can also result from a strike, the outbreak of war, or from export or import bans. The seller can also be liable for 'external' impediments if it would have been reasonable for it to have 'taken these into consideration' upon conclusion of the contract. The seller is also liable if it failed to take reasonable measures to prevent the impediment (or its consequences) from arising. It should be noted that the seller can protect itself against a recognisable impediment by securing a waiver in the contract for such a circumstance or, if this is not possible, by refusing to conclude the contract.

Thus the fault principle is disappearing in its general form, but its exit should not be mourned. It is true that German law clings to this principle more closely than other legal systems, and it is also correct that its use is sometimes defended with the argument that it has an inherently greater legal-ethical persuasion than the guarantee principle.[52] But that does not sit well together with the recognition that, in important cases, German law has ignored the fault principle in favour of a stricter liability, and that in practice it is often given short shrift when it matters. If in a contract a party has not just promised best efforts, but the achievement of a specific result, it is preferable from a legal-ethical perspective that the party should be held to its promise, even if it later transpires that it has promised more in the contract than it can actually deliver.

---

[51] BGH 24 Mar. 1999, BGHZ 141, 129, 134. For extensive details concerning art. 79 CISG, see, for example, P Schlechtriem and U Schroeter, *Internationales UN-Kaufrecht* (6th edn, 2016) mn. 644ff; P Winship, 'Exemptions under art. 79 of the Vienna Sales Convention' (2004) 68 *RabelsZ* 495, both with extensive evidence.

[52] See CW Canaris, 'Die Reform des Rechts der Leistungsstörungen' [2001] *JZ* 494, 506. See also D Medicus, 'Voraussetzungen einer Haftung wegen Vertragsverletzung' in J Basedow (ed), *Europäische Vertragsrechtsvereinheitlichung und deutsches Recht* (2000) 179, 187: the argument is that strict liability can sometimes result in 'unreasonable hardship', such as where the owner of a small company becomes ill and is thus unable to perform the promised services. But even in this case, one should ask if the risk of illness could not be better borne by the service provider than the client. In a case where the client knows that the promised works can only be carried out by the other party and by no one else, the *Cour de cassation* has assumed that the service provider has assumed an *obligation de résultat* but, exceptionally, that the illness constituted a case of *force majeure*. See Ass.plén. 14 Apr. 2006, Bull.cass. 2006 no. 5 and, in detail, Ranieri (n 21) 590ff.

C. Link Between Non-Performance and Damage

If the debtor has failed to perform, it must in principle compensate the creditor for all resulting harm. But that applies only in so far as there is sufficient linkage between the non-performance of the contract and the harm suffered. This is doubtful mainly in two sets of circumstances. The first concerns damage 'caused' by the non-performance, but which is so far removed from it that it is questionable whether the debtor should be held liable for compensation.[53] The other case concerns damage that is not due (or only partly due) to the debtor's non-performance, but entirely or partly due to the creditor's own actions. This may be because the creditor has failed to take steps that a reasonable person would have undertaken in order to mitigate damage that has already taken place, or to avoid such damage in the first place.

I. Liability for remote damage

The debtor is not liable to pay damages for harm caused to the creditor if it can be shown that, upon closer analysis, the harm is not really the consequence of the debtor's breach. Examples would be if a hotel guest demands damages for bodily injury after falling down some hotel steps, or a patient is damaged by a false diagnosis from a doctor. The hotel owner will not be liable if it can show that the guest fell down the steps and was hurt because of a heart attack rather than because the steps were faulty. And the doctor will not be liable to pay damages to the patient if it can be shown that even if the diagnosis had been correct, the damage could not have been averted. The hotel owner and doctor have not correctly performed their contracts, but the non-performance did not cause the harm for which damage is being sought.

Even if there is the required causal link between non-performance and harm, this in itself is not sufficient for the debtor to be liable. There are types of harm that would not have occurred if due performance had been made, but which are so loosely and indirectly linked to the non-performance that for normative reasons it is doubtful whether they can be attributed to the debtor. This is well illustrated by a much-discussed example debated by Ulpian and in even greater detail by Pothier.[54] It has also been used as the basis for a rule in the *Code civil*. If a seller has sold a cow, in full knowledge that it is sick, it is liable to reimburse the buyer not only for the value of the sick cow, but also for the value of a healthy cow that was infected by the sick cow. But this is where the seller's liability stops. It is not responsible for the damage caused to the buyer because it can no longer use its land due to the animals dying. And the seller

---

[53] Take the case allegedly decided in the seventeenth century in which 'a man going to be married to an heiress, his horse having lost a shoe on the journey, employed a blacksmith to replace it, whose work was so lacking in skill that the horse was lamed and, the rider not arriving in time, the lady married another, and the blacksmith was held liable for the loss of the marriage.' See *British Columbia Saw Mill Co. Ltd. v. Nettleship* (1868) L.R. 3 C.P. 499 (508) and Treitel (n 9) no. 20-082. No legal system would today award the rider damages against the blacksmith 'for the loss of the marriage'. What are the grounds on which damages for breach of contract should be limited in this and other cases?

[54] Ulpian D. 19, 1, 13 pr. and RJ Pothier, 'Traité des obligations' no. 166f, reprinted in RJ Pothier, *Traités de droit civil et de jurisprudence française* vol. I (2nd edn, 1781).

is most certainly not liable if the buyer become insolvent, is unable to pay its debts, and its farm is seized by creditors and subsequently sold at a knock-down price to a third party. In the opinion of Pothier, this damage is only indirectly linked to the delivery of the sick cow. So art. 1231-4 *Code civil* (previously art. 1151) states that the debtor, even if it committed a '*faute lourde ou dolosive*', will only be liable for the damage '*qui est une suite immédiate et directe de l'inexécution*'.[55] There is a further limitation of liability that applies only in the normal case where the debtor's non-performance was not based on bad faith or dishonesty. In that case, art. 1221-3 *Code civil* (previously art. 1150) provides that the debtor will not be liable for damages which were neither foreseen nor foreseeable at the time the contract was concluded.

A similar rule on remoteness of damage has also applied in England since the decision in *Hadley* v. *Baxendale*.[56] The plaintiff owned a flourmill. Its iron shaft broke, and this was given to the defendants for transportation to the manufacturer so that a new shaft could be made on the basis of the broken part. Due to a mistake by the transport company, the transport was delayed. The mill was unable to operate for a long time, and the plaintiff claimed damages from the transporter. The claim failed. In the opinion of the court, compensation must be paid for damages arising 'according to the usual course of things' as a consequence of non-performance, including such damage as 'may reasonably be supposed to have been in the contemplation of both parties at the time they made the contract as the probable result of the breach'. The standstill at the mill was not seen as a 'usual' consequence of the delayed delivery; the defendant was also not liable as, under the circumstances, it was the plaintiff and not the defendant who at the time the contract was drawn up should have taken into account that the mill would be unable to operate during any delay.

This rule also applies if when the contract was concluded the parties were able to consider not the scope, but the *type* of damage resulting from non-performance. So if a seller has promised immediate delivery of a machine part (knowing that the part would be used by the buyer to operate washing machines), if delivery is delayed for five

---

[55] The limitation of liability to foreseeable damage has been taken up by many legal systems (see below, n 60). Sometimes, however, a debtor will also be liable for unforeseeable damage if it has acted with gross negligence. See art. 1225 *Codice civile* and art. 1107 Spanish Civil Code which impose liability for unforeseeable damage if the debtor acted maliciously. In other legal systems, the debtor can also be punished with particularly extensive liability if it acts deliberately or with gross negligence. This is the case in Austria (see §§ 1323f. ABGB); in Switzerland, the judge can also take the 'degree of culpability' into account when deciding how much damages to award (art. 43 I, 99 III OR). See also art. 9:503 PECL and art. III.-3:703 DCFR. Such punishment of the debtor may be worth considering if the harm to the creditor results from a tort, but not if it results from non-performance of a contractual obligation. After all, the reason behind contractual liability for damages is not to deter the debtor from particularly reprehensible conduct, but to make it liable for the breach of what it promised in the agreement. See below, p. 264.

[56] (1854) 9 Exch. 341, 156 Eng.Rep. 145. There is some indication that in delivering this judgment the judge not only knew about the French foreseeability rule, but also used it as guidance as it was a 'sensible rule'. *Hadley* v. *Baxendale* has often been discussed from an historical, economic, and comparative law perspective. See, for example, R Danzig, '*Hadley* v. *Baxendale*: A Study in the Industrialization of the Law' (1975) 4 *J Leg Stud* 249; F Faust, '*Hadley* v. *Baxendale*: An Understandable Miscarriage of Justice' (1994) 15 *Journal of Legal History* 41; AWB Simpson, 'Innovation in 19th Century Contract Law' (1975) 91 *LQR* 247, 278; F Faust, *Die Vorhersehbarkeit des Schadens gemäß Art. 74 Satz 2 UN-Kaufrecht (CISG)* (1996) 198ff; U Huber, *Leistungsstörungen* vol. II (1999) § 39 I 2; J Gordley, 'The Foreseeability Limitation on Liability in Contract' in A. Hartkamp et al. (eds), *Towards a European Civil Code* (4th edn, 2011) 699; Treitel (n 11) s. 127ff.

months the seller must compensate the buyer for the usual profit it would have earned if the contract has been performed properly. But the seller would not have to reimburse the buyer for unusual profit, such as where the buyer could have concluded a particularly favourable contract with a third party if delivery had been made on time. The seller would not know about these special profit opportunities when the contract was concluded, nor could it have been aware of them.[57] French courts have come to similar conclusions in many cases where a transport company is held liable for loss or damage to goods, but asserts the defence that the goods had an unusually high value: if the company had not been told about the value of the goods and this was not foreseeable for it, liability would be excluded under art. 1231-3 *Code civil* (formerly art. 1150).[58] The foreseeability rule has also been followed by other legal orders, and also by the CISG and the international sets of rules.[59]

Are there economic reasons that justify the foreseeability rule? It provides a desirable incentive for the creditor to notify the debtor prior to the contract that the level of damages could be high. The debtor may refuse to enter into the contract. But if the debtor does wish to conclude the contract, this will be on the basis that it knows the scope of the threatened risk, and will be able to assess the cost of averting it. On this basis, the debtor will be able to correctly price the cost of performance or negotiate a limitation of liability. If the debtor were required to compensate the creditor in full even though it knew nothing about the high amount of damages it might have to pay, it would need to raise the price for *all* customers. Creditors with the high potential loss would be cross-subsidised by the other customers, since they would have to pay the same price, but would nonetheless be able to demand particularly high damages in case of non-performance.

Under these circumstances, it is not entirely surprising that German law does not recognise the foreseeability rule, but still manages to reach similar results via different paths. In particular, the creditor's claim, or at least the scope of the claim, may be restricted if the injured party 'fail[s] to draw the attention of the obligor to the danger of unusually extensive damage' and the obligor 'neither was nor ought to have been aware of the danger' (§ 254(2) sent. 1 BGB). Differently than under the Common Law and French law, this is not justified by the *debtor* being unable to foresee the risk without being informed of it by the creditor, but because it is the creditor who, by its failure to pass on the information, breached a duty of care owed to the debtor and has thus itself caused all or part of the damage suffered.[60] There is no material practical difference here.

---

[57] *Victoria Laundry (Windsor) Ltd. v. Newman Industries Ltd.* [1949] 2 KB 528.
[58] See, for example, Civ. 3 March 1897, D.P. 1898.1.118; Com. 9 July and 23 Dec. 1913, D.P. 1915.1.35; Com. 6 Jan. 1970, Bull.cass. 1970.IV. no. 6. In other cases, the refusal to award damages is (also) justified on the basis that the harm is not a '*suite immédiate et directe*' of the non-performance: see Req. 18 May 1915, S. 1917.1.38; Civ. 16 May 1922, S. 1922.1.358; Com. 30 June 1969, Bull.cass. 1969.IV. no. 249.
[59] See, for example, art. 1225 *Codice civile* and art. 1107 Spanish Civil Code, and also art. 74 sent. 2 CISG; art. 9:503 PECL; art. 7.4.4 PICC; art. III.-3:703 DCFR; art. 161 CESL.
[60] See BGH 29 Jan. 1969, [1969] *NJW* 789: a hotel guest can also be partly liable by handing over his car to the hotel owner for safekeeping, but not mentioning that there is a collection of gold watches in the boot. This does not mean that the damages resulting from the theft of the watches falls entirely to the hotel guest. The issue of if and how much damages will be due depends on the circumstances and 'in particular, to what extent the damage has been caused by one party or the other'. See also OLG Hamm 28

In other cases under German law, the liability of the debtor is limited with the help of *Adäquanztheorie* (theory of adequate causation), by which the debtor is not liable for damages which a neutral observer would conclude could be expected 'only under especially unique, rather improbable and, in the general course of things, very exceptional circumstances'.[61] This theory is largely based on the entirely indeterminate criterion of *Wahrscheinlichkeit* (probability) of the damage and is thus largely rejected by the academic literature.[62] It is increasingly being supplemented—or even replaced—by the *Schutzzwecktheorie* (protective purpose theory). It first determines the obligation which the debtor undertook to perform in the contract. The debtor will then be held liable only for those damages which are within the 'protective purpose' of the assumed obligation. The degree of 'probability' or 'foreseeability' of the damage is not relevant, but only whether or not the damage belongs to the type of damage which the proper performance of the debtor's obligations was intended to prevent.[63]

More recent English cases also indicate that the rule in *Hadley* v. *Baxendale* is normally followed, but only if the contract itself does not show that there shall be no liability for the type of damage in question, even though it may have been quite foreseeable for the debtor.[64] So if an expert valuer has drawn up a valuation report for a bank and has been careless in setting the value of a property too high, the valuer must compensate the bank for any damage suffered if it lends too much money on the basis of that valuation. But will the expert valuer also be liable to compensate for any additional damage resulting from a general fall in property prices after the report has been drawn up? The answer here is that the valuer is not liable, because correct construction of the contract requires the valuer to conduct the valuation with care, but not to assume the risk of a general fall in property prices, even if he or she might have foreseen this risk at the time the contract was concluded and the bank would not have lent any money if the report had been so drafted.[65]

Feb. 1989, [1989] *NJW* 2066; OLG Hamm 17 June 1996, [1998] *NJW-RR* 380; see also (in cases of failure to provide information about the unusually high value of goods to be transported) BGH 1 Dec. 2005, [2006] *NJW-RR* 1108; BGH 20 July 2006, [2007] *NJW-RR* 28.

[61] BGH 9 Oct. 1997, [1998] *NJW* 138, 140; BGH 16 Apr. 2002, [2002] *NJW* 2232, 2233.

[62] See, in detail, H Oetker in *Münchener Kommentar zum BGB* (6th edn, 2012) § 249 BGB mn. 103ff.

[63] See, for example, BGH 3 Dec. 1991, [1992] *NJW* 555, 556: 'It is recognised that the breach of a legal obligation only leads to compensation for the damage that compliance with the obligation is intended to prevent. It applies not only to tort law, but also to contract law; here, too, the type and formation of damage must be derived from the area of risk that the unfulfilled obligation was intended to prevent.' See also BGH 6 June 2002, [2002] *NJW* 2459, 2460; BGH 13 Feb. 2003, [2003] *NJW-RR* 1035.

[64] See Lord Hoffmann in *Transfield Shipping Inc.* v. *Mercator Shipping Inc.* [2009] 1 AC 61 (HL). The question of whether the debtor is liable for a particular type of damage under the foreseeability rule, or whether it is *not* liable (even though the damage was foreseeable) depends on 'what these parties contracting against the background of market expectations ..., would reasonably have considered the extent of the liability they were undertaking' (no. 23).

[65] *South Australia Asset Management Corp.* v. *York Montague Ltd.* (n 42). The case is not much different from the example set out by Lord Hoffmann on p. 213 of the judgment: a mountaineer wanted to undertake a difficult mountain ascent and asked his doctor in advance if he would be able to make the trip with his injured knee. Even if the doctor dealt with the inquiry recklessly and answered that the patient could undertake the trip, the doctor was not liable for damages suffered by the mountaineer not because his knee gave way, but because he was injured by a rock-fall. The doctor would also not be liable if a correct recommendation concerning the knee would have stopped the patient from undertaking the trip in the first place. The 'protective purpose' of the obligation taken on by the doctor in giving advice was not to guard against all hazards of climbing in the mountains.

II. Contributory responsibility of the creditor

If the debtor has not performed the contract, it must compensate the creditor for the damage it has suffered. But what if the creditor is also partly responsible for the damage occurring in the first place? It may also be the case that the damage occurred without the creditor being responsible, but it has since failed to take steps that would have mitigated the level of damage (or even prevented the damage from occurring). The creditor may also have taken steps that have made the damage worse.

In earlier years, a claim for damages by the creditor would have been excluded if it also bore some responsibility for the damage and thus (in part) caused the damage. The only exception in favour of the creditor was if the debtor had acted deliberately. A division of liability in proportion to the degree of responsibility for causing the damage was not recognised,[66] and did not begin to be relaxed until the nineteenth century. First of all, Austria determined in § 1304 ABGB that 'if an injured party is jointly liable for damage', the damage is to be split 'proportionately' between the parties. Similarly, art. 6:101(1) BW states that damage is to be divided between the injured person and the liable person when it is 'caused as well by circumstances which are attributable to the injured person himself'. The division is then based on the proportion of the damage 'attributable' to the parties. The approach is stated even more succinctly in art. 44 OR: the court may reduce compensation to the injured party, or even dispense with it entirely, where the damage was caused or worsened by circumstances 'attributable' to the injured party. But § 254 BGB seems to indicate that the injured party's claim for damages can only be excluded or limited where there is *Mitverschulden* (contributory negligence).[67] But one should not be misled here. On the one hand, the term *Verschulden* (fault) under § 254 BGB does not carry the same meaning as fault towards a third party under § 276 BGB.[68] On the other hand, it is acknowledged that under § 254 BGB the injured party must tolerate a reduction, or even exclusion, of its claim for damages if it has not acted culpably, but is responsible for the damage for other reasons—because the damage can be attributed to the injured party or it is in some way held liable for that damage.[69] Some legal systems also attempt to distinguish cases where the contributory responsibility of the injured party relates to the *origination* of the damage, or where the injured party failed to mitigate the damage. This distinction does not have any real impact, and it always turns on implementation of the same

---

[66] See R Zimmermann, *The Law of Obligations, Roman Foundations of the Civilian Tradition* (1990) 1010ff, 1047ff.

[67] See also, for example, art. 1227 *Codice civile*; art. 300 Greek Civil Code; art. 570 Portuguese Civil Code

[68] Liability to a third party means that somebody breaches an obligation owed to the third party. On the other hand, § 254 BGB concerns damage to oneself: anyone who contributes to a damage suffered by himself, or fails to mitigate or avert such damage, does not breach a *duty*, but merely an *Obliegenheit*, since his own claim against the liable party will be reduced or even excluded.

[69] This applies where the responsibility of the injured party is not based on his or her fault, but on other reasons. Take the example of a carrier who had to deliver goods to a client and whose vehicle was damaged because it was not informed of the dangers of the premises. The carrier can demand damages from the client but, even if the carrier's actions were not negligent, it must offset the 'operational risk' inherent in using its vehicle. Pursuant to § 7 of the Road Traffic Act (StVG), this operational risk would mean that it would be strictly liable for damage caused to a third party. It also means that its own claim for damages against the client will be mitigated even though it did not act negligently.

basic principle. Nevertheless, one can differentiate between 'giving rise' to the damage or 'exacerbating' it (see art. 44 OR). The first subsection of § 254 BGB also sets out the basic principle of splitting damages, and subsection 2 says that this 'also applies' if the injured person has failed to warn the obligor of 'the danger of unusually extensive damage' or has failed to reduce or avert the damage.[70] The injured party will be held jointly responsible in such cases where its actions to avert or reduce the damage differ from how a reasonable person would have acted in their own interest under the same circumstances. It is self-evident that this approach gives judges a wide discretion.

French law does not have a general statutory rule governing contributory liability of the injured party, but the courts still manage to come to a similar result. The debtor can avoid or reduce liability by showing that the damage is based on a *faute de la victime*—for example, where a train passenger has suffered damage during a journey but the train operator can show that the passenger had been careless and had caused the damage himself, or contributed towards the damage.[71] If the injured party has failed to warn the other party of the risk of a particularly high potential damage when the contract was concluded, a claim for damage is excluded or reduced in Germany under § 254 BGB. The position is the same in France, because failing to pass on such information means that the high level of damages is not foreseeable, and liability is thus excluded pursuant to art. 1231-3 *Code civil*.[72] In addition, many advocate that the points that have already been adopted by the judiciary should be expanded into a general rule that requires the injured party to minimise the damage where possible under the circumstances, and threatens a reduction in the claim for damages if it fails to take these steps.[73]

England also does not have a general rule, with cases falling into two categories. In the first, the defendant asserts that the injured party has failed to take reasonable measures that would have mitigated the damage, or took steps that (because they made the damage worse) should not have been taken. In the second set of cases, the defendant says that the culpable actions of the injured party made it (partly) responsible for causing the damage.

In the first set of cases, the injured party has a duty to mitigate, and must act as a reasonable person would have acted under the same circumstances to reduce the damage. So if a buyer has purchased foodstuffs but breached its duty to accept them, the seller may not just let the food rot and demand damages from the buyer. Instead, the seller must seek to sell the goods elsewhere. The principle of mitigation of damage may also require a buyer seeking damages from the seller for its breach of not

---

[70] The basic rule governing the splitting of damages also applies if the injured party has failed to mitigate the level of damages. So if non-performance of a contract by the debtor would cause damage of 500, and the creditor has not taken steps to reduce the damage by 100, it depends on the circumstances whether the debtor's liability will be reduced by 100 (to 400) or by a lesser sum (to 410 or 420, for example). This is based on the wording of § 254 BGB and case law. See, for example, BGH 24 July 2001, [2001] *NJW* 3257, 3258.
[71] See, with examples from case law, Terré, Simler, and Lequette (n 3) no. 584.
[72] See above, n 58.
[73] See Terré, Simler, and Lequette (n 3) no. 597; B Fages, 'Einige neuere Entwicklungen des französischen allgemeinen Vertragsrechts im Lichte der Grundregeln der Lando-Kommission' (2003) 11 *ZEuP* 514, 521.

delivering them at the agreed time to conclude an alternate transaction with a third party in order to be able to fulfil its own supply obligations to its customers.[74] Similar is the situation where a seller has not made the agreed delivery and is instead offering the buyer an alternative delivery or the delivery of similar goods. The buyer is not obliged to accept the alternative offered, but if the buyer rejects it, this can result in a reduction of its claim for damages against the seller, provided that a reasonable person in the same situation as the buyer would have accepted the offer and would thus have reduced the damage.[75] It should also be noted that the injured party's claim for damages would be reduced by the full amount that the mitigation would have entailed had it been undertaken.[76]

In the second group of cases, a law dating back to 1945 expressly states that an injured party's claim for damages can be reduced by its contributory negligence if the debtor's liability is based on a tort.[77] But what if the injured party asserts a claim against the other party for breach of contract? It is generally assumed that in such cases the damages can only be reduced for contributory liability if two conditions are met: the debtor must not be strictly liable for its failure to achieve the promised result, but must only have promised to carry out the customary degree of care necessary to achieve the purpose of the contract.[78] Furthermore, if it had failed to do so, the debtor must also be liable to the creditor in tort. Such is the case if a bank commissions a valuation report on a property from an expert, and now seeks to assert a claim for damages against the valuer because his or her report is incorrect due to the failure to exercise the necessary due care. The valuer will be liable in damages for breach of contract, but also, although the bank suffered only financial damage, under the tort of *negligence*.[79] The valuer may therefore seek to defend the claim by asserting that the bank was also negligent, perhaps because it should not have mortgaged the property for other reasons, and was culpable in failing to take these reasons into account. There is often criticism that this approach is excluded in other cases.[80]

Unfortunately, the international sets of rules fail to agree on a uniform solution that covers the whole scope of the debtor's liability. It would have been useful, as the same question comes up again and again in this area: by how much can the injured party's claim be reduced if both parties carry some degree of responsibility for the damage? Instead, there is a special rule (as in English law) only for the case where the injured party's conduct contributed to the other party's non-performance or the resulting damages.[81] There is also another rule that wholly excludes the injured party's claim for damages to the extent to which it could have mitigated the damages by reasonable

---

[74] See below, nn 92ff.   [75] *The Solnit* [1983] 1 Lloyd's Rep. 605.
[76] See *British Westinghouse Co. v. Underground Electric Railways Co. of London Ltd.* [1912] AC 673, 689: an injured party must take all reasonable steps necessary in order to mitigate a loss. If it fails to do so, its claim for damages will be reduced by the *full amount* by which such steps would have reduced the loss.
[77] S. 4 Law Reform (Contributory Negligence) Act 1945.   [78] See above, nn 42–45.
[79] See chapter 3 above, n 84; chapter 4 n 71.
[80] See Treitel (n 9) no. 20-105ff; E McKendrick, *Contract Law* (8th edn, 2009) no. 20.12.
[81] See art. 9:504 PECL: The non-performing party is not liable 'to the extent that the aggrieved party contributed to the non-performance or its effects'. See also art. III.-3:704(1) DCFR and art. 162 CESL. Article 7.4.7 PICC is more precise: the damages payable to the aggrieved party can be reduced to the extent that its own conduct, or an event for which it bears the risk, has contributed to the damage.

steps.[82] This must be contrasted with the solution presented by many continental legal systems, which is that if the injured party fails to take reasonable steps to reduce a claim by €100, it is possible to also reduce its damages by €100. But it is also possible to split the damage. Take the case where the debtor, by causing the damage deliberately or through a palpable breach of its contractual obligations brought the injured party into such a pressurised situation that it was forced to act quickly, and thereby negligently failed to reduce the damage by €100: should the debtor not in this case be restricted to reduce its liability for damages by *less* than €100?[83]

D. Nature and Extent of Damages

I. Liability for expectation interest

A party that has failed to perform its obligations under a contract and is therefore liable in damages to the other party must pay an amount of money that would bring the other party into the same position it would have been in if the contract had been fulfilled. This basic rule is universally recognised. It is based on the idea that the party that has given a binding contractual promise has raised an expectation in the other party that the promise will be met. If the debtor does not meet the promise, it must compensate for the expectation interest of the other party by paying the money that the other party would have received had the contract been performed.[84] Application of this innocuous principle results in many cases in a satisfactory result, but sometimes causes considerable problems, as illustrated by the following examples.

Non-performance of the contract usually causes a loss for the creditor, but may often result in an *advantage* that must be offset against the claim for damages. If a buyer who has not received delivery of goods from the seller is able to obtain the same goods in a covering transaction from a third party at a higher price, the advantages and disadvantages of the two transactions (the non-performed contract of sale and the covering purchase performed) must be calculated and offset against each other. The buyer will then only be able to claim damages if the difference from the two transactions

---

[82] See art. 9:505(1) PECL; art. 7.4.8(1) PICC; art. III.-3:705(1) DCFR; art. 77 CISG; art. 163 CESL.

[83] With extensive comparative law references, see also H Koziol, 'Rechtsfolgen der Verletzung einer Schadensminderungspflicht, Rückkehr der archaischen Kulpakompensation?' (1998) 6 ZEuP 593; A Keirse, 'Why the Proposed Optional Common European Sales Law Has Not, But Should Have, Abandoned the Principle of All or Nothing: A Guide to How to Sanction the Duty to Mitigate the Loss' [2011] ERPL 951.

[84] See also *Robinson v. Harman* (1848) 1 Ex. 850, 855: 'The rule of the common law is, that where a party sustains loss by reason of a breach of contract, he is, so far as money can do it, to be placed in the same situation, with respect to damages, as if the contract had been performed.' The same formula can also be found in art. 9:502 sent.1 PECL; art. 7.4.2(1) PICC; art. III.-3:702 sent. 1 DCFR; art. 74 sent. 1 CISG; art. 160 CESL. That damages must always be payable in the form of money is not self-evident under German law. Under § 249 BGB (see also § 1323 ABGB; art. 43 OR), damages may also take the form of *Naturalherstellung*, which means that the debtor must 'restore' the position in which the creditor would find itself if the agreement had been performed. The practical importance of this is slight, because 'restoration' is often not possible, or can only be effected at disproportionate expense, or is insufficient to compensate the creditor and it is therefore demanding monetary damages pursuant to § 251 BGB. This is to be distinguished from the case where the injured party is not asking for damages for non-performance, but is demanding performance of the contract. See above, chapter 12.

results in a loss. What if the debtor has failed to perform the contract, but the creditor benefits from other advantages which means that the losses resulting from the non-performance do not arise, or are subsequently mitigated or reduced to zero? Must the creditor tolerate these advantages being offset, or can it retain the advantages and still demand that the debtor pay the full amount of damages for non-performance? What if, for example, a tenant vacating a property fails to carry out the agreed renovations, but this does not result in a loss for the landlord because the new tenant will carry out the renovations at its own cost? The *Bundesgerichtshof* held that the tenant had to pay the landlord the renovation cost; a *Vorteilsausgleichung* (balancing of interests, *compensatio lucri cum damno*) was thus denied.[85] Similarly, a company which had agreed to deliver equipment to a client, but had negligently caused the client's premises to burn down, must reimburse its client for all damages, including the cost of building a new factory. The company could not rely on the client's advantages resulting from the fact that its operating costs in the new factory were much lower than in the old factory.[86]

Expectation interest also includes the disadvantages suffered by a creditor if it has made arrangements after concluding the contract in the belief that the contract will still be performed; when this does not take place, the arrangements are meaningless. So if a musical producer advertises that a certain star will be appearing in a production, and the star cancels without reason at the last minute, the producer can claim from him or her not only the *lost profit*,[87] but also compensation for losses caused by frustrated advertising costs. It may also be the case that the non-performance results in no losses for the creditor (or only insignificant losses) or that the losses are

---

[85] BGH 15 Nov. 1967, BGHZ 49, 56. On this (controversial) decision, see H Oetker in *Münchener Kommentar zum BGB* (6th edn, 2012), § 249 mn. 263. The same question is also often raised in English court decisions; see, in detail Treitel (n 9) no. 20-037ff. In *Redford v. De Froberville* [1978] 1 All ER 33, the court decided in the same manner as the BGH. But see also the decision in *Tito v. Waddell (No. 2)* [1977] Ch. 106, 328ff: The plaintiff owner of a small Pacific island had given the defendant mining company the right to extract phosphate on the island. The contract stated that before handing the island back to the owners, the mining company must restore and replant the land. Although the mining company failed to do so, the claim for damages for restoration and replanting was dismissed, because during the thirty years of the contract the plaintiffs had since moved to another island, had become successful farmers, and had no real intention of returning. See also *Ruxley Electronics and Construction Ltd. v. Forsyth* [1996] AC 344 (also discussed above, pp. 207f.): A building contractor had built a defective swimming pool for a client. But the contractor was not required to compensate the client for the (unreasonably high) costs of remedying the defect, but had only to reimburse the (much lower) damages suffered by the client for the loss of amenity in using the defective swimming pool.

[86] See *Harbutt's 'Plasticine' Ltd. v. Wayne Tank and Pump Co. Ltd.* [1970] 1 QB 447. See also *British Westinghouse* (n 76): the plaintiff delivered faulty turbines that the defendant—reserving its claim for damages—first installed, but then replaced several years later with modern turbines. The more modern turbines brought advantages for the defendant since they required less coal to run than the turbines had they been delivered by the plaintiff in the agreed condition. The House of Lords found that the plaintiff need pay only for the damage suffered by the defendant until such time as the new turbines had been installed. It is true that the defendant installed the new turbines only because it was unhappy with the performance of the faulty turbines supplied by the plaintiff. There was thus a 'causal link' between the plaintiff's breach and the installation of the new turbines. Even so, the plaintiff did not have to pay for the new turbines since their operational advantage was much greater than the loss incurred. See Treitel (n 9) no. 20-010ff. and 20-104 and (for a comparative perspective) Treitel (n 11) s. 149f.

[87] Proving lost profit can be difficult. See below, pp. 268ff.

so uncertain or speculative that the creditor finds it hard to prove them. In such cases, the creditor may limit its claim to compensation for lost expenses. It is not then claiming the expectation interest, but the reliance interest, since it wishes to be put into the position it would have been in if the contract had not been concluded, arrangements had not been made, and it had not suffered the related loss. This is normally regarded as permissible. For example, art. 109(2) OR expressly states that after termination of the contract the creditor can 'claim damages for the lapse of the contract' and demand restoration of the position it was in before the contract had been concluded.[88] In Germany, decisions of the courts following the same approach have meanwhile found a statutory basis in § 284 BGB. Under this provision, the creditor can waive its claim for damages for non-performance and instead 'demand reimbursement of the expenses which he has made and in all fairness was entitled to make in reliance on receiving performance'.[89] Nor is it a defence for the debtor to say that the creditor's reliance interest is higher than its expectation interest.

II. Calculating damages for non-performance of contracts of sale

The calculation of damages has a particular significance if a buyer does not accept the delivered contractual goods or the seller delivers goods which are not in line with the contract and, as a consequence, the seller or the buyer has terminated the contract. In such cases, they can demand damages from the counterparty for non-performance, but how are the damages calculated? For the *buyer*, calculation of damages is based on the difference between the value of the goods had they had been delivered in the agreed condition, and the price payable under the contract. For the *seller*, calculation of damages is based on the fact that the goods which the buyer did not accept and are thus still in the seller's possession have a lower value than the sale price under the contract. So both cases turn on determination of the value of the goods after termination of the agreement. There are two methods of calculation, which in German are called *konkrete Schadensberechnung* (concrete calculation of damages) and *abstrakte Schadensberechnung* (abstract calculation of damages). The first method is used where a substitute transaction has indeed been carried out. Damages will be calculated according to the second method if no such transaction took place (or is not pleaded by the claimant) and the claimant relies instead on the 'current price' normally paid for the performance agreed but not rendered.

---

[88] See BG 22 Sept. 1964, BGE 90 II 285, 294.
[89] On earlier case law, and criticism of the new provision of § 284 BGB, see Huber (n 56) § 39 II. Under English law, the creditor may also decide whether it wants to claim expectation interest or reliance interest. If it chooses the latter, it may also be possible to claim reimbursement of expenses made *before* conclusion of the contract. See Treitel (n 9) no. 20-023f, 20-031ff; McKendrick (n 80) no. 20.7. See also *McRae v. Commonwealth Disposals Commission* (1951) 84 CLR 377 (also discussed above, p. 155): the defendant sold the plaintiff salvage company a shipwreck that was stated to be at a particular location. In fact, the wreck did not exist. The court upheld the contract. The court dismissed the salvage company's claim to the extent to which damages were sought for the profit it would have made if the wreck had existed and had been salvaged. This profit was speculative. But the salvage company could claim damages for the expenses incurred in fitting out its ship in preparation for the salvage operation.

Both methods of calculating damages are widely recognised.[90] If a buyer decides on the concrete method, it must assert and (if they are disputed) prove the facts showing the price it had to pay for the goods under the substitute transaction with a third party. In France, the new rule under art. 1221 *Code civil* will be interpreted as allowing a buyer who has not received delivery to conclude a substitute transaction—even without any prior sanction by the court—and demand that the seller compensate it for the resulting costs (less the savings on the unpaid contract price).[91] The position is the same in Germany. Also, pursuant to art. 7:37 BW, where the buyer has concluded a *dekkingskoop* and acted reasonably, it is entitled to demand that the debtor pay the difference between the contractual price and the price of the substitute transaction. This naturally also applies if the *seller* demands damages. In both cases, the innocent party's right to recover *higher* damages is unaffected (art. 7:38 BW).

There are often reasons that make the concrete method of damage calculation less attractive or even impossible. For example, the injured party may in such cases fear that the other party will claim contributory liability—for example, by asserting that the conclusion of the substitute transaction has been delayed and thus increased the damage unnecessarily.[92] Sometimes the aggrieved party sees a disadvantage in having to provide a court with documents to evidence the substitute transaction, and these documents may reveal internal company information, calculation bases, and business contracts to the other party. If the creditor is a trader that transacts similar deals for goods of the same type on a daily basis, it may be difficult to prove that the substitute transaction upon which its claim is founded is directly attributable to the transaction that the debtor has failed to perform.

For this reason, the creditor is often best advised to calculate its loss using the abstract method. This involves demanding the difference between the contractual price and the price that would have been achieved by a hypothetical substitute contract for purchase or sale at the time the original contract was terminated. It avoids the practical pitfalls of a concrete calculation of damages. Perhaps this is the reason why English law does not specifically exclude the concrete method, but usually proceeds along the basis that '[w]here there is an available market for the goods in question, the measure of damages is prima facie to be ascertained by the difference between the contract price and the market or current price of the goods'.[93] The creditor can select this option even if it has actually concluded a substitute transaction, perhaps at a lower

---

[90] See arts. 75 and 76 CISG; arts. 9:506 and 507 PECL; arts. 7.4.5 and 6 PICC; arts. III.-3:706 and 707 DCFR; arts. 164 and 165 CESL. See also the comparative law approach to concrete and abstract calculation of damages in Treitel (n 11) s. 102.

[91] On the earlier rule under art. 1144 *Code civil*, see Terré, Simler, and Lequette (n 3) no. 1116.

[92] See BGH 17 Jan. 1997, [1997] *NJW* 1231: the seller demanded damages from a buyer who had purchased a property for DM 800,000 but had not gone through with the transaction due to lack of money. The seller then sold the property to a third party for DM 500,000 and asked the buyer to pay damages in the amount of DM 300,000. The buyer was allowed by the court to say that the seller would have been able to achieve a higher-priced substitute transaction at an earlier point in time. For a critical view, see Huber (n 56) § 35 VI 3. The same question also comes up in English law. See Treitel (n 9) no. 20-099, and (for a comparative law perspective) Treitel (n 11) s. 147: '[O]n a buyer's failure to accept or a seller's to deliver in accordance with the terms of the contract, the aggrieved party cannot recover loss due to market movements after the time when he ought to have gone into the market to make a substitute contract.'

[93] See s. 51(3) Sale of Goods Act 1979.

price than the current market price. Dutch law also allows buyers and sellers to use both methods of calculation (art. 7:36 and 37 BW). A similar approach is taken under § 376(2) and (3) HGB, which expressly allow the use of both methods of calculation.[94] Although § 376 HGB applies only to sales contracts between business firms in which 'time is of the essence', there is no reason why the abstract method of calculating damages stated in (2) should not also be allowed in other cases, in particular for transactions that do not involve a sale of goods but some other sort of transaction—provided that a current market price can be determined for the performance not provided by the debtor.[95] So if somebody buys goods for €100 but does not accept them although they are offered in the agreed condition and at the agreed time, the seller may terminate the contract and ask for damages of €20 if the 'current price' of the goods is €80 at the date of termination. This amount is the minimum damages that the seller can demand. It is entitled to do so even if it did conclude a substitute transaction and used special business contracts to secure a price of €90. Nor does it make a difference if the seller did not sell the goods at the market price of €80, but held on to them, speculated on rising prices and eventually sold them to a third party at a price of €90 or more. Even in these cases, the seller must be entitled to claim damages of €20 from the original buyer using the abstract method of calculation: 'What the seller really does with the goods is none of the buyer's business.'[96] It is correct that art. 76 CISG, the international sets of rules, and art. 165 CESL do not allow use of the abstract method of calculation when a substitute transaction has actually been made, but there is no good reason for such a restriction.

III. Liability for lost profits and lost expectations

The debtor is also required to pay damages where the creditor has lost profits that it would otherwise have made but for the non-performance of the debtor.[97] In France, the damage must be *'une suite immédiate et directe'* of the non-performance of the contract, but no one doubts that this requirement can also be filled by a *préjudice futur*.[98] However, the judge must be sufficiently certain that the creditor would have achieved such a hypothetical profit, and the amount of that profit. Under English law, it is sufficient for the judge to have found it 'more likely than not' that there would have been a profit.[99] In countries in continental Europe, however, judges must be 'certain'

---

[94] The concrete method (based on the result of another sale or purchase) is generally admitted even where the substitute transaction is the contract by which the buyer resold the goods (not delivered by the seller) to one of its own clients. For details, see Huber (n 56) § 38 III 1.

[95] See Huber (n 56) § 38 II 2 (p. 237) and § 38 III 3 (pp. 248f.).

[96] See Huber (n 56) § 38 II 2 (p. 238). It is argued that a buyer, if sued for the minimum damages of €20, should be allowed to prove that the seller did conclude a substitute transaction at a higher price than €80. Such proof is difficult because the buyer has no overview of the internal workings of the seller's business. Moreover, it would be inappropriate if the buyer were able to avail itself of the fact that the seller had utilised special business contracts in securing the substitute transaction or had speculated at its own risk.

[97] See, for example, § 252 sent.1 BGB; art. 6:105(1) BW; §§ 1324f. ABGB.

[98] See Terré, Simler, and Lequette (n 3) no. 700.

[99] The judge must decide 'on a balance of probabilities'. See, for example, *Allied Maples Group Ltd. v. Simmons & Simmons* [1995] 1 WLR 1602 (CA). Under art. 6:105(1) BW, the judge can make a decision about damage that has not yet revealed itself by weighing up the arguments in favour of and against the possibilities.

of facts on which they rely, although what is needed is only a 'degree of certainty useful for practical daily life [that] silences doubt without excluding it entirely'.[100] There is, however, an exception to this general rule in § 252 sent. 2 BGB which provides that it is sufficient for the recovery of lost profits if the claimant can show profit 'that in the normal course of events ... could probably be expected'.[101]

It follows that a claim must not be allowed if the claimant cannot show with sufficient certainty that the non-performance of the contract has caused the lost profit for which it is claiming reimbursement. So if an architect has entered a competition tendered by a town, and the town accepts the submissions of forty-two entrants but incorrectly rejects the architect's submission for being entered too late, the architect cannot claim payment of the prize money that would be paid out to the winner. It is not at all certain whether the architect's entry would have won if the submission had been accepted.[102] The situation is no different if a claimant seeks reimbursement for stolen items from a company that has installed a faulty security system that failed to inform the police that a burglary was under way. Here, too, it is by no means certain whether the items would not have been stolen as well if the security system had worked and the police had turned up.[103] However, the claimant in these cases might get a better result by arguing that it has lost the opportunity of earning a profit or avoiding a loss. The claimant's aim then would not be to secure the prize money or the value of the stolen items, but a lower amount that reflected the judge's assessment of the probability that the claimant had been deprived of the opportunity of winning the prize or avoiding the theft. German courts do not allow this approach, but follow a strict all-or-nothing principle that allows the claimant full damages only if the evidence shows that the profit (or averted loss) was sufficiently certain. If this proof cannot be provided, the claimant gets nothing.[104] English law[105] and French law[106] take a completely different approach. It is often not easy to determine whether the opportunity concerned is sufficiently tangible and concrete, and what value it may have under the circumstances.

---

[100] See, for example, BGH 17 Feb. 1970, BGHZ 53, 245, 256.

[101] Under art. 9:501(2b) PECL, future loss 'which is reasonably likely to occur' can give entitlement to damages. See also art. III.-3:701(2) DCFR. Article 7.4.3(1) PICC requires 'a reasonable degree of certainty', but if this is not present, under subsection (3) 'the assessment is at the discretion of the court'.

[102] See BGH 23 Sept. 1982, [1983] *NJW* 442.

[103] See Civ. 17 May 1988, Bull.cass. 1988.I. no. 148; Civ. 6 Oct. 1998, Bull.cass. 1998.I. no. 276.

[104] See BGH 23 Sept. 1982 (n 102) and the critical observations by H Kötz and HB Schäfer, *Judex oeconomicus* (1993) 266. This approach is vehemently criticised in academic commentary. See, in particular, H Fleischer, 'Ersatz für verlorene Chancen im Vertrags- und Deliktsrecht' [1999] *JZ* 766; G Wagner, 'Neue Perspektiven im Schadensersatzrecht' in *Verhandlungen des 66. Deutschen Juristentages* (2006) A 53; G Mäsch, *Chance und Schaden* (2004). See also N Jansen, 'The Idea of a Lost Chance' (1999) 19 *OJLS* 271; H Koziol, 'Schadensersatz für den Verlust einer Chance?' in *Festschrift für Hans Stoll* (2001) 233; T Kadner Graziano, '"Alles oder nichts" oder anteilige Haftung bei Verursachungszweifeln?' (2011) 19 *ZEuP* 171; L Khoury, 'Causation and Loss of Risk in the Highest Courts of Canada, England and France' (2008) 124 *LQR* 103.

[105] See, for example, *Chaplin v. Hicks* [1911] 2 KB 786 (CA), where the promoter of a beauty contest denied the claimant the opportunity to enter the contest. See also *Kitchen v. Royal Air Force Association* [1958] 1 WR 563 (CA) and *Allied Maples Group Ltd. v. Simmons & Simmons* (n 99), where a firm of solicitors denied its clients the opportunity of pursuing a promising claim or negotiations with third parties. On this, see also K Oliphant, 'Loss of Chance in English Law' [2008] *ERPL* 1061.

[106] An overview of the extensive French case law on liability for the '*perte d'une chance*' can be found in Terré, Simler, and Lequette (n 3) no. 701.

But such difficulties are by no means insurmountable, and the case law in England and France shows that there are no obvious reasons why the solution should not be left to the courts.[107]

IV. Liability for disgorgement of profits

In principle, the creditor can only demand damages where it suffered a loss as a consequence of the debtor's non-performance. What about cases where the creditor has *not* suffered a loss, but the debtor has gained a profit by not performing the contract? Can the creditor require disgorgement of the profit?

A liability to disgorge profits may arise from special statutory provisions. Whilst bound by a contract of employment, an employee must not conclude transactions for his or her own account in the area of business of the employer. If the employee breaches this obligation, the employer (regardless of whether or not it has suffered a loss) can require the employee to hand over the profit made through the unauthorised transaction.[108] The practical importance of § 285 BGB is much wider.[109] It applies mainly in cases where a seller has sold a particular item to a buyer at market price, and then sells and delivers it to a second buyer for a higher price. In such a case, the first buyer can no longer demand *performance* from the seller, because delivery is now impossible or only possible at an unreasonably high cost.[110] A *claim for damages* is also not of much use to the first buyer, because it bought at market price and can buy the goods elsewhere for the same price. But § 285 BGB allows the first buyer to demand that the seller pays the price received from the second buyer, less the (lower) price the first buyer would have had to pay to the seller but has now saved (§ 326(3) BGB). This allows the first buyer to 'skim off the profit' (*den Gewinn abzuschöpfen*) accrued by the seller from the second sale of the same goods. This can perhaps be best explained by the idea that while the seller still owns the goods sold to the first buyer, it does so only as its *Treuhänder* or trustee. If the seller breaches this trust relationship by selling the

---

[107] Damages may also be allowed under art. 7.4.3(2) PICC 'for the loss of a chance in proportion to the probability of its occurrence'. There is dispute about the question of whether a patient can claim damages as compensation for a lost opportunity to be healed if a doctor fails to perform a contract or commits a tort against the patient. French courts allow such damages, but English courts do not. See on the one hand Civ. 29 June 1999, *JCP* 1999.II.10138, n. P Sargos; on the other hand *Gregg v. Scott* [2005] 2 AC 176: G Mäsch, '*Gregg* v. *Scott*—Much Ado About Nothing' (2006) 14 *ZEuP* 656. There is no question that the cases of medical liability differ from cases in which the claimant was deprived of an opportunity to make a profit or avoid a loss. In the latter case, the claimant's loss is clearly attributable to the defendant's non-performance, and since the claimant's loss is certain, there is 'only' the question of measuring it. But if in the case of the medical treatment the patient would have survived in only half the cases, it is quite uncertain to which half of these cases the patient would belong. If the patient dies, is it as a result of the medical malpractice, or would the patient have died anyway even if the treatment had been carried out correctly? It is questionable whether this difference should have legal consequences. For arguments in support of this, see Fleischer (n 104) 771ff. and for arguments against, see Wagner (n 104) A 57ff; Mäsch (n 107) 656ff; Kadner Graziano (n 104) 183ff.

[108] See the position under German law in accordance with §§ 60, 61 HGB. The same applies if a partner undertakes unauthorised transactions within the sphere of business of the other partners of the company; see §§ 112ff. HGB and § 88 AktG.

[109] See also art. 1259 *Codice civile*.   [110] See above, chapter 12.D (pp. 212ff.).

item to the second buyer, any resulting profits must be disgorged to the first buyer.[111] The question of whether the creditor can also skim off the debtor's profit in other cases is currently the matter of vibrant discussion, not least because it was so held by the House of Lords in the landmark case of *Attorney-General* v. *Blake*. The defendant in this case worked for the British Secret Intelligence Service and had given an undertaking to his employer—the British Crown—not to divulge any official information gained as a result of his employment. Many years later, he penned a successful autobiography that made some of this information public. The House of Lords upheld the Crown's application for an account of the author's profit. The Crown had suffered no tangible loss due to Blake's breach of contract, but its claim for 'restitutionary damages' was upheld, because the defendant was deemed a trustee of the information he received during the course of his employment and therefore had to hand over any profit made from a breach of this fiduciary trust. Another ground was that the Crown had a legitimate interest in ensuring that information remained secret, and secret service employees must not have a financial incentive to publish such information.[112] Academic literature takes the approach that any profit gained as a result of a breach of contract must be disgorged if 'the debtor has deliberately ignored its obligations to the creditor'.[113] The rule in art. 6:104 BW is quite uncertain, stating that, if the debtor derived a profit from having committed a tort or a breach of its contractual obligations, the court 'may' evaluate the creditor's damages 'according to the amount of that profit or part thereof'.[114]

V. Liability for intangible loss

Intangible losses are disadvantages that cannot be quantified by objective measures, because their importance is heavily dependent on sentiments, attitude, feelings, frame of mind, or sensibility of the person affected. It can involve losses such as bodily pain, a permanent disability, grief or distress, or loss of social reputation. The affected person can also miss out on opportunities such as no longer being able to feel happiness, satisfaction, or comfort, or no longer being able to experience them as expected. That some legal orders are reluctant to allow monetary compensation for such immaterial disadvantages is mainly based on two reasons. Determining the level of monetary compensation is difficult, because the weight placed on the disadvantage differs from

---

[111] See *Lake* v. *Bayliss* [1974] 1 WLR 1073: after conclusion of a contract for the sale of property, the seller holds the property as trustee for the buyer. If the seller then sells the property a second time, the price received must be passed on to the first buyer, even if the first buyer has suffered no, or only insignificant, damage. For details, see Treitel (n 9) no. 20-003ff.

[112] *Attorney General* v. *Blake* [2001] 1 AC 268 and in detail in K Rusch (2002) 10 *ZEuP* 122. The House of Lords overturned the decision of the Court of Appeal (*Attorney General* v. *Blake* [1998] Ch. 439); see R Bollenberger (2000) 8 *ZEuP* 893.

[113] See Wagner (n 104) A 83ff, A 97.

[114] For a comparative law discussion about liability to disgorge profits, see Rusch (n 112); K Rusch, 'Restitutionary Damages for Breach of Contract: A Comparative Analysis of English and German Law' (2001) 118 *S.Afr. LJ* 59; R Bollenberger, *Das stellvertretende Commodum* (1999); P Schlechtriem, *Restitution und Bereicherungsausgleich in Europa* vol. II (2001) 191ff; T Helms, *Gewinnherausgabe als haftungsrechtliches Problem* (2007); J Köndgen, 'Immaterialschadensersatz, Gewinnabschöpfung oder Privatstrafen als Sanktionen für Vertragsbruch' (1992) 56 *RabelsZ* 696.

person to person, and there is no 'market' on which supply and demand result in a general 'price' paid for the intangible losses or gains described above. It is also argued that allowing monetary compensation for claimants will give an incentive for people to fake disadvantages and cry crocodile tears before the courts in order to give foundation to—or even inflate—their claims.

Some countries have differing rules to compensate for intangible loss that depend on whether the claimant is basing the claim on non-performance of a contract or in tort. Here the claimant must choose which route offers the better chances of success. The position is different in France, where for a long time the courts have held that where there is a contractual relationship between the claimant and the defendant, the claimant's action for damages can *only* be heard under the rules of contract law.[115] In practice, this is not really important, since the question of what constitutes damage (*dommage*) is the same in contract and in tort,[116] and because compensation for intangible damage (*dommage moral*) is particularly generous in both fields. *Dommage moral* is not only payable where the claimant suffers pain as a consequence of bodily harm and is paid a sum of money—called *Schmerzensgeld* in Germany—as a compensation for that pain and suffering. French law also places great emphasis on the question of whether the claimant, presuming his or her health has been restored, is still able to enjoy the same zest for life or is prevented from taking part in social activities—such as a musician no longer being able to play the piano, or a person no longer being able to play their favoured sport. How far the courts are prepared to go is shown in the case where the defendant was responsible for the death of the claimant's favourite horse. It makes no difference whether the defendant has to pay damages for breach of contract or in tort. Even if the defendant breached a contractual obligation to exercise care in looking after the horse, it is required not only to compensate for the cost of buying a new horse, but must also compensate for the intangible loss '*que lui causait la perte d'un animal auquel il était attaché*'.[117] Similarly, a funeral parlour that breaches its contract to deliver the body of a deceased person on time must pay the deceased's relatives compensation for the intangible damage they suffer from the funeral having to be cancelled.[118]

German law takes a much more reserved approach. For a long time, it has been carrying out a rearguard action against the traditional approach (which dates from Roman law), whereby there is no monetary compensation where someone's honour or physical integrity has been damaged.[119] The German Civil Code was unable to follow this ungenerous position, and § 253(1) BGB stated—and still states—that non-pecuniary loss can only be compensated for in cases stipulated by law. But such provisions can only be found in tort law, and then only where the intangible damage

---

[115] On the principle of *non-cumul des responsabilités contractuelle et délictuelle*, see above, n 26.
[116] A certain difference is that the debtor, whose liability is founded in a breach of contract, need only compensate for 'foreseeable' damage. See art. 1231-3 *Code civil* and above, section C.I = pp. 257ff.
[117] Civ. 16 Jan. 1962, Bull.cass. 1962.I. no. 33 = D. 1962, 1999, n. R Rodière.
[118] Trib.civ. Seine 20 Dec. 1932, p. 1932.2.144, and in detail Terré, Simler, and Lequette (n 3) no. 562.
[119] See, for example, Zimmermann (n 66) 1090ff; N Jansen, 'Konturen eines europäischen Schadensrechts' [2006] JZ 160, 166ff.

is based on bodily harm.[120] The courts have gone beyond the statutory provisions in granting a claimant compensation if he or she has suffered intangible damage following a breach of their *allgemeines Persönlichkeitsrecht* (general right of personality). The legislature then moved the battle lines a little in 2002 when it decided that compensation could also be awarded for intangible damage resulting from a breach of contract. In these cases, however, as in cases where the defendant committed a tort, intangible losses are only compensable if they result from 'an injury to body, health, freedom or sexual self-determination' or (it must be added) from a violation of a person's general right of personality.[121] Since 1979, the German Civil Code has been a little more generous in cases where the defendant is a tour operator: it must compensate a customer for intangible loss if the cancellation or significant impairment of the travel caused the customer to have spent his or her holiday leave 'to no avail'.[122] Of course, there are other contracts that present similarly good reasons why intangible losses should be recognised. It is, of course, not sufficient that someone is merely disappointed or sad that the counterparty has not performed the contract. But there are some contractual obligations where, under the special circumstances of the case, performance of the contract is (also) intended to protect one of the parties from the occurrence of certain intangible losses. Take the case where, for example, a hotel offers a newly married couple on a certain day a 'wedding breakfast in the fireside salon', or where an undertaker offers to provide a funeral service at a certain time for the deceased's relatives: if the fireplace salon is in use by other guests, or the undertaker forgets that the funeral is on a particular day, the debtors should compensate for intangible losses suffered by the married couple or the deceased's relatives. German law does not go this far, at least not yet.[123] Academic commentators have suggested that as a default rule § 253(2) BGB

---

[120] Article 2059 *Codice civile* also originally stated that intangible loss could only be compensated for when based on criminal actions of the defendant. But the Italian courts have gone beyond this position and assume a '*danno biologico*' or '*danno esistenziale*' if someone's health or wellbeing in terms of personal development in the social environment are impeded, including when such damage is a result of a breach of contract. See Cass. 11 Nov. 2008, Nr. 26973, [2009] Foro it. 120 and in detail (including a comparative perspective) G Christandl, 'Das italienische Nichtvermögensschadensrecht nach 2008' (2011) 19 *ZEuP* 392. Under art. 6:106(1) BW, liability to compensate for intangible loss is only allowed if deliberately caused by the defendant, or if the claimant has suffered bodily harm or harm to his or her honour or reputation, or if '*op andere wijze in zijn persoon is angetast*'.

[121] See § 253(2) BGB and in detail and with a comparative perspective in G Wagner, 'Ersatz immaterieller Schäden: Bestandsaufnahme und europäische Perspektiven' [2004] *JZ* 319; Wagner (n 104) A 51ff; F Maultzsch, 'Der Schutz von Affektionsinteressen bei Leistungsstörungen im englischen und deutschen Recht' [2010] *JZ* 937.

[122] See § 651f(2) BGB. The European Court of Justice has interpreted art. 5 of the Package Travel Directive 90/314/EEC of 13 June 1990 as meaning that if the holiday is cancelled or defective, the travel company must compensate the customer for intangible losses suffered. See Case C-168/00, ECJ, 12 March 2002, *Leitner* v. *TUI*, I-2631.

[123] See OLG Saarbrücken 20 July 1998, [1998] *NJW* 2912: a bride has no right to compensation if she suffers a nervous breakdown because a hotelier could not provide the promised fireplace salon at the time of the wedding. Similarly, there is no compensation for a patient who fails to be given the promised 'clinic stay in a wonderful countryside environment'; or where a yacht is not delivered for a sailing trip on the Baltic Sea. Both cases fail to meet the requirements of § 651f BGB. See BGH 21 May 1981, BGHZ 80, 366; BGH 29 June 1995, BGHZ 130, 128. See also BGH 9 July 2009, [2009] *NJW* 3025: by giving incorrect advice that she had incurred an existence-threatening obligation, a lawyer caused his client to suffer a nervous breakdown. She demanded damages from the lawyer on the basis of a breach of contract. While the BGH held that her health had been harmed, her claim was nonetheless rejected on the ground that the 'protective purpose' of the contract (see above, n 63) was the client's wealth and not her health. The

could be contracted out by the parties, and that judicial construction of the contract could thus find that it was intended to create certain intangible advantages which, if not brought about, could lay the basis for liability for the ensuing intangible losses.[124]

English case law shows that this question is sometimes difficult to answer, but the problems are not insurmountable. In England, the general principle is that the intangible losses of the claimant are not to be compensated for by money if caused by the defendant's breach of contract. So if a lawyer instructed by a client to prepare for the purchase of a property makes one mistake after another, the client cannot ask for compensation merely because he became anxious about the deal, feared the worst, and suffered 'mental distress'. The lawyer had committed serious breaches of contract, but this is an 'incident of commercial life which players in the game are expected to meet with mental fortitude'.[125] But the situation is different if a travel package is being sold to enable the client to have an enjoyable time during the short period of his holiday, and the holiday arrangements turn out to be so dreadful that the client is deeply disappointed.[126] The situation is also different if a woman asks a lawyer to protect her from unlawful harassment by a third party[127] or to make sure that a child in her custody is not wrongfully abducted overseas by her husband.[128] If the lawyer's mistake is instrumental in bringing about the situation he was asked to prevent, the lawyer must compensate the client for the mental stress involved under the circumstances. In the case of child kidnapping, the compensation has been set at £20,000. A contract with a real estate broker can have the purpose of finding a property that will allow the client to enjoy a feeling of calmness and happiness. In *Farley v. Skinner*,[129] a real estate broker had offered his client a 'gracious country residence'. As the house and land were near to Gatwick Airport, the client had instructed the broker that he was looking for

---

decision would have been different if a client had been jailed due to a mistake by his or her criminal lawyer: on the one hand, the client's unfounded incarceration is an injury to his or her 'freedom' (see above, n 121), and on the other hand the proper performance of the lawyer's activities should (also) include protecting the client from being jailed without cause.

[124] It has been suggested that the legislature could intervene. Under the suggestion by Wagner (n 104) A 53, § 253 BGB should be amended so that compensation could be paid if the purpose of the contract is the protection or support of intangible interests (*der Schutz oder die Förderung der immateriellen Interessen*) of a contractual partner.

[125] *Johnson v. Gore Wood Co.* [2002] AC 1, 49.
[126] *Jarvis v. Swans Tours Ltd.* [1973] 1 All ER 71 (CA).
[127] *Heywood v. Wellers* [1976] QB 446.
[128] *Hamilton Jones v. David & Snape* [2004] 1 All ER 657.
[129] [2002] 2 AC 732. In *Watts v. Morrow* [1991] 1 WLR 1421, a property surveyor had negligently failed to inform his client that the property he wanted to buy was in need of considerable repairs. He had to pay compensation for the fact that during these repairs the client had to live in the house and suffered 'physical inconvenience and discomfort' as well as 'mental suffering directly related to that inconvenience and discomfort' (1425). See also *Ruxley Electronics* (n 85). Here a client whose building contractor had built a defective swimming pool was not able to claim damages for the cost of having a new pool installed by another company, but only £2,500 for the 'loss of amenity'. A German court would have come to the same decision: the client would have no right to subsequent performance (*Nacherfüllung*) against the building contractor (§ 275(2) BGB), but a right to claim damages or reduce the agreed fee. The amount of damages or fee reduction would be fixed by taking into account that the client was able to use the pool despite its defect, and was thus able to mitigate the damages according to § 254(2) 1 BGB. In the result, he would only be allowed to claim damages or reduce the fee in an amount equivalent to the loss of amenity in using a swimming pool that was not quite perfect. See also P Schlechtriem, *Schuldrecht, Besonderer Teil* (6th edn, 2003) mn. 435.

a peaceful and restful property, and that he should check whether the property was likely to be affected by aircraft noise. The broker failed to do this, and informed the client that he should not worry about this issue. The client bought the property for a reasonable price, and suffered no financial loss. Nevertheless, the broker had to pay the client the sum of £10,000 to compensate for the intangible losses caused by aircraft noise. There is for these reasons much in the suggestions put forward in the international sets of rules that compensation should also be available for 'non-pecuniary loss'.[130]

VI. Agreements on limitation of damages

Sometimes agreements are made whereby a party agrees to pay a certain amount of money to the other party if there is non-performance. Generally, it is the innocent party that has an interest in such an agreement because it can thereby avoid the difficulties of proving the damages caused by the other party's non-performance, or of resisting the other party's allegation that the damages claimed were too remote, not foreseeable, speculative, or intangible. The validity of such agreements is supported by the principle of freedom of contract. But they are not without dangers. A debtor may accept them without taking the trouble of making any serious check in the optimistic hope that it will be able to perform as agreed and everything will work out in a satisfactory manner. The creditor is well aware of this fact, may even speculate on the debtor's rashness, and therefore has an incentive to set the sum at a high level, thus putting the debtor under significant pressure. If the debtor is unable to fulfil the contract despite this pressure, the creditor may then demand payment of a sum that is much higher than the actual damage suffered. In effect, we are facing a conflict of interest: on the one hand, such provisions are sensible and desirable as they simplify damage regulation, make the downside of non-performance clear to the debtor, and ease pressure on the courts. On the other hand, debtors must be protected from the danger of misuse of such provisions.

All legal systems use two terms to describe such agreements. On the one hand, there are provisions whose purpose is to make a reasonable estimate of the damages in case of non-performance of the contract and avert any dispute between the parties over their exact amount. These are referred to as liquidated damages clauses. On the other hand, the parties can also agree to a penalty clause (*Vertragsstrafe, clause pénale, clausula penale*). Its main purpose is to put the debtor under financial pressure to perform the contract properly. However, it is difficult to differentiate between these two types of clauses and the consequences of classifying an agreement as one or the other.[131]

The penalty clause is a venerable form of contractual agreement known already under Roman law.[132] Its purpose was not only to determine the amount of damages

---

[130] See art. 9:501(2a) PECL; art. 7.4.2(2) PICC; art. III.-3:701(3) DCFR.

[131] Of the extensive literature on this subject, see M Baum, 'Vertragsstrafe' in *Max Planck Enc.* (2012) 1701ff; Treitel (n 11) s. 164ff; I Steltmann, *Die Vertragsstrafe in einem Europäischen Vertragsrecht* (2000); HN Schelhaas, *Het boetebeding in het Europese contractenrecht* (2004); L Miller, 'Penalty Clauses in England and France' (2004) 53 *ICLQ* 79.

[132] See Zimmermann (n 66) 95ff; R Knütel, *Stipulatio Poenae, Studien zur römischen Privatstrafe* (1976); RP Sossna, *Die Geschichte der Begrenzung von Vertragsstrafen* (1993).

to be paid to the creditor, but to make sure the debtor undertook a certain action. If, for example, the debtor had promised the creditor to pay money to a third party or to confer on it some other benefit, the third party could not itself force the debtor to perform: *alteri nemo stipulari potest*.[133] One way to get around this rule was the debtor's promise to pay the creditor a penalty should it fail to confer the agreed benefit to the third party. This is the reason why most continental legal systems deal with contractual penalties in a separate section of their codes, and not where they are today important, namely for damages for non-performance.[134]

Normally, the predetermined sum that the debtor must pay in case of non-performance will be higher than the damage actually suffered by the creditor. If the situation is not so, one can question whether the creditor may only demand the fixed sum or if it may decide to assert its claim for damages using the normal applicable rules. What the parties have agreed is decisive. If there is nothing in their agreement, some legal systems limit the creditor's claim to the agreed amount,[135] while others give the creditor a choice between both possibilities, and even permit it to demand the penalty and also assert a claim for any further damage it may have suffered.[136]

What is of great practical importance is the fact that all continental systems (quite differently than the Common Law) have binding statutory provisions that enable the court (mostly only on application by the debtor, but sometimes at its own discretion) to lower the agreed sum if it is unreasonably high (*unverhältnismäßig hoch* or *manifestement excessive*).[137] Sometimes this authority applies both to clauses on liquidated damages and penalty clauses,[138] while it is limited to penalty clauses in other legal systems (such as Germany and Switzerland). However, the court has no power to lower the sum agreed in a penalty clause if both parties are business people (§ 348 HGB).

The question of whether or not a provision constitutes a contractual penalty turns in German law on whether the amount has been fixed in an attempt to coerce the debtor by putting it under effective pressure to perform the contract properly.[139] This criterion is not satisfactory, because 'each liquidated damages clause also exerts a pressure to perform correctly, and each contractual penalty also simplifies damage settlement' and 'a limitation following these parameters is hardly likely to lead to convincing

---

[133] See chapter 17.A = pp. 319ff.
[134] See, for example, §§ 339-345 BGB; arts. 158-163 OR; arts. 1382-1384 *Codice civile*; arts. 6:91-94 BW. Article 1231-5 *Code civil* now takes a different approach.
[135] See art. 1382(1) *Codice civile*. Article 6:92(2) BW states that the penalty clause replaces the claim for damages, but art. 6:94(2) BW allows the obligee to demand more than the contractual penalty 'if it is evident that equity so requires'.
[136] See § 340(2) BGB and § 1336(3) ABGB. Article 161(2) OR states that if the loss exceeds the penalty the creditor 'may claim further compensation only if he can prove that the debtor was at fault'.
[137] § 343 BGB; § 1336(2) ABGB; art. 163(3) OR; art. 1231-5(2) *Code civil*; art. 1384 *Codice civile*; § 36 Scandinavian Contract Law (Denmark, Sweden, Finland); art. 6:94(1) BW; art. 409 Greek Civil Code; art. 1154 Spanish Civil Code (see S Leible, 'Die richterliche Herabsetzung von Vertragsstrafen im spanischen Recht' (2000) 8 *ZEuP* 322). This judicial power was not recognised under Roman law (see Zimmermann (n 66) 106ff.), has only become established in the face of considerable resistance, and was not introduced in France until 1972, and until 1992 in the Netherlands.
[138] See art. 1231-5(2) *Code civil*; art. 6:94 BW (and for a comparative perspective H Schelhaas, 'The Judicial Power to Reduce a Contractual Penalty' (2004) 12 *ZEuP* 386).
[139] As under standing case law. See, eg, BGH 25 Nov. 1982, [1983] *NJW* 1542.

results'.¹⁴⁰ Nevertheless, the distinction between liquidated damages clauses and penalties is of great practical importance. One reason already referred to is that the court is only allowed to lower the agreed sum if it is a penalty. The other reason is that such agreements are often made by standardised terms forming part of one party's general terms of business. In that case, penalty clauses are always invalid, while liquidated damages clauses are invalid to the extent to which the agreed sum 'exceeds the damage expected under normal circumstances'; they are also invalid if they do not expressly inform the customer of its right 'to show that damage ... has either not occurred or is substantially less than the agreed sum'.¹⁴¹ These strict provisions governing the validity of standard terms and conditions apply only if the debtor that is to pay the predetermined amount is a consumer. In business-to-business contracts, the general rule is that such clauses will be valid if they are reasonable under the circumstances (§§ 307, 310(1) BGB).¹⁴²

The Common Law also differentiates between penalties and liquidated damages. Penalties are always invalid, even in business-to-business transactions. But an agreement on liquidated damages, by which the debtor undertakes to pay the creditor a genuine pre-estimate of any loss likely to be sustained by him as the result of the breach, will be valid. The Common Law does not recognise an authority of the court to lower or set aside a contractually agreed sum of damages if it considers the amount to be unreasonably high. Thus it has adopted an all-or-nothing approach: either the provision is invalid as it is a penalty clause, with the result that the creditor can only demand damages in accordance with the general rules. Or it is a liquidated damages clause and is valid. The difference is thus of considerable practical importance. The British Supreme Court discussed the issue in detail in a leading case from 2015.¹⁴³ There was no support for doing away entirely with the difference between penalties and liquidated damages. But the difference will no longer turn on whether the agreed sum is so high that it must be seen as having been made '*in terrorem* of the offending party'. Now a penalty requires that the debtor agreed to pay a sum of money that is 'unconscionable' or 'extravagant' because it is beyond the bounds of any reasonable interest that the creditor may have in proper performance of the contract.

How might a European solution be formulated? There is much to be said in favour of the approach currently followed in France and the Netherlands, and mirrored in

---

¹⁴⁰ As correctly argued by W Wurmnest in *Münchener Kommentar zum BGB* (6th edn, 2012) § 309 no. 5 BGB mn. 6.

¹⁴¹ See § 309 nos. 5 and 6 BGB. There was no need for the German legislature to introduce the difference between a contractual penalty and lump-sum damages. Pursuant to art. 3(3) and Annex 1e of the Unfair Terms Directive 93/13/EEC, the German government was only required to implement a law that held standard terms and conditions to be invalid if they 'requir[e] any consumer who fails to fulfil his obligation to pay a disproportionately high sum in compensation'.

¹⁴² See Wurmnest (n 140) § 309 no. 6 BGB mn. 19ff.

¹⁴³ *Cavendish Square Holding BV v. Talal el Makdessi, ParkingEye Ltd. v. Beavis* [2015] UKSC 67. The Supreme Court judgment deals with two appeals. One was an appeal from a claimant who had parked his car in a parking garage. He had agreed 'not to park [his] car for more than two hours and, upon any breach of that obligation, to pay a sum of £85'. The Supreme Court held this clause to be valid. Neither was it void as a penalty under the general rules. Nor could the claimant as a consumer assert that the clause 'contrary to the requirements of good faith ... causes a significant imbalance in the parties' rights and obligations' (see art. 3(1) EC Directive 93/13/EEC as implemented by art. 5(1) of the Unfair Terms in Consumer Contracts Regulations 1999).

the international sets of rules, where no difference is drawn between a penalty and liquidated damages. The rules combine both under the term 'agreed payment for non-performance'. But at the same time, they give the court the power to reduce an amount determined to be 'grossly excessive' to a 'reasonable amount'.[144] English law would find it difficult to accept this solution. If penalties and liquidated damages clauses were treated on the same footing, the difficulties of drawing a line between the two types of clause would evaporate. But the price to be paid for this would be to create legal uncertainty elsewhere, since the courts would have to be given the power to reduce the agreed sum to an acceptable amount even if both parties were business firms. This power would not sit well with the traditional scepticism that English judges have with the idea of recognising a contract as valid, but then going over the heads of the parties by modifying its content so that it becomes reasonable.

---

[144] See art. 9:509 PECL; art. 7.4.13 PICC; art. III.-3:710 DCFR.

15
The Effect of Unexpected Circumstances

A. Introduction	279
B. Solutions	280
I. French law	280
II. German law	281
III. English law	285
C. International Sets of Rules	288

A. Introduction

Sometimes there is an unexpected change in circumstances after the contract has been concluded. Such change may in some cases make it *impossible* for the debtor to perform the contract—for example where a specific object was sold, but destroyed before delivery, or where a factory which was to produce the goods accidentally burns down, or where the ship to be chartered is requisitioned by the state. But suppose the unexpected change of circumstances now not exactly renders it impossible for the debtor to perform the contract, but makes performance so much more difficult or so vastly more expensive that the two sides of the contract are now quite out of proportion: what is to be done in such cases of 'distortion of parity'? And what is to be done in cases of 'frustration of purpose' where, for example, one party under the contract is to pay a sum of money and can easily do so, but finds that the other party's counterperformance has now been rendered valueless by subsequent unexpected events?

It is sometimes difficult to draw a line between circumstances that render the performance of the contract impossible and those that render it more onerous or more costly or frustrate the purpose of the transaction. No such distinction is needed in English law because, as we shall soon see, its doctrine of frustration is applied to both types of cases. Continental legal systems and the international sets of rules form a separate category for cases in which intervening events make performance more difficult for the debtor or render performance pointless for him or her. French law refers in these cases to *imprévision*, Italian law to *eccessiva onerosità*, German law to *Störung der Geschäftsgrundlage*, and Dutch law to *onvorziene omstadigheden*. Sometimes reference is made to a *clausula rebus sic stantibus*, and sometimes—as in Denmark and Sweden—it is said that the basis of the contract has disappeared.[1]

---

[1] See in detail E Hondius and HC Grigoleit (eds), *Unexpected Circumstances in European Contract Law* (2011): this book sets out the rules by which seventeen European legal systems address the problem of unexpected circumstances. It also looks in detail how fifteen different sets of circumstances would be dealt with by each of the different legal systems. See also the review by H Kötz (2013) 77 *RabelsZ* 865. There is a vast amount of academic literature on this subject. See, for example, H Rösler, 'Hardship in German Codified Private Law in Comparative Perspective to English, French and International Contract

It goes without saying that the parties have very good reason to agree on clauses by which the risk of a 'subsequent change in circumstances' is allocated to one or the other party. It is equally clear that such clauses take precedence over the general rules to be discussed below. These rules are therefore mere default rules which will apply only to the extent to which the parties have not made other contractual arrangements. This does not mean, however, that these rules have no practical importance. Experience suggests that parties are sometimes not sufficiently sophisticated or too careless of their own interests to include *force majeure* clauses, hardship clauses, or other clauses to the same effect. Even where such clauses are agreed, they may not cover all eventualities or run into some other unforeseen difficulty.

B. Solutions

I. French law

Every discussion on this topic in France starts with a famous decision of the *Cour de cassation* of 6 March 1876.[2] In a contract dating back to the middle of the sixteenth century, a party agreed to deliver water for a certain price so that the counterparty could irrigate agricultural land. Around 300 years later, the water supplier sought to increase the price for the water because the value of the currency had changed, staff costs had increased considerably, and the contract price was no longer sufficient. Both lower courts upheld the claim and increased the price by a reasonable amount. But the *Cour de cassation* rejected the claim because it is not the function of the court '*de prendre en considération le temps et les circonstances pour modifier les conventions des parties et substituer des clauses nouvelles à celles qui ont été librement acceptées par les contractants*'. French law has upheld this decision for a long time,[3] even in cases where a party's participation in the contract was made more difficult not by currency devaluation but also by other circumstances.[4] It is true that the strict prohibition of a

---

Law' (2007) 15 *ERPL* 483; H Rösler, 'Change of Circumstances' in *Max Planck Enc.* (2012) 163; F Ranieri, *Europäisches Obligationenrecht* (3rd edn, 2009) 815ff; M Mekki and M Kloepfer-Pelèse, 'Hardship and Modification (or "Revision") of the Contract' in A Hartkamp et al. (eds), *Towards a European Civil Code* (4th edn, 2011) 651; E McKendrick (ed), *Force Majeure and Frustration of Contract* (2nd edn, 1995); GH Treitel, *Frustration and Force Majeure* (3rd edn, 2014); A Janzen, 'Unforeseen Circumstances and the Balance of Contract: A Comparison of the Approach to Hardship in the UNIDROIT Principles and the German Law of Obligations' (2006) 22 *JCL* 156; SH Jenkins, 'Exemption for Non-Performance: UCC, CISG, UNIDROIT Principles, A Comparative Assessment' (1998) 72 *Tul. LR* 2015. In contrast to art. 79 CISG, the PECL follow the distinction made in continental legal systems between cases of 'impossibility' and 'hardship'. See art. 8:108 (dealing with cases in which non-performance is caused by an 'impediment') and art. 6:111 (dealing with cases in which performance has become 'more onerous' for the debtor). The same approach was taken by the PICC (see art. 6.3.3. and art. 7.1.7) and the DCFR (see art. III.-3:104 and art. III.-1:110). See also below at pp. 288ff.

[2] D.P.1876.1.197 (*Canal de Créponne*) and for details, see W Doralt, 'Der Wegfall der Geschäftsgrundlage: Altes und Neues zur *théorie de l'imprévision* in Frankreich' (2012) 76 *RabelsZ* 761.

[3] See the literature cited in F Terré, P Simler, and Y Lequette, *Droit civil, Les obligations* (11th edn, 2013) no. 466. After the two World Wars, special statutory provisions came into force that divide the risk of currency devaluation reasonably between the parties.

[4] Exceptionally, in proceedings before the administrative court a court can increase the price if a company has a fixed-price contract with a public authority to carry out work on roads or railways, or to supply gas, water, or electricity. If the court would not be allowed to adjust the contractual price in such cases, there would be a danger that the company could become insolvent as a result of the

révision pour imprévision has often been criticised. A cautious step in that direction was taken by the *Cour de cassation* when it decided that if a party's performance is made more difficult by a significant change in circumstances, the other party must in good faith undertake negotiations to adjust the contract.[5] In the end, however, as part of the reform of the French law of obligations, the old prohibition of any *révision pour imprévision* was dropped, and replaced by a new rule in art. 1195 *Code civil*.[6] It applies in cases where there is an unexpected change in circumstances after conclusion of the contract that makes its performance much more difficult for one of the parties, provided that neither party has under the contract assumed the risk of such circumstances arising. In such a case, the affected party can request the counterparty to negotiate an adjustment of the contract. If such renegotiation is refused, or the parties cannot agree on an adjustment of the contract, they can either agree on its termination on the agreed terms, or reach a *commun accord* to ask the court for an adjustment. It is only if the parties are unable to agree on such a step within a reasonable time that each party can alone and by itself apply to the court to either modify the contract in light of the changed conditions, or to terminate it '*à la date et aux conditions qu'il fixe*'. There is no doubt that an agreed adjustment of the contract is preferable to an adjustment fixed by the court. But there is the question of whether the procedure set out in art. 1195 *Code civil* is perhaps not too complicated.

II. German law

The drafters of the German Civil Code deliberately ignored a rule that would have allowed debtors to regard a contract as invalid or requiring adjustment if performance were to become especially difficult due to a change in circumstances after the contract had been concluded. No basis for such a rule could be found in classical Roman law. It is only later that the doctrine of *clausula rebus sic stantibus* was developed by Canon law,[7] adopted by the Glossators, and then by *Grotius* and *Pufendorf*, and finally enacted by legislation influenced by Natural Law. There was little sympathy for this rule among most German authors in the nineteenth century. An exception is *Bernhard Windscheid*, who thought that each contract is based on the parties' 'assumption' that the circumstances under which it is concluded will not change too much.[8] In discussions about the drafting of the German Civil Code, the argument that won the day was that a party's 'assumption' cannot be distinguished from a mere one-sided motive

---

strict adherence to the unchanged contract. Thus it is in the public interest not to endanger the supply of important utilities to the general public. See Conseil d'État 30 March 1916, D.P. 1916.3.25 and 9 Dec. 1932, D.P. 1933.3.17.

[5] See, for example, Civ. 16 March 2004, D. 2004, 1754.

[6] See, for example, B Fauvarque-Cosson, 'Le changement de circonstances' [2004] *RDC* 67; P Ancel and R Wintgen, 'La théorie du "fondement contractuel" (*Geschäftsgrundlage*) et son intérêt pour le droit français' [2006] *RDC* 897, but also (with some reservation) Terré, Simler and Lequette (n 3) no. 470f. and YM Laithier, 'L'incidence de la crise économique sur le contrat dans les droits de *common law*' [2010] *RDC* 407. See also Doralt (n 2) 768f.

[7] See R Zimmermann, *The Law of Obligations, Roman Foundations of the Civilian Tradition* (1990) 579ff; Ranieri (n 1) 815ff.

[8] *Lehrbuch des Pandektenrechts* (1865) §§ 97ff.

not incorporated in the contract, and that Windscheid's theory would endanger the security of commerce.⁹

It soon became clear, however, that the choice by the legislature would not long survive intact when it came up against real-life facts. After the outbreak of the First World War in particular, there were many cases in which the unexpected consequences of the war meant that sellers were finding it so difficult to procure and deliver goods that it was doubtful whether they could be held bound to their contracts. At first, the *Reichsgericht* helped out with the assumption that the mere increased difficulty of performance could be treated as if performance of the contract had become *wirtschaftlich unmöglich* (economically impossible) for the seller. So if a seller was unable to deliver foreign raw materials because their import had been made much more difficult or even interrupted by the wartime blockade of German ports, the delivery was deemed to be a *wirtschaftliche Unmöglichkeit*. This impossibility was not time-limited (for the duration of the war), but a permanent impossibility because 'the economic conditions under which delivery might take place after the war has ended would be entirely different after several years of war from those existing during peacetime when the contracts had been concluded'.¹⁰ Consequently, if delivery were impossible, sellers would neither be liable for specific performance of the agreement or for damages, since they were not 'responsible' for the impossibility of delivering the goods. More difficult issues were posed by cases where the seller was able to procure the goods, but at higher cost because they had become scarce during wartime and prices had risen considerably. The *Reichsgericht* again used the concept of *wirtschaftliche Unmöglichkeit* in these circumstances, but only on condition that the 'procurement of the product ... is bound up with such extreme difficulty that these difficulties are equivalent to impossibility in the generally accepted sense'.¹¹ The *Reichsgericht* then abandoned *wirtschaftliche Unmöglichkeit* and turned instead to a concept coined by Paul Oertmann's *Lehre von der Geschäftsgrundlage* (doctrine of the basis of the transaction). The first time it came up was in a case where a seller had at the normal price sold a property that he still had to procure from the current owner, which was a company in liquidation. The process took a long time. Inflation meant that property prices increased by a huge amount in the intervening period, and the seller no longer wanted to complete the sale under the original conditions. The *Reichsgericht* accepted the argument in principle. The *Geschäftsgrundlage* or 'basis of the transaction' was the common assumption held by both parties at the date of the contract that the value of the currency would be more or less stable. Rampant inflation had led to a disappearance of the basis of the transaction. This did not automatically give the seller the right to withdraw from the contract. First, it had to ask the buyer to raise the purchase price: 'Not until the buyer rejects the approach is he free. This follows from § 242 BGB, whereby the primary consideration of the debtor is to act according to the requirements of good faith'.¹² From here it was just a small step to the famous decision of the *Reichsgericht* that practically prohibited

---

⁹ *Protokolle der Kommission für die zweite Lesung des Entwurfs des BGB* vol. II (1897) 690f.
¹⁰ RG 22 Oct. 1918, RGZ 94, 68, 69f. See also RG 4 Feb. 1916, RGZ 88, 71; RG 27 Mar. 1917, RGZ 90, 102.
¹¹ See RG 23 Feb. 1904, RGZ 57, 116, 118f. See also RG 25 Feb. 1919, [1919] JW 499 and (restrictive) RG 21 Mar. 1916, RGZ 88, 172.
¹² RG 3 Feb. 1922, RGZ 103, 328.

property owners from buying off mortgages with virtually worthless paper money. Instead mortgage lenders were granted claims against property owners for payment of an additional amount intended to equalise the effects of inflation.[13]

Since that time, the German courts have heard countless cases where the judges have considered whether to modify or terminate a contract due to loss of the basis of the transaction. The requirements have been laid down in summarised form in § 313 BGB enacted in 2002. Admittedly, this provision is what German lawyers call a *Generalklausel*—a provision couched in very indefinite terms to which flesh must be added by judicial decisions in individual cases. The courts have said that the basis of the transaction is the 'common understanding of the parties at the time the contract was concluded of the presence or future occurrence of certain circumstances to the extent that the intent of the parties is built on such perceptions'. The parties do not have to have an exact meeting of minds on this point, provided that one party's understanding of the basis of the transaction was, or should have been, clear to the other party and that party raised no objections.[14] When there has been a 'significant' change of the basis of the transaction, the disadvantaged party can ask the court to modify the contract if it is no longer 'conscionable' (*zumutbar*) to bind it to the contract in its original form. Under § 313 BGB, this depends upon the 'individual circumstances, particularly the contractual and statutory allocation of risk'. If it is not possible for the court to adjust the contract, or if an adjustment would not be 'conscionable' for one of the parties, a right to terminate the contract or to cancel a continuing obligation *pro futuro* can also be considered.[15]

It is only through an analysis of the case law that some light may be shed on what the vague formulations of § 313 BGB actually mean. What seems to be highly important in many cases is that no party can rely on a change of the 'basis of the transaction' if that change results from the facts for which the party bears the risk under the

---

[13] RG 28 Nov. 1923, RGZ 107, 78. It was not until after this decision that the legislature took action, passing the *Aufwertungsgesetz* (Revaluation Act) in 1925. See RG 10 Feb. 1926, RGZ 112, 329 and RG 30 Jan. 1928, RGZ 119, 133.

[14] These formulations can be found in the case law. See, for example, BGH 21 July 2010, [2010] *NJW* 2884. Pursuant to § 313(2) BGB, there can also be a change to the basis of the transaction if 'material conceptions that have become the basis of the contract are found to be incorrect'. This covers circumstances where the parties have mistakenly assumed something that turns out not to have been correct *at the time the contract was concluded*, or mutual mistake. See chapter 9.C.VI = p. 166.

[15] Similar rules can also be found in the statutes and case law of many continental legal orders. See, for example, art. 1467ff. *Codice civile* (on this, see C Reiter, *Vertrag und Geschäftsgrundlage im deutschen und italienischen Recht* (2002)); art. 6:258ff. BW; art. 437 Portuguese Civil Code (on this, see A Pinto Monteiro and J Gomez, 'Rebus Sic Stantibus—Hardship Clauses in Portuguese Law' (1998) 6 *ZEuP* 319); art. 388 Greek Civil Code (on this, see P Papanikolaou, 'Rebus Sic Stantibus und Vertragskorrektur auf Grund veränderter Umstände im griechischen Recht' (1998) 6 *ZEuP* 303); art. 357 Polish Civil Code. Austria and Switzerland do not have an express statutory provision, but their courts follow the decisions of German courts in this area, though Swiss courts say that a party insisting on the original terms of the contract despite a significant change in the circumstances acts 'in abuse of the law' and therefore violates the general principle laid down in art. 2(2) Swiss Civil Code. For a critical view, see E Kramer, 'Neues zur clausula rebus sic stantibus' (2014) 110 *SJZ* 273. In Scandinavian countries, the courts reach the same results. Contractual agreements, even if individually negotiated, may also be amended or modified under § 36 Contract Law if a party insists on them despite a significant change in the circumstances. See B Lehrberg, 'Renegotiation Clauses, the Doctrine of Assumptions and Unfair Contract Terms' (1998) 3 *ERPL* 265. The whole topic is discussed in detail with many references in Ranieri (n 1) 815ff. and in particular by Hondius and Grigoleit (n 1) 55ff.

express or implied terms of the properly construed contract. So where a building contractor had been awarded a tender for €15 million to recultivate a site previously used for lignite mining, it could not later complain that its original price calculation was based on a third-party offer to provide cheap electricity and that this offer had lapsed because the tender was not awarded to the contractor until much later than expected, so that it had to pay €1.8 million more for electricity than assumed.[16] A company offering district heating at the same price as the state-run district heating company could not seek relief because the price of heating oil used in its business rose dramatically as a consequence of the 1973 oil crisis. Nor could it argue that the price at which the state-run company was able to supply heating was kept artificially low by subsidies paid by the state for political reasons.[17] Similarly, an oil trader that contracted to deliver heating oil at a particular price bore the risk that the oil would become scarce after the contract was signed and that its price would rise considerably.[18] And the lessee of a run-down hotel who suffered from a strong drop in demand for rooms, changed travel habits and increased demand for more luxurious accommodations cannot argue a change in the basis of the transaction and thus reduce lease payments by half, as these circumstances are 'all risks that fall to [him]'. They are 'in principle not suitable grounds for a claim that there has been a change in the basis of the transaction', even if the disappointment suffered by the lessee results in 'consequences that threaten the existence of the business'.[19]

The courts take a similarly strict view in cases where a party agreed a price for the other party's performance but now argues that due to a change in circumstances the purpose can no longer be achieved which the performance was originally thought to serve. Generally, each party to a contract—whether a buyer contracting for the delivery of goods, or a tenant who takes on the lease of a property—bears the 'utilisation risk' that it will no longer be able to use the other party's performance in the way which it—and perhaps also the counterparty—had in mind at the date of the contract. Someone buying a silver breadbasket as a wedding present for his son bears the risk that the wedding may be called off and there will no longer be any use for the basket. Similarly, if someone buys land in the hope of his planning application being approved by the planning authorities, he cannot rely on a change in the basis of the transaction if no authorisation is given.[20] It falls upon the buyers in these cases to ensure that this risk is transferred to the seller, and if there is no such (express or implied) agreement, the default rule must be that the buyers bear the 'utilisation risk' and must therefore pay the agreed price even though they can no longer use the object for the intended

---

[16] BGH 10 Sept. 2009, [2010] *NJW* 519.   [17] BGH 25 May 1977, [1977] *NJW* 2262.
[18] BGH 8 Feb. 1978, [1978] *JZ* 235. The trader had contracted to deliver goods and had therefore also taken on the procurement risk (see chapter 14.B.I = p. 244). The BGH rejected the trader's appeal on the basis of a change in the 'basis of the transaction' because the trader had recognised the danger of a further rise in prices at an early stage, but had failed to take out a low-priced hedging transaction to cover the price rise in the hope that prices would fall.
[19] BGH 19 Apr. 1978, [1978] *NJW* 2390. See also BGH 21 Sept. 2005, [2006] *NJW* 899: if someone has leased rooms for gambling premises in a shopping centre that had not yet been built, that party bears the risk that after it has been built the shopping centre will not be as popular with customers as envisaged by the parties. This is also not a ground to successfully argue a change in the 'basis of the transaction'.
[20] BGH 1 June 1979, BGHZ 74, 370.

purpose. Of course, there may be exceptions. The *Bundesgerichtshof* considered a case in which a company contracted to produce 600 drill hammers that both parties knew to be technically outdated and could only be exported by the buyer into the Eastern zone of Germany that was (at that time) still occupied by the Soviet Union. When exports to the Eastern zone turned out to be no longer possible due to the effects of the Berlin blockade, the buyer sought to escape from the contract. Even though there were good reasons why the utilisation risk should only be borne by the buyer, the *Bundesgerichtshof* accepted that the assumption of the parties that the drill hammers would be exported into the Eastern zone had become the basis of the transaction and that the contract thus needed to be modified to the new circumstances. The buyer had to pay a quarter of the agreed price to compensate the producer for any costs incurred during the production of some of the drill hammers.[21]

III. English law

If, after a contract has been concluded, circumstances arise that prevent a party from performing, or considerably change performance, or make it much more difficult, under English law that party can rely on the *doctrine of frustration*. If the party successfully argues that the doctrine applies, this means that the occurrence of such circumstances puts an end to the contract and excludes all contractual remedies, in particular any claim for damages for breach of contract.

The doctrine of frustration does not only apply if there has been a change in circumstances which makes performance more difficult or destroys the purpose which the agreement was originally intended to serve; it also applies if the change in circumstances has rendered performance *impossible*. Continental legal orders give relief in these cases provided that the debtor can prove that it was not 'responsible' for the change in circumstances or that the promised result was made impossible by *force majeure*.[22] In England, the doctrine of frustration will be applied in cases of impossibility as well, and commentators have indeed said that '[s]upervening impossibility of performance is the most obvious ground of frustration'.[23] This is illustrated by the case of *Taylor* v. *Caldwell*.[24] The plaintiff hired the defendant's music hall for concerts on four future dates. Before the first of these concerts, the hall was accidentally destroyed by fire, and the plaintiff claimed damages for the loss he had suffered by reason of the non-occurrence of the concerts. The claim failed because the contract of

---

[21] BGH 16 Jan. 1953, [1953] *MDR* 282. Another result was reached by the Swiss Federal Court in BG 13 Apr. 1943, BGE 69 II 139: At the end of 1939, a Swiss arms producer contracted with the French government to deliver certain weapons for the French army. He needed some special parts to fulfil the contract, so on 4 June 1940 he placed an order for them with the plaintiff. Both parties knew what these parts were for, and what the current French military situation was, but when armistice occurred between Germany and France sooner than was expected, the arms manufacturer repudiated the contract. The plaintiff's claim for damages for the ensuing loss was successful. The German case law on frustration of a contract is discussed in detail in T Finkenauer in *Münchener Kommentar zum BGB* (6th edn, 2012) § 313 BGB mn. 252ff.
[22] See above, chapter 14.B = p. 244.
[23] GH Treitel, *The Law of Contract* (13th edn, by E Peel, 2011) no. 19-008.
[24] (1863) 122 Eng.Rep. 309 and see chapter 14.B.III = p. 252.

hire was construed to have an implied term that 'the parties shall be excused in case ... performance becomes impossible from the perishing of the [music hall] without default of the contractor'. The doctrine of frustration has also been applied in many other instances of impossibility, such as where a seller agreed to deliver goods that were unique or had to be supplied from a specified stock of goods: in these cases, sellers were not liable for damages if the unique goods[25] or the stock from which they were to be supplied[26] were destroyed after the contract had been concluded. The doctrine does not apply if the seller is responsible for the loss of the items, nor if the items are destroyed after the loss risk has already been transferred to the buyer even though it had not yet taken possession.[27] In all these cases, everything turns on whether the debtor has assumed the risk of impossibility under the contract, or whether it has been assumed by the other party. A seller who has contracted to deliver goods to a buyer by ship to a specific harbour at a particular time cannot rely on frustration if it turns out that, for reasons beyond its control, it cannot charter suitable shipping capacity and thus the delivery has become impossible.[28] On the other hand, a contract can be terminated for frustration if a pianist has undertaken to perform at a concert on a particular day, but cannot perform due to illness.[29] A contract will also be frustrated if the seller is forbidden under the Trading with the Enemy Act 1939 to perform as agreed, or where a shipowner cannot deliver a ship to a charterer because it has sunk before the delivery date or has been seized by the State. A party that has chartered a ship for six months need not pay the full price if the shipowner makes the ship available at the agreed port on the agreed date, but the charterer cannot load the vessel because the port is closed for months due to a strike.[30]

The frustration doctrine is also applied in cases where the debtor's performance is not impossible, but because of a change in circumstances performance has now become extremely expensive, or can only be carried out if the debtor can overcome extreme unexpected difficulties. However, the contract is only deemed to be frustrated in such cases if performance by the debtor under the new circumstances would be 'a thing radically different from that which was undertaken by the contract'.[31] It has also been said that the new circumstances must 'be of a character and extent so sweeping that the foundation of what the parties are deemed to have had in contemplation has disappeared, and the contract itself has vanished with that foundation'.[32] It is not

---

[25] See s. 7 Sale of Goods Act 1979: A contract of sale for 'specific goods' is then invalid if the contract has been concluded and 'subsequently the goods, without any fault on the part of the seller or buyer, perish before the risk passes to the buyer'.

[26] *Howell v. Coupland* (1876) 1 QBD 258 and see Treitel (n 23) no. 19-023ff.

[27] Such as where the goods have been destroyed or damaged after the seller has already handed them over to a carrier for transportation to the buyer. See above, chapter 13.D.II = pp. 227f.

[28] *Lewis Emanuel & Son Ltd. v. Sammut* [1952] 2 Lloyd's Rep. 629.

[29] *Robinson v. Davison* (1871) LR 6 Ex. 269.

[30] *Pioneer Shipping Ltd. v. BTP Tioxide Ltd., The Nema* [1982] AC 724.

[31] *Davis Contractors Ltd. v. Fareham Urban DC* [1956] AC 696, 729 per *Lord Radcliffe*. In this case, a building contractor had promised to build seventy-eight houses, but did not want to perform the contract because it could not hire sufficient trained workers and would need twenty-two months to complete the contract instead of the eight months envisaged. This meant that the contractor would have considerably higher costs. Nevertheless, the House of Lords held the contract to be valid.

[32] *F.A. Tamplin Steamship Co. Ltd. v. Anglo-Mexican Petroleum Products Co. Ltd.* [1916] 2 AC 397, 406 (per Lord Haldane).

important which of these formulations is chosen. What is important is whether the change in circumstances has resulted in a situation that is commonly regarded as still lying within the *risk sphere* of the party trying to escape from the contract. In that case, the party will not be allowed to rely on the frustration doctrine.

The doctrine also applies if a party has entered into a contract to buy goods or services, and now argues that due to a subsequent change of circumstances the goods or services no longer meet the original purpose which that party—and perhaps also the other party—had in mind when the contract was concluded. *Krell* v. *Henry*[33] is perhaps the most famous case on the subject. The plaintiff had a house on the route of King Edward VII's coronation procession and he hired it to the defendant for the day. The coronation procession was cancelled due to the King's ill health, and the hirer refused to pay the hire. The owner's claim was rejected: the rule in *Taylor* v. *Caldwell* is not only applicable if it is impossible for the debtor to perform, but if 'the event which renders the contract incapable of performance is the cessation or non-existence of an express condition or state of things, going to the root of the contract, and essential to its performance'.[34] The case law shows, however, that contracts are rarely set aside for a frustration of purpose, as this requires not only that the purpose of the agreement must be known to both parties but also that the party relying on the doctrine must not have assumed the 'risk' of this purpose being frustrated. So if goods are bought which the buyer intends to export to a specific country, he must bear the risk of being denied the necessary government export approvals. When somebody buys land for redevelopment purposes, he must pay the agreed price of £1.7 million even though the authorities tell him on the day after the contract was signed that the buildings on the land were listed as being of special architectural interest, so that redevelopment became more difficult or impossible and the market value slumped to £200,000. It is true that when the contract was signed, *both* parties had expected that the land would not be given protected status. On the other hand, the buyer must have been aware that the risk of being able to redevelop the land was his, that it was only he who would be affected by a decision making redevelopment more difficult, and that it was therefore for him to secure (and pay for) a contractual right to terminate the contract or ask for a renegotiation of the price if he were prevented from putting the land to the intended use.[35]

---

[33] [1903] 2 KB 740.

[34] The case would also have been decided in the same way in Germany. It is only a question of judicial taste whether the holding of the parade is made the 'basis of the transaction', or if instead it is assumed that the landlord did not just rent out the apartment but rented out an apartment with a view of the parade. In the latter case, it would have been impossible for the landlord to perform: whether he would then lose the right to the rental sum (§ 326(1) BGB) or may retain it (§ 326(1) BGB) depends on the decisive question of which party has assumed the risk of the parade actually taking place. That this is the landlord results from the fact that the parties would have not agreed differently if this matter had been brought up during contract negotiations. It is for this reason that the matter may have to be decided differently when the plaintiff, a commercial operator, agreed to make his ship available to the defendant on the day on which King Edward VII was to review the British fleet. The review by the King was cancelled, but the court held the defendant to the contract. He was able to enjoy the trip and see the fleet, so that despite the cancellation of the review the contractual purpose of the agreement could still be achieved in part. See *Herne Bay Steamboat* v. *Hutton* [1903] 2 KB 683.

[35] *Amalgamated Investment & Property Co. Ltd.* v. *John Walker & Son Ltd.* [1977] 1 WLR 164 and in detail in Treitel (n 23) no. 19-043.

The fact that the change in circumstances leads one party to pay considerably more than expected has in general no impact on the validity of the contract. It does mean that the party has made a bad deal, but the purpose of the frustration doctrine is not 'to relieve the contracting parties of the normal consequences of imprudent bargains'.[36] No party can escape an improvident bargain when the circumstances responsible for causing the performance to become more expensive fall within that party's risk sphere. The strictness with which the English courts regard this question is shown in the case where a seller claimed that performance of a contract to deliver 300 tonnes of Sudanese peanuts *cif* Hamburg had been made much more difficult because, contrary to the expectations of both parties, the Suez Canal had been blocked due to a war between Israel and Egypt. The goods could now only be transported via the Cape of Good Hope, which would double the transportation costs of delivering the goods to Hamburg. The court found the contract to be valid. The quality of the peanuts would not be affected by the longer journey, and the buyer did not care how the carrier transported the goods or when they arrived in Hamburg.[37]

English case law sometimes throws up decisions that may seem unfair. But they reflect the interests of those parties attracted by the commercial court system in London—large, and often international, companies. The legal system presents these companies with a strong incentive to contract out of the frustration doctrine by making express agreements to allocate risk if performance of the contract becomes impossible (or just more expensive), such as in case of war, strikes, natural catastrophes, import or export bans, or other hardship situations. The strict line taken in the case law also has the reverse effect in that the English courts, knowing that the use of such agreements is widespread, are loath to allow parties recourse to the frustration doctrine if they could have protected themselves by making such an agreement at the outset, but failed to do so.

C. International Sets of Rules

Where a debtor claims that a change of circumstances should free it from liability for breach, the international sets of rules distinguish two types of cases. In the first, the changed circumstances present an *impediment* that makes performance impossible for the debtor.[38] In the other line of cases, the changed circumstances make performance *more difficult*.[39] In the latter cases, the court can only terminate or modify the

---

[36] *Pioneer Shipping* (n 30) 752 (per Lord Roskill).
[37] *Tsakiroglou & Co. Ltd.* v. *Noblee Thörl GmbH* [1962] AC 93. See also *Ocean Tramp Tankers Corp.* v. *V/O Sovfracht* [1964] 2 WLR 114: a party had chartered a ship for a journey from Genoa to ports in India, agreeing to pay a certain amount per day for the hire of the ship. The charterer tried, unsuccessfully, to argue that performance of the contract had become much more difficult as the closure of the Suez Canal meant that the journey took 138 days instead of the planned 108 days.
[38] See art. 8:108 PECL; art. 7.1.7 PICC; art. III.-3:104 DCFR.
[39] Article 6:111 PECL; art. 6.2.1ff. PICC; art. III.-1:110 DCFR; art. 89 CESL. However, the difference between an impediment and a difficulty in performance can be difficult to define: 'Of course there is sometimes a very fine line between a performance which is only possible by totally unreasonable efforts, and a performance which is only very difficult even if it may drive the debtor into bankruptcy. It is up to the court to decide which situation is before it' (art. 6:111 PECL Comment A). Article 79 CISG determines exemption from liability only for the case where a debtor cannot perform a contract due to an impediment. But prevailing opinion says that art. 79 CISG can also be applied if the debtor's performance is

contract if the changed circumstances make performance for the debtor *excessively onerous*[40] or if they have such a strong impact 'that it would be manifestly unjust to hold the debtor to the obligation'.[41] Sometimes a contract can only be terminated or modified for hardship if the change in circumstances 'fundamentally alters the equilibrium of the contract'.[42] The rules also all state that a party cannot complain that performance has become more difficult if that party has in the contract assumed the risk of that change occurring or if, at the time of the agreement, the party should have reasonably taken into account the possibility of a change in circumstances, and protected itself by making an appropriate agreement on risk allocation.

These formulations are general and imprecise; and national statutes—if indeed they address the issue at all—are equally offering no more than very general principles. The basic question is in each case to determine the party that must bear the risk of a change of circumstances. If the contract contains no express agreement to this effect—and such agreements always take precedence, unless they contravene binding legal provisions and are thus invalid—there is a *gap* in the contract that must be closed by judicial interpretation. The court will examine how the parties would have allocated risk if they had addressed the issue when concluding the contract.[43] Mention should be made of the solution in art. 89(2a) CESL, which states that where performance has become 'excessively onerous' for one party because of a change in circumstances, the court may adapt or terminate the contract but only with the aim of bringing it into accordance with 'what the parties would reasonably have agreed at the time of contracting if they had taken the change of circumstances into account'. Of course, it is not easy to determine what the parties would reasonably have agreed. But one should assume that they would have agreed on the most advantageous—in effect the most efficient—solution by imposing the risk in question on the party that would have been able—at lower cost than the other party—to avert the risk, to lower the probability of its materialisation, or to take steps (including taking out insurance) to protect itself against the consequences of the change in circumstances.

If the debtor claims that performance has been made significantly more difficult due to a change in circumstances, the court can terminate the contract 'at the date and on terms to be determined by the court'.[44] The court can also maintain the contract and 'adjust' it in such a way that it takes account of the new circumstances 'in a just and equitable manner'. This power for the court to modify a contract can be found in all continental legal systems that address such issues, and it now also applies under French law (art. 1195 *Code civil*). English law takes another position. The adjustment of a contract must have a basis in the agreement of the parties, and if there is no

---

made more *difficult* by a change in circumstances. See P Schlechtriem and U Schroeter, *Internationales UN-Kaufrecht* (6th edn, 2016) mn. 678ff. However, it will be a rare event for a seller to be allowed to amend the original selling price on the grounds that the price it has to pay to procure the goods from a third party or transport them to the buyer has risen since the contract was concluded. Performance has become more difficult, but the risk of rising prices is to be 'taken into account upon conclusion of the contract' by the seller, and thus cannot free him from liability to perform the contract at the original price.

[40] Article 6:111 (2) PECL; art. 89 CESL. [41] Article III.-1:110 (2) DCFR.
[42] Article 6.2.2 PICC.   [43] See Kramer (n 15) 276ff.
[44] See art. 6:111(3) PECL; art. 6.2.3(4) PICC; art. III.-1:110(2) DCFR; art. 89a(2) CESL.

such agreement, it is not the function of the court to go above the heads of the parties to impose an agreement that it considers appropriate. It follows that if the conditions for frustration are present, a contract will always be invalid under English law, and does not give rise to a claim for damages for breach of contract.[45] However, if the parties have before the change in circumstances already begun to perform the (still valid) contract, the court may make an order for the reasonable restitution of what has already been performed.[46]

It is self-evident that parties will usually start to negotiate with each other if one of them says that performance of the contract has been made significantly more difficult by a change in circumstances. It hardly ever happens that one of the parties goes straight to court, or waits until the other party starts legal proceedings. This is because parties are usually interested in maintaining business relationships. In practical terms, they seek repeat business transactions and if settlement of a particular transaction throws up problems, they will seek to come to a mutual arrangement with each other.

It is remarkable, if rather implausible, that the international sets of rules go one step further by making it an *obligation* of the parties 'to enter into negotiations with a view to adapting the contract or ending it', and that they only allow the court to modify a contract if the parties have actually negotiated with each other and have failed to come to an agreement on modification within a reasonable deadline.[47] They also specify that the court should be able to award damages against a party it considers responsible for refusing to enter into negotiations or which it has broken off 'contrary to good faith'.[48]

No one disputes that it is better to settle the problem of a change in circumstances by agreement, rather than by judicial fiat. Nor does anyone dispute that the parties are entitled, and sometimes well advised, to agree a contractual obligation to negotiate in the event of a change in circumstances. But it is doubtful whether the introduction of a *duty* to negotiate makes sense (even where the contract contains no such clause) and will not merely lead to empty formalities. What will happen, for example, in the

---

[45] The same decision has to be made, if one accepts the prevailing opinion that art. 79 CISG also covers a change in circumstances. If the requirements of art. 79 CISG are met in such a case, the debtor will be freed of its liability to pay damages for non-performance. Judicial modification of the contract would be excluded since national legal systems, should they provide for such modification, would allow art. 79 CISG to take precedence. See Schlechtriem and Schroeter (n 39) mn. 681f.

[46] See s. 1(3) Law Reform (Frustrated Contracts) Act 1943; Treitel (n 23) no. 19-090ff. and E McKendrick, *Contract Law* (8th edn, 2009) no. 14.17. The same principle of judicial restraint also applies in England for penalty clauses: they will always be invalid, and the judicial reduction of a penalty to a reasonable level is excluded. See chapter 14.D.VI = p. 277.

[47] See arts. 6:111(2) and (3) PECL; art. 6.2.3 PICC; art. 89(1) and (2) CESL.

[48] See art. 6:111(3) PECL. In France, too, the prevailing opinion is that if the court has determined a '*changement de circonstances imprévisible*', it may award damages against a party if it has refused to negotiate over a modification of the contract or broken off such negotiations without good cause. How is the court to decide if a party has broken off negotiations too quickly, without good reason, out of opportunism, or in bad faith? How would the court calculate damages on this basis? It is also rather implausible that art. 1195 *Code civil* does not only oblige the parties to negotiate about a modification of the contract but requires them, if such negotiations have failed, either to reach another agreement on the termination of the contract, or to reach a *commun accord* on the involvement of the court. It is only when no such agreements have been made that *one* individual party becomes entitled to apply to the court for the contract to be modified.

typical case where a seller refuses to deliver because it had to procure the goods from a third party at a price that was 70 per cent higher than the price originally envisaged?[49] In this case, the seller will take the initiative to suggest that the buyer pay a higher price than agreed in the contract. Even if the buyer wishes to stand by the contract, and thus regards the proposal as unjustified, it will not be allowed to simply say 'No'. Under the international sets of rules, the buyer is under a duty to actually negotiate—if need be 'for show' or by jumping through the hoops of formality—since this is the only way the buyer can be sure to avoid the risk of being held liable for having refused to negotiate. One should also bear in mind that negotiations always take place 'in the shadow of the law'. Both parties will take account of the likely judicial decision and then only agree to a negotiated settlement if it is no worse than the outcome they would expect to achieve in court. These are the reasons, and not the bad faith of a party, that usually lead to parties refusing to negotiate or breaking off negotiations. So if in the above example the buyer refused to increase the agreed price, or broke off negotiations with the seller, the court must immediately be in a position to decide whether or not an adjustment of the contract was justified so as to allow for the price increase suggested by the seller. It makes no sense for the court to defer this decision *ad calendas graecas* and concentrate on the buyer's reasons for refusing or breaking off negotiations and, depending on the result of these deliberations, decide whether or not the buyer should have to pay damages on that basis.[50]

---

[49] This was the case in the much-discussed decision of the Belgian *Cour de cassation* of 19 June 2009 (*Scafom International BV v. Lorraine Tubes SAS*, CISG online Nr. 1963). The court correctly assumed that art. 79 CISG was applicable in cases in which one party's performance had become more difficult. But the court was not correct in deciding that a price rise of 70 per cent was an 'impediment' outside of the seller's control. Nor was it correct to assume that art. 79 CISG was 'incomplete', and that the gap should be closed pursuant to art. 7(2) CISG by recourse to art. 6.2.3 PICC, which had the result that the buyer was under a 'duty' to negotiate over the modification of the original contract. See Schlechtriem and Schroeter (n 39) mn. 682; I Schwenzer, 'Die clausula und das CISG' in *Festschrift für Eugen Bucher* (2009) 723; D Philippe, 'Renégociation du contrat en cas de changement de circonstances dans la vente internationale' [2011] *RDC* 963; see also the extensive discussion of the judgment in J Dewez, C Ramberg, R Momberg Uribe, R Cabrillac, LP San Miguel Pradera, 'The Duty to Renegotiate an International Sales Contract under CISG in Case of Hardship and the Use of the Unidroit Principles' (2011) 19 *ERPL* 101–54.

[50] § 313 BGB allows the court to modify the contract in the event of a change in circumstances, but does not oblige the parties to carry out negotiations about an adjustment of the contract. This is largely supported in the academic literature, but it is disputed. See J Lüttringhaus, 'Verhandlungspflichten bei Störung der Geschäftsgrundlage' (2013) 213 *AcP* 266 referring to BGH 30 Sept. 2011, BGHZ 191, 139. There may be exceptional cases in which obligations from a long-term contract (such as a contract of employment, partnership agreement, or distributorship agreement) can no longer be performed by one party due to a change in circumstances: in such cases, a party's categorical refusal to enter negotiations about an adjustment of the contract may be a reason for its liability in damages. See, for example, Com. 3 Nov. 1992, *JCP* 1993.II.22164, n. G Virassamy = [1993] *Rev trim civ* 124, n. J Mestre.

16

Agency and Representation

A.	Historical Development and Economic Importance	293
B.	Statutory Representatives	297
C.	Grant, Extent, and Termination of Authority or the Power to Represent	298
	I. Grant	298
	II. Implied grant	299
	III. Formalities	300
	IV. Extent	301
	V. Self-dealing by agent	303
	VI. Termination	305
	VII. Revocability	305
D.	Dealing without Authority	307
	I. Ratification	307
	II. Apparent or ostensible authority	308
	1. Giving the appearance of authority	308
	2. Justifiable reliance by the third party	310
	III. Liability of the supposed agent	311
E.	The Effects of Agency	312
	I. Disclosed agency	312
	II. Undisclosed agency	314
	1. Claims by the principal	315
	2. Claims by the third party	317

A. Historical Development and Economic Importance

A developed economic system that depends on the division of labour for the production of goods and services has to allow contracts to be negotiated and concluded by persons other than the parties themselves, or else it cannot function at all. An individual craftsman might start off by personally ordering all the raw materials he needs and making all the contractual arrangements by which he disposes of his goods and services. But sooner or later, as his business grows, he will have to have others do the negotiations for him, for his suppliers and customers will be more numerous and further away, and the negotiations will call for special skills. The entrepreneur who delegates the procurement of materials to a member of his staff, the heirs who commission an auctioneer to sell off inherited property, the landowner who has a factor run his estate, the manufacturer whose distributive chain includes independent salesmen as well as staff of his own: all these people—who for one reason or another cannot or will not act personally—expand their sphere of activity by engaging others to effect contracts with third parties and do everything incidental to such contracts, and these intermediaries act 'for them', 'on their account', 'as agent', or 'in their interest'. Such intermediaries all have a good deal in common: they facilitate the business activity of the person who retains them, and do so pursuant to a mandate, power, or authority which has been given to them.

This gives only the barest outline of the subject matter of this chapter. Since the various interests involved come into conflict, jurists need to have rules that are much more detailed, as well as concepts to help them put these rules into an intellectually satisfying order.

Roman law had no general concept of what we call agency or representation, the idea of one person acting for another. Partly this is because Roman jurists were temperamentally averse to systematisation, but mainly it is because they never broke away from the traditional idea that while Roman citizens could generate rights and liabilities for themselves personally by the contracts they made, they could not do so for third parties. This may be connected with the fact that in ancient Rome legal obligations could arise only from formal acts such as the incantation of prescribed formulaic words, and so could affect only those who personally did the acts.

This idea lost ground as Roman law increasingly accepted the validity of formless transactions,[1] but the jurists were able to stick to their traditional principle by finding other ways of meeting the need for people to be able to create rights and duties in others. Thus it had always been accepted that the *paterfamilias* could acquire ownership and other rights through members of his household, children, or slaves. This acquisition did not result from any power granted by the *paterfamilias* to his dependants, but rather from the structure of Roman society: the dependants had the 'status' of an extension of the *paterfamilias*, and indeed he owned whatever belonged to them. The *paterfamilias* was not originally liable for the debts contracted by his dependants, but the praetor made an increasing number of exceptions to this principle. If the *paterfamilias* set up one of his family to manage a ship or a shop or other business, business creditors could look to the *paterfamilias* for payment of their debts. So where a dependant was granted a *peculium* or fund to manage, the *paterfamilias* was liable up to the amount of that *peculium*. In both cases, the liability of the *paterfamilias* was additional to that of the dependent trader, for Roman law never accepted that an obligation could arise exclusively in the person on whose account or on whose behalf another was acting: 'Direct representation does not appear anywhere. It is a juridical marvel.'[2]

It took the natural lawyers to make this marvel possible. They were able to see the problem in quite a new light since they had discovered a new non-Roman principle—the concept of the autonomy of the parties—which they held to be the foundation of contract law. Hugo Grotius held that a promise could be made 'in the name of the person who was to receive the thing' and that in such a case ownership vested immediately in the person 'in whose name' the acquisitive transaction was made.[3] Christian

---

[1] See above, pp. 106ff.

[2] E Rabel, 'Die Stellvertretung in den hellenistischen Rechten und in Rom' in *Atti del congresso internazionale del diritto romano* (1934) I, 235, 238 = HG Leser (ed), *Gesammelte Aufsätze* (1971) 492. For details of Roman law and its development, see R Zimmermann, *The Law of Obligations, Roman Foundations of the Civilian Tradition* (1990) 45ff. with numerous references.

[3] *De iure belli ac pacis libri tres*, book II ch 11 § 18.

Wolff took the matter a step further: he held that a contract made by a mandatary or procurator within his mandate could not only confer rights on his principal, but also impose liabilities on him directly.[4] This was the basis on which the natural law codes built: contractual rights and duties could be created in P as a result of A's negotiating a transaction with T provided that A was empowered by P to do this and that A effected the transaction 'in the name of' P, that is, the contract must have been made *in P's name*. This rule was laid down clearly and precisely by Pothier,[5] and then incorporated into the *Code civil*, which in art. 1984 defines agency or the management of affairs as a transaction '*par lequel une personne donne à une autre le pouvoir de faire quelque chose pour le mandant et en son nom*'.[6]

From the requirement that the agent must contract with the third party 'in the name' of his principal, one could easily infer that if the agent, though acting within his powers, does *not* deal in the name of his principal, then the principal is entirely unaffected by the transaction if the agent does not make it known or knowable that the transaction is in law that of the principal.

Yet can it be right to draw such a sharp distinction between acting in one's own name and acting in the name of someone else? In both cases, the agent is acting in the interest of his principal, on his behalf, and pursuant to his instructions. Besides, the economic aim is the same in the two cases. When a person tasks an art dealer to acquire a specified painting from a third party, their purpose is that the principal becomes the owner of the painting, pays the price, meets the dealer's outgoings, and pays a fee. Whether or not the dealer lets the seller know that it is acting for someone else, named or unnamed, does not affect the achievement of this purpose in the least.

The Common Law speaks of agency in both cases, and regards the 'law of agency' as covering the legal relationships that arise when one person is used by another to perform certain tasks on his behalf.[7] Different interests are admittedly in play and different rules are required, depending on whether the third party knew or could have known that he was making a contract with someone other than the person he was negotiating with. But common lawyers see the situations as being alike, in that that person is negotiating with him at the instance of and in the interest of another. By contrast, lawyers on the Continent tend to draw a very sharp distinction between acting in someone else's name and acting in one's own name, and to hold that in the latter case the principal acquires no direct contractual claims against the third party, and the third party acquires none against the principal. The sharp distinction is not always easy to draw and cannot, as we shall see, be completely maintained. After all, from an economic point of view there is little difference between acting in one's own name and acting in the name of another. We shall accordingly deal with both situations here,

---

[4] *Institutiones iuris naturae et gentium* (1761) § 380 and 381. For details see H Coing, *Europäisches Privatrecht*, vol. 1: *Älteres Gemeines Recht* (1985), 429f.

[5] *Traité des obligations* (1761) no. 74 and 75.

[6] § 5ff. I 13 Prussian ALR and § 1002 ABGB are similar.

[7] GHL Fridman, *Law of Agency* (7th edn, 1996) 11 defines agency as 'the relationship that exists between two persons when one, called the *agent*, is considered in law to represent the other, called the *principal*, in such a way as to be able to affect the principal's legal position in respect of strangers to the relationship by the making of contracts or the disposition of property'.

encouraged by the realisation that in recent efforts to unify the law in this area the notion of representation is given a similarly wide scope. This is also the path taken by the international sets of rules.[8]

Another insight has helped to systematise the relevant rules and improve their legislative formulation, at least in continental systems. This has to do with the relation between the contract that links principal and agent, and the transaction whereby the former grants the latter the power to represent it in transactions with third parties. At one time these were not distinguished: people thought that every power rested on, or was even identical with, a contract of agency, and must stand or fall with it. Thus the Prussian ALR (§ 5 I 13), the *Code civil* (art. 1984), and the Austrian ABGB (§ 1002) treat the principal's contract with the agent and his grant of the power to represent him as being the same.

Jhering[9] was the first to point out that one must distinguish between the underlying contract—which may be an employment contract, a partnership agreement, or agency agreement—and the grant of the power to act as agent. Laband[10] went so far as to say that the two were entirely distinct and independent, that a clear distinction must be made between the question of the scope and duration of the power granted (which the agent *could* use to affect the principal either way), and the other question whether there was a contract between the parties (and thus what the agent *should* do according to its terms). After winning its spurs in Germany, this doctrine has made a 'triumphal progress' into modern codes.[11] In practical terms cases are decided much the same way whether one accepts it or not, but it has had the result that the rules regarding the grant, scope, duration, and termination of the agent's power are kept quite separate from the rules regarding the content of the contract between agent and principal. This is so not only in textbooks and learned writings but also in codes, where they appear in different sections. It is not only the case for the German Civil Code: its example has been followed in the Swiss Law of Obligations (1911), the Swedish Contract Law (1915)

---

[8] See art. 3:101f. PECL; art. 2.2.1 PICC; art. II.-6:105f. DCFR and below, pp. 312ff. See also J Kleinschmidt, 'Representation' in *Max Planck Enc.* (2012) 1455; MJ Bonell, 'Agency' in A Hartkamp et al. (eds), *Towards a European Civil Code* (4th edn, 2011) 515. The Convention on Agency in the International Sale of Goods (Geneva 1983) (hereinafter the 'Geneva Convention', not yet in force) also delineates its scope in art. 1(1) as follows: 'This Convention applies where one person, the agent, has authority or purports to have authority on behalf of another person, the principal, to conclude a contract of sale of goods with a third party' and art. 1(4) provides that this is 'irrespective of whether the agent acts in his own name or in that of the principal'. On this, see J Bonell, 'The 1983 Geneva Convention on Agency in the International Sale of Goods' (1984) 32 *Am J Comp L* 717 (with the text of the Convention at 751ff.); M Evans, 'Rapport explicatif sur la Convention sur la représentation en matière de vente internationale de marchandises' [1984] *Rev dr unif* 72; H Hanisch, 'Das Genfer Abkommen über die Stellvertretung beim internationalen Warenkauf' in *Festschrift Giger* (1989) 251; HA Stöcker, 'Das Genfer Übereinkommen über die Vertretung beim internationalen Warenkauf' [1983] *WM* 778; C Mouly, 'La convention de Genève sur la représentation en matière de vente internationale' [1983] *Rev int dr comp* 829.

[9] R von Jhering, 'Mitwirkung für fremde Rechtsgeschäfte' in *Jherings Jahrbücher* 1 (1857) 273.

[10] P Laband, 'Die Stellvertretung bei dem Abschluss von Rechtsgeschäften' (1866) 10 *ZHR* 183.

[11] W Müller-Freienfels, *Die Vertretung beim Rechtsgeschäft* (1955) 2, giving extensive references to the laws of the many countries which have adopted the distinction between contract and grant of agency. See also F Ranieri, *Europäisches Obligationenrecht* (3rd edn, 2009) 489ff. The Common Law is not familiar with this distinction. It has nonetheless been held that a power to act on behalf of a principal will arise even though the contract between principal and agent is unenforceable because of a want of consideration or the agent's minority. See R Munday, *Agency* (2nd edn, 2013) no. 2.02, 2.07, 8.13f.

that was subsequently adopted by other Nordic countries, the Greek Civil Code (1940), the Italian *Codice civile* (1942), the Portuguese Civil Code (1966), and the Dutch Civil Code of 1992.[12]

B. Statutory Representatives

The power to make contracts on behalf of and in the interest of another, whether in his name or not, generally results from an explicit and intentional grant of such power by the other party. But not always: such power may be accorded by a statutory text, regardless of the will of the party represented. In continental legal systems, this statutory power is conferred by the legislature where a person lacks full contractual capacity, such as a minor or a person who has mental health issues. Parents are granted extensive rights to represent their minor children, and so is the guardian of a child whose parents are dead or unable to look after him or her. There are also many other situations, such as bankruptcy or succession, where rights of management and disposition have to be conferred on someone other than the owner. The notion of statutory representation also applies to those who act as the representative bodies of legal persons. While the scope and duration of the powers of all such statutory representatives are laid down in detail by legal provisions, it is accepted that in the absence of applicable provisions, the general rules on agency, though primarily designed for agency created by the will of the principal, may be applied by analogy by the courts.

It is a remarkable fact that the notion of statutory representation as a general device to enable incapacitated persons to take part in legal life is entirely lacking in English law;[13] only in a few disparate cases does one person become agent for another by force of law. Even parents have no general power to represent their children in law or litigation.[14] The 'parental responsibility' conferred on parents by s. 3(1) of the Children Act 1989 is defined as 'all the rights, duties, powers, responsibilities and authority which by law a parent of a child has in relation to the child and his property'. But the law refrains from stating what these rights may be, and the courts will have to decide the matter from case to case, depending on whether the issue is the management of the child's property, consent to medical treatment, or representing the child as claimant or defendant in a civil case in court.[15] The validity of a minor's contract does not depend on whether a statutory representative consented to it, but basically on whether or not it is for the minor's benefit.[16] A minor who owns land or other property needs someone else to manage and dispose of it, but this need not be a parent as statutory representative.

---

[12] It has long been recognised in France that *mandat et représentation* were to be distinguished. See, for example, F Terré, P Simler, and Y Lequette, *Droit civil, Les obligations* (11th edn, 2013) no. 173ff; M Mekki, Mandat, in Juris-classeur civil art. 1984–1990 *Code civil* (2009) Fasc. 10 no. 5 und 11. It is only in the course of the recent reform of the French law of obligations that a new section on *répresentation* was introduced by arts. 1153–1161 *Code civil*.

[13] See the remarks of Müller-Freienfels (n 11) 166ff.

[14] Unlike in France (art. 389 *Code civil*), eg, or Germany (§ 1629 BGB).

[15] On this, see S Cretney, J Masson, and R Bailey-Harris, *Principles of Family Law* (7th edn, 2003) no. 18-001.

[16] See GH Treitel, *The Law of Contract* (13th edn, by E Peel, 2011) no. 12-001ff.

Under the Common Law, people who want to give property to a child or leave it by testamentary disposition generally do it by transferring the property to a trustee. This trustee acquires the legal title and the power to manage and dispose of the assets, with the child being the equitable owner whose only claim is to the proceeds of the property in accordance with the instructions of the testator or donor.[17] If children are involved in litigation—perhaps against the trustee who has failed to hand over the trust proceeds or has otherwise misbehaved—they are usually represented by their parents, not by reason of their being statutory representatives but because the court nominates them for this purpose as the child's 'next friend' (or 'guardian *ad litem*' if the child is being sued) if this seems the right thing to do in the circumstances of the case.[18]

C. Grant, Extent, and Termination of Authority or the Power to Represent

In this section, we shall ask how a power of representation or authority to act for another is granted (see sections I–III below) and inquire about its possible scope (sections IV–V) and its termination (sections VI–VII). It must be remembered throughout that in continental systems the power of representation (*Vertretungsmacht, pouvoir de représentation, potere di rappresentanza*) refers to the situation where one person is empowered to create rights and obligations for another only when he or she is acting in the name of that other. On the other hand, when one speaks of an agent having authority from the principal in the Common Law, this means that the agent may act on behalf of the principal whether or not he discloses that he is acting as agent.

I. Grant

The power to act as agent or representative is normally granted by means of an appropriate declaration by the principal; in Germany the power is called *Vollmacht* (see § 166(2) BGB). In England, agreement between principal and agent is required. In continental legal systems, the agreement of the agent is also almost always present in practice, though not required by law and not always express.[19] Even a minor may be granted the power to act as agent, provided he or she is of sound mind; this is stated explicitly in many systems,[20] and is accepted in the absence of any statutory provision.[21]

---

[17] If, as often happens, the parents are nominated trustees, they manage the property not as a child's statutory representatives but as owners of the legal title in their own name but in trust for the child.

[18] See Rules of the Supreme Court, Order 80 rule 2(1).

[19] Under § 167(1) BGB and art. 217 Greek Civil Code, the power of agency is conferred when the appropriate declaration of the principal reaches the agent; whether the power exists if the agent then disclaims the power is a purely theoretical question.

[20] § 165 BGB; art. 3:63(1) BW; art. 1389 *Codice civile*; art. 213 Greek Civil Code; art. 263 Portuguese Civil Code; art. 100 Polish Civil Code. Article 1716 Spanish Civil Code provides that a minor may be an agent, from which it is inferred that a contract negotiated by the minor in the name of the principal is also valid. Under art. 1160 *Code civil*, the powers of an agent '*cessent s'il est atteint d'une uncapacité*' It seems to follow that such powers will arise if the principal knew about the agent's minority when he granted them. On the position taken by the French courts before the recent reform of contract law, see Civ. 5 Dec. 1933, D.H. 1934, 49 and Mekki (n 12) Fasc. 20 no. 5.

[21] Fridman (n 7) 59; Treitel (n 16) no. 16-012.

One apparent exception to the proposition that the grant of power to act as agent requires the consent of the parties, if not a valid contract, is what in Germany is called *Außenvollmacht*, where such power is granted by a declaration addressed to the third party with whom the negotiations are to take place.[22] One should not make too much of this, however, for even though the agent may acquire this power without knowledge of this, it cannot actually act as agent and so create rights and liabilities in the principal until it knows about and accepts the power.

II. Implied grant

The power to act as agent is often made by an express verbal or written declaration by the principal. But such declaration is not necessary. It is enough if the facts allow one to infer with sufficient certitude that the principal intended to confer such authority. In such cases one speaks of implied authority, or says that the grant of the power to act as agent is implicit in the principal's conduct.[23]

When the owner of a business appoints a manager, or a developer appoints an architect to oversee its building plans, they are empowered to act as agents even if nothing is said about the subject. Another question is what the scope of such power may be (to be discussed below). Furthermore, where the power has been conferred expressly it may be inferred from the circumstances that the manager was to have authority to enter transactions other than those actually mentioned.[24]

Everyone agrees on one very important matter: the appointment of a person to a particular position which cannot be properly performed without entering into certain types of transaction automatically confers authority to act as agent in such transactions. As s. 10(2) of the Swedish Contract Law states, a person who 'as employee or otherwise by contract with another accepts a position which by law or usage carries the legal power to act in the name of another ... is treated as empowered to enter transactions within the scope of such power'. Several jurisdictions have provisions which attach such powers to particular positions: the German Commercial Code refers to the 'manager of a shop or open warehouse',[25] the Italian *Codice civile* to the *institore* or business manager,[26] and the Swiss Law of Obligations to a person appointed 'either to run a whole business or certain parts of a business'.[27] The same is true in English law, for 'every agent has implied authority to do everything

---

[22] As in § 167 BGB; art. 33(3) OR; art. 217(1) Greek Civil Code.

[23] This is express in art. 3:61(1) BW. See also BG 15 May 1973, BGE 99 II 39, 41; Civ. 27 Mar. 1979, Bull. cass. 1979.I. no. 102. See also art. 9(1) Geneva Convention (n 8).

[24] See Fridman (n 7) 69: 'Every agent has implied authority to do everything necessary for, and ordinarily incidental to, carrying out his express authority according to the usual way in which such authority is executed.' To the same effect are art. 1155(2) *Code civil*, art. 1708(1) *Codice civile* and art. 9(2) of the Geneva Convention (n 8): 'The agent has authority to perform all acts necessary in the circumstances to achieve the purposes for which the authorisation was given.'

[25] § 56 HGB. See too § 1030 ABGB; art. 97 Polish Civil Code.   [26] Article 2204 *Codice civile*.

[27] Article 462 OR; § 54 HGB.

necessary for, and incidental to carrying out his express authority according to the usual way in which such authority is executed'.[28]

III. Formalities

Although generally the grant of authority to an agent may be effected without any special formality—in principle it can even be done verbally—important exceptions are to be found in all systems.

Laws often lay down that for specified types of transaction the agent's authority must have been granted in a particular form. For example, under art. 493(6) of the Swiss Law of Obligations, an agent's 'power to give a guarantee' requires the same form as the guarantee itself—it must be in writing and state in figures the maximum sum guaranteed.[29] In England, an agent's authority must be in writing in order to create or dispose of an interest in land on behalf of the principal.[30] Occasionally, written form is required for the grant of a general authority.[31]

Of particular interest are formal requirements laid down in general terms. Thus art. 1985 *Code civil* renders art. 1359 (formerly art. 1341) applicable to verbal contacts of agency (including the grant of authority) so that if the transaction exceeds €1,500 in value, the evidence of witnesses is inadmissible and a document is required, though not necessarily a notarial one. It is true that this rule does not apply between merchants, and that its scope has been considerably limited in other ways (see above, pages 78f.), but it nevertheless constitutes a powerful incentive to put grants of authority into writing.

Many systems provide that the grant of authority must be in the form required for the transaction which the agent is to effect.[32] In Germany, courts have reached the same conclusion even though § 167(2) BGB provides otherwise by stating that for an effective grant of authority 'the declaration is not required to be in the form laid down for the legal transaction to which the authority relates'. Notwithstanding this clear wording, the courts insist that if the grant of authority exposes the principal to an obligation similar to that which would arise under the main transaction, the formalities required for the transaction entered into must also be observed in the grant of authority to enter into it. This is especially the case if the purpose of the formality is to warn of the obligation being undertaken or, *a fortiori*, to ensure the involvement of an independent legal expert (such as a notary) who can instruct on its legal consequences. Thus a notarial act under § 311b BGB is required for the grant of a power to conclude a contract of sale or purchase of landed property if the grant is irrevocable and the agent

---

[28] Fridman (n 7) 69. See also art. 3:201(2) PECL; art. 2.2.2(2) PICC; art. II.-6:104(2) DCFR.

[29] This does not apply to a 'general power whose extent is determined by law' such as that of a *Prokurist* or a *Handlungsbevollmächtigter*: BG 8 Feb. 1955, BGE 81 II 60, 62.

[30] Law of Property Act 1925, ss. 53(1), 54. Compare § 27(2) Swedish Contract Law, whereby the authority to sell or charge land must be in the form required for such transactions.

[31] Article 99(2) Polish Civil Code.

[32] Article 1392 *Codice civile*; art. 217(2) Greek Civil Code; art. 262(2) Portuguese Civil Code; art. 99(2) Polish Civil Code. There is no such general rule in the BW, but see art. 3:260(3) BW whereby the grant of authority to create a mortgage requires the same form as the mortgage itself.

is empowered to buy or sell it for itself;³³ the same applies for an irrevocable grant of power to give a guarantee, for which written form is required under § 766 BGB.³⁴ The courts in Austria decide likewise when the purpose of the requisite formality is to ensure that the parties are serious, rather than simply to provide evidence of their agreement.³⁵ The situation is similar in France. If a formality is intended to protect a certain person, where the contract is to be signed by a representative the form requirements must be met by the power issued to that representative.³⁶

IV. Extent

Although there may be a dispute about *whether* any power of representation was granted, more commonly the question is as to its *extent*. Here again, it depends in principle on the expressed intention of the party for whom the agent was to act. If the extent of the power is unclear, the expressed intention will be construed in accordance with general principles. If it is communicated to the agent in person (in Germany, *Innenvollmacht*), the question will be how the agent would reasonably understand it. If the expression is directed to third parties (in Germany, *Außenvollmacht*), their view and that of the business circle to which they belong will be relevant. Similar principles apply to grants of authority in England.³⁷

If this were so without qualification, the extent of an agent's authority could often only be ascertained by asking the principal or construing the grant. This would be most unsatisfactory, especially in commerce, where contracts are generally made through agents rather than with principals personally, and it is particularly undesirable that there should be any doubts about the agent's authority to act. Many systems have accordingly enacted rules that specify which powers attach to holders of certain common trade occupations, often adding that any restrictions on such authority either do not affect those who contract with such persons, or affect them only under certain conditions.

In Germany, Austria, and Switzerland, the *Prokurist* is equipped by statute with extensive powers of representation. A person appointed as *Prokurist* for a company has power to bind it to all contracts of the types in which such a firm engages, apart from selling or charging landed property.³⁸ A person who is appointed as a *Handlungsbevollmächtigter* 'to engage in transactions of a specified type appertaining

---

³³ BGH 23 Feb. 1979, [1979] *NJW* 2306. Swiss law is different: although sales of land must be notarised just as in Germany and for the same reasons (art. 216 OR), authority to enter such a contract needs no form, BG 1 Apr. 1958, BGE 84 II 151, 157; BG 29 May 1973, BGE 99 II 159, 161f. In England, where sales of land must be made in written form, authority to enter them may be given verbally; see Fridman (n 7) 56f. and above, n 30.

³⁴ BGH 29 Feb. 1996, BGHZ 132,119,125.

³⁵ OGH 26 Jan. 1963, [1964] *JBl* 101; OGH 29 Apr. 1970, [1970] *JBl* 423.

³⁶ See Terré, Simler, and Lequette (n 12) no. 110; Mekki (n 12) Fasc. 20 no. 35. Sometimes the formal requirements for issuing a power of attorney are derived from the fact that French law sometimes requires the contract between principal and agent to be in a particular form, such as the contract giving the representative the power to sell land: see Mekki (n 12) Fasc. 20 no. 31. Finally, the written form of the authority may be useful because the proof by witnesses of a merely verbal authority may be excluded (see above, p. 300).

³⁷ See Fridman (n 7) 64ff.   ³⁸ §§ 48ff. HGB (also in effect in Austria); art. 458ff. OR.

to a trade' has power that extends to all the acts which 'engaging in transactions of that type normally entails'.[39] In England, mercantile agents may 'in the ordinary course of business of a mercantile agent' make dispositions of goods in their possession belonging to the principal as if they were 'expressly authorised', even if they are not.[40] Very extensive powers are granted in Germany to partners in a partnership (*Personengesellschaft*), to the managing director of a company with limited liability (*GmbH*), and to the directors of a public corporation (*Aktiengesellschaft*).[41]

In all such cases, the third party can rely on the negotiator having the authority attributed to the agent by law without being affected by any 'internal' limitation put on the agent's statutory authority by the principal—unless the third party was acting 'in bad faith', that is, knew of the limitation or was unaware of it through carelessness.[42] A person who buys or acquires an interest in goods belonging to the principal can rely on the authority of a mercantile agent acting in the ordinary course of business if

> the person taking under the disposition acts in good faith, and has not at the time of the disposition notice that the person making the disposition has not authority to make the same (Factors Act 1889, section 2(1)). It is sometimes laid down that limitations affect the third party only if it was grossly negligent,[43] and often, when the statutory authority is described as illimitable, one has the impression that no limitation could ever affect the third party, even if it was acting in bad faith.[44]

Yet here the courts have imposed limits. The case of *collusion* is clear: even if a transaction falls within the powers of the agent, it is invalid if the agent has colluded with the third party to cause deliberate harm to the principal.[45] It is more difficult when the third party had no actual knowledge that the agent, by concluding the transaction in breach of the principal's instructions, was abusing its authority (consciously or not, and whether or not for personal advantage). In a Swiss case, an agent had been granted in writing an unlimited power to sell a piece of land. Despite a verbal instruction *not* to sell it to a particular person, he proceeded to show that very person his written authority and then sell him the land. The *Bundesgericht* held that the buyer 'could not rely on the written power which he had been shown if, without engaging in anything that can be called collusion, he nevertheless knew, or would have known if taking proper care, that the agent was abusing his authority'.[46] German courts seem

---

[39] § 54 HGB; art. 462 OR; art. 97 Polish Civil Code. See also § 69ff. German Insurance Contracts Act (VVG) as to the extent of the authority of an insurance agent, and § 10(2) Swedish Contract Act on the authority of a person placed in a 'position' by the head of a business (see above, p. 299).

[40] Factors Act 1889, s. 2(1); for details, see Fridman (n 7) 290ff.

[41] See, for example, § 126 HGB, § 35 GmbHG, § 78 AktG.

[42] See, for example, § 54(3) HGB, § 11(1) Swedish Contract Law. Under art. 1156(1) *Code civil*, a transaction concluded by a representative without authority or beyond his or her authority may nonetheless be set up against the principal if the third party 'a *légitimement cru en la réalité des pouvoirs du représentant, notamment en raison du comportement ou des déclarations du représente.*'

[43] For example § 69(2) sent. 2 of the German Law on Insurance Contracts (VVG).

[44] This is laid down as to the *Prokura* (§ 50 HGB) and as to partners and the representative bodies of companies (§§ 126(2) HGB, 37(2) GmbHG, 82 AktG).

[45] BGH 6 May 1999, BGHZ 141, 357; BGH 17 May 1988, [1989] *NJW* 26; Civ. 9 June 1958, Bull.cass. 1958.I. no. 295; Civ. 11 Dec. 1950. Bull.cass. 1950.I. no. 254.

[46] BG 20 Mar. 1951, BGE 77 II 138, 143.

to require rather more than this before they hold a transaction invalid for abuse of authority. If the third party did not actually know of the abuse, the agent's conduct must have been such as was bound to arouse suspicion.[47] They are even stricter when the power abused is illimitable, such as that of the *Prokurist* or the managing director of a GmbH. Here the agent must have acted *deliberately to the disadvantage* of the principal, though it suffices, incongruously enough, that 'the third party should have realised this if he had shown the requisite care'.[48]

Other systems have no special rules for abuse of authority, doubtless because they do not make the distinction so sharply drawn in Germany between the agent's powers *vis-à-vis* third parties and its duties towards the principal. It is true that in France a transaction is invalid where the agent has deliberately gone against the interests of its principal, but it was said to be invalid not because an existing power was abused, but because the agent had no *mandat* and consequently no power to enter into such a transaction.[49] There is now a special rule in art. 1157 *Code civil* under which the principal may invoke the invalidity of any transaction concluded by an abuse of the agent's authority if the third party was aware of the abuse or could not have been unaware of it.

V. Self-dealing by agent

The benefits of engaging an agent are offset by one major drawback, namely the risk that it may use the power for its own benefit rather than to advance the interests of the principal, as instructed. Rules to invalidate such self-serving transactions are therefore to be found in all systems.

In England, an agent owes the principal a comprehensive fiduciary duty, which means 'that the agent must not let his own interests conflict with the obligations he owes to the principal'.[50] Accordingly, the principal may disavow any transaction made by the agent with itself, with a nominee, with a relative, with itself in his capacity as agent for someone else, or under other circumstances in which a conflict may exist between its own interests and those of its principal. The only exception is when the agent has kept the principal fully informed about the proposed transaction, and has obtained agreement; this is required even if the transaction is actually beneficial to the principal, or thought by the agent to be so.[51]

---

[47] BGH 25 Oct. 1994, BGHZ 127, 239; BGH 29 June 1999, [1999] *NJW* 2883.
[48] So held in BGH 25 Mar. 1968, BGHZ 50, 112 (*Prokura*); but see BGH 5 Dec. 1983, [1984] *NJW* 1461 (managing director of a GmbH).
[49] See Req. 14 Apr. 1908, DP 1908.1.344; Civ. 29 Nov. 1972, Bull.cass. 1972.III. no. 647; Civ. 9 June 1958, Bull.cass. 1958.I. no. 295.
[50] Fridman (n 7) 175. See in detail S Festner, *Interessenkonflikte im deutschen und englischen Vertretungsrecht* (2006).
[51] The details are in Fridman (n 7) 175ff; Treitel (n 16) no. 16-095ff. The problem of a conflict of interest is addressed in detail in art. 3:205 PECL; art. 2.2.7 PICC; art. II.-6:109 DCFR. The principal may avoid a contract concluded by an agent if the third party knew or could not have been unaware of the conflict between the agent's and the principal's interest. Such a conflict of interest is presumed where the agent also acted as agent for the third party, or concluded the contract with itself in its personal capacity. The principal cannot avoid the contract if it knew or should have known about the agent's actions, or if the agent had told the principal about the transaction and the principal failed to object within a reasonable time.

In most continental legal systems, there are legal provisions which invalidate transactions that the agent makes 'in the name of the party represented with himself in his own name or as representing some third party'.[52] This does not apply where the principal has given consent to the transaction or, as under art. 1395 *Codice civile*, 'the content of the contract is such that there is no possibility of a conflict of interest'[53] or, as the Swiss courts hold, 'the transaction by its nature excludes the risk of prejudice to the party represented'.[54] These rules make the validity of the transaction in each case turn on the court's decision whether or not there was a conflict of interest. By contrast, § 181 BGB invalidates transactions whenever the agent has contracted with itself (or with itself as agent for another). The courts agree that the policy of § 181 BGB is to prevent 'the representation by one and the same person of different conflicting interests ... for such self-dealing always involves a risk of conflict of interest and of harm to one or other party'.[55] This is not what § 181 BGB actually says, for the draftsmen wanted to avoid introducing the unclear idea of 'conflict of interest' with the attendant lack of legal certainty. In the event, the courts have constantly been occupied with the question of the validity of a contract which falls within the wording of § 181 BGB but excludes the possibility of any conflict of interest,[56] as well as with the converse question of whether a contract may not be invalid for conflict of interest although it does not fall within the wording of § 181 BGB.[57]

Certain types of intermediary, such as the *Kommissionär* (commission agent) in Germany, typically act on behalf of the principal in their own name rather than in that of the principal. Continental systems require special rules for this. Here, too, there is a danger of a conflict of interest, especially when the commission agent buys goods it is supposed to be selling for the principal, or supplies the goods it is supposed to be buying. Such transactions are valid only in very exceptional cases, such as where the commission agent can prove that the price charged or credited to the principal was the current market price.[58]

---

[52] § 181 BGB; art. 1395 *Codice civile*; art. 235 Greek Civil Code; art. 108 Polish Civil Code. In France, art. 1156 *Code civil* (see above, n 42) would apply if it is assumed that an agent acting in a conflict is acting '*sans pouvoir ou au delà de ses pouvoirs*'. There are also special provisions, such as art. 1596 *Code civil*, which provides for the invalidity of a contract made at a public auction whereby an agent personally or through a nominee buys property which he was to sell on behalf of his principal. The courts apply this by analogy to purchases outside public auctions. See Paris 12 Nov. 1964, D. 1965, 415; Civ. 27 Jan. 1987, Bull. cass. 1987.I. no. 32 and Terré, Simler, and Lequette (n 12) no. 182.

[53] Much the same are art. 3:68 BW; art. 108 Polish Civil Code.

[54] BG 30 Sept. 1963, BGE 89 II 321, 326. See also OGH 16 Sept. 1971, SZ 44 no. 141; OGH 9 Apr. 1981, SZ 54 no. 57.

[55] BGH 19 Apr. 1971, BGHZ 56, 97, 101.

[56] For example, where the sole proprietor of a GmbH enters into a transaction with himself. On the validity of such a contract, see BGH 19 Apr. 1971 (n 55). For more detail, see H Kötz, *Vertragsrecht* (2nd edn, 2012) mn. 455ff.

[57] In one case, an agent provided security for his personal debt by giving a guarantee in the name of the principal, and the Reichsgericht held that § 181 BGB was not applicable since the agent had contracted not with himself, but with his creditor (RG 14 June 1909, RGZ 71, 219, 220). This narrow view only avoids being damaging because the principal can avoid liability under the guarantee on the ground that the agent has abused its authority, provided it can prove that the creditor knew of the abuse or could hardly avoid suspecting it.

[58] See, for example, § 400ff. HGB; art. 436ff. OR; § 40ff. Swedish Law on Mercantile Agents of 18 Apr. 1914 (adopted in essence by Denmark and Norway); art. 1735 *Codice civile*; arts. 7:409 and 410 BW. France

VI. Termination

The power to make contracts for a principal ends when the principal revokes the power, the agent disavows it, or the period for which it was granted has expired. It also ends, subject to contrary provision, when the underlying contract comes to an end, whether by rescission, cancellation, lapse of time, discharge through performance, or collapse of the basis of the transaction.[59] So too in England, when it concerns the ending of authority of an agent.[60] The power of agency also normally ends on the death or incapacity of the agent. The same is true where the principal dies or becomes incapacitated,[61] unless the principal grants an authority to outlast death, as quite often happens. Where there is no such agreement, there is often a legislative provision to the effect that the power remains valid as regards urgent business until revoked by the heirs. Agency is also ended by the bankruptcy of the principal.[62]

Contracts made by an agent with a third party after the expiry of its power of agency generally have no effect on the principal, unless the principal has by words or conduct induced the third party to believe that the power continued to exist. This happens, for example, when at the end of the agency the principal fails to demand the return of the document evidencing the grant of power, thus creating the danger that the agent will continue to proffer the document and make further contracts.[63] In all such cases, the third party's reliance on the survival of the agency is protected until it learns of its expiry, whether from the principal or in some other way.[64] The same rule applies in England.[65]

VII. Revocability

According to art. 2004 *Code civil*, the principal may terminate the mandate, and consequently the power to act as agent, at any time, '*quand bon lui semble*'. There is

---

has no special statutory provision, but the courts have developed a similar rule: see G Ripert, R Roblot, P Delebecque, and M Germain, *Traité de droit commercial* vol. II (15th edn, 1996) no. 2647ff.

[59] § 168 BGB; art. 35 Swiss Law of Obligations; § 1020f. ABGB; art. 2003 *Code civil*; art. 3:72 BW; art. 218, 222 Greek Civil Code; art. 1732 Spanish Civil Code; art. 265 Portuguese Civil Code.

[60] See Fridman (n 7) 389ff.

[61] For details, see Fridman (n 7) 406ff; § 168, 672, 675 BGB; § 1022, 1025 ABGB; art. 2003 *Code civil*; art. 35 OR; art. 3:72f. BW; § 21f. Swedish Contract Law; art. 222 Greek Civil Code; art. 101(2) Polish Civil Code.

[62] Fridman (n 7) 398ff; § 115ff. InsO; § 1024 ABGB; art. 35 OR; art. 3:72 BW; § 24 Swedish Contract Law.

[63] Statutes often specify that at the end of the agency the principal may demand the return of the document or, if need be, have it officially declared invalid; see § 175f. BGB; § 16f. Swedish Contract Law; art. 36 OR; art. 3:75 BW; art. 2004 *Code civil*; art. 1397 *Codice civile*; art. 227 Greek Civil Code; art. 267 Portuguese Civil Code; art. 102 Polish Civil Code.

[64] See §§ 170–173 BGB; art. 34(3) OR and BG 15 May 1973, BGE 99 II 31, 45; § 1026 ABGB; §§ 12–16, 19f. Swedish Contract Law; art. 2005 *Code civil*; art. 1396 *Codice civile*; art. 224 Greek Civil Code; art. 266 Portuguese Civil Code. Likewise art. 19 Geneva Convention (n 8). Under art. 3:209 PECL; art. 2.2.10 PICC; art. II.-6:112 DCFR an agent's authority continues until the third party knew or ought to have known that it has been brought to an end.

[65] See *Drew v. Nunn* (1879) 40 LT 671: 'If the agent has been held out as having authority to the third person, and the latter acts with the agent before he has received any notice of the authority having ceased, the principal is still bound upon the ground that he made representations upon which the third party had a right to act, and cannot retract from the consequences of those representations' (Brett LJ at 673). See the details in Fridman (n 7) 402ff.

good sense in such a rule. The principal engages the agent in order to extend its range of activity; when it no longer has any such interest, it should be free to terminate the agency. Another issue is whether the agency is made permanent if the principal renounces his right to revoke, or makes it irrevocable in writing. One consideration is that if an agency—especially one with wide powers—is made irrevocable, it puts the principal into long-term dependence on the agent. That is doubtless why art. 34(2) OR provides that 'any advance waiver of this right by the principal is void'.

This surely goes too far. All other European systems accept that grants of the power of representation may be irrevocable, and reduce the inherent risk by providing that where a power is stated to be irrevocable, the principal may still revoke it if there is good reason, *'wichtiger Grund',*[66] a *'cause légitime reconnue en justice',*[67] a *'justa causa',*[68] or *'gewichtige redenen'.*[69] It is generally a good ground for revocation that the agent has abused its authority, broken its contract, or otherwise betrayed the trust reposed in it.

A power of agency may sometimes be treated as irrevocable although not expressly so described. It is important to know when this is. Take the case of a seller, which cannot unilaterally relieve itself of the contractual obligation to transfer the goods. The same must be true when instead of transferring the goods under the contract of sale, the seller grants the buyer a power to dispose of them to a third party or even to acquire them itself by 'self-dealing'. Here the agent's special contractual right and interest should render the grant of power irrevocable.

The various legal systems in Europe agree in substance, but differ in wording. In England, it is said that an authority cannot be revoked where it is 'coupled with an interest held by the agent'.[70] Article 3:74(1) BW provides that a grant of agency may be irrevocable when the transaction envisaged is 'in the interest of the representative or a third party'.[71] When art. 218 Greek Civil Code states that a power 'exclusively in the interests of the principal' is always revocable,[72] we may infer *e contrario* that it may be irrevocable if it serves the interests of the agent as well. In France, where the distinction between the grant of agency and the underlying contract is not sharply drawn, the discussion centres on the question whether, contrary to art. 2004 *Code civil*, the *mandat* is irrevocable. The courts regularly hold that a *mandat d'intérêt commun*, where the transaction is also in the interests of the agent, is always irrevocable. The mere fact that the agent could earn a fee is not enough for this purpose. But it is different in the case of a commercial agent who has invested heavily in reliance on the continuation of the agency, setting up a distribution system and creating a network of customers.[73]

---

[66] BGH 12 May 1969, [1969] *WM* 1009; BGH 8 Feb. 1985, [1985] *WM* 646.
[67] Com. 10 Nov. 1959, *JCP* 1960.II.11509; Com. 20 May 1969, Bull.cass. 1969.IV. no. 186.
[68] Article 265(3) Portuguese Civil Code. [69] Article 3:74(4) BW.
[70] See Treitel (n 16) no. 16-110ff; Fridman (n 7) 389f.
[71] Likewise art. 1723(2) *Codice civile* and art. 265(3) Portuguese Civil Code. In Germany, the courts require a 'particular interest of the agent in the transaction to be executed' before the grant of agency will be held irrevocable: see, eg, BGH 8 Feb. 1985 (n 66); BGH 13 May 1971, [1971] *WM* 956.
[72] So also BGH 13 May 1971 (n 71).
[73] For details, see Mekki (n 12) Fasc. 10 no. 70ff. The mere fact that the agent could earn a fee is not enough for this purpose. See Civ. 11 June 1969, Bull.cass. 1969.I. no. 223; likewise Treitel (n 16) no. 16-111; Fridman (n 7) 390 and RG 25 Sept. 1926, [1929] *JW* 1139. It is otherwise when the agent's interest in the transaction is 'equal' to that of the principal, the gain to be split between them (RG, ibid.).

Then revocation of the *mandat* and its associated power of agency are permissible, but the principal will have to pay the agent damages suffered due to the revocation.[74]

D. Dealing without Authority

Transactions concluded by an agent or representative with no authority to do so generate no rights or liabilities in the principal. The principal can, however, adopt or ratify such a transaction with the same effect as if the agent had originally been authorised (section I below). Even in the absence of such ratification, there may be special reasons for preventing the principal from raising the defence of the agent's lack of authority (section II below). If not, the question arises whether the third party can look to the supposed agent (section III below).[75]

I. Ratification

It is accepted throughout Europe that a transaction entered into by a representative without authority (*falsus procurator*) can be ratified by the party represented.[76] This applies whether the representative had no authority at all, or simply exceeded the authority it had. Ratification need not be express: it may be effected by '*tous actes, faits et circonstances qui manifestent de la part du mandant la volonté certaine de ratifier*'.[77]

These rules also apply in England where an agent lacks the requisite authority to conclude the transaction,[78] provided that he made it clear that it was acting 'as agent' so that the third party was aware that it was acting for a particular identifiable principal. If, failing this, the third party supposed the agent to be acting on its own account although was actually acting for the principal (undisclosed agency), the undisclosed principal cannot ratify.[79]

A transaction entered into by a *falsus procurator* starts off in a state of ambivalence, since it is not clear whether or not it will be ratified. The third party may curtail the period of ambivalence by setting a time within which the person for whom the *falsus procurator* was acting must ratify the transaction, if it is to do so at all.[80] Even if no such time is set, the party represented must decide within a reasonable period, for otherwise it could speculate on market movements at the expense of the third party.

---

[74] Civ. 11 June 1969 (n 73); Civ. 17 March 1987, Bull.cass. 1987.I. no. 94; Com. 17 May 1989, Bull.cass. 1989.IV. no. 157. See Mekki (n 12) Fasc. 10 no. 70ff.

[75] See in detail D Busch and LJ Macgregor (eds), *The Unauthorized Agent, Perspectives from European and Comparative Law* (2009).

[76] § 177(1) BGB; art. 38(1) OR; § 1016 ABGB; art. 3:69(1) BW; art. 1156(3) *Code civil*; art. 1399(1) *Codice civile*; art. 229 Greek Civil Code; art. 1259(2) Spanish Civil Code; art. 268(1) Portuguese Civil Code; art. 103 Polish Civil Code. Compare art. 15(1) Geneva Convention (n 8) and art. 3:207 PECL; art. 2.2.9 PICC; art. II.-6:111 DCFR.

[77] Civ. 2 Dec. 1935, D.H.1936, 52.   [78] See Fridman (n 7) 84ff; Treitel (n 16) no. 16-042ff.

[79] *Keighley, Maxstead & Co. v. Durant* [1901] AC 240, on which see Fridman (n 7) 89ff; Treitel (n 16) no. 16-045.

[80] See § 177(2) BGB; art. 38(2) OR; art. 3:69(4) BW; art. 1399(4) *Codice civile*; art. 229 sent. 2 Greek Civil Code; art. 268(3) Portuguese Civil Code; art. 103(2) Polish Civil Code. Under art. 1158 *Code civil*, the third party may request the principal in writing '*dans un élai qu'il fixe et qui doit être raisonnable, que le représentant est habilité à conclure cet acte*'.

If the third party was unaware of the agent's lack of authority, it can withdraw from the contract at any time until ratification takes place.[81] Here English law differs. In *Bolton Partners* v. *Lambert*,[82] an agent had purchased land on behalf of his principal. When it appeared that the agent had acted without authority, the seller withdrew from the contract. The principal then ratified the authority, and the court held the contract good: the principal's ratification had retroactive effect and validated *ab initio* the contract made by the agent.[83]

This ruling is rather unsatisfactory. It is also incongruous, for elsewhere in English law ratification is not made retroactive to the time of the transaction. Suppose, for example, that an agent buys property without authority and then a third party acquires a conflicting interest in the property from the seller: subsequent ratification does not affect the third party's right.[84] Again, suppose that an offer which has to be accepted within a certain period is accepted in time by a *falsus procurator* and then ratified out of time by the principal; here it is agreed that there is no contract.[85]

II. Apparent or ostensible authority

The third party normally has no claims against the principal if the agent with whom it effected a transaction had no authority. But as we have seen, such a claim does lie if the principal ratifies what the intermediary has done, or if the principal has created a situation in which the agent appeared to have authority and the third party concluded the transaction with the agent in justified reliance on such appearance. In this case, if the third party can show that the agent had ostensible or apparent authority (*Anscheinsvollmacht, mandat apparent*), the principal is liable as if it had actually granted the authority in question.

1. Giving the appearance of authority

The first requirement is that the principal has created by speech or conduct a situation in which the third party was justified in supposing that the apparent agent was empowered to act as the principal's representative in transacting as it did. Such an appearance can be created if the principal equipped the intermediary with a document evidencing the agency without making it sufficiently clear that it was subject to limitations, or if the principal was aware that the intermediary was dealing with third parties and did not intervene when it could have done so. Here the principal is liable

---

[81] § 178 BGB; art. 3:69(3) BW; art. 1399(2) *Codice civile*; art. 230 Greek Civil Code; art. 1259(2) Spanish Civil Code; art. 268(4) Portuguese Civil Code. See also art. 15(2) Geneva Convention (n 8).

[82] (1889) 41 Ch.D. 295.

[83] The decision has been much criticised, and has been severely restricted by subsequent case law. Certainly the rule does not apply if the agent disclosed its deficient authority and the transaction was made 'subject to ratification'. See *Watson* v. *Davies* [1931] 1 Ch. 455 and the extensive treatment by Fridman (n 7) 97ff; Treitel (n 16) no. 16-050ff.

[84] Fridman (n 7) 97f. Likewise § 177(1), 184(2) BGB; art. 1399 *Codice civile*; art. 268(2) Portuguese Civil Code.

[85] Civ. 18 Apr. 1934, *Gaz Pal* 1934.1.970; BGH 13 July 1973, [1973] *NJW* 1789; *Dibbins* v. *Dibbins* [1896] 2 Ch. 348.

to the third party who dealt with the supposed agent on the faith of appearances.[86] The same is true when the principal has placed the intermediary in a position which by trade custom or general practice entails some power of agency. Here, too, the principal is barred from arguing against the third party that in fact he gave the intermediary less than the normal power, or none at all. The final case of apparent authority is where the third party was aware that authority had been granted, but not aware that it was no longer in force, and justifiably relied on its continuing in force.[87]

For many years, the French courts attributed the liability which arose from *mandat apparent* to a fault on the part of the principal, and held that the person who intentionally or carelessly permitted the continued appearance of authority when there was no underlying *mandat* was liable in tort for the consequent harm. The *Cour de cassation* then decided that liability under a *mandat apparent* could arise even if there was no culpable behaviour on the part of the defendant, provided that the third party had acted in justifiable reliance on the existence of a sufficient power of agency, with reliance being justifiable when the circumstances were such that the third party need make no further inquiries.[88] This has now been laid down in art. 1156 *Code civil*, which provides that the principal will be bound by the agent's action if the third party 'legitimately believed' in the existence of a power of agency on the basis of the principal's behaviour or statements. The cases say that the principal must not be '*complètement étranger à l'apparence alléguée*', and have held that there is no *mandat apparent* when a negotiable instrument was signed by a *falsus procurator* who had no position in the defendant's business and of whose existence the defendant was unaware.[89]

In the English cases also, 'apparent authority' is held to exist only where the principal has put the agent into a position 'which in the outside world is generally regarded as carrying authority to enter into transactions of the kind in question'.[90] Sometimes, indeed, it is said that the apparent authority of the agent must be the principal's fault,

---

[86] See Ranieri (n 11) 500. German and Swiss law have a word for this—*Duldungsvollmacht*, agency by acquiescence—while the French speak of *mandat apparent* in this case also. See BGH 4 July 1966, [1966] *NJW* 1915 (a wife who left her business in the hands of her husband was liable for the business debts he incurred); BGH 15 Dec. 1955, [1956] *NJW* 460; BG 19 Jan. 1993, BGE 119 II 23; BG 16 March 1995, BGE 121 III 69; BG 21 Mar. 1995, BGE 121 III 176; Civ. 18 Jan. 1977, Bull.cass. 1977.III. no. 26; Civ. 15 Mar. 1984, Bull.cass. 1984.IV. no. 106. English courts also regard it as a case of apparent authority when 'the agent has had a course of dealing with a particular contractor and the principal has acquiesced in this course of dealing and honoured transactions arising out of it' (*Armagas Ltd.* v. *Mundogas S.A.* [1986] 2 All ER 385, 389ff. per Lord Keith). See Fridman (n 7) 111ff; Treitel (n 16) no. 16-020ff. Such instances of acquiescence as well as the other instances given here are sometimes treated not as examples of apparent authority but of real authority, conferred by an 'implied' grant or through conduct by the principal. The boundaries between *Duldungsvollmacht* and *Anscheinsvollmacht*, like those between *mandat apparent* and *mandat tacite* or *implied authority* and *apparent authority* are fluid. It is really a question of juristic taste whether or not one treats it as a pure fiction to say that particular conduct on the part of the principal falls within an implied grant of authority: the critical question in all cases is how a reasonable and bona fide third party would and must reasonably interpret the situation as presented.

[87] See above, n 65.

[88] Ass.plén. 13 Dec. 1962, D. 1963, 277, n. J Calais-Auloy = *JCP* 1963.II.13105, n. P Esmein. See for detail Mekki (n 12) Fasc. 50 no. 70ff.

[89] Com. 12 Dec. 1973, Bull.cass. 1973.IV. no. 361; Com. 27 May 1976, D.S. 1977, 421, n. JP Arrighi. See also J Kleinschmidt, 'Stellvertretung in Deutschland und Frankreich, Perspektiven für eine Rechtsvereinheitlichung' (2001) 9 *ZEuP* 697, 723ff.

[90] *Armagas Ltd.* v. *Mundogas S.A.* (n 86) at 389, per Lord Keith.

whether intentional or negligent.[91] German courts also require that the principal knew or ought to have known of the agent's unauthorised dealings, and that a reasonable person in the principal's place would have corrected the situation.[92] This means only that the principal must or should have been aware of the circumstances that gave rise to the appearance of the apparent power or authority, and not that the principal can escape liability by proving that it was not at fault in not realising that there was a risk of harm to third parties.

2. Justifiable reliance by the third party

Necessary though it is that the principal has caused the appearance of authority, this is not sufficient to render it liable. In addition, the third party must have relied on that appearance, the reliance must have been justifiable, and caused the third party to enter the transaction.[93] There is accordingly no liability when the third party saw through the appearances and realised the truth of the matter. If it was mistaken, the question is whether a reasonable person in the circumstances would have believed in the existence of authority without further inquiry, or would have asked to see the agency agreement or checked with the supposed principal. Whether such precautions are indicated in a particular case may depend on many factors: customary practice in the relevant branch of commerce; whether the deal had to be closed quickly; whether it was a perfectly ordinary transaction or one involving much money; whether or not the third party was experienced in business; how time-consuming and complicated inquiries would be; how great the risk to be allayed by such inquiries; and whether the supposed agent had such an obvious interest in the transaction that the third party's suspicions should have been aroused.

The reason that all courts take the same factors into account is that they are all asking the same question, namely whether the risk inherent in having business done through intermediaries is one which should be borne by the principal or the third party. Legal systems tend to regulate the matter so that liability (and consequently an incentive to avoid it) is imposed on the party who could avoid the risk at least expense. That is why a comparison is made between the precautions that the principal would need to take in order to avoid the appearance of authority, and the precautions that the third party would have to take in order to ascertain the truth of the matter. One could hazard a guess that the reason the courts in Europe reach very similar conclusions is because, consciously or intuitively, they engage in this comparison and decide for or against apparent authority on the basis of the results.

---

[91] See Fridman (n 7) 118. Treitel (n 16) no. 16-024 mentions no such requirement.
[92] BGH 12 Feb. 1952, BGHZ 5, 111, 116; BGH 12 Mar. 1981, [1981] *NJW* 1727, 1728.
[93] There is an excellent formula for this in the BW: under art. 3:61(2) the principal cannot invoke absence of authority when '[the third party] assumed and in the given circumstances reasonably could have assumed on the basis of a statement or the behaviour of [the principal] that an adequate authority for representation was granted'. See on this HR 27 Nov. 1992, [1993] *Ned Jur* 287. A similar rule may be found in art. 14(2) of the Geneva Convention (n 8). According to art. 3:201(3) PECL, a person is to be treated as having been granted authority 'if the person's statements or conduct induce the third party reasonably and in good faith to believe that the apparent agent has been granted authority for the act performed by it'. Similarly art. 2.2.5(2) PICC; art.II.-6:103(3) DCFR; art. 61 CEC.

III. Liability of the supposed agent

When a party negotiating a deal makes it clear that it is acting as agent or representative, it thereby asserts or implies that it has the appropriate authority to bind the principal. If this is not so, the party is liable to the counterparty in damages, unless the counterparty was or could have been aware of the lack of authority. While there is agreement on the principle, there is some variation in detail.

In English law, the liability of the intermediary is particularly strict, for every agent gives the third party an 'implied warranty of authority'. Unless the third party knew or should have realised that the intermediary had no authority or was exceeding that authority, it can sue the agent for damages for breach of warranty. This liability attaches to the agent even if it was entirely free from fault in supposing that it had the requisite authority.[94] Indeed, the agent must even meet the third party's performance interest, and pay monetary damages to the third party to put it in the position it would have been in had the supposed authority been present. This liability is thought by many commentators to be too strict, and they suggest that perhaps the warranty should be reduced to a duty that the agent take care to verify the agent's authority.[95]

Most continental systems are less severe, and make the agent liable for the third party's performance interest only when the agent was actually aware of the lack of authority. If the agent erroneously supposed it had such authority, it is liable only for reliance damages—it must meet the expenditure incurred by the third party in the belief in the existence of a valid contract, or the loss of the chance of making another favourable contract in lieu.[96] Swiss law has a flexible solution. According to art. 39 OR, the purported agent is liable only for the third party's reliance interest, but 'on grounds of equity' it can be made liable in damages up to the performance interest if at fault in supposing itself authorised.[97]

There are no special provisions in the French Civil Code on the liability of an agent that exceeds its authority. The third party's claim for damages will therefore be based on the agent's tort under art. 1240 (formerly art. 1382) *Code civil*. This requires some fault on the agent's part, but some cases have held that the agent impliedly guaranteed its authority.[98]

The purported agent will often escape liability even where the third party was not at fault in believing the asserted authority to be present, for if there was apparent authority the third party can sue the principal and this excludes the liability of the purported agent.[99]

---

[94] *Collen* v. *Wright* (1857) 120 Eng.Rep. 241; *Yonge* v. *Toynbee* [1910] 1 KB 215. Equally strict is art. 16 of the Geneva Convention (n 8); art. 3:204 PECL; art. 2.2.6 PICC; art. II.-6:107(2) and (3) DCFR; and probably § 25 Swedish Contract Law and art. 3:70 BW.

[95] See Treitel (n 16) no. 16-077.

[96] This liability attaches even if the agent was free from fault in supposing he had authority; see § 179 BGB; OGH 19 Nov. 1975, [1978] *JBl.* 32, 35; art. 1398 *Codice civile*; art. 231 Greek Civil Code; art. 103(3) Polish Civil Code.

[97] See BG 10 June 1980, BGE 106 II 131, 132.   [98] Dijon 19 May 1931, D.H. 1983, 405.

[99] See *Rainbow* v. *Hawkins* [1904] 2 KB 322; BGH 20 Jan. 1983, BGHZ 86, 273.

E. The Effects of Agency

If a representative or agent negotiates a deal within the power or authority conferred by the principal, its legal effects largely depend on whether or not the agency was disclosed. The difference is widely recognised, and is referred to using terms such as disclosed agency or undisclosed agency, *direkte Stellvertretung* or *indirekte Stellvertretung*, *représentation parfait*, or *représentation imparfaite*. Disclosed agency is when the agent discloses during the negotiations that it is acting as agent for another (see section I below). It is undisclosed when the agent makes no such indication and the third party therefore assumes, or can properly by reason of the circumstances assume, that the agent is acting on his own account (see section II below).

I. Disclosed agency

It is accepted that when the agent discloses the fact of its agency, the contract arises directly between the third party and the principal. Accordingly, all claims lie between the principal and the third party; they do not affect the agent.[100] The Common Law follows the same principle, for where there is a disclosed agency 'a direct contractual relationship [is thereby created] between principal and third party'.[101]

Continental systems treat agency as disclosed only if the agent acts 'in the name of' the principal, but this does not mean that the precise name of the particular principal has to be stated when the deal is closed. It is sufficient if the third party was made aware by all the circumstances that rights and liabilities were to attach to a principal and not to the agent.[102] In the Common Law also, agency is disclosed not only when the principal is actually named, but also when it is agreed that it will be named later or that its identity will emerge from what follows.[103] If it is not clear whether the agent was acting for a principal or on its own account, all legal systems look to the agreement of those negotiating the deal, ambiguous though it may be, as well as to the customary practices in that branch of trade and the interests of the parties. The following cases may serve as illustrations.

---

[100] § 164(1) BGB; § 1017 ABGB; art. 32(1) OR; art. 3:66(1) BW; § 10(1) Swedish Contract Law; art. 1154(1) *Code civil*; art. 1338 *Codice civile*; art. 211 Greek Civil Code; art. 95(2) Polish Civil Code.

[101] Fridman (n 7) 216.

[102] See also art. 12 Geneva Convention (n 8). This states that disclosed agency is 'where an agent acts on behalf of a principal within the scope of his authority and the third party knew or ought to have known that the agent was acting as agent'. Pursuant to art. 3:102 PECL, 'where an agent acts in the name of a principal ... [there is] direct representation', but it is not relevant whether or not the principal's identity is revealed to the third party until later. But there is 'indirect representation' if an intermediary acts on instructions and 'on behalf of, but not in the name of, the principal' (and is therefore referred to as an intermediary, and not as an agent). This applies also if the third party 'neither knows nor has reason to know that the intermediary acts as an agent'. The PICC make a similar differentiation between disclosed and undisclosed agency. See art. 2.2.3(1); art. 2.2.4(1) and Bonell, 'Agency' (n 8) 523ff.

[103] Here the Common Law speaks of an 'unnamed principal'; see Treitel (n 16) no. 16-054. Continental systems also accept that where the agent overtly acts as such the contract may be with a principal not yet named. See, for example, BG 19 Dec. 1934, BGE 60 II 492; BGH 23 June 1988, [1989] *NJW* 164, 166; and Mekki (n 12) Fasc.10 no. 20 (*déclaration de command*).

Ships' agents normally act for a shipowner, so that the shipowner becomes party to the contract even if the agent does not reveal the shipowner's name. Exceptionally, however, the ships' agent may step beyond its normal role and make a contract with a shipowner on behalf of a shipper, but then it must reveal what it is doing or will be held liable.[104] In *Universal Steam v. McKelvie*,[105] a charterparty for the carriage of coal in which the party was 'James McKelvie & Co., charterers' was signed 'for and on behalf of James McKelvie & Co. (as agents)'. The shipowner's claim against James McKelvie & Co. failed, for the defendant had effected the charter not for itself but 'as agents' on behalf of the Italian consignee of the cargo as principal. Under certain circumstances, an agent openly acting for a principal, who thereby becomes bound and entitled under the contract, may also be held to be a party. It was so decided in *The Swan*,[106] where the owner of a vessel had handed it over for management to a company of which he was the sole director. He signed a contract for the repairs needed by the vessel expressly as director of the company, but the court held that in view of the special circumstances he himself, as the person known to own the vessel, was liable for the cost of repairs alongside the company, now in liquidation. The *Bundesgerichtshof* decided likewise in 1965.[107] A dairy firm contracted with a haulier to collect milk from the farmers in a specified area, and in doing so contracted as agent for the farmers. The court nevertheless held that the dairy was also liable for the transportation costs, for it must have realised that the haulier had a 'justified interest in not having to deal separately with each farmer, calculating quantities collected and distances covered'. A person who orders flight tickets from a travel agency for a party of ten acts 'in his own name' only for his own flight, and as agent for the other travellers in the party, even if he or she alone signs the order form as customer.[108] Where a bank makes a loan 'in the name of a group of banks', it can be taken that it alone is the contractor, especially if at the time of the contract the membership of the group of banks is not yet fixed.[109]

The third party very generally has a great interest in knowing with whom it is contracting. That is why there is disclosed agency only when the third party realised or ought to have realised to whom the obligations were to attach. An exception can, however, be made in cases where the identity of the other party to the contract is a matter of indifference. In such cases, when the agent has contracted in the interest and on the account of its principal, the contract may be with the latter even though the third party could have no means of knowing the principal existed.[110] There is not much

---

[104] OLG Hamburg 8 Oct. 1981, [1983] VersR 79.
[105] *Universal Steam Navigation Co. v. James McKelvie & Co.* [1923] AC 492.
[106] [1968] 1 Lloyd's Rep. 5. [107] BGH 1 Dec. 1965, LM § 164 BGB no. 26.
[108] BGH 6 Apr. 1978, LM § 164 BGB no. 43. See also R Bork, *Allgemeiner Teil des Bürgerlichen Gesetzbuchs* (4th edn, 2016) mn. 1382ff.
[109] BG 19 Dec. 1934 (above, n 103) 501: 'The formula ["in the name of a group of banks"] normally indicates direct representation, but this is rebuttable if the other party can prove that in the particular case the formula meant something else and that the rights and duties under the contract attach to the purported agent personally.'
[110] See art. 32(2) OR: if the agent gave no indication that he was acting for a principal, the principal nevertheless becomes party to the contract if the third party 'did not care with whom the contract was made'. In Germany, this is called *Handeln für den, den es angeht* (acting for whom it may concern); see Bork (n 108) mn. 1397ff.

II. Undisclosed agency

A *verdeckte Vertretung* or undisclosed agency exists when the third party did not and could not know at the time of the conclusion of the contract that the party it was dealing with was contracting for the account of someone else, and thought it was contracting with the person it was dealing with. To this we must add the case, of great importance on the Continent, where a commission agent (*commissionnaire, Kommissionär*) makes deals on behalf of its principal. The third party will very often know that the commission agent is acting as agent and may even know for which principal, but in accordance with mercantile practice familiar to both parties it is the commission agent who becomes party to the contract. This is often laid down in statutes to the effect that the commission agent's business is 'to buy or sell goods or instruments in its own name but for the account of another' (the *committant*).[111] This means that the commission agent becomes a party to the contract even if the other party knew that it was entered into on behalf of a principal.[112] These are often said to be instances of indirect representation, *mittelbare Vertretung, indirekte Vertretung*, or *mandat sans représentation*.[113]

In cases of undisclosed agency, all European legal systems agree on the principle that contractual relations arise only between the third party and the undisclosed agent. Only the agent can have a claim against the third party, regardless of whether that claim concerns the payment of money, or delivery of goods sold, or performance of promised services. The undisclosed principal can only have such a claim if and when the agent has transferred or assigned such claims.[114]

The Common Law goes much further. If a third party concludes a contract with a person who is in fact an agent acting within the scope of his authority, the principal may sue the third party on this contract, even if the third party was unaware of the

---

[111] See § 383 HGB; art. 94 *Code de commerce*; art. 1731 *Codice civile*; § 4 Swedish Law on Commission Agents and Salesmen of 18 Apr. 1914 (adopted by Denmark and Norway). The freight forwarder (*Spediteur, commissaire de transport*) who typically acts in its own name in arranging for the carriage of other people's goods becomes a party to the contract; see § 407 HGB; art. 96 *Code de commerce*; art. 1737 *Codice civile*.

[112] Article 1705 *Codice civile* is explicit. Article 2.2.3(2) PICC deals with the commission by stating that relations *only* arise between the agent and the third party if, on the one hand, the third party knows for whom the agent is acting and, on the other hand, the agent 'with the consent of the principal undertakes to become the party of the contract'.

[113] See, in detail D Busch, *Indirect Representation in European Contract Law* (2005). There is also indirect representation if someone is acting in its own name, but as a frontman, *Strohmann* or *prête-nom* in the interest of and for the account of a hidden backer or *Hintermann*. French law gives third parties a choice: the third party can stick with the *prête-nom* as party to the contract, but may also treat the contract concluded like a fictitious transaction (*Scheingeschäft*) and claim against the hidden backer. See Mekki (n 12) Fasc. 10 no. 8; Civ. 8 July 1992, JCP 1993.II.21982, n. G Wiederkehr.

[114] A principal will often have a right to assignment on the basis of the agency contract that it has concluded with the agent. The assignment can be an advance assignment, namely occur at a time when the agent has not even concluded the contract with the third party. See pp. 343ff.

agency. Conversely, the third party can also sue the principal (once he learns of its existence).

Contractual claims can therefore be made by and against a party who was neither involved in the formation of the contract nor mentioned by the party negotiating it, a party of whose involvement the third party had and could have no suspicion. As has often been noted, even by common lawyers, this is difficult to reconcile with the general rules about the scope of contractual obligations.[115]

How well do these common law rules of undisclosed agency adjust the interests of the principal and the third party? There are really two questions: what protection does the third party have when it is sued by the undisclosed principal (see subsection 1 below)? And what happens when the third party, instead of demanding performance from the agent with whom it has been dealing, seeks performance from the principal (see subsection 2 below)?

1. Claims by the principal

The third party may be unpleasantly surprised to find a total stranger demanding performance simply on a showing that the contract was entered into on its behalf. How are the third party's interests to be protected?

First, the third party may claim that its agreement with the agent excludes any claim by the principal. Such exclusion may arise from the circumstances. In *Said* v. *Butt*,[116] the plaintiff was determined to attend a theatre première, but as the theatre management was ill disposed towards him and would never sell him a ticket, he got a friend to buy a ticket for him. This was a waste of money, since the defendant manager of the theatre refused him admission on the night of the play. The court rejected the plaintiff's argument that he was entitled to admission as the undisclosed principal of the friend who bought the ticket for him. The rule may be formulated as follows: if it emerges from the construction of the contract that the third party had a justified interest in knowing to whom it was to be obligated, the undisclosed principal has no claim.[117]

In addition, the third party may raise against the undisclosed principal any defences it could use against the agent. In particular, it is a defence that the third party has already rendered performance to the agent in the belief that it was his creditor. The third party can set off against the undisclosed principal any debts due from the agent,

---

[115] See, for example, F Pollock in (1887) 3 *LQR* 358, 359: 'The plain truth ought never to be forgotten that the whole law as to the rights and liabilities of an undisclosed principal is inconsistent with the elementary doctrines of the law of contract. The right of one person to sue another on a contract not really made with the person suing is unknown to every legal system except that of England and America.' Much ingenuity has been deployed in trying to justify this anomaly in the Common Law. In particular, see W Müller-Freienfels, 'Die "Anomalie" der verdeckten Stellvertretung (undisclosed agency) des englischen Rechts' part I (1952) 17 *RabelsZ* 578 and part II (1953) 18 *RabelsZ* 12; Fridman (n 7) 253ff; all with references to the extensive literature.
[116] [1920] 3 KB 497.
[117] See Treitel (n 16) no. 16-056ff. with references to many other decisions.

provided, in both cases, that the defence arose before the third party knew or could know that a principal might lurk undisclosed behind the agent.[118]

In this respect, as will be seen, the situation is just as if the agent had *assigned* its claim to the principal and the principal was suing as assignee. In fact, the interests of the parties in the two cases are comparable, since in both of them the third party is being sued by a creditor with whom it originally had no relationship. Indeed, Common Law commentators have suggested that the undisclosed principal's right to take legal action rests on an assignment, resulting directly by law and not from any act of the agent.[119] A similar point was made by the eminent English judge who stated that the rules on undisclosed principals were designed to simplify proceedings by sidestepping the need for the principal to sue the agent for its consent to the principal's suit against the third party.[120]

Thus the Common Law is not so very different from the continental systems, where admittedly one starts from the viewpoint that if the intermediary acts in its own name, only it may sue on the contract. However, art. 401(1) OR lays down that '[w]here the agent acting on the principal's behalf acquires claims in his own name against third parties, such claims pass to the principal provided he has fulfilled all his obligations towards the agent under the agency relationship.' Here one sees the legislature approving a *cessio legis* (legal assignment) of the kind inferred by common lawyers as an explanation of the undisclosed principal's right to sue. The Romanistic legal systems reach the same conclusion when they grant the principal an *action directe* against the third party.[121] Nordic countries have a very carefully tailored rule. The principal of a commission agent may exercise against the third party claims on the contract which the agent entered in its own name but on the principal's behalf 'if the third party is in breach of his obligations under the contract, or the commission agent has failed to account or acted improperly as regards the principal, or is insolvent'.[122]

---

[118] Ibid. no. 16-060.

[119] For example, AL Goodhart and CJ Hamson, 'Undisclosed Principals in Contract' (1931) 4 *Camb. LJ* 320, 351f.; see also Fridman (n 7) 257.

[120] See Lord Diplock in *Freeman & Lockyer* v. *Buckhurst Park Properties* [1964] 2 QB 480, 503: 'It may be that this rule relating to "undisclosed principals", which is peculiar to English law, can be rationalised as avoiding circuity of action, for the principal could in equity compel the agent to lend his name in an action to enforce the contract against the contractor, and would at common law be liable to indemnify the agent in respect of the performance of the obligations assumed by the agent under the contract.'

[121] This is done by art. 1705(2)(2) *Codice civile*. In France, there is much dispute amongst the commentators as to whether the principal may have an *action directe* against the third party. The courts have not come to a conclusive decision on the matter. See, for example, B Starck in J Hamel (ed), *Le contrat de commission* (1949) 157, 164ff; R Houin and M Pédamon, *Droit commercial* (9th edn, 1990) no. 615; Ripert, Roblot, Delebecque, and Germain (n 58) no. 2635; A Jauffret and J Mestre, *Droit commercial* (23rd edn, 1997) no. 760; Mekki (n 12) Fasc. 10 no. 14. However, in the case of a commission sale it is permitted by way of an *action oblique* for the principal to make a claim directly against the buyer if it has not yet paid the commission agent. See Mekki (n 12) Fasc. 10 no. 14. In Germany, the principal needs an assignment of the agent's claims before it can claim against the third party, but there is no difficulty in effecting such an assignment, which is perfectly normal and can be arranged in advance, at the time the agency contract is concluded.

[122] Before the principal can claim against the third party, it must have performed all its own obligations towards the commission agent, or have given security for such performance, and have informed the agent of its intention to proceed against the third party. If the third party has already rendered performance to the agent, 'he is never bound to perform again on the demand of the principal, unless when performing he knew or should have known that it was the principal who was entitled to proceed against him on the contract'. For the details, see § 56ff. of the Swedish Law (n 111). To similar effect is art. 7:412(1) BW:

All legal systems agree on the special situation where an agent acting in its own name but on behalf of a principal has become insolvent. Anything due from the third party enures not to the agent's creditors, but to the principal for whom the agent was acting. In English law, this is already implicit in the fact that the undisclosed principal can sue the third party directly; indeed, this is said to be one of the reasons behind undisclosed agency. In continental legal systems, it is done by giving the principal a privileged claim to the agent's rights against the third party.[123]

2. Claims by the third party

In English law, there is no doubt about the third party's right to sue the principal, except in the unusual case where it emerges from the contract (implicitly or explicitly) that the agent alone should be liable. Otherwise, once the third party has learnt of the principal, it can choose whether to take action against the principal or the agent. But once a definitive decision has been made, such as by taking action against the agent after learning of the principal, legal action cannot be taken against the other.[124]

If the undisclosed principal acquires ownership in goods which the agent bought on its behalf, it can hardly complain of being sued directly by the third party for payment of the price. But suppose that the principal has already paid the agent and the agent has failed to transfer the money to the third party. Does the principal have to pay again? The courts say that in principle it must do so, since it belongs to the principal's sphere of risk if the agent it has chosen breaks their contract and diverts to its own purposes the money the principal has provided.[125]

The third party has no such right in continental legal systems, even where conversely the principal has or may have a direct claim against it, or such a claim is at least possible.[126] This is justifiable, as everyone must bear the risk of the possible insolvency

---

any principal (and not just the principal of a commission agent) can transfer the agent's rights to itself by a written document if the agent is in breach of its obligations to the principal or has gone bankrupt. See also art. 3:301 PECL: a contractual relationship only arises between the third party and the intermediary if the intermediary was acting in its own name, or the third party neither knew or had no reason to know that the intermediary was acting on the instructions of a principal. Nevertheless, the principal can make a direct claim against the third party if the intermediary has become insolvent, or it has not performed a significant term relating to its agency agreement with the principal (art. 3: 302 PECL). In practical terms, the *principal* can make a direct claim against the third party if it does not receive the promised performance. However, the third party can defend the claim against the principal with all objections that would have been available had he been sued by the intermediary. See also art. 13 of the Geneva Convention (n 8). By contrast, art. 2.2.4 PICC excludes a direct claim by the principal against the third party; see Bonell, 'Agency' (n 8) 524ff; A Hartkamp, 'Indirect Representation According to the PECL, the UNIDROIT Agency Convention and the Dutch Civil Code' in *Festschrift Drobnig* (1998) 45; S Kortmann, 'Indirect Representation According to the DCFR' (2016) 24 *ERPL* 489.

[123] In Germany and the Nordic countries, this admittedly applies only where the agent is a commission agent; see § 392(2) HGB, § 57(2), § 61 Swedish Law (above, n 111). Other legal orders give the same protection in all cases of undisclosed agency. See art. 401 OR, arts. 121(1), 122 French Law on Insolvency of 25 Jan. 1985; art. 1707 *Codice civile*.

[124] For details see Treitel (n 16) no. 16-075; Fridman (n 7) 267.

[125] See for details Treitel (n 16) no. 16-064; Fridman (n 7) 266f.

[126] See Ripert, Roblot, Delebecque, and Germain (above, n 58) no. 2658 and Trib.de commerce Paris 25 Sept. 1985, [1986] Sem.Jur. (Cahiers de droit de l'entreprise no. 3) 10. In this case, a purchasing syndicate called Cedac ordered goods from the defendant at the instance of retailer members, and when Cedac became insolvent the suppliers claimed the price of the delivered goods from the individual retailers, but

of the person they deal with. If a party knows when concluding the contract that the person it is dealing with is acting for a principal, it may seek to arrange by agreement that any claims can also be levied against the principal. But if the party only learns of the existence and identity of the principal later, it is far from clear why the party should have the benefit of a right to sue the principal as well, and thus elide the risk of the insolvency of the counterparty it dealt with. What can be said for this position is that principal and agent are closely linked, the former having chosen the latter to promote its interests by doing deals with third parties, and that by implicating the agent in the business the principal created a risk that the agent's contractors may be damaged by the agent's insolvency.

Who should bear the risk of the undisclosed agent becoming insolvent or causing a breach of contract: the third party or the principal? Article 3:303 PECL decides this question the same way as the Common Law—to the disadvantage of the principal and in favour of the third party. If the third party does not receive performance from the intermediary, either because it has become insolvent or has breached the contract, it can assert a claim directly against the principal. But the principal's liability is restricted: it can exercise the defences that would have been available to the intermediary if the third party had taken action against it. Above all, the principal can also rely on those defences that it would be able to avail itself of in any claim against the intermediary.[127] So if the principal has appointed a commission agent to purchase goods, and has already paid the agent for those goods, if the commission agent becomes insolvent after delivering the goods to the principal, the third party seller can make a claim against the principal for the purchase price. But the third party will not get far with this claim, as the principal can raise all defences it would have had if the commission agent had brought a claim for the purchase price. Having prepaid the price, the principal would neither be liable to the commission agent nor to the third party.

---

their claim was dismissed: '*les ventes devant être considérées comme contractées directement entre Cedac agissant en qualité de commisionnaire et les fournisseurs, ce qui n'autorise pas ces derniers à se retourner vers les détailleurs avec lesquels ils n'ont pas de lien de droit*'.

[127] See also art. 7:413 BW and art. 13(2) of Geneva Convention (n 8).

17

Contracts for the Benefit of Third Parties

A. Historical Development and Economic Importance	319
B. Requirements	323
I. The intention of the parties	323
II. Contracts protective of third parties	325
III. Claims by third parties not based on contractual intention	328
1. *Action directe*	328
2. Contract chains	329
IV. Limitations of liability and third parties	331
C. Effects	332
I. Rights of the promisee	332
II. Defences available to the promisor	333
III. Modification or termination of third party rights	334

A. Historical Development and Economic Importance

'*Le contrat ne crée d'obligations qu'entre les parties.*' So says art. 1119 *Code civil*, and indeed it seems obvious. When two parties make a contract, such as contract of sale, it seems perfectly reasonable that they and they alone should acquire rights and duties under that contract. Of course, the parties may agree that each may perform by rendering performance to someone else. This makes no difference. If the buyer is to pay the price to the seller's bank or the seller is to deliver the goods to one of the buyer's customers, the obligation is still owed only to the other party to the contract, not to the third party. This must be distinguished from the case where the parties agree that the third party, although a stranger to the formation of the contract, should not only receive the promised performance but also be entitled to demand performance in its own right.

The need for contracts that give a third party a personal claim to performance is clearest where the promisee wants to be assured of the future maintenance of members of his or her family. Arrangements for the devolution of a farm provide an example. When an ageing farmer decides to transfer his farm to one of his sons on condition that that son make provision for his siblings in cash or kind, it is not enough that the farmer himself can take legal action against the son for performance. He needs to be sure that after his death the siblings themselves, as beneficiaries of the son's promise, are entitled to take legal action against their brother if necessary. It is much the same when the buyer of a business undertakes, as part of the price, to pay an annuity to the seller's widow or children, or when a partnership agreement provides that on the death or departure of one of the partners the others should pay certain sums to his relatives or accept his widow into the partnership.

Insurance, however, is the classic instance of a contract under which the rights of third parties must be recognised. The sum to be paid by the insurer on the occurrence of the insured event is often payable not to the insured but to a third party—the beneficiary named by the insured in a life policy or, in the case of cargo insurance, the owner of the goods at the time of the loss or damage.

There are, however, many other types of contract where persons other than the contractors themselves would benefit from proper performance, and the question is whether they too should be treated as contracts for the benefit of those third parties so as to give them a right of action. When a landlord engages a contractor to install central heating or air-conditioning, the tenant will often have an interest in the prompt and proper performance of the work contracted for, but it is quite another question whether this interest should receive legal recognition. If the installation is defective or delayed, can the tenant claim damages from the contractor on the basis that the contractor's duty to perform was owed to it as well as to the landlord who was paying for the work? If a landlord agrees with the present tenant that if the tenant sells its business the buyer may continue on the premises, can the buyer sue the landlord to have the lease continued, or for damages if the premises are let to someone else? Third parties may also have an interest in contracts of sale, as well as contracts for work or leases. If blood bought by a hospital is tainted by a virus, can a patient who suffers in consequence take action against the supplier, although it sold the blood to the hospital and not to the patient?[1]

Nowadays, nearly all European legal systems have rules which determine when a third party may bring a claim for performance of a contract or damages for breach. These rules are the product of a long historical process. Germany accepted third-party rights in contracts in the nineteenth century; in some other countries the development is not yet complete. Among the obstacles to be overcome in this process was the idea that a contract was a *vinculum iuris* between the parties who made it, such that it seemed impossible that any third party should acquire rights under it. The third party had no claim in classical Roman law—*alteri stipulari nemo potest* (Ulpian D.45,1,38,17). Indeed, even the promisee had no claim, since a claim presupposed an interest in the claimant and what interest did the promisee have in a performance that was to be rendered to someone else? This particular obstacle could be overcome by stipulating a penalty if the promisor failed to render performance to the third party, but even then only the promisee had a claim, not the third party.[2] Late classical law did eventually allow the third party to claim, but only in special cases, the most important of which was *donatio sub modo*, whereby if a person received a gift on condition that he render some performance to a third party, the third party was granted an *actio utilis* against him.

Both the basic principle and its exceptions and limitations were included in the *Corpus Iuris*, and the consequent flood of interpretational disputes occupied both

---

[1] See Civ. 17 Dec. 1954, JCP 1955.II.8490, n. R Savatier, where in a similar case the plaintiff's claim was allowed. See also below, pp. 323ff.

[2] For details see R Zimmermann, *The Law of Obligations, Roman Foundations of the Civilian Tradition* (1990) 34ff, especially at 38f, and H Kötz in *Int.Enc.Comp.L.* vol. VII ch 13, 4ff.

commentators and practitioners well into modern times.³ However, the natural lawyers succeeded in eviscerating the basic Roman principle by insisting that the nature and scope of the legal consequences of a contract should be determined by the will of the parties—a view that still has great force today. If the parties really wanted to vest an actionable right in a third party, they could do so. The limitation that the third party must have 'accepted' the right so accorded was maintained. The Prussian ALR provided in § 74(1)(5) that a party not implicated in the formation of a contract could acquire a personal right under it, but only when he had 'acceded to the contract with the consent of the principal parties' (§ 75). Ten years later, the French *Code civil* followed Roman law more closely. According to the former art. 1121, a '*stipulation au profit d'un tiers*' was valid only if, along with his request for performance to the third party, the promisee made a gift to the promisor (*donatio sub modo*), or else requested some performance to himself (which would give him an interest in performance). The courts proceeded to ignore these limitations, with the result that in modern French law the only question is whether the parties intended to equip the third party with a right of action. This has meanwhile been stated expressly in art. 1205 *Code civil*. It is now clear that the third party's right is created merely by the agreement of the parties. It is therefore irrelevant whether or not the third party agreed with, or even knew anything about, the agreement made by the parties in his or her favour.⁴ In Germany, there was a long dispute over whether the third party's agreement was necessary before it acquired a right. It was finally decided not to be necessary, so now all that is required under § 328 BGB—as under art. 112(2) OR or (after the revision of 1916) § 881(2) ABGB—is that the parties should have intended the third party to have this right. The right cannot, however, be forced upon the third party: if it is rejected, it is treated as never granted.⁵

English law is different. Until 1999, it was firmly established that a third party could not acquire an actionable right from a contract to which it was not a party, even if the parties seriously intended that the third party should benefit and the claim was legitimate and plausible. This was based on the doctrine of privity that only a person who is a party to a contract can sue on it. In England, the doctrine of consideration was also used to deny a third party's right to sue on a contract to which it was not a party.⁶ Under this doctrine, a party can only acquire rights to performance if it has provided or promised consideration in return. But a third party does not perform or promise anything in return for the benefit it will receive under the contract, and thus cannot require performance from the party making the promise. That the doctrine of privity has managed to survive so long in English law is due,

---

³ See Zimmermann (n 2) 41ff; H Coing, *Europäisches Privatrecht*, vol. 1: *Älteres Gemeines Recht* (1985) 424ff; II, 452ff; E Schrage (ed), *Ius Quaestium Tertio* (2008).
⁴ See now arts. 1205–1209 *Code civil* in the form enacted as part of the recent reform of the French law of obligations.
⁵ See § 333 BGB; art. 1411(3) *Codice civile*; art. 413 Greek Civil Code; art. 447 Portuguese Civil Code. See also art. 6:110(2) PECL; art. 5.2.6 PICC; art. II.-9:303(1) DCFR; art. 78(4) CESL. Under art. 6:253(1) BW, by contrast, 'acceptance' by the third party is required before it acquires a right. However such acceptance is presumed if the right is granted irrevocably and gratuitously, the third party was aware of it and did not object (art. 6:253(4)).
⁶ See above, pp. 53f.

on the one hand, to the legislature creating exceptions for important cases. Under s. 11 Married Women's Property Act 1882, a life insurance policy taken out by one spouse in favour of the other spouse or their children creates a trust in favour of the beneficiaries named in the contract, who thereby also acquire rights as against the insurer.[7] While upholding the doctrine of privity in principle, English courts have made many inroads into it with exceptions and limitations, so that many commentators and judges have criticised the rule as outdated.[8]

The foundation had thus been laid for the Contracts (Rights of Third Parties) Act 1999. The Act gives third parties their own rights of claim in contracts concluded by other parties, but only under certain conditions. Those conditions are met, firstly, if the parties to the contract have 'expressly' named the third party as a beneficiary. Secondly, a third party may also enforce a term of the contract if the term 'purports to confer a benefit on [the third party]' even though it is not expressly named. This will not apply if the party against which the third party seeks to enforce a claim can prove that 'on a proper construction of the contract it appears that the parties did not intend the term to be enforceable by the third party'. In the end, it comes down to interpretation and construction. How the English courts will proceed is still unclear, due to a lack of a ruling on this matter.[9] The wording of the statute leaves no doubt that, on the one hand, the third party's right to enforce the contract includes its right to invoke any remedy based on its breach (such as a claim for damages). On the other hand, a party may, if sued by the third party, rely on all defences available to it had it been sued by the other party. There are also detailed rules on the conditions under which the right

---

[7] That the third party is a beneficiary who has its own claims against an insurer as trustee has been a long-standing rule of the law of trusts. Statutory provisions have also given third parties rights as beneficiaries in other types of insurance contract; see GH Treitel, *The Law of Contract* (13th edn, by E Peel, 2011) no. 14-128ff; E McKendrick, *Contract Law* (8th edn, 2009) no. 7.21. Another exception can be found in s. 56 Law of Property Act 1925, which applies to contracts by which the parties have conveyed land or transferred some other interest in land or other property: if in such a case the parties agreed that the ownership or the other interest should be acquired by a *third party*, this party will indeed acquire the right 'although he may not be named as a party to the conveyance or other instrument'. See Treitel (n 7) no. 14-136ff.

[8] In *Swain* v. *Law Society* [1983] 1 AC 598, 611, Lord Diplock said that the total exclusion of a third party's right to sue on a contract made by others was 'an anachronistic shortcoming that has for many years been regarded as a reproach to English private law'. See also Steyn LJ in *Darlington BC* v. *Wiltshier Northern Ltd.* [1995] 1 WLR 68, 77: '[W]e do well to remember that the civil law systems of other members of the European Union recognize such contracts. That our legal system lacks such flexibility is a disadvantage in the single market. Indeed it is a historical curiosity that the legal system of a mercantile country such as England ... has not been able to rid itself of this unjust rule deriving from a technical conception of a contract as a purely bilateral *vinculum juris*'.

[9] One can assume that the specified conditions are not met, and thus third parties will not acquire rights of their own in two important cases. One case is known in Germany and Austria as *Vertrag mit Schutzwirkung für Dritte* (contract protective of third parties; see below, p. 325). The other case is where contracts are 'linked' or form a 'chain of contracts'. Take the case where an owner of land contracts with main contractor A to construct a building, and A then agrees with the subcontractor B to prepare certain building work. Both A and B know that the owner has an interest in making sure the building work is carried out correctly, and the owner may even be named in the contract between A and B. However, unless special agreement is reached it is assumed that the owner will have no rights against B under the contract between A and B if B fails to perform correctly. See Treitel (n 7) no. 14-099; McKendrick (n 7) no. 7.6.

given to the third party can be subsequently modified or withdrawn by the parties to the contract.[10]

B. Requirements

I. The intention of the parties

Whether or not a contract confers rights on a third party depends on the intention of the parties. This universally recognised proposition is sometimes expressed formally: art. 112(2) OR provides that the third party may 'compel performance where that was the intention of the contracting parties'.[11]

The requisite common intention of the actual parties is also sufficient by itself to create a right in the third party. It is true that the former art. 1121 *Code civil* laid down further requirements, but the courts have long since dispensed with them. As the insurance business began to boom in the mid-nineteenth century, there was considerable pressure in France to make life policies enforceable as contracts for the benefit of third parties. Likewise, where the former art. 1121 required that the promisee must have stipulated for something for itself, it was enough that it obtain a *profit moral* from the promisor's performance to the third party, such as the payment of the insured sum to the beneficiary of the policy.[12]

The creation of a right enforceable by the third party need not be explicit: it may just be inferred with sufficient certainty from what the parties have expressed, from the purpose of the transaction, and from other circumstances of the case. Legislatures have sometimes tried to assist the courts by raising presumptions for different types of case. Thus § 330 BGB provides that 'in case of doubt' the third party acquires a right if it is named as beneficiary in a life insurance or annuity contract. So, too, when the transferee of a farm or business[13] promises the transferor to confer a benefit on a third party, usually a relative of the transferor, by way of 'compensating' him or her for the loss of inheritance expectancies on the transferor's death.

These cases involve promises to provide support for a third party, usually a family member. It is more difficult when a third party wishes to enforce a contract of sale, lease, carriage, or warehousing entered into by others. It is not enough that the actual parties were aware of the third party's interest: it must have been their express or

---

[10] See below, pp. 332ff.
[11] Equally clear is § 881(2) ABGB and art. 411 Greek Civil Code. See also art. 6:110(1) PECL; art. 5.2.1 PICC; art. II.-9:301 DCFR; art. 78(1) and (2) CESL. For detail, see Kötz (n 2) s. 22ff; S Whittaker, 'Privity of Contract and the Law of Tort' (1995) 15 *OJLS* 327; R Wintgen, *Etude critique de la notion d'opposabilité: Les effets du contrat à l'égard des tiers en droit français et en droit allemand* (2004); S Vogenauer, 'Contract in Favour of a Third Party' in *Max Planck Enc.* (2012) 385; S Vogenauer, 'The Effects of Contracts on Third Parties' in S Vogenauer, J Cartwright, and S Whittaker (eds), *Reforming the French Law of Obligations* (2009) 235.
[12] Under art. 1411(1) *Codice civile*, the promisee must have an 'interest' in the benefit to the third party, and under art. 441 Portuguese Civil Code an interest 'which deserves legal protection'. But in practice this means no more than that the contract must be valid in accordance with general principles. See Cass. civ. 12 July 1976 no. 2663, [1977] *Rep.* 1731, where it was held that an interest of the promisee which is '*meramente morale*' is sufficient.
[13] RG 16 Oct. 1905, [1905] *JW* 717.

implied intention to grant the third party the right to enforce specified performance and/or damages for breach.

For example, a builder that contracts with a partnership to construct a building and fails to complete on time may be sued for damages by one of the partners if the builder knew that the partner was to set up a medical practice there and had a particular interest in its speedy completion.[14] The purchaser of a plot of land who builds above a certain height in breach of his promise to the developer may be sued by neighbours who, to his knowledge, purchased from the same developer in reliance on the developer's assurance that the plots would have a 'view uninterrupted by building'.[15] When a seller of a business agrees with the buyer to find jobs for any employees rendered redundant by the reorganisation of the business, it can be inferred that the employees in question are to have a claim against the seller.[16] If a wholesale dealer in precious stones places gems sent to him for appraisal by a jeweller in a strongbox rented from a bank, the jeweller can sue the bank if it is at fault in letting them be stolen. In France, such a claim is based on a contract for the benefit of third parties,[17] and the decision would be the same in Germany if at the time of making the contract the bank was aware that the wholesaler would store other people's goods in the strongbox.[18] Even in England, the owner of the deposited jewels could sue, but not as beneficiary of the contract of safekeeping. It could sue because, in renting the strongbox from the bank with the knowledge and approval of the jeweller, the wholesaler could be seen as acting as the jeweller's agent, and the jeweller would have a claim as undisclosed principal even if the wholesaler did not disclose that it was acting as the jeweller's agent (see above, pages 314ff.).

It will have been seen that the concept of the contract for the benefit of third parties is used in very various types of situation involving quite different interests, and also that its limits are not very clearly defined. The basic principle that a third party's right may arise from the agreement of the parties permits a finding of an 'implied agreement' whenever this seems reasonable in view of the interests involved. This is shown by the fact that third party rights are recognised more widely in some legal systems

---

[14] Civ. 14 June 1989, Bull.cass. 1989.I. no. 243 = (1990) 89 *Rev.trim.dr.civ.* 71, n. Mestre. See also the overview of French case law in C Larroumet, *Droit civil, vol. III: Les obligations, Le contrat, Effets* (6th edn, 2007) no. 802.

[15] See BGH 26 Nov. 1974, [1975] *NJW* 344. The neighbours are protected almost as if the defendant's land were burdened with an easement in their favour. The *Cour de cassation* decided otherwise in Civ. 29 Mar. 1933, D.H. 1933, 282, criticised by H Mazeaud, L Mazeaud, and F Chabas, *Leçons de droit civil, vol. III.1: Obligations, Théorie générale* (9th edn, 2006) no. 754.

[16] Com. 14 May 1979, D. 1980, 157, n. C Larroumet. If the buyer has to compensate the redundant employees because the seller fails to meet its obligation, the buyer has a claim against the seller that it can set off against the price.

[17] Com. 15 Jan. 1985, D. 1985.I.R. 344. See also Civ. 21 Nov. 1978, *JCP* 1980.I.19315, n. R Rodière: A contract for the carriage of money between a bank and a security firm may be for the benefit of the customer whose money is being carried.

[18] See BGH 10 May 1984, [1985] *NJW* 2411 (contract protective of third parties, on which see text immediately below). If the bank had no such knowledge, the same solution could be reached in a different way, through *Drittschadensliquidation* (liquidation of third-party damage): a person who entrusts a third party's goods to another for safe keeping can sue the other party for the loss resulting from the breach of duty, even though the loss is actually suffered not by him, but by the *owner* of the goods. The owner is a third party to the contract who can only sue when this claim is assigned to him.

than in others, especially in systems where inadequate protection is offered by the law of tort.

A decision of the *Cour de cassation* in 1932 offers a good example. The court held that a contract for the carriage of persons could be for the benefit of third parties so as to allow the traveller's relatives to sue the carrier in their own right if he suffered a fatal accident *en route*. The carrier is strictly responsible for the contractual claim unless there is *force majeure*.[19] The decision has attracted criticism by commentators in France on the ground that the parties to the contract had no such intention. Today, there is no longer any need for relatives to assert claims in contract because the carrier is regarded as *gardien* of the vehicle and thus liable in tort under art. 1242(1) (formerly art. 1384(1) *Code civil*), which imposes strict liability on the carrier. In addition, motor vehicle accidents are now covered by the law of 5 July 1985 to improve the position of victims of motor vehicle accidents, which introduced a special no-fault liability regime to compensate victims. So there was no longer any need for the courts to deem survivors to be third party beneficiaries of the contract of carriage by means of an '*opération mentale purement fictive, inventée pour les besoins de la cause*'.[20]

II. Contracts protective of third parties

In Germany, the contract for the benefit of third parties has proved extremely useful in filling gaps in the law of tort. A decision of the *Reichsgericht* in 1930 paved the way. A tenant contracted for the repair of a gas stove he had brought into the house. The repairs were badly done, the stove exploded, and a cleaning woman engaged by the tenant suffered personal injuries. The *Reichsgericht* granted her claim for damages against the repairman on the basis of contract, since his contract of repair with the tenant 'included a contract for the benefit of the plaintiff as well'.[21] Today we would say that this was not a 'true' contract for the benefit of a third party—after all, the plaintiff could not sue the repairman for actual performance, that is proper repair of the stove—but rather a *Vertrag mit Schutzwirkung für Dritte* (contract protective of third parties), since the repairman's duty to take care in the repair of the oven was a duty also owed to the plaintiff, and one for breach of which he must be liable to her in damages. This does not mean that if A breaches a contract made with B, any third party may sue A if it suffered damage as a result of A's breach. The courts seek to limit the circle of protected third parties by requiring a particularly close relationship or 'proximity' between the third party and B, so that A's breach of contract ordinarily and foreseeably would lead to damage to the third party. The courts also require B to have a *schutzwürdiges Interesse* (protectable interest) for the benefit of the third party. Finally,

---

[19] Civ. 6 Dec. 1932, D.P. 1933.I.137, n. L Josserand = S. 1934.1.81, n. P Esmein. However, such claims are only open to third parties to whom the deceased owed a statutory duty of maintenance, so his sister was not included, even if the deceased had actually maintained her. See Civ. 24 May 1933, D.P. 1933.I.137, n. L Josserand.

[20] See Josserand (n 19) 138; see also Larroumet (n 14) no. 803.

[21] RG 10 Feb. 1930, RGZ 127, 218, 221.

all this must be *recognisable* for A, so that it knows or should know that it would also be liable to the third party in case of breach of contract.[22]

German law is generous in admitting contractual claims for damages mainly because such claims often do not generate the desired result if founded solely in tort. So if someone slips on an escalator while in a department store, or on a salad leaf on the floor, a claim in tort may fail because the defendant department store operator may be able to rely on § 831 BGB and escape liability by proving that it exercised due care in the supervision of its agents. In other cases, the tort claimant may not be able to show that the defendant store was negligent. If the claimant can rely on a contractual claim for damages, it is in a much better position because § 831 BGB would be inapplicable and it would be for the defendant to show that due care was exercised. Contractual claims can also be pursued if the parties have merely an *intention* to conclude a contract and the defendant's duty to prevent accidental harm to the plaintiff is based on the parties' pre-contractual relationship. In addition, a third party may rely on the protective effect that the contract or the 'pre-contractual relationship' may offer. So if the fourteen-year-old son accompanies his mother to the department store and has injured himself by slipping on the floor, he has a contractual claim for damages against the department store operator. His mother may not yet have concluded a contract with the store (ie bought anything), but at least had the intention of doing so, and the son can take advantage of the protective effect of this pre-contractual relationship as a third party.[23]

But what about situations where the claimant's claim for compensation is for harm which is not personal injury or property damage but pure economic loss? Here the matter is less clear. The typical case is where a credit institution, accountant, architect, or other expert professional undertakes to give information or an opinion on the financial status or solvency of a firm or the value of some object. If such information

---

[22] See H Kötz, *Vertragsrecht* (2nd edn, 2012) mn. 514ff. and extensive case law. See RG 26 Nov. 1936, [1937] *JW* 737 (contract between municipality and owner of house for the supply of drinking water affords protection to tenants injured by drinking lead-infected water); BGH 7 Nov. 1960, BGHZ 33, 247 (contract between company and supplier of concrete slabs gives protection to company's employees injured by their faulty installation); BGH 23 June 1965, [1965] *NJW* 1757 (contract between hotel and club for the hire of a hall for a party is protective of club members who slip and fall on over-polished floor); BGH 22 Jan. 1968, BGHZ 49, 350 (lease of business premises is protective of those whose goods the lessee allows to be brought onto the premises and which are damaged there owing to a defect in the premises). French courts decide likewise: Civ. 13 Oct. 1987, *JCP* 1987.IV.391 (contract between hotel and organiser of educational course gives rise to a contractual claim by a participant whose clothes are stolen owing to negligent supervision of cloakroom). See also OGH 29 Apr. 1981, [1982] *JBl* 601 (contract for levelling of ground prior to construction of road protects the electricity company whose high-tension mast on the premises is damaged by the works). See also OGH 20 Nov. 1997, [1998] *JBl* 655 (contract between lessor and cleaning company gives protection to lessees and their family members, but not to guests visiting the lessees or persons temporarily present in the lessees' apartment).

[23] See BGH 28 Jan. 1976, BGHZ 66, 51. Such artificial constructs are not required in legal systems where the law of tort functions well, either because they do not allow the defendant to escape liability by proof that its agents were duly supervised, or because they assume strict liability independent of proof of fault where the claimant's accident relates to a defect of the defendant's building or services. This is the approach followed under Swiss and Italian law (art. 58 OR; art. 2051 *Codice civile*), and by French law if the defendant is a *gardien du sol* and thus subject to strict liability under art. 1242 (formerly: art. 1384) *Code civil*. See in detail F Ranieri, *Europäisches Obligationenrecht* (3rd edn, 2009) 1345ff; K Zweigert and H Kötz, *An Introduction to Comparative Law* (Tony Weir tr, 3rd edn, 1998) § 41 II; H Kötz and G Wagner, *Deliktsrecht* (13th edn, 2016) mn. 319ff.

is false through negligence, the person contracting for the information can naturally sue for breach of that contract. But what if that information comes into the hands of a third party that relies on the information to its detriment? In Germany, the third party cannot sue in tort since, subject to a few exceptions, tort claims lie only in respect of corporeal harm or damage to property.[24] The contract protective of third parties can help to fill this gap, if there is one. The court can hold that a third party may come within the scope of a contract to provide information if the informant could have known that the information provided was also destined for a third party, which would change its position in reliance on it.[25] In other countries, the third party may be able to sue in tort—in France because art. 1240 (formerly: art. 1382) *Code civil* provides for the compensation for all harm caused by fault, including pure economic loss.[26] In England, it can take action because, although liability in the tort of negligence generally requires corporeal or physical harm, an exception permitting recovery of 'mere pecuniary loss' has been made precisely for the case of misleading information negligently provided. For example, if a surveyor retained by a building society to inspect a dwelling knows that his report will get into the hands of the eventual purchaser, he will be liable in the tort of negligence if through his carelessness the report is false and the purchaser suffers harm by buying the house in reliance on it. The same is true even if the buyer never sees the report, but infers its favourable contents from the fact that the building society was ready to lend the purchase money.[27] These rules have now been extended from cases of erroneous information to cases where a professional service has been poorly rendered. Take the case that a lawyer retained to draw up a will giving succession rights to a third party makes a mistake, with the result that the will is invalid as drafted, the legal heir takes the estate, and the intended beneficiary gets nothing. The disappointed legatee can sue the lawyer for damages—in Germany because the contract between testator and lawyer is one with protective effects for the third party,[28] and in England because the lawyer has breached a duty of care owed to the third party.[29]

---

[24] One of the exceptions is § 826 BGB, which makes a person liable for harm, including 'pure economic loss', intentionally caused by immoral conduct. Informants whose misconduct is particularly gross can also be held liable under § 826 BGB; see, for example, BGH 17 Sept. 1985, [1986] *NJW* 180. See generally on tort liability for pure economic loss in German law Kötz and Wagner (n 23) mn. 164, 430ff. and, on a comparative basis, WH van Boom, H Koziol, and CA Witting (eds), *Pure Economic Loss* (2004); M Bussani and V Palmer (eds), *Pure Economic Loss* (2003); G Wagner, *Grundstrukturen des Europäischen Deliktsrechts* (2003) 189, 229ff.

[25] See, for example, BGH 28 Apr. 1982, [1982] *NJW* 2431; BGH 2 Nov. 1983, [1984] *NJW* 355; BGH 23 Jan. 1985, [1985] *JZ* 951; BGH 26 Nov. 1986, [1987] *NJW* 1758.

[26] Thus one need not be a customer to sue a bank under art. 1240 (formerly: art. 1382) *Code civil* for providing inaccurate information: see Req. 2 Dec. 1930, *Gaz.Pal.*1931.1.38. See also Com. 9 Jan. 1978, Bull.cass. 1978.IV. no. 12; Com. 17 Oct. 1984, *JCP* 1985.II.20458, n. A Viandier.

[27] *Smith* v. *Eric S. Bush* [1990] 1 AC 831; *Yianni* v. *Edwin Evans & Sons* [1982] 1 QB 438. On the liability in negligence of an accountant for an erroneous audit report, see *Caparo Plc* v. *Dickman* [1990] 2 AC 605.

[28] BGH 6 July 1965, [1966] *JZ* 141, n. W Lorenz. Likewise BGH 11 Jan. 1977, [1977] *NJW* 2073: if a lawyer drafts a settlement on divorce so badly that the children it is supposed to favour do not benefit, the children may sue the lawyer for damages as third parties protected by the contract.

[29] See *White* v. *Jones* [1995] 2 WLR 187 (HL). A client had instructed a solicitor to draw up a will to benefit the claimants, who were the testator's daughters. A mistake by the solicitor meant that the will was not drawn up in time before the testator died. The daughters received nothing and took legal action for damages against the solicitor. In an interesting passage, Lord Goff examined the question of whether the contract between the client and lawyer had a protective effect with respect to the

III. Claims by third parties not based on contractual intention

We have seen that the third party can acquire a personal right under a contract if this was the express or implied intention of the parties. There are also cases, especially in the Romanistic legal family, where in the absence of any such intention third parties are granted contractual rights, either by the legislature or the judiciary.

1. Action directe

In French law, a creditor may bring a direct claim against the person indebted to the debtor to the extent of anything still owed by both of them. This is called the *action directe*.[30] For example, if a building firm has not been paid by the site owner, those builders who worked on the construction but have not been paid by the building firm have a direct claim against the site owner.[31] Likewise, a building subcontractor who has not been paid by the main contractor, which is perhaps now insolvent, can take action against the site owner who has not yet paid the main contractor.[32] A lessor that is owed rent by a lessee may make a direct claim against the sub-lessee,[33] and a principal can sue a sub-agent to whom its agent has delegated the contracted task.[34] A particularly important example of the *action directe* is the claim brought by an accident victim against the tortfeasor's liability insurer. Here the legislature ratified a result originally reached by the courts on the ground that a liability insurance policy constitutes a contract for the benefit of the third party victims of the insured.[35] Where

---

claimants, thus giving them a claim in contract (as in BGH 6 July 1965, n 28). In the end, Lord Goff decided, along with the majority of the court, that the claim must be founded in the tort of negligence, thus finding in favour of the claimants. See T Weir, 'A damnosa hereditas' (1995) 111 *LQR* 357; R Zimmermann, 'Erbfolge und Schadensersatz bei Anwaltsverschulden' (1996) 4 *ZEuP* 672. The liability of a notary or other expert in tort to third parties in the Netherlands is also based on art. 6:162 BW. See HR 23 Dec. 1994, [1996] *NedJur* 627; HR 15 Sept. 1995, [1996] *NedJur* 629 and N Jansen and AJ van der Lely, 'Haftung für Auskünfte: Ein Vergleich zwischen englischem, deutschem und niederländischem Recht' (1999) 7 *ZEuP* 229.

[30] See C Jamin, *La notion d'action directe* (1991). See now art. 1341-1ff. *Code civil*.
[31] Article 1798 *Code civil*; art. 1676 *Codice civile*; art. 1597 Spanish Civil Code; art. 702 Greek Civil Code.
[32] Article 12 of L. 75-1334 of 31 Dec. 1975 '*relative à la sous-traitance*'. The decision of the *Cour de cassation (Chambre mixte)* of 30 Nov. 2007, D. 2008, 5, n. X Delpech, states that provided the building work is being carried out in France, art. 12 of the law is a *loi de police*, allowing the subcontractor to take an *action directe* against the site owner even if its contract with the main contractor or the contract between the main contractor and the site owner is subject to the law of another jurisdiction. See J Bauerreis, 'Direkter Zahlungsanspruch des Subunternehmers gegen den Auftraggeber nach französischem Recht unabhängig von der durch die Parteien getroffenen Rechtswahl' (2011) 19 *ZEuP* 406.
[33] Article 1753 *Code civil*; art. 1595 *Codice civile*; art. 1552 Spanish Civil Code; art. 1063 Portuguese Civil Code.
[34] Article 1994(2) *Code civil*; art. 1705(2) *Codice civile*; art. 1722 Spanish Civil Code; art. 716(3) Greek Civil Code; art. 399(3) OR. French courts have applied the same idea in reverse: the subagent can claim its expenses not only from the agent who hired it, but directly from the principal: see Civ. 27 Dec. 1960, *Gaz Pal* 1961.1.258. Swiss courts decide otherwise: BG 8 May 1915, BGE 41 II 268, 271.
[35] Now art. L 124-3 *Code des assurances*. The same practical result emerges from art. 3:287 BW which gives the victim a *voorrecht* to the tortfeasor's claim for an indemnity from his liability insurer, a claim which the victim can make good without being affected by the rights of third parties.

the claimant is the victim of a traffic accident, the direct action against the motorist's liability insurer is now law throughout Europe.[36]

2. Contract chains

Courts in France have long held that the buyer of goods that is injured by a latent defect in them has a direct action in damages against the manufacturer. Although the goods may have passed from hand to hand before reaching the injured party, so that there are no contractual relations between the injured party and the manufacturer, there is agreement that the claim is based on an *action directe*. Its basis, however, is much disputed. Several commentators have read a '*stipulation pour autrui*' into the contract between the manufacturer and the party it sells it to, whereby the manufacturer guarantees not only to its immediate buyer but also to all future buyers that there are no hidden defects in the goods. Others say that the eventual claim is implicitly assigned by each buyer to the next in line, or that the claim is attached to the goods (an *accessoire* within the meaning of art. 1615 *Code civil*) and runs automatically with them to whoever becomes their owner.[37]

In recent years, French courts have greatly expanded the scope within which third parties can bring contractual claims. Until recently, it seemed as if a claim for damages might be qualified as *contractuel* notwithstanding the absence of direct contractual relations between the parties to the litigation if both of them had made contracts with other people which, though distinct in law, formed part of an economic complex which could be described as a *groupe de contrats* or an *ensemble contractuel*. Take the case of a building project where the site owner contracts with a main contractor, it subcontracts to a subcontractor, and the subcontractor subcontracts again to a supplier of building materials. If the supplier delivers defective building materials or the subcontractor does defective work, and the defects are later put right at the expense of the site owner, the site owner can of course claim damages from the general contractor if the relevant conditions are met. But what if the general contractor is insolvent, or the claim against it is time-barred? Can the site owner then take legal action directly against the supplier or the subcontractor? Since there are no direct contractual links between the parties, one would suppose that the claim must be in tort. Such a claim would be successful, since art. 1240 (formerly: art. 1382) *Code civil*, which covers *tout dommage*, would permit the recovery by the site owner of its pure economic loss, provided it can establish some *faute*.[38] But to allow such short-circuiting by the law of tort would pervert the contractual allocation of risks between the various parties,

---

[36] See art. 6 of the Annex to the European Agreement of 20 Apr. 1959 on mandatory liability insurance for motor vehicles (BGBl. 1965 II 282). See also § 115(1) German Insurance Contract Act (VVG); s. 148 Road Traffic Act 1988.

[37] On these various 'theories', see n. P Malinvaud, note to Civ. 5 Jan. 1972, *JCP* 1973.II.17340; JS Borghetti, 'Breach of Contract and Liability to Third Parties in French Law: How to Break the Deadlock?' (2010) 18 *ZEuP* 279, 284ff.

[38] The courts decide otherwise in Germany (BGH 30 May 1963, BGHZ 39, 366) and, after many a twist and turn, in England (*Murphy* v. *Brentwood DC* [1990] 2 All ER 908 (HL)). Both jurisdictions come to the same result, but via different paths: in the end, the site owner has no claim in tort so long as the claim is for pure economic loss.

and also permit the appropriate time-bar to be sidestepped. The *Cour de cassation* therefore decided in numerous cases that while the direct action was permissible, the claim must be qualified as contractual despite the absence of direct contractual links between the parties to the lawsuit. As a result, plaintiffs could not claim in tort[39] and defendants could invoke all the defences arising from either of the two contracts which they respectively made with the middlemen.[40]

This line of cases was criticised on the ground that it was inconsistent with the principle of *relativité des contrats* laid down in art. 1199 (formerly: art. 1165) *Code civil*, and that the concept of *groupe de contrats* lacked rigorous definition. The *Cour de cassation* has now indeed changed course, and has decided that no contractual claims lie between site owner and subcontractor, and that consequently the site owner can only claim damages in tort for the harm suffered due to the subcontractor's faulty work—which means that the claimant must evidence fault. It follows that the subcontractor cannot defend a claim in tort by the site owner by invoking arguments it could have used to defend a claim in contract against the main contractor.[41] But that was not all. Individual chambers of the *Cour de cassation* decided that the third-party claim must be made in tort, but is already founded if it can show that its harm was caused by the defendant's breach of a contract made with another party.[42] Although this rule might be said to remove all limits to claims by third parties, it was followed by the *Cour de cassation* in another plenary decision. The claimant was a retailer whose shop was in premises rented from the company Myr'ho. The claimant said the premises were badly maintained and that his business was suffering harm as a consequence. He sought damages not from his contractual partner Myr'ho, but from the owner of the building that had let out the entire complex to Myr'ho (including the rooms used by the claimant). The *Cour de cassation* allowed the retailer's claim, with the rather succinct reasoning that 'a third party making a claim in tort can rely on a breach of contract if it has caused damage to the third party'.[43]

---

[39] This follows from the doctrine of *non-cumul*, whereby concurrence of contractual and tortious claims is prevented: a possible contractual claim always bars a possible claim in tort. See the thorough discussion of the doctrine of *non-cumul* by G Viney, *Introduction à la responsabilité* (3rd edn, 2008) no. 216ff.

[40] See, for example, Civ. 29 May 1984, D. 1985, 213, n. A Bénabent = *JCP* 1985.II.20387, n. P Malinvaud; Ass.plén. 7 Feb. 1986, D. 1986, 293, n. A Bénabent = *JCP* 1986.II.20616, n. P Malinvaud. See also Civ. 8 Mar. 1988, *JCP* 1988.II.21070, n. P Jourdain: The camera shop to which the plaintiff sent some film for development sent it on to the defendant firm, which lost it. Although there was no direct contractual link between plaintiff and defendant, the plaintiff's claim was classified as contractual, with the result that the defendant was allowed to invoke defences arising under *both* contracts. See also Civ. 21 June 1988, D. 1989, 5, n. C Larroumet = *JCP* 1988.II.21125, n. P Jourdain, in which the same result was reached: the airplane which the plaintiff had entrusted to the managers of an airfield was damaged when a tractor purchased by the airfield suffered a mechanical failure while being used to tow the plane down a runway. When the owner of the plane sued not only the airfield, with which it had a contract, but also the manufacturer of the tractor and the supplier of the defective component, his claim against the two latter firms was characterised as contractual because the contracts between the four firms involved constituted a *groupe de contrats*.

[41] Ass.plén. 12 July 1991, *JCP* 1991.II.21743 (arrêt *Besse*), n. G Viney = D. 1991, 549, n. J Ghestin. See also C Jamin, D. 1991 Chron. 257; C Larroumet, *JCP* 1991.I.3531; P Jourdain, D. 1992 Chron. 149; C Witz and G Wolter, 'Missbräuchliche Vertragsklauseln auf dem Prüfstand der französischen Gerichte' (1993) 1 *ZEuP* 360; Borghetti (n 37) 286f.

[42] Civ. 18 July 2000, Bull.cass. 2000.I. no. 221; but see also Com. 18 Oct. 2002, *JCP* 2003.I.152, n. G Viney.

[43] Ass.plén. 6 Oct. 2006, D. 2006, 2825 (arrêt *Myr'ho*), n. G Viney. For a critical view, and with references to the extensive literature, see Borghetti (n 37) 289ff.

This ruling takes the *Cour de cassation* far away from the rules under which third parties are treated in other jurisdictions.[44] Under English law, the claimant will only have a claim in tort. But when the claim is for pure financial loss, the claim will only be allowed if the court can find that the defendant owed the third party a duty of care, and that this duty has been negligently flouted.[45] The third party will have a claim under contract in German law, but only if certain conditions are met, under which exceptionally a *Vertrag mit Schutzwirkung für Dritte* can be accepted.[46] Under French law, however, the impression is given that any party which is in breach of a contract may be open to direct action not only from its contractual partner, but from any third party that has suffered damage as a result of the breach. One might ask if anything remains of the original art. 1165 *Code civil*: '*Les conventions n'ont effet qu'entre les parties contractantes.*'

IV. Limitations of liability and third parties

Under a contract for the benefit of third parties, the third party generally acquires a right to *sue* one of the parties, but can it also acquire a *defence*? Can the parties equip the third party with a shield as well as a sword?

The law reports in England and Germany suggest that the problem arises most frequently in cases of carriage. Carriers of goods normally limit or exclude their liability to the shipper in the event that goods are lost or damaged. Carriers often hand the cargo over to another carrier for all or part of the route, and have the goods handled by contracted cargo handlers or storage companies. If the shipper whose goods are damaged sues not the carrier it contracted with but others who were involved in getting the goods delivered, the question arises whether they can avail themselves of limitations of liability contained in the contract of carriage. The same question arises when the shipper sues not the firms themselves but one of their employees, such as the captain, the stevedore or the crane driver.

English courts have often supported the third-party effect of such rules excluding or restricting liability, though they have often had to resort to some artificial legal reasoning. It was impossible to hold that the third party was protected because the parties so intended, since that would conflict with the dogma 'that no one can enforce a contract to which he was not a party'.[47] So the English courts had somehow to construct contractual relations between the shipper and the third party. They held that the carrier, by limiting or excluding its liability, was also acting as 'agent' for third parties,

---

[44] Note that the cases decided by the *Cour de cassation* do *not* concern those cases where the harm to the third party results from faulty characteristics of *goods* that have come into its possession after a chain of contractual transactions: Here the third party will have a claim in *contract* against any company that has manufactured the goods or distributed them in a chain of contracts. See, for example, Civ. 28 Apr. 1998, Bull.cass. 1998.I. no. 104 and above, p. 329. While the third party's claim is described as 'contractual', this does not mean that a French court is allowed to base its international jurisdiction over the third party's claim against a German manufacturer on the ground that (under art. 5(1)a Brussels I Regulation) it must decide on a 'contractual claim'. See ECJ 17 June 1992, [1992] Slg. I-3967 (*Handte/TMCS*).

[45] See, for example, the decisions listed in nn 27 and 29 above, and see also *Simaan General Contracting Co. v. Pilkington Glass Ltd. (No. 2)* [1988] QB 758.

[46] See text to n 22f. above.   [47] See *Adler v. Dickson* [1955] 1 QB 158, 181 per Lord Denning.

or that the exemption clause was an implied offer made by the shipper to the third party which the latter accepted, also by implication.[48] The Contracts (Rights of Third Parties) Act 1999 now offers a more simple approach. Section 1(6) of the Act states that a third party is entitled to the benefit of an exemption clause in contracts made between others. But this applies only if the requirements of the Act are satisfied, that is where the contract expressly specifies the third party as a beneficiary, or the contract can be construed that it 'purports to confer a benefit on [the third party].'

Article 6:253 of the Dutch Civil Code expressly states that a contract can provide a third party not only with a right to performance, but also a right 'to invoke the contract in another manner', in particular to rely on an exemption clause in a contract made by others. German courts reach the same result. A provision in a contract of carriage that 'all claims against the shipowner are time-barred after six months' may be invoked not only by the shipowner but also by any other carrier it has subcontracted to carry out the transportation, and also their crews.[49] The question whether employees may invoke an exemption clause in their employer's contract is of some practical importance. The Dutch Civil Code gives a positive answer: art. 6:257 BW provides that an employee may do so 'as if he himself was a party to that agreement' regardless of whether or not the wording of the clause gives express exemption to the employee.[50] German courts reach the same result in the absence of any such statutory basis. If a security firm contracts to guard a building site subject to an exemption of liability for harm 'due to the servicing or guarding of machines, ovens, boilers or heating appliances', a claim by the builder against the individual watchman will be dismissed—not because the words of the clause cover him, but because it emerges from the circumstances that the security firm had an interest, as the builder knew, in having the clause cover their staff.[51] Of course every party that makes a contract for work, carriage, warehousing, or safeguarding with an independent contractor knows that the service will actually be rendered by employees rather than the firm itself. It would be absurd if the party or its insurer could sidestep an agreed and valid exemption clause simply by suing the contractor's employees under the general rules of the law of tort.

C. Effects

I. Rights of the promisee

A party that by contract undertakes to render performance to a third party certainly becomes the third party's debtor, but not its contractor. While the third party may

---

[48] See, for example, *Elder Dempster & Co.* v. *Paterson, Zochonis & Co.* [1924] AC 522; *Scruttons Ltd.* v. *Midland Silicones* [1962] AC 446; *The Eurymedon* [1975] AC 154; and in detail Treitel (n 7) no. 14-064ff.

[49] BGH 21 Oct. 1971, [1972] *VersR* 40; likewise BGH 7 July 1960, [1960] *VersR* 727, 729; BGH 28 Apr. 1977, [1977] *VersR* 717.

[50] Article 6:257 applies only to subordinate assistants in the contractual enterprise (*ondergeschikte*). Comparable rules apply in favour of independent contractors retained by the main carrier or warehouser. See art. 7:608 and 8:71, 362ff BW.

[51] BGH 7 Dec. 1961, [1962] *NJW* 388. Likewise BGH 12 Mar. 1985, [1985] *VersR* 595: a clause which restricts a builder's liability to cases of intentional wrongdoing or gross negligence may be invoked by its employees. The same rule can be found in art. 5.2.3 PICC; art. II.-9:301(3) DCFR; art. 78 (2) CESL, but not (apparently by inadvertence) in art. 6:110 PECL.

acquire rights under this agreement, the question remains what rights the *promisee* has against the promisor.

It is generally recognised that, in the absence of contrary agreement, the promisee may demand that the promisor render the promised performance to the third party.[52] Equally, the promisee may claim damages for the loss it suffers as a result of the promisor's failure to render performance to the third party, or rendering it late. The promisee may also invoke the promisor's non-performance as a defence, and withhold its own performance until the promisor does perform. It may be a question, however, whether the promisee can terminate the contract, or withdraw from it on the ground of the promisor's breach, and so terminate the third party's right to performance. In principle this is allowed. If the buyer has promised the seller to pay one half of the price to a third party, the buyer seller must be able to terminate the contract or exercise other rights if the seller committed a fraud or delivered defective goods. Nor does the buyer need the assent of the third party, even when the third party's right to receive one half of the price has become irrevocable (below, pages 334ff.).

II. Defences available to the promisor

The third party's right derives from and depends on the contract made between promisor and promisee. It follows that the promisor can raise against the third party any defences that it could invoke against the promisee if sued for performance.[53] Thus, if the third party in the case above claimed the part of the price it was to receive, the buyer could raise the defence that the contract remained unperformed and withhold payment until the seller did perform. The buyer can refuse payment altogether if it has avoided the contract or withdrawn from it. Of course, the defences must arise from the contract that gave the third party its rights. If they are *'extérieurs au contrat générateur de la stipulation pour autrui',*[54] they are not available to the promisor. Thus the promisor cannot set off against the third party a claim it has against the promisee arising from some other matter,[55] though it may set off a claim arising directly from any legal relationship it has with the third party.

---

[52] Civ. 12 July 1956, D. 1956, 749, n. J Radouant; Com. 14 May 1979 (n 16); § 335 BGB; § 881(1) ABGB; art. 112(1) OR; art. 6:256 BW; art. 410 Greek Civil Code; art. 444(2) Portuguese Civil Code.

[53] Com. 25 Mar. 1969, Bull.cass. 1969.IV. no. 118; Civ. 7 Mar. 1989, *JCP* 1989.IV.170; Civ. 29 Nov. 1994, Bull.cass. 1994.I. no. 353; § 334 BGB; § 882(2) ABGB; art. 1413 *Codice civile*; art. 414 Greek Civil Code; art. 449 Portuguese Civil Code; art. 393(3) Polish Civil Code. See also art. 5.2.4 PICC; art. II.-9:302(b) DCFR; art. 78(3)(b) CESL. There may be special cases which call for a different result. Thus in BGH 17 Jan. 1985, BGHZ 93, 271, a holiday tour operator had chartered seats on an airline for specified flights from Frankfurt to the Caribbean and sold them on to customers. The operator failed to pay the sum agreed in the charter and was now insolvent, but the airline was nevertheless held liable to the customers as third-party beneficiaries of the charter.

[54] Larroumet (n 14) no. 820.

[55] BGH 27 Feb. 1961, [1961] *MDR* 481, 482. Here there is a clear difference from assignment: if the third party acquires its right not directly under a contract for its benefit but derivatively as assignee, its claim is subject to a set-off in respect of counterclaims however arising, provided that they existed at the time the debtor learnt of the assignment.

III. Modification or termination of third party rights

Many years may elapse between the formation of a contract and the moment when the third party seeks to assert its rights under it, so one needs to know whether the right the third party acquired on formation can subsequently be modified or terminated.

Most European legal systems start from the rule to be found in the French *Code civil*, whereby the third party's right can only be revoked if the third party has not yet 'accepted' it. An 'acceptance' may be made by a declaration addressed either to the promisee or the promisor (art. 1206(2) and (3) *Code civil*). Likewise art. 112(3) OR provides that the third party's right becomes irrevocable as soon as he informed the promisor 'that he wishes to make use of his right'.[56]

However, this principle is often restricted in the important case where the third party is entitled to performance only after the death of the promisee, often by a special rule that (in the absence of a contrary provision) the promisee can modify or cancel the right of the third party even if the latter has already declared that it wishes to exercise it.[57] Article 112(3) OR is held not to be mandatory—the parties can agree that the third party's right may be revoked notwithstanding its declared acceptance.

By contrast, the French courts apparently regard art. 1206(2) (formerly: art 1121 sent. 2) *Code civil* as mandatory, and apply it rather strictly. This applies in particular to life insurance contracts, since art. L 132-8 *Code des assurances* states that once the original beneficiary has expressed 'acceptance', he or she cannot be replaced. One might therefore suppose that an insured or other promisee could only revoke a nomination if the beneficiary had been kept entirely in the dark. In practice, this is not quite so. For one thing, the beneficiary has to manifest 'acceptance' by actually placing his or her name on the policy, by writing in appropriate terms to the insurer, or by paying the premiums. Simple acquiescence of nomination does not suffice. Also, even when the beneficiary has duly accepted, the insured—and this would apply equally to promisees under other contracts—may exceptionally be able to revoke the nomination. This is so in the (hopefully rare) case where the beneficiary has sought to end the life of the insured,[58] as well as where the benefit was by way of gift and the beneficiary has proved grossly ungrateful or has failed to satisfy the conditions attached.[59] Indeed art. 1096 *Code civil*, which provides that gifts between spouses are inherently revocable, has led the courts to hold that where the insured has nominated his or her spouse as beneficiary and this has been duly accepted, the insured may nevertheless revoke the gift at any time.[60]

---

[56] Likewise art. 1411(2) sent. 2 *Codice civile*; art. 1257(2) Spanish Civil Code; art. 448(1) Portuguese Civil Code; art. 412 Greek Civil Code; art. 6:253(2) BW; art. 393(2) Polish Civil Code. Under s. 2(1) of the Contracts (Rights of Third Parties) Act 1999, a third party's right to enforce a term of the contract may not without its consent be varied or extinguished by the parties if 'the third party has communicated his assent to the term to the promisor'. This is merely a default rule that does not apply if the parties have expressly reserved a right to rescind or vary the contract without the consent of the third party (s. 2(3) of the Act).

[57] Thus art. 1412(1) *Codice civile*; art. 448(1) Portuguese Civil Code.

[58] Article L 132-24 *Code des assurances*.

[59] See art. 953 *Code civil* and Civ. 8 July 1991, Bull.cass. 1991.I. no. 230.

[60] Poitiers 17 Jan. 1962, [1963] *RGAT* 54; Nîmes 20 Dec. 1978, [1979] *RGAT* 355. But see also Civ. 13 May 1998, Bull.cass. 1998.I. no. 170. It is doubtful what consequences result from the amendment of art. 1096 *Code civil* by which the rights of a spouse to revoke gifts have been considerably restricted.

In the light of this, it seems better not to lay down any binding rules, but to leave it to the parties to decide whether the third party's right may be modified or terminated. This is the solution adopted by German law. The question 'whether the contractors are to have the power to cancel or alter the third party's right without his consent' is one for the parties to agree, and if they make no express arrangement it depends 'on what can be inferred from the circumstances, in particular the purpose of the contract' (§ 328(2) BGB).[61] More specific rules are suggested by the international sets of rules. Pursuant to art. 6:110(3) PECL, the promisee can no longer deprive the third party of its rights after the third party has received notice from the promisee 'that the right has been made irrevocable'. Nor can the right be withdrawn or varied if the third party informed one of the parties that it 'accepted' the rights. Such 'acceptance' need not be express and can be seen in the fact that the third party took action in reliance on its right and made this known to the promisor or promisee. Article 5.2.5 PICC simply says that the third party's rights may only be modified or revoked until it 'has accepted them or reasonably acted in reliance on them'.[62]

---

[61] There is a special rule in §§ 331(1) BGB, 159 German Insurance Contracts Act for the case where performance to the third party is not to be made until after the promisee has died. This is the case with a life insurance contract. Unless otherwise agreed, the third party is only to receive the right to performance once the promisee has died. It follows that until this event occurs, the promisee may at any time replace the third party by another beneficiary, even if the third party knows of the future benefit and accepted it in some way. Article 1411f. *Codice civile* reaches the same result: if the third party will not receive performance until after the death of the promisee, then the promisee may revoke the promised benefit, even if it has already been accepted, unless the promisee has waived the right of revocation in written form.
[62] A similar rule can be found in s. 2(1) Contracts (Rights of Third Parties) Act 1999.

18
Assignment

A. Historical Development and Economic Importance	337
B. Requirements for an Effective Transaction	340
I. Substantive validity	341
II. Non-assignable rights	342
1. Rights to wages, maintenance, and support	342
2. Personal rights	342
3. Parts of debts	343
4. Future debts	343
5. No-assignment clauses	346
III. Formal requirements	348
IV. Priorities	350
C. Effects	352
I. Between assignor and assignee	352
II. Protection of the debtor	353
1. Payment to the original creditor	353
2. Defences available to the debtor	353
3. Waiver of defences by debtor	354

A. Historical Development and Economic Importance

In an economy based on money and credit, rights arising from contracts must be freely transferable. Just as an owner can transfer or convey chattels, so should a creditor be able to transfer, assign, or cede (the terms are interchangeable) intangible rights with the effect of making the transferee creditor in its place. The economic purpose of an owner transferring a receivable is usually to sell the receivable to another. If A does not have the money to settle a debt to B, on account of payment A can transfer to B a receivable owed to A from a third party C. An assignment of rights can often be for the purpose of providing collateral security for a debt—for example, when a bank lending money to a customer accepts as security an assignment of the claims that the customer has against third parties. Nowadays, whole packages of claims may be sold or transferred as security in a single transaction; credit institutions often take a bulk assignment of hundreds of claims at a time as security from those who borrow from them.

This is what happens in factoring contracts, which are made when manufacturers or dealers need to secure cash at the present time with respect to amounts due from customers who have yet to settle their accounts and where due dates may vary considerably. They sell their accounts receivable to a factor for rather less than the nominal value, the difference representing the interest the factor forgoes on the cash advanced, its trouble in collecting the debts, and sometimes the risk of default. Factoring contracts and credit security contracts are often very complex, but we need not go into details here, since our interest lies in the keystone of such arrangements—the legal institution of assignment or transfer of debts.

Nowadays, the rules for the transfer of debts are quite practical, but this took a long time to come about. The original principle in ancient Roman law and medieval Common Law was that a contract right was something so highly personal as to be inseparable from the actual relationship between creditor and debtor. As time went by, however, both Roman law and the Common Law developed rules that went some way to meeting the ever-more imperative need to recognise such transfers.[1] The Romans first accepted that by making the chosen transferee a *procurator in rem suam*, the creditor could empower him to sue the debtor in his own name and keep the proceeds. The disadvantage of this solution was that the creditor could revoke the power at any time until the lawsuit was started and claim the debt himself, for it was still owed to him, or release the debtor for payment or otherwise. In imperial times, the transferee's position was strengthened. He was given a personal *actio utilis* in certain cases: first, where the right was part of a succession he had bought; then where the debt was part of a dowry; and finally where he himself had received the debt from the creditor by purchase or gift. By the time of Justinian, therefore, it was accepted in substance that debts were transferable, since practically every transferee was given an *actio utilis*— a claim of his own against the debtor—provided only that the creditor and he had agreed, for whatever reason, on the transfer. It does, however, seem that notice to the debtor, a *denuntiatio*, was required.

All would have been well if the *Corpus Iuris* had simply enacted this culminating principle, but the jurists charged by Justinian with the selection and ordering of the texts included all the different techniques that their predecessors had *successively* thought up, so that it looked as if these different solutions had featured *simultaneously* in Roman law. Attempts to harmonise these different techniques provoked endless dispute until well into the nineteenth century. As late as 1850, the dominant view among Pandectists was that debts were not properly transferable, the *actio utilis* of the assignee being explained on the basis that the creditor had simply given him power to claim the debt rather than transferred the debt itself. Eventually, the Pandectists accepted that debts could be freely transferred, and this approach was adopted in the German Civil Code (§§ 398 ff.). Today, it is recognised throughout Europe that contract rights are transferable in the sense that the new creditor takes the place of the old and can enforce the right against the debtor in just the same way.

Like Roman law, the Common Law started out by regarding intangible rights as inalienable but, in unconscious mimesis of Roman law, it later came to hold that the intended transferee could claim the debt if the creditor granted him a power of attorney.[2] But such a power could be revoked, as in Roman law, and lapsed if the grantor died or became bankrupt. So in the early seventeenth century the courts of Equity

---

[1] On what follows, see R Zimmermann, *The Law of Obligations, Roman Foundations of the Civilian Tradition* (1990) 58ff; K Luig, *Zur Geschichte der Zessionslehre* (1966) 2ff; also H Kötz in *Int.Enc.Comp.L.* vol. II ch 13, 60ff.

[2] For the details, see SJ Bailey, 'Assignment of Debts in England from the Twelfth to the Twentieth Century' (1931) 47 *LQR* 516 and (1932) 48 *LQR* 248, 547.

came to the rescue and granted the transferee a claim of his own, provided it was clear that the parties really wanted the right to be transferred.[3]

If the transferability of contract rights is now widely recognised, legal systems differ as to when and how the debtor is to be apprised of the transfer. Of course, it makes sense for the assignee to inform the debtor of the transfer, otherwise there is a danger that a debtor unaware of the assignment will settle the obligation with the assignor, thus leaving the assignee empty-handed. Another issue is whether informing the debtor not only makes sense from the assignee's point of view, but is actually *required*. The view in France since the sixteenth century has been that if the assignee sued the debtor, it had to prove that the debtor had been shown the document of transfer or had it formally served on him by a court official. From this, it was only a short step to holding that the assignee should only be considered as the new creditor if the debtor had been given formal notice of the assignment.[4] This rule found its way into the *Coutume de Paris* (art. 108), was endorsed by Pothier,[5] and finally adopted in the old art. 1690 *Code civil*.[6] During the *ius commune*, the Dutch and German courts were less strict, but there were dissentient voices on the matter, and even Windscheid upheld the view that a transfer only took effect *erga omnes* when the transferee had informed the debtor of the transfer or taken legal action against him.[7] Windscheid's view, however, could not prevail against the dominant view that ultimately found its way into the BGB in § 398 sent. 2, whereby the new creditor steps into the shoes of the former creditor as soon as the transfer is agreed between them. There is no need for the debtor to know about the assignment.

It cannot be denied that national legal systems still contain some rules on assignment that date back to earlier times, and that are now obsolete and no longer meet the needs of modern business practice. It is also doubtful in some legal systems whether and on what conditions 'future' receivables can be assigned. There is also a lack of clarity about what are the consequences if creditor and debtor have agreed that a receivable will not be assignable. Is an assignment under these circumstances valid or not? All these rules sit uneasily with the fact that receivables are now an important economic asset that must often be realised by their owners before maturity, and that they are often assigned to banks in great volumes for the purpose of

---

[3] These rules applied only to 'equitable assignments' where the assigned right would be implemented by a court of Equity—for example, where the debtor was a trustee who had to perform certain services for the creditor on the basis of a trust relationship. For other claims (legal choses of action), the old rule was that the claim against the debtor must be made jointly by the assignor and the assignee. This was replaced by what is now called a 'statutory assignment' (see now s. 136(1) Law of Property Act 1925), which allows the assignee to make a claim directly against the debtor if the assignment is in writing signed by the assignor and notice has been given in writing to the debtor. If any conditions of a 'statutory assignment' are not present (particularly if the assignment is made verbally or has not been notified to the debtor), it can still be valid as an 'equitable assignment'. For details, see GH Treitel, *The Law of Contract* (13th edn, by E Peel, 2011) no. 15-009ff. These rules have long since been abandoned in other jurisdictions of the Common Law and will not be considered further here.

[4] See H Coing, *Europäisches Privatrecht, vol. 1: Älteres Gemeines Recht* (1985), 447; II, 470.

[5] 'Traité du contrat de vente' in M Bugnet (ed), *Oeuvres de Pothier* (1847) vol. III no. 554-7.

[6] This rule led to many practical difficulties, and for this reason was supplemented by special legislation—in particular the *Loi Dailly* (see below)—and finally replaced by an entirely new regime in arts. 1321–1326 *Code civil*. See art. 1701-1 *Code civil*.

[7] B Windscheid, *Lehrbuch des Pandektenrechts* (1865) § 331.

securing loans, or sold to factoring companies.[8] For this reason, many legal orders have passed special regulations that treat the commercial transfer of receivables differently than envisaged in the unchanged general rules of assignment. A particularly notable example is the *Loi Dailly* introduced in France in 1981.[9] The commercial assignment of receivables also often has an international character, because creditor and debtor or transferor and transferee have their registered offices in different countries. Two international agreements have attempted to find harmonised solutions for the resulting problems: the UNIDROIT Convention on International Factoring of 28 May 1988[10] and, above all, the United Nations Convention on the Assignment of Receivables in International Trade of 12 February 2001.[11] This Convention also contains rules that go far beyond the rules on assignment of receivables contained in the national legal systems. The same applies for the international sets of rules that aim to harmonise the law of assignment, and are also guided by the idea of taking account of the interests of the commercial parties in having a modernisation of the law in this area.

B. Requirements for an Effective Transaction

The purpose of transferring a right is to make the transferee creditor, and this aim is achieved—and the transfer is effective—when the right leaves the estate of the transferor, thereby ceasing to be available to its creditors, and the transferee becomes the owner of the right. This aim may be wholly or partially frustrated in several ways. For one thing, the assignment itself may be defective, either void *ab initio* or subject to annulment by one of the parties (see section I below). For another, although the parties' agreement may be invulnerable, the right sought to be assigned may be intrinsically non-transferable, either by law or because it was so agreed between the original creditor and debtor (see section II below). Furthermore, there may be certain formalities to be observed, neglect of which may invalidate the assignment completely or else

---

[8] A further source of large-scale assignments is with respect to securitisation transactions (in Germany: *Forderungsverbriefung*, in France: *titrisation*): Great volumes of receivables are sold and transferred from their creditors to an independent legal entity without the debtor having any knowledge of this transaction. The legal entity issues securities, uses the income generated to pay the assignors, and services the securities with the payments received from the assignors when the receivables are paid by the debtors. The purpose of such transactions is to free the assignors from the risk of collecting the receivables for a relatively low amount.

[9] The rules of the *Loi Dailly* have since been incorporated into the *Code monétaire et financier*. See art. L 313-27ff. (see below, p. 348), and with respect to *titrisation* art. L 241-43ff. Similar laws have also been adopted in Italy. See also A Salomons, 'Deformalisation of Assignment Law and the Position of the Debtor in European Property Law' [2007] *ERPL* 639.

[10] The Factoring Convention has been ratified by Germany and entered into force, although only in relation to relatively few countries. See the German Law of 25 February 1988, BGBl 1998 II 2375.

[11] The United Nations Convention on the Assignment of Receivables in International Trade (CARIT) is not yet in force. It is reprinted in (2002) 10 *ZEuP* 860. Both this Convention and the Factoring Convention (referred to in n 10) are examined in detail by E Schütze, *Zession und Einheitsrecht* (2005) and C Rudolf, *Einheitsrecht für internationale Forderungsabtretungen* (2006). See also H Eidenmüller, 'Die Dogmatik der Zession vor dem Hintergrund der internationalen Entwicklung' (2004) 204 *AcP* 457; S Bazinas, 'Der Beitrag von UNCITRAL zur Vereinheitlichung der Rechtsvorschriften über Forderungsabtretungen' (2002) 10 *ZEuP* 782.

render it ineffective against the debtor and other third parties, while remaining valid between assignor and assignee (section III below). Finally, we must mention the rules relating to priority, for if the creditor assigns the same right to two parties in succession, conflicts may arise between them (section IV below).

I. Substantive validity

Like any other contract, an assignment can be invalid by reason of illegality or immorality. It is also invalid if the transferor lacked capacity or was not properly represented at the time of the act. It is the same if the agreement was tainted by mistake or deceit so as to enable the transferor to avoid the contract. The general rules as to the invalidity of contracts are applicable in all these cases.[12] Here it makes little actual difference whether one distinguishes, as most European systems do, between the assignment and the underlying transaction; whether one distinguishes them but regards them as so intertwined that they stand or fall together; or whether (as in Germany) one makes a strong distinction of principle between them, but admits that the ground of invalidity of one very commonly renders the other invalid as well.

We shall here consider only those grounds of invalidity that are specific to assignment—the first being that the right involved is the subject of litigation.

For a long time, the transfer of rights was regarded with suspicion. The fear was that people might make a business out of buying up contested rights cheaply and then pursuing the debtor. The *Code civil* stopped short of invalidating the transfer of contested rights, but lays down a rule, based on the *lex Anastasiana* (C.4.35.22), that the purchaser of a contested debt cannot claim from the debtor any more than he paid the creditor for it (art. 1699 ff. *Code civil*).[13] The aim of this rule was '*pour mettre un frein à la cupidité des acheteurs de droits litigieux, et pour arrêter les procès*',[14] and for the same reason an assignment is void if made to a lawyer or other legal functionary engaged in the courts where the claim is or can be heard.[15]

There are no such provisions in Germany, Austria, or Switzerland, where it is thought sufficient to apply to assignments the general rules as to the nullity of legal acts which infringe legal prescriptions or moral precepts. Thus an assignment may be ineffectual where its purpose is to enable the transferee to engage in conducting litigation (which is reserved to lawyers duly licensed to practise law), or where it is known that the transferee is insolvent and therefore unable to meet the costs of the debtor if its claim were to be unsuccessful.[16]

---

[12] See above, chapters 5ff.
[13] See also art. 1535f. Spanish Civil Code. See also in detail F Terré, P Simler, and Y Lequette, *Droit civil, Les obligations* (11th edn, 2013) no. 1296.
[14] Pothier (n 5) no. 590.
[15] Article 1597 *Code civil*; art. 1261 *Codice civile*; art. 1495(5) Spanish Civil Code; art. 579f. Portuguese Civil Code. In the Netherlands, art. 3:43 BW invalidates such transfers of all property, not just of contract rights.
[16] See BGH 18 Sept. 1959, [1959] *MDR* 999; BGH 18 Apr. 1967, BGHZ 47, 364; BGH 6 Nov. 1973, [1974] *NJW* 50; OGH 13 June 1956, [1957] *JBl* 215; BG 27 July 1961, BGE 87 II 203.

II. Non-assignable rights

1. Rights to wages, maintenance, and support

Rights designed to provide an individual with a minimum of means of support cannot be transferred. This is generally accepted as regards claims for wages, maintenance, support, and for social security payments, and is often laid down in statutory form—sometimes in the form that such claims are not subject to execution and to the extent they are not, they are also non-transferable.[17]

2. Personal rights

An assignment has the effect of presenting the debtor with a new creditor without its consent. The debtor may well be indifferent as to whom performance is to be rendered, especially if it consists of the payment of money, but sometimes the debtor has a considerable interest in dealing exclusively with the original creditor. If so, it can protect against any change of creditor by stipulating that the claim be non-transferable (see below, pages 346f.). Even if the debtor fails to secure such an agreement, the courts will treat a claim as non-transferable if they think that the debtor's expectation that it be liable only to the original creditor deserves protection. Sometimes claims which are 'of a highly personal nature'[18] or 'closely connected'[19] to the identity of the creditor or 'adherent'[20] to it are rendered non-transferable by statutory provision. When § 399 BGB says that claims are non-transferable when 'performance cannot be made to a person other than the original obligee without a change of its contents', it means the same thing. English courts also refuse to treat rights as transferable 'if it is clear that the debtor is willing to perform only in favour of one particular creditor'.[21]

It follows that if the person who has promised to render services has a reasonable interest in rendering them only to the party he or she contracted with, then the right to receive such services cannot be transferred without consent. Thus, if the publishing house selected by an author by reason of its high standing, special expertise, or other qualification sells the business, the author can refuse to deal with the buyer.[22] Special rules apply when an employer transfers its undertaking, stemming in part from the EC Directive on Transfer of Undertakings of 14 February 1977.[23] These rules provide that the firm taking over a business becomes a party to all employment contracts subsisting at the time of the takeover. As to other contracts, since anyone who lets or leases an asset generally relies on the personal qualities of the person who is to use it,

---

[17] See, for example § 400 BGB; art. 325 OR; § 293ff Austrian Law of Execution; art. 7A:1638g BW; Terré, Simler, and Lequette (n 13) no. 1278; Treitel (n 3) no. 15-066 and 15-068.
[18] Article 1260 *Codice civile*; § 6:194(3) Hungarian Civil Code; art. 509(1) Polish Civil Code.
[19] Article 465 Greek Civil Code; art. 577 Portuguese Civil Code. [20] § 1393 ABGB.
[21] Treitel (n 3) no. 15-051. See also art. 11:302 PECL; art. 9.1.7(2) PICC; art. III.-5:109 DCFR.
[22] See § 613(2), 664(2) BGB; *Griffith v. Tower Publishing Co.* [1897] 1 Ch. 21.
[23] EC Directive 77/187/EEC of 14 February 1977 (O.J. 1977 L 61/26), transposed into § 613a BGB in Germany, into the Transfer of Undertakings (Protection of Employment) Regulations (SI 2006/246) in Britain, and into the *Code du travail* art. L 122-12-1 in France. In fact, what is involved here is not the assignment of a right but the transfer of the contract as a whole.

the latter's rights are not transferable.²⁴ But a buyer's right to delivery of the goods and a customer's right to have a piece of work done or improved may be assigned unless the debtor would find performance to the assignee more burdensome or riskier, or if performance would be turned into '*etwas anderes*' (something other) than what was originally undertaken.²⁵

3. Parts of debts

The debtor may be put in a difficulty if only part of the debt is assigned, or if it is assigned to several assignees jointly so that each of them becomes entitled to part of it. Having to deal with more than one creditor may put the debtor to the extra expense of having to dispute the amount due more than once, and there is also a risk of inconsistent judgments if separate actions can be brought by different assignees.

Nevertheless, it is generally accepted that where the claim itself is divisible, such as a money debt, it may be transferred in part.²⁶ The risk of conflicting judgments can be avoided by allowing the debtor to insist that all assignees join in the legal action.²⁷ By contrast, the extra expense must be borne by the debtor, unless this would be unacceptable for some particular reason. The *Bundesgerichtshof* so decided in a case where an employer contested the validity of a partial assignment of an employee's claim for wages, saying that the company had 8,000 employees and the expense would be intolerable if each of them could assign rights in divided parts. The court rejected the argument: employees had an interest in being able to transfer part of their right to wages, and if the employer wished to protect itself, it could have a term prohibiting assignment included in the individual contracts of employment or in the collective bargaining agreement (see below, pages 346f.).²⁸

4. Future debts

Can a debt that will only become actionable in the future be transferred before the due date? And what of a debt not yet in existence, but expected to arise in the future?

In times gone by, it was thought to be a 'legal impossibility' to transfer a debt which did not yet exist—*nemo plus iuris transferre potest quam ipse haberet*. Furthermore,

---

²⁴ See H Mazeaud, L Mazeaud, J Mazeaud, and F Chabas, *Leçons de droit civil, vol. III.1: Obligations, Théorie générale* (9th edn, 2006) no. 1258; G Roth in *Münchener Kommentar zum BGB* (6th edn, 2012) § 399 mn. 24ff.
²⁵ See BGH 24 Oct. 1985, BGHZ 96, 146, 149 (claim to remedy a defect by repair held transferable). On the transferability of a buyer's claim for delivery, see *Kemp* v. *Baerselman* [1906] 2 KB 604 and BG 17 Dec. 1968, BGE 94 II 274 (transferability denied); *Tolhurst* v. *Associated Portland Cement* [1903] AC 414 (transferability accepted).
²⁶ This is express in art. 577(1) Portuguese Civil Code; art. 456(2) Greek Civil Code. See also Roth (n 24) § 398 mn. 46ff. Also, partial assignment is permissible under art. 11:103 PECL as long as 'the assignor is liable to the debtor for any increased costs which the debtor thereby incurs'. See also art. 9.1.4(1) and art. 9.1.8. PIC; art. III.-5:107(1) and (3) DCFR.
²⁷ This is the way the Common Law deals with the problem: see Treitel (n 3) no. 15-013. Other jurisdictions do not have such special rules, since the debtor is protected by the general rules of procedure as regards notification and joinder.
²⁸ BGH 20 Dec. 1956, BGHZ 23, 53, 56.

the transfer of mere 'expectancies' was regarded as probably speculative and doubtfully serious. There was the further risk that if a debtor that got into serious difficulties could transfer all future rights, this might impair its personal and economic liberty. As against this, modern business urgently requires that future debts be transferable, especially as security, and the validity of such assignments is now widely accepted.

Everyone agrees, however, that a global assignment of future debts is invalid if it would have the effect of virtually incapacitating the assignor by rendering it economically impotent. So individuals cannot assign all the wages they might ever earn, but this is not because these are future debts, but rather because such an assignment would be offensive to public order and good morals for the reason given, or else because those rights were to serve the assignor's basic needs and are therefore non-transferable.[29]

A debt may be constituted but not yet enforceable, because the due date has not arrived, because its amount is not yet determined, or because it is subject to a condition not yet fulfilled. Nevertheless, everyone agrees that such a debt may be assigned. A builder or a seller can assign a right to the fee or price even if—the building not having been started yet, nor the goods delivered—any claim they brought could be met with the defence that it was not yet due. The assignment does not prejudice the debtor because this defence, just like any other defence good against the assignor, can also be set up against the assignee.

By contrast, there is some doubt about the case where at the time of the purported transfer the debt has not yet been constituted. German lawyers use the term *Vorausabtretung* to describe a situation where a party that has not yet entered a contract of sale, lease, or services assigns the potential right to the price, rent, or fee. The general approach is to ask whether the debt is sufficiently 'identified' or at least 'identifiable'; if the latter, then the approach is whether it is enough that it be identifiable at the time it arises. In Germany, the courts have accepted this last position, so that the transferee of a debt proleptically assigned acquires the debt as soon as it comes into existence, provided that at that time its identity and scope sufficiently answer the contractual description of the rights the parties intended to assign. It follows that such rights that have not yet come into existence for the transferor at the time of the assignment are assignable, even though the contract from which they are to be derived has not yet been signed and it may not even be clear at this time who the debtor will be or what amount the debt will have. But, of course, the assignee only acquires the debt once it comes into existence and when the contract of assignment clearly shows that the parties intended this particular debt to be assigned. German courts have therefore accepted the validity of assignments of future rights which the assignor will acquire by way of the future sale of certain goods, the future provision of certain services, or the

---

[29] See above, pp. 110ff. and BG 13 Mar. 1958, BGE 84 II 355, 366f; BG 11 Dec. 1986, BGE 112 II 433, 436; *King v. Michael Faraday & Partners* [1939] 2 KB 753; and Treitel (n 3) 15-066. In Switzerland, a recent amendment to art. 325 OR provides that a transfer of future wages made by way of security for the performance of obligations is invalid. The same applies if the transferor assigns all current and future rights to a bank as collateral for a loan. Such an assignment of collateral is invalid if it unduly restricts the economic freedom of the assignor, or if it is clear from the outset that there is an obvious imbalance between the loan granted and the value of the assets transferred as collateral. See Roth (n 24) § 398 mn. 129ff. An assignment by way of collateral can also be invalid if the same right that has been assigned to the bank has also been assigned in advance by the same assignor by way of an extended reservation of title (see n 64).

future lease of certain premises, although it is not known at the time of the assignment who will buy the goods, who will order the services, or who will rent the premises and thus become the debtor of the assigned claim.[30]

It is doubtful whether other legal systems are as generous as Germany with respect to the assignment of future debts. It is sometimes permitted but is not regarded as effective *erga omnes* until the debtor is informed of the assignment or unless the assignment is registered officially, or if it is specifically identified by some overt 'sign' or 'mark'.[31] In France, the *Cour de cassation* heard a case where someone bought property on the basis of a loan made by a bank and secured not only by a mortgage on the property but also by the assignment of future rents the lender would receive from the tenant of the property. When the lender became insolvent, the bank sued the tenant. This action was dismissed by the appeal court on the ground that the claim against the tenant was neither sufficiently certain nor ascertainable at the time of assignment. The *Cour de cassation* overturned the decision. Future or possible claims could also be assigned but only '*sous la réserve de leur suffisante identification*'; this check had not been made and would have to be repeated.[32]

The Common Law starts from the principle that the assignee can only become owner of the right assigned if the right existed at the time of the assignment. But this does not mean that an agreement by which the assignor transfers a future right is without legal effect. If the agreement amounts to a valid contract—in particular, if the transferee provided some consideration for the promise to transfer—it is 'converted' into a valid assignment as soon as the assigned debt comes into existence.[33]

The doctrinal and policy objections to the transferability of future rights have thus all faded away in the face of 'the overwhelming practical needs of commerce and banks in particular'.[34] All international sets of rules have taken this into account. Article 11:101(1) PECL expressly states that claims can be assigned if they are derived from a 'future contract', provided that the future claim 'can be identified as the claim to which the assignment relates' at the time it comes into existence (or at another time agreed *inter partes*).[35] The same applies with respect to

---

[30] See, for example, BGH 25 Oct. 1952, BGHZ 7, 365; BGH 7 Dec. 1977, BGHZ 70, 86; BGH 15 Mar. 1978, BGHZ 71, 75. See in detail Roth (n 24) § 398 mn. 79ff. See also BG 12 May 1987, BGE 113 II 163.

[31] See also below, pp. 348ff.

[32] Civ. 20 Mar. 2001, JCP 2002.II.10124, n. I Goaziou = D. 2001, 3110, n. L Aynès. Article 1231(2) *Code civil* now states that rights are assignable regardless of whether they are '*présentes ou futures, déterminées ou déterminables*'. It is also clear that the assignment of a future right becomes valid, as between the parties as well as against third parties, only '*au jour de sa naissance*' (art. 1323(3) *Code civil*). It is not quite clear, however, under what conditions the future right is sufficiently 'identifiable' or 'ascertainable' at the time of the assignment. According to Terré, Simler, and Lequette (n 13) no. 1278, there must be some sign of its existence: it must exist '*en germe*', and it seems that claims derived from a '*contrat non encore souscrit*' are not assignable. The new Hungarian Civil Code states expressly that future rights are assignable only if they can be derived from a relationship 'existing' at the time of the agreement (§ 6:194(1)).

[33] *Tailby v. Official Receiver* (1888) 13 App.Cas. 523, 543; Treitel (n 3) no. 15-025.

[34] As stated by the Obergericht Zürich, see BG 11 Dec. 1986 (n 29) 435.

[35] Article 11:102(2) PECL. For the case where the same claim is assigned multiple times by the same party, the principle of *prior tempore potior iure* applies (see below, p. 350). As to the date of the (competing) assignments, art. 11:202(2) PECL provides that an assignment of a future claim takes effect 'from the time of the agreement to assign or such later time as the assignor and assignee agree'. See also art. 9.1.5 PICC and art. III.-5:106(1) and III.-5:114(2) DCFR.

the United Nations Convention on the Assignment of Receivables in International Trade.[36]

5. No-assignment clauses

A debtor often has good reason to conclude an agreement prohibiting the creditor from assigning its contractual claims, or to only allow such assignment with the express consent of the debtor. A debtor will have particular interest in securing a no-assignment clause when it wishes to have dealings only with the creditor and no other, or when it wishes to avoid the trouble of dealing with assignments or partial assignments and keep its settlement of claims clear and transparent. Many legal systems thus proceed from the principle that contractually agreed prohibitions on assignment are valid. The conclusion is that an assignment made in the face of such a prohibition is not just invalid as between creditor and debtor but is absolutely invalid *erga omnes*—with the consequence that creditors of the assignor can assert that an assignment is invalid, that an (apparently assigned) claim is still owned by the assignor and can then be claimed from him or be attributed as an asset in case of his insolvency. This viewpoint is followed in Germany, Austria, and Switzerland in particular.[37] In Italy, the prohibited assignment is only invalid if the assignee knew about the prohibition.[38]

There is a high price to pay for accepting prohibitions on assignment as valid. They are not easy to justify, at least with respect to claims for money, on the sole ground of the debtor's interest in keeping the settlement of its debts clear and easy. The debtor does not need the protection of a no-assignment clause if it pays the creditor at a time at which it knows nothing about the assignment (see below, page 353). If the debtor has been informed about assignments, it must indeed incur the additional expense of keeping track of them, and it is true that no-assignment clauses, if valid, would

---

[36] See art. 8 CARIT (n 11) and Schütze (n 11) 156ff. See also the Factoring Convention (n 10). It applies only to cases where a seller assigns claims to a factoring company arising from contracts of sale with non-consumers that have already come into existence or will come into existence in the future. Where future claims are assigned, they transfer to the factoring company either at the time of the assignment or 'when they come into existence ... [and] can be identified to the contract' (art. 5(a)); for details, see Rudolf (n 11) 246ff.

[37] See § 399 BGB and BGH 14 Oct. 1963, BGHZ 40, 156, 160; BGH 27 May 1971, BGHZ 56, 228, 230f; BGH 1 Feb. 1978, BGHZ 70, 299, 301. See also art. 164 OR and BG 25 Apr. 1986, BGE 112 II 241. See also OGH 16 Jan. 1984, [1984] *JBl* 311. Contractually agreed prohibitions on assignment are also generally accepted as valid in the Netherlands (art. 3:83(2) BW) and in England. See *Helstan Securities Ltd.* v. *Hertfordshire County Council* [1978] 3 All ER 262, 265f; *Linden Gardens Trust Ltd.* v. *Senesta Sludge Disposals Ltd.* [1994] 1 AC 85, 104ff. This has been widely criticised. See R Goode, 'Inalienable Rights?' (1979) 42 *Mod. LR* 553; R Munday, 'Prohibitions Against Assignments of Choses in Action' (1979) 38 *Camb. LJ* 50; B Allcock, 'Restrictions on the Assignment of Contractual Rights' (1983) 42 *Camb. LJ* 328; R Goode, 'Contractual Prohibitions Against Assignment' [2009] *LMCLQ* 300. The Law Commission has proposed a rule under which no-assignment clauses would be invalid with respect to claims against companies (Law Commission Report No. 296, Company Security Interests (2005) mn. 4.35ff.). See also with further references M Armgardt, 'Die Wirkung vertraglicher Abtretungsverbote im deutschen und ausländischen Privatrecht' (2009) 73 *RabelsZ* 314.

[38] See art. 1260(2) *Codice civile*; art. 577(2) Portuguese Civil Code. Germany and Switzerland also rely on the assignee acting in good faith, but only in the rare case where the debtor has produced a document which records its debt but does not mention the no-assignment clause and where the assignor presented this document to the assignee who did not know (or could not reasonably be required to know) about the no-assignment clause. See § 405 BGB; art. 164(2) OR.

save it that expense. Should the principle of freedom of contract not allow the debtor to save that expense by agreeing with creditors on a no-assignment clause? Freedom of contract must be restricted, however, where it leads to agreements that will seriously affect the legitimate interests of *third parties*. This is the case here, because if no-assignment clauses were valid, receivables would in effect become *res extra commercium*, that curtail the circulation of money rights, inhibit the readiness of credit institutions and factoring firms to accept assignments of receivables, and hobble the economically desirable provision of credit.

Many countries have thus passed special laws in recent years to set strict limits to the validity of contractually agreed prohibitions on transfer of claims. Such agreements have always been regarded with some scepticism in France.[39] A law from 2001 specifically states that prohibitions on assignment are ineffective if they are in respect of commercial monetary transactions.[40] In Germany, since 1994 a special provision of the Commercial Code (§ 354a) has stated that any assignment made despite a prohibition on assignment is valid if the assigned claim is based on a commercial transaction or is made against the state.[41] A rule introduced in Austria in 2005 as § 1396a ABGB also states that contractually agreed prohibitions on assignment with respect to 'monetary claims from commercial transactions' are invalid.[42]

Thus there are major obstacles to the validity of contractually agreed prohibitions on assignment. A similar view is taken by the international sets of rules. Anyone assigning a claim to an assignee in contravention of a prohibition on assignment may be liable to the debtor for breach of contract.[43] But this prohibition will not prevent the assignee from acquiring the claim, either because such prohibition is generally invalid,[44] or because it is invalid at least in cases when the assignment refers to a future monetary claim that will derive from the contract concluded with the debtor.[45]

---

[39] In an older decision, the *Cour de cassation* found such a prohibition to be invalid because it contravened the general principle of free transferability of goods (*principe de libre disposition des biens*); see Civ. 6 June 1853, D.P. 1853. I. 191.

[40] See now art. L 442-6 (II c) *Code commercial*. The same applies if a claim agreed to be non-assignable is assigned by the assignor under the rules of the *Loi Dailly*; see Com. 21 Nov. 2000, Bull.cass. 2000. IV. no. 180 = D. 2001 Actualité jurispr. 123, n. V Avéna-Robardet. Under the general rules, however, no-assignment clauses seem to be valid. While art. 1321(4) *Code civil* states that assignments are valid without the debtor's consent, this does not apply (and the debtor's consent is necessary) if the assignor's claim has been agreed to be 'incessible'.

[41] However, a no-assignment clause is valid if it refers to a bank's claim against the debtor for the repayment of a loan. In other cases, while the assignment is valid despite the no-assignment clause, the debtor will be discharged if it chooses to pay the assignor. The debtor is also entitled to claim damages from the creditor if the latter breached the no-assignment clause and thus caused harm to the debtor.

[42] However, this does not apply if the prohibition on assignment is 'individually negotiated and in consideration of all the circumstances the creditor is not grossly disadvantaged'. No-assignment clauses are also invalid under § 6:195(/1) of the new Hungarian Civil Code of 2013. The debtor is therefore liable to the assignee, but may claim damages from the assignor for foreseeable harm caused by its breach of the no-assignment clause. See F Szilágyi, 'Das Zessionsrecht im neuen Zivilgesetzbuch Ungarns' (2015) 23 *ZEuP* 52, 57f.

[43] See art. 11:301(2) PECL; art. 9.1.9 (1 sent. 2) PICC; art. III.-5:108(6) DCFR.

[44] Article 9.1.9 (1 sent. 1) PICC.

[45] Articles 11:203 and 11:301(1c) PECL. A similar rule can be found in art. 9 CARIT (n 11); see in detail Schütze (n 11) 183ff. and Eidenmüller (n 11) 464ff. Similarly also art. 6(1) and (3) Factoring Convention (n 10). Under art. III-5:108 DCFR, prohibitions on assignment are invalid in principle. But in these cases and if certain conditions are met, the debtor can also discharge its obligations be performing for its creditor.

III. Formal requirements

An assignee is not likely to be satisfied with a purely verbal assignment, as assignment will have to be proven before the debtor will pay. Accordingly, the assignee always insists not only on receiving the documents evidencing the debt,[46] but also demands a written statement of the assignment itself[47] or that the assignment be documented in writing. Yet it is not only the parties that have an interest in the assignment being recorded in written form. There is a public interest in the avoidance of disputes over the question whether and when an assignment has taken place. Accordingly, it is widely laid down that the assignment agreement or transfer by the assignor must be in writing.[48] It also applies in France for assignments under the *Loi Dailly*, which requires a dated written list of assigned claims (*bordereau*) to be prepared and given to the assignee.[49] The international sets of rules contain only a general provision whereby the contract of assignment requires no special form.[50]

The written-form requirement for the contract of assignment does not protect the assignee from the danger that the assignor may have previously assigned or mortgaged the same claim to another party and no longer owns the claim. For an assignment to be valid as against third parties, many legal systems thus require the assignment to be made evident in some form, for example by requiring that formal notification of the assignment is made to the debtor. German law has not followed this path. Pursuant to § 398 BGB, a claim is transferred to the assignee by the contract of assignment. The debtor need not be informed, with the consequence that any payment made to the assignor will discharge the debtor even though it was made after the assignment, provided that the debtor knew nothing of the assignment at the time of payment (see pages 353ff.). Other legal systems do not take this view. In Austria, an assignment made to provide security for the assignee's right against the assignor is valid only if the debtor has been informed of it, and if the parties want the assignment to be silent, that is to keep it secret from the debtor, it must be documented in a written contract of assignment and also recorded by way of a special notice in the assignor's accounting.[51] The

---

[46] See § 402 BGB; art. 6:143 BW; art. 1262 *Codice civile*; art. 170(2) OR; art. 456 Greek Civil Code; art. 586 Portuguese Civil Code, all of which entitle the assignee to demand that the assignor deliver any documents evidencing the debt and any information needed for its collection.

[47] § 403 BGB and art. 457 Greek Civil Code grant the assignee the right, on payment of the costs, to demand a declaration of assignment officially certified.

[48] Article 165(1) OR and BG 23 Jan. 1962, BGE II 18. On 25 May 1979 (BGE 105 II 83), the court held that it is not enough for the seller to copy to the assignee an invoice stating that payment is to be made to the latter. Elsewhere an assignment has to be in writing (art. 3:94(1) BW; art. 1322 *Code civil*; art. 511 Polish Civil Code). In England also, a 'statutory assignment' must be in writing, but in the absence of writing it may be saved as an 'equitable assignment'. See above, n 3.

[49] See *Code monétaire et financier* art. L 313-23.

[50] See art. 11:104 PECL; art. 9-1.7(1) PICC; art. III.-5:110(1) in conjunction with art. II.-4:101 DCFR. Of course, this means only that the assignor and assignee cannot assert that a contract of assignment is invalid because the assignment was only made verbally or the intent of the parties can only be ascertained from the circumstances.

[51] See, eg, OGH 7 Sept. 1978, SZ 51 no. 121; OGH 1 Mar. 1989, SZ 62 no. 32; OGH 28 Oct. 1997, [1998] *JBl* 105 (standing case law).

law of the Netherlands also requires a notarised or registered private deed for a 'silent assignment'.[52] Formal requirements were particularly strict under the former French law. The old art. 1690 *Code civil* provided that assignments operated only as between the assignor and the assignee and that—as against the debtor, and more significantly as against the assignor's creditors—the assignee became entitled to the debt only if a court official had been dispatched to the debtor to intimate the fact (*signification*), or the debtor had declared its *acceptation* to the assignee by notarial act. These formalities made it difficult, if not impossible, to use assignments in the way now required by commerce, especially where a whole package of debts is to be sold to a factor for cash, or transferred to a bank as security. Courts in France have therefore weakened the burdensome requirements of art. 1690 in many respects. There was '*une tendance constante au recul du formalisme de l'article 1690*'.[53] A major contribution to the '*déclin de l'article 1690*'[54] was made by the legislature itself. Under the *Loi Dailly*,[55] passed in 1981 to facilitate the granting of credit to businesses, a special procedure was made available for the assignment to banks of money debts arising from commercial transactions. According to the provisions of this law, such claims are acquired by the bank as assignee without the understanding or knowledge of the debtor as soon as the assignor and the bank have agreed on the assignment and the bank has received a list (*bordereau*) of the assigned claims. As a result, if the assignor becomes insolvent after the list has been provided, its creditors must accept that its claims have already been transferred to the bank as assignee and no longer count as the assignor's assets when insolvency proceedings open. After the *Loi Dailly* was able to prove its worth in practice over a longer period, there was general acceptance that the general assignment rules of the *Code civil* should be updated. This has now been carried out. Article 1322 *Code civil* now provides that an assignment must be effected in writing, and that it is at the date of execution of this writing that the assigned right vests in the assignee—not only as between the assignor and the assignee, but also as to third parties. This effect also applies if the debtor knows nothing of the assignment, as well as if it knew of the assignment but did not agree with it.[56]

In summary, two purposes are served by the formalities required for the validity of assignments. First, to prevent disputes about when, if at all, a debt was transferred; this is why it is often a prerequisite that the transfer be recorded in writing and dated. The second reason is to enable the transferee of the debts to ascertain whether they are still fully vested in the transferor. In theory, the transferor may ask the debtor to find out whether it thinks it is indebted to the assignor or to some other party. This was the approach on which the former French law was based. It is impracticable, partly because the debtor is not bound to respond quickly, fully, and accurately to whoever claims to be the assignee, partly because it does not work when tradesmen want to

---

[52] See art. 3:94(3) and (4) BW.
[53] Mazeaud and Chabas (n 24) no. 1268-2.   [54] Terré, Simler, and Lequette (n 13) no. 1283.
[55] Law no. 81-2 of 2 Jan. 1981. See now *Code monétaire et financier* art. L 313-27ff.
[56] If the debtor knew nothing of the assignment, and thus performs its obligations to the creditor, this will discharge its obligation even though the creditor had assigned the claim and was therefore no longer entitled to demand performance from the debtor. See art. 1324(1) *Code civil*.

transfer a great many debts all at once, or do not wish to divulge to the debtor, for the time being, the fact that the debt due has been assigned. How can a bank or other assignee ensure in these cases that the debt has not already been assigned to someone else? The best solution is probably the introduction of a system under which a publicly available register would be created, and an assignment would only be valid after it has been duly registered.[57]

IV. Priorities

Courts often have to deal with disputes over priorities of claims, typically when a creditor purports to transfer a debt first to A and then to B. If both A and B claim payment, the wise debtor will pay the sum into court and leave it to the purported assignees to sort out the conflict of priorities. If the debtor has paid B in ignorance of the assignment to A, its liability is discharged, and A can claim the proceeds from B on the basis of its priority claim. Similar conflicts arise when the assigned debt has been attached by one of the assignor's creditors or is claimed as part of the distributable assets in the assignor's bankruptcy.

Such disputes are resolved by applying the principle of chronological priority, *prior tempore potior iure*: the first to acquire the right obtains priority over anyone who acquires or attaches the right subsequently. The result can also be explained on the basis that once the assignor has effected a transfer, it no longer has any entitlement which can be attached or which could, in the absence of any principle of good faith, be transferred to anyone else.

The critical thing, then, is to determine the moment when all the prerequisites of a valid transfer are satisfied, including any formalities that may be required. Thus, if the validity of an assignment depends on an entry in a register or being recorded in the assignor's books, then the date of the registration or record is determinative. If the same debt is transferred to two banks by *bordereau* under the *Loi Dailly*, the bank whose *bordereau* bears the earlier date has priority, and may claim the proceeds from the other bank if the debtor has paid it.[58] The same rule is now stated in the new art. 1325 *Code civil*: in the case of successive assignments, the competition is resolved in favour of the assignee to which the assignment was first made.

A similar rule applies in England. While the validity of an assignment does not necessarily depend on any notice to the debtor,[59] it is clear that a wise assignee will

---

[57] Such a system of registration has been discussed for a long time. A model can be found in the United States, where such a system has been in place for many years. See art. 9 Uniform Commercial Code and Schütze (n 11) 28ff. Under English law, a 'general assignment of book debts' is only valid as against insolvency creditors of the assignor if the assignment is recorded in a public register: See s. 344 Insolvency Act 1986; s. 395f. Companies Act 1986. Book IX of the DCFR also envisages such a registration system which would take priority over the general rules on assignment of claims: see art. III.-5:103(1) DCFR. See, for example, Eidenmüller (n 11) 475ff; EM Kieninger, 'Die Zukunft des deutschen und europäischen Mobiliarkreditsicherungsrechts' (2008) 208 *AcP* 182.

[58] See art. L 313-27 *Code monétaire et financier*; Com. 28 Oct. 1986, Bull.cass. 1986.IV. no. 194 = D. 1986, 592, n. M Vasseur = *JCP* 1987.II.20735, n. J Stoufflet; Com. 7 Dec. 2004, Bull.cass. 2004.IV. no. 3213 = D. 2005, 230, n. C Larroumet; Terré, Simler, and Lequette (n 13) no. 1302.

[59] No notice is required in an 'equitable assignment', see above, n 3.

give such notice if only because that is the only way it can prevent the debtor from being discharged by paying the assignor. But giving notice has another advantage, for if a debt is transferred for consideration successively to different persons, the rule in *Dearle* v. *Hall*[60] gives priority to the assignee that—in ignorance of any prior assignment—first gives notice to the debtor. Such notification entitles the assignee to claim and keep the debt with no need to disgorge the proceeds to the prior assignee. The same approach is reflected in art. 11-401(1) PECL: if the creditor assigns the same rights to A and then to B, then B will have priority if the debtor first learns of the assignment to B.[61]

The situation is different in those legal systems that—like Germany—require no more than a valid assignment between assignor and assignee for the assignment also to be effective as against third parties. It follows that the debt will be acquired only by the assignee that was first to conclude the contract of assignment; the assignee that purportedly acquires the same debt subsequently will be left empty-handed.[62] If the debtor pays the second assignee, its obligation will be discharged if it believes the assignee to be the creditor. But that does not mean that the second assignee will be allowed to keep the debt paid—it will have to pay this out to the first assignee.[63] These rules also apply if the same future debt has been assigned twice *in advance*. As soon as the debt comes into existence, here too the debt will pass to the first assignee.[64]

---

[60] (1828) 38 Eng.Rep. 475, 492. § 31(2) Swedish Law on Negotiable Instruments is to the same effect.

[61] This applies only if, at the time the assignment was made to B, B did not know or could not have known of the earlier assignment to A. See also art. III.-5:120(1) DCFR. On the other hand, the assignee always has priority if after the time the assignment has taken effect the same claim is attached by the assignor's creditors or insolvency procedures are opened over the assignor's estate. See art. 11-401(3) and (4) PECL.

[62] Therein lies the difference between those legal systems that, in case of multiple assignments of the same right, give priority to the assignee that can show that its assignment was notified to the debtor first. This difference was seen as unbridgeable in the CARIT discussions (n 11); thus art. 22 CARIT states that the matter is determined by the national rules applicable in the jurisdiction where the assignor is domiciled. See in detail Schütze (n 11) 282ff. For the same reason, art. 9.1.11 PICC addresses only the question of protection of the debtor, not which of several assignees will have priority over the claim; see. F Mazza in S Vogenauer, *Commentary on the PICC* (2nd edn, 2009) art. 9.1.11 no. 1-3.

[63] The basis for this claim is unjustified enrichment: in receiving from the good faith debtor a payment which extinguishes the entitlement of the first assignee, the second assignee has obtained something at the latter's expense which it may not retain. See § 816(2) BGB and BGH 16 Dec. 1957, BGHZ 26, 185, 193; BG 4 Nov. 1930, BGE 56 II 363; BG 1 Mar. 1984, BGE 110 II 199; OGH 11 July 1985, [1986] *JBl* 235, 236f; OGH 30 Mar. 2004, [2004] *JBl* 641. See also art. 1325 *Code civil*. In England, the payment received by the second assignee will be held by it on 'constructive trust' for the first assignee. See Goode, 'Contractual Prohibitions Against Assignment' (above, n 37) 316ff. and the comparative discussion by F Ranieri, *Europäisches Obligationsrecht* (3rd edn, 2009) 1238ff.

[64] German courts have made a very significant inroad into the priority principle in cases where a seller of goods assigns the future right to the price both to a bank and to the party who supplied the goods. Here the supplier wins even if the assignment to the bank was made earlier in time. The preference given to the later assignment is justified by holding the prior assignment of the future debt void under § 138 BGB as contrary to good morals, for it will inevitably force the customer to breach its contract with the bank if, as the bank knew or should have known, it could only obtain supplies on terms obliging it to assign to the supplier the right to claim the price on resale which it had already assigned to the bank ('extended reservation of title'). See BGH 30 Apr. 1959, BGHZ 30, 149; BGH 8 Oct. 1986, BGHZ 98, 303, 314 (standing case law). The same rule should also apply if the (earlier) assignment in favour of the bank clashes with a (later) assignment in favour of a factoring company, provided that the factoring company can in the event of the debtor's inability to pay take recourse against the assignor. See BGH 14 Nov. 1981, BGHZ 82, 50, 61.

C. Effects

I. Between assignor and assignee

There remains the question what obligations may arise between assignor and assignee when the agreement does indeed effect a change of creditor. If the debt assigned does not exist or cannot, by reason of the debtor's insolvency, be collected, what rights has the assignee against the assignor? These rights and duties are not generated from the assignment as such, which is simply the transfer of the debt, but from the underlying transaction.[65] But since that underlying transaction may not spell out such rights and duties or even allow them to be inferred by constructive interpretation, every system provides *règles supplétives* or default rules to fill the gap.

Generally, the assignee may require the assignor to deliver up the documents evidencing the debt assigned and provide the information needed to claim the debt.[66] Furthermore, in the absence of contrary indications, the transfer carries with it any existing security rights, such as pledge interests in moveables, mortgages on immoveables, and claims against sureties and guarantors.[67] If the contract between assignor and debtor contains an arbitration clause, it is generally accepted that the assignee is bound by that clause and may invoke it.[68]

Can the assignee sue the assignor if it can obtain no satisfaction from the debtor? If the assignment is gratuitous, the answer is negative.[69] But where assignment is made pursuant to a sale or other transaction for consideration, the basic rule is that the assignor guarantees the existence (*Verität*), but not the collectability (*Bonität*) of the debt assigned.[70] Occasionally, one finds a provision that if the seller of a debt does guarantee the solvency of the debtor, it is presumed to guarantee the debtor's solvency only at the time of the assignment, not thereafter, and is liable only up to the amount it received for the assignment.[71] But all these rules are subject to derogation by the parties and may be ousted by their agreement. In addition, the assignor may well be liable for breach of contract in accordance with general rules. In France and Italy, it

---

[65] See above, n 7.   [66] See above, n 46.

[67] Article 1321(3) *Code civil*; art. 1263 *Codice civile*; art. 1528 Spanish Civil Code; art. 582 Portuguese Civil Code; art. 458 Greek Civil Code; art. 6:142 BW; § 401 BGB; art. 170(1) OR; art. 509 Polish Civil Code. See also art.11:201 PECL; art. 9.1.14 PICC; art. III.-5:115 DCFR; art. 10 CARIT (n 11) and in detail in Schütze (n 11) 202ff.

[68] See BG 25 Jan. 1977, BGE 103 II 77; BGH 2 Mar. 1978, BGHZ 71, 162; BGH 20 Mar. 1980, BGHZ 77, 32, 35f; OGH 16 Jan. 1936, SZ 18 no. 12; Civ. 5 Jan. 1999, Bull.cass. 1999.I. no. 1; Civ. 20 Dec. 2001, *JCP* 2002.IV.1209; Civ. 28 May 2002, *JCP* 2002.IV.2221 and Terré, Simler, and Lequette (n 13) no. 1290; *The Leage* [1984] 2 Lloyd's Rep. 259.

[69] Unless the assignor expressly undertook liability or was acting in bad faith; see art. 1266(2) *Codice civile*; § 523 BGB; art. 171(3) OR.

[70] Article 1326(1) *Code civil*; art. 1266 *Codice civile*; art. 1529 Spanish Civil Code; art. 587 Portuguese Civil Code; art. 467 Greek Civil Code; § 437 BGB; art. 171 OR; art. 516 Polish Civil Code; § 9 Swedish Law on Negotiable Instruments. In Austria, the assignor is liable also for the collectibility of the debt, provided there are no contrary indications (§ 1397 ABGB). A comprehensive treatment of liability of the assignor in relation to the assignee can be found in art. 11:204 PECL; art. 9.1.15 PICC; art. III.-5:112 DCFR; art. 12 CARIT (n 11) and in detail in Schütze (n 11) 233ff.

[71] Details in art. 1326(3) *Code civil*; art. 1267 *Codice civile*; art. 1529(2) Spanish Civil Code; art. 468 Greek Civil Code; § 1397 ABGB; art. 173 OR.

is said that the assignor is always *garant de son fait personnel*, or liable *per il fatto proprio*.[72] This means that even if the seller has excluded or limited its liability should the debt not exist or not be collectible, it will nevertheless be liable in damages if it subsequently accepts payment from the debtor or releases the debtor from the debt, or gives it time to pay. That would constitute a breach of the obligation flowing from the contract of sale not to do anything, which might prejudice the buyer's ability to realise the debt assigned to it.

II. Protection of the debtor

Recent developments tend to dispense, at any rate in the commercial sphere, with the need for the debtor to be apprised of assignments. But even where notice is required, *consent* is not. This means that a new creditor can be forced upon the debtor without its consent, and even against its will. There must, therefore, be rules to prevent the debtor being prejudiced by such a change of creditor.

1. Payment to the original creditor

Suppose the debtor pays the old creditor after the assignment has taken place, or obtains a release or time to pay or some other favour. Can the debtor rely on such dealings when sued by the assignee?

The general rule is that if any such agreements are made between the debtor and the assignor before the debtor learned of the assignment, the assignee is bound by them.[73] In order to fix the debtor with knowledge in this context, it must have been made unambiguously clear, generally by a document sent by the assignee, that the change of creditor has taken place, and perhaps also that in future payment must be made to the new creditor only.[74] In case of successive assignments of the same debt, the debtor who pays a subsequent assignee will be released from liability if it was unaware of the earlier assignment.[75]

2. Defences available to the debtor

The debtor may challenge the assignee's standing to sue by asserting that the assignment was defective and the assignee is thus not the assignee of the claim.

---

[72] See Mazeaud and Chabas (n 24) no. 1275; art. 1266(1) *Codice civile*.

[73] § 407 BGB; art. 167 OR; § 1395f. ABGB; art. 1324(2) *Code civil*; § 29 Swedish Law of Negotiable Instruments. English law is to the same effect: see Treitel (n 3) no. 15-037ff. If notice to the debtor is a requisite for the validity of an assignment, the time of notice is determinative of the question in the text. See art. 1527 Spanish Civil Code; art. 512 Polish Civil Code. Article 11:303(1) PECL states that the debtor is bound to pay the assignee 'if and only if [the debtor] has received a notice in writing either from the assignor or the assignee which reasonably identifies the claim which has been assigned and requires the debtor to give performance to the assignee'. Consequently, if the debtor gives performance to the *assignor*, it will be discharged 'if and only if the performance is given without knowledge of the assignment'. See art. 11-303(4) PECL and similar provisions in art. 9.1.10 PICC; art. III.-5:118 DCFR; and art. 17 CARIT (n 11).

[74] See OGH 27 Mar. 1979, [1979] EvBl. no. 189; *James Talcott Ltd. v. John Lewis & Co.* [1940] 3 All ER 592 (CA); OLG Bremen 23 Oct. 1986, [1987] *NJW* 912; HD 30 Jan. 1986, [1986] NJA 44.

[75] See § 408 BGB and art. 167 OR.

But even a valid assignment must not be allowed to restrict the debtor's defences and counterclaims that it would have enjoyed against the creditor but for the assignment. So the debtor may assert defences against the assignee that would have been open to it as against the assignor—such as the debt never arose, that it has lapsed, that a period of grace was allowed, that it is now time-barred, or that for some other reason it is not actionable.[76] A frequent saying in the Common Law is that 'the assignee stands in the shoes of the assignor' or that 'the assignee takes subject to equities'.[77] The occasional provision that the debtor can only use defences that were already 'founded' does not mean that every element of a particular defence must have been in existence at the time of the assignment. For example, if a building company assigns its right to receive payment for work to be done and the assignee sues the site owner, the latter can defend on the ground that the work was badly done and that it has suffered a loss in consequence. And it can set off the amount of the loss against the assignee's claim even though the builder's breach of contract did not occur until after the assignment. It is enough that the contract that generated the debt assigned was also capable of generating a defence, even one which would be fully constituted only after the assignment had taken place.[78]

As to set-off, any debt which the debtor could have set off against the assignor may be set off against the assignee, provided that at the time the debtor became aware of the assignment or received the notice of assignment it was able to exercise the set-off as against the assignor. However, there are sometimes restrictions. Pursuant to § 406 BGB, set-off is excluded if the debtor only obtained knowledge of the set-off claim after it became aware of the assignment; it is also excluded if the set-off claim *becomes due* only after the debtor became aware of the assignment and later than the assigned claim.[79]

3. Waiver of defences by debtor

These rules for the protection of the debtor mean that there is a considerable risk that the assignee may well be unable to collect on the debt assigned. This risk is

---

[76] § 404 BGB; art. 169 OR; § 1396 ABGB; art. 6:145 BW; art. 1324(2) *Code civil*; § 27 Swedish Law on Negotiable Instruments; art. 463 Greek Civil Code; art. 585 Portuguese Civil Code; art. 513 Polish Civil Code. See also art. 11.307(1) PECL; art. 9.1.13 PICC; art. III.-5:116(1) DCFR; art. 18(1) CARIT (n 11).

[77] See *Business Computers Ltd. v. Anglo-African Leasing Ltd.* [1977] 1 WLR 578, 582; *The Raven* [1980] 2 Lloyd's Rep. 266.

[78] RG 11 Nov. 1913, RGZ 83, 279; BGH 26 June 1957, BGHZ 25, 27, 29; BGH 23 Mar. 2004, [2004] *NJW-RR* 1347, 1348; Obergericht Zürich 6 Dec. 1940, (1942) 41 *BlZüRspr.* no. 65; OGH 19 Mar. 1963, [1963] *JBl* 530; OGH 8 Jan. 1980, SZ 53 no. 1. The same is true of assignments in France pursuant to the *Loi Dailly* (n 9): Com. 9 Feb. 1993, Bull.cass. 1993.IV. no. 51.

[79] See also art. 169 II OR; art. 6:130(1) BW; § 28 Swedish Law on Negotiable Instruments; art. 463(2) Greek Civil Code; art. 513(2) Polish Civil Code and the French cases cited in Terré, Simler, and Lequette (n 13) no. 1291 and 1302. In England, the rule is 'that a debt which accrues due before notice of an assignment is received, whether or not it is payable before that date, ... may be set off against the assignee'; see *Business Computers Ltd. v. Anglo-African Leasing Ltd.* (n 77). There is some doubt what the conditions of a sufficient 'accrual' or 'maturity' of the debtor's right are, and whether the debtor may set off a claim arising from a contract with the assignor other than, but sufficiently close to, the contract on which the assigned claim was based. See Treitel (n 3) no. 15-039ff. and art. 11-307 PECL; art. 9.1.13(2) PICC; art. III.5:116(3) DCFR; art. 18(1) and (2) CARIT (n 11).

diminished if the assignor concludes a contractual clause with the debtor whereby the debtor agrees not to raise certain defences against it, and consequently not against the assignee. Such waivers are valid in principle, including as against an assignee, as they are made at a time before assignment or before the debtor is aware of it. It should be noted that such waivers of defences usually form part of standard terms and conditions and are thus subject to the rules and controls governing such clauses.[80] They are always invalid if a consumer in a credit agreement waives the right to defend any claim by the lender (and its assignees) with defences and set-off which the borrower is entitled to assert.[81]

If the waiver is given only later, at the request of the assignee on informing the debtor of the assignment, its effect depends on how it is interpreted. The courts are distinctly debtor-friendly here, and hold in particular that the debtor can be taken to waive only such defences as it was (or should have been) aware of when it gave the waiver.[82]

---

[80] Such clauses are often invalid as against consumers. See, eg, § 309 nos. 2 and 3 BGB; art. 6:236f. and art. 6:237g BW.

[81] See art. 17 of EU Directive 2008/48/EEC of 23 April 2008 on consumer credit agreements (O.J. 2008 L 133/6).

[82] See BGH 18 Oct. 1972, [1972] *NJW* 29; BGH 25 May 1973, [1973] *NJW* 2019, BGH 23 Mar. 1983, [1983] *NJW* 1903; OGH 27 May 1982, [1983] *JBl* 29; OGH 21 Feb. 1985, [1986] *JBl* 175. The case is similar if the debtor, at the request of the assignee that has acquired the claim under the parameters of the *Loi Dailly*, declares *acceptation* of the assignment (art. L 313-29 *Code monétaire et financier* and Terré, Simler, and Lequette (n 13) no. 1302).

Index

acceptance 17f., 25
  by conduct 26ff.
  declaration of 25f.
  delayed 31f.
  expiry of time for 22
  qualified acceptance 29ff.
acquis communautaire 10, 14
action directe 328f.
agency
  apparent or ostensible authority 308ff.
  dealing without authority 307ff.
  deceit practised by agent 182
  disclosed 312ff.
  extent of powers 301ff.
  formalities 300f.
  grant of authority 298f.
  historical development and economic
    importance 293ff.
  implied grant 299f.
  justifiable reliance by third party 310
  liability of supposed agent 311
  ratification 307f.
  revocability 305ff.
  self-dealing 303f.
  statutory 297f.
  termination 305
  undisclosed 314ff.
agreements to agree 43ff.
Anscheinsvollmacht 308
anticipatory non-performance 228
assignment
  defences available to the debtor 353f.
  formal requirements 348ff.
  future debts 343ff.
  historical development and economic
    importance 337ff.
  international agreements 340
  no-assignment clauses 346f.
  non-assignable rights 342ff.
  obligations between assignor
    and assignee 352f.
  parts of debts 343
  payment to the original creditor 353
  personal rights 342f.
  priorities 350f.
  protection of the debtor 353ff.
  requirements for an effective transaction 340f.
  rights to wages, maintenance, and support 342
  substantive validity 341
  waiver of defences by debtor 354f.
assumpsit, writ of 50f.
astreinte 200f.
attribution 244ff.
authority, ostensible 308ff.

bargain principle 6
battle of the forms 30
breach of contract
  damages 242ff.
  efficient breach 212ff.

brewery contracts 45, 118, 121, 149, 231
business-to-business contracts 136ff.

Canada 13
cancellation rights 8, 9
capacity 24f., 51, 118, 297, 341
carriage of goods 331f.
causa 51
cause 51f., 71, 109, 306
CISG *see* UN Sales Law
civil codes 2f., 8, 11, 198ff.
claims for performance 197f.
  Common Law 202ff.
  continental law 198ff.
  efficient breach of contract and 212ff.
  harmonised rules in Europe 205ff.
  impossibility of performance 206f.
  personal performance 208
  substitute transaction 209
  supplementary performance 207, 210f., 217
  timely claim 209
  unreasonably high cost 207f.
codification 11
collateral duties 106ff.
comfort letters 34ff.
commencement de preuve par écrit 55, 79, 82ff.
commission agent 304, 314ff.
Commission on European Contract Law 3
Common European Sales Law (CESL),
  proposal for 10f., 14
Common Law 8, 202ff.
common mistake 166f.
competition, restraints on 45, 119ff.
confirmatory note 28
consent 17f., 31, 129, 176, 180, 297
consideration 6, 22, 28, 51f., 53f., 63ff., 69ff., 80, 321
constructive interpretation 100ff., 103ff.
  collateral duties 106ff.
  implication of terms by default rules 102f.
consumer associations 136f.
consumer protection 9, 10, 133, 136, 140
contract
  collateral duties 106ff.
  concurrence with tort *see* tort claims
  definiteness of 41ff.
  economic analysis of 5ff., 212
  fairness in 34, 36, 109, *see also* unfair
    contract terms
  formation 18f.
  freedom of 6f., 33, 102, 109, 112ff., 133, 135,
    192, 275, 347
  interpretation *see* interpretation
  justice of 34, 36
  long-term 118f.
  modification 63ff.
  pre-contract 34
  termination *see* termination
  third parties *see* third party rights
  validity 6f.
  welfare state and 122

contract chains 329ff.
contra proferentem rule 100, 135
contributory negligence 261ff.
credit agreements 36, 84, 355
criminal sanctions 145f.
cross-border transactions 11, 12f.
culpable conduct 35
culpa in contrahendo 33, 37f., 38, 88, 180, 184

damages 38, 202f., 241f.
   agreements on limitation 275ff.
   attribution 244ff.
   breach of contract 252ff.
   contracts of sale 212f., 266ff.
   contributory responsibility
     of the creditor 261ff.
   deceit 184
   disgorgement of profits 270f.
   efficient breach of contract 212ff.
   expectation interest 264ff.
   fault principle 244ff., 256
   intangible loss 271ff.
   international rules 254ff.
   liability for remote damage 257ff.
   limitation of 275ff.
   liquidated 275ff.
   lost profits and lost expectations 268ff.
   nature and extent of 264ff.
   non-performance of the contract 242f., 257ff.
   *obligations de moyens/obligations
     de résultat* 248ff.
death of offeror 24f.
debts, assignment of *see* assignment
deceit
   claims for damages 184
   duties to inform 175ff.
   elements 173ff.
   non-disclosure 175ff.
   by third party 182ff.
declaration of acceptance 17f., 25f.
deeds 77
default rules 102f.
defective performance 233ff.
definiteness 41ff.
   agreements to agree 43ff.
   unilateral price-fixing 45ff.
delayed performance 229ff.
detrimental reliance 86ff.
directives 9f.
disclosure, duty of 176, 180ff.
disgorgement of profits 270f.
dispositives Recht 102
distance-selling contracts 194f.
division of labour 5f.
doorstep selling 192f.
Draft Common Frame of Reference (DCFR) 10, 14
duress 113f.
   elements 185ff.
   exploitation and 185
   by third party 188f.
duties to inform 175ff.
duty of care 33f., 37, 62f., 259, 327, 331

earnestness, test of 49ff.
economic duress 113

economic order 5ff.
   agency and 293ff.
   assignment and 337ff.
   efficiency 212
   third party rights 319ff.
efficient breach of contract 212ff.
employees
   non-compete agreements 119
   protection of 103
enforcement of contracts lacking
     requisite form 84ff.
Enlightenment 14
equivalence, principle of 111, 140
   see also laesio enormis
error 155f.
estoppel *see* promissory estoppel;
   proprietary estoppel
EU Commission 10, 12
European Parliament 1f.
European private law 2f., 5
European Union contract law 8ff.
executed gifts 54ff.
expectation interest 264ff., 268ff.
exploitation 185
expression 91f., 97

factoring 337, 340
fair dealing 34, 36
falsa demonstratio 93
fault principle 244ff., 256
fiduciary duty 181, 271, 303
force majeure 201, 226, 244, 249ff., 253
foreseeability of damage 259ff.
formalities 73ff.
   enforcement and 84ff.
   gifts 53, 80
   guarantees 61, 80ff.
   land contracts 83
forms, battle of 30
fraud 174
freedom of contract 6f., 33, 102, 109, 112ff.,
     133, 135, 192, 275, 347
frustration 226, 246, 252, 279, 285ff.

general principles 4, 14f.
gifts 52ff., 80
good faith 34, 36, 38
gratuitous transactions 60ff.
group actions 146f.
guarantee
   contracts of 61
   formality 61, 80ff.
   non-performance and 246f.
   offensiveness 115f.
   quality guarantee 247f.
guardianship 114, 181, 297

harmonisation 1f., 12ff.
   claims for performance 205ff.

illegality 109, 122ff.
   restitution and 125ff.
immorality 109, 111, 116f.
   restitution and 125ff.
implied terms 8, 31, 41, 101ff., 222, 254

impossibility of performance 206f., 226ff.
in pari delicto 127
incapacity 24f.
incomplete performance 231ff.
informal promissory gifts 56ff.
information, duty to give 180
intangible loss 271ff.
intention
    to be bound 19ff.
    defects in 150
    to enter a legal obligation 66ff.
    expression and 91ff., 97
interpretation 91
    constructive 100ff., 103ff.
    implication of terms by default rules 102f.
    intention and expression 91ff., 97
    maxims 98ff.
    objective 92, 93ff.
invalidity
    enforcement of contracts lacking requisite form 84ff.
    partial 121f., 143ff.
    sanctions 80ff.
    unfair, illegal, and immoral contracts 110
invitation to treat 20f., 23

laesio enormis 111f.
land, sales of 83
letter of intent 34
liability 32ff.
    limitations of 331f.
liberalism 6, 112
limitation of damages 275ff.
limitations of liability 331f.
liquidated damages 275ff.
loan agreements 193f.
long-term contractual relationships 118f.
lost profits 268ff.

mailbox rule 23, 26
maintenance payments 57ff.
management of affairs, contracts for 62
memorandum of understanding 34
minors, capacity of 297
misconduct 36
misrepresentation 150f., 164f., 173, 181ff.
mistake 149ff.
    causality 158
    caused by the other party 163ff.
    claims by buyer for non-conforming goods 152ff.
    development of European law 167ff.
    effecting avoidance 171f.
    existence of a contract 151f.
    historical background to the doctrine 155f.
    liability 152ff.
    motive 159f.
    negligence 162ff.
    offer to make good 163
    primacy of the contract 168f.
    as to the qualities of the thing or person 156ff.
    recognisable 165f.
    risk in transactions 162
    shared 166f.
    as to value 161
modification of contracts 63ff.
motive 159f.

Nachfrist 223f., 226, 228ff., 243
national laws 1, 9f., 12, 15
negligence 37, 62, 107, 135, 137, 162ff., 173, 179f., 245ff., 263
    contributory 261ff.
negotiations, breaking off 32ff.
nemo auditur 125ff.
non-compete agreements 119ff.
non-disclosure 175ff.
non-performance
    anticipatory 228
    attribution 244ff.
    damages 242f., 257ff.
    fault principle 244ff., 256
    see also termination
notarial documents 77
nudum pactum 50

objective interpretation 92, 93ff.
obligations de moyens/obligations de résultat 248ff.
offensive contracts 110, 116
offer 17ff.
    definiteness 19
    effect 21
    to make good 163
    refusal or failure to accept 21f.
    revocation 22ff., 63
    termination 21ff.
oral evidence, exclusion of 78ff.

pacta sunt servanda 51
partial invalidity 121f., 143ff.
partial termination 232f.
paternalism 76f., 112
Patronatserklärung 34
penalties 276ff.
performance
    claims *see* claims for performance
    commencing 26f.
pledges 56f.
pre-contract 34
price-fixing 45ff.
Principles of European Contract Law (PECL) 3f., 11, 14
priority of claims 350f.
profits
    disgorgement of 270f.
    lost 268ff.
promissory estoppel 64
promissory gifts 56ff.
property, contracts for the use of 61f.
proprietary estoppel 86ff.
protection of consumers 9, 10, 133, 136, 140

qualified acceptance 29ff.

règles supplétives 8, 102, 352
reliance
    agency and 305ff., 310f., 324, 327
    detrimental 37, 86ff., 327

reliance (cont.)
  interest 36, 38, 266
  protection of 23f., 32, 56ff., 62, 92, 97, 150f., 156, 164ff., 171f., 184, 189
remote damage 257ff.
representation see agency
restitution 125ff., 237ff.
revocation see withdrawal
risk 8f., 22, 31f., 62, 80ff., 86, 88f., 99, 101, 103, 105ff., 116f., 162, 176, 183f., 194, 203, 218, 224, 230f., 281
  agency and 303ff., 317
  allocation 132f., 139, 141ff., 182, 227f, 283ff., 329
  assignment and 343f., 354
  CISG 235, 239
  foreseeability 259ff.
  mistake and 150, 153ff., 159, 161f.
  procurement risk 246ff.

sanctions 78, 84
  exclusion of oral evidence 78ff.
  invalidity 80ff.
seriousness, indicia of 49ff.
services rendered 59f.
silence, acceptance as 271
specific performance 202ff., 212ff.
standard terms 9, 11, 30f., 97, 132f., 134, 139f.
statutory representatives 297f.
stipulation 17, 49, 74
substitute transaction 209
supplementary performance 207, 210f., 217

tenants, protection of 39, 127, 181, 198f., 265, 320
termination 215f., 243
  anticipatory non-performance 228
  basic requirement 224ff.
  defective performance 233ff.
  delayed performance 229ff.
  English law 220ff.
  French law 219f.
  German law 223f.
  impossibility of performance 226ff.
  incomplete performance 231ff.
  interests of the parties 216ff.
  natural law 218f.
  partial termination 232f.
  restitution 237ff.
  Roman law and Canon law 218
third party rights
  action directe 328f.
  claims not based on contractual intention 328f.
  contract chains 329ff.
  contracts protective of third parties 325ff.
  defences available to the promisor 333
  historical development and economic importance 319ff.
  intention of the parties 323ff.
  limitations of liability 331f.
  modification or termination of rights 334f.
  rights of the promisee 332f.
timeshare contracts 193f.
tort claims
  concurrence 330
  English law 33f., 37, 50, 62, 71, 107, 184, 202, 213, 263
  European private law 2, 3
  French law 33, 38, 108, 250, 272, 309, 311, 325, 328f.
  third party rights and 325ff.
transaction costs 12, 31, 101, 133, 137, 141

UN Sales Law 13, 18ff., 93, 154, 206ff., 224f., 234ff., 255ff.
undisclosed principal 307, 314ff., 324
undue influence 114f., 181, 185ff.
undue restraints on personal or economic freedom 117f.
  long-term contractual relationships 118f.
  non-compete agreements 119ff.
  partial invalidity 121f.
unexpected circumstances 279f.
  English law 285ff.
  French law 280f.
  German law 281ff.
  international rules 288ff.
unfair contract terms 131ff.
  administrative controls 147f.
  contracts between businesses 136ff.
  criminal sanctions 145f.
  definition of unfairness 140ff.
  group actions 146f.
  inequality between performance and counterperformance 110ff.
  judicial control 134ff.
  legislative options 136ff.
  partial invalidation 140ff.
  preventive control 145ff.
  standard terms and individually negotiated terms 139ff.
UNIDROIT 4, 340
unilateral price-fixing 45ff.
United States 13
utilitarianism 7

validity 5f.
  balance between performance and counterperformance 110ff.
  see also invalidity

welfare state 122
withdrawal
  basis and reasons for 192ff.
  consequences of revocation 195f.
  distance-selling contracts 194f.
  loan agreements 193f.
  right of 191f.
  timeshare contracts 193f.
writs 50f.

EUROPEAN CONTRACT LAW